This "O-P Book" is an Authorized Reprint of the Original Edition, Produced by Microfilm-Xerography by University Microfilms, Inc., Ann Arbor, Michigan, 1964

THE OPENING OF THE MISSISSIPPI

A STRUGGLE FOR SUPREMACY
IN THE
AMERICAN INTERIOR

THE OPENING OF
THE MISSISSIPPI

A STRUGGLE FOR SUPREMACY

IN THE

AMERICAN INTERIOR

BY

FREDERIC AUSTIN OGG

INSTRUCTOR IN HISTORY IN INDIANA UNIVERSITY

New York
THE MACMILLAN COMPANY
LONDON: MACMILLAN & CO., LTD.
1904

All rights reserved

To My Wife

COPYRIGHT, 1904,
BY THE MACMILLAN COMPANY.

Set up, electrotyped, and published February, 1904.

Norwood Press
J. S. Cushing & Co. — Berwick & Smith Co.
Norwood, Mass., U.S.A.

PREFACE

This book is intended primarily to be a history of the discovery, exploration, and contested rights of navigation of the Mississippi River prior to the final securing of American supremacy by the closing events of the War of 1812. As such, however, it inevitably appears here and there to have been broadened into an attempted history of the entire Mississippi Valley. The author disclaims any purpose to deal with so large a subject, except in so far as has seemed necessary in order to give his more restricted narrative its true setting.

In writing the earlier history of the Mississippi an effort has been made to place due emphasis on two most important aspects of it — the diplomatic and what may perhaps be called the physiographic. Not until after the second American war for independence did the ownership and control of the Mississippi cease to be the subject of almost perennial diplomatic negotiation. The purchase of Louisiana, whose centenary is about being celebrated, was but an incident — a most important one, to be sure — of that prolonged negotiation. Four nations — Spain, France, England, and the United States — were from time to time involved in it, and no account of the development of the great Middle West is complete without a careful survey of its devious courses.

The close relation coming more and more to be recognized as existing between the geography of a country and the history of its inhabitants impels a consideration of the Mississippi as the great trade and travel artery of the American interior. Together with its tributaries, it furnished the most inviting pathway for the early explorer, the missionary, the trader, and the settler. It was, of course, because of its extreme economic importance that the river was so keenly contended for by rival nationalities and influenced so greatly the transforming of the inland wilderness into one of the choicest of dwelling-places for mankind.

Among the more recent writers whom I have consulted to advantage in the study of my subject, those to whom I am chiefly indebted are carefully indicated in foot-notes throughout the book. It is a pleasant duty, however, to make special mention of Mr. Henry Adams's monumental *History of the United States during the Administrations of Jefferson and Madison*, which has been invaluable, not merely for the scholarly and original ideas which it contains, but for numerous references opening the way to material otherwise in danger of being overlooked. It is truly said that history can never be written in its final form, but Mr. Adams's volumes surely fall as little short of finality as is possible for a work of their kind. The writer has been stimulated by the spirit of this great work as much as he has been aided by information drawn from it. Other secondary authorities which should not be passed without mention in this connection are Bancroft's *History of the United States*, McMaster's *History of the People of the United States*, Miss Grace King's

PREFACE

New Orleans, Binger Hermann's *The Louisiana Purchase*, James K. Hosmer's *Short History of the Mississippi Valley* and *The Louisiana Purchase*, Theodore Roosevelt's *Winning of the West*, Charles Gayarré's *History of Louisiana*, Justin Winsor's *Narrative and Critical History of America*, *Cartier to Frontenac*, *The Mississippi Basin*, and *The Westward Movement*, and John Fiske's *New France and New England*.

Various sorts of original materials — correspondence, memoirs, contemporary historical writing, and state papers — have been drawn upon at every stage of the preparation of the book. These are all referred to in the footnotes. Those used most frequently are R. G. Thwaites's edition of the *Jesuit Relations*, J. G. Shea's collection of narratives in his *Discovery and Exploration of the Mississippi Valley*, B. F. French's *Historical Collections of Louisiana*, E. B. O'Callaghan's *New York Colonial Documents*, the writings of George Washington, Benjamin Franklin, James Madison, Rufus King, John Adams, John Jay, Thomas Jefferson, and James Monroe, the *Secret Journals of Congress*, Martens's *Collection of the Principal Treaties concluded by the Powers of Europe*, Margry's *Découvertes et Établissements des Français dans l'Ouest et dans le Sud de l'Amérique Septentrionale*, Charlevoix's *Histoire Générale de la Nouvelle France*, the *Correspondance* of Napoleon, the *Mémoires* of Lucien Bonaparte, Richardson's *Messages and Papers of the Presidents*, the *Executive Journal*, the *Annals of Congress*, and, — most important of all, — the *American State Papers, Foreign Relations*.

Among the many persons to whom I am indebted for valuable assistance in the preparation of this book, I cannot refrain from making mention of Professor Albert Bushnell Hart, of Harvard University, Mr. Dudley O. McGovney, also of Harvard, Mr. Thomas J. Kiernan, Superintendent of Circulation in the Harvard University Library, and Mr. James Lyman Whitney, of the Boston Public Library.

FREDERIC AUSTIN OGG.

BLOOMINGTON, INDIANA,
September 1, 1903.

CONTENTS

CHAPTER		PAGE
I.	The Importance of the Mississippi Valley	1
II.	The Spanish Discovery of the Mississippi	8
III.	The Search of the French for the Mississippi	45
IV.	La Salle and the Opening of the Great West	81
V.	The Exploration of the Upper Mississippi	133
VI.	The Beginnings of Louisiana	169
VII.	The Struggle of the English and French for Possession	214
VIII.	English and Spanish Neighbors after 1763	294
IX.	The Navigation of the Mississippi, 1783–1795	400
X.	Napoleon and the Louisiana Country	460
XI.	The Louisiana Purchase	495
XII.	Congress and the Problems of National Expansion	539
XIII.	Establishing the American Régime	575
XIV.	The Territory of Orleans and the New Louisiana	608
INDEX		657

THE OPENING OF THE MISSISSIPPI

A STRUGGLE FOR SUPREMACY IN THE AMERICAN INTERIOR

CHAPTER I

THE IMPORTANCE OF THE MISSISSIPPI VALLEY

THE history of the world is in no small degree the history of its great river valleys and of the civilizations that have flourished in them. In ancient times the chief prerequisite to a people's prosperity was the possession of a fertile and well-watered habitation, such as a great river valley affords, and even to-day there is nothing of a material sort which is more conducive to human progress and happiness, unless perchance it be the possession of good harbors and an abundant entrance to the high seas. For, while we have grown away from the limitations in skill and inventiveness which bound the Egyptians so slavishly to the beneficence of the Nile, or the Babylonians to that of the Euphrates, we too have a vast population to feed, we too want fertile soil, easily tillable ground, and an abundant water-supply.

From the earliest history of our country the river valleys have been chiefly sought for habitation. Not only did the early Spanish, and particularly the early French, explorers and colonizers follow the watercourses, but the English also showed an unmistakable propensity to exploit and utilize first the lands that had been prepared for them by the great rivers of the country. The Cavaliers of Virginia lined the fertile banks of the James and its tributaries with their broad plantations, and made the rivers almost their only highways of trade and social intercourse. The valley of the Potomac received the first settlers of Maryland, and that of the Delaware and Susquehanna those of Pennsylvania. New York's history was begun at the mouth of the Hudson. When the Massachusetts colonies began to overflow, it was to the broad and beautiful valley of the Connecticut that the emigrants turned their steps. And the early settlers of the farther south kept closely to the larger streams — the Cape Fear and Roanoke in North Carolina, the Ashley and Cooper in South Carolina, the Savannah in Georgia, and the St. John's in Florida.

And when the Englishman had possessed himself quite thoroughly of the lands lying between the Atlantic and the headwaters of the Susquehanna, the Potomac, and the James, by natural impulse he took up the line of march again toward the west into new river valleys, and eventually into the greatest of them all. Crossing the Alleghanies, he stood upon the threshold of the most magnificent heritage that has ever been vouchsafed to an enterprising people. Before him stretched to the Gulf, to the Rockies, and to the Great Lakes, an area of more than a million and a quarter square miles, whose economic possibilities no like region in all the world can equal. In respect simply to fertility and luxuriance of vegetation the valley of the Amazon, of course, excels that of the Mississippi. But climatic conditions in the former case almost

completely offset any advantages the region may claim as an abode for mankind. The distinguishing characteristic of the Mississippi Valley is its rare combination of beneficent features in the absence of unfavorable ones. In richness of soil, variety of climate, number and value of products, facilities for communication, and general conditions of wealth and prosperity, the Mississippi Valley surpasses anything known to the Old World as well as the New. Of course, there are most excellent agricultural regions in Europe and Asia and Africa, but on a scale by no means so extensive as the Mississippi Valley, and without many of the collateral advantages which render this region preeminently adapted to the development of the highest type of civilization. In the economy of the world's life for a region merely to yield food for the support of a dense population is certainly much. But for it to do so under conditions that stimulate to energy, thrift, and culture on part of its inhabitants is infinitely more.

The area of the Mississippi Valley may be stated roughly at a million and a quarter square miles. All the great countries of central Europe — Germany, Austria-Hungary, France, and Italy — could be set down in it, and yet there would be much room to spare. As a recent writer has said, almost every rood of its space "can be made to furnish a home and sustenance, if not to the farmer, at any rate to the ranchman or the miner"; and it is worthy of note that this region is rapidly becoming the greatest home of English-speaking peoples on the globe. Compared with the population which it is capable of supporting, that which it has at present is sparse. From the statistics of the last census it appears that 40,413,051 people now live in the broad central plain between the Rockies and the Alleghanies — 52.9 per cent of the total population of the country. Justin Winsor, in his *Westward Movement*, some years ago affirmed that the Mississippi basin can easily maintain 200,000,000 people — a density about seven times that of this same region to-day, or about equal to that of the state of Connecticut. More recently Professor Albert Bushnell Hart, in an article in *Harper's Magazine*, has placed the figure as high as 350,000,000, which would mean a density practically equal to that of Massachusetts to-day. When the possibilities of intensive farming are taken into account, even the latter estimate seems quite within the bounds of reason. Hitherto there has been, and even yet is, such a superabundance of land in the Middle West that there has generally prevailed a luxurious carelessness in the utilization of it, such as fills the European small farmer with surprise. Except to the few who actually sit down to estimate what our numbers must be four or five hundred years hence, the fear of overcrowding which has long haunted the peoples of the Old World is here all but unknown.

It is quite probable that by the time the population of the Mississippi Valley shall have doubled, as it has done every quarter of the past century, that of the East and West will be found to have increased in like proportion. But one thing is certain — it is the Mississippi Valley that must ever continue to provide food for the growing population, not merely within its own borders, but throughout the entire country. This means that the region must permanently retain its agricultural character. Measured

by the value of products, the United States as a whole, since the decade from 1880 to 1890, has passed from the character of an agricultural to that of a manufacturing nation. But in the Mississippi Valley this transition can and must never occur — at least until that far distant day when the limits of agricultural enterprise shall have been reached. For a long time to come the growth of cities must not progress faster than in a certain proportion to the increase of the farming population. It seems hardly necessary to remark that this does not mean any retarding of the substantial progress of culture and better living. As time goes on and inventions multiply, the city will possess fewer and fewer advantages over the country. Even now in many parts of the Mississippi Valley rural mail delivery, good roads, telephones, daily newspapers, and the consolidation of schools have rendered rural life but slightly less desirable in some particulars, and vastly more desirable in a good many others, than life in the cities. Indeed it may well be that not the least of the benefits to be conferred upon the world at large by the Mississippi Valley and its people will be the practical demonstration of how agricultural life can be freed from most, if not all, of the inconveniences which have been supposed to be inevitable to it, and which have been so largely responsible for the undue crowding of the people into cities in our day.

The Mississippi Valley has long been what clearly it is at present — the most interesting and in some respects the most important theatre of our national life. The movement into it of the pioneers from Virginia and Pennsylvania and New England; the encounters with the Indians and with the French; the rivalry with the Spanish neighbors on the southwest; the purchase of the great western half of the valley from France just a hundred years ago; the memorable migrations of the first half of the nineteenth century which gave it its population; the great question of slavery extension in the territories created from it; the struggle of civil war upon its soil and for the settlement of its problems; and finally its marvellous development under the fostering of a reunited nation, — all these things, and very many more, have not so much contributed to our history as constituted the main body of it. Here it is that democratic government is being put to the supreme test of efficiency over a widely extended domain, and here again it is that the problems of capital and labor, science and invention, and the diffusion of an educated citizenship, are most pressing for solution. The future of the nation may be taken to lie closely along the course marked out by the men of the Middle West.

The ligaments by which nature has bound this great region together are streams of water — chiefly the Mississippi and its tributaries. This noble river, with its affluents, direct and indirect, said to be more than 100,000 in number, constitutes the third largest drainage system in the world. The length of the main stream is more than 2500 miles, and the volume of water which it discharges into the sea is second only to that of the Amazon and greater than that of all European rivers combined (leaving only the Volga out of account), being estimated at not less than 139 cubic miles annually. It and its tributaries provide somewhat over 16,000 miles of navigable water —

more than any other river system except the Amazon. Truly it merits the name bestowed upon it in early times by the Chippewa Indians — *May-see-see-bee*, "The Father of Running Waters."

The Mississippi is interesting, however, not so much on its physical as on its political and economic side. As the key to the control of the Middle West the river has had a most important part in determining the history of the great American interior. It has been the fortune of few rivers or other physical features of the globe to appear as continuously in the annals of discovery and diplomacy. From the earliest discovery by the Spanish, probably in the second quarter of the sixteenth century, until the superfluous victory of General Jackson at New Orleans in 1815, the control of the great river seemed never quite permanently settled. Three of Europe's most powerful nations contended long and vigorously for the maintenance of their authority over greater or lesser portions of its basin; and when the American Revolution created a new power, with its frontiers resting on the eastern bank of the river, the problem of possession became, if anything, more complicated than before. It was not until more than a decade after the United States had secured all the remaining contiguous territory by purchase (except the disputed region of West Florida) that the great river and its valley became integral parts of the American nation, no longer to furnish fuel for international rivalries and subjects for perennial diplomatic negotiation.

CHAPTER II

THE SPANISH DISCOVERY OF THE MISSISSIPPI

THERE is no way of assuring ourselves just when the people of Europe began to discern that the land which Columbus had discovered was not Asia. It would seem that very few expeditions thither must have convinced at least the voyagers who actually took part that the landfall was neither the desired Cathay nor India. The gold-roofed houses and heaps of sea-shore treasure with which these countries were said to abound were nowhere apparent. In their visits to the islands of the West Indian group Columbus and his companion adventurers found tropical fruits and fertile soil and curious natives, but no gold. The earliest explorations on the mainland yielded results no less unsatisfactory.

Vague rumors were repeatedly encountered to the effect that still farther to the west there were lands fully as rich as the most vivid Spanish imagination had ever conceived. This delusion was not infrequently fostered by the natives in order to induce the Spanish invaders to seek other fields. Of course the search, except in Mexico and Peru, was from the outset illusory. It reminds one of the childish pursuit of the pot of gold at the rainbow's end. But very many decades elapsed after the first discovery by Columbus before the Spaniards ceased to think

THE SPANISH DISCOVERY OF THE MISSISSIPPI

that by going westward from Florida they must sometime, somewhere, come upon the fabled wealth of the Indies. For a great while it was with them a question merely of distance and direction.

It was in search of these western seats of wealth, or at least a passage to them, that the early Spanish navigators began first to push their way into the Gulf of Mexico, then supposed to be some part of the great Indian Ocean south from Asia. If we are to believe a considerable amount of testimony which has come down to us, the first European to sail in the waters of the Gulf was Americus Vespucius, a Florentine sailor in the Spanish employ, who, as pilot of the expedition of Pinzon and Solis, in 1497–1498, visited the coast of Honduras, rounded Yucatan, spent some time among the hospitable natives of the Tampico region on the Mexican coast, skirted the northern shores of the Gulf eastward to Florida, and finally returned to Cadiz by way of Chesapeake Bay and the Bermudas. On this expedition no discoveries then regarded as important were made, and so little is known about it that there has been perhaps no more disputed subject in all the history of American exploration.[1] If Vespucius really effected his reputed

---

[1] There is no satisfactory book in English on Vespucius and his reputed discoveries, though John Fiske deals with the subject quite well in his *Discovery of America*, II. 25–175. Sydney Howard Gay's chapter in Winsor's *Narrative and Critical History of America* (Vol. II. Ch. II.) is far below the average of the monographs in that great work. Mr. Winsor's critical notes, however, are excellent. Francisco Adolpho de Varnhagen's collection of French and Portuguese monographs, published at Vienna, is so valuable that, as Mr. Fiske declared, "No one who has not mastered it in all its details is entitled to speak about Vespucius." Other important works on the subject are John Boyd Thacher, *The Continent of America*,

circuit of the Gulf he must have beheld lands not seen subsequently by Europeans before 1513 and 1519. It may even be that the mouth of the Mississippi was sighted by him, but there is no evidence whatever to lead us to think so. Certainly no practical results followed the expedition.

Columbus, on his fourth voyage, in 1502, planned to reach the Cochin-Chinese coast far to the south, in the vicinity of the Malay Peninsula, and so took a southwesterly course, which landed him on the shores of Honduras.[1] The Indians told him of a great sea to the southward — the Pacific Ocean, of course — and declared that, being once embarked on it, the Ganges might be reached in ten days. They told him, too, of a narrow passage to the southeast, which unfortunately he understood to be a passage of water, *i.e.* the Strait of Malacca, instead of what it really was — a passage of land, *i.e.* the Isthmus of Darien. The remainder of the expedition was consumed in a vain search for this passage, and for gold. M. Henry Harrisse, the greatest of our authorities on the beginnings of the exploration period of American history, thinks that before Columbus died he understood that the continent which he had discovered was not any part of Asia, and that the Spanish government was

---

Part III., and Henry Harrisse, *Americus Vespucius*, the latter, however, being merely a book review. The letters of Vespucius have been translated several times, notably by Clements R. Markham [published by the Hakluyt Society]. The narrative of the voyage of 1497–1498 is reprinted in the *Old South Leaflets*, No. XXXIV.

[1] The best accounts of this voyage are those by Winsor in his *Christopher Columbus*, Chs. XII.–XIV., and by John Boyd Thacher in his *Christopher Columbus*, II. Chs. C.–CXI.

convinced of this as early as 1501. But the generally prevailing view is rather that Columbus thought only that he had failed to reach those parts of the Asiatic continent where treasure abounded, and that further search would certainly open up a way into the waters on the Indian coast.

Our knowledge of Spanish exploring enterprise and achievement prior to 1511 is extremely unsatisfactory. We have only intimations of numerous voyages concerning which we know next to nothing. For instance, in April, 1495, Ferdinand and Isabella published a decree authorizing any person to equip an expedition for the purpose of discovering "new isles and continents in the Indian Ocean." We are told by a contemporary chronicler, Peter the Martyr,[1] that a number of sea-captains availed themselves of the opportunity thus offered. It is just possible that some of these penetrated the waters of the Gulf far enough to behold the mouth of the Mississippi, but there is absolutely no evidence that such was the case. Beginning, however, with Ponce de Leon's expedition from Porto Rico to Florida in 1513, we have a considerable number of chronicles and so-called histories from which to draw information. Many of these are of uncertain reliability, and many are known to be utterly untrustworthy; but judicious and painstaking use of them has doubtless brought us fairly near the truth — as near, at any rate, as we are likely ever to be.

It is agreed by practically all students of the subject that the Spaniards had no knowledge of the Mississippi prior, in any event, to the year 1519. If Vespucius or any

---

[1] Peter the Martyr, *Decades*, published in 1511. There is an elaborate account of Peter the Martyr in Thacher, *Christopher Columbus*, I. 3–95.

other of the earlier voyagers saw the river, the fact either was not reported or was entirely overlooked by the chroniclers of the time. In 1517 Francisco Hernandez de Córdova was put in command of an expedition sent out by Diego Velasquez, governor of Cuba, toward the southern coasts of the Gulf for the purpose of slave-catching in the region of Honduras.[1] Córdova is declared by the contemporary Spanish historian and philanthropist, Las Casas, to have been "very prudent and courageous, and strongly disposed to kill and kidnap Indians."[2] Doubtless it was chiefly the latter quality that recommended him to the service of Velasquez. The chief pilot of the expedition was Antonio de Alaminos, who had been with Columbus on his fourth voyage, and more than a hundred soldiers were sent to assure the success of the undertaking. Córdova sailed from Santiago in February, nominally for the purposes of discovery, since slave-hunting expeditions were illegal. After cruising a considerable distance along the Yucatan coast, inhabited by the bitterly hostile Mayas, Córdova's vessels met with injury from storms so that the sailors were compelled to land.[3] A treacherous attack from the Indians so weakened and disheartened the men that the few who remained were glad enough to give up all hope

---

[1] Dr. J. G. Shea affirms that Córdova's original destination was the Bahama Islands, but that he was carried by storms upon the coast of Yucatan, which country then received the name it has since borne. Winsor, *Narrative and Critical History*, II. 236.

[2] Las Casas, *Historia de las Indias*, tom. IV. p. 369.

[3] Another account is that exhaustion of the water supply caused the landing. Fiske, *Discovery of America*, II. 242. This, however, seems to have been the occasion of another and equally disastrous landing, on the Florida coast on the return to Cuba. See Shea, in Winsor, *Narrative and Critical History*, II. 236.

of securing slaves and sail again for Cuba at the earliest opportunity. Córdova soon died of his wounds.[1]

In the course of a few months Alaminos, the pilot of this disastrous expedition, made his way to the island of Jamaica and to the home of the wealthy governor, Francisco de Garay. The pilot's heart was still set upon steering a way through a "western passage" into the waters of the Indian, and he talked so eloquently of the advantages to arise from such an achievement that Garay was at last persuaded to undertake its accomplishment. Garay had been a companion of Columbus on the latter's second voyage, in 1493, and was deeply interested in everything pertaining to navigation and discovery. In the account which Alaminos gave of the gorgeous dress of the Mayans and their "strange-looking pyramids or towers, ascended by stone steps," the governor discerned striking indications that at least the threshold of the much-desired Orient had been reached.

Permission to engage in the exploration of the mainland and the search for the western passage was obtained from the priors of the Order of St. Jerome, then the governors of the Indies,[2] and an experienced navigator by the name of Alonso Alvarez de Pineda was put in command of the expedition. The *real cédula* granted by the Regents in the absence of the Spanish king, Charles V., by which Garay was subsequently authorized

---

[1] The following year the governor's nephew, Juan de Grijalva, was sent to the Yucatan coast with a force of 250 picked soldiers to avenge the outrages of the Mayas. A battle was fought in which the natives were roundly beaten. Grijalva continued exploration along the coast westward, possibly as far as the Panuco River.

[2] Winsor, *Narrative and Critical History*, II. 237.

to colonize the northern coast of the Gulf,[1] states that the expedition of Pineda consisted of four vessels fitted out entirely at Garay's expense.[2] It is said to have numbered 270 men, with a good supply of horses and provisions. The route followed is uncertain, but the farthest point reached by the voyagers is known to have been the mouth of the Panuco River, about fifty miles from the present site of Vera Cruz.[3] Landing at this place near the end of August, 1519, Pineda's men fell in with the followers of Cortés, whose explorations had already been in progress several months. Cortés challenged the right of Garay to advance into the territories thus preempted, but his opposition was silenced by the information that the Spanish government had specifically sanctioned the enterprise.

One of the most controverted subjects in early American history is the precise course and achievements of this Pineda voyage. Until about twelve years ago it was generally assumed by writers that the enterprise took its greatest claim to distinction from the fact that it culminated in the discovery of the Mississippi River. More recent critical study of the evidence in hand, however, especially on the part of Dr. Walter B. Scaife and Mr. Peter J. Hamilton, has gone far toward discrediting the old assumption and transferring the honor of the Mississippi discovery from Pineda to his later fellow-countryman, Hernando de Soto. It may be well to set forth the

[1] In 1521.   [2] Henry Harrisse, *The Discovery of North America*, 164.
[3] Barnard Shipp, *Hernando de Soto and Florida*, Ch. III. Many of the conclusions arrived at by this author have been superseded, but the chapter referred to contains transcripts of much original material on the expedition of Francisco de Garay to Panuco.

basis of the old view, and then state the grounds of objection to it. According to such eminent authorities as Henry Harrisse, Justin Winsor,[1] John G. Shea, and John Fiske, it was sometime during the course of Pineda's voyage that the original discovery of the Mississippi occurred.[2] The account in the *real cédula* before mentioned says that while navigating the Gulf the adventurers entered a river, "very large and very full," where they tarried forty days while repairs were being made on their vessels. There is much doubt as to whether this discovery was made on the westward voyage or on the return. In Garay's letters patent it is stated that after entering the Gulf, Pineda's vessels found it impossible to emerge by way of the northeast on account of "the country of Florida found by Ponce de Leon." Turning about, they struck a due westerly course along the northern shore of the Gulf. As the voyage progressed the sailors examined carefully "the country, rivers, harbors, inhabitants, and all that which deserved to be noted on the said coast." When the followers of Cortés were encountered in the Tampico region, Pineda's men set up a monument to mark the limits of their explorations, and then turned to retrace their course. They had sailed westward a distance of more than three hundred leagues, taking possession in the name of Castile of all the lands which they sighted.

[1] It is but fair to note that in the later course of his studies Mr. Winsor came to refer to Pineda's alleged discovery of the Mississippi as at least an unsettled question. *Narrative and Critical History*, II. 292.

[2] Las Casas, in his *Historia de las Indias*, conveys the idea that the Mississippi had been discovered in 1518 by Diego de Camargo, in charge of an expedition sent out by Garay. Harrisse has shown this to be false. *The Discovery of North America*, 163.

"They then turned back with the said ships," continue the letters patent, "and entered a river which was found to be very large and very deep, at the mouth of which they say they found an extensive town, where they remained forty days and careened their vessels. The natives treated our men in a friendly manner, trading with them, and giving what they possessed."[1] This river, according to the old view, was the Mississippi, called by the Spaniards the Rio del Espíritu Santo, or the River of the Holy Ghost.[2] Pineda's party ascended the stream a distance of six leagues, and saw on its banks, in that short space, no fewer than forty Indian towns and villages "covered with reedes," besides the large settlement at the river's mouth.[3]

From this account it would appear that the Mississippi was discovered on the return voyage, or in other words, when the expedition was sailing from the west toward the east. But in the sworn testimony of Garay, found in the Archives of the Indies, it is represented that Pineda's discovery was made "in navigating from north and east to south and west."[4] Fortunately we still possess the map made by Pineda's pilots and sent by Garay to the Regents in 1519-1520, when petitioning for the privilege of colonizing the recently discovered countries.[5] On this map is found a legend which reads, "*From here, Francisco Garay commenced discovering.*" It is placed to the east from the

---

[1] Harrisse, *The Discovery of North America*, 164.

[2] The name was evidently given by Garay. Winsor, *Narrative and Critical History*, II. 237, note.

[3] Harrisse, *The Discovery of North America*, 168.   [4] *Ibid.*, 168-169.

[5] This map is reproduced in A. J. Weise's *The Discoveries of America to the Year 1525*, opp. p. 278.

Rio del Espíritu Santo in about the locality of the Appalachicola. The line of discovery follows the coast thence toward the west and southwest until, after having passed the Mississippi's mouth, it ends in the Tampico region on the Mexican shore.[1] The sworn testimony of Garay, taken in conjunction with the map, makes it highly probable, under the old view, that the discovery of the Mississippi was effected during the westward voyage, perhaps as early as May or June, 1519. According to Harrisse's interpretation of the tangled testimonies that have come down to us, Pineda's expedition sailed from Jamaica in February or March, went not north by the windward passage, but west between Cuba and Yucatan, bore then toward the northeast until the Florida coast was reached, and being unable to find an outlet in that direction, cruised first northwest, then west, and finally southwest, along the Gulf shore. The Mississippi was sighted on the westward voyage, though it may well have been seen again on the return; for in Harrisse's opinion it is quite impossible to tell whether the expedition retraced its earlier course or sailed back straight across the Gulf from Mexico to Jamaica.[2]

Such are the speculations of those who accept the theory of the Mississippi's discovery by Pineda. The objections to this view may be summarized as follows: (1) there is no evidence that the name Espíritu Santo was applied by Pineda or his immediate companions to any specific stream of water; (2) the contemporary writer Navarrete, in his

[1] Harrisse, *The Discovery of North America*, 170.
[2] *Ibid.*, 173. See an argument for the discovery by Pineda in Henry L. Reynolds, "The Discovery of the Mississippi," in the *Magazine of American History*, XXII. 37-41.

account of the expedition of Pineda,[1] makes no mention of the Espíritu Santo, but speaks merely of the discovery of "a river of very great volume" — a phrase applied by the Spaniards with utter lack of discrimination to streams as insignificant as the St. John's and the Panuco; (3) the mention of a large town (*un gran pueblo*) at the mouth of the river in question precludes the Mississippi, for all other accounts of the region in this early period go to show that these lands, by reason of their swampy and unattractive character, were not only uninhabited but well-nigh uninhabitable; (4) the statement that there were forty villages on the lower banks of the river likewise argues against the Mississippi, for it seems clear that Soto's retreating band twenty-four years later found no such inhabitants or trace of them; (5) the ascent of the Mississippi could hardly have been accomplished by Pineda's ocean-going vessels. Nine years later Narvaez's ships, small though they were, could not effect an entrance, and in 1699 the French under Iberville found it necessary to explore the mouth of the stream with improvised boats of very diminutive size; and (6) contemporary maps contain the name Espíritu Santo, but applied in every case to a pear-shaped bay utterly unlike the mouth of the Mississippi.[2]

Having shown with apparent conclusiveness that Pineda's

---

[1] Martin Fernandez de Navarrete, *Colección de los viages y descubrimientos que hicieron por mar los Españoles desde fines del siglo XV.* tom. III. pp. 64–69.

[2] For a very illuminating discussion of the whole subject, especially of the unwarranted identification of the Rio del Espíritu Santo with the Mississippi, see Dr. Walter B. Scaife's *America: Its Geographical History*, Supplement. [Johns Hopkins University Studies in Historical and Political Science, Extra Volume XIII.]

discovery of the lower Mississippi cannot be squared at all with contemporary evidences, the critics have gone on to demonstrate with equal cogency that what the Spanish navigator really discovered and explored was Mobile Bay and Mobile River, and that it was these that the early sixteenth-century cartographers intended to designate by the name of Espíritu Santo. The location of the name on the maps of the time, the close correspondence of the descriptions with facts ascertained from other sources, and the numerous improbabilities of the Mississippi discovery, combine to render this newer view the only one easily tenable.[1] There is nothing in all the body of contemporary testimony which conflicts with it in the least; there are many things which seem to make it inevitable. Under these circumstances the historian can do nothing but reject the old for the new. It is possible, of course, that Pineda passed close by the Mississippi's mouth, but if he did, no genuinely trustworthy record of the fact has survived. In all probability he was utterly unaware of the great river's existence.

The Gulf coast region sighted in 1519 was given the name Amichel. On their return Pineda's men told great stories about its wealth, — how the land "fairly glistered" with gold, how the houses of the natives were filled with treasure, and how the people wore gold ornaments in their noses and ears. They had tales to tell, too, of tribes of giants and of pygmies which they had encountered.

---

[1] A recent and careful statement of the Mobile theory is in Peter J. Hamilton's *Colonial Mobile*, Ch. II. See also Jacob V. Brower's "The Mississippi River and its Source," in *Minnesota Historical Collections*, VII. 16–20.

The natives they reported generally to be very friendly, ready to trade, and quite willing to embrace the Christian faith. These optimistic views were evidently not shared by Garay, for we find him declaring that he "thought the coast to be very lytle hospitable, because he saw tokens and signes of small store of golde, and that not pure."[1] On a map made in 1529 the Spanish cosmographer Ribero designated the region of the Espíritu Santo as "too far from the tropics" to abound in gold.

Nevertheless Garay sent several more expeditions into the Gulf. The first of these was led by Pineda in 1520. But this time the intrepid adventurer met death at the hands of the Indians before being able to accomplish anything of note. The same year four caravels were sent out under Diego de Camargo to occupy a post near the Panuco. The expedition was mismanaged and strife with Cortés's men caused a speedy abandonment of the enterprise. In 1523 Garay fitted out a fleet of thirteen vessels, carrying nearly a thousand soldiers, with which he proposed personally to undertake the conquest of Amichel. At the last moment, however, his troops prevailed upon him to sail instead to Panuco, where in a few months Cortés captured such of the company as had survived the storms and shipwrecks encountered on the Mexican coasts. Garay himself was killed in a conflict with Cortés.

"To Alonzo Alvarez Pineda alone," concludes Harrisse, "belongs the merit of having discovered and ranged before any other Spanish captain the shores of the Gulf of Mexico which now form part of the United States."[2]

---

[1] Reported by Peter the Martyr.
[2] Henry Harrisse, *The Discovery of North America*, 167.

Several important results followed this accomplishment. In the first place, the mouths of two of the greatest southward flowing rivers, the Alabama and the Tombigbee, were discovered and marked off for Spanish possession. Not until the beginning of the last century was the claim founded on Pineda's discovery really given over. Pineda's voyage also revealed the uselessness of the search for a western passage through the Gulf of Mexico. The chart prepared by Garay from Pineda's reports showed that the Gulf "bendeth like a bow" and that a line drawn from Yucatan to southern Florida would " make the string to the bow." Thus was Florida proved not to be an island, as Ponce de Leon had considered it, but rather "by huge, crooked windings and turninges to bee joyned to this maine continent of Tunustitan" (Yucatan). Nevertheless, the exact nature of Pineda's achievements not being generally understood, the search for the western passage through the Gulf was renewed many times in subsequent generations.

The stories which became current concerning the discoveries of Pineda and the conquests of Cortés fired the imaginative Spaniards with fresh zeal. Without waiting to inquire why Pineda's men had not themselves carried away some of the treasure which they declared to be so abundant among the Indians of the Espíritu Santo, other Spaniards set to work to organize expeditions of conquest and duplicate in the lands north of the Gulf the career of Cortés in the south. Of most note among these was Pamphilo de Narvaez, an adventurer of very mediocre character and ability, but of unlimited cupidity, who in 1526 obtained from Charles V. a grant of authority to subdue all the territory between the Atlantic and the River of Palms — practically the entire northern coast of the Gulf — and to establish at least two towns and two fortresses therein. He had some time before been sent to displace Cortés, but had been ignominiously put to defeat by the Mexican conqueror, so that he now was animated not only by the motive of gold-seeking but also by that of reputation-repairing. In an official document he styles himself in his new capacity "Governor of Florida, Rio de las Palmas, and Espíritu Santo" — all the territory as yet claimed by the Spaniards in North America, except Mexico. His expedition sailed out of the Guadalquivir, June 17, 1527, spent the following winter in southern Cuba, and on April 14, 1528, reached the American continent in the vicinity of Tampa Bay. It had been intended not to effect a landing until the Rio de las Palmas had been reached; but, by reason of the incompetence of the pilots, the voyagers were glad to seek respite from the sea by tarrying awhile in Cuba. The landing on the Florida coast was likewise unexpected, being occasioned by storms.

Directing his ships to meet him at the harbor of St. Mark's,[1] agreed upon by the pilots as a suitable anchorage, Narvaez, with three hundred men, struck into the interior of the country, May 1, 1528.[2] It was now for

---

[1] In Apalachee Bay. The knowledge of the pilots was of course very vague, being based wholly on hearsay. Buckingham Smith, *The Relation of Cabeza de Vaca*, Ch. V.

[2] For a recent account of the expedition of Narvaez, and also that of Cabeza de Vaca, which followed, see Woodbury Lowery's *The Spanish Settlements within the Present Limits of the United States*, 172–213 [Putnam, 1901]. See also Theodore Irving's *The Conquest of Florida*, Ch. II. — an older book — and Barnard Shipp's *Hernando de Soto and*

the first time that the lands north of the Gulf were traversed to any considerable distance by men of European origin. The journey westward through the virgin wilderness, as might be supposed, was not an easy one. The natives were treacherous, food was scarce, and fever disabled many of the men. "Toiling on through swamps and forests, wading the lagoons, crossing rivers by swimming and on temporary rafts, harassed continually by an enemy, with whom suddenness and secrecy of attack were the first arts of war, their courage and their hopes were only sustained by some vague reports from prisoners of gold to be found in a distant district called Apalache."[1] On the 25th of June, after nearly two months of marching, the town of Apalache was reached. It proved to be a mere hamlet of forty wretched huts, in the middle of a dense swamp, from which the Indians had fled, leaving behind only women and children. Nevertheless Narvaez's men "gave thanks to God," for in the village they found maize with which to appease their hunger, and in the neighborhood game was discovered to be abundant. The party remained in Apalache twenty-five days. During that time the Indians recovered from their fright and returned to attack the intruders and burn the wigwams in which they had taken shelter. Hostility developed so strongly that the Spaniards dared not wander any distance

---

Florida, Ch. VI. On the disputed question of the landing-place of Narvaez, see Appendix J. in Lowery. The proclamation issued at Tampa Bay by Narvaez in taking possession of the country for the crown of Castile is given in Lowery, 178-180. A most important original source of information on the whole subject is *The Relation of Cabeza de Vaca*, translated by Buckingham Smith, and published at New York in 1871.

[1] Gay, Bryant's *Popular History of the United States*, I. 153.

from the camp, lest they be shot down or captured for torture. Such exploration as could be risked soon demonstrated that the stories of gold were the sheerest hoax, and that, instead of being wealthy, the surrounding country was as poverty-stricken as any the adventurers had yet traversed.[1]

Impelled by disease, disappointment, and danger, the unfortunate company pressed on until it reached St. Mark's, on a bay which Narvaez styled Bahia de Caballos.[2] The fleet which had been instructed to advance to that point was nowhere to be found.[3] In this contingency there was manifestly but one thing to be done. Three months of bitter experience suggested strongly that a return into the wilderness would be equivalent to suicide. Another fleet must be constructed in which to escape from the pestilential country and reach the long-desired goal. The 250 men who survived set to work laboriously to build five rude boats in lieu of the much better ones they had lost. "They knew not how to construct, nor were there tools, nor iron, nor forge, nor tow, nor resin, nor rigging, nor any man who had a knowledge of their manufacture; and, above all, there was nothing to eat while building for those who should labor." But despair forced invention. Stirrups, spurs, and other iron

---

[1] Smith, *The Relation of Cabeza de Vaca*, Chs. VI. and VII.

[2] "Bay of Horses," because while building boats there the men lived chiefly on horse-flesh. Smith, *The Relation of Cabeza de Vaca*, Ch. VIII.

[3] The vessels had failed to find the harbor which the pilots had agreed with Narvaez to seek, and had returned to Tampa Bay. For nearly a year they continued to cruise along the Gulf coast, but without encountering the slightest trace of the land expedition.

articles were wrought into saws, axes, and nails. Pine resin was gathered for use as pitch. Seams were calked with the fibre of the palmetto. Cordage was manufactured from the tails and manes of the horses. The shirts of the men supplied material for sails. By killing their horses and catching shell-fish the toilers managed to subsist until they should be ready to put to sea, although forty died of disease and hunger, besides the many who were slain by the Indians.

September 22 the wretched survivors crowded into their five frail barks, and in them set out to complete the westward journey to the River of Palms. Lack of skill in seamanship, the necessity of landing frequently to obtain food and water, and the insubstantial character of their vessels compelled the voyagers to keep close to the shore. "Enduring always the extremity of suffering from cold, and wet, and hunger, they were buffeted when on the sea by storms, and repulsed by the Indians when they attempted a landing."[1] Their only hope was to reach the Spanish colony at Panuco. After more than a month's perilous voyaging, on the 30th of October, the little vessel commanded by Cabeza de Vaca sailed out into the placid waters of the easternmost mouth of the Mississippi. It was noted that the volume of water entering the Gulf was such that the current preserved its freshness for many miles out to sea, and the famished soldiers were delighted to find that a supply of drinking water was to be had without going on shore.[2] In the midst of a little group

---

[1] Gay, Bryant's *Popular History of the United States*, I. 155. Smith, *The Relation of Cabeza de Vaca*, Ch. IX.

[2] Smith, *The Relation of Cabeza de Vaca*, Ch. X.

of islands a league from the river's mouth the storm-beaten ships at length found secure anchorage.

One of the most serious needs which the voyagers had experienced was fuel with which to parch their corn. By reason of their fear of Indian attacks they had hitherto been prevented from remaining long enough on land to secure a supply, even if they had had means of transporting it, and it was now hoped that a short ascent of the river might be made and the desired fuel obtained. Several efforts in this direction, however, proved futile. A north wind was blowing, and the current of the stream was so strong that the vessels could make little headway. They succeeded only in getting within a mile and a half of land, where a sounding of thirty fathoms was made without touching bottom. Two days the men labored, only to find that they were but wasting their time and strength. Finally two of the five boats capsized, and all the men they carried, including Narvaez, were lost. The remaining vessels became separated, though all ended by putting out to sea again toward the west. Storms arose, and on the 6th of November Cabeza de Vaca's boat was driven ashore in the vicinity of Galveston Bay. At least one other of the three was wrecked at the time, and the fate of the remaining one, together with its crew, has ever since been in doubt. The almost incredible journey subsequently accomplished by Cabeza de Vaca and three companions, from the Texan coast to Culiacan on the Pacific, a distance of nearly two thousand miles, is one of the most striking incidents in all the history of exploration and adventure.[1]

---

[1] A detailed account of the great adventure is in Smith's translation of *The Relation of Cabeza de Vaca*, Ch. XV. *et seq.* A brief secondary

Thus the expedition of Narvaez resulted only in suffering and disaster, brought on largely by the rashness and ignorance with which it had been undertaken. Little or nothing was added by it to the Spaniards' geographical knowledge, except indirectly through the wanderings of Cabeza de Vaca. No gold had been found, nor any reliable traces of it. Nevertheless, the disappointments and sufferings of the explorers were but dimly understood in Europe, and the romance of discovery was even yet but slightly tarnished. The relation of Vaca's travels had only the effect of further stimulating Spanish zeal. If the continent was so very large, as Vaca had proved it to be, there manifestly remained yet vast unexplored regions, and in these regions must be the riches of which so many rumors had been heard. In 1537 Vaca returned to Spain, where he was welcomed as the "Columbus of the continent." The account of his adventures which he placed in the hands of the king naïvely implied that the lands north and west of the Gulf of Mexico were beyond compare the richest in the world.[1]

Within two years thereafter, Francisco Vasquez Coronado, with the largest band of Spanish adventurers yet mustered in America, was on his way from Culiacan northeastward into the very heart of the continent. After

---

account is in Lowery's *The Spanish Settlements within the Present Limits of the United States*, 198–212. An extract from Cabeza de Vaca's *Relation of the Journey to New Mexico* is reprinted in the *Old South Leaflets*, No. XXX. See Ad. F. Bandelier's "Alvar Nunez Cabeza de Vaca" in the *Magazine of Western History*, IV. 327–336.

[1] *Relation of the Invasion and Conquest of Florida by the Spaniards under the command of Fernando de Soto. Written in Portuguese by a Gentleman of the Town of Elvas*, Ch. II.

suffering the great disappointment of finding that the Seven Cities of Cibola, reported to abound in silver and gold, were really only little squalid villages built on the highlands, Coronado's party, in 1540–1541, pressed on probably as far as the region now known as Kansas. Several streams were discovered which were conjectured to flow into the Espíritu Santo. Perhaps not one of the explorers of the time was more ambitious or more persevering than was Coronado, and certainly no one conducted an expedition toward the interior with half the courage and ability. But of course the effort to open up a northern Peru was fruitless, and Coronado returned to Mexico only to be disgraced and deprived of his governorship of New Galicia.

Meanwhile, as a result of Cabeza de Vaca's tales a still greater undertaking was preparing. Hernando de Soto of Xeres, a companion of Pizarro in the conquest of Peru, having asked Charles V. for permission to conquer Florida at his own expense, had been appointed at the same time Governor of Cuba, Adelantado of Florida, and Marquis of certain parts of the lands to be conquered. Soto was exceedingly wealthy and was said to have "passed all other Captaines and principall persons" in bravery in the Peruvian expedition, from which he had but recently returned. "When he led in the van of battle," says an old chronicler of his exploits, "so powerful was his charge, so broad was the bloody passage which he carved out in the ranks of the enemy, that ten of his men-at-arms could with ease follow him abreast." He was a typical example of the ambitious adventurer who left Spain with nothing but blade and buckler, and re-

turned in a few years from America laden with riches and honors, and more ambitious than ever. When applying at court for his appointment he was careful to appear with a numerous band of followers and to make a lavish and impressive display of his wealth. Since it was a matter of common knowledge that his good fortune had come from participation in the conquest of America, the announcement of his new plans aroused widespread interest and excitement. The flower of Spanish chivalry gathered about him, eager to share in the new enterprise and have a part in its gains. The enthusiasm was raised to the highest pitch when it became known that Cabeza de Vaca had applied for Soto's position; for it was reasoned that Cabeza doubtless desired the post because he knew from observation the wealth of the countries in question. Six hundred Spaniards "in doublets and cassocks of silk, pinct and embroidered" and Portuguese "in the equippage of soldiers in neat armor"[1] were selected and carried to Cuba — "as high-born and well-trained men as ever went forth from Spain to win fame and fortune in the New World."[2] From Havana, May 1,

---

[1] *Relation of the Invasion and Conquest of Florida by the Spaniards under the Command of Fernando de Soto. Written in Portuguese by a Gentleman of the Town of Elvas.* This is the source from which our account of Soto's expedition has been mainly drawn. It was translated into English and printed at London in 1686. Another English version of this work is entitled "Virginia richly valued, by the Description of the Main Land of Florida her next Neighbor," translated by Richard Hakluyt and published in the *Force Tracts*, Vol. IV. 9–132. Hakluyt's translation of the narrative is printed also in B. F. French, *Historical Collections of Louisiana*, Part II. pp. 113–220. The name of the author will probably never be known.

[2] Winsor, *Narrative and Critical History of America*, II. 245.

1539, in a fleet of nine vessels, the adventurers set out for the land of their hopes. After a twelve days' sail they disembarked on the Florida coast, on a bay which was given the name Espíritu Santo.[1] Full of confidence in the success of the undertaking, Soto sent most of the ships back to Cuba, and with somewhat more than five hundred men, two or three hundred horses, and a number of bloodhounds, struck off toward the north through the wilderness.

The company numbered more men than had that of either Cortés or Pizarro, but no such good fortune awaited it. The march was but a melancholy repetition of that of Narvaez twelve years before.[2] Much excellent agricultural country was found, but it was not this that the Spaniards were seeking. As for gold, there was none — scarcely any longer even rumors of it. The Indians were generally hostile, always suspicious; and as food ran low Soto's men had to depend upon overawing and robbing

---

[1] Because it was discovered on the day of the Feast of Pentecost. Winsor, *Narrative and Critical History of America*, II. 245. For a discussion of the question of Soto's landing, see Mr. Buckingham Smith's paper "Espíritu Santo" appended to his *Letter of De Soto*," p. 51, Washington, 1854. Some have held that the landing was at Tampa Bay, *e.g.* H. H. Bancroft, *North Mexican States*, I. 600.

[2] The details of it are carefully stated in *The Relation of the Gentleman of Elvas*, Ch. VIII. *et seq.* For general accounts see Lowery, *The Spanish Settlements within the Present Limits of the United States*, Ch. IV.; Grace King, *De Soto and his Men in the Land of Florida*; Barnard Shipp, *De Soto and Florida*; Theodore Irving, *The Conquest of Florida*; Lambert A. Wilmer, *The Life, Travels, and Adventures of Ferdinand de Soto*; Albert J. Pickett, *Invasion of the Territory of Alabama by One Thousand Spaniards under Ferdinand de Soto*; and John W. Monette, *History of the Discovery and Settlement of the Valley of the Mississippi*, I. 10–64.

the natives for subsistence. The treatment accorded the Indians by the Spaniards was almost unspeakably cruel and treacherous. The barbarism of the invaders was scarcely a whit surpassed by that of the natives. One Indian guide was burned alive because he indiscreetly declared he knew of no country where gold was abundant; another had to have "a gospell said over him" at frequent intervals to prevent his feigning madness and running away. At each town which the explorers visited Soto demanded of the cacique, or head chief, maize for his men and horses, and Indians to carry baggage and do the menial work of the camp. Usually the chief was compelled to accompany the expedition until the next town was reached, when he might return. Most of those who were given to the Spaniards as temporary servants became permanent slaves.

The first few weeks' march, through the present states of Florida, Georgia, and Alabama, were sufficient to reveal to the adventurers the perils which they might expect from hunger, disease, and attacks by the natives.[1] At Caliquen, in the hope of rescuing a captured cacique, the Indians made a desperate onslaught on the Spanish camp. They failed in their purpose, but set an example which other similarly afflicted tribes were not slow to emulate. So tedious was the march that it was not until the last of October that the Apalache country was reached, where a side expedition sent under Añasco discovered the spot where Narvaez's men more than a decade before had built their little fleet. The winter of 1539–1540 was spent in

[1] On Soto's route through Georgia, see Jones, *History of Georgia*, Ch. II.; through Alabama, Pickett, *History of Alabama*, I. Ch. I.

camp not far from the harbor of St. Mark's. Early the next spring the march was resumed toward the northeast. The perilous wanderings, endless encounters with the natives, disappointments, and sufferings, which their travels brought the party throughout the summer of 1540 would be wearisome to relate. At last, late in October, a descent of the Alabama brought the wanderers to the junction of that river with the Tombigbee, near Mobile Bay. There all the pent-up fury of the Indians broke afresh upon the intruders, culminating in the battle of Mavila,[1] which has been well characterized as one of the bloodiest ever fought on our soil between white and red men in the early days.[2] Mavila was an Indian village of considerable size and, being well palisaded, the natives believed it capable of being defended against the Spaniards. Accordingly when Soto and his attendants entered it in their accustomed lordly manner, they were given a haughty reception. As soon as one of the visitors resented this by striking a native with his cutlass, the battle was on. Five of the invaders were killed in attempting to escape from the town. Led by Soto, the main body of the Spaniards, who had remained outside the palisade, assaulted the town with sword in one hand and torch in the other. Soon the houses were in flames, and the battle was turned to a slaughter of the escaping Indians. Esti-

---

[1] The river and city of Mobile take their name from this Indian village. The exact location of Mavila is in dispute. It was probably on the Alabama River at what is now called Choctaw Bluff, in Clarke County.

[2] Winsor, *Narrative and Critical History of America*, II. 249. For a good brief account of the battle of Mavila, see Peter J. Hamilton, *Colonial Mobile*, Ch. III. The original account is in *The Relation of the Gentleman of Elvas*, Chs. XVIII.-XX.

mates vary, but it seems that as many as 6000 Indians perished, while the loss of the Spaniards was very considerable — about eighty-two killed and every survivor more or less wounded.[1] One early writer tells us that at nightfall only three Indians remained alive, two of whom were soon killed fighting; the last hung himself from a tree in the palisade with his bowstring.[2]

The proximity of Pensacola harbor was now made known to Soto, but though his vessels were already awaiting him there, he was not ready to return, or even to send back a report. Fearing mutiny, he was careful to conceal from his followers the opportunity which they now had to escape from the wilderness. Yet undaunted and unconvinced, he set off from Mavila toward the northwest into the valley of the Yazoo, in the northern part of Mississippi, where the winter of 1540–1541 was spent. Food was plentiful, but the discontent of the soldiers was such that only a man of Soto's domineering energy could have held them from deserting the enterprise. Late in April, after a disastrous renewal of hostilities on part of the Indians, the march was resumed toward the northwest diagonally across the present state of Mississippi to about the thirty-fifth parallel — the boundary line between the

[1] Hamilton, *Colonial Mobile*, 16. Shea, following Biedma, says that only twenty Spaniards were killed; Winsor, *Narrative and Critical History of America*, II. 249.

[2] Luys Hernandez de Biedma, *Relación del suceso de la jornado que hizo Hernando de Soto*. Quoted in Winsor, *Narrative and Critical History of America*, II. 249. A copy of the original Spanish manuscript of this chronicle is in the Lenox Library at New York. The work was published by Buckingham Smith in 1857 from the original manuscript in the Archivo General de Indias at Seville. It may be found in French, *Historical Collections of Louisiana*, Part II. pp. 97–109.

states of Mississippi and Tennessee. Seven days sufficed to bring the Spaniards to the banks of the greatest river they had ever seen — the Mississippi, or, as Soto's men called it, the Rio Grande (Great River). The stream was described as "half a league over, so that a man could not be distinguished from one side to the other; it was very deep and very rapid, and being always full of trees and timber that was carried down by the force of the stream, the water was thick and very muddy. It abounded with fish, most of which differed much from those that are taken in the rivers of Spain."[1]

The Indians in the vicinity seem to have been moved more by curiosity than hostility in their treatment of the visitors. The inhabitants of one village were so terrified by a rumor that Soto intended to attack them that they gathered all their portable belongings and withdrew to the other side of the river. At length the Spaniards made their way down the east bank of the stream to the lowest Chickasaw landing, a little below the thirty-fifth parallel, where they made ready for the crossing.[2] Nearly a month's delay was occasioned by the fact that the Indians had no boats strong enough to transport horses, so that the Spaniards had to construct barges for the purpose. While engaged in this work they were frequently visited by the curious natives, and Aquixo, the leading potentate in the lands across the river, undertook with all the barbaric splendor he could command to produce upon the

[1] *Relation of the Gentleman of Elvas*, 112. See Buckingham Smith, *De Soto*, 101-105 and 249-250.

[2] This is the point generally agreed on by students of the subject, though some writers have adopted other theories. See Winsor, *Narrative and Critical History*, II. 292.

strangers a lasting impression of his dignity and power. "A multitude of people from the western banks of the river," says Bancroft, in describing the scene, "painted and gaily decorated with great plumes of white feathers, the warriors standing in rows with bows and arrows in their hands, the chieftains sitting under awnings as magnificent as the artless manufactures of the natives could weave, came rowing down the stream in a fleet of two hundred canoes, seeming to the admiring Spaniards like 'a fair army of galleys.'"[1] The great cacique, Aquixo, who came with this spectacular expedition, carried gifts of fish and fruits and bread, and professed the heartiest friendship for the Spaniards; but the latter deemed his motives to be only those of treachery, and slew all of his followers who sought to effect a landing. By their uniform cruelty toward the natives, as on this occasion, the Spaniards persistently defeated their own ends, and added to their already too numerous difficulties the most ruinous of them all.

After crossing the river Soto turned northward toward New Madrid. Progress was at first very difficult on account of the forests and wet bottom lands, but in a few days higher ground was reached and the expedition paused to recuperate. The Spaniards were here given the unusual experience of being welcomed and worshipped by the natives as children of the sun. And when Soto set up a cross on one of the little artificial hills on which the caciques were accustomed to build their houses,[2] they

---

[1] Bancroft, *History of the United States* (Centenary ed.), I. 46–47. Smith, *The Relation of the Gentleman of Elvas*, Ch. XXII.

[2] "The caciques of this country make a custom of raising, near their

brought to him two blind men to be healed. Instead of the desired healing, a sermon was preached to them in which they were admonished to "demand of the Lord who was in Heaven all that they might stand in need of." History does not record in what measure the blind men were able to appreciate this homily as a substitute for the expected restoration of sight. There does not seem to have been any general disappointment, however, as we learn that a few days later a chieftain of the vicinity manifested his good will by selling his two sisters to Soto for wives at the goodly price of a shirt apiece.

The most northerly point reached by the explorers seems to have been Pacaha, which unfortunately cannot now be identified, but was probably not far south of the mouth of the Ohio. The reconnoitring party sent out in this direction brought back a report that the country was but very sparsely inhabited, but that it fairly swarmed with herds of bison, whose robes "were very convenient against the cold of that country because they made a good furr, the hair of them being as soft as sheep's wool."[1] After forty days the march was resumed toward the northwest, and subsequently toward the south. Just when Soto's men were at the northernmost limit of their journeying, in the summer of 1541, they must have been so near the party of Coronado that, as a recent writer has suggested, an Indian

---

dwellings, very high hills, on which they sometimes build their huts. On one of these we planted the cross, and went with much devotion on our knees to kiss the foot of it." Biedma, *Narrative of the Expedition of Hernando de Soto*; in French, *Historical Collections of Louisiana*, Part II. p. 105. These hills were doubtless the "mounds" built by the earlier natives.

[1] Smith, *The Relation of the Gentleman of Elvas*, 115 et seq.

runner in a few days might have carried tidings between them. Coronado actually heard of Soto's proximity, and sent a letter of greeting which, however, failed to reach its destination.[1]

Advancing in a generally southerly direction through a fertile, well-watered, and thickly populated country, the wanderers at length emerged from the forests near the site of modern Little Rock in Arkansas. The winter of 1541–1542 was spent probably in the valley of the Washita, some two hundred miles west from the Mississippi. The winter was long and severe, and the sufferings of the Spaniards were intense. During the three years which had elapsed since the landing at Espíritu Santo 250 of Soto's followers had perished, and 150 horses. Even the dauntless leader was forced at last to acknowledge that the expedition was a failure. Disappointment and chagrin took the place of courage and hope. Gold-hunting was forgotten; escape from the wilderness became the one purpose.

Early in March, 1542, the party advanced down the Washita in the hope of reaching the sea, where boats might be constructed, after the plan of Narvaez, and a return to Cuba thus made possible. The marshes and bayous of the Red River were soon encountered, after which it was only with the greatest difficulty that the Spaniards could make any progress. At length, on Sunday, April 17, 1542, they emerged on the banks of the Mississippi at the point where the Red joins the larger stream. The distance to the mouth of the Mississippi was anxiously inquired of the natives, but not one of them

[1] Winsor, *Narrative and Critical History of America*, II. 292.

could tell. Evidently, thought the Spaniards, it must be considerable. The chief of the surrounding province, which bore the name of Guachoya, declared that the lower banks of the river were only an uninhabited waste. In the hope that this might not be true, Soto despatched a company of nine men to descend the river and bring back a report of the character of its lower course. After spending eight days in advancing little more than thirty miles, they returned with the disheartening information that the bayous, marshes, and dense woods almost precluded the possibility of land travel in that direction.[1]

The situation was precarious. The men were fast falling sick by reason of the climate, food was scarce, the way of escape was unknown, and the Indian chief to whom the "children of the sun" applied for aid astutely imposed as a condition of giving it that Soto prove his divine origin by drying up the river. The outcome may be fitly told in the words of the Gentleman of Elvas, who was a member of the unfortunate expedition. "The Gouvernor," he says, "fell into great dumps to see how hard it was to get to the sea; and worse, because his men and horses were every day diminished, being without succour to sustaine themselves in the country: and with that thought he fell sick . . . being euill handled with fevers, and was much aggrieved, that he was not in case to passe presently the River and to seeke him, to see if he could abate that pride of his, considering the River went now very strongly in those parts ; for it was neare half a league broad, and sixteen fathoms deep, and very furious, and ranne with a great current; and on both sides there were many Indians

[1] Smith, *The Relation of the Gentleman of Elvas*, Ch. XXVIII.

and his power was not now so great, but that hee had
neede to helpe himselfe rather by flights than by force."[1]

A malignant fever hastened the end. ". . . the 21
of May," continues our chronicler, "departed out of this
life, the valorous, virtuous, and valiant Captaine, Don
Fernando de Soto, Gouvernour of Cuba, and Adelantado
of Florida: whom fortune advanced as it vseth to doe
others, that he might have the higher fal. He departed
in such a place, and at such a time, as in his sicknesse he
had but little comfort: and the danger wherein all his
people were of perishing in that Countrie, which appeared
before their eyes was cause sufficient, why euery one of
them had need of comfort, and why they did not visit nor
accompanie him as they ought to have done."[2]

At the time of the death of their leader the party was
still near the mouth of the Red. Soto's body was buried
first in the ground in the gateway of the camp; but as
some Indians were observed to contemplate the freshly
turned earth and exchange signs with one another, and as
the Spaniards wished to keep up as long as possible the illusion of their own divine, and hence immortal, nature, the
body was taken from the grave, and at midnight silently
committed to the waters of the great river.[3] The curious

---

[1] "Virginia richly valued, by the Description of the Main Land of
Florida, her next Neighbor," etc., in Richard Hakluyt, *The Principall
Voyages, Navigations, Traffiques, and Discoveries, of the English Nation*
(London, 1609), II. 1–131 *passim*. Quoted in Albert Bushnell Hart,
American History Told by Contemporaries, I. 59. Or, Smith, *The Relation of the Gentleman of Elvas*, Ch. XXX.

[2] Smith, *The Relation of the Gentleman of Elvas*, 157. Reprint from
the *Relation* in the *Old South Leaflets*, No. XXXVI.

[3] "Assoone as he was dead, Luis de Moscoso commanded to put him
secretly in an house, where hee remained three daies: and remoouing

Indians were told that the lord for whom they inquired had "ascended into the skies for a little while" and would "soon be back."

Before his death Soto, at the solicitation of his followers, had designated his successor. The choice had fallen upon Luis de Moscoso, and all the soldiers had taken a solemn oath to obey him. Soto's lingering pride and ambition having been put to rest, the question was now even more than before simply one of escape. Thinking that on the whole travelling by land was safer than by the river, the party made an extensive detour through the region of Arkansas, harassed as ever by hunger, fevers, and treachery of the natives. After wearing themselves out by marching and countermarching in the deep forests, they determined to return to the Mississippi and follow its current as the only sure means of reaching the sea. After a journey characterized by almost untold hardship, they once more stood upon the banks of the great river, in December, 1542, at Minoya, a few miles above the mouth of the Arkansas. They were now considerably farther from the sea than they had been at the time of Soto's death.

Amid frequent attacks from the natives, and with

him from thence, commanded him to bee buried in the night at one of the gates of the towne within the wall. And as the Indians had seene him sick, and missed him, so did they suspect what might bee. And passing by the place where hee was buried, seeing the earth mooved, they looked and spake one to another. Luys de Moscoso vnderstanding of it, commanded him to bee taken vp by night, and to cast a greate deale of sand into the mantles, wherein hee was winded up, wherein hee was carried in a canoe, and throwne into the middest of the riuer. . . ." *The Gentleman of Elvas*, Hakluyt's translation, as before, *Force Tracts*, IV. 97.

malarial diseases threatening to exterminate the entire company, Moscoso's men set to work to construct boats in which to make the journey to the Gulf. Owing to the scarcity of materials and the crudeness of their tools, the work was very tedious and wearisome. The horses had to be killed and their flesh dried to provide food. The few poverty-stricken Indians of the neighborhood were robbed of the scanty provisions they had, so that many of them died of starvation. At last seven small barges were completed for the carrying of the 372 men who remained.[1] The craft were necessarily very frail, and a heavy wind must have capsized them. But fortunately the weather continued favorable after the embarkation, July 2, 1543, and the trip to the Gulf — a distance of about five hundred miles — was successfully accomplished in just seventeen days.

No time was to be lost, because food was running very low and the Indians were increasingly hostile. As soon, therefore, as the Gulf was reached the voyagers turned westward, travelling at such speed as they could and keeping generally within sight of the shore line. Fifty days' sailing brought the survivors — now reduced to 311 — to a place of security, and on the 10th of September the seven weather-worn barks were steered into the mouth of the hospitable Panuco River. Six days afterward the exhausted sailors were in the Spanish settlement at Tampico. "Haggard, gaunt, half-naked, having only a scanty covering of skins, looking more like wild beasts than men, they kissed the ground when they landed among their countrymen, and on bended

[1] Smith, *The Relation of the Gentleman of Elvas*, Ch. XXXV.

knees, with hands raised above them, and their eyes to heaven, remained untiring in giving thanks to God."[1]

After Soto's expedition Spanish exploring enterprise languished. More than two hundred years elapsed before we hear of any further attempt on part of the Spanish government to possess the region about the Mississippi. During the next two or three decades after Soto there were a few expeditions undertaken by private individuals for the exploration of Florida, but without exception their ending was disastrous. For very many decades the Mississippi country continued untrodden by the Spaniard. Successive failures to find the coveted gold on the northern shores of the Gulf led to the centring of attention almost exclusively on the countries farther south where it had been repeatedly demonstrated that the precious metals did exist. Already, too, the Spanish nation was entering upon its long and fatal decline. Greed for wealth without labor, absolutism in government, and bigotry and intolerance in religion were crushing out the best part of Spanish life and energy. Those who had grown rich by plunder in America returned to Spain to waste their ill-gotten treasure in extravagant living. Of the rest of the people, those who were best fitted to perpetuate Spanish glory and achievement were systematically persecuted on religious or political grounds, and rendered wholly incapable of service to the state. By the end of the sixteenth century the era of Ponce de Leon and Narvaez, of Coronado and Soto, had passed completely.

---

[1] Gay, Bryant's *Popular History of the United States*, I. 170; Smith, *The Relation of the Gentleman of Elvas*, Chs. XLI. and XLII.

THE SPANISH DISCOVERY OF THE MISSISSIPPI

After all has been said, there remains considerable difference of opinion as to who of the Spaniards is most properly to be considered the discoverer of the Mississippi. Some look upon Pineda's possible visit to the river's mouth in 1519 as amounting to a discovery. Others, accepting the story of Cabeza de Vaca that in the course of his wanderings, on the 30th of October, 1528, he crossed one of its mouths, deem the honor of the discovery to belong to this famous adventurer.[1] And perhaps a greater number of people, if asked who discovered the Mississippi, would reply by the name of Soto.

In a very real sense the discovery of the Mississippi River, just as that of the American continent, can be regarded as progressive, so that all these explorers, and quite a number more, had more or less part in it. It may be that Pineda was the first to see the waters of the great river, but if so he comprehended not at all the vast extent of the stream and its drainage system. There can be no doubt that both Narvaez and Cabeza de Vaca were at the Mississippi's mouth, but there is no evidence that they had any appreciation of its importance. Unquestionably it was Soto who first explored the river's banks to any considerable distance, and it must have been by him and his men that the first approach toward an

---

[1] Mr. Buckingham Smith spent much time in the study of Cabeza de Vaca's wanderings, and was convinced that not only was this story true, but that Vaca had also crossed the river much farther north. At one time Mr. Smith thought the passage of the Mississippi to have occurred as far north as the southern boundary of Tennessee, but in later writings he tracked the traveller nearer the Gulf. See Winsor, *Narrative and Critical History of America*, II. 287.

adequate conception of the magnitude and importance of the Mississippi was made. As has been said, for more than two centuries nothing further was learned by the Spaniards concerning the river, so that such knowledge as they possessed of it must have been lost except for the dust-covered narratives of the Gentleman of Elvas and his contemporaries. The opening of the Mississippi to the knowledge and use of the world remained to be accomplished by another people, the French, who in turn were to give way to still another before the valley of the "great water" should be occupied and utilized. Nevertheless the Spaniard had yet much to do in shaping the history of the Mississippi before the final triumph of the Anglo-Saxon in the Middle West.

CHAPTER III

THE SEARCH OF THE FRENCH FOR THE MISSISSIPPI

EXCEPT as a basis for subsequent territorial claims, the discovery of the Mississippi by the Spaniards might as well never have occurred. The Spaniard came to the Mississippi country for gold, and, not finding it, withdrew in ill-concealed disgust. The primeval wilderness which had been the scene of his eager search, his perilous adventures, and his crushing disappointments, was left without any other memorial of him than new-made graves and here and there a wooden cross or a forgotten utensil. The whole work of discovery had to be wrought out anew nearly a century and a half later, and this time by the efforts of a different people and from an entirely different direction. The glory of revealing to the world the nature and extent of the Mississippi and its great drainage system remained for the fur-trader and missionary from New France. The Spaniards had never consciously searched for the river and had almost no appreciation of its value when they did happen to stumble upon it. The French, on the other hand, sought the Mississippi in a large measure for its own sake, being drawn thither by a desire for more extended trade routes and better facilities for the carrying of the gospel to the remoter Indian tribes. The story of the French discovery of the Mississippi is therefore the story of a persevering search which was finally rewarded by the attainment of its object, and not that of a series of accidents, as in the case of the Spanish discovery.

The search for the Mississippi may be said to have been begun by the French about the year 1634. In that year the enterprising explorer of the St. Lawrence, Samuel de Champlain, desiring to prove whether a western passage to the "Sea of China" might not be discovered by way of the upper Ottawa, despatched an intrepid adventurer by the name of Jean Nicolet on a westward journey whose ultimate goal, if all things went well, was to be the "great salt sea" between America and Asia. Stories were current among the Indians to the effect that far to the west there was a hairless and beardless people who travelled in enormous canoes, and who had come into their present habitations from a land bordering on a great body of water that was not fresh. Champlain was curious to know what foundation there might be for such rumors, and whether profitable trade routes might be opened up for the French in this direction. Nicolet had been in America since 1618, and under the guidance of Champlain had spent most of his time among the Ottawas and Nipissings, acquainting himself with the Indian language and character.[1] He was therefore eminently prepared, not merely by his qualities of endurance and hardihood, but also by his familiarity with the speech and mode of life of the natives, to undertake just such a mission as Champlain had in mind.

---

[1] Benjamin Sulte, *Mélanges d'Histoire et de Littérature*, 426, 436 (Ottawa, 1876). R. G. Thwaites [editor], *The Jesuit Relations and Allied Documents*, VIII. 295-296.

Starting from Three Rivers, on the upper St. Lawrence, probably about the first of July, 1634,[1] Nicolet ascended the Ottawa, and journeyed on by way of Lake Nipissing and the Georgian Bay into the Huron country where seven Indians were secured as guides. In the expectation of coming among Orientals, and with the purpose not to appear too foreign when he should arrive there, the thoughtful traveller had taken care to include in his supplies a Chinese gown of damask, "all strewn," according to the chronicler, "with flowers and birds of many colors."[2] After traversing the eastern and northern shores of Lake Huron, Nicolet's party at length arrived at Sault Ste. Marie at the southeastern extremity of Lake Superior, a

---

[1] The date has been in doubt, but Sulte, in his "Notes on Jean Nicolet" (printed in the *Collections of the Wisconsin Historical Society*, VIII. 188-194), seems to have established at least the reasonableness of the view that Nicolet left Three Rivers in the company of Brebeuf and Daniel, two priests who are known to have started for their missions July 1, 1634. Earlier writers, and some less scholarly ones to-day, assign Nicolet's expedition to 1639. Even John Fiske does this (*The Discovery of America*, II. 532). See the account by Barthélemy Vimont in the *Jesuit Relations* (1642-1643), XXIII. 275-279; also C. W. Butterfield's monograph, *The History of the Discovery of the Northwest by John Nicolet* [Cincinnati, 1881]. In addition to these works the following may be referred to for general discussions of the Nicolet expedition: J. V. Brower, "The Mississippi River and its Source," *Minnesota Historical Collections*, VII. 40-46; Henri Jonan, "Jean Nicolet" (trans. by Grace Clark) in *Wisconsin Historical Collections*, XI. 1-22; and Benjamin Sulte, "Les Interprètes du temps de Champlain," in *Memoirs of the Royal Society of Canada*, 1883. In the *Wisconsin Historical Collections*, XI. 23-25, is an excellent Nicolet bibliography prepared by C. W. Butterfield. A brief, popular account is in Thwaites, *Story of Wisconsin*, Ch. I.

[2] This is the conjectural explanation of Parkman, *La Salle and the Discovery of the Great West*, p. xxiv. It may be that Nicolet had no such romantic idea, but expected merely to appeal with his robe to the Indian's love of finery.

point beyond the furthest reach of previous exploration. Turning again toward the south the travellers followed the coast of the northern peninsula of Michigan as far as the Straits of Mackinaw. This latter point is indeed one of the most strategic in all the interior of the American continent;[1] but Nicolet and his men did not appreciate it as such because Lake Erie was not then known to exist, and the all-water route from the interior to the Gulf of St. Lawrence was still a matter of the sheerest speculation.

From Mackinaw Nicolet continued to skirt the shore of Lake Michigan until he had reached the southern extremity of Green Bay. There he encountered the friendly Winnebagoes and, dressed in his gaudy Chinese robe, which served excellently to inspire admiration, gave them their first exhibition of fire-arms. We may well believe the effect to have been startling. Says a contemporary chronicler: "No sooner did they perceive him than the women and children fled, at the sight of a man who carried thunder in both hands, — for thus they called the two pistols that he held. The news of his coming quickly spread to the places round about, and there assembled four or five thousand men. Each of the chief men made a feast for him, and at one of these banquets they served at least six score beavers."[2] The Winnebagoes, being of

---

[1] R. G. Thwaites, "The Story of Mackinac," *Wisconsin Historical Collections*, XIV. 1–16; Van Fleet, *Old and New Mackinac*, Ann Arbor, 1870.

[2] Barthélemy Vimont, *Relation . . . en l'année MDCXL.* (Vols. XVII.–XX. in Thwaites's edition). Vimont succeeded Le Jeune as Superior of the Jesuit Order in New France in 1639. Although his name appears on the title-page of the *Relation* for 1640, it is probable that he

the Dacotah stock, spoke a language unintelligible to Nicolet, but when he ascended the Fox River to the country of the Algonquin Mascotins (in the region of Green Lake County, Wisconsin) he found once more a people whose speech he readily understood. From them he learned many things of interest. Most important was the information that off toward the south, a three days' journey, was a "great water" which might be reached by ascending the Fox still farther, crossing a short portage, and then descending a stream tributary to the "great water." The manner in which the Indians spoke of the "great water" conveyed the impression that it was a sea rather than a river; and forty years more were to elapse before the Fox-Wisconsin route was to be traversed, and the real character of the "great water"—which was of course the Mississippi—made known.

We cannot tell definitely why Nicolet did not attempt to make the passage. Perhaps he felt that in learning authoritatively, as he thought, of the close proximity of the sea, he had accomplished the work which his master had given him to do. After visiting the country of the Illinois tribe to the southward, he returned down Green Bay, receiving friendly attention from the Pottawattomies on the western shore of Lake Michigan, passed again through the Huron country, joined the usual summer trading expedition down the Ottawa, and reached Three Rivers in July, 1635, after an absence of almost precisely one year. He was rewarded by being made commissioner and interpreter at Three Rivers, but his achieve-

merely edited the volume and transmitted it to Paris for publication. See Thwaites, *Jesuit Relations*, XVIII. 2..

ments fell far short of being appreciated at their full importance. Champlain died in the year of Nicolet's return, and for a long time to come there was no man of like energy in control of French exploring enterprises in America. Had Champlain lived, Nicolet's exploration would doubtless have been followed up at once, and the Mississippi might well have been discovered within very few years. But as it was, five years elapsed before even an account of the expedition was embodied in the records of the Jesuits.[1] Scientific interest perished for a time with Champlain. The Mississippi remained merely the rumored "great water," understood by the French to be nothing more or less than the sea intervening between America and the Chinese coast.[2]

Missionary spirit, however, remained to impel westward movements. In 1641 Fathers Raymbault and Jogues visited the Indians in the vicinity of Sault Ste. Marie at the eastern outlet of Lake Superior, and preached to audiences numbering two thousand or more. Ten times as many redskins were then at the Sault as usual, because the Pottawattomies had fled thither from their more southerly homes, which were being overrun by wandering bands of Iroquois. The priests heard numerous rumors of a great body of water off to the west and of an exceedingly vigorous people — the Sioux of later

[1] In the volume for 1640, whose title-page bears the name of Barthélemy Vimont. Winsor, *Narrative and Critical History of America*, IV. 302.

[2] Nicolet himself was drowned in the St. Lawrence in 1642 while returning from an errand of mercy to Quebec. Thwaites, *Jesuit Relations*, XXIII. 275.

times — dwelling upon its banks. Raymbault died at the Sault,[1] having, as Vimont says in his *Relation*, "had his path diverted from China to heaven." In August, 1642, Father Jogues was captured by the Mohawk tribe of Iroquois, along with twelve canoes of Hurons, and carried away to the region of Lake Champlain to endure a year of captivity.[2] The mission at Sault Ste. Marie lingered on, but the ravages of the Iroquois prevented communication between it and the eastern settlements for several years.

In 1649 the entire tribe of Hurons was dispersed by the advance of the hostile Iroquois.[3] Many of the refugees wandered westward into the Green Bay district, and even as far as the Mississippi. For a time the Iroquois war rendered exploring enterprises quite out of the question and the work of the missionaries extremely precarious. "One by one," says a recent writer, "the Jesuit missions in the Huron country succumbed to the onslaughts of the dreaded foes. St. Joseph, St. Ignace, Ste. Marie, all fell to rise again beyond Lake Huron; and by the middle of the seventeenth century

---

[1] Thwaites, *Jesuit Relations*, XXIII. 273. This is Winsor's view, *Cartier Frontenac*, 160. Mr. Charles Moore, in his *Northwest under Three Flags*, 8, asserts Raymbault's death to have occurred at Quebec.

[2] Jogues was rescued by the Dutch in 1643. He was sent to France, but returned to America a year later, only to become a martyr in the Iroquois-Huron war in 1647. Father Jogues's account of his experiences among the Iroquois may be found in the *Collections of the New York Historical Society*, Second Series, III. Part I. 173 *et seq*. An interesting extract is in Hart, *American History Told by Contemporaries*, I. No. 40. Parkman, *The Jesuits in North America*, Ch. XVI.

[3] See the graphic account of this movement in Parkman, *The Jesuits in North America*, Ch. XXVII.

all that great stretch of country from the St. Lawrence to the Straits of Mackinaw was debatable territory, traversed alike by white man and red only at the constant risk of ambush and battle."[1] But since the work of the Jesuits had been most successful among the Hurons, this movement had not a little to do ultimately with enticing the missionaries into the remote West, in order to follow up their unfortunate converts and at the same time spread the Christian religion in parts hitherto unknown.[2]

By the middle of the century fresh rumors were afloat, based on the tales of the Indians, concerning the "great water" in the West. The *Jesuit Relation* of 1654 speaks of the sea separating America from China as being only a nine days' journey from Green Bay. Likewise it was reported that the sea was very narrow and easy of passage. Many stories were current which seemed to confirm this idea. Among them was that of a Jesuit missionary, Father Grelon, who, after serving at a mission on Lake Huron, had been stationed in Chinese Tartary and had there encountered a woman who had belonged to his congregation in Canada. The accepted explanation was that she had been sold from tribe to tribe until she had passed from America into Asia — a consummation which certainly strengthened the theory that the two continents were quite near each other.

---

[1] Moore, *The Northwest under Three Flags*, 8.

[2] "On the Condition of the Huron Nation, and of its Latest Defeat by the Iroquois," Thwaites, *Jesuit Relations*, XLV. (1659-1660), 241-261. The handful of Wyandots, now in Kansas, is all that remains of the great Huron tribe. Parkman, *The Jesuits in North America*, Ch. XXXII.

Once again the spirit of adventure was stirred, and scientific and commercial interests came to the reënforcement of religious zeal. In August, 1654, two French traders penetrated the region west of Lake Michigan, returning two years later with a goodly stock of furs and an abundance of stories regarding the geography of the West. It is conjectured that these two men were Medard Chouart, Sieur de Grosseilliers, and Pierre d'Esprit Radisson, who at any rate are known a little later to have engaged in similar undertakings.[1] In 1656 a party of thirty Frenchmen set out for Lake Superior, but found the trip impracticable owing to the hostility of the Iroquois.

In 1658-1659 Grosseilliers spent several months trading and exploring on the shores of Lake Superior. The Sioux Indians, among whom he lived, told him of a great river some distance south whose valley their own people occupied. In the spring of 1659 Grosseilliers returned to the St. Lawrence, whence he, together with his brother-in-law Radisson and a number of Huron guides, started off again within a few weeks for Lake Superior. They explored the southern shore of the lake as far west as La Pointe — the site of the present city of Ashland. "They were fortunate enough," says the *Relation* of 1659-1660, "to baptize there two hundred little children of the Algonquin nation, with whom they first made their abode. These children were the victims of disease and famine; and forty went straight to heaven, dying

---

[1] This is Sulte's view, supported by Winsor, *Cartier to Frontenac*, 183. For adverse arguments see Henry C. Campbell, "Radisson and Grosseilliers," in *American Historical Review*, V. 226-237.

soon after baptism."[1] During the winter season the two Frenchmen made many excursions among the surrounding tribes, finding among others a remnant of the Hurons, who had been compelled to bury themselves in the forests beyond the reach of Iroquois fury. "These poor people," says the *Relation*, "fleeing and pushing their way over mountains and rocks, through these vast, unknown forests, fortunately encountered a beautiful river, large, wide, deep, and worthy of comparison, they say, with our great river St. Lawrence."[2]

The latter part of the explorers' travels is involved in much doubt. "We weare," says Radisson, "4 moneths in our voyage wthout doeing any thing but goe from river to river. We mett severall sorts of people. We conversed wth them. By the persuasion of some of them we went into ye great river that divides itself in 2, where the hurrons [Hurons] wth some Ottanake and the wild men (Indians) that had warrs wth them had retired. There is not great difference in their language as we weare told. This nation have warrs against those of forked river. It is so called because it has 2 branches, the one towards the west, the other towards the south, which, we believe, runns towards Mexico, by the tokens they gave us."[3] The identity of these rivers is uncertain. It is difficult to make the description apply in any

---

[1] Thwaites, *Jesuit Relations*, XLV. 235.

[2] *Ibid.*, XLV. 235.

[3] *Voyages of Peter Esprit Radisson, being an Account of his Travels and Experiences among the North American Indians from 1652 to 1684*, pp. 167–168. Transcribed from the original manuscripts in the Bodleian Library and the British Museum. Published by the Prince Society, Boston, 1885.

way to the Mississippi unless, as John Fiske suggests, the rivers meant were the Mississippi and the Missouri.[1] This would involve conceding that Radisson and Grosseilliers were the discoverers of the Mississippi — a conclusion far from being accepted by most students of the subject. Some have even gone so far as to maintain that Radisson's account is a pure fabrication.[2] This seems quite unwarranted, though we must suppose it to be as full of errors as it is of incongruities. A manuscript prepared merely from memory and occasional hasty notes, as it was, could hardly be otherwise. On the whole, it is safest to conclude that the travellers encountered only some of the eastern tributaries of the Mississippi. While they must have been at no great distance from the main stream, their narrative could hardly have left so much doubt about the matter if they had really seen it. At any rate, we know that after leaving the "Forked" River, the explorers traversed the entire region about the western end of Lake Superior, and that they heard from the natives many things which tended strongly to confirm their belief that the China Sea was not far distant.

[1] John Fiske, *New France and New England*, 101. Gideon D. Scull, in his introduction to the Prince Society edition of the *Voyages*, declares it a fact that "during the third voyage Radisson and his brother-in-law went to the Mississippi River in 1658-1659." One's opinion on the question will be determined almost wholly by his interpretation of Radisson's obscure language.

[2] H. C. Campbell, "Radisson and Grosseilliers," *American Historical Review*, V. 226-237. R. G. Thwaites, "The Third Voyage of Radisson," *Wisconsin Historical Collections*, XI. 66, accepts the theory of Radisson's discovery of the Mississippi. See Mr. Campbell's illuminating paper on "Radisson's Journal: its Value in History," in *Proceedings of the State Historical Society of Wisconsin at its Forty-third Annual Meeting*, held December 12, 1895.

In the summer of 1660 they returned to Three Rivers with a flotilla of sixty canoes laden with furs.[1]

In August of the same year Grosseilliers, accompanied by several traders and an aged Jesuit missionary, René Ménard, made another trip to Lake Superior. The expedition was successful from the commercial, though not from the religious, point of view. The priest, Ménard, set out from the southern shore of Lake Superior to visit a remnant of the Hurons in central Wisconsin, and was never seen again by the French. His fate is unknown, but at least one writer[2] avers that the Mississippi was discovered in the course of his wanderings. It may have been so, but evidence is almost wholly lacking. Grosseilliers and his party returned to Three Rivers in 1663.

The *Relation* of 1659–1660 contains an interesting narrative of a Jesuit Father (probably Gabriel Druillettes) who had recently met and conversed with a converted Indian after the latter had spent two years in wandering through the region of Lake Superior and Hudson Bay. The account is a characteristic bit of geographical speculation of the time. "The Savages," it goes on to say, "dwelling about that end of the lake Superior which is

---

[1] A carefully annotated reprint of Radisson's third and fourth *Voyages*, prepared by R. G. Thwaites, is in *Wisconsin Historical Collections*, XI. 64–96. See sketches of Radisson and Grosseilliers by Edward D. Neill in *Minnesota Historical Collections*, V. 401–403; *Wisconsin Historical Collections*, IX. 292–298; and *Magazine of Western History*, VII. 412–421; also by Henry C. Campbell in *Parkman Club Publications*, No. II. [Milwaukee, 1896].

[2] Nicholas Perrot, in his *Memoirs*. Perrot was one of the better class of French adventurers in the West. On Ménard's career, Thwaites, *Jesuit Relations*, XLVIII. 115–143. See also H. C. Campbell's monograph on Ménard, *Parkman Club Publications*, No. XI. [Milwaukee, 1897].

farthest distant from us, have given us entirely new light, which will not be displeasing to the curious, touching the route to Japan and China, for which so much search has been made. For we learn from these peoples that they find the Sea on three sides, toward the South, toward the West, and toward the North; so that, if this is so, it is a strong argument and a very certain indication that these three Seas, being thus contiguous, form in reality but one Sea, which is that of China. For,—that of the South, which is the Pacific sea and is well enough known, being connected with the North Sea, which is equally well known, by a third Sea, the one about which we are in doubt,—there remains nothing more to be desired than the passage into this great Sea, at once a Western and an Eastern sea. Now we know that, proceeding Southward for about three hundred leagues from the end of Lake Superior, of which I have just spoken, we come to the bay of St. Esprit,[1] which lies on the thirtieth degree of latitude and the two hundred and eightieth of longitude, in the Gulf of Mexico, on the coast of Florida; and in a southwesterly direction from the same extremity of Lake Superior, it is about two hundred leagues to another lake, which empties into the Vermilion Sea on the coast of New Granada, in the great South Sea. It is from one of these two coasts that the Savages who live some sixty leagues to the West of our Lake Superior obtain European goods, and they even say that they have seen some Europeans there."[2]

Meanwhile, during the earlier years of the decade from

[1] Equivalent to the Spanish Espíritu Santo. On the Franquelin map of 1684 it appears at what is now Mobile Bay.
[2] Thwaites, *Jesuit Relations*, XLV. 221–223.

1660 to 1670 French enterprises in the New World were taking on a new lease of life. This was due in part to Louis XIV.'s assumption of personal control of the French government, and also in perhaps a greater measure to the elevation of the energetic Colbert to the comptrollership of finance and the ministry of marine in France. By Colbert's influence Jean Baptiste Talon, a man of ability almost equal to that of Colbert himself, was appointed intendant of New France, and Daniel de Rémy, Sieur de Courcelles, governor. Courcelles was not particularly interested in geographical questions, but for nearly a decade Talon was to be the guiding genius of French exploration in the American interior. For the first time since the days of Champlain the leading authority[1] in the French colonies looked upon the Far West as worthy of exploration and occupation at any cost. Talon was from the first determined to follow up the explorations made by Nicolet a generation before. His plans embraced the opening of all the West by French activity and the actual establishing of French rule over all the interior. His purposes in this direction were so pronounced that when the Spaniards heard of them they greatly feared the carrying of the French colors down the Mississippi Valley all the way to the Gulf — a consummation actually attained a little later, though not under Talon's administration. Talon also urged upon King Louis the necessity of taking time by

[1] The intendant was an officer charged with the duty of keeping watch on the governor's actions and enforcing a system of detailed regulations in the colony. The office, when filled by a man of Talon's energy and ability, was second to none in importance. Talon's commission and instructions as intendant are printed in O'Callaghan, *New York Colonial Documents*, IX. 22–29.

the forelock and adopting measures whereby to thwart the proposed extension of the English colonies beyond the Alleghanies.

In 1665 Father Claude Allouez, one of the most vigilant of the Jesuits in America, accompanied a party of Frenchmen to the Superior region and founded the mission of the Holy Spirit at La Pointe.[1] Rumors of the "great water" were soon heard from the surrounding Chippewas, and it was now that the name by which we know the river began to take form. Allouez's phonetic rendering of the name of the tribes said to live along the river's banks was "Missipi," and the stream was thus designated by him in his correspondence. Curiously enough, the missionary believed that the river flowed into the Chesapeake Bay, or Sea of Virginia as it was then called. On one of his numerous excursions about the western end of Lake Superior, Allouez encountered a party of Sioux who said that they came from a region forty or fifty leagues in the direction of the "Missipi," and that beyond their country there was just one other people before the China Sea was reached.

In 1669 Allouez was displaced at La Pointe by Jacques Marquette, a priest who the year before had established the first mission in what is now the state of Michigan, on

---

[1] The Indian name of the place was Chagwamegan, which means "on the long, narrow point of land." It was upon this site that René Ménard had established his unsuccessful mission five years before. See "Of the Mission of Pointe du Saint Esprit in the Country of the Outaouac Algonquins," Thwaites, *Jesuit Relations*, LII. 199-213; Allouez's description of Lake Superior, *Jesuit Relations*, L. 265-267; Pierre Margry, *Découvertes et Établissements des Français dans l'Ouest et dans le Sud de l'Amérique Septentrionale*, I. 59-72; and Thwaites, "The Story of La Pointe," in *How George Rogers Clark Won the Northwest, and Other Essays in Western History*.

the south side of the Sault, and who was soon to be made famous by his explorations and adventures in the West. Allouez in this same year founded the mission of Francis Xavier among the Pottawattomies on Green Bay, having been induced to go there, it is said, not merely for the sake of ministering to the Indians, but also to exercise a repressive influence upon the lawless *coureurs-de-bois* who had assembled there in considerable numbers.[1] Some months later, in company with another missionary, Father Dablon, he ascended the Fox and crossed to the head of the Wisconsin. But again the passage to the Mississippi by this inviting route failed to be completed. Allouez knew, as Nicolet certainly did not, that the Wisconsin led directly to the great river. He records, indeed, that it was only a six days' journey from the point he reached to the "Messisipi." There are some older authorities who avow that Allouez did reach the Mississippi; but a similar claim is made by somebody for almost every missionary and explorer in the West from Nicolet down, and all are alike without foundation until we come to Joliet and Marquette in 1673. In the *Relation* of 1669–1670 we read that the "Messisipi" was more than a league wide, that it flowed from north to south, that the Indians had never descended to its mouth, and that there was still doubt as to whether it flowed into the Gulf of Florida or into that of California.[2]

The winter of 1669–1670 Marquette spent at La Pointe. The Sioux Indians, by whom he was frequently visited, professed to live on the banks of the great river, and Marquette, who was a priest but something more, was stirred

[1] Thwaites, *Jesuit Relations*, LIV. 305.   [2] *Ibid.*, 137.

by a great ambition to journey to the river and find out the actual facts regarding its size, direction, and commercial value. Allouez had adopted the view that the river flowed into the Atlantic, but Marquette thought it flowed into the Pacific through the Gulf of California. "If I get the canoe which the Indians have promised to make me," he boldly declared on one occasion, "I intend with another Frenchman, who can speak with these lower people in their own tongues, to navigate this stream and come in contact with these lower tribes, and so decide the question of the ultimate direction of this great river's flow."[1] A war between the Hurons and the Sioux, however, produced such disturbed conditions that the plan was for the time abandoned.

The *Jesuit Relation* of 1670–1671 says that there is no longer doubt that the Mississippi (its modern spelling had now come into use) flowed either into the Vermilion Sea or the Gulf of Mexico, "since what is known of great rivers in that direction, is that they flow into one or the other of these seas." The *Relation* continues: "The Indians say that for more than three hundred leagues from its mouth it is wider than the St. Lawrence at Quebec, and that it flows through a treeless prairie-land where the only fuel is turf or dried excrements. As it nears the sea, the woods again grow, and in this region the inhabitants seem like the French, have houses in the water, and cut trees with large knives. All along the

[1] Letter of Father James Marquette to the Father Superior of the missions, in Thwaites, *Jesuit Relations*, LIV. 189–191. For a sketch of Marquette's experiences at La Pointe, see Thwaites, *Father Marquette*, Ch. VIII.

river from the Nadouesse [Sioux] to the south there are many tribes of different customs and tongues, and they make war on each other."[1]

The war between the Sioux and the Hurons obliged Marquette instead of seeking the Mississippi to follow his Huron protégés eastward in the year 1670. Thereafter we find him at Sault Ste. Marie, and a year later at the Straits of Mackinaw, where he established the mission of St. Ignace. June 14, 1671, in the course of an imposing ceremony at Sault Ste. Marie, the French took formal possession of all territory "from the North to the South Sea, and westward to the ocean" — an area as utterly enigmatical as that specified in the "sea to sea" charters of the English.

The ceremony, which was under the management of Simon François Daumont, Sieur St. Lusson, as the agent of Talon, was one of the most notable in the history of the country. For months Nicholas Perrot had been working among the tribes of the Green Bay region, inducing them to send representatives, and with such success that as many as sixteen or seventeen agreed to do so.[2] The ceremony was preceded by several weeks of feasting, games, and mock fights, designed to win the sympathy of the natives, and enlist their support in the great scheme which the French were preparing to execute. At length,

---

[1] Thwaites, *Jesuit Relations*, LV. 207–209.

[2] The "Procès Verbal" of Talon mentions by name fourteen nations. The Hurons and Ottawas, at a later time, conferred with the French and assented to the arrangement. Winsor, *Narrative and Critical History of America*, IV. 175, note. The "Procès Verbal" is given in the *Wisconsin Historical Collections*, XI. 26. On Perrot's labors among the Wisconsin Indians, see *Wisconsin Historical Collections*, XVI. 32–50.

on the 14th of June, in the midst of a great concourse of painted and gaudily dressed savages, gathered on the crest of a hill overlooking the rapids of the Sault, signatures were affixed and marks were made to a document which claimed for Louis XIV. all the North American continent, from the Arctic Ocean to the Gulf of Mexico, and from the coast of Labrador westward to the "salt sea," with a fine disregard of all such trivial matters as conflicting English and Spanish claims. A wooden cross was set up, and the Frenchmen solemnized the occasion by chanting a hymn in Latin. Beside the cross was erected a post bearing the *fleur-de-lis* of France; and as a symbol of the possession assumed, St. Lusson took from the ground a piece of sod and held it aloft toward the heavens. It was felt, however, as John Fiske says, that all this pageant would be incomplete without a speech that would stir the hearts of the Indians, and Father Allouez, the orator of the day, knew "how to tell them what they could appreciate."[1]

Some parts of the speech are so characteristic that they call for quotation. Allouez's main endeavor was to impress his hearers with the magnitude of the French power, in doing which he gave the following description of the monarch whose ensign had just been borne aloft beside the cross: "He lives beyond the sea; he is Captain of the greatest Captains, and has not his equal in the world. All the Captains you have ever seen, or of whom you have ever heard, are mere children compared with him. He is like a great tree, and they, only like little plants that we tread under foot in walking. . . . When

[1] John Fiske, *New France and New England*, 108.

he says 'I am going to war,' all obey him; and his ten thousand Captains raise companies of a hundred soldiers each, both on sea and on land. Some embark in ships, one or two hundred in number, like those that you have seen at Quebec. Your canoes hold only four or five men — or at the very most, ten or twelve. Our ships in France hold four or five hundred, and even as many thousand. Other men make war by land, but in such vast numbers that, if drawn up in a double file, they would extend farther than from here to Mississaquenk, although the distance exceeds twenty leagues. When he attacks, he is more terrible than the thunder: the earth trembles, the air and the sea are set on fire by the discharge of his Cannon; while he has been seen among his squadrons all covered with the blood of his foes, of whom he has slain so many with his sword that he does not count their scalps, but the rivers of blood which he sets flowing. So many prisoners of war does he lead away that he makes no account of them, letting them go about whither they will, to show that he does not fear them. No one dares make war upon him, all nations beyond sea having most submissively sued for peace. From all parts of the world people go to listen to his words, and to admire him, and he alone decides all the affairs of the world. What shall I say of his wealth? You count yourselves rich when you have ten or twelve sacks of corn, some hatchets, glass beads, kettles, or other things of the sort. He has towns of his own more in number than you have people in all these countries five hundred leagues around; while in each town there are warehouses containing enough hatchets to cut down all your forests, kettles to cook all your moose, and

glass beads to fill all your cabins. His house is longer than from here to the head of the Sault [more than half a league], and higher than the tallest of your trees; and it contains more families than the largest of your Villages can hold."[1] For vividness and force this speech has few equals, at least among the efforts of sober churchmen.

As has been said, it was the chief ambition of the intendant Talon to solve the problem of the river system of the West. Colbert at the French court was equally interested, for a time at any rate, in this matter, and lent his assistance to every scheme of exploration which seemed at all feasible. He was especially desirous that the Mississippi be found to flow into the Gulf of California, so that it might constitute an outlet to the China Sea. Lest, however, the river should be found to flow throughout all its course toward the south, the Spanish government was given to understand that if the French flag should some day appear in the Gulf of Mexico it was not to be disregarded with impunity.

In April, 1672, Louis de Buade, Comte de Frontenac, was appointed governor and lieutenant-general of New France.[2] When he arrived, in late autumn, he at once fell to quarrelling with Talon, and the latter was soon recalled. Already, however, the unfortunate official had advised the new governor to send Louis Joliet on an exploring expedition toward the Mississippi, and the plan was put into

[1] Thwaites, *Jesuit Relations*, LV. 109–113.
[2] Louis XIV.'s instructions to Frontenac are in O'Callaghan, *New York Colonial Documents*, IX. 85–89. The best account of Frontenac's interesting career in America is in Parkman, *Count Frontenac and New France under Louis XIV.*

speedy execution.[1] Joliet was a man of roving disposition, a successful trader, and just the sort of person to undertake any adventurous enterprise that offered. He was a native of the colony, having been born at Quebec in 1645, ten years after the death of Champlain. He was a man of good education, excellent judgment, though possessed of the spirit of the adventurer rather than that of the student. In 1669 he had engaged in a search for a copper mine on Lake Superior, and in 1671 had been a companion of St. Lusson at the planting of the arms of France at Sault Ste. Marie. To the home government Frontenac wrote that Joliet had promised to penetrate the interior of the continent as far as the Mississippi by way of Green Bay, and that he would in all probability prove once for all that the great river flowed into the Gulf of California.

Joliet set out on his ambitious expedition in August, and by December 8 had reached Mackinaw, then known as Michillimackinac.[2] There the winter and spring were

[1] In Charlevoix, *Histoire Générale de la Nouvelle France* (trans. by J. G. Shea), III. 179, it is asserted that Talon had commissioned Marquette to undertake the exploration of the West. This is erroneous. Joliet was the governmental agent, Marquette a mere associate. Jared Sparks, *Robert de la Salle*, 4, and other older writers allowed themselves to be led astray by Charlevoix, who though always interesting was not always accurate.

[2] On the expedition of Joliet and Marquette the following authorities may be cited: Parkman, *La Salle and the Discovery of the Great West*, Ch. V.; Thwaites, *Father Marquette*; Samuel Hedges, *Father Marquette*; Winsor, *Cartier to Frontenac*; Monette, *History of the Valley of the Mississippi*; Charlevoix, *Histoire Générale de la Nouvelle France*; Le J. P. Brucker, *Jacques Marquette et la Découverte de la Vallée du Mississippi*; Alfred Hamy, *Au Mississippi: La Première Exploration* (1673). The leading original sources of information are: *The Jesuit Relations*; Margry, *Découvertes et Établissements des Français dans l'Ouest et dans le Sud de l'Amérique Septentrionale*; French, *Historical*

spent in completing preparations. A goodly supply of Indian corn and smoked buffalo meat was provided for the trip. All possible information regarding the country to be traversed was obtained from the Indians and a map was constructed for a guide. Marquette was still in charge of the Jesuit mission at Mackinaw, but despite all the vicissitudes of his life among the fugitive Hurons, had never outgrown his desire to seek a field of labor even less promising in some respects among the Illinois who were known to live in close proximity to the Mississippi. The missionary therefore joined himself with the adventurer, and when on May 17, 1673, Joliet set out anew toward the goal of his ambition, he had as his friend and confidential companion the man whose name has ever since been linked with his own in the annals of western discovery.

The first Indians encountered were the Folles-Avoines, or the nation of the *wild oats*, a small tribe to whom Marquette was already known by reason of a previous visit. "I acquainted them," says Marquette in the account which he subsequently wrote of the expedition, "with my design of discovering other nations, to preach to them the mysteries of our holy religion, at which they were much surprised, and said all they could to dissuade me from it. They told me I would meet Indians who spare no strangers, and whom they kill without any provocation or mercy; that the war they have one with the other would expose me to be taken by their warriors,

Collections of Louisiana and Florida; Shea, *Discovery and Exploration of the Mississippi Valley;* Le Clercq, *Premier Établissement de la Foi dans la Nouvelle France;* and the *Wisconsin Historical Collections.*

as they are constantly on the lookout to surprise their enemies. That the Great River was exceedingly dangerous, and full of frightful monsters who devoured men and canoes together, and that the heat was so great that it would positively cause our death. I thanked them for their kind advice, but told them I would not follow it, as the salvation of a great many souls was concerned in our undertaking, for whom I should be glad to lose my life. I added that I defied their monsters, and their information would oblige us to keep more upon our guard to avoid a surprise. And having prayed with them, and given them some instructions, we set out for the Bay of Puan (Green Bay), where our missionaries had been successful in converting them."[1]

The party, numbering seven in all, made its way in two canoes into Green Bay, following the same course as had Nicolet nearly forty years before. Marquette tried to satisfy himself as to the reason for the name "Fetid" which these waters had long borne, but was unable to arrive at any more satisfactory conclusion than that it was "on account of the quantity of slime and mud there, constantly exhaling noisome vapors which cause the loudest and longest peals of thunder that I ever heard."[2] During the first week in June the Fox River was ascended, though not without some difficulty on account of the rocks and rapids in its upper waters. This brought

---

[1] Father James Marquette, *The Discovery of Some New Countries and Nations in North America in 1673.* Translated by J. D. B. De Bow in French, *Louisiana Historical Collections*, Part II. 281. Thwaites, *Jesuit Relations*, LIX. 93.

[2] "Narrative of Father Marquette," Shea, *Discovery and Exploration of the Mississippi Valley*, 237.

the voyagers among the Mascotins, or Fire Nation, where Marquette was "extremely consoled to see a beautiful cross planted in the midst of the town, adorned with several white skins, red belts, bows and arrows which these good people had offered to the Great Manitou to thank him for having had pity on them during the winter."[1] The sachems of the tribe were assembled, and Joliet explained his commission to discover new countries and Marquette declared his purpose to "illumine them with the light of the gospel." The Indians proved very hospitable, readily consenting to furnish the travellers with two guides to set them on their way toward the great water. When, however, on the 10th of the month the Frenchmen and these two guides embarked from one of the villages to continue their journey into parts unknown, the inhabitants of the place could not restrain their expressions of astonishment at the boldness of the travellers. Finding them determined to go in spite of all warnings, the natives told Joliet and Marquette that three leagues farther up the Fox they would come upon the head waters of a river which flowed into the Mississippi, and that they should follow this stream "west-southwest" in order to reach the desired goal.[2] These directions brought the voyagers to the Fox-Wisconsin portage — a region so full of swamps and lakes

---

[1] French, *Historical Collections of Louisiana*, Part II. 283. Thwaites, *Jesuit Relations*, LIX. 103. Nicolet had visited the Mascoutins (Mascotins) in 1634, and several missionaries, among them Marquette himself, had appeared in their villages from time to time thereafter. The cross may have been erected by Allouez and Dablon in 1667.

[2] "Narrative of Father Marquette," Shea, *Discovery and Exploration of the Mississippi Valley*, 238.

that, as Marquette says, had the guides not been familiar with the country the party must have become greatly confused. "The river upon which we rowed and had to carry our canoes from one to the other, looked more like a corn-field than a river, insomuch that we could hardly find its channel." The canoes had to be borne on the backs of the guides a distance of about two and a half miles over a portage which in times of flood becomes a stream joining the head waters of the Fox and the Wisconsin, and thereby connecting the St. Lawrence drainage system with the Mississippi. When the canoes were floated on the waters of the Wisconsin the guides returned to their homes (having gone as far as their knowledge extended), "leaving us alone," says Marquette, "in an unknown country, having nothing to rely upon but Divine Providence."

"Before embarking," continues Marquette's account, "we all offered up prayers to the Holy Virgin, which we continued to do every morning, placing ourselves and the events of the journey under her protection, and after having encouraged each other, we got into our canoes." The trip down the river brought to view many things of interest to the Frenchmen — a luxuriant vegetation of strange trees and plants, enormous herds of buffaloes, and beetling bluffs affording scenery of the rarest ruggedness and beauty. Navigation was not so easy, however, because of the number of sand-bars and islands covered with grape-vines. Marquette called the stream the "Mesconsing," but its name was subsequently given as "Ouisconsin" by the explorer Hennepin, from which the modern name is directly derived.

June 17 the curiosity of a generation of Frenchmen was rewarded. On that day the little fleet of Marquette and Joliet, just a month after starting from Mackinaw, floated out upon the placid waters of the Mississippi.[1] Despite all the contradictory views that have been set forth by various students of the subject at different times, we may regard this event as constituting quite certainly the real discovery of the Father of Waters by the French. By it the mystery of the "great water" was cleared up, so far at least as to show that this expression actually denoted a large southward flowing river, as the Indians had declared. The river at the point first viewed is walled in, as one writer has described it, "by picturesque bluffs, with lofty limestone escarpment, whose irregular outline looks like a succession of the ruined castles and towers of the Rhine." By reason of its being thus comparatively narrow, the explorers were probably disposed to be just a bit disappointed in the "great water" until they made a sounding and discovered it to be nineteen fathoms deep. A few miles below the mouth of the Wisconsin the river widens, as Marquette takes care to tell us, nearly three-quarters of a league, and assumes the aspects more characteristic of it in its lower course. Joliet bestowed upon the stream the name La Buade, in honor of Frontenac, while Marquette, with true religious instinct, preferred to designate it Conception. As yet the explorers knew almost as

[1] In his *Narrative* Marquette simply says, "We safely entered Missisipi on the 17th of June, with a Joy that I cannot express." Thwaites, *Jesuit Relations*, LIX. 107. See J. G. Shea, "Address on the Discovery of the Mississippi, read on the Bi-centennial of said Discovery, June 17, 1873," in *Wisconsin Historical Collections*, VIII. 111-122.

little, of course, of the real extent of the river and of the vast area drained by it, as had Soto and his companions a century and a quarter before.

Bearing in mind that it was chiefly the direction and outlet of the stream that the authorities wanted to know, Joliet and Marquette determined to pursue their investigations exclusively toward the south. They therefore set out to descend the river, floating leisurely along by day and resting at anchor in mid-stream by night. Within a week they had reached a village of the Illinois tribe where they were well entertained, and also warned against demons who were said to dwell along the river farther south. These warnings, as the earlier ones, were ignored with what the Indians regarded as the most consummate foolhardiness, and the voyage was eagerly resumed. The appearance of the country traversed now began to change, and the adventurers were in no wise lacking in entertainment. "There were scarcely any more woods or mountains," says Marquette. "The islands are covered with fine trees, but we could not see any more roebucks, buffaloes, bustards, and swans. We met from time to time monstrous fish, which struck so violently against our canoes, that at first we took them to be large trees, which threatened to upset us. We saw also a hideous monster; his head was like that of a tiger, his nose was sharp, and somewhat resembled a wildcat; his beard was long, his ears stood upright, the color of his head was gray, and his neck black. He looked upon us for some time, but as we came near him our oars frightened him away. When we threw our nets into the water we caught an abundance of sturgeons, and

another kind of fish like our trout, except that the eyes and nose are much smaller, and they have near the nose a bone three inches broad and a foot and a half long, the end of which is flat and broad, and when it leaps out of the water the weight of it throws it upon its back. . . . As we were descending the river we saw high rocks with hideous monsters painted on them, and upon which the bravest Indians dared not look. They are as large as a calf, with head and horns like a goat; their eyes red; beard like a tiger's, and a face like a man's. Their tails are so long that they pass over their heads and between their fore legs, under their belly, and ending like a fish's tail. They are painted red, green, and black. They are so well drawn that I cannot believe they were drawn by the Indians. And for what purpose they were made seems to me a great mystery."[1]

The fish which so astonished the travellers was a variety of swordfish, now quite rare. And the animal paintings on the cliffs were but expressions, familiar enough to-day, of the mingled religious and artistic temperaments of the natives.

Some time after passing the mouth of the Illinois, the voyagers came upon the mouth of another great river, — the *Pekitanoni*, as the Indians called it, or the Missouri, as it is known to us. Marquette says that while he and his companions were discoursing upon the monsters they had seen, they began to hear a great rushing and bubbling of waters, and to see small islands of floating trees coming down the mighty tributary from the west with

---

[1] "Narrative of Father Marquette," Shea, *Discovery and Exploration of the Mississippi Valley*, 253–254.

such rapidity that they dare not at first trust themselves to go near it. The waters of the Missouri were found to be too muddy for drinking, and it was noted that they so discolored the Mississippi as greatly to enhance the dangers of navigation. Marquette determined at some future time to ascend the stream and find whither it led. The Indians informed him that "by ascending this river for five or six days, one reaches a fine prairie, twenty or thirty leagues long. This must be crossed in a northwesterly direction, and it terminates at another small river on which one may embark, for it is not very difficult to transport canoes through so fine a country as that prairie. This second river flows toward the southwest for ten or fifteen leagues, after which it enters a lake, small and deep, which flows toward the west, where it falls into the sea." "I have hardly any doubt," concludes Marquette, "that it is the Vermilion Sea, and I do not despair of discovering it some day, if God grant me the grace and the health to do so, in order that I may preach the gospel to all the peoples of this New World who have so long grovelled in the darkness of infidelity."[1]

Meanwhile the voyage was continued toward the south. It was now dawning upon the adventurers that the Mississippi flowed into the Gulf of Mexico, and when they passed the mouth of the Ohio[2] and reached that of the Arkansea, or Arkansas, the fact was assured to their minds beyond doubt. The Indians in the Arkansas region

---

[1] "Narrative of Father Marquette," Shea, *Discovery and Exploration of the Mississippi Valley*, 249. Thwaites, *Jesuit Relations*, LIX. 143.

[2] The Ohio was then known by its Indian name *Ouabouskigon*, or "The Beautiful."

told them that it was but a ten days' voyage to the mouth of the river, from which testimony the distance was estimated to be considerably less than it really is — nearly eight hundred miles. Here the travellers began to hear of the Europeans to the south and southwest, and that farther down the river the natives had firearms brought in through trade with foreigners. The farther the voyage was continued the more numerous became the evidences of the proximity of the Spaniards. Joliet and Marquette began seriously to deliberate as to whether they should venture any lower. Since the latitude 33° 40' had been reached and the Gulf was thought to be not more than a two or three days' journey distant, they decided that it was time to turn about in their course.[1] Curiosity to behold the lower stretches of the river was overcome by dread of the long ascent on the return and also by fear of capture by the Spaniards. "We considered," says Marquette, "that the advantage of our travels would be altogether lost to our nation if we fell into the hands of the Spaniards, from whom we could expect no other treatment than death or slavery; besides, we saw that we were not prepared to resist the Indians, the allies of the Europeans, who continually infested the lower part of this river."[2]

Having, therefore, assured themselves of the direction

---

[1] Father Anastasius Douay, a companion of La Salle a few years later, in his *Narrative* denies that Joliet and Marquette descended the Mississippi below Cape St. Anthony. There was apparently no reason but jealousy for this assertion. See Shea, *Discovery and Exploration of the Mississippi Valley*, 222.

[2] "Narrative of Father Marquette," Shea, *Discovery and Exploration of the Mississippi Valley*, 256.

and outlet of the river[1] — the matters which Frontenac was chiefly desirous of knowing — the voyagers turned back from the Arkansas, July 17, just a month after their first view of the Mississippi, and commenced the laborious trip up-stream. When the mouth of the Illinois was reached, the Indians of the neighborhood persuaded the Frenchmen that a quicker and easier return could be effected by way of that river and Lake Michigan. The Illinois Indians proved very hospitable and besought Marquette to remain among them as a religious teacher. For the present the condition of his health, as well as other considerations, forbade the priest's accepting the invitation, though he promised to return at some future time. From the Illinois the travellers passed finally into the Des Plaines River. An elevation about forty miles southwest of Chicago to which Joliet gave his own name is the only landmark which still preserves any of the many names bestowed by him and his companion during the course of this trip. The Chicago portage — between the head waters of the Chicago and Illinois rivers — was passed, and by the end of September the familiar waters of Green Bay were reached. The journey had covered in all about two thousand five hundred miles and had been accomplished in almost exactly four months.[2]

[1] Says Marquette, "The Mississippi undoubtedly had its mouth in Florida or the Gulf of Mexico and not on the east, in Virginia, whose seacoast is at 34° north, which we had passed, without having as yet reached the sea, nor on the western side, in California, because that would require a west or west-southwest course, and we had always been going south." Shea, *Discovery and Exploration of the Mississippi Valley*, 256.

[2] The following table of distances is taken from French, *Historical Collections of Louisiana*, Part II. 297 : —

Marquette remained at Green Bay to recover from the malaria contracted on the lower Mississippi, and Joliet pressed on to Quebec, which he reached the following summer. In the ascent of the St. Lawrence the box of papers and records which he was carrying was lost by the capsizing of his canoe, and Joliet himself barely escaped. The loss of these papers has been a serious detriment to the untangling of the history of the French discoveries in the Northwest.[1] From memory their author constructed a map which is probably the first to mark the course of the Mississippi on a basis of discovery rather than mere conjecture.[2] While the extreme southern portion of the river had not actually been viewed by the explorers, their conclusions regarding it amounted for all practical purposes to absolute knowledge. They had at least established the unwelcome fact that its outlet was into the Gulf of Mexico and not into the Gulf of California — and hence the China Sea — as had been hoped. In view of the loss of Joliet's narratives it is peculiarly fortunate that those of Marquette have come down to us.[3] They

From Green Bay (Puans) up Fox River to the portage, 175 mi.
From the portage down the Wisconsin to the Mississippi, 175 mi.
From the mouth of the Wisconsin to the mouth of the Arkansas, 1087 mi.
From the Arkansas to the Illinois River, 547 mi.
From the mouth of the Illinois to Chicago, 305 mi.
From Chicago to Green Bay by the lake shore, 260 mi.   Total, 2549 mi.

[1] Joliet did what he could to repair the loss by writing out a narrative based on his recollections. This is to be found in two forms in Margry, *Découvertes et Établissements des Français*, I. 259-270.

[2] Reproduced in Thwaites, *Jesuit Relations*, LIX. 86, and in A. P. C. Griffin, *The Discovery of the Mississippi; a Bibliographical Account*, frontispiece. Cf. Marquette's map, *Jesuit Relations*, 108.

[3] They were sent by the author to Dablon at Quebec, who used them in his *Relation* and transmitted a copy to Paris. The original manu-

have been drawn upon almost exclusively for our account of the entire expedition.

In 1674 Marquette, recovered in health as he thought, returned from Green Bay to the Illinois country to establish the mission of the Immaculate Conception. Again falling sick, he was forced to suspend his labors and withdraw toward the north. The winter of 1674–1675 was spent with the Indians on or near the present site of Chicago.[1] The following spring he attempted further missionary effort in the region of Kaskaskia, but was compelled by renewed illness to return by way of the portage to the shore of Lake Michigan where, May 19, 1675, he was overtaken by death.[2] No greater grief could have come to the Frenchmen whose cheery companion he had been alike in days of hardship and of triumph, or to the Indian peoples all through the district between Lakes Superior and Michigan and the "great water," to whom he had commended himself in an unusual degree as a friend, teacher, and devoted minister. Although but thirty-eight years old at the time of his death, he had been a priest twenty-one years, and no one had so stamped his personality upon the fortunes of the French nation and the Christian religion alike in the Northwest. In 1677 some Ottawa Indians exhumed the body which had

script had a long and eventful history before it came into the possession of Dr. Shea, who gave it its first publication in English. Appendix to *The Discovery and Exploration of the Mississippi Valley.*

[1] "Father Marquette at Chicago," from Marquette's *Narrative* and Dablon's *Relation, Old South Leaflets*, No. XLVI. See article on "Early Visitors to Chicago" in the *New England Magazine*, April, 1902, by Edward G. Mason, President of the Chicago Historical Society.

[2] Marquette's "Precious Death in the Heart of the Forest," Thwaites, *Jesuit Relations*, LIX. 191-201.

been buried at Green Bay, and a "melancholy procession of thirty canoes accompanied the remains to St. Ignace," where beneath the chapel of the mission they were given their final resting-place.[1] Marquette's boundless patriotic and religious zeal made him little less than a martyr to the interests of the nation of which he was a citizen and of the religion to which he had consecrated his life. The state of Wisconsin did a fitting thing some years ago when it placed in the Capitol at Washington a statue of the faithful priest and explorer.

For some years after the return of Joliet and Marquette exploration in the direction of the Mississippi languished. Louis XIV. had given Frontenac to understand that French enterprise in America might need to be directed toward ends other than westward discovery and that all projects for the opening of the Mississippi country should be held in abeyance. Frontenac was not so greatly interested in such matters, anyway, as Talon had been, especially after the disappointment of finding that the Mississippi led only into a hostile Spanish country and did not afford the long-desired passageway to the oceans bordering on the Indies. So when, a little later, Joliet desired to establish a trading post on the Mississippi,

[1] Thwaites, *Jesuit Relations*, LIX. 201-203. Shea, *History of the Catholic Church in Colonial Days*, 319. The chapel of St. Ignace was burned in 1705. Not until 1877 were the remains rediscovered and honored with a monument. For an account of the finding of the chapel and burial-place by Mr. Patrick Murray, see Samuel Hedges, *Father Marquette; his Place of Burial at St. Ignace*, Ch. XVI.; George Duffield, "The Recent Discovery of the Long Lost Grave of Père Marquette," *Report of the Pioneer Society of the State of Michigan*, II. 134-145; and J. G. Shea, "Romance and Reality of the Death of Marquette, and the Recent Discovery of his Remains," in the *Catholic World*, II. 267-281.

he received no encouragement from the governor; and from Colbert, the minister of marine, he received an unqualified prohibition. The king's great military projects were now absorbing all the energies of France, war was threatening between the English and French colonies in America, and altogether the outlook for western exploration and settlement was anything but bright.

Nevertheless, the man who was to make the Mississippi a French river from its source to its mouth was already preparing for his work, and the time of its accomplishment was not far distant.

CHAPTER IV

LA SALLE AND THE OPENING OF THE GREAT WEST

RÉNÉ-ROBERT CAVELIER, Sieur de La Salle,[1] was descended from an old and wealthy burgher family whose ancestral estates were in the vicinity of Rouen in Normandy. Not much is known regarding the early life of the man. We cannot even tell definitely the year of

---

[1] By far the best work on La Salle is Parkman, *La Salle and the Discovery of the Great West*. Jared Sparks's *La Salle* in the Library of American Biography, second series, I., is exceedingly readable, but not wholly trustworthy. Other authorities are: Winsor, *Cartier to Frontenac* and *Narrative and Critical History of America*; Monette, *History of the Valley of the Mississippi*; Thomas Falconer, *On the Discovery of the Mississippi*; William Kingsford, *History of Canada*; Bancroft, *History of the United States*; Gabriel Gravier, *Nouvelle étude sur Cavelier de La Salle* [Rouen, 1885]; Parkman, "Cavelier de La Salle," in the *North American Review*, CXXV. 427-438; and Joseph Wallace, *Illinois and Louisiana under the French Rule*. Source materials on La Salle are, for the most part, abundant. They are to be found mainly in French, *Historical Collections of Louisiana*; Thwaites, *Jesuit Relations*; Margry, *Découvertes et Établissements des Français dans l'Ouest et dans le Sud de l'Amérique Septentrionale*; J. G. Shea, *Early Voyages Up and Down the Mississippi, The Discovery and Exploration of the Mississippi Valley*, and *A Description of Louisiana by Father Louis Hennepin*; *The Relation of the Discoveries and Voyages of Cavelier de La Salle from 1679 to 1681*, trans. by Melville B. Anderson and published by the Caxton Club of Chicago; Charlevoix, *Histoire Générale de la Nouvelle France*; and the *Wisconsin Historical Collections*. There is a bibliography of La Salle literature, by Cyrus K. Remington, published in the Ninth Annual Report of the Commissioners of the State Reservation at Niagara, 1893.

his birth, though it is generally given as 1643. Father Hennepin, subsequently famous for his exploration of the upper Mississippi, informs us that ten or twelve years of La Salle's boyhood were spent in a seminary of the Jesuits where he received an excellent education, according to the standards of the time. Having thus entered upon preparation for a churchly career, he had forfeited his share of his father's property, so that when he found the life of the Jesuit not to his liking and withdrew from the order, he was under the necessity of making his own way in the world. Because of the unreliableness of Father Hennepin's narratives several modern writers have been inclined to doubt La Salle's early connection with the Jesuits, there being little or no corroborative evidence. But there seems to be no good reason why in this case at least we may not accept the venerable priest's statement. Certain it is that throughout all his later career there was an antipathy between La Salle and the Jesuits which may well have been caused by the circumstances under which the young man turned his back upon the order. This antipathy is attested by the fact that in all his exploring expeditions La Salle was accompanied by Sulpitians and not by Jesuits, and by the further fact that throughout the voluminous *Relations* of the Canadian Jesuits, La Salle and his achievements were treated with manifest contempt.[1]

Granting that La Salle was brought up as a Jesuit, it is not difficult to see why he did not remain one. His adventuresome disposition, love of independent action,

[1] See Jacker, "La Salle and the Jesuits," in *American Catholic Quarterly Review*, III. 404-420.

and impatience with all forms of control, caused him to
chafe unbearably under the restrictions of church vows.
He was just the sort of man to whom the free, wild life
of the frontiersman would appeal, and it is not at all surprising that while yet a young man, perhaps not over
twenty-three years old, he decided to cast in his fortunes
with the settlers of the western world. This was about
the year 1667. Probably the most immediate object in
view was the accumulation of wealth by engaging in the
Indian trade, although, as John Fiske reasonably supposed,
La Salle before his coming to America may well have entertained a more or less definite purpose of participating
in exploring enterprise.[1] At any rate, such a purpose
must soon have been formed, for almost upon landing
the young adventurer began the study of the Indian
languages with a zeal which clearly bespoke an anticipated need for such knowledge. From the priests of the
Sulpitian order in New France, of whom his brother was
one, La Salle secured the grant of a seigniory at the
head of the rapids above Montreal.[2] The place was
admirably located for the fur trade, and from the first
the energetic and shrewd young seignior prospered abundantly. A palisaded village was laid out, settlers were
attracted by grants of farm and pasture lands, and trading excursions were made in all directions among the

[1] Fiske, *New France and New England*, 110.

[2] Montreal had been founded by priests of the Sulpitian order not far
from the time when La Salle was born. The order's incorporated seminary was now the feudal lord of a large landed property in the vicinity.
La Salle's grant was several miles from the city. The exact location of
his homestead is in doubt. On La Salle and the Sulpitians, Parkman,
La Salle and the Discovery of the Great West, Ch. II.

Indian tribes. All the while La Salle was learning lessons in navigation, commerce, Indian lore, and outdoor science, which were to serve him well in larger undertakings.

The life of the frontier seignior, however, strenuous enough for most men, was not so for La Salle, who was ever a better explorer than colonizer. His natural ambition, augmented by pondering the exploits of Columbus, Soto, and Cortés, overleaped the Sulpitian settlements at Montreal and longed to express itself in enterprises that would startle the world. This was before the explorations of Joliet and Marquette, so that the theory that the "great water" led to the South Sea, and therefore to China and the Indies, was not yet exploded. From some Seneca Indians who visited his post in the winter of 1668–1669 La Salle received information which convinced him that there was an almost continuous waterway westward across the continent to the sea. The Senecas told him of a great river whose source was in their country (western New York and Pennsylvania), and which flowed to the southwest for such a distance that as much as eight or nine months would be required for a canoe to follow it to the sea. This rumor had a very real basis of fact, for the Allegheny, Ohio, and lower Mississippi, taken together, compose precisely such a stream as the Indians described. From the great length attributed to it La Salle conceived that it must flow into the Gulf of California, and hence afford the long-desired outlet to the South Sea and China. Even if this should fail, beyond the Great Lakes, he thought, there must be

rivers leading to the China Seas, or possibly another series of lakes which would render communication easy and direct. So infatuated with this conception did he become that he forthwith christened his Montreal settlement La Chine, as if it were but the stepping-stone to the much-desired goal.[1]

With little loss of time preparations were begun for an expedition in the direction of the South Sea. La Salle proposed to cross into the land of the Senecas and follow the reputed watercourse until he should satisfy French curiosity completely on the subject. From Courcelles, the governor of New France, residing at Quebec, letters patent were secured authorizing the holder to make discoveries in the western country, and commending him to the consideration of the English in Virginia or the Spanish in Florida or any other Christian people that might be encountered. La Salle was himself quite uncertain whither his expedition might eventually go; consequently in making contracts with those who were to accompany him he was careful to stipulate that his men should follow him faithfully either north or south. An independent expedition which was being planned by the Sulpitians for the carrying of the gospel to some Indian tribes in the Northwest was merged, by order of Courcelles, with that of La Salle — hardly an auspicious move for the success of either enterprise.

---

[1] Désiré Girouard, *Les Anciens Forts de La Chine et Cavelier de La Salle* [Montreal, 1891]. It should be observed that some recent Canadian authorities hold that the name La Chine was applied to La Salle's Montreal seigniory only by scoffers after the failure of the Ohio expedition.

July 6, 1669, La Chine was sold to aid in defraying the costs of the undertaking, showing that its founder was bent heart and soul upon the immediate execution of his new purpose. On the same day the start was made up the St. Lawrence with twenty men and seven canoes, and a number of Senecas for guides.[1] From the St. Lawrence the little flotilla passed out upon the broad, glassy expanse of Lake Ontario. Coasting along the southern shore of the lake it reached Irondequoit Bay, where a landing was effected just thirty-five days after the start from La Chine. La Salle, Galinée, and a few others made a twenty-mile trip inland to one of the principal Seneca villages, where they hoped to secure guides for the later stages of the exploration. Much difficulty was experienced in communicating with the Indians, though they prepared for their visitors a great entertainment, the main feature of which was six hours of torturing a captive whom La Salle tried in vain to rescue. At length an interpreter who had served some recent Jesuit visitors to the place was found and the natives were apprised of the Frenchmen's desires. Upon learning that the white men proposed to descend the Ohio, the hosts became profuse in their warnings against

[1] The chief authority for the events of the expedition is the journal of Galinée, now preserved in a Paris library. Galinée was one of the Sulpitians with whose enterprise that of La Salle had been merged. The map which he made in 1670 is the earliest that survives which undertakes to show explicitly the region of the upper lakes. There is a copy of it in the library of Harvard University. See map and comment on it in Winsor, *Cartier to Frontenac*, 220-222. Galinée's journal is printed in Margry, *Découvertes et Établissements des Français*, I. 112-166, and there are extracts from it in Berthold Fernow, *The Ohio Valley in Colonial Days*, Appendix A.

the wicked Indians who dwelt in that direction. "They would furnish no guides nor be in any way instrumental in leading their beloved friends into such unseemly dangers."[1] And that was all the satisfaction the visitors could get. Manifestly the Senecas, who were animated by the eternal Iroquois antipathy toward the French, were opposed to the travellers passing through their country. This attitude became the more apparent when finally one of the Indians came forward with a proposal to lead the party by an entirely different route so that it could reach the Ohio eventually, but at a much lower point than had been intended. Having seen enough to make their blood run cold, La Salle and his companions were quite ready to accept this offer and return to their canoes on the lake shore.[2]

As the expedition continued westward past the mouth of the Niagara, the travellers heard the distant roar of the cataract, but did not turn aside to investigate the cause of it. Galinée's mention of it in his narrative is the earliest we have, except from Indian sources. At the western end of the lake, where they were hospitably entertained by the natives, they were told by a Shawnee prisoner that it was a six weeks' journey to the "great water" and that he could easily lead them there. La Salle secured the captive's release and gladly accepted his services. Here, too, the party fell in with Joliet and his companion, Peré, who had been sent out by Talon to investigate the copper deposits near Lake Superior and were now returning with

---

[1] Fiske, *New France and New England*, 112.

[2] Orsamus H. Marshall, "The First Visit of De La Salle to the Senecas, made in 1669," in *Historical Writings*, 187–235.

their report. La Salle was much interested in Joliet's account of his travels, but saw in it no reason for changing his opinion that the passage for which he was searching lay farther to the south, terminating in the Vermilion Sea, or Gulf of California. The Sulpitian missionaries were more attracted by Joliet's story. When he described the wickedness of the Pottawattomies, they speedily came to the conclusion that there could be no people down the Ohio who stood in such immediate need of salvation. They therefore resolved to abandon the Ohio expedition, and since La Salle refused to do so, there was nothing for the company to do but separate. Guided by a map which Joliet left with them, the Sulpitians made their way to Sault Ste. Marie, where they were so coolly received by the Jesuits that they decided eventually to forego the whole enterprise and return to Montreal. It should be said, however, in extenuation of their faint-heartedness, that in a storm which broke up their boats all their sacred vessels and other ecclesiastical belongings were destroyed, so that they did not deem themselves capable thereafter of establishing missions.

The subsequent course of La Salle in the Ohio expedition cannot be definitely determined. Because of Galinée's withdrawal, our one reliable source of information fails at this point. There is a theory that he went southward with his surviving band of followers, discovered the Ohio in 1670, descended it to the Mississippi, and again in 1671 reached the Mississippi by way of Lake Michigan, the Chicago portage, and the Illinois.[1] This sweeping

---

[1] This view is upheld in the "Histoire de Monsieur La Salle," printed in Margry, *Découvertes et Établissements des Français*, I. 103-166. This

claim is but poorly supported. Practically all first-class students of the subject regard it as a mere invention, or at best a bad piece of bungling due to contemporary geographical ignorance. Owing to a total lack of trustworthy evidence, this is the obscurest period in La Salle's life. It is all but assured, as Parkman thought, that La Salle did reach the Ohio at this time, and perhaps descended it as far as the site of Louisville, but it is far from probable that he saw the Mississippi.[1] A decade and more was to elapse before he should sail on the broad waters of that stream. The real discoverer, as has already appeared, was not to be La Salle at all, but Marquette, together with Joliet, whose great work was to be accomplished four years later.

Without speculating any further on a matter which, after all has been said, is just as uncertain as before, we may conclude that except for the increased knowledge and experience which it brought its leader, this first expedition of La Salle was an almost unqualified failure. We know that it was so regarded by his contemporaries, and that the name La Chine now came to be employed derisively by those who had had no faith in the enterprise from its beginning.[2] For the first time, but not the

work contains what purports to be some recorded conversations of La Salle at Paris, in 1678, concerning the latter part of the Ohio expedition. Circumstances surrounding the paper, however, are so suspicious that it can be given but very slight credence. See the excellent discussions of the whole subject in Winsor, *Cartier to Frontenac*, 222–228, and Parkman, *La Salle*, 21–27.

[1] Charles Whittlesey, "Discovery of the Ohio River by Robert Cavelier de La Salle, 1668–1670," in *Western Reserve and Northern Ohio Historical Society Tracts*, No. 37; Kingsford, *History of Canada*, I. 406–409; and C. W. Butterfield, "History of Ohio," in the *Magazine of Western History*, III. 695–708.

[2] "In these later days, this name of ridicule has been made good by

last, the intrepid adventurer was baffled. His Montreal seigniory was gone and he had nothing to show for it. However, a new field was being opened for his genius, and La Salle knew no such thing as despair.

In 1672, by order of Count Frontenac, successor of Courcelles in the governorship of New France, a fort of earth and palisade of wood was built at the eastern end of Lake Ontario, near the site of the present town of Kingston, as a stronghold against the hostile Iroquois. The fort was known at first as Cataraqui, but subsequently as Frontenac. La Salle, ever alive to strategic advantages, perceived the importance of the place both as a trading post and as a base of operations in the work of western discovery. Accordingly he set about securing control of the fort. After winning the favor of Frontenac he went to France, in 1674, and made his request of Louis XIV. and Colbert so effectively that letters patent were issued granting the government and property of Fort Frontenac with the seigniory of a tract of land around it, on condition that the holder rebuild the fort with stone, maintain a garrison there at his own expense, and clear certain portions of the neighboring territory. A title of nobility was also conferred by the king.[1]

The next two years were spent by La Salle at Fort

---

the passage across La Salle's old possessions of the Canadian Pacific Railway, England's new way to China." — Moore, *The Northwest under Three Flags*, 29.

[1] La Salle's petition for the control of Fort Frontenac is printed in O'Callaghan, *New York Colonial Documents*, IX. 122. The terms of the grant are given in Margry, "Lettres de Cavelier de La Salle," in *Découvertes et Établissements des Français*, II. 10-12, and in the *New York Colonial Documents*, IX. 123-126.

Frontenac. The fort was reconstructed, forests were cleared away, fields were planted, a school was established by the Recollect missionaries, and ships were built with which to navigate the lake in the pursuit of trade. Yet La Salle was no more satisfied than he had been with the life at La Chine six or seven years before. Marquette and Joliet had in the meantime actually discovered the Mississippi, and the guardian of Fort Frontenac was fired with a new ambition to carry on the work they had so auspiciously begun. His dreams embraced not only exploration, but also the founding of colonies and the extension of the French domain throughout the West. "Nor were his visions of China and Japan grown dim or less attractive. He still hoped to find a passage to those distant countries from the head waters of the Mississippi. His achievements at Fort Frontenac were only preparatory to the grand enterprise upon which he had so long set his heart."

In 1677 La Salle was again in France. This time he had a different sort of request to make of the king. What he wanted now was not a grant of land, but authority to explore the Mississippi country and open up new trade routes to the West. It having been all but proved by the voyage of Marquette and Joliet that the Mississippi flowed into the Gulf of Mexico, La Salle now proposed to follow the stream to its mouth and find whether it might not be more practicable to maintain commerce with the interior by means of the Mississippi than by the Great Lakes and the St. Lawrence. He showed that the staples of trade in this region — such as furs, wool, and buffalo hides — were bulky, and their carriage would be greatly facilitated if an all-water route could be found. He asked for the right to establish posts toward the south and west for a period of five years, and offered himself to bear all the expenses of the work.[1]

La Salle's plans were really as far-sighted as they were ambitious. It was his idea that France should no longer delay in assuming possession of the Mississippi Valley as against the counter claims of both the English and the Spanish. He would therefore establish military stations all along the river, and an especially strong one near the mouth. He would see to it that the Indians of all this vast region were swayed by French policies, and that the commerce of the interior should be developed as rapidly as possible to insure speedier settlement. This was indeed the very line of action — especially as to the posts and relations with the Indians — which France subsequently adopted in her great contest with the English for the possession of the Middle West. It is greatly to La Salle's credit that he was among the first to perceive that in such action lay the only hope of the French to make good their inchoate claims to the valley of the Father of Waters. As history proved, the undertaking was too vast to be accomplished by the small population and limited resources of the French in America; but if the attempt was to be made at all, the plan outlined by La Salle was certainly the best one available.

Such an opportunity as that afforded by La Salle's project for the extension of French dominion and prestige

[1] "Memoir of Robert Cavelier de La Salle on the Necessity of Fitting out an Expedition to take Possession of Louisiana," in French, *Historical Collections of Louisiana*, I. 25-34.

in the New World was not to be treated lightly. Louis XIV.'s ministers were enthusiastic in support of the scheme. Accordingly, May 12, 1678, new letters patent were granted by the king.[1] In these it was stated that because of gratitude for the grantee's faithful execution of the agreement of three years before, and because "there is nothing we have more at heart than the discovery of this country," full permission was granted "to endeavor to discover the western part of our country of New France, and, for the execution of this enterprise, to construct forts whenever you shall deem it necessary." It was understood that the work was to be done within five years.

In August, 1678, La Salle sailed from Rochelle. While in Paris he had been joined by a remarkable man who was ever after to be his most faithful companion and lieutenant. This was Henri Tonty, the son of a refugee Italian living in Paris whose name is kept alive by the *tontine* form of insurance. Tonty had seen several years of service in the French army, and was a man of scarcely less energy, courage, and resolution than La Salle himself.[2] In his youth he had one of his arms shot off in battle. The missing member was replaced with one of iron, over which a glove was always worn. Before Tonty had long been in

---

[1] The letters patent are given in translation in the Appendix to Sparks's "La Salle," *American Biography*, I. 181-183; also in O'Callaghan, *New York Colonial Documents*, IX. 127, and in French, *Historical Collections of Louisiana*, I. 35-36. For an excellent account of La Salle's "Grand Enterprise," see Parkman, *La Salle*, Ch. VIII.; and for his western explorations in general, Kingsford, *History of Canada*, I. Chs. IX. and X., II. Chs. VI. and VII.

[2] On the career of Tonty, see Henry E. Legler, *Chevalier Henry de Tonty; his Exploits in the Valley of the Mississippi*, Parkman Club Publications, No. 3 [Milwaukee, 1896].

America this peculiarity became known to the Indians who universally referred to him as "Iron Hand." On the return from France a large quantity of supplies was brought out — anchors, cordage, sails, and other materials for the construction of vessels for lake navigation. Several pilots, mariners, and ship-carpenters were also brought over. Quebec was reached in September, and without loss of time the journey was completed to Fort Frontenac, where the ensuing weeks were to be spent in making preparations for the anticipated expedition of the following year.[1]

Preparations were also to be made at the same time farther west. November 18 Tonty, with a party of workmen, sailed in a brigantine of ten tons to the vicinity of Niagara, having as one object the establishing of a fort at the mouth of the Niagara River, and as another the construction of a vessel in the waters above the falls in which the party might travel upon Lake Erie the following spring. An attempt was made by these forerunners to secure the good-will of the neighboring Senecas, but with only indifferent success. Besides Tonty there was another member of this advance guard who was to become famous in the annals of western discovery. This was the Flemish friar Louis Hennepin, a man possessing many admirable qualities, but bearing in these latter days a reputation much tarnished by his notorious mendacity. We shall have more to say con-

---

[1] "Narrative of the First Attempt by M. Cavelier de La Salle to explore the Mississippi." Drawn up from the manuscripts of Father Zenobius Membré, a Recollect, by Father Crétien Le Clercq. Translated in Shea, *Discovery and Exploration of the Mississippi Valley*, 89 et seq.

cerning him in a later chapter; for the present it is important merely to note that Hennepin was probably the first European to behold America's greatest natural wonder — Niagara Falls. Certainly he was the first to make a sketch of them for publication.[1] In his *Description de la Louisiane*, published at Paris in 1683, he made mention of the falls as follows: "Four leagues from Lake Frontenac [Ontario] there is an incredible cataract or waterfall, which has no equal. The Niagara River near this place is only the eighth of a league wide, but it is very deep in places, and so rapid above the great fall that it hurries down all the animals which try to cross it, without a single one being able to withstand its current. They plunge down a height of more than five hundred feet, and its fall is composed of two sheets of water and a cascade, with an island sloping down. In the middle these waters foam and boil in a fearful manner. They thunder continually, and when the wind blows in a southerly direction, the noise which they make is heard for from more than fifteen leagues."[2]

Meanwhile La Salle had left Fort Frontenac and was cruising along the southern shore of Lake Ontario. He thus encountered the Senecas before joining his own men, and succeeded better than had Tonty in explaining to their satisfaction his purposes in exploring the West.

---

[1] The sketch was published at Utrecht in 1697 in *Nouvelle Découverte d'un très grand Pays, situé dans l'Amérique*, an account of Hennepin's travels in America. It is reproduced in Winsor, *Cartier to Frontenac*, 261; also in the *Narrative and Critical History of America*, IV. 248. It is extremely important as a basis for comparing the contour of the falls to-day with that of two and a quarter centuries ago.

[2] Shea, *A Description of Louisiana by Father Louis Hennepin*, 71–72.

January 20 he was with his outpost at Niagara, having brought with him the remaining materials necessary to the construction of the new ship. In or near the mouth of Cayuga Creek a shipyard was improvised, and thither, a distance of twelve miles, the lumber, anchors, and masts were transported by land.[1] Leaving Tonty to oversee the work, La Salle returned to Fort Frontenac by a perilous overland trip, only to find himself attacked by his creditors and other enemies of his enterprise.

By May the new vessel was ready to be launched. She was of fifty tons burden and carried five guns. Since she bore at her prow a grotesque griffon, representing an attempt to imitate the family arms of Count Frontenac, she retained the name *Griffon* which the builders had bestowed upon her. During the summer the work of fitting continued until early in August, when all was in readiness for the departure of the expedition. On the 7th of the month, amid a discharge of guns, and with the crew chanting the *Te Deum*, La Salle started for — he knew not what, except that the most easy passage into the Mississippi was the main object of desire.[2] By the 23rd the waters of Lake Huron had been entered. After weathering a storm which called out many a vow to St. Anthony of Padua, the little vessel was anchored

[1] Mr. O. H. Marshall of Buffalo, whose name is connected with many studies in the history of the Niagara region, was the first to point out this spot as corresponding best to the contemporary descriptions. The exact place of the shipyard is in some doubt, but the general location is quite certain. Mr. Marshall's *The Building and Voyage of the Griffon* is printed as Number I. of the publications of the Buffalo Historical Society; also in his *Historical Writings*, 73-121. Another treatise on the subject is Cyrus K. Remington, *The Ship-yard of the Griffon* [Buffalo, 1891].

[2] Shea, *A Description of Louisiana by Father Louis Hennepin*, 90.

four days later in the harbor at St. Ignace, in the straits of Mackinaw, where there was already a French mission. In a few days La Salle proceeded to Green Bay, where some of the men sent ahead had collected a goodly store of furs. With these the *Griffon* was loaded, and on the 18th of September the ship was started back to Frontenac with her valuable cargo. It was hoped by La Salle that the revenue from these furs would appease his hungry creditors and keep them from seizing his property on the St. Lawrence during his absence. The sending of them, however, was a violation of his patent; for by the terms of this instrument he was in no case to divert Indian traffic from Montreal.[1]

As soon as the *Griffon* was well under way La Salle and his men started in bark canoes for the southern end of Lake Michigan. The objective point was the mouth of the St. Joseph River — then known as the Miami. Tonty was to advance directly thither along the eastern shore of the lake, while La Salle himself was to traverse the western and southern coasts. It was expected that by the time the party was ready to cross to the Kankakee and thence to the Illinois, the *Griffon* would have returned with fresh supplies and articles for trade. La Salle's trip along the Wisconsin shore of the lake was accomplished with extreme difficulty, owing to the heavy cargoes of his canoes and the scarcity of food, so that it was not until November 1, 1679, that the mouth of the St. Joseph was reached. Tonty encountered difficulties almost as great, and did not arrive until three weeks later than La Salle. Much to the latter's disappointment, Tonty brought no

[1] French, *Historical Collections of Louisiana*, I. 25.

news of the *Griffon*. Two men were at once despatched to Mackinaw to guide the expected vessel, on her return from Niagara, to the fort at the mouth of the St. Joseph.

As a matter of fact the ill-fated ship was never to be heard of again. What became of her cannot be definitely known. Soon after her start from Green Bay to Mackinaw a gale swept the northern part of the lake, and even then La Salle was led to fear greatly for her safety. Probably under the weight of her cargo she foundered and none of her crew survived.[1] At any rate she never reached Mackinaw. In later times La Salle professed to believe that the pilot of the vessel had played false and had carried her out of her course with the intention of selling her to the English. We have no reason other than La Salle's suspicion, however, for thinking that such was the case.

December 3 La Salle, with eight canoes and thirty-three men, struck off into the interior, following the course of the St. Joseph into northern Indiana.[2] A portage of five miles, discovered only after much search, enabled the party to embark on the upper Kankakee. The three-hundred-mile voyage down this river was unmarked by important incidents, although the travellers were several times threatened with starvation, due to the scarcity of buffalo and other game in the winter season. Passing out of the Kankakee, the voyagers continued their journey on the broader waters of the Illinois.

[1] Certainly the crew did not contain half La Salle's party, as John Fiske would have us believe. *New France and New England*, 126. Winsor says there were seven men on board. *Cartier to Frontenac*, 263.

[2] Bartlett and Lyon, *La Salle in the Valley of the St. Joseph* [South Bend, 1899].

Diligent rummaging in a deserted village of the Ottawas brought to light a large store of buried corn, from which La Salle felt constrained to "borrow" about fifty bushels as a relief from animal diet. Fortunately, when the owners were encountered a few days later, he was able to make satisfactory explanations.

Meanwhile trouble was brewing. In the first place, the Illinois Indians were far from enthusiastic in their reception of the Frenchmen.[1] La Salle endeavored to impress them with the benefits which would come to them by reason of the present expedition, such as better trading facilities, and an opportunity to learn of the true God; but the wily natives were far from being convinced. Their attitude was generally that of sullen and ill-concealed suspicion. Despite La Salle's protestations to the contrary, they persisted in believing that in some way the coming of the French was connected with the much-dreaded renewal of the Iroquois invasion of the West. Moreover, La Salle's own men were showing unmistakable signs of disaffection. The mystery of the *Griffon*, the hardships of the expedition, and the threatening manner of the Indians, worked together to discourage and even frighten all except the most daring. Six of them deserted at once, including two carpenters on whom much depended.

To make matters worse, Nikanape, brother of the great chief of the Illinois, and a man of much influence in the Peoria region, made a long speech at a banquet served to the Frenchmen in his own home, in which he set forth

[1] Margry, "Lettres de Cavelier de La Salle," *Découvertes et Établissements des Français*, II. 32–50.

with terrifying eloquence the perils to be anticipated by the voyager on the Mississippi. Many other adventurers, he said, had met their end in the attempt to reach the mouth of the "great water." The banks were inhabited by a strong and fearless race of men who delighted in putting to death every stranger who came among them. The waters swarmed with crocodiles, serpents, and all manner of terrible monsters. No boat but the very largest and strongest could pass in safety the many rapids and falls in the river. And even if these dangers could be survived, there was no possible escape from destruction in the great whirlpool at the mouth of the river, to which the rapidly accelerated current inevitably bore the luckless adventurer.[1] La Salle argued as best he could against the verity of these reports, and quoted other Indian informants to the contrary of Nikanape's statements, but the mischief was done. The crafty host had succeeded only too well in frightening the prospective travellers to the Gulf.

Knowing that idleness bred discontent, the dauntless leader set his disaffected followers to work at the construction of a fort near the present site of Peoria. The name given the place was Crêvecœur, "Broken Heart," — whether as an expression of disappointment, or merely in honor of Louis XIV.'s capture of a fort by that name in the Netherlands in 1672, cannot be determined.[2] The

---

[1] Shea, *A Description of Louisiana by Father Louis Hennepin*, 167.

[2] Jared Sparks, in his *Life of La Salle*, says the name was given as "a memorial of the sadness he [La Salle] felt at the loss of his vessel." *American Biography*, I. 56. This view is borne out by Father Crétien Le Clercq's narrative, which says that La Salle called the fort Crêvecœur "on account of the many disappointments he had experienced, but which

building of a vessel of forty tons for the navigation of the lower Illinois and the Mississippi was also begun. Despite the defection of the carpenters, the work was pushed so rapidly that in six weeks' time the fort was complete and the ship ready for the masts and rigging. The fears of the men were somewhat allayed by La Salle's wringing from a young Illinois the truth about the lower Mississippi. Possessed of such information, the tactful French leader was thereafter able to contradict successfully the flagrant and purposeful misrepresentations of the jealous natives.

Although La Salle was bent personally upon following the Mississippi to the Gulf, he determined to send out a side expedition to explore the upper course of the great river. One of the men, by the name of Michel Accau, was put in command of this expedition, and the priest Hennepin and another man, Picard du Gay, were detailed to accompany him. On the 29th of February, 1680, the little party dropped down the Illinois, and began its long and eventful journey. The recital of its achievements must be reserved for another chapter.

A few days later La Salle, with five companions and two canoes, started on a return trip to Fort Frontenac. Crèvecœur and its little garrison were left under the command of the faithful Tonty. La Salle wished, before going further with his undertaking, to set his affairs in better

---

never shook his firm resolve." Shea, *Discovery and Exploration of the Mississippi Valley*, 96. On the other hand, in editing this narrative, Shea doubted if "any but a foolish leader could have so clearly emphasized his misfortunes, when his querulous adherents needed so much to be inspirited." See Winsor, *Cartier to Frontenac*, 266, and Parkman, *La Salle*, Ch. XIII.

order at Frontenac; and besides, he must have anchors and other equipment for the new vessel built on the Illinois. He also wished to clear up the mystery which still remained regarding the fate of the *Griffon*. The journey was one of extreme difficulty, accomplished as it was in the treacherous weather of early spring. By the end of March the St. Joseph had been reached, and there the certain failure of the *Griffon* was first learned. Traversing southern Michigan to the Detroit River, and thence by way of Lakes Erie and Ontario, the wearied travellers at last reached Fort Frontenac on the 6th of May. They had covered a thousand miles in sixty-five days.

La Salle found his business interests in a sorry condition.[1] Trusted agents had misappropriated his funds. A rumor of his death had been given credence, and a forced sale of his goods had been held. A vessel from France, carrying a cargo belonging to him and valued at $30,000 in money of to-day, had been wrecked in the St. Lawrence without anything being saved. Misfortunes had crowded thick and fast upon every enterprise in which he was interested. Had not Governor Frontenac continued to have faith in him, he must have been compelled to abandon his western explorations, or at least return to them empty handed. As it was, after two months he found himself ready to set out again for Fort Crèvecœur.

But now came bad news from that direction. When passing up the Illinois on his way to Frontenac, La Salle had observed the strategic point known as Starved Rock,

---

[1] Margry, "Lettres de Cavelier de La Salle," *Découvertes et Établissements des Français*, II. 167.

and had sent back an order to Tonty to use part of his men in fortifying it. The order had been executed, and Tonty himself had taken up his abode at the new fort. But very soon the men left at Crêvecœur, freed from restraint, decided that they had had enough of frontier life, mutinied, and destroyed the stockade. This disaster was followed by an invasion of the Illinois country by the Iroquois, and it was only by the most remarkable self-possession and effrontery that Tonty and his five companions at the so-called "Rock Fort" came through the conflict alive.[1] They saw that to remain on the Illinois was folly, so, embarking in canoes, they made their way as speedily as possible to Lake Michigan, whose shores they followed northward from the Chicago portage until at last, famished, exhausted, and ill, they were given a hospitable reception in a Pottawattomie village near Green Bay.[2]

Only the news of the revolt at Crêvecœur had reached La Salle at Frontenac. The Iroquois invasion occurred after Tonty's messengers had left the Illinois country. So that at the very time that Tonty was on the west bank of Lake Michigan, hastening northward (November and December, 1680), La Salle was on the east bank, supposing him still to be at Starved Rock and pressing on to his relief. La Salle's return had been by way of Mackinaw, the St. Joseph, the Kankakee, and the Illinois. From the

[1] On Tonty and the Iroquois, Parkman, *La Salle*, Ch. XVI.
[2] Father Zenobius Membré, "Narrative of the Adventures of La Salle's Party at Fort Crêvecœur, in Illinois," Shea, *Discovery and Exploration of the Mississippi Valley*, 147 et seq. A. A. Graham, "The Story of Starved Rock on the Illinois," in the *Magazine of Western History*, I. 213-230.

St. Joseph he was accompanied by only five Frenchmen and an Indian. Starved Rock was found inexplicably unoccupied. A little farther on the Illinois country was reached — now a horrible scene of desolation, such as the Iroquois were only too generally accustomed to leave behind them on their expeditions of conquest. Crèvecœur was in ruins, though the hull of the vessel built the year before was still on the stocks. The loss of his outposts on the Illinois must have seemed to La Salle an all but overwhelming climax to the long series of reverses he had encountered in the last twelvemonth.

Meeting with no opposition, seeing, indeed, scarcely a human being, the little band continued to descend the Illinois, until, in the early days of December, 1680, La Salle was rewarded by his first glimpse of the Father of Waters.[1] This was interesting enough, but it was no discovery. With his bark canoes and his mere handful of men, the intended trip down the river could not yet be made, so there was nothing to do but turn back and renew the effort to secure adequate equipment for the undertaking. Lest Tonty and his men might have preceded the present party, a letter was tied to a tree at the junction of the Mississippi and Illinois. Then the lonely travellers began the long and toilsome return voyage.

The winter of 1680–1681 was spent by La Salle in the Miami country, southeast of Lake Michigan. No one knew better than he that precious time was being lost, but there seemed to be no other way for it. "I am disgusted

---

[1] "Relation du Voyage de Cavelier de La Salle du 22 Août, 1680, à l'Automne de 1681," in Margry, "Lettres de Cavelier de La Salle," *Découvertes et Établissements des Français*, II. 115–135.

at being always compelled to make excuses," he wrote to a friend, "but I hope you will get other information of how things are going on here, beside what the Jesuits give you." In March, 1681, he again went westward into the Illinois country, in the hope of bringing about a league of the Illinois with the Miamis against the Iroquois. It was while on this trip that he received the very welcome intelligence from a band of Foxes that Tonty was among the Pottawattomies at Mackinaw. Hastening northward, he found his long-lost lieutenant, as the Foxes had said he would, and in June the two set out on a thousand-mile canoe trip to Frontenac.

After two months' work at repairing his credit and securing supplies, La Salle started anew upon the execution of his cherished scheme of descending the Mississippi to the Gulf. Twenty-three Frenchmen and thirty-one New England Indians (Mohegans and Abenakis) accompanied him, and many recruits were gathered on the way. November 3 the party was at Fort Miami at the St. Joseph's mouth. The Indians had insisted on taking their women with them, and there were ten of these and also three children. It is uncertain whether they went with the expedition all the way to the Gulf.

On the 21st of December the party left Fort Miami in two divisions. One led by Tonty and the Recollect missionary Zenobius Membré, from whose narrative most of our information regarding the expedition is drawn, sailed around the head of Lake Michigan to the "divine river," called by the Indians *Checagou* [Chicago]. The other, led by La Salle himself, went by land to the same point, arriving early in January. Dragging their canoes and supplies on sledges, the travellers ascended the frozen Chicago, crossed the portage to the Illinois, and finally made their way to the site of Crêvecœur. Below this point the river was open so that the canoes could be launched. On the 6th of February the voyagers found themselves floating on the waters of the Mississippi. After a delay of a week, caused by the dangerous ice-floes borne down from above, a start was made down the river.[1]

In a short time the mouth of the Missouri was reached.[2] The travellers were amazed, as Joliet and Marquette had been, at the volume of muddy water poured by that stream into the Mississippi. Membré says in his account that the quantity of sediment brought in by the Missouri was such that the waters of the larger stream were never clear thereafter to the Gulf, "although seven other rivers of clear water were discharged into it." The Indians assured La Salle that by ascending the Missouri ten or twelve days a lofty range of mountains would be reached, from whose crests great ships were to be descried on the distant sea. About the middle of February the mouth of the Ohio was passed, but, as Justin Winsor has pointed out, La Salle does not seem to have recognized the stream

[1] Father Zenobius Membré, "Narrative of La Salle's Voyage down the Mississippi," Shea, *Discovery and Exploration of the Mississippi Valley*, 166. La Salle's own account of the descent of the river is in Margry, "Lettres de Cavelier de La Salle," *Découvertes et Établissements des Français*, II. 164–203. Another account is in the Memoir of Sieur de Tonty, in French, *Historical Collections of Louisiana*, I. 52 *et seq.*

[2] At this point La Salle wrote a letter — to whom is not known — describing the journey to the Missouri. It is printed in Margry, II. 164–180, and in translation in the *Magazine of American History*, II. 619–623.

as one he had seen before.[1] If he had ever been on the Ohio at all, it must have been in the region of eastern Kentucky, and likely enough he thought the river flowed thence southward directly to the Gulf.

The Indians along the Mississippi's course were not numerous and were generally quite hospitable. La Salle always used extreme caution, and several times averted probable trouble by simply allowing the natives to see that he was prepared for resistance. Food was abundant and easily obtained in exchange for trinkets which the Frenchmen had been careful to bring from Montreal and Frontenac, and there were enough new plants and animals to be seen and strange Indian customs to be observed to relieve the journey of monotony.

On the 14th of March, when the voyagers were in the Arkansas region, a landing was effected for the purpose of taking possession of the country in the king's name.[2] A cross was planted, together with the royal arms, and to the curious crowd of natives whom the coming of the strangers attracted, Father Membré managed to communicate a few of the cardinal facts of the Christian religion, though he had to depend wholly on improvised signs. "I took occasion," he writes, "to explain something of the truth of God, and the mysteries of our redemption, of which they saw the arms. During this time they showed that they relished what I said, by raising their eyes to heaven and kneeling as if to adore. We also saw them rub their hands over their bodies after

---

[1] Winsor, *Cartier to Frontenac*, 291.
[2] Margry, "Lettres de Cavelier de La Salle," *Découvertes et Établissements des Français*, II. 181–185.

rubbing them over the cross. In fact, on our return from the sea, we found that they had surrounded the cross with a palisade."[1]

A week later, after travelling three hundred miles farther, the Frenchmen found themselves among the Taensas, who dwelt "around a little lake formed in the land by the river Mississippi." Tonty was sent to the chief's village with presents and offers of peace. Not only were these thankfully accepted, but the chief insisted on making a visit to La Salle. "Two hours before the time," says Membré, "a master of ceremonies came, followed by six men. He made them clear the way he [the chief] was to pass, prepare a place, and cover it with a delicately worked cane mat. The chief, who came some time after, was dressed in a fine white cloth, or blanket. He was preceded by two men, carrying fans of white feathers. A third carried a copper plate, and a round one of the same metal, both highly polished. He maintained a very grave demeanor during the visit, which was, however, full of confidence and marks of friendship."[2] Such regal dignity on the part of a chieftain of eight miserable mud villages must have seemed ludicrous to the Frenchmen, but consideration for their own safety doubtless enabled them fairly well to maintain their composure during the ordeal.

Membré's description of the lower Mississippi country is genuinely interesting and in the main quite true to fact. "When you are twenty or thirty leagues," he says, "below the Maroa [midway between the mouths

---

[1] "Narrative of Father Membré," Shea, *Discovery and Exploration of the Mississippi Valley*, 170.

[2] "Narrative of Father Membré," Shea, *ibid.*, 171.

of the Illinois and the Ohio], the banks are full of canes until you reach the sea, except in fifteen or twenty places where there are very pretty hills, and spacious, convenient landing-places. The inundation does not extend far, and behind these drowned lands you see the finest country in the world. Our hunters, French and Indian, were delighted with it. For an extent of at least two hundred leagues in length, and as much in breadth, as we were told, there are vast fields of excellent land, diversified here and there with pleasing hills, lofty woods, groves through which you might ride on horseback, so clear and unobstructed are the paths. These little forests also line the rivers which intersect the country in various places, and which abound in fish. The crocodiles are dangerous here, so much so that in some parts no one would venture to expose himself, or even put his hand out of his canoe. . . . You meet prairies everywhere; sometimes of fifteen or twenty leagues front, and three or four deep, ready to receive the plough. The soil excellent, capable of supporting great colonies. Beans grow wild, and the stalk lasts several years, always bearing fruit; it is thicker than an arm, and runs up like ivy to the top of the highest trees. The peach trees are quite like those of France, and very good; they are so loaded with fruit that the Indians have to prop up those they cultivate in their clearings. There are whole forests of very fine mulberries, of which we ate the fruit from the month of May; many plum trees and other fruit trees, some known and others unknown in Europe; vines, pomegranates, and horse-chestnuts are common. They raise three or four crops of corn a year. . . . I saw some ripe, while more was sprouting. Winter was known only by the rains."[1]

The mouth of the Red River was reached by La Salle's party on the last day of March. April 2 the canoes were fired upon by the hostile Quinipissas, but without suffering harm. Four days later a point was reached where the river divides into three branches, in reality its three main mouths. La Salle followed the western one, Tonty and Membré the middle one, and Dautray the eastern. Before many miles had been covered the voyagers began to observe unmistakable evidence that the sea was not far distant. The water, from being entirely fresh, became first brackish, then quite salt. In a few hours the explorers were gladdened by their first sight of the broad ocean. So far as we can tell, this was the earliest occasion on which men of French nationality had been permitted to look out upon the inner waters of the great Gulf, so long the haunt exclusively of the gold-seeking Spaniard. The three bands were again brought together, and the next two days, March 7 and 8, were spent in exploring the mouths of the river and searching for a suitable spot for the ceremony which was to constitute a fitting culmination to the enterprise.

This ceremony was performed April 9, 1682. Except for the absence of the natives, it was not unlike that at Sault Ste. Marie almost eleven years before. In a dry place beyond the reach of inundations a column and a cross were set up in token of the French possession now established in the lower Mississippi Valley. To

[1] "Narrative of Father Membré," Shea, *Discovery and Exploration of the Mississippi Valley*, 179-182.

the column were attached the arms of France, with the inscription : —

LOUIS LE GRAND, ROI DE FRANCE ET DE NAVARRE, RÈGNE; LE NEUVIÈME AVRIL, 1682.

The whole party, under arms, chanted the *Te Deum*, the *Exaudiat*, and the *Domine salvum fac Regem;* and then after a salute of guns and cries of "Vive le Roi," La Salle delivered a formal speech in which he christened the Mississippi Valley "Louisiana."[1] Possession was taken of all the lands drained directly by the Mississippi, together with all their "nations, people, provinces, cities, towns, villages, mines, minerals, fisheries, streams, and rivers." Protest was formally entered against "all those who may in future undertake to invade any or all of these countries, people, or lands, to the prejudice of the right of his Majesty, acquired by the consent of the nations" named in the earlier parts of the address. After more shouts of "Vive le Roi" a leaden plate was buried at the foot of the tree to which the cross was attached, bearing on one side the French arms, and on the other a statement in Latin to the effect that La Salle, Tonty, and their companions were the first white men to navigate the Mississippi from the Illinois

[1] Sparks doubted whether La Salle originated the name. In his *Robert de La Salle*, he says : "It has been said that the name Louisiana was first given to the country by La Salle on the present occasion. This is possible; yet, as Hennepin's *Description de la Louisiane* was printed the same year, it is more probable that the name had before been used, or at least spoken of as appropriate. La Salle does not profess, in the *Procès Verbal*, to give a new name, but seems rather to employ it as one already existing." *American Biography*, I. 104. It should be noted, however, that Hennepin's *Louisiane* did not appear until January, 1683.

to the Gulf. "Whereupon the ceremony was concluded with cries of 'Vive le Roi.'" A full account of the proceedings, including a draft of La Salle's speech, was drawn up, certified by a notary, and signed by thirteen principal persons of the company.[1]

The geographical terms employed by La Salle in his speech give only a very vague idea of what he really meant by Louisiana. Two years after this expedition, however, a map-maker by the name of Franquelin, who lived at Quebec and carefully recorded the progress of western discovery, marked off on his map of the Mississippi Valley the great region which was by that time included in the French claim.[2] On the southwest it extended to the Rio Grande; on the west and northwest, to the Rockies; on the north, to a rather vague watershed south of the Great Lakes from central Minnesota to the Alleghanies; on the east, to the latter range of mountains; and on the south, to the northern limits of Spanish Florida and the western coasts of the Gulf. All in all, it was an area of hardly less than 150,000 square miles — one of the most magnificent in resources in the world.

Of course, according to the tenets of modern international law, such a sweeping claim would be clearly inadmissible. The best authorities in this field are agreed

---

[1] For La Salle's "Procès Verbal" of the taking possession of Louisiana, see French, *Historical Collections of Louisiana*, I. 45; also the Appendix of Sparks, *American Biography*, I. 194-202.

[2] The original of this map has been lost. The so-called Parkman copy is in the Archives of the Marine in Paris. See the reproduction in Winsor, *Cartier to Frontenac*, 294, and an account of Franquelin and his map in Parkman, *La Salle*, Appendix, p. 455.

that discovery confers no title at all, except at best an inchoate one, unless followed within reasonable time by actual settlement.[1] Two centuries ago, however, this principle was not so clearly established, and greed for territory, together with gross geographical ignorance, led to the setting up of absurdly extravagant claims whenever a new quarter of the globe was to be possessed by one or more of the powers of Europe. The theory then proceeded upon was that the discovery of a river, and particularly of a river's mouth, gave a title to all the lands of the interior drained by that river and its tributaries. As late indeed as 1803, when the controversy concerning the Louisiana boundary was raging at Paris and Madrid, Monroe and Livingston, the American negotiators of the purchase, held steadfastly to the proposi-

---

[1] "It has now been long settled that the bare fact of discovery is an insufficient ground of proprietary right. It is only so far useful that it gives additional value to acts in themselves doubtful or inadequate. . . . An inchoate title acts as a temporary bar to occupation by another state, but it must either be converted into a definitive title within reasonable time by planting settlements or military posts, or it must at least be kept alive by repeated local acts showing an intention of continual claim. . . . When territory has been duly annexed, and the fact has either been published or has been recorded by monuments or inscriptions on the spot, a good title has always been held to have been acquired as against a state making settlements within such time as, allowing for accidental circumstances or moderate negligence, might elapse before a force or a colony were sent out to some part of the land intended to be occupied; but that in the course of a few years the presumption of permanent intention afforded by such acts has died away, if they stood alone, and that more continuous acts or actual settlement by another power become a stronger root of title." Hall, *International Law* [4th ed.], 106. See also Wheaton, *International Law*, 240 et seq.; Pomeroy, *Lectures on International Law*, Ch. III.; and Walter B. Scaife, "The Development of International Law as to Newly Discovered Territory," in the *Papers of the American Historical Association*, IV. 267–293.

tion that "when any European nation takes possession of any extent of seacoast, that possession is understood as extending into the interior country to the sources of the rivers emptying within that coast, to all their branches and the country they cover." That the territory taken under control was already inhabited by native races was not considered a bar to occupation by Europeans. The natives were heathens, and the theory prevailed that it was the divine prerogative of Christian peoples to assume sovereignty over them and their lands. The American Indians were regarded as abundantly compensated by the opportunity thus afforded them to acquire civilization and become believers in the true God. The Spanish explorers and colonizers invariably refused to recognize that the Indian had any inherent right to his land, and the French as a rule pursued the same course. The English government usually acted on this policy, though in the practice of the settlers the Indians were generally dealt with as owners of the soil competent to grant the tenure of it after a more or less improvised legal fashion.[1]

It was quite impossible that La Salle and his contemporaries should have any very definite conception of the extent of Louisiana. The head waters of the Mississippi were unknown, and likewise the length and direction of such of the more important tributaries as the Missouri, Ohio, Arkansas, and Red. Yet it was understood that the area

[1] On the European conceptions of Indian land tenure, see George E. Ellis, *Red Man and White Man in North America*, Chs. IV. and VI.; P. A. Bruce, *Economic History of Virginia*, I. 493 *et seq.*; James Kent, *Commentaries on American Law*, III. 377-400. See especially Chief Justice Marshall's decision in the case of Johnson v. McIntosh (1828), in Freeman Snow, *Cases and Opinions on International Law*, 6.

of the valley must be very great, and it was already a well-determined plan of the French that every square mile of it should be kept out of the grasp of the rival Englishman and Spaniard. As we shall see, it was because of no lack of effort on the part of La Salle that his people failed in this purpose.

Lack of provisions dictated that La Salle's men should not tarry long at the Mississippi's mouth. As soon as the ceremony of assuming possession was completed, the homeward voyage was commenced. Relations with the Indians on the return trip were generally quite similar to those sustained on the way down the river. Some tribes were as friendly as could be desired; others, as the Quinipissas, were disposed to make trouble. There was at least one open combat, and a very narrow escape from another. When the party was within a hundred leagues of the Illinois its intrepid leader fell sick. Tonty was sent ahead to carry the news of the discovery to Mackinaw, while for forty days his chief lay at Fort Prudhomme,[1] hovering between life and death. Due to the careful nursing of Membré and others the illness did not prove fatal, and by the end of July the patient had recovered sufficiently to move slowly on toward the settlements. At the end of September the St. Joseph River was reached. "He thus finished," he says in closing the report which he prepared for transmission to France, "the most important and difficult discovery which has ever been made by any Frenchman, without the loss of a single

---

[1] A stockade on the third Chickasaw bluff, built on the downward voyage, and named in honor of a member of the party who, after being lost for a time in the forest, found his way back to his comrades at this point.

man, in the same country where Jean Ponce de Leon, Pamphile de Narvaez, and Ferdinand de Soto, perished unsuccessful with more than two thousand Spaniards. No Spaniard ever carried through such an enterprise with so small a force, in the presence of so many enemies. But he has gained no advantage for himself. His misfortunes and the frequent obstacles in his way have cost him more than two hundred thousand livres. Still he will be happy if he has done anything for the advantage of France, and if his endeavors may win for him the protection of Monseigneur."

Though suffering a weakness which did not pass away for four months or more, La Salle lost no time in cementing the friendship of the Miamis and Illinois with the French, making many long and dangerous trips in the furtherance of this precautionary work. Already his scheme for the establishing of French colonies on the Mississippi had taken definite shape. Wishing to make a speedy and correct report of his achievements to the home government, he despatched Father Membré to Quebec, where the missionary arrived just in time to take passage for France in the ship that carried back the retiring governor, Count Frontenac. The French capital was reached late in December. Besides the report, Membré carried with him La Salle's outline of a plan for colonizing both the upper and lower Mississippi and thus preparing to meet any subsequent aggressions of the English or Spanish. Already Tonty had been sent back into the Illinois country with a new colony. Starved Rock had become Fort St. Louis — the outpost of French civilization in the Great West and the centre of influence from

which the surrounding Indians were to be kept on good terms with the French during the interval that must elapse before there could be an extensive settlement of the latter in the region.

Late in the summer of 1683, leaving Tonty in charge of his interests in the West, La Salle journeyed to Quebec, and thence took passage for France, where he arrived December 23. His plans for colonization were growing upon him to such an extent that he felt it necessary to enter personally upon the task of enlisting the French government in the enterprise. Moreover, the new governor, La Barre, was trying to influence the king against La Salle by making it appear that the latter had precipitated the recent Iroquois war and was perverting his royal commission for the purposes of mere trade.[1] La Salle wished to ward off this attack by a personal defence before the king. He found this in no wise hard to do. The French monarchy was in the heyday of its successes, and large projects for its aggrandizement in foreign lands were never more favorably contemplated than now. The returned explorer was received with the greatest distinction by both the king and Seignelay, son of Colbert, now minister of marine, and La Barre was forcefully ordered to cease his backbitings.

It will be remembered that, when asking state aid in his

---

[1] Margry, "Lettres de Cavelier de La Salle," *Découvertes et Établissements des Français*, II. 337, 348; Parkman, *La Salle*, 297–305; Kingsford, *History of Canada*, II. 111. The instructions issued to Le Febvre de La Barre as governor and lieutenant of New France were dated May 10, 1682. They are printed in O'Callaghan, *New York Colonial Documents*, IX. 167-168. See La Barre's charges against La Salle in the *New York Colonial Documents*, IX. 211.

projects for the opening of the Mississippi on the occasion of his former visit to France, in 1678, one of La Salle's main arguments had been that trade with the interior could be carried on more expeditiously by way of the Gulf of Mexico and the lower Mississippi than by way of the Great Lakes. As the explorer's work had proceeded during the past five years this idea had become a much stronger one with him, and his plans had been enlarged proportionally. He had soon discerned that it was not enough merely to descend the great river to its mouth and demonstrate the ease of its navigation. If the French were really to profit by the discovery, settlements must be established, colonies planted as posts of exchange, and a French population developed after the nature of that in the Canadian country. The proximity of the Spaniards, both in Florida and Mexico, and the vague but persistent claim they maintained over the entire northern shore of the Gulf, likewise pointed to the wisdom of an early colonization of Louisiana by the French.

When, therefore, La Salle, early in 1684, presented himself at the French court, it was with a definite scheme for the immediate establishment of a French colony sixty leagues above the mouth of the Mississippi. Despite La Barre's strenuous efforts to bring the explorer into discredit with King Louis and his ministers, the proposed plan was at once adopted. The opportunity to clinch the French claim to the Louisiana country and at the same time to thwart the suspected designs of the Spaniards was too good to be missed. Relations between France and Spain at the time were much strained, and the colonizing of the lower Mississippi gave promise of some very effec-

tive blows at the Spanish domination in southwestern America. According to La Salle's representations, the natives were incensed at Spanish insolence and were quite ready to welcome French settlement. Fifteen thousand fighting men could be counted on, it was said, from among the river tribes, while as many as four thousand warriors could easily be brought down from the Illinois country.[1] Without doubt the thirty silver mines of the Spanish in New Biscay could be made French property, and this would be but a beginning. It thus appears that La Salle's plans and enterprises were tinged with the same romantic colors that had long characterized those of the Spaniards.

Seignelay easily won the king to a policy of generosity in dealing with La Salle, and, whereas only a single vessel had been asked with which to carry two hundred men to the Mississippi's mouth, it was determined that four ships, one of which (the *Joly*) was a frigate of thirty-six guns, should be employed in the enterprise. The government undertook to furnish munitions and supplies in whatsoever quantity they were needed.[2] La Salle was to be in supreme command, and to him was issued a new commission, authorizing him to establish colonies anywhere in Louisiana, and to rule over all the vast territory from Lake Michigan to the bounds of Mexico.

July 24, 1684, the expedition started.[3] La Salle's hopes

---

[1] Margry, "Lettres de Cavelier de La Salle," *Découvertes et Établissements des Français*, II. 359–369; Parkman, *La Salle*, Ch. XXIII.; Kingsford, *History of Canada*, II. 117–127.

[2] Margry, *ibid.*, 377–388. La Salle's commission is in O'Callaghan, *New York Colonial Documents*, IX. 225.

[3] Father Crétien Le Clercq, "The Account of La Salle's Attempt to reach the Mississippi by Sea, and of the Establishment of a French

were high. It seemed that after multiplied failures and disappointments success was about to be achieved. A region half as large as Europe was on the point of being secured for all time for the French people. In the company being transported to the New World were the 200 soldiers that had been asked for, and besides these about 280 colonists,—men, women, and children, mostly picked up by La Salle's agents in the streets of Rochelle. It was intended that after the proposed settlement near the mouth of the river had been made, others should very soon be established on its banks farther toward the north.

But again we encounter a saddening story of misfortunes, an aggregation of mistakes and disasters which speedily worked ruin to La Salle's fondest dreams. In the first place, the colonists were mostly vagabonds and beggars, quite devoid of the industry and skill so necessary to settlers in a wilderness country. From the narrative of Father Le Clercq we gather that La Salle's agents shared the universal delusion that any sort of people were good enough for colonists. After speaking of two or

Colony in St. Louis Bay;" Joutel, "Historical Journal of Monsieur de La Salle's Last Voyage to discover the River Mississippi." These are the most available narratives. They are printed, respectively, in Shea, *Discovery and Exploration of the Mississippi Valley*, 185–196, and French, *Historical Collections of Louisiana*, I. 85–193. Other interesting documents on the subject are in Margry, II. 392 *et seq.* Still another very important source is the *Relation du voyage entrepris par feu M. Robert Cavelier, Sieur de La Salle, pour découvrir dans le Golfe de Mexique, l'embouchure du fleuve de Missisipi. Par son frère, M. Cavelier.* This is a report said to have been drawn up by La Salle's brother at the instance of M. de Seignelay, minister of marine. It is incomplete, and hence not so satisfactory as the narratives of Joutel and Le Clercq. A translation of it is in J. G. Shea, *Early Voyages up and down the Mississippi*, 15–42.

three men of excellent character who accompanied the expedition, the pious father exclaims, "Would to God the troops and the rest of the crew had been as well chosen! Those who were appointed, while M. de La Salle was at Paris, picked up 150 soldiers, mere wretched beggars soliciting alms, many too deformed and unable to fire a musket. The Sieur de La Salle had also given orders at Rochelle to engage three or four mechanics in each trade; the selection was, however, so bad that when they came to the destination it was seen that they knew nothing at all."[1]

Moreover, Beaujeu, a captain of the royal navy who had been placed in command of the *Joly*, despised La Salle because of the latter's ignorance of naval affairs, and from first to last there was nothing but jealousy and distrust between these two leaders of the expedition.[2] Before the ocean had been crossed this same spirit came to animate both the crews and the soldiery. The horrors of disease on shipboard added to the discontent. Finally, when, on November 25, the three vessels which had survived an attack by the Spaniards left St. Domingo, a fog arose and separated them for several weeks. The *Aimable*, with La Salle on board, sighted the mainland December 28, probably in the vicinity of Atchafalaya Bay, about a hundred miles west of the Mississippi delta. Unfortunately La Salle took this bay to be that of Apalachee, which is

---

[1] "Narrative of Father Le Clercq," Shea, *Discovery and Exploration of the Mississippi Valley*, 188.

[2] See the letters of Beaujeu printed in Margry, II. 395-410, 436-453, and 564-572; Parkman, *La Salle*, 331-340; Kingsford, *History of Canada*, II. 124-142.

three hundred miles east of the Mississippi.[1] He therefore directed the sailors to proceed westward along the shore in search of the great river. On they went, until by January 6 they had reached an opening in the coast which seems to have been Galveston Bay. Fearing that Beaujeu, in command of the *Joly*, had passed the *Aimable*, La Salle continued yet farther along the Texas coast, probably as far as Matagorda Island. The surmise proved correct, and in a short time the missing vessel was encountered. Then broke out a war of words between Beaujeu and La Salle, which, to say the least, did not improve the spirits of the disappointed and restless colonists.

In despair of finding the desired location for his colony, La Salle determined to effect a landing, establish a settlement, and continue the search for the Mississippi at a later time. A camp was built and the people made as comfortable as possible. Still misfortunes came thick and fast.[2] The *Aimable* foundered in plain sight of the disheartened colonists. The Indians stole and murdered and burned. Disease carried off the settlers at the rate of five or six a day. Beaujeu, sent out to explore the

---

[1] La Salle's mistake arose from misinformation received at St. Domingo to the effect that the Gulf Stream ran with incredible rapidity toward the Bahama Channel, so that the westward voyager would make progress much more slowly than was apparent. "Narrative of Father Le Clercq," Shea, *Discovery and Exploration of the Mississippi Valley*, 190. Parkman, *La Salle*, Ch. XXIV.

[2] Our chief source of information on the vicissitudes of La Salle's colony is the "Journal Historique" of Joutel, in French, *Historical Collections of Louisiana*, I. 85-193. Joutel was a nephew of La Salle and a member of the colony at Fort St. Louis. A portion of an interesting map of the Mississippi country prepared by him is reproduced in Winsor, *Cartier to Frontenac*, 318-319, from a copy in the Boston Public Library.

coast and ascertain the whereabouts of the Mississippi, continued his voyage to Mobile Bay, and then set sail for France.[1] By midsummer there were only 180 souls left at the new southern "Fort St. Louis."[2]

Three times during the years 1685–1687 did La Salle strike out into the wilderness at the head of a band of the hardiest survivors, in the hope that he might be able to reach the Mississippi and communicate with the French of the Great Lake region. It was only by this means that he could expect to secure the aid for his wretched colony which Beaujeu's treachery and the hostility of the Jesuits were withholding from it. The last of these attempts was made in January, 1687.[3] By that time the colony had been reduced to forty men, women, and children, and was in immediate danger of annihilation from starvation, or the Indians, or both. During the closing days of 1686 it was determined to divide the colonists about equally, and while half remained at the fort, the rest should make one more effort to traverse the two thousand miles that separated them from aid and sympathy. Twenty of the

---

[1] Margry, *Lettres de Cavelier de La Salle*, 577–588; Parkman, *La Salle*, 362–367; Joutel, "Journal Historique," in French, *Historical Collections of Louisiana*, I. 110.

[2] The exact location of this Fort St. Louis is somewhat uncertain. General J. S. Clark, a recent investigator of the topography of the region, believes that the fort was on the Garcitas River, five miles from its entrance into Lavaca Bay. See Winsor, *Cartier to Frontenac*, 317.

[3] "Narrative of La Salle's Attempts to ascend the Mississippi in 1687, by Father Anastasius Douay, Recollect." Inserted by Le Clercq in his "Narrative," and printed in Shea, *Discovery and Exploration of the Mississippi Valley*, 197–229. Douay, of whom comparatively little is known, was one of the survivors of the expedition of 1687. See Joutel's interesting account, in French, *Historical Collections of Louisiana*, I. 130 *et seq.*

strongest survivors were selected for the trip, and five horses were procured from the Indians to be used as pack animals. Among those who were to accompany La Salle were his brother, John Cavelier, their two nephews, Joutel and Moranget, Father Anastasius Douay, the surgeon, Liotot, and a freebooter by the name of Duhaut. With proper provision for food and shelter, such a journey through the Southland might be accomplished to-day with little discomfort; but La Salle's party had no shoes, only sail-cloth clothes, no boats except improvised ones of skin to ferry them across the swollen rivers, a food supply that was always uncertain and often positively inadequate, and no waterproof tents. There was constant danger of attack from the Indians, and besides, the relations of the members of the party were anything but harmonious. Among other quarrels, that of Duhaut and Liotot with the leader's nephew, Moranget, seemed most threatening of disaster.

By reason of all these deterring conditions the expedition made very slow progress. It was nearly two months before the region of the Trinity was reached. By this time the jealousies and disappointments of the travellers were ready to break out in open mutiny. Angered by a just but hotly delivered reproof from Moranget, Duhaut and Liotot resolved upon the assassination of the boy. An Indian guide, Nika, and La Salle's servant, Saget, were also marked out for death. On the night of the 15th of March the dastardly work was done by Liotot while Duhaut and another confederate by the name of Heins kept watch. La Salle was six miles away and did not join the company until three days later. Father Douay accompanied the weary explorer on the walk back to

camp, and has left us a record of their conversation on religious themes, as well as the sadness which so changed La Salle's demeanor from what it usually was. When confronted by their chief and asked concerning the whereabouts of his nephew, the murderers, embittered by their jealousies and failures, added the culmination to their crimes. Duhaut fired his gun, and La Salle fell. The great leader lingered an hour before death, during which Douay administered as best he could the comforts of the gospel. At last all was still. At the age of forty-three one of France's most valiant empire builders lay dead in the heart of the inland wilderness.[1] "Thus," says Douay, "died our wise commander, constant in adversity, intrepid, generous, engaging, dexterous, skilful, capable of everything. He who for twenty years had softened the fierce tempest of countless savage tribes was massacred by the hands of his own domestics, whom he had loaded with caresses. He died in the prime of life, in the midst of his course and labors, without having seen their success."

The party now succumbed to the terrorizing rule of Duhaut. For several days the men ranged aimlessly among the Indians, at length falling in with some deserters from one of La Salle's earlier expeditions. One of these con-

---

[1] Joutel's account of the death of La Salle, translated from his "Journal," is to be found in the *Magazine of American History*, II. 753, and in French, *Historical Collections of Louisiana*, I. 143. Parkman declares it marked by "sense, intelligence, and candor." Father Douay had an unequalled opportunity to know the facts. His account is reported in Le Clercq's "Narrative," printed in Shea, *Discovery and Exploration of the Mississippi Valley*, 197 *et seq*. See Benjamin Sulte, "La Morte de Cavelier de La Salle," in Royal Society of Canada, *Mémoires*, ser. 2, vol. 4, sec. 1, pp. 3–31 [Ottawa, 1898]; Parkman, *La Salle*, Ch. XXVII.; Kingsford, *History of Canada*, II. 155–159.

spired with Heins, and in a quarrel Duhaut and Liotot were shot, thus paying an early penalty for the assassination of La Salle. The little company broke in pieces. The lawless element, led by Heins, wandered off to live among the Indians, and what their after history was no one knows. The others — six in all — led by Joutel and Father Douay, pressed on toward Canada. By obtaining horses from the natives they were able to make very good time.[1] On the 24th of July, more than four months after the death of La Salle, they were overjoyed to come out of the wilderness upon the banks of the long-sought Mississippi, near the point of its junction with the Arkansas. Still more delighted were they to find there a cottage built on the French fashion and surmounted by a cross. How it happened to be there demands a word of explanation.

The return of Beaujeu to Rochelle about two years before had first brought to France the intelligence that La Salle's colonizing expedition had gone astray. As soon as Tonty, in command at Fort St. Louis on the Illinois, became aware of his friend's misfortunes, he resolved upon a rescuing expedition to the Gulf. In February, 1686, he started down the river with a band of French and Indians to join his old commander. Of course, when the Gulf was reached, La Salle was nowhere to be found, as Tonty had no idea that the colony was at such a distance from the river's mouth. Returning, he left several men as an outpost at the mouth of the Arkansas, hoping that they would learn something as to the whereabouts of La Salle

[1] Joutel's detailed narrative of the journey is in French, *Historical Collections of Louisiana*, I. 145-174.

and his followers. It was two of these who now extended much-needed hospitality to Joutel and his companions.

After a few days of rest and rejoicing the wanderers commenced the ascent of the Mississippi. The rest of the trip was over a route already familiar to the French, and was accomplished without special incident. When Tonty's fort on the Illinois was reached, about the middle of September, the commander was found to be absent on a campaign against the Senecas.[1] The joy at their appearance was so great that the men foolishly forebore to minimize it by telling of La Salle's death. Rather they represented themselves as merely the forerunners of their chief, who might be expected to arrive in due time fresh from his successes in the south. Leaving this impression, the travellers continued on their way as far as the Chicago River. There the lake was found so rough that it was decided to return to Fort St. Louis [Starved Rock] to spend the winter. By the time the post was again reached Tonty had returned. Having begun a course of deception, there was nothing to do but follow it up. Tonty was therefore assured of La Salle's safety and given to understand that the great leader would certainly make his appearance the following spring. Before suspicions were aroused the falsifiers were again well on their way to Canada. Instead of La Salle, however, Couture — one of the Frenchmen stationed at the mouth of the Arkansas — came up the river early in 1688 and revealed the truth. The following December, Tonty, with eight companions, set out to rescue the remnant of La Salle's colony. But the loss of

---

[1] Joutel's narrative, in French, *Historical Collections of Louisiana*, I. 183.

several of his men compelled him to turn back without reaching the Gulf, although he was absent from his post nearly a year.

Meanwhile Joutel and the other members of his party had passed safely through Canada without telling what they knew, and had reached France. It was only after they were safe in the home land that they confessed the truth regarding the fate of their commander. It is impossible, of course, to justify their conduct in this respect, particularly as an earlier confession at Tonty's fort might have made possible the saving of the survivors on the Gulf. It is not easy even to assign motives for the continued duplicity of the men, except perhaps in the case of John Cavelier, the brother of La Salle.[1] It is said that he desired to prevent the announcement of his brother's death until he could secure some property against seizure by La Salle's creditors. Keenly disappointed in the outcome of the project, King Louis could not be induced, even by the forcible arguments of Joutel, to renew the undertaking, or even to make any effort to rescue the unfortunate colonists on the Gulf. The only result of the news was a royal order that the murderers of La Salle be apprehended. As a matter of fact, no one was ever called to account legally for the crime, though, as we have seen, the two men most responsible for it had long since fallen victims to the anarchic violence which they had themselves instituted in killing their leader.

[1] Joutel simply says that he and his companions were unwilling that the Indians should be emboldened in their relations with the French by reason of the intelligence of La Salle's death. French, *Historical Collections of Louisiana*, I. 175.

The fate of the Texan colony is soon told.[1] Ever since the landing of La Salle's expedition in 1684, the Spaniards had been searching along the coasts with a view to ascertaining the location and strength of the trespassing colony. They had uniformly failed to find it, however, despite the fact that they early encountered the wrecked vessels in the vicinity of Galveston. It was through a Frenchman, probably a deserter from La Salle's company, that the desired information was finally obtained. Under his guidance a band of Spanish soldiers was despatched from New Leon to capture the colony. When they arrived at the fort, some months after La Salle's final departure from it in January, 1687, they found it deserted and in ruins. A short distance off lay the bodies of three of the soldiers. From the Indians it was learned that two of the Frenchmen survived and were living with the members of a distant tribe. Under a pledge of good treatment these were sent for. When they arrived they had horrible tales to tell of smallpox and of slaughter by the savages, by which the colony had been exterminated. A few others who had deserted the colony at various stages of its existence subsequently fell into the hands of the Spaniards, all with the same stories of suffering and hardship.[2]

The first attempt of the French to take actual posses-

---

[1] The Spanish account of the end of the colony is translated from Barcia's "Ensayo cronologico de la Florida," in Shea, *Discovery and Exploration of the Mississippi Valley*, 208-210, note. Another Spanish account is printed in French, *Historical Collections of Louisiana*, II. 293-295. See Parkman, *La Salle*, Ch. XXIX.

[2] Two of these men eventually escaped to France. Their testimony in regard to the fate of the colony is given in Margry, *Découvertes et Établissements des Français*, III. 610-621.

sion of the Mississippi Valley had ended in failure and ignominy. This had been due to a combination of unfavorable conditions and events, beginning with the quarrels of La Salle and Beaujeu and ending with the mutiny of the colonists. Even if the Mississippi had been reached, as was intended, the colony could hardly have been a success, owing to the unfitness of the settlers. Likewise Louis and his ministers were too much preoccupied with European affairs to give the requisite attention to the interests of France in America. A single failure, such as that of La Salle, was sufficient to cut off royal patronage absolutely. French settlement of Louisiana was at this stage very similar to the English settlement of the Atlantic seaboard in the days of Raleigh and Queen Elizabeth. Only through some very bitter experience was the method of effectiveness being worked out for the benefit of future generations.

After two decades of hazardous endeavor in behalf of his country's interests on the American frontier, La Salle lay a martyr alike to his own ambition and the glory of the Bourbon dominions. "Thus," says John Fiske, " was cut short the career of the man whose personality is impressed in some respects more strongly than that of any other upon the history of New France. His schemes were too far-reaching to succeed. They required the strength and resources of half a dozen nations like the France of Louis XIV. Nevertheless the lines upon which New France continued to develop were substantially those which La Salle had in mind, and the fabric of a wilderness-empire, of which he laid the foundations, grew with the general growth of colonization, and in the next cen-

tury became truly formidable. It was not until Wolfe climbed the Heights of Abraham that the great ideal of La Salle was finally overthrown."[1]

Despite his failures, the achievements of La Salle had indeed been sufficient to warrant this tribute. His contemporaries, especially those who were associated most closely with him in his great enterprises, were not slow to recognize in him the most dauntless of explorers and far-seeing of empire builders. In his narrative of the descent of the Mississippi, in 1682, Father Membré says, "Our expedition of discovery was accomplished without having lost any of our men, French or Indian, and without anybody's being wounded, for which we were indebted to the protection of the Almighty, and the great capacity of Monsieur de La Salle."[2] In his account of the expedition of 1686 in search of the Mississippi, Father Douay declares, "It would be difficult to find in history courage more intrepid or more invincible than that of the Sieur de La Salle; in adversity he was never cast down, and always hoped with the help of heaven to succeed in his enterprises, despite all the obstacles that rose against them."[3]

As Father Douay asserted, one may search a long while in the annals of discovery and exploration before finding another man who accomplished so much in the face of such constant and disheartening reverses. It was, perhaps, no great feat to follow the Mississippi to the sea after Marquette and Joliet had already gone as far as the

---

[1] Fiske, *New France and New England*, 132.

[2] "Narrative of Father Membré," Shea, *Discovery and Exploration of the Mississippi Valley*, 183.

[3] "Narrative of Father Douay," Shea, *ibid.*, 206.

Arkansas. It *was* a great feat to reach the Mississippi at all after undergoing all the ill luck and disappointments that were crowded into the decade of La Salle's life immediately prior to 1682. It did not require unusual genius to lead out to the New World such a colony as landed at Matagorda in 1685; but to fight so desperately as did La Salle for the life of the settlement called for a strength of character and heroism rare indeed among the seventeenth-century advance agents of Europe in America.

Two estimates of the man by modern historians may be quoted in closing this chapter. Says George Bancroft, "For force of will and vast conceptions; for various knowledge and quick adaptation to untried circumstances; for energy of purpose and unfaltering hope, — this daring adventurer had no superior among his countrymen."[1] And James K. Hosmer, "For all the qualities of rugged manhood, courage, persistency that could not be broken, contempt of pain and hardship, in the story of America he has never been surpassed, and seldom paralleled."[2]

[1] Bancroft, *History of the United States* (Centenary ed.), II. 342.
[2] Hosmer, *Short History of the Mississippi Valley*, 40.

CHAPTER · V

THE EXPLORATION OF THE UPPER MISSISSIPPI

IN the opening of the North American continent the Frenchman had this great advantage over some of his rivals, — that he entered the land from the right direction and at a very strategic point. The first important expedition which the French sent out to the New World — that of Jacques Cartier in 1534 — brought them at once to the mouth of the St. Lawrence and set them on the most inviting path to the vast interior. From this vantage point the way was easy and inevitable. With but two breaks, each of a very few miles, the waterway was absolutely continuous all the distance up the St. Lawrence, through the Great Lakes, into the eastern tributaries of the Mississippi, and finally down the long stretch of that noble stream to the Gulf. The English colonists on the seaboard ascended the affluents of the Atlantic only to be brought up short within a little time against a great mountain barrier. Farther to the north the French found nothing more serious to impede the way than occasional rapids and easy portages. As a consequence of this, and of the further fact that by nature the Frenchmen who came to America were of a more roving and venturesome disposition than the English, their explorations moved much more rapidly. They covered ground a score of times as fast, and had ranged and mapped the country continuously from Labrador to the Gulf of Mexico before the English yet knew the upper courses of even the James, the Hudson, and the Connecticut.

Their movements were also strikingly unlike those of the Spanish. The Spaniard in America thought little of colonization and much of plunder and conquest. It was not scientific curiosity, nor missionary zeal, nor commercial enterprise, that had prompted the expeditions of Leon and Cortés, of Narvaez and Soto. These heroic but misguided adventurers sought the New World only because they had been led to believe that they would find fabulous wealth in it — wealth ready to hand, and not requiring to be wrung from the soil or laboriously wrought out from the resources of the country. In his explorations the Spaniard moved by land and not by water. He expected by traversing the wilderness to come the more quickly upon the treasure he was seeking. De Leon, Narvaez, Soto — all wore their followers to a pitiful remnant by dragging them through the swamps and forests of the southern United States, exposing them to every peril of disease and Indian attack, and cutting them off entirely from outside aid and support. On the other hand, the Frenchman kept close to the watercourses, by which his travels were materially facilitated. Moreover, he did not contemplate forcible conquest — was not expecting to find any treasure for which conquest would be worth while. His interests in the American interior were in part those of the missionary, in part those of the thrifty trader, and in no small degree those of the mere adventurer, who loves for their own sake the excitements

and vicissitudes of the explorer's life. He therefore moved, not in cumbersome military divisions, but singly or in companies of from two to a dozen. Only very rarely did death or other serious misfortune overtake him. In the single expedition of Soto probably a number of Spaniards perished greater than that of all the Frenchmen who died by violence or accident on the American frontiers during the seventeenth century. For the Spaniard the Mississippi, instead of being a highway of exploration and discovery, became merely a luckily found road of escape from the torments of the wilderness. In the unfortunate methods and false ideals pursued by him, as well as his blunted geographical perception, must be found the reasons why the subsequent work of the French was not forestalled and the banner of Castile carried along the waterways from south to north through the very heart of the continent a century and a quarter before any Frenchman had ever looked upon the "great water."

From Montreal and Quebec the stream of French enterprise flowed westward, first by the Ottawa Valley to the Huron country, and later thither by the line of the lower Great Lakes. The hostile Iroquois nation in western New York served as a buffer in that direction, and long kept the French and English from coming into contact in the region of the upper Ohio. With the exception of La Salle's shadowy expedition down the Ohio in 1670, we hear of no noteworthy efforts on part of the French before the end of the seventeenth century to enter that part of the continent. Long after Michigan, Wisconsin, Illinois, and the Mississippi shores all the way to the Gulf were well known the valley of the Ohio remained a *terra incognita*.[1] It was eventually the English from across the Alleghanies, rather than the French, who explored and opened it to settlement.

Whatever route the French trader or missionary took from the St. Lawrence colonies to the West brought him inevitably to Mackinaw, from which point the lines again diverged. He might press on westward by way of the Sault and enter the Lake Superior region, or he might turn southward in the direction of Green Bay and southern Lake Michigan. If he wished to reach the Mississippi there were several ways of doing so. He might ascend the Fox River from Green Bay, cross the grass-choked portage to the Wisconsin, and follow that stream to its junction with the larger one, as had Marquette and Joliet in 1673. Or he might turn from southwestern Lake Michigan into the Chicago River, and by a portage at its head reach the upper Illinois, as had La Salle on one of his trips. Or, as La Salle did on another occasion, he might ascend the St. Joseph from southeastern Lake Michigan, cross in northern Indiana to the Kankakee, and follow that stream to the Illinois and eventually arrive at the desired destination.[2]

The pathway to the far Northwest was Lake Superior. On account of the fact that the French first sought the West by way of the Ottawa Valley, Lake Superior was

---

[1] For example, on the notable map constructed at Paris in 1682 by Father Hennepin — a map designed to show all that was known of the North American interior — Lake Erie is carried as far south as the latitude of the Ohio, and of this river there is not the slightest trace. See a reproduction of the map in Winsor, *Cartier to Frontenac*, 279.

[2] On the portages of the Mississippi basin, see Archer B. Hulbert, *Historic Highways of America*, VII. Ch. IV.

pretty thoroughly explored before as much could be said for two or three of the more eastern lakes — indeed before even the existence of Lake Erie was understood.[1] On a map prepared by Champlain in 1632, we are given the first cartographical intimation of a "Grand Lac" beyond the Saut du Gaston, or Sault Ste. Marie.[2] In 1634 Nicolet reached the Sault, being probably the first European to do so, but was apparently indifferent to the waters which lay beyond. There is no doubt that Grosseilliers spent the winter of 1658-1659 on the southern shore of the lake, where from the neighboring Sioux he heard of the great river to the West. The following summer, as has been elsewhere related, Grosseilliers, with his brother-in-law Radisson, explored the lake to its western extremities, spending considerable time in the vicinity of modern Duluth, where they were again among the Sioux. In 1665 Father Allouez had founded the mission of the Holy Spirit at La Pointe, and bestowed the name "Tracy" upon the lake in honor of Marquis de Tracy, then lieutenant general of New France. In 1669 Allouez had been displaced by Marquette, who remained at La Pointe until the Sioux drove the Hurons eastward the following year. It was at the Sault gateway that St. Lusson took possession of the Great Lake country in 1671. The *Jesuit Relation* of 1672 contained the earliest complete map of the lake, and one it must be said whose accuracy is truly remarkable.[3] The first important ex-

---

[1] Arthur Harvey, "The Discovery of Lake Superior," in the *Magazine of American History*, XIII. 573-581.

[2] This map is reproduced in Winsor, *Cartier to Frontenac*, 142-143.

[3] *Ibid.*, 208-209, and in Thwaites, *Jesuit Relations*, LV. 94. Winsor declares that it is doubtful if any better was engraved at that day. "It

ploring enterprise in which Joliet had engaged was an expedition to Lake Superior in 1669, under Talon's direction, to investigate the truth of current rumors regarding deposits of copper in the vicinity of the lake.

All the visitors to the Superior region from Grosseilliers on had become more or less acquainted with the Sioux, from whom they heard many interesting things regarding the lands lying back from the lake and extending to the shores of the yet undiscovered "great water." It must be remembered that one of the chief interests of the French officials was to open up a westward route to the China Sea. So far as could be known there might be still more great lakes west of Superior, and these might well lead all the way across to the desired outlet. The region beyond Superior was therefore regarded as well worth exploring on this account alone. Especially keen was the interest in this direction after the descent of the Mississippi by Marquette and Joliet in 1673; for that expedition disappointed the long-cherished hope that the river would be found to flow southwestward into the Gulf of California. If a water passage to the China Sea was yet to be found, it must be by some other route, and of the possible ones remaining, that directly west from Lake Superior seemed on the whole the most promising.

In 1678, about the time that La Salle was securing his patent from the crown for the establishing of a system of forts in the Illinois country, a cousin of Tonty, named Daniel Greysolon du Lhut (or Duluth), was given permission by Frontenac to go on a voyage of discovery in

was certainly a surprising improvement upon what the leading cartographers of Europe at this time were letting pass for the geography of the region." *Cartier to Frontenac*, 207.

the then unexplored region inhabited by the Sioux and Assineboines in northern and central Minnesota. Duluth was a typical forest wanderer, apparently but little interested in trade or missions, but always ready for an enterprise promising adventure. When times grew dull in America, he returned to France to take part in King Louis's campaigns, and after the life of the soldier lost its novelty and charm, he once more set his face toward the tempting wilderness of the New World. On the 1st of September, 1678, with three Frenchmen and three Indians, he set out from Montreal for Lake Superior.[1] The winter was spent somewhere in the vicinity of Lake Huron, and as early the next spring as the weather would permit, the journey was continued past Mackinaw in the direction of Sault Ste. Marie. On the 5th of April the party was within three leagues of the Sault. At that time Duluth despatched a letter to Frontenac in which he expressed his intention to take formal possession of the Sioux country in the name of the king of France, and thus forestall aggressions in that quarter by the Spaniards

[1] Among general accounts of Duluth's expedition may be mentioned: Edward D. Neill, *History of the Minnesota Valley*, Chs. IV. and V.; an anonymous sketch in *Minnesota Historical Collections*, I. 314–318; Winsor, *Cartier to Frontenac*, Ch. XII., and *Narrative and Critical History of America*, IV. Chs. V. and VII. *passim;* and Parkman, *La Salle*, 255–262. It should be observed that historical estimates of Duluth have usually been based on information drawn from the reports of his arch enemy, the intendant, Du Chesneau, and are therefore rather too unfavorable. For the correction of the intendant's bias it is necessary to resort to Duluth's "Mémoire sur la Découverte du Pays des Nadoussioux dans le Canada," written in 1685, and published in Harrisse, *Notes pour servir à l'Histoire de la Nouvelle France*, 177–181. A translation of this "Mémoire" is in J. G. Shea, *Hennepin's Description of Louisiana*, 374–377.

from the Gulf or by the English from the Hudson Bay region.[1] This purpose was executed July 2. On that day, according to a letter to Frontenac, he "caused his Majesty's arms to be planted in the Great Village of the Nadoussioux, called Kothio, where no Frenchman had ever been, nor at Sougaskicons and Houetbatons, 120 leagues distance from the former, where he also set up the king's arms in 1679."[2] The first ceremony occurred among the Isanti Sioux who dwelt in the Mille Lacs region about seventy miles west of Lake Superior, the latter one not far from the shores of Sandy Lake on the upper Mississippi. September 15 a meeting of the Sioux and Assineboines was held near the head of Lake Superior[3] for the purpose of giving Duluth an opportunity to mediate between the two peoples in the settlement of some of their perennial quarrels. According to his later account, his efforts on this occasion were entirely successful and the warring peoples were "reunited together."[4] The Assineboines were originally but an alienated band of Sioux, so perhaps the work of conciliation was not so very difficult.

In the summer of 1679 one of the Frenchmen, Pierre Moreau, alias La Taupine, who had accompanied Duluth to the Sioux country, returned to Quebec, boasting of his success in trading for furs among the Ottawas. By the French law the *coureurs-de-bois*, to which class Duluth and his companions clearly belonged, were forbidden to trade

[1] O'Callaghan, *New York Colonial Documents*, IX. 795.

[2] *Ibid.;* Duluth's "Mémoire," in Shea, *Hennepin*, 375.

[3] Apparently on the site of the Fort William of the old Northwest Company. Winsor, *Narrative and Critical History of America*, IV. 182.

[4] Duluth's "Mémoire," in Shea, *Hennepin*, 375.

with the Indians, though of course the prohibition was regularly evaded. On being arrested by the order of the intendant, Moreau coolly produced a special license from Governor Frontenac, permitting him and his comrades of the Duluth expedition to engage in the fur trade, at least among the Ottawas. This episode operated greatly to inflame the lawful traders of New France against the governor, and it was openly asserted by his enemies that the whole object of Duluth's visit to the West was to open up a clandestine trade for the governor's advantage. In a letter to Seignelay, the French minister of marine, under date of November 10, 1679, the intendant, Du Chesneau, declared that the incorrigibility of the *coureurs* had "reached such a point that every body boldly contravenes the King's interdictions." Frontenac was directly accused of being wholly responsible for the miscarriage of the law, inasmuch as he issued special exemptions whenever it was to his interest to do so. A brother-in-law of Duluth was said to be the agent through whom the governor and his most notorious ally in the West reached agreements regarding the division of the spoil.[1] There can hardly be any doubt that Frontenac marred his administration by a certain amount of such illicit conduct, though not likely to the extent his accusers would have us believe.

During the summer of 1680, Duluth busied himself with an attempt to reach the Sioux villages by a water route, having gone thither heretofore by land.[2] With an Indian

---

[1] O'Callaghan, *New York Colonial Documents*, IX. 131-136; Parkman, *Frontenac and New France*, 56.

[2] Duluth's "Mémoire," in Shea, *Hennepin*, 375.

interpreter and four Frenchmen he made a start from the mouth of the Bois Brulé River which flows into Lake Superior, eight leagues distant from the western end of the lake, near the eastern line of Douglas County, Wisconsin. This stream was a narrow one with its course much obstructed by fallen trees and beaver dams, so that progress on it was slow. When its upper waters were reached, the travellers dragged their two canoes across a short portage to the upper Lake St. Croix, from which they passed directly into the St. Croix River. This led them to the Mississippi at Hastings, Minnesota, a short distance below St. Paul. On arriving among the Sioux, Duluth received the rather surprising intelligence that a party of their warriors had gone down the river to hunt, in company with a number of visiting Europeans. The question which at once presented itself was, Who were these Europeans? There were several possibilities, and the descriptions given by the Indians were not sufficient to identify them.[1] They might, of course, be only other *coureurs-de-bois*. Yet they might also be Spaniards or Englishmen, betokening a rival movement to secure possession of the country. In this latter case Duluth might not have been any too soon in setting up the banner of King Louis at Mille Lacs. It appears that Duluth, when starting from Lake Superior, had determined upon the plan of continuing his explorations westward in search of a passage to the China Sea, and thus fulfilling the real purpose of his visit to the West.

---

[1] This view, *i.e.* that Duluth was in doubt as to the nationality of the Europeans, is that held by Winsor. *Cartier to Frontenac*, 274. Neill, however, assumes that Duluth understood that they were Frenchmen. Winsor, *Narrative and Critical History of America*, IV. 184.

He firmly believed that in twenty days he could reach the Gulf of California. This project was now to be given over for the time being, however, until it should be learned who these Europeans were of whose late presence the Indians told. Two of the men were therefore left at the mouth of the St. Croix in charge of the provisions and articles for trading which the party carried, while Duluth with the other two started down the river in pursuit of the hunting expedition which the Europeans were reported to be accompanying. It is now necessary to explain who these Europeans were and how they happened to be in the Sioux neighborhood in the summer of 1680.

It will be remembered that during the course of La Salle's hazardous operations in the Illinois country in the winter of 1679-1680, a side expedition had been sent out under Michel Accau to explore the waters of the upper Mississippi. With Accau went two companions — Antoine Augel, commonly known as Picard du Gay, and Father Louis de Hennepin, a Recollect of the Province of St. Anthony in Artois. Our knowledge of the enterprise comes wholly from the narratives of Father Hennepin, and for this reason the expedition is generally associated with his name.

Hennepin is an interesting, though not an altogether attractive, personality. He was a Flemish friar of the Franciscan order and a man of no less venturesome disposition than La Salle himself. Coming to Quebec in 1675, he had entered upon a career fraught with perils which he seems habitually to have made little attempt to avoid. His first undertaking in the New World was characteristic, being nothing less than a winter pilgrimage into the very heart of the hostile Iroquois country. It was he, together with Tonty, whom La Salle had sent out from Fort Frontenac in 1678 as his advance agent in the Niagara region. He it was who wrote the first description of Niagara Falls and made the first map of their vicinity, and he participated in the construction of the first boat ever built on the Great Lakes by Europeans. And when the country north from the Illinois to Lake Superior was to be explored in 1680, it is small wonder that this intrepid priest was selected as one of the party to do the work. In years subsequent to his American career Hennepin acquired an unenviable reputation for mendacity, but no one ever successfully imputed his hardihood and bravery.

Hennepin and his two comrades set out from Fort Crêvecœur on the last day of February, 1680.[1] The Illinois — or Seignelay, as it was then called — was descended without important incident. The travellers noted that it was "as deep and broad as the Seine at Paris," having a current so sluggish, by reason of the flatness of the country, that it was not perceptible except in time of great rains.[2] This was, of course, before La Salle had yet gone below Crêvecœur, and the lower Illinois had afforded a

[1] General accounts of Hennepin's explorations are in Parkman, *La Salle*, Chs. XVII. and XVIII.; Kingsford, *History of Canada*, I. Ch. X.; Winsor, *Cartier to Frontenac*, Chap. XII., and *Narrative and Critical History*, IV. Ch. V.; *Minnesota Historical Collections*, I. 302–313; VI. (the Hennepin bi-centenary papers and speeches), and VIII. 223–240 (paper on *Hennepin as Discoverer and Author*, by Samuel M. Davis), Neill, *History of the Minnesota Valley*, Ch. IV., and *History of Minnesota*, Ch. VI.

[2] "Narrative of Father Hennepin," Shea, *Discovery and Exploration of the Mississippi Valley*, 108. This "narrative" forms the latter half of Hennepin's *Description of Louisiana*, previously referred to.

pathway for European explorers on but one former occasion, *i.e.* the return of Joliet and Marquette in 1673. When within two leagues of the Mississippi, Hennepin encountered the Tamaroa Indians, who were incensed at the white men's refusal to go with them to their village farther down on the west bank of the larger stream. Escaping the pursuit of these outraged natives, the Frenchmen arrived at the mouth of the Illinois on or near the 8th of March. It was noted especially that in the angle north of the Illinois there were fields of black earth, the end of which could not be seen, all ready for cultivation, which would be very advantageous for the existence of a colony. For three days the floating ice in the Mississippi prevented a continuation of the journey northward. But at last the current was clear enough to be breasted with safety by the small canoes. The river was found to be "almost everywhere a short league in width, and in some places two or three"; also "divided by a number of islands covered with trees, interlaced with so many vines as to be almost impassable." Many large tributaries were observed — the Des Moines, the Iowa, the St. Peter's, the Wisconsin, the Chippewa, and others. Some of them were ascended short distances to determine their direction and navigability.

On the 11th of April, when near the mouth of the Black River, the voyagers fell in with a party of 120 Sioux coming down the river "with extraordinary speed" to make war on the Illinois, Miamis, and Tamaroas. The Indians at first discharged a shower of arrows, but when some of the older men saw Hennepin with the calumet of peace in his hands, they prevented the younger bloods from following up their advantage. Nevertheless, the savages leaped from their canoes, seized the French, and were handling them vigorously, until the latter made them presents of smoking tobacco, axes, and knives. Upon this the victims were graciously given to understand that their lives were their own, for a few hours at least. At night the peace calumet was returned to Hennepin, and the worst was expected. "Our two boatmen," says the priest, in his narrative, "were resolved to sell their lives dearly, and to resist if attacked; their arms and swords were ready. As for my own part, I determined to allow myself to be killed without any resistance, as I was going to announce to them a God who had been falsely accused, unjustly condemned, and cruelly crucified, without showing the least aversion to those who put him to death."[1] In the morning, however, the chiefs had no worse news to announce than that they had decided to discontinue their expedition against their southern neighbors, and were proposing to carry their newly found friends back with them to their northern homes. The Sioux had already profited by the extension of French trade in their country, and doubtless considered it the part of wisdom to refrain from the deeds of violence which their first instincts prompted.

Accordingly, when Hennepin and his comrades continued their journey up the Mississippi, they went in the rôle of prisoners. Far from being assured of their future safety, they were as careful as possible to do nothing which would arouse the suspicion or hatred of their

[1] "Narrative of Father Hennepin," Shea, *Discovery and Exploration of the Mississippi Valley*, 116.

captors. Hennepin had no small difficulty in securing opportunities to say his prayers. Neither people could understand a word of the other's language, but it was noted that when the Indians saw the priest moving his lips at his devotions, they displayed unmistakable signs of displeasure. Accau and Picard, whose piety was not conspicuous enough to bring them into danger, remonstrated with the more conscientious Hennepin, declaring that unless he stopped saying his breviary they would all be killed. After vainly trying to elude the gaze of the savages long enough to perform his wonted acts of worship, he finally adopted the scheme of disarming their suspicion by chanting the litany of the Virgin, since they were discovered to be extremely fond of singing.

For nineteen days the voyage was continued, covering a distance which the Frenchmen estimated at 250 leagues. Hennepin tells us that the Indians "rowed with great rapidity from early in the morning till evening, scarcely stopping to eat during the day." He says further: "The outrages done us by these Indians during our whole route was incredible, for seeing that our canoe was much larger and more heavily laden than theirs, and that we could not go faster than they, they put some warriors with us to help us row, to oblige us to follow them. These Indians sometimes make thirty or forty leagues, when at war and pressed for time, or anxious to surprise some enemy."[1] Navigation was rendered the more difficult and dangerous, of course, by reason of the fact that the river was still filled with floating ice from the spring thaw.

[1] "Narrative of Father Hennepin," Shea, *Discovery and Exploration of the Mississippi Valley*, 117.

All the time there was a portion of the party which clamored for the Frenchmen's death. Especially threatening was one chief whose son had been killed by the Miamis, and who was enraged at Hennepin for having been the cause, albeit a very unwilling one, of the Sioux band's turning aside from the war of vengeance. "He wept through almost every night him he had lost in war, to oblige those who had come out to avenge him, to kill us and seize all we had, so as to be able to pursue his enemies." At Lake Pepin, near modern Red Wing, the inconsolable chieftain's grief was so conspicuous that the Frenchmen bestowed upon this beautiful expanse of the river the name Lake of Tears.[1] Hennepin says that the chief shed tears all night long, or when himself tired of his lacrymose exertions, compelled his surviving son to take up the demonstration of sorrow, "in order to excite his warriors to compassion, and oblige them to kill us and pursue their enemies to avenge his son's death." But better counsels still prevailed. "Those who liked European goods were much disposed to preserve us, so as to attract other Frenchmen there and get iron, which is extremely precious in their eyes, but of which they knew the great utility only when they saw one of our French boatmen kill three or four bustards or turkeys at a single shot, while they can scarcely kill only one with an arrow."[2]

Near the present site of St. Paul the canoes were

[1] Parkman attributed the name Pepin to the fact that one of Duluth's four companions was known by it. *La Salle*, 257. This is possible, of course, but by no means assured.

[2] "Narrative of Father Hennepin," Shea, *Discovery and Exploration of the Mississippi Valley*, 117–118.

hidden in the brushwood, and the Sioux with their captives pressed on by land along the valley of the Rum River in the direction of Mille Lacs. Hennepin, Accau, and Du Gay were distributed to three heads of families to take the places of three of their children who had been killed in war. The march overland was a striking demonstration of the physical superiority of the Indian over the European. Day after day, from dawn until two hours after nightfall, the exhausted Frenchmen were compelled to keep pace with their swift-limbed captors. "I was so weak," says Hennepin, "that I often lay down on the way, resolved to die there rather than follow these Indians. To oblige us to hasten on, they often set fire to the grass of the prairies where we were passing, so that we had to advance or burn." After five or six days of this sort of thing the party reached the chief village of the Sioux, where, after barbarous ceremonies which the Frenchmen thought portended their death, it dispersed. Each of the white men was carried away by the chief who had adopted him, and for three months they saw but little of each other.

Although the circumstances of Hennepin's trip through southern Minnesota were thus hardly compatible with sight-seeing, he did not fail to be impressed with the natural beauty and wealth of the region. "Nothing is wanting," he writes, "that is necessary for life." He describes with much enthusiasm the sweeping prairies, reaching far as eye could see, the mines of copper, coal, and slate, the vast forests to be cleared, the great variety of fish inhabiting the lakes and streams, and the fertility of the soil, producing Indian corn, squashes, melons, turnips, wheat, cabbages, parsnips, and numerous other vegetables. Among other noteworthy products he speaks especially of the frogs which "are seen there, of strange size, whose bellowing is as loud as the lowing of cows." The district which he saw in part is that commonly known to-day as the Lake Park region. Explorers and travellers, beginning with Hennepin, have long vied with each other in setting forth the attractiveness of the lakes, prairies, and forests of this country. In later times the Park region has become a thickly settled one — a veritable garden, and at the same time one of the world's finest fishing preserves and lake and summer resorts.

The occasion of reunion of the three captives was a buffalo hunt down the river — the self-same hunt of which Duluth was to hear a little later. The start was made early in July, 1680, with a party of 250 warriors. Accau and Du Gay had no trouble in gaining permission to go along with the expedition, but Hennepin came near being left behind. At the last moment he persuaded two braves to admit him to their canoe on condition that he earn his passage by bailing out the leakage. When the hunters reached the mouth of the St. Francis they allowed Hennepin and Du Gay to make their way ahead down the Mississippi to the mouth of the Wisconsin, where La Salle had promised to have some Frenchmen in waiting for the relief of the explorers.[1] Accau refused to accompany

[1] This is the first we hear of this arrangement, but Hennepin clearly states it as a fact. "Narrative," Shea, *Discovery and Exploration of the Mississippi Valley*, 133.

them, and the Indians seem to have thought that he remained behind as a sort of hostage for the return of his colleagues.

It was now July, and life on the upper Mississippi was really far from unpleasant. In their bark canoe the voyagers floated leisurely with the current of the great river, stopping occasionally to supply themselves with game and wild fruits for food. After some days of travelling they came upon the picturesque falls near Minneapolis, one of the finest pieces of scenery in all the great Northwest. "These falls," says Hennepin, "I called St. Anthony of Padua's in gratitude for the favors done me by the Almighty through the intercession of that great saint, whom we had chosen patron and protector of all our enterprises." The falls are described in Hennepin's narrative as forty or fifty feet in height, divided in the middle by a rocky island of pyramidal form, and surrounded by fascinating scenery. Since that day the contour of the falls has greatly changed. They are now precipitous rapids rather than an abrupt cataract. Moreover, they have moved back up the river more than a fifth of a mile — a recession of about three and a half feet a year. Geologists estimate that they have been not less than eight thousand years cutting their way from Fort Snelling, where the cataract was first established, to their present position. A remnant of the island which divided the fall when Hennepin saw it, as Goat Island now divides Niagara, can be observed to-day a thousand feet or more below.[1]

---

[1] Interesting sketches and maps of the Falls of St. Anthony were left by a long succession of subsequent explorers of the Northwest, especially

The Indians knew the cataract as *Owah-menah*, or Falling Water; and as Hennepin and Du Gay came in sight of it, they observed one of them in a near-by oak, weeping bitterly, with a well-dressed beaver robe which he was offering as a sacrifice to the Spirit of the Falls. By a curious coincidence it was reserved for Hennepin, who probably first heard the roar of Niagara and who made the first map locating that great natural wonder, also to discover and name the only cataract of any consequence in the vast interior of the continent. In our day, of course, the Minnehaha fall far eclipses that of St. Anthony in beauty and fame, and one may well be surprised that Hennepin nowhere mentions it, although he passed the mouth of the creek which rushes over it, and not more than a short mile away. It should be remembered, however, that in its wild, primitive state St. Anthony was doubtless far grander than Minnehaha. Early explorers always referred to Minnehaha as the Little Fall, and it was not until its immortalizing by Longfellow's *Hiawatha* that it was redeemed from insignificance. It may be, of course, that Hennepin neither saw nor heard of Minnehaha.

Carrying their canoe around the Falls of St. Anthony, the two Frenchmen embarked in the placid water below

---

Carver in 1766, Pike in 1805, Long in 1817 and 1823, Schoolcraft in 1820 and 1832, and Featherstonehaugh in 1835. Stephen H. Long's "Voyage in a Six-oared Skiff to the Falls of St. Anthony in 1817" is printed in the *Minnesota Historical Collections*, II. 9–87. The records of Carver's and Pike's explorations are in the same volume, pp. 349–416. In a supplement to the *Annals* of the Minnesota Historical Society [St. Paul, 1850] is a general survey of early visits to the falls, prepared by Edward D. Neill.

and continued their journey to Lake Pepin. Food became scarce, and on one occasion two days were passed without any sort of sustenance. A buffalo, shot while swimming across the river, broke the fast, and fish dropped from the claws of eagles came to the pious Hennepin as a veritable godsend. July 11 the voyagers were overtaken by a band of Sioux hunters, among whom Hennepin was surprised to find his foster-father. Hennepin's departure from the Indian settlements having been against this chieftain's will, there was some reason to fear such a meeting. The Indian, however, proved friendly, and merely gave his "beloved son" an invitation to remain in his company throughout the hunt. The proffer was received with due expressions of appreciation, but gracefully declined. The Sioux then went on their way, after which Hennepin and Du Gay continued down the river, "running great risk of perishing a thousand times."

The hunting expedition had broken up into several smaller parties, who were scouring the country in search of buffalo and incidentally looking out for demonstrations from the hostile Illinois and Miamis. Scarcely a day passed on which the Frenchmen did not encounter one or more of these parties, and finally they decided to assure themselves of food by keeping all the time in close range of the provident redskins. One day there was a great alarm raised in the camp where Hennepin and Du Gay were sojourning. Says the priest in his narrative: "The old men on duty on the top of the mountains announced that they saw two warriors in the distance. All the bowmen hastened there with speed, each trying to outstrip the others. But they brought back only two of their own women, who came to tell them that a party of their people, when hunting at the extremity of Lake Condé (Superior), had found five spirits (so they call the French), who, by means of a slave, had expressed a wish to come on, knowing us to be among them, in order to find out whether we were English, Dutch, Spaniards, or Frenchmen, being unable to understand by what roundabout way we had reached those tribes."[1]

The "five spirits" were, of course, Duluth and his men, who had but recently reached the Mississippi at the mouth of the St. Croix, and who were now trying to learn the identity of the Europeans, of whose proximity the Indians told. Hennepin's curiosity was likewise aroused by the reports borne by the two squaws; and when the hunt was ended, and the Indians started on their northward trip home, he resolved to accompany them. He hoped thus to join the yet unknown party of French. By some Indians whom he had commissioned to visit the Wisconsin's mouth, he had already been informed that there were no Frenchmen there, such as La Salle had promised to send, so that Hennepin felt abundantly justified in foregoing a return directly to Crêvecœur, and in casting in his fortunes with the explorers of the Lake Superior district.

His hopes were soon realized. July 25 the party of Duluth was encountered, and the problem on both sides was solved. Just where the meeting occurred cannot be ascertained. In one edition of his narrative Hennepin tells us that the place was 220 leagues from the Sioux country, which would be below the Illinois, and is mani-

---

[1] "Narrative of Father Hennepin," Shea, *Discovery and Exploration of the Mississippi Valley*, 139.

festly incorrect; in another he substitutes 120 for 220, which would bring the meeting just below the Wisconsin. If our information as to Duluth's movements is at all well founded, it is quite impossible to see how he could have been so far south at this time. In the present state of our knowledge (and we are hardly likely ever to be better informed upon this point) the whole matter is in doubt, and any statement affecting assurance would be mere folly.[1]

Although the purpose for which he had started from Lake Superior had in no wise been accomplished, Duluth now declared himself ready to return to the settlements. From his correspondence it appears that Hennepin's recital of his adventures among the Sioux had not a little to do with this change of plan. In a letter to Seignelay, written after Duluth was again in France, he said: "My design was to push on to the sea in a west-northwesterly direction, which is that which is believed to be the Red Sea [Gulf of California] whence the Indians who had gone to war on that side gave salt to three Frenchmen whom I had sent exploring, and who brought me said salt, having reported to me that the Indians had told them that it was only twenty days' journey from where they were to find the great lake, whose waters were worthless to drink. They had made me believe that it would not be absolutely difficult to find it, if permission were given to go there. However, I preferred to retrace my steps,

---

[1] See Shea, 139-140. Duluth, after he returned to France, wrote a letter to Seignelay, in which he made it appear that at the time of the meeting Hennepin was a prisoner; but La Salle, who probably got his information from Accau, refused to believe this. Winsor, *Narrative and Critical History of America*, IV. 184. Thwaites, in *Hennepin's New Discovery*, I. XXXI., accepts Duluth's representation.

exhibiting the just indignation I felt, rather than to remain, after the violence which they had done to the Reverend Father [Hennepin] and the other two Frenchmen who were with him, whom I put in my canoes and brought back to Michelimakinak."[1]

The Sioux were given to understand that the French proposed to return to the St. Lawrence simply in order to obtain the necessary equipment for the establishing of missions. Consent was readily given by the grand chief, who, according to Hennepin's statement, took pencil and paper and traced the easiest route to be followed in making the trip. Using this guide, the party of eight dropped down the Mississippi to the mouth of the Wisconsin, ascended that stream, crossed the portage to the Fox, and came out on Green Bay, where they found a company of *coureurs-de-bois*, engaged, as usual, in an illegal traffic with the natives. "We remained two days to rest," writes Hennepin, "sing the *Te Deum*, high mass, and preach. All our Frenchmen went to confession and communion, to thank God for having preserved us amid so many wanderings and perils."[2] By trading a gun for a larger canoe the party was able to set out across Lake Michigan for Mackinaw, which was reached in time to spend there the winter of 1680–1681. When the Hurons were told of the distance to which the Frenchmen had travelled, they declared it clearly proved that, while they were themselves mere men, the French were spirits, for the latter had gone fearlessly everywhere,

[1] Duluth's "Mémoire," Shea, *Hennepin*, 377.
[2] "Narrative of Father Hennepin," Shea, *Discovery and Exploration of the Mississippi Valley*, 142.

while an attempt to do such a thing on their part would have meant certain death from the strange nations of the West.

Although terminating in a manner very different from that which La Salle had intended, Accau's (or Hennepin's) expedition had been a success. Many hundred miles of the Mississippi's course now became known to Europeans for the first time. The banks of the great river had been continuously explored from the mouth of the Illinois to the mouth of the Rum — from 39° to nearly $45\frac{1}{2}$°. Much invaluable information had been obtained concerning the products, climate, and inhabitants of the Minnesota country; in fact, it may truly be said that Hennepin was the first European to give a clear account of the great Northwest.

In May, 1681, Duluth reached Quebec, only to be arrested by the intendant, Du Chesneau, for engaging in illegal trade. He protested that his career in the West had been purely that of an explorer and peacemaker among the natives, but to no avail. Even Frontenac, who was feeling the pressure of public sentiment, was constrained to keep his friend in prison in the castle at Quebec until a grant of amnesty could be received from the king.[1] After his release Duluth, along with Frontenac, Perrot, and other leading spirits of the colony, continued to be inveighed against by the intendant. The additional charge was preferred that they were diverting

---

[1] The amnesty was general, applying to all who were suspected of being *coureurs-de-bois*. Governor Frontenac was authorized to issue yearly twenty-five licenses to as many canoes, each carrying three men, to trade among the Indians.

the fur trade from New France to the English colonies because it was more profitable in that quarter. In 1682 Frontenac was recalled. His departure for France was soon followed by that of Duluth, whose American career, however, was yet far from an end.

In the meantime Hennepin had also gone east from Mackinaw, and after spending some weeks at Frontenac, Montreal, and Quebec, had finally sailed for France in the early summer of 1681. The following year was spent by him, probably in the monastery at Saint-Germain-en-Laye, in writing a narrative of his adventures and achievements in America. The account was published at Paris early in January, 1683, under the title, *Description de la Louisiane nouvellement découverte au Sud-Ouest de la Nouvelle France*.[1] The book was accompanied by a notable map, designed to show all that was known of the North American interior.[2] On this map the Mississippi was traced with remarkable accuracy as far south as the site of modern St. Louis; beyond that point its probable course to the Gulf was marked with a dotted line. Hennepin's zeal for Recollect successes at the expense of the Jesuits led him to place on his map a mission of his order far to the north of the Mississippi's source, though from subsequent revisions of the map this mark of audacity was prudently withdrawn. Hennepin's idea of the Great

---

[1] Copies of all of Hennepin's books are rare. The *Description* may be found in the Boston Athenæum, the Library of Congress, the Carter-Brown Library at Providence, the Harvard College Library, and the Lenox Library at New York. A translation of it was published by J. G. Shea at New York in 1880.

[2] Reproduced in Winsor, *Narrative and Critical History of America*, IV. 249, and *Cartier to Frontenac*, 279.

Lake and Ohio Valley region was much confused. He knew no such thing as the Ohio River, and Lake Erie was extended so far southward as to comprehend all the present state of Ohio and much of the surrounding territory. This ignorance was rather remarkable in view of the fact that Hennepin had so long been in company with La Salle, who had certainly traversed Lake Erie, if not the Ohio, in 1670.

In 1697 appeared a new book from the pen of Hennepin. Its author had in the meantime incurred the displeasure of the Provincial of his order by refusing to return to America, and had thrown himself upon the favor of William III., king of England, whose acquaintance he had formed at The Hague. The new work — *Nouvelle Découverte d'un très grand Pays, situé dans l'Amérique, entre le Nouveau Mexique et la Mer glaciale* it was called — was printed at Utrecht and bore a fulsome dedication to King William.[1] It was, in fact, only an enlargement of the *Description*, but in it the author went on to explain that at the time of the earlier writing he was not at liberty to tell all that he knew, and that now he had a supplementary account to render. This additional information proved to be startling enough. Its substance was that when the writer and his two companions descended the Illinois in the spring of 1680, they did not at once turn northward on the waters of the Mississippi, but rather southward, going indeed all the way to

---

[1] Copies are in the Boston Athenæum, the Carter-Brown Library, and the Harvard College Library. The second English edition of this work, edited by R. G. Thwaites, has recently been reprinted in two volumes by A. C. McClurg & Co., Chicago.

the Gulf, and that only after this great feat had been accomplished did they ascend the Mississippi, fall in with the Sioux, and sustain the fortunes and misfortunes related in the narrative of 1683. To bear out his revelation the writer accompanied his book with a revised map, on which the Mississippi was represented throughout its entire course to the Gulf.[1] Hennepin alleged that he had been prevented from making public his descent of the Mississippi at an earlier date because of the enmity of La Salle, who wished to be considered the original explorer by reason of the expedition of 1682.

This story of the ambitious friar represents the most reckless mendacity. No one at all informed as to the conditions of river navigation at the time could be expected to believe it. According to the dates given by Hennepin himself, he would have had to travel thirty-two hundred miles in thirty days — a rate of more than double the best that any western explorer had yet been able to make. In his earlier narrative he had written what may well have been the truth: "We had some design of going to the mouth of the river Colbert, which more probably empties into the Gulf of Mexico than into the Red Sea; but the tribes that seized us gave us no time to sail up and down the river."[2] The astounding claim to a descent of the Mississippi in 1680 was on the face of it all but incredible. In 1698 its author, recognizing its weakness, sought to add to it the quality of reason by yet another book — the *Nouveau Voyage*

---

[1] This map is reproduced in Thwaites, *Hennepin's New Discovery*, I. 23.

[2] "Narrative of Father Hennepin," Shea, *Discovery and Exploration of the Mississippi Valley*, 118.

d'un Pais plus grand que l'Europe[1] — in which he vigorously denied that the distance from the Illinois to the Gulf was what La Salle had declared it to be. Moreover, he juggled the dates of the *Description* so as to allow forty-three days instead of thirty for the journey to and from the river's mouth. The result was a confusion of dates and evidence such as scarcely accomplished, even for the time, the object which the unscrupulous friar had in mind.

To the charge of attempted deception must be added also that of plagiarism. The portion of the *Nouvelle Découverte* which has to do with the lower Mississippi is closely copied after the journal kept by Father Membré during La Salle's voyage in 1682.[2] Hennepin was, of course, driven to this ruse by the necessity of lending plausibility to his description of a country which he had never seen. He indeed made a bold effort to cover up his ruthless conduct by charging Le Clercq, the editor of Membré's journal,[3] with having made free use of an earlier paper left by Hennepin at Quebec, and for more than a century many people believed the story. It remained for Jared Sparks, in his *Life of La Salle*, to make a thorough exposure of the trick. In the light of Sparks's researches, as well as those of Shea and Parkman,[4] it

---

[1] Copies in the Boston Athenæum and the Carter-Brown Library. The London edition of the work is reprinted in Thwaites, *Hennepin's New Discovery*, Vol. II.

[2] On the authorship of this narrative, see Winsor, *Cartier to Frontenac*, 286.

[3] In *Premier Établissement de la Foi*, published in 1691. This work had been suppressed by the government, hence was almost unknown, and could be used by a plagiarist with the greater impunity.

[4] For Shea's masterful statement of the case, see his *Discovery and Exploration of the Mississippi Valley*, 99-106.

appears that Hennepin's claim to priority in the exploration of the lower Mississippi must certainly be considered one of the most gigantic frauds in American history. Far from having its intended effect, the deception has reacted against the name of Hennepin until some students of the period have even gone so far as to stamp the friar's narratives pure fabrications from beginning to end.[1] While this represents an extreme of criticism, it nevertheless but emphasizes the fact that whatever Hennepin says, regarding his own exploits at least, must be verified before being fully accepted. As this is generally impossible, we are left in a very unsatisfactory position with respect to all his achievements from the time he left Crèvecœur in the spring of 1680 until he reached Quebec about a year later.

The only defence that has ever been set up for Hennepin is that he was the victim of unscrupulous publishers, who inserted the passages from Membré merely to create a sensation and so enhance the sale of the friar's books. But in view of the numerous editions of the *Nouvelle Découverte* issued during the author's lifetime, each containing the offensive claims, and in view, further, of the utter absence of evidence that Hennepin attempted to set the matter right, such defence cannot be deemed very satisfactory.[2] There is abundant proof that the geogra-

---

[1] Shea did this in his earlier writings. Subsequently he changed his point of view, and regarded Hennepin as the victim of circumstances and only in part responsible for the exaggerated statements of his achievements. See the Introduction to his translation of the *Description* (1880).

[2] Winsor, *Cartier to Frontenac*, 285–286. See a paper by E. D. Neill on the writings of Hennepin, read before the Minnesota Historical Society in November, 1880.

phers of his own time did not believe the story. Condone the offence as we may, there has been neither charity nor indifference enough on the part of succeeding generations to prevent Hennepin's name passing into history under a heavy cloud.

After Hennepin, French operations on the upper Mississippi were rather desultory. Such effort as was made in that direction had a twofold object — to suppress the unlicensed *coureurs-de bois*, and to fortify the region against English aggression from the Hudson Bay district. In 1685 Denonville, who had that year assumed the governorship of New France, despatched Nicholas Perrot to take command in the Sioux country and establish outposts of French authority.[1] Perrot had been in charge of French interests at Green Bay, and was a man of wide acquaintance with western affairs. Upon crossing to the Mississippi he built one post near the mouth of the Wisconsin, and another one on the shores of Lake Pepin, known as Fort St. Antoine. From the Sioux he heard of a people to the west who used horses and looked like Frenchmen — evidently the Spaniards of New Mexico. He heard also of the English on Hudson Bay, who

---

[1] For Perrot's career on the upper Mississippi, see *Minnesota Historical Collections* for 1864, pp. 9-20, and for 1867, pp. 22-31, and E. D. Neill, *History of the Minnesota Valley*, Ch. V. In the *Wisconsin Historical Collections*, XVI. 143-160, is a translation of La Potherie's account of Perrot in Wisconsin in his *Amérique Septentrionale*, II. 244-276. See also Gardner P. Stickney, *Nicholas Perrot; a Study in Wisconsin History*, in the Parkman Club Publications, No. 1 [Milwaukee, 1895]. Perrot left a journal in which were recorded the incidents of his life in America from 1665 to 1726. It was edited and annotated in Paris in 1864 by Father Tailhan under the title, *Mémoires sur les mœurs et coutumes et religion des sauvages de l'Amérique Septentrionale*.

were described as men who lived in houses that walked on the water. At the same time that Perrot was erecting stockades on the Mississippi, De Troyes and Iberville, two agents of the Canadian Company of the North, were ranging the south shores of Hudson Bay and capturing some of the English forts. These, however, were given back by a treaty signed between the two powers at Whitehall, November 16, 1686. During the years 1688 and 1689, Perrot was especially active in exploring the country west of Lake Superior and winning, or terrifying, the natives to friendship with the French. May 8, 1689, occurred another of those spectacular ceremonies by which the French were accustomed to impress the Indians with the majesty of King Louis, and at the same time announce to the world another extension of the Bourbon dominion. On that day at the post of St. Antoine on Lake Pepin, a little distance above the mouth of the Chippewa, formal possession was taken of the rivers St. Croix, St. Pierre, and the region of Mille Lacs. Duluth had already taken such possession, but in matters of this kind a duplication was not considered out of the way.

The next Frenchman of note who visited the upper Mississippi after Perrot was Le Sueur, who indeed had been with Perrot on the occasion of assuming possession in 1689. In 1695 he established a post on Lake Pepin to serve as a base of operations in his search for copper mines on the upper banks of the St. Peter. Five years later he was a member of Iberville's ocean expedition to the mouth of the Mississippi. With a party of twenty men he pushed his way once more up-stream to Lake Pepin,

determined to make another attempt to secure information regarding the "green earth" which had long been reported to be abundant in some parts of the Northwest.[1] By September, 1700, the Falls of St. Anthony had been passed and the St. Peter — now known as the Minnesota — entered. One of the St. Peter's tributaries, called indiscriminately the Blue Earth and the Green River,[2] was followed to a point somewhat above 44° north latitude, where a stockade was built in October, 1701, known as Fort d'Huillier. An adjoining mine was worked profitably and a goodly stock of furs collected. In May, 1702, a number of canoes were loaded with the furs and "green earth" to be transported to the settlements. A small garrison was left at the fort, while the rest of the men made their way back down the Mississippi to the colony which had by this time been established in the vicinity of its mouth. A series of misfortunes resulted in Le Sueur's never seeing his mine again. In a few months the Sioux

[1] Such scant information as we have regarding Le Sueur's expedition comes from the journal of a carpenter by the name of Penicaut, who was one of Iberville's party, and from a narrative supposed to have been compiled by Benard de La Harpe, a French officer of high standing who came to Louisiana in 1718. The latter document is printed in B. F. French, *Historical Collections of Louisiana*, Part III. pp. 19 *et seq.*, and in J. G. Shea, *Early Voyages up and down the Mississippi*, 89–111. Extracts from it are given in Hart, *American History told by Contemporaries*, II. 313–315. Penicaut's "Relation" is given in Margry, *Découvertes et Établissements des Français dans l' Ouest et dans le Sud de l'Amérique Septentrionale*, V. 375–586, and in partial translation in *Minnesota Historical Collections*, III. 4–12. On Le Sueur, see also *Minnesota Historical Collections*, I. 319–339; Neill, *History of the Minnesota Valley*, Ch. VII., and *Wisconsin Historical Collections*, XVI. 173, 177–200.

[2] In the narrative of La Harpe the "Blue River" is given as equivalent to the Minnesota, but the greatest confusion prevailed regarding the name.

attacked the fort, and expelled its defenders. Thus the enterprise was early brought to naught, though its prospects of success were for a little time such as to lead Governor Callières at Quebec to protest vigorously to the ministry against the diversion of western traffic from the St. Lawrence to the Mississippi. There is a story to the effect that at about the same time an explorer by the name of Du Charleville endeavored to reach the head waters of the Mississippi in order to extend trading connections, and that he went a hundred leagues beyond the Falls of St. Anthony, where he met a party of Sioux hunters who influenced him to turn back by representing that the distance from the falls to the source was fully as great as that from the falls to the sea.

The journal kept by Le Sueur during his northern explorations contains a very interesting account of his contact with the Sioux. "He then entered Blue River," runs the narrative, "so called from some mines of blue earth which he found on its banks. At this place he met nine Scioux, who told him this river came from the country of the West. He built a post here, but finding that his establishment did not please the Scioux of the East, as well as the neighboring tribes, he had to tell them that his intentions were only to trade in beaver skins, although his real purpose was to explore the mines in this country, which he had discovered some years before. He then presented them with some powder, balls, knives, and tobacco, and invited them to come to his fort, as soon as it was constructed, and he would tell them the intention of the king his master. The Scioux of the West have, according to the accounts of those of the East, more than

a thousand huts. They do not use canoes or cultivate the land, but wander in the prairies between the upper Mississippi and the Missouri, and live by hunting. All the Scioux say they have three souls, and that after death the good one goes to a warm country, the bad one to a cold country, and the third watches the body. They are very expert with their bows. Polygamy is very common among them. They are extremely jealous, and sometimes fight duels for their wives. They make their huts out of buffalo skins, sewed together, and carry them with them. Two or three families generally live together. They are great smokers. They swallow the smoke, but some time after they force it up from their stomach through their nose. . . . On the 1st of December they invited M. Le Sueur to a great feast which they had prepared for him. They made a speech, and presented him with a slave and a sack of oats."[1]

For a long time to come nothing more was added to the knowledge of the French regarding the upper course of the Mississippi and the surrounding country. Traders and missionaries continued to make frequent visits to the regions which Duluth, Hennepin, Perrot, and Le Sueur had explored, but they only traversed territory already more or less familiar. In 1703 the cartographer Delisle published a map of the upper Mississippi, based on the reports of the explorers named, and also on Indian tales which were transmitted to him through the same channels. On this map the source of the Mississippi was put at the

---

[1] Quoted from Le Sueur's "Journal" in La Harpe, "Historical Journal of the Establishment of the French in Louisiana." Printed in French, *Historical Collections of Louisiana*, Part III. 19-28 *passim*.

parallel 49°, in a swampy district where there was a network of lakes and connecting streams. Three of these lakes were shown, from which the river was said to take its beginning. For more than three-quarters of a century this conception was the generally prevailing one. As late as 1782 it involved in confusion the settlement of boundaries by the negotiators of the treaty of peace between the United States and Great Britain. There were, of course, not a few variations, such as that of the Dutch geographer Schenck, who carried the source of the stream as far north as 55°; but, as Justin Winsor facetiously remarks, there was about as little warrant for these "as the French traders wandering among the upper Sioux had when they detected Chinese sounds in the savage gutturals." For that matter, any seventeenth or eighteenth century attempt to fix definitely the source of the Mississippi must have been subject to liberal revision. As yet, conjecture and Indian representations served instead of actual exploration to determine ideas on the subject. It remained until comparatively late in the nineteenth century for the maze of waterways of northern Minnesota to be sufficiently untangled to establish clearly the exact spot where the great river starts on its twenty-five-hundred-mile course to the Gulf.

CHAPTER VI

THE BEGINNINGS OF LOUISIANA

AS the seventeenth century drew to a close there came a succession of events in Europe which went far toward shaping the destiny of the Mississippi Valley. Chief among these was the English Revolution of 1688–1689. The last two Stuarts — Charles II. and James II. — were pensioners of the French court, and had persistently refused to allow England to be embroiled in conflict with the Bourbon monarchy. The bold aggressions of Louis XIV. on the continent were more or less secretly connived at, and French colonial aggrandizement in foreign lands, chiefly America, was scrupulously respected. With the accession of William of Orange in 1689, however, all was changed. The man who for years had been the hope of Europe in resisting the imperial ambitions of the French king now became the sovereign of a people already long desirous of engaging on the side of the Dutch and Germans against King Louis. The deposition of the Stuarts cleared the way for England to step boldly forth as the unquestioned leader of the opposition. William III. as king of England meant inevitable and immediate war between the English and the French.

The struggle which began in 1689 in the War of the Palatinate may be regarded as having lasted almost precisely a century and a quarter. Professor Seeley in his

Expansion of England has well termed this long deadly contest a second Hundred Years' War. Not, of course, that fighting was continuous during all the period; there were many decades during which not a blow was struck and one time of peace which lasted more than twenty-five years. From this point of view the conflict may be considered a series of outbreaks of hostility, of quite unequal length and severity, opening with the War of the Palatinate, 1689-1697, known in America as King William's War, and closing with the great Napoleonic War from 1803 to 1815. But in a very real sense the struggle was continuous from the capture of French Port Royal by Sir William Phips and his Massachusetts fleet in 1690 to the final overthrow of Napoleon at Waterloo in 1815. Whatever the conditions giving immediate occasion to the successive conflicts of the series, — whether Louis's devastation of the Palatinate, Frederick the Great's aggressions in Austria, or Napoleon's threatened consolidation of Europe, — so far as England and France were concerned the underlying cause of them all was the perennial rivalry of the two powers for colonial empire. From this it followed that the French and English fought, not merely on the battlefields of Europe and on the high seas, but also in whatever part of the globe their peoples came in contact. The outbreak of war in Europe was the unfailing signal for the renewal of hostilities in the colonies in both India and America. Altogether the struggle was one such as the world had rarely, if ever, witnessed. When it was little more than half over (treaty of Paris, 1763), France had lost and England had won. Thereafter the energies of the former power were directed toward the recovery of

that which had been lost, and those of the latter toward the maintenance of that which had been gained.

From the year 1689 the story of the Mississippi country must be considered in the setting just indicated. La Salle's descent of the Mississippi occurred just seven years before the opening scene in that great drama of the nations, and his death came two years too early to allow him actually to witness it. But the ardent explorer had been far too shrewd not to foresee in a large measure what was coming. No one understood better than he the meaning of the slow, steady, substantial advance of the Anglo-Saxon along the Atlantic seaboard. No one detected more quickly than he the signs of Anglo-Saxon ambition in the direction of the Mississippi. It was because of this, as much as for personal reasons, that he had so strongly urged upon the French ministry the wisdom of an early colonization of Louisiana. Already by the time of the ill-fated settlement at Fort St. Louis, the Indians were passing the word westward from tribe to tribe that a new race of "pale faces," neither Spanish nor French, was making its appearance in the person of traders and adventurers on the western slopes of the Alleghanies. It was folly to hope that the French claim to so extensive and magnificent a region as Louisiana would long remain uncontested. La Salle met his death in a futile attempt to establish a pioneer stronghold at the mouth of the great river he had explored, but not before he had pointed out the policy by which alone his country could be assured of permanent prestige in the interior of America.

During the decade which followed La Salle's death, nothing further in the way of colonization on the Mississippi was attempted. Louis was busy with his European wars, and the man who was eventually to take up La Salle's work and carry it to a successful conclusion was still occupied with the English-French controversies in the Hudson Bay region. As a trade route from the interior, however, the Mississippi was rapidly gaining at the expense of the St. Lawrence. With one exception, all the royal orders of the time recognized the Mississippi as the only legitimate route from the Illinois and Lake Superior country to the sea. That exception was a special grant made to Tonty in 1699, allowing him to send two canoes and twelve men yearly from the St. Lawrence to his headquarters at Starved Rock on the Illinois. Even this privilege was withdrawn three years later, and Tonty was compelled to direct his energies toward the south. So far as trade with Europe was concerned, the Mississippi route was unquestionably the better one. The portages by which the Great Lakes were reached, while not long, were extremely annoying, and traffic by these northern passages was exceedingly slow and expensive.

In December, 1697, a *Memoir* written by Sieur de Rémonville, a friend of La Salle, appeared in Paris urging upon the government the importance of colonizing Louisiana.[1] This paper, setting forth in glowing terms as it did the natural beauties and resources of the country, and depicting the greediness of both the Spanish and the English to possess it, made a strong impression popularly, and stirred the court to renewed activity. Some years earlier

---

[1] Margry, *Découvertes et Établissements des Français*, IV. 19–43. The "Memoir" is translated in French, *Historical Collections of Louisiana*, New Series, I. 1–16.

Tonty had asked permission to follow up the discoveries of La Salle about the Mississippi's mouth, and only two months before the publication of the *Memoir* Sieur de Louvigny had proposed the establishment of a colony in the same region as a base of operations against the Spanish in Mexico,[1] but both offers had been ignored by the government. "I begin by telling you," wrote the minister of marine to a certain M. Ducasse, governor of St. Domingo, April 8, 1699, "that the king does not intend at present to form an establishment at the mouth of the Mississippi, but only to complete the discovery in order to hinder the English from taking possession there."[2] Now, however, that De Rémonville was telling of a rumor that William Penn, the governor of Pennsylvania, had already despatched fifty men to found a settlement on the Wabash, as a step preliminary to an advance upon the Mississippi, even Louis and his ministers felt that the time for more decisive action on their part had come. "Although the route is long and difficult," wrote De Rémonville, "the English, who are not easily discouraged when the subject of extending their commerce is in question, will, without doubt, surmount all difficulties, if time is given them." An English colony might well have to be counterbalanced by a French one. Doubtless the king was the more easily inclined to this view by the fact that the peace of Ryswick had recently brought a respite from both his European and colonial wars.

De Rémonville's *Memoir* was addressed to Louis de

---

[1] Margry, *Découvertes et Établissements des Français*, IV. 9-18.
[2] *Ibid.*, 294. Quoted in Winsor, *Narrative and Critical History of America*, V. 13.

Phelypeaux, Comte de Pontchartrain, minister of marine. It so happened that just before its receipt Pontchartrain's son and successor, Jerome, had been considering an appeal from Pierre Le Moyne, Sieur d'Iberville, asking the government's aid in a colonizing project in lower Louisiana.[1] Although the king had at first been disposed to turn a deaf ear toward the suppliant, the revelations of De Rémonville and the enthusiasm of the petitioner did not fail of effect upon him. "The grandeur of the scheme," says one writer, "began to attract his attention. It was clear that the French had not only anticipated the English in getting possession of the upper waters of the great river, but their boats had navigated its current from source to mouth. If they could establish themselves at its entrance, and were able to control its navigation, they could hold the whole valley. Associated with these thoughts were hopes of mines in the distant regions of the upper Mississippi which might contribute to France wealth equal to that which Spain had drawn from Mexico. Visions of pearl-fisheries in the Gulf, and wild notions as to the value of buffalo-wool, aided Iberville in his task of convincing the court of the advantages to be derived from his proposed voyage."[2] The outcome was that he was specially commissioned by the government to execute the plans in which La Salle had failed.

Iberville was the eldest son of a burgher of Dieppe, Charles Le Moyne, who in 1641 had come to Canada to

---

[1] Iberville's letter to Pontchartrain, June 18, 1698, outlining his plan, is printed in Margry, *Découvertes et Établissements des Français*, IV. 51–57.

[2] Andrew McFarland Davis in Winsor, *Narrative and Critical History of America*, V. 15.

cast in his fortunes with the Jesuits. Until the time of his petition in the interest of the proposed Louisiana colony, Iberville and his youngest brother Bienville had been leaders in the French conflict with the English on the St. Lawrence and in the Hudson Bay region.[1] In the winter of 1694-1695, and again in 1697, we encounter the elder brother at the head of very successful expeditions sent out from Quebec against the English forts on Hudson Bay. It was the treaty of Ryswick, which closed the war of King William in 1697, that took from him his business and caused him to turn his attention toward a new field.

Late in 1697 Iberville repaired to France to make ready his expedition to Louisiana. A company of two hundred soldiers and colonists — men, women, and children — was speedily gathered at Rochelle, comprising on the whole much better pioneer material than La Salle's company thirteen years before.[2] Among those who chose to be identified with the new undertaking was Father Anastasius Douay, who was one of the survivors of La Salle's unfortunate colony, and was able therefore to bring to the enterprise some very valuable knowledge concerning the lands bordering the Gulf. Two ships were obtained, the *Badine* and the *Marin*, and lest they should be attacked by English or Spanish buccaneers they were to be convoyed through American waters by the *François*, a vessel of fifty guns. The start was made from Brest, October 24, 1698.[3] St.

---

[1] Winsor, *Narrative and Critical History*, IV. 161, 223, 230, 243.

[2] Letter of Iberville to Pontchartrain, June 18, 1698, in Margry, *Découvertes et Établissements des Français*, IV. 58-62. Iberville's instructions are in Margry, IV. 72-75.

[3] The main sources of information on the expeditions of Iberville are as follows: (1) the "Relation" of Penicaut, a carpenter who remained

Domingo was reached December 4. Here the expedition halted to obtain rest and refreshment and await the arrival of the tenders carrying provisions and other supplies.[1] January 1, 1699, the voyage was resumed, and in three weeks the coast of the mainland was reached in the vicinity of the island of St. Rosa, just below Pensacola. The distant fort, recently established by three hundred Spaniards from Vera Cruz, was sighted, but entrance to the harbor was forbidden by the governor.[2] Perhaps the French did not greatly care to tarry there, since they would certainly have been asked some rather embarrassing questions with reference to their purpose in seeking the waters of

in Louisiana until 1721. This is published in Margry, *Découvertes et Établissements des Français*, V. 375–586, and in translation in French, *Historical Collections of Louisiana*, New Series, I. 35–175; (2) the "Narrative" of Iberville in French, *Historical Collections of Louisiana*, New Series, I. 19–31, and Iberville's letters and reports in Margry, IV. *passim;* (3) the *Journal Historique de l'Établissement des Français à la Louisiane*, attributed to Benard de La Harpe, but evidently a compilation [Paris, 1831]; (4) a "Memoir" attributed with doubtful correctness to Georges Marie Butel Dumont, printed in French, *Historical Collections of Louisiana*, V. 1–122; (5) Pierre François Xavier de Charlevoix, *Histoire et description générale de la Nouvelle France*, translated by J. G. Shea, in six vols.; (6) M. de Sauvole, "Journal Historique de l'Établissement des Français à la Louisiane," in French, *Historical Collections of Louisiana*, III. 223–240; and (7) Le Page du Pratz, *Histoire de la Louisiane*. Du Pratz was in the Louisiana colony from 1718 to 1734. Modern accounts are in Monette, *History of the Mississippi Valley*, I. Ch. V.; King and Ficklen, *History of Louisiana*, 26–86; Hamilton, *Colonial Mobile*, Chs. VI.–XII.; W. G. Brown, *History of Alabama*, Ch. II.; Gayarré, *History of Louisiana*, I. 30–115; and Martin, *History of Louisiana*, I. Ch. VII.

[1] Letter of Ducasse to Pontchartrain, January 13, 1699, in Margry, *Découvertes et Établissements des Français*, IV. 92–95.

[2] Penicaut and other French authorities state that Pensacola had been established only a few months, though the Spaniard Barcia, in his *Ensayo cronologico* (p. 316), says it was founded in 1696.

the Gulf. Before the departure from Rochelle rumors had been rife that an expedition was being fitted out in London for the purpose of establishing a colony of French Protestants on the lower Mississippi. Iberville had warned Pontchartrain of the fact, and had asked that he be " instructed " to proceed to the mouth of the Amazon so that, if challenged by the English at sea, he could produce evidence which would deceive them into thinking that the French were intending merely to invade Spanish territory. Although provided with papers for this purpose, it was clearly understood by all parties concerned with the expedition that the mouth of the Mississippi was to be sought, and some spot commanding it to be fortified. No other nation was to be permitted at any hazard to effect a settlement there.

From Pensacola the ships were directed westward along the Gulf coast on their hundred-and-fifty-mile sail to the mouth of the Mississippi. Mobile Bay was passed, January 31, and Ship Island, about eighteen miles southeast of modern Mississippi City, was arrived at ten days later. This island is one of a series which runs parallel with the general trend of the coast at a distance of from ten to thirty miles out, and encloses a sound which affords safe anchorage for smaller craft. Huts were erected on the island, and Iberville, fearing that he might pass the river's mouth in the way that La Salle was supposed to have done, determined to make careful search along the neighboring shores for the desired haven. Three-fourths of the colonists remained on the island while the rest accompanied their chief. Soon the Pascagoula River was discovered, and from a wandering band of Bayagoula Indians it was learned that the "great river" was only a little farther west.[1] Guided by this information, and also by the driftwood and turbid waters which everywhere abounded, Iberville, with his brother Bienville and forty-eight other men, sought the mouth of the main stream, which they entered successfully, March 2.[2] They were thus the first Frenchmen to enter the river from the sea.

Ascending its broad waters, the voyagers continued their explorations past the present site of New Orleans, and reached the village of the Bayagoulas, just below the river which has since been named in honor of the leader of this expedition. Here the party was entertained right royally with a feast and a liberal exchange of presents. When the chief of the tribe asserted that the blue serge cloak which he wore had been given him by a Frenchman named Tonty, the explorers were much more confident that the river on which they were was really the Mississippi. Observation of the lands and peoples along the stream verified Membré's narrative of La Salle's voyage in 1682, though it very naturally did not altogether square with the account given in Hennepin's *Nouvelle Découverte* recently published in Paris. The crafty friar had necessarily done his filch-

---

[1] Margry, *Découvertes et Établissements des Français*, IV. 155.

[2] The number of men is uncertain. Iberville himself states it in one place as thirty-three and in another as forty-eight. Winsor, *Narrative and Critical History of America*, V. 17. Charlevoix says that Iberville sought the Mississippi with "the Sieur de Sauvole, ensign on a vessel of the line, his own brother De Bienville, a midshipman, a Recollect Father, forty-eight men on two Biscayennes, and provisions for twenty days." Shea, *Charlevoix's History of New France*, V. 120.

ing without much discernment, and had ruined everything by his occasional attempts to elaborate upon his material. Iberville's men confirmed the suspicion which not a few cartographers in Europe were beginning to cherish — that Hennepin's "narrative" was a wholly fictitious one.

Whether, as Bancroft held, Iberville ascended the Mississippi to the mouth of the Red — a distance of some two hundred miles, as the crow flies — cannot now be known definitely.[1] At any rate, his return to the Gulf was by a slightly different route. Acting on the advice of the Indians, it was decided that four of the party should leave the main stream about the vicinity of Baton Rouge and make their way back to the sea by a watercourse more to the east. This company was led by Iberville himself. Descending by way of the bayou Iberville, it passed through Lakes Maurepas and Pontchartrain to the bay which was henceforth known as St. Louis.

The main division of the band, under command of Bienville, followed the route by which the stream had been ascended. While in the region near the Red, Iberville had been told by the natives of a chief near the mouth of the "great water" who possessed a letter, or "speaking bark," left in his keeping by Tonty many years before. On the return voyage Bienville spared no effort to find this missive, which if found would be an incontestible proof that the river was indeed no other than the Mississippi. In the vicinity of the lower

---

[1] Bancroft, *History of the United States* [Centenary edition], II. 364.

delta a proclamation was issued offering a hatchet to the Indian who should produce the desired document. The plan was effective, and in a little time the letter was in Bienville's hands. It was found to have been written fifteen years before, when its author had been on the point of turning to ascend the Mississippi after an ineffectual search for La Salle's supposed colony at the river's mouth. The Indian who had faithfully preserved it all these years had been instructed by Tonty to deliver it to the first Frenchman who should enter the river. La Salle, of course, had never appeared there, yet curiously enough Tonty's instructions were quite literally executed.[1]

Bienville reached Ship Island only a few hours after Iberville. Tonty's letter was produced, and called forth a general expression of assurance that the colonists were really in the region they had set out to seek. It was also reported that Sauvole, another brother of Iberville,[2] had marked off a spot on the east bank of the river about twenty-five leagues above its mouth, sufficiently elevated to be above the overflow, and therefore well adapted for the establishing of a colony. This site, not immediately taken possession of, became ultimately the location of the city of New Orleans.

Upon returning to Ship Island after his six weeks' exploring tour, Iberville at once began preparations for the intended settlement. One of the ships had already

---

[1] The letter is quoted in part in Margry, *Découvertes et Établissements des Français*, IV. 190.

[2] Hamilton in his *Colonial Mobile*, 32, doubts this relationship though it is affirmed by Gayarré, *History of Louisiana*, I. 58.

THE PARTITIONING OF NORTH AMERICA AT THE BEGINNING OF THE EIGHTEENTH CENTURY.

returned to France, and the other was awaiting leave to go. The permanent location of the colony must be speedily determined, else the settlers would be left with no means of transporting their cannon and other heavy equipment from the island. Careful search along the shore of Mississippi Sound failed to reveal any very desirable situation, but it was finally decided that the colony should be established at the head of the little bay of Biloxi. A greater mistake could hardly have been made. The colonists were simply set down on the burning, barren sand, where agriculture was impossible and comfortable living equally out of the question. It would have been far better, as the event proved, if the colony had been established farther inland, where there were better soil, water supply, and sanitary conditions, as would have been the case on the site which Sauvole had marked off. But Iberville wished the settlement to be just as near the mouth of the river as the flood season would allow, and an inland town, he thought, would be in greater danger of attack by the Indians.

At the head of Biloxi Bay, therefore, within the limits of the present state of Alabama, was erected a stronghold with four bastions and twelve cannon, surrounded by a nine-foot palisade, known as Fort Maurepas, to serve as a visible token of French jurisdiction all the way from the Rio del Norte to the Spanish outpost at Pensacola.[1] The settlement itself was called Biloxi, and included at

---

[1] Hamilton, *Colonial Mobile*, 32. The fort was named in honor of Count Maurepas, a son of the younger Pontchartrain. See a lively sketch of this notable member of Louis XIV.'s official family in Gayarré, *History of Louisiana*, I. 43–49.

the outset, besides the soldiery, just ninety people. Those who did not belong to the garrison built their little huts close under the fortification, sacrificing all consideration of comfort to that of safety. After the guns, forges, and heavy stores had been laboriously transferred by ferry from Ship Island, and a sufficient number of houses had been built to accommodate the people, Iberville prepared to return to France to secure further governmental support for his enterprise. Sauvole was placed in charge of the colony, with Bienville, still a mere lad of eighteen, as deputy. May 3, 1699, the *Badine* and the *Marin* sailed from Ship Island. During the voyage Iberville busied himself with the preparation of a report to be presented to Pontchartrain.[1] In it he dealt in a most merciless manner with Hennepin, declaring that such suffering and lack of success as the expedition had incurred had been due to the time spent in fruitless search for things which had no existence except in the lying Recollect's imagination.

From the beginning the colony at Biloxi utterly failed to prosper. Even before Iberville had left, some renegade Spaniards had fired the Frenchmen's imaginations with a description of the gold and other treasure to be found in lands lying off to the west. The settlers were far from industrious, though it must be said that their location rendered industry all but useless. The heat was oppressive, the water nauseating, food scarce and of poor quality. A score of Canadians, who had been ministering to the Taensas and Tonicas in the region of the Arkansas, made their way down the Mississippi and joined the colony;

---

[1] This report, dated July 3, 1699, is printed in French, *Historical Collections of Louisiana*, New Series, I. 19-31.

but as they brought no supplies they were hardly a welcome addition.

The summer of 1699 was spent by Bienville in exploring the network of streams comprising the delta. One day, about the middle of September, he was surprised to encounter an English vessel of twelve or fifteen guns commanded by a Captain Barr [1] whose acquaintance he had already made in the Hudson Bay country. This ship was one of two which had been sent out by Daniel Coxe, a New Jersey proprietor, for the purpose of exploring the Mississippi's mouth and ascertaining the navigable passages to the interior. After a series of transfers the patent of "Carolana," first issued by Charles I. to Sir Robert Heath in 1627, had recently fallen into the possession of Coxe. This patent conferred the proprietorship of the Carolina coasts between parallels 31° and 36°, together with "all the lands lying westward to the sea." In more recent times it had been understood by the holders of the patent that the Spanish possessions at St. Augustine and in New Mexico were to be exempted, but no attention had been given to conflicting French claims in the region of the Mississippi. Coxe determined to found a state in the remoter parts of his domain, and had made public a scheme for securing it financially by organizing a stock company with eight thousand shares at five pounds each.[2] As a

---

[1] The name is sometimes given as Bank. Winsor, *The Mississippi Basin*, 45.

[2] See Coxe's "Description of the English Province of Carolana, by the Spaniards called Florida, and by the French La Louisiane," in French, *Historical Collections of Louisiana*, II. 223–276. The "Description" was compiled from memoirs and journals placed in Coxe's hands by his agents sent into the Mississippi Valley.

beginning of the enterprise he had fitted out two armed vessels in 1698 and started them for the lower Mississippi. A company of French Huguenots and Englishmen had been sent with the expedition to found the proposed colony, but a halt having been made at Charleston, the prospective colonists concluded not to go farther, so that but one ship, with only crew enough to manage it, actually reached the intended destination. The point in the river where the vessel was met by the French is still known as the English Turn. It is eighteen miles below New Orleans. Captain Barr was not greatly interested in the mission on which he had been sent, and readily assented to the French claim of prior possession set up by Bienville, though he intimated that he might sometime be seen again upon the river. The story that Bienville boldly deceived the English captain by telling him that the Mississippi was still farther west and that the French already had a chain of settlements along the stream he was then exploring may be true, but evidence is very unsatisfactory.[1] Nothing of importance came of the incident, but it was regarded by the French as of weighty significance in confirming suspicion of English territorial designs in the Mississippi Valley. Since in England King William was declaring in council that he would " leap over twenty stumbling-blocks rather than not effect a settlement on the banks of the Mississippi," it is clear that such sus-

[1] In most of the popular histories it is stated without mention of its doubtful character; as in Gay, Bryant's *History of the United States*, II. 523, and Maurice Thompson, *Story of Louisiana*, 30. It is based on the so-called La Harpe journal, French, *Historical Collections of Louisiana*, III. 17, and a statement in François-Xavier Martin's *History of Louisiana*, 149.

picion was not without considerable reason. In 1722 a son of Coxe, who had inherited "Carolana," and was trying to induce emigration thither, published journals and maps in which the claim was made that his father's ship, commanded by Captain Barr, had been the first sea-going vessel to enter the Mississippi, and that therefore the English should be deemed the discoverers and rightful possessors of the river. The first part of the claim was probably well founded, but the second was manifestly absurd. Surely the French title was not vitiated by the fact that La Salle and Iberville had navigated the lower Mississippi in mere boats rather than in "ships."

Iberville returned to his colony December 7, 1699, — not a day too soon, for fever and famine had left but 150 of the colonists and soldiers alive, and these were almost ready for desertion or mutiny. He brought a welcome supply of provisions and 60 new settlers, and was armed with a commission to ascertain by exploration what "furs, ores, pearls, etc." were to be obtained in Louisiana, and to find out whether silk might be profitably grown there.[1] Early in the next year a party including Iberville and the geologist Le Sueur again made an ascent of the Mississippi. Hearing of the English visit to the vicinity, Iberville was determined to establish another base of resistance to such aggressions. On a plot of higher ground, about fifty-four miles from the Gulf, and about half as far south from the site of New

---

[1] Iberville's instructions for this second stage of his Louisiana enterprise are given in Margry, *Découvertes et Établissements des Français*, IV. 348-354. Iberville's journal of the expedition is in Margry, IV. 395-431.

Orleans, Fort La Boulaye was built.[1] It was to be garrisoned by a company of men under command of Bienville. In February, while work on the palisades was still in progress, Tonty surprised the laborers by suddenly appearing with several canoes of peltry which he had gathered on a trading expedition among the Arkansas.[2] A few weeks later Le Sueur set out upon his trip up the Mississippi to search for "green earth" in the Minnesota country. The results of this venture have been told in the preceding chapter.

After the departure of Le Sueur, Iberville followed leisurely up the Mississippi, with the intention of visiting the Taensas and other peoples of whom Tonty told. From the Bayagoulas he obtained the startling information that the Chickasaws were securing firearms from the English. He heard, too, that Le Sueur had encountered a Carolina trader at the mouth of the Arkansas. It was coming to be so that at every turn the Frenchmen in the West were confronted with additional evidence that a great conflict was brewing. By the establishments at Biloxi and La Boulaye the French had committed themselves irrevocably to a policy of colonization on the Mississippi. While King Louis long remained comparatively indifferent, the broader views of his ministers

---

[1] At the foot of a leaden cross erected near the fort was affixed a leaden plate bearing the inscription: —

D. O. M.

THE FRENCH FIRST CAME HERE FROM CANADA UNDER M. DE LA SALLE, 1682. FROM THE SAME PLACE, UNDER M. DE TONTY, IN 1685. FROM THE SEA COAST, UNDER M. D'IBERVILLE, IN 1700, AND PLANTED THIS CROSS FEB. 14, 1700.

[2] Margry, *Découvertes et Établissements des Français*, IV. 364.

and the greater enthusiasm of the merchant class assured the permanency of the plan. But the English were hardly less vigilant and active. Though more than half a century was yet to elapse before their great swarming from the seaboard colonies across the Alleghanies into the Ohio and lower Mississippi valleys, already their advance agents were trading, exploring, and threatening in all the eastern half of Louisiana.[1]

When Iberville's party reached the Red River, Bienville made a detour along the course of that stream to ascertain whether the Indian reports of Spanish settlements on its banks were well founded. Nothing of a corroborative nature was discovered, although on account of the swamps and unusual wetness of the spring season it was not possible to explore as far as had been intended.[2]

On the day that Bienville started up the Red River, Iberville began the return from the country of the Natchez to Biloxi. He was confident, without exploring farther, that the Mississippi Valley possessed abundant resources, and that the French claim to it must be maintained at all hazards. Feeling that he could accomplish more in the rôle of petitioner at the court than in that of explorer, he again sailed for France, late in May, 1700, leaving Sauvole and Bienville in charge of the colony.[3]

---

[1] In Iberville's report to Pontchartrain, September 7, 1700, particular stress is laid on the increasing danger from the English. Margry, IV. 370–377.

[2] Interesting passages from Bienville's journal of this expedition appear in Grace King, *Sieur de Bienville*, Ch. VIII. The journal is printed in Margry, IV. 432–443.

[3] Iberville's instructions to Sauvole, May 26, 1700, in Margry, *Découvertes et Établissements des Français*, IV. 462–466.

Meanwhile the Mississippi as a trade route continued to grow in favor. The transfer of Father Pinet's mission, in the autumn of 1700, from old Kaskaskia on the Illinois to the site of the modern town of that name on the peninsula between the Kaskaskia River and the Mississippi, greatly facilitated commerce by providing an excellent place of deposit and exchange. Kaskaskia speedily became the most important intermediate point in the traffic of the French up and down the river. The growth of the Mississippi trade was further encouraged by Governor Callière's execution of the king's order to reduce the number of posts in the Great Lake region so as to lessen the expense of garrisons. The bushrangers turned to Kaskaskia, and other settlements which soon grew up, for markets, and the Louisiana colony profited in proportion.

Soon after Iberville's departure for France, in 1700, Biloxi was visited by Don Francisco Martin, the Spanish governor of Pensacola. He came to enter protest against the French settlements on the lower Mississippi. The entire Gulf shore, from Mexico to Florida, he said, belonged of right to the Spaniards, and they could not be expected to stand idly by and see their territory wedged apart by French colonial ambition. This was but a threat, yet it furnished another reason for grave concern on part of those who had the projects of France in Louisiana at heart. Danger from the Spanish seemed even more imminent than from the English. On the return voyage to Pensacola, however, the governor's ships were wrecked, and such of the crews as survived were compelled to make their way

back to Biloxi as best they could in the humiliating rôle of suppliants.[1]

While in Paris, during the years 1700 and 1701, Iberville was urged by the court officials to undertake the conquest of those parts of Spanish America which were contiguous with Louisiana, both on the east and west. He readily agreed that this policy was a wise one, but declared that the government should first make the French position on the lower Mississippi more secure by sending additional settlers, cannon, ammunition, and general supplies. Iberville seems always to have been really more interested in repelling the English than the Spanish. He returned to the colony in December, 1701,[2] but only for a few weeks, hastening back to Europe the following March. When he came to the colony it was to find it on the point of being moved from Biloxi to the head of Mobile Bay. The climatic conditions at Biloxi were threatening to exterminate the settlers unless some such change was made. Sauvole had been numbered among the victims of the fever epidemic of the previous summer, and Bienville had been called from La Boulaye to assume charge of the older post. The surviving colonists at both places were in a wretched condition.[3] Instead

---

[1] In Margry, *Découvertes et Établissements des Français*, IV. 539-582, there is an extensive collection of letters, memoirs, and other documents pertaining to the rivalry of the Spanish and French on the Gulf coast during the years 1700-1702. Especially important are Iberville's memoirs on the English, Spanish, and French interests about the Gulf, the Spanish Junta's memoir, and Pontchartrain's reply to the representations of the Junta.

[2] Documents relative to Iberville's third expedition to Louisiana are printed in Margry, IV. 482-523 *passim*.

[3] In 1700 Father James Gravier, one of the first Jesuit missionaries

of attempting to better their state by agriculture, they engaged almost solely in fishing, hunting, and fitting out expeditions for the discovery of mines. All the time important explorations were being made in the great region now occupied by the states of Louisiana, Mississippi, Alabama, Arkansas, and Tennessee; but interesting as were the results, they scarcely operated to make the lot of the settlers more endurable. Submitting to the inevitable, Iberville formally authorized the abandonment of Biloxi, though he remained in America no longer than was necessary simply to see the new location at Mobile occupied. Along with his discouraging description of conditions in lower Louisiana he carried back to France bad news also from the upper Mississippi country, — Le Sueur's settlement at Fort d'Huillier on the Green River had been attacked by the Indians and completely broken up. Hoping that the recital of these reverses would stir the ministry to greater activity in behalf of Louisiana, Iberville, in the spring of 1702, again presented himself at court.

But the indefatigable colonizer's career was nearing an end. When, in the summer of 1703, he had his affairs in shape again to go to America, he found himself too worn by his labors to do so. He lived three years longer, and grew strong enough again to command a fleet in an expedition to drive the English from the West Indies. But it was while engaged in this enterprise that death overtook him, July 9, 1706, at Havana. He did not see

among the Illinois, made a voyage down the Mississippi and visited the French settlements at its mouth. His description of their condition is in Shea, *Early Voyages up and down the Mississippi*, 152-162.

his colony after 1702. Although his interest in its welfare never flagged, probably his disheartenment at the ministry's shortsightedness and parsimony made him feel that there was nothing more which he could do. In 1703 Pontchartrain had made him "Commander of the Colony of the Mississippi,"[1] but as the appointment carried with it no material concessions, such as would aid in developing the resources of the colony, the recipient regarded it as little less than mockery. Bienville continued in command until 1708, and under his direction the original settlements were all transferred to Mobile.

Iberville belonged to that extremely limited class of men, headed by La Salle, whose wide experience and personal observation enabled them to foresee the trend of subsequent events in the great American interior. For a time after La Salle's death Iberville seems almost alone to have discerned the essential weakness of the French colonial policy. Over and over again he attempted to demonstrate to the court that the agriculturist and not the hunter, nor even the trader, must be chiefly favored if the French were to resist successfully the advancing Englishman. In his opinion French possession of Canada and Louisiana could be maintained only by developing a numerous population in these regions — a population not of *coureurs-de-bois* and transient gold-seekers, but of farmers and artisans permanently attached to the soil. It was in this way that the English had made sure their hold upon the Atlantic seaboard, and it was in this way that they were certain sometime to contend for the valleys of the Ohio and the Mississippi. But at the dis-

[1] Margry, *Découvertes et Établissements des Français*, IV. 632.

tance of Paris the situation was viewed under distorted aspects. The aggressions of the English were minimized and affairs closer home were deemed of greater importance. It was only when, half a century later, France found herself stripped of all her American dominion that she saw fully the wisdom of Iberville's advice and the folly, as a recent writer has put it, of "sacrificing an imperial future in pursuing the phantom of an imperial present."[1]

Meanwhile the base of the colony was shifted from the inhospitable Biloxi, which, however, was not entirely abandoned, to Mobile Bay. Iberville's earlier explorations in the latter region had revealed its fertility and healthfulness, and there are reasons for thinking that when a change became inevitable, it was he who selected the new location.[2] The Spaniards at Pensacola protested against the removal because it brought their rivals several leagues nearer, but threats were without effect and the order for the evacuation of Biloxi was definitely issued, December 17, 1701. The exact site of the new settlement — Fort St. Louis, as it was called — has been much disputed. Probably the truth has been arrived at by Mr. Peter J. Hamilton who, on the basis of Iberville's journal, the account by Penicaut, Indian tradition, and physical remains, has fixed the location at the Twenty-seven Mile Bluff, on the right bank of the Mobile River, about fifty miles above its mouth. The work of removal from Biloxi was hastened as much as possible. As soon as the erection of a fort and barracks was well under way, Bienville

---

[1] George P. Garrison, *Texas*, 37.
[2] This is Hamilton's view, *Colonial Mobile*, 37.

went out to establish peaceful relations with the Mobiles, Alabamas, and other neighboring tribes. It was his intention to win the firm allegiance of these powerful peoples, not merely as a matter of protecting the Mobile settlement from their ravages, but also to erect them into a strong barrier against the English on the site of Georgia and the Carolinas. In this he was, for a short time, very successful. Several chiefs of the Choctaws and Chickasaws were led to visit the new fort and there receive presents and sign treaties, every effort being made meanwhile to impress them with the wealth and power of the French. The Choctaws and Chickasaws were promised that if they would expel the English from their lands, the French would make the Illinois cease war upon them and would establish a trading station, where they could obtain all kinds of goods in exchange for skins of beef, deer, and bear. "Thus," says Hamilton, "was the first Mobile founded. It was to guard the Mississippi entrance, be the capital of vast Louisiana, the meeting-place for the Indian tribes south of the Great Lakes, and the point from which English influence, not only in the Alabama regions, but in all the Mississippi and Ohio valleys, was to be overthrown;"[1] in other words, to serve as the key to the control of the great Middle West by French authority.

The six years of Bienville's administration were filled with hardship and disaster. The colony failed to increase materially in either numbers or prosperity. In Europe the War of the Spanish Succession was absorbing all the energies and resources of the French monarchy, and as a consequence very little effort was made to relieve bad

[1] Hamilton, *Colonial Mobile*, 43.

conditions in Louisiana. The Indians of the upper Mobile country were restless, and there was increasing evidence that they were being prompted to an attitude of suspicion and hostility by the English. No one could tell when the Virginians or the Carolinians might appear on the lower Mississippi and force the issue of possession. While civilities were, from time to time, exchanged between the half-famished colony at Mobile and the scarcely more prosperous Spanish settlement at Pensacola,[1] it was still uncertain how long the alliance of France and Spain in the European war would continue to make possible such friendly relations between their colonies in America.

Fever and famine united to make life at Mobile all but unendurable and death doubly horrible and real. So monotonous and fruitless was the existence of the colonists that a contemporary chronicler epitomizes the history of more than a twelvemonth by saying, "During the rest of this year, and all of the next, nothing new happened except the arrival of some brigantines from Martinique, Rochelle, and Santo Domingo, which brought provisions and drinks which they found it easy to dispose of."[2] In 1704, during a lull in the struggle with England and Austria, the French government bestirred itself to the

[1] For example, Penicaut in his journal relates the following: "On the 7th of January, 1706, Don Señor Guzman, governor of Pensacola, came to pay a visit to M. de Bienville at the fort, where he remained four days, during which time he was feasted by the French; and, on his return to Pensacola, he ordered his aide-de-camp to distribute among the soldiers of the garrison a thousand dollars in presents, and requested M. de Bienville, as a favor, to set at liberty all the prisoners." French, *Historical Collections of Louisiana*, New Series, I. 98.

[2] Winsor, *Narrative and Critical History of America*, V. 24.

extent of equipping and sending to the colony a vessel laden with supplies and carrying seventy-five soldiers and four priests. But the result was such as absolutely to discourage any further effort of the sort. The vessel arrived at Mobile in July, when the colony was in the throes of one of its most serious epidemics of fever.[1] So many of the crew died that it became necessary for twenty of the soldiers to assist in taking the ship back. Of those who remained, in two months' time thirty had died, along with many victims among the older settlers, including the veteran Tonty who had joined the colony in 1702. The only bright side to the coming of the vessel was the fact that it brought two nuns and twenty-three girls. The latter speedily found husbands among the residents of the colony, and the gloom of colonial life was relieved somewhat, as one writer says, by a merry month of weddings.[2] An official despatch on the condition of the colony in 1704 runs as follows: "180 men capable of bearing arms; two French families with three little girls and seven little boys; 6 young Indian boys, slaves, from fifteen to twenty years of age; a little of the territory around Fort Louis (Mobile) has been cultivated; 80 wooden houses, of one story high, covered with palm leaves and straw; 9 oxen, five of which belong to the king; 14 cows; 4 bulls, one of which belongs to the king; 6 calves; 100 hogs; 3 kids; 400 hens."[3]

---

[1] Winsor holds the view that the disease — yellow fever it seems to have been — was contracted by the soldiers by reason of a landing at St. Domingo. The matter is of comparative unimportance, as the malady was already by no means unknown at Mobile. Winsor, *The Mississippi Basin*, 64.

[2] Penicaut's journal in French, *Historical Collections of Louisiana*, New Series, I. 95. [3] William G. Brown, *History of Alabama*, 37.

Until his death in 1706, Iberville remained nominally "commander" of the Mississippi colony, and even in his absence this fact had a restraining influence upon the disaffected. When, however, the tidings of his death at Havana reached the colony, the position of Bienville became increasingly unenviable. "This melancholy news," says Penicaut, "fell like a dark cloud over the colony, and destroyed, for a while, all their hopes of receiving any further assistance from France, until a treaty of peace should be negotiated in Europe."[1] Religious factions, quarrelling bushrangers, and the irritating espionage of the commissary of marine, Nicolas de La Salle, reduced the lieutenant's station to one of a mere cringing, helpless advocate of civil peace. His friends fell away, his enemies increased. The representations of the latter at court resulted in the unfortunate official's recall, on the ground that his administration had been a failure. It does not admit of doubt that Bienville in his dismissal was wronged. Bad as conditions in the colony certainly were, it was gross injustice to fix the blame upon one who had labored as faithfully as had Bienville. Under the most adverse circumstances he seems to have done all that any one could have done for the good of the settlement. The causes of failure lay deeper than men generally perceived.[2]

For some months after Bienville's removal the colony was under the charge of Diron d'Artaguette, who bore the title of *commissaire-ordonnateur*[3] — or commissary of ma-

[1] French, *Historical Collections of Louisiana*, New Series, I. 97.

[2] For a general survey of Bienville's character and services, see Grace King, *Sieur de Bienville*, in the "Makers of America" series.

[3] Bienville received information of his removal, February 25, 1708, but D'Artaguette did not arrive at Mobile to take charge of the colony until

rine. Hitherto the incumbent of this office had been vested merely with the control of public property and the right to attest the public acts of the governor, but now he was to assume for a time full charge of the colony's affairs. The removal of Bienville, in whom the majority of the colonists had implicit confidence, marked the beginning of a still more humiliating stage in Louisiana history. The great far-sighted enterprises of Iberville were forgotten. There was no longer so shrewd and enthusiastic an official in the colony. As Hamilton well says: "The great policy of Iberville for wholesale rearrangement of Indians dropped out of view, and what was actually accomplished was to maintain Mobile as a point of observation and influence, the port for a large but ill-organized trade among the Gulf and Mississippi River savages. A few interior trading-posts there were, but for the present no other colonies, and the agricultural resources of the country were almost entirely neglected." [1]

Early in 1709, by reason of an unusual rise of the Mobile River, the colony at Fort Louis came near suffering a disastrous end. The town was flooded and for a time cut off by the waters which completely encircled Twenty-seven Mile Bluff. This event forced the conclusion that the colony's location was an unfortunate one and should be changed before further danger arose. Once again, therefore, Bienville — at that time still the *de facto* head of the settlement — began preparations for a transplanting of the unpleasantly migratory French citadel on the

---

early in January, 1711. Penicaut, in French, *Historical Collections of Louisiana*, New Series, I. 99, 107.

[1] Hamilton, *Colonial Mobile*, 56.

Gulf. Some land farther down the river which had been given to a band of fugitive Choctaws was selected, and on it was begun the erection of a new Fort Louis. The Choctaws were moved to Dog River, and thus the site of the modern city of Mobile was cleared for its new tenants. Work on the Fort was continued for more than a year, so that the removal of the colonists could not take place until late in 1710.[1] The old location was entirely abandoned.

In May, 1710, by a governmental order, Lamothe Cadillac, who had been in charge of the post at Detroit, was transferred to the French colony on the Gulf. Cadillac was a man of such restless energy that he had outgrown the constraints of the northern colonies and was thought to be just the person to bring life and vigor to the dormant settlement at Mobile. The ministers at Paris failed to see that the unsatisfactory state of the Louisiana colony was due much more to their own indifference and lack of support than to inefficient leadership in America. Being obliged to go to his new post by way of France, Cadillac did not reach it until May, 1713, three years after his appointment. Besides another consignment of marriageable young ladies, he brought with him the news of the treaty of Utrecht in closure of the War of the Spanish Succession. This latter might mean greater liberality on the part of the court in its dealings with the colony, but it might also mean an end to friendly relations with Pensacola.

[1] Penicaut's journal, in French, *Historical Collections of Louisiana*, New Series, I. 103. For an account of the removal of the colony and a contemporary description of the newly established Fort Louis, see Hamilton, *Colonial Mobile*, Ch. X. Hamilton enters into a detailed discussion of the exact site of Bienville's town relative to the present city of Mobile.

On his arrival Cadillac found that, though the colony now numbered about four hundred whites and twenty negro slaves, it was even farther from prosperity than a decade before. Many of the better settlers, who survived the fever, either returned to France or went farther up the Mississippi and Mobile rivers in search of more favorable conditions of livelihood. It had been learned that the inland missions, such as Kaskaskia, Peoria, and Vincennes, offered inducements to colonists far in advance of anything to be found in the Gulf region. Both agriculture and trade were prosperous there, while on the Gulf they were failures. It was but natural that the settlers should desire to escape from the horrors of their life in the semitropics and seek more beneficent abodes in the Illinois and Miami country. The constant drain thither of the Mobile settlement's best men was one of the problems with which Bienville and D'Artaguette had vainly wrestled.

On the coming of Cadillac a patent was made public which deeply concerned the welfare of the colony. This was a royal grant to one Antoine Crozat, bestowing upon him exclusive control of the trade of Louisiana for a period of fifteen years.[1] Crozat was a leading French merchant upon whose purse Louis had drawn heavily during his later wars. It was in partial payment of his loans to the

---

[1] The patent granted Crozat is printed in French, *Historical Collections of Louisiana*, III. 38-42. On Crozat's Louisiana enterprise, see Martin, *History of Louisiana*, I. Ch. VIII.; Hamilton, *Colonial Mobile*, Ch. XI.; Monette, *History of the Mississippi Valley*, I. Ch. V.; Brown, *History of Alabama*, Ch. III.; Winsor, *Narrative and Critical History*, V. 28-31, and *The Mississippi Basin*, Ch. IV.; Gayarré, *History of Louisiana*, I. 102-191 *passim*; Pickett, *History of Alabama*, I. Ch. V.; and Wallace, *History of Illinois and Louisiana under French Rule*, Ch. XII.

crown that the grant of exclusive trading rights in Louisiana was extended. In this patent an attempt was made to define in a general way the extent of the Louisiana territory. The region was described as containing all the lands between Carolina and New Mexico, extending from the Gulf northward to the Illinois. On the east it embraced the basin of the St. Jerome, or Ohio, and on the west that of the St. Pierre, or Missouri. No claim was set up to territory beyond the source of the Missouri. In general, then, Louisiana was now understood to comprise all the Mississippi Valley except that part of it lying east of the river and north of the Illinois. It is not to be understood, of course, that France had abandoned her claim to this latter district. It was simply attached for the time being, not to Louisiana, but to New France.[1] There was no effort in Crozat's patent to define boundaries more accurately than has just been indicated. In fact, the French government was always averse to specific definition. In 1715 the cartographer Delisle was respectfully requested to remove from his map the line of dots which marked the borders of Louisiana, for the reason that the court "wished it left indefinite, and did not want French maps to be quoted by foreign nations against us."[2]

Crozat had been given a complete monopoly of trade in all this vast district. By the patent, King Louis had forbidden " all persons and companies of all kinds, whatever their quality and condition, and whatever the pre-

[1] In September, 1717, when Crozat gave up his patent and was succeeded by the Company of the West, Illinois was detached from New France and again incorporated with Louisiana.

[2] Winsor, *The Mississippi Basin*, 86.

text might be, from trading in Louisiana under pain of confiscation of goods and ships, and perhaps of other and severer punishments." As soon as possible after receiving the grant, September 14, 1712, Crozat set to work to develop the rudimentary commerce of the country. He had been given not only the right to trade, but also that of opening and working mines, making concessions of land to settlers, establishing manufactures, and overseeing explorations. He had also been given a monopoly of the slave trade in the province. By 1713 his agents were in America, ready for their work.

It is not too much to say that Crozat accomplished more toward the exploration of the Mississippi Valley in a year than had been accomplished altogether since the death of La Salle. Posts were established on all the important rivers, and explorers were sent out in every direction to search for mines and waterways. Among the many trading posts established along the lower Mississippi, the one located on the site of modern Natchez was easily the most important. There was just one thing which kept Crozat's scheme of commercial exploitation from being a grand success. That was the rivalry of the English. Just as the fur trade down the Mississippi was reaching a scale never known, or scarcely contemplated, before, the English trader began to break across the Alleghanies and offer the Indians higher prices for their peltries. Even as far south as the Red River these aggressors were active. Moreover, the *coureurs-de-bois*, always ready to subserve their own interests, regardless of those of their country, were readily induced by better prices to send their stores of fur to Charleston and Pensacola, instead of down the Mississippi. And, to make matters worse, the Spanish buccaneers played into the hand of the English by attacking Crozat's peltry-laden vessels as they sailed out of the Gulf. With no competitors in the colony, Crozat found his expected gains thwarted by those outside.

Most noteworthy among the explorations engaged in by Crozat's agents were those in the Red River country with the purpose of opening up trade with the Spaniards of the Southwest. In 1716 Juchereau de Saint-Denys, a former lieutenant-general of Montreal, under the joint direction of Crozat and Cadillac, ascended the Red and crossed nearly to the Rio Grande. He returned with the conviction that the Spaniards would welcome any attempt of the French to extend commercial relations in that direction, though the confiscation of the goods which he sent into the Rio Grande Valley a few months later hardly bore out his opinion. Saint-Denys's operations on the Mexican frontier were very romantic, even to the extent of including a love affair between the gallant adventurer and a daughter of Raimond, the commander of the Spanish troops at the mission of Saint Jean Baptiste, on the banks of the Rio Grande. The net result, however, was simply to impress the Spaniards with the advisability of renewed activity in the Texas country to insure possession against the French on the east.

[1] Penicaut's journal, in French, *Historical Collections of Louisiana*, New Series, I. 114-128; La Harpe's (?) journal, French, *ibid.*, III. 47-48, 63; Le Page du Pratz, *History of Louisiana*, 8-13; and Shea, *Charlevoix's History of New France*, VI. 19-24. See the full account of Saint Denys and his exploits, in Winsor, *The Mississippi Basin*, 90-98; also in George P. Garrison, *Texas*, Ch. V.

Late in 1716 Cadillac was recalled from the governorship of Louisiana. His haughty, imperious disposition had made him generally unpopular. Aside from ascending the Mississippi to the Illinois in a vain search for silver mines, and sending Bienville to suppress the hostilities of the Natchez,[1] he had done little during his administration except send in complaints to the ministry at Paris. Probably those to whom the complaints were addressed agreed with Crozat when he wrote, "I am of the opinion that all the disorders in the colony of which M. de la Mothe [Cadillac] complains proceed from his own maladministration of affairs."[2] The new governor sent out was one L'Epinay. The abilities of Bienville seem by this time to have been better recognized, inasmuch as the control of the colony was left in his hands during the interim of six months between Cadillac's recall and L'Epinay's arrival.

The following year was marked by Crozat's surrender of his patent. He was discouraged with the results of his efforts in America, and decided to give up the monopoly.[3] It was well for the future interests of Louisiana that he did so, for, while many trading-posts were established under his direction, the work of colonization had

---

[1] Bienville, with the title "Commandant of the Mississippi and its Tributaries," was for the time stationed at Natchez with a garrison. For contemporary accounts of this first Natchez war, see Le Page du Pratz, *History of Louisiana*, 41–49; M. de Richebourg, "Mémoire sur La Première Guerre des Natchez," in French, *Historical Collections of Louisiana*, III. 241–252; Martin, *History of Louisiana*, I. Ch. VIII.; Shea, *Charlevoix's History of New France*, VI. 28–31.

[2] Winsor, *Narrative and Critical History of America*, V. 30.

[3] Penicaut's journal, in French, *Historical Collections of Louisiana*, New Series, I. 135.

languished. Crozat had been interested solely in commerce, not in establishing an agricultural population. In 1717 it is estimated that there were not more than seven hundred French people in Louisiana.

As soon as Crozat gave back his charter, the privileges which had belonged to him under its provisions were conferred upon a new organization known as "The Company of the West," or more commonly, "The Mississippi Company."[1] This company owed its origin to an attempt to relieve France from the extreme financial embarrassments which Louis XIV. had brought on her by his wars. Its capital stock was to be 100,000,000 livres, divided into shares of 500 livres each. The government guaranteed an income of four per cent on the capital invested. The company was to continue twenty-five years, and during that time it should enjoy a monopoly of the commerce of the colony, the proprietorship of all lands improved, the ownership of all mines, as well as absolute control of all the colony's affairs. During the continuance of the charter, property in Louisiana

---

[1] Letters Patent granted by Louis XV. to the Company of the West, August, 1717, in French, *Historical Collections of Louisiana*, III. 49-59. On the organization and operations of the Company of the West, see Martin, *History of Louisiana*, I. Ch. IX.; Monette, *History of the Mississippi Valley*, I. Chs. VI.-VIII.; Hamilton, *Colonial Mobile*, Ch. XII.; Pickett, *History of Alabama*, Ch. VI.; King and Ficklen, *History of Louisiana*, Ch. XII.; King, *Sieur de Bienville*, Chs. XX.-XXIV.; Gayarré, *History of Louisiana*, I. 191-233; Wallace, *History of Illinois and Louisiana under French Rule*, Ch. XIII.; Winsor, *The Mississippi Basin*, Ch. V., and *Narrative and Critical History*, V. Ch. I.; Perkins, *France under the Regency*, Chs. XIII.-XV.; and Anon., *A Full and Impartial Account of the Company of Mississippi projected and settled by Mr. Law* [London, 1720]. There is a detailed bibliography of Law and the Mississippi Company in Winsor, *Narrative and Critical History*, V. 75-77.

was to be exempt from taxation. Practically the only obligation assumed by the company was to settle six thousand white persons and three thousand negro slaves within the prescribed twenty-five years. Bienville, now entirely vindicated of the earlier charges of incompetency made against him, was to serve as governor-general of the province and act as local agent of the company.

At the head of the list of directors nominated by the king stood the name of the Scotch adventurer, John Law, who was to have a notable, if not a very glorious, part in the development of the Louisiana territory. Law was a professional gambler and roustabout, but possessed of a keen mind and a winning personality. After failing in an attempt to induce the Scottish Parliament to adopt one of his pet schemes for a paper currency, he passed over to France in 1716, where the death of Louis XIV. the previous year had thrown wide the flood-gates of speculation and financial recklessness. It promised to be a fertile field for a man of Law's tastes and genius. On his arrival in Paris he sought Philip, Duke of Orleans, the Regent in the infancy of Louis XV., with a proposition to relieve conditions by establishing a royal bank of issue. The Regent was properly suspicious, but finally gave permission for the founding of a private bank under the special patronage of the government. With this institution Law was compelled to be content for the time being, hoping, however, to see it transformed into a regular royal bank according to his original plan. Although the bank was not based on principles of recognized soundness in finance, it prospered even beyond its founder's expectation, and in the course of a few months had so commended itself to the Regent that all limit upon its power to issue bills was removed, and it was formally converted into the Banque Royale.

By Law's leadership in both enterprises the fortunes of the bank and of the Mississippi Company were bound together. For a time the success of the one augured well for the success of the other. As soon as banknotes began to flow from the presses, emigrants began to turn their faces toward Louisiana. In February, 1718, three vessels were despatched by the company, bearing a large number of troops and colonists.[1] With this beginning the work of settlement continued, until within five years not fewer than seven thousand whites and six hundred negroes had been brought over. Every effort was made to develop the resources of the country. Engineers were appointed to oversee the construction of public works, the mouth of the Mississippi was mapped and equipped with diminutive lighthouses, the adjacent coasts were carefully surveyed, and land was parcelled out in concessions to large numbers of expectant fortune-finders.[2] It must be said that many of the immigrants were of an undesirable character. The delusion still lingered that criminals and paupers were

---

[1] Penicaut's journal, in French, *Historical Collections of Louisiana*, New Series, I. 137.

[2] Penicaut, in French, *Historical Collections of Louisiana*, New Series, I. 140 and III. 78. See especially Le Page du Pratz, *History of Louisiana*, 13-30. Du Pratz was one of the *concessionnaires*, his grant being in the vicinity of New Orleans. The account which he gives of his taking possession of it is full of interest.

good enough material for the making of successful colonies. The company at first exercised little discretion in respect to the settlers it sent out. It was a question of numbers, not character. Vagrants and convicts, "the scum of Europe," as a contemporary described them, made up far too large a proportion of the accessions to the colony.

Early in 1719 there was a renewal of the war between England, Holland, France, and the Empire, on the one side, and Spain on the other, ostensibly to compel the last-named power to observe the provisions of the peace of Utrecht of six years before. As soon as the news reached Mobile, Bienville organized a force to surprise Pensacola. After a brief contest the place was captured and its garrison sent to Havana. The Spaniards seized the vessels which carried the prisoners and turned the tables by retaking the fallen fort. Upon the arrival of some more ships from France, Bienville repeated the operation, in September, 1719. But in 1721, when Philip of Spain ceased resistance and became a member of the alliance, the much-beleaguered post was given back to its founders.[1] Aside from these little skirmishes which the colonists felt themselves obligated to engage in when the mother countries were at war, the Spanish and French in the Gulf region managed to give each other wide enough berth to insure peace and quiet. Successive efforts of the French in 1720 and 1721 to establish themselves on

[1] On the captures of Pensacola, see Penicaut's journal, Chs. XIV.–XVI., in French, *Historical Collections of Louisiana*, New Series, I. 145–162; Dumont's memoir in French, *ibid.*, V. 4–9; Le Page du Pratz, *History of Louisiana*, 111–117; and Shea, *Charlevoix's History of New France*, VI. 42–67.

the disputed Texan coast failed, mainly on account of the hostility of the Indians.

Meanwhile the most notable of all French settlements in the Gulf district had been made. In the course of their earlier explorations, Bienville and Sauvole had marked a spot on the eastern bank of the Mississippi, about eighty miles from its mouth, which seemed an especially desirable location for a trading-post and colony. At this place the banks were not more than ten feet above the level of the stream, but everywhere else they were even less elevated. In the morass of the delta the securing of a safe and dry location was no easy matter. In February, 1718, a force of mechanics and convicts was sent to clear the ground and build the first storehouses and traders' cabins. "The first act of his [Bienville's] administration," says Penicaut, "was to make arrangements to remove the headquarters of the colonial government from the sterile lands of Biloxi, Mobile, and St. Louis bays, to the rich country bordering on the Mississippi, the site for which he had selected, and sent workmen and laborers there the year before [1718], to lay the foundation of the future capital of Louisiana. They removed the trees and bushes, traced the streets and squares, and dug drains around each, to carry off the waste water from the overflowings of the river in high water; and also threw up an embankment in front and around the city to protect it from inundation."[1] There is a longer and more interesting contemporary account of all this in the memoirs attributed to George Marie Butel

[1] Penicaut's journal, in French, *Historical Collections of Louisiana*, New Series, I. 138.

Dumont, which is well worth quoting. "While the concessionnaires," it says, "thus dispersed in different places in that vast province, were engaged in forming their establishments, the commandant, now left alone at Old Biloxi, with the troops and officers of the company, thought of making a more stable and solid establishment in the country than any that had yet been formed for the colony. With this view he selected a tract thirty leagues above the mouth of the river, and sent the Sieur de la Tour, chief engineer there, to choose in that tract a place fit for building a city worthy of becoming the capital and headquarters, to which all the rising settlements might have recourse to obtain aid.

"The Sieur de la Tour was no sooner arrived at the place, then consisting only of some unimportant houses, scattered here and there, formed by voyageurs, who had come down from Illinois, than he cleared a pretty long and wide strip along the river, to put in execution the plan he had projected. Then, with the help of some piqueurs, he traced on the ground the streets and quarters which were to form the new town, and notified all who wished building sites to present their petitions to the council. To each settler who appeared they gave a plot ten fathoms front by twenty deep, and as each square was fifty fathoms front, it gave twelve plots in each, the two middle ones being ten front by twenty-five deep. It was ordained that those who obtained these plots should be bound to enclose them with palisades, and leave all around a strip at least three feet wide, at the foot of which a ditch was to be dug, to serve as a drain for the river water in time of inundation. The Sieur de la Tour deemed these canals, communicating from square to square, not only absolutely necessary, but even to preserve the city from inundation raised in front, near a slight elevation, running to the river, a dike or levee of earth, at the foot of which he dug a similar drain.

"All were engaged in these labors, and several houses or cabins were already raised, when about the month of September a hurricane came on so suddenly, that in an instant it levelled houses and palisades. With this impetuous wind came such torrents of rain that you could not step out a moment without risk of being drowned. A vessel, called the *Adventurer*, lay at anchor before the town, and though all sails were reefed, and the yards and vessel well secured to the shore by cables, and in the river by anchors, it was full twenty times in danger of going to pieces or being dashed on the shore. In fact, this tempest was so terrible that it rooted up the largest trees, and the birds, unable to keep up, fell in the streets. In one hour the wind had twice blown from every point of the compass. On the third day it finally ceased, and they set to work to repair the damage done. Meanwhile the new city began to fill up with inhabitants, who insensibly began to abandon New Biloxi [Fort Louis] to come and settle there; at last the commandant himself went there with his council and troops, leaving only an officer with a detachment at New Biloxi to guard the post, and direct vessels coming from France to the residence of the colony. When the foundation of the new capital, which took the name of New Orleans, was laid, the houses, as I have said, were mere palisaded cabins, like those of Old and New Biloxi; the only difference being that in the latter

places the posts were pine, while at the capital they were cypress. But since they began to make brick there, no houses but brick are built, so that now the government-house, church, barracks, etc., and almost all the houses are brick, or half-brick and half-wood."[1] In such a way began the city of New Orleans.

With every passing month the Mississippi bubble grew in magnitude. Law's financial devices were as popular and delusive as they were then novel. Shares in the Company of the West rose rapidly in value, going even beyond ten thousand francs. Values of land in Louisiana were grossly exaggerated, and the rush to acquire allotments correspondingly increased. Maps were abundant bearing the legend "this region is full of mines," sprinkled liberally over them. Ore and ingots were produced at the mint in evidence, though they probably came from Mexico or Peru. Money was plentiful, the spirit of speculation was rife, and nobody dreamed of a collapse. The Banque Royale was free to issue unlimited quantities of notes; the company existed to draw them into circulation. Investors came from all parts of Europe. "Paris," says an English pamphleteer of the time, "like the temple of fortune among the heathen, is resorted to by innumerable crowds of every nation, quality, and condition, and the dirty kennel of Quinquempoix has for some time been

---

[1] Dumont's "Memoirs" in French, *Historical Collections of Louisiana*, V. 23-25. On the founding of New Orleans, see Dumont, *Mémoires Historiques sur la Louisiane*, II. 39-46; Le Page du Pratz, *Histoire de la Louisiane*; French, *Historical Collections of Louisiana*, III. 179-182; Grace King, *New Orleans*, Ch. III.; and Gayarré, *History of Louisiana*, I. 233-286. In Shea, *Charlevoix's History of New France*, VI. 40, there is an interesting plan of the early city.

more frequented than the Royal Exchange of London." It is estimated that at the end of 1719 there were five hundred thousand foreigners in Paris, who had been attracted thither solely by the unusual opportunities that were offered for speculation. The capital stock of the company came to be stated at the enormous figure of 3,000,000,000 livres.

In 1720 the end came. In January of that year Law became comptroller-general of the kingdom, and in the following month the Banque Royale was absorbed by the company. But already the structure had commenced to crumble. The more conservative investors had begun to ask to have their stock converted into coin or real estate in France. This was obviously out of the question. The company made desperate efforts to save itself. Edicts were issued compelling the acceptance of its notes in the payment of debts and securities, and others demonetizing gold and silver. Under Law's direction a royal decree was promulgated for the purpose of reducing values. But these expedients, of course, only made the situation worse, revealing as they did the embarrassment of the company's sponsors. Confidence gave place to distrust, and the whole project went down in utter ruin. Law endeavored wildly to ward off the crash, but, finding himself quite unable to accomplish anything, was glad to escape the fury of a Parisian mob and seek asylum in Belgium.

For a time the bursting of the bubble disgraced Louisiana in the eyes of Europe. The mask of romance and splendor which had been made to adorn the colonization of the Mississippi Valley was rudely torn away. "Instead

of the splendid visions of opulence, the disenchanted public would now see only unwholesome marshes, which were the tombs of immigrants; its name was a name of disgust and terror." Yet the colony was entirely too strong and valuable to be abandoned. The failure of Law's schemes merely meant that the French settlement of the Great West would proceed hereafter by slower but saner methods.

CHAPTER VII

THE STRUGGLE OF THE ENGLISH AND FRENCH FOR POSSESSION

AS early as 1720 the issue between the French and the English in the Mississippi Valley was pretty clearly defined. During the half-century which had elapsed since the expedition of Joliet and Marquette, enough had been seen of the great region from the Illinois to the Gulf to convince both peoples of its eminent desirability for possession. As yet the English had contented themselves with reiterated assertions of their wholesale claims through the American interior, and had made no concerted effort to explore, much less to colonize, beyond the Alleghanies. Traders who traversed the western country, however, kept them fairly well informed as to its resources, and also as to the activities of other Europeans in that direction. The time had not yet come for the swarming of the English from their seaboard homes, but some of the more far-sighted among them conceived already of an impending conflict, and by a few it was deemed highly expedient that steps be taken without further delay to circumvent their ambitious rivals.

Among these seers of the first quarter of the eighteenth century was Lieutenant-Governor Alexander Spotswood of Virginia. In 1716, with his party of fifty "Knights

of the Golden Horseshoe," he had set out from the capital at Williamsburg to explore the sources of the James, Potomac, and other rivers which for a hundred years had formed the great highways of Virginian travel and trade in the tide-water districts. Another object was to examine the passes of the Appalachian barrier and find whether a good trade route might not thus be opened from the English colonies to the Great Lakes. The James River was ascended by the party in thirty-six days "to the very head, where it runs no bigger than a man's arm, from under a large stone" on the crest of the Appalachian range.[1] Seven miles farther the travellers came upon the Susquehanna, which they named the Euphrates. There "the Governor buried a bottle and a paper enclosed, on which he writ that he took possession of this place in the name of and for King George the First of England. We had a good dinner, drank the king's health in champagne, and fired a volley."[2] Convinced that the desired portal to the western trade had thus been found, Spots-

---

[1] Journal of John Fontaine, quoted in Winsor, *The Mississippi Basin*, 130. Fontaine was one of Spotswood's companions on the trip. His rather slender journal (printed in Maury, *Huguenot Family*, New York, 1872) is practically our only authority for the expedition, aside from Spotswood's report and letters. The latter are published in the *Virginia Historical Society Collections*, New Series, Vol. II. For general accounts of Spotswood's expedition, see Winsor, *The Mississippi Basin*, 127-135, and *Narrative and Critical History*, V. Ch. IV.; Edward Ingle, "Governor Spotswood's Horseshoe Campaign in 1716, as related to the romance of Cathay," in the *Magazine of American History*, XVII. 295-307; Robert Beverly, *Virginia*, Preface; W. A. Caruthers, *Knights of the Horseshoe*; R. A. Brock's Introduction to the Official Letters of Spotswood in *Virginia Historical Society Collections*, New Series, Vol. I.; Fiske, *Old Virginia and her Neighbors*, II. Ch. XVII.; and Charles Campbell, *History of Virginia*, 378-410.   [2] Journal of John Fontaine.

wood led his party back to Williamsburg and proceeded to formulate a report to the English Lords of Trade.

This report is an interesting document, revealing as it does the views and plans of the most ambitious executive in the English colonies respecting the French rivalry for the possession of the interior. "Having for a long time endeavored," he writes, "to inform myself of the situation of the French to the westward of us, and the advantages they reap by an uninterrupted communication along the lake, I shall here take the liberty of communicating my thoughts to your lordships, both of the dangers to which his Majesty's plantations may be exposed by this new acquisition of our neighbors, and how the same may be best prevented. I have often regretted that after so many years as these countries have been seated, no attempts have been made to discover the sources of our rivers, nor to establishing correspondence with those nations of Indians to the westward of us, even after the certain knowledge of the progress made by the French in surrounding us with their settlements." After asserting that Lake Erie was but a five days' march from mountain peaks seen by the explorers, Spotswood went on to state the problem of the English in this western country as follows: "The British plantations are in a manner surrounded by the French commerce with the numerous nations of Indians settled on both sides of the lakes. They may not only engross the whole skin trade, but may, when they please, send out such bodies of Indians on the back of these plantations as may greatly distress his Majesty's subjects here. Should they multiply their settlements along these lakes so as to join their dominions of Canada to their new

colony of Louisiana, they might even possess themselves of any of these plantations they pleased. Nature, 'tis true, has formed a barrier for us by that long chain of mountains which runs from the back of South Carolina as far as New York, and which are only passable in some few places; but even that natural defence may prove rather destructive to us, if they are not possessed by us before they are known to them. To prevent the dangers which threaten his Majesty's dominions here from the growing power of these neighbors, nothing seems to me of more consequence than that now while the nations are at peace, and while the French are yet incapable of possessing all that vast tract which lies on the back of these plantations, we should attempt to make some settlements on the lakes and at the same time possess ourselves of those passes of the great mountains which are necessary to preserve a communication with such settlements."[1]

It was Spotswood's idea that by pressing through the Alleghany passes to the country about Lake Erie the English would be enabled to cut the French line of communication from Canada to Louisiana. He was an ardent champion of the "sea to sea" charters, and it was he more than any one else who formulated Virginia's great claim to the Northwest — a claim adhered to with steadfast persistence until after the close of the Revolution. As he interpreted the Virginian charter, it marked off for English possession all the region of the Great Lakes from Erie westward, as well as most of the lands in the upper Mississippi Valley. As late as 1720 he was ignorant of

[1] Official Letters of Alexander Spotswood, *Virginia Historical Society Collections*, New Series, II. 295.

much that the French had done to assure permanent possession in this quarter. "In the space westward of us," he writes, "I do not know that the French yet have any settlements, nor that any other European nation ever had. Neither is it probable that the French from their new plantations will be able in some years to reach the southern boundaries mentioned in the charter of Virginia."[1] And although he held that the French establishments on the lower Mississippi were in territory rightfully belonging to the Carolinas, he seems to have been satisfied that a little more activity of the English in the direction of Lake Erie would effectually prevent the permanent encroachment of French colonization. His views were essentially narrow, yet rather more intelligent than those of most of his contemporaries.

On the whole the prospect of French possession in the Mississippi Valley was at this time quite good. The bursting of the Mississippi bubble had far more serious effects in France than in America. The net result of the whole ill-fated enterprise of Law was to settle in Louisiana not fewer than six or seven thousand people. A population had been gained, by however questionable a process, and a population that for the most part reconciled itself in time to the disappointments incident to the failure of Law and the first untrained contact with the American wilderness, and remained to become the progenitors of a very important element of the inhabitants of the lower Mississippi Valley. By the time that Spotswood was writing that he knew of no French settlements in or west

[1] Spotswood to the Lords Commissioners of Trade, May 20, 1720. *Virginia Historical Society Collections*, New Series, II. 336.

of the great Virginia territory, the Mississippi, between the Illinois and the Red, was fast coming to be lined with French missions and trading-posts.[1] In the spring of 1720 Pierre Dugué Boisbriant, a cousin of Bienville and commander in the Illinois district, completed a strong fort sixteen miles north of Kaskaskia, and named it Fort Chartres in honor of the Regent of France.[2] This post was destined to distinction forty years later, as it was the last point at which the French flag was hauled down east of the Mississippi. The next year Kaskaskia was elevated to the dignity of a parish, an act indicative of its growing importance. About this time Pierre François Xavier de Charlevoix, a Jesuit priest in the employ of the Regent, made a tour of the French settlements in the West for the express purpose of observing their number and strength and communicating the facts to the home government.[3] From his reports we are able to ascertain

[1] Richard B. Haughton, "The Influence of the Mississippi River upon the Early Settlement of its Valley," in *Mississippi Historical Society Publications*, IV. 465-483.

[2] At the time of its construction the fort seemed to stand upon solid foundations. A half century later, however, when it was held by the English, a springtime freshet compelled its permanent abandonment. See a very interesting paper by Edward G. Mason on "Old Fort Chartres," in *Illinois in the Eighteenth Century* (Fergus Historical Series, No. 12) [Chicago, 1881]. The same paper is in Mason, *Chapters from Illinois History*, 212-250. Another valuable paper by the same author is "Kaskaskia and its Parish Records," in the *Magazine of American History*, VI. 161-182.

[3] Charlevoix had been specially commissioned by the Regent, the Duke of Orleans, to ascertain all that could be known concerning the long-sought route to the China Sea. He landed in Canada in 1720. An account of his travels was published twenty-four years later in his very important work, *Histoire et description générale de la Nouvelle France avec le journal historique d'un voyage fait par ordre du roi dans l'Amé-*

quite definitely the position of the French on the Mississippi at the time under consideration. Besides Fort Chartres and Kaskaskia, he describes a settlement at Cahokia at the mouth of the Illinois, now more than a score of years old, and another in its incipient stages at Natchez. Many more were being planned and some were already being marked on the maps as sure to be established soon. While New Orleans was described as a hundred cabins for the troops, irregularly placed, a storehouse of wood, two or three mean dwellings, and an unfinished warehouse, the day was predicted when it would become an opulent town, the capital of a rich colony. Under date of January 10, 1722, Charlevoix writes in his journal as follows: "I am at length arrived in this famous city which they have called *la Nouvelle Orléans*. . . . This city is the first which one of the greatest rivers of the world has seen raised on its banks. If the eight hundred fine houses and the five parishes which the newspapers gave it some two years ago are reduced at present to a hundred barracks placed in no very great order, to a great storehouse built of wood, to two or three houses which would be no ornament to a village of France, and to the half of a sorry storehouse which they agreed to lend to the lord of the place, and which he had no sooner taken possession of, but they turned him out to dwell under a tent; what pleasure, on the other side, to see insensibly increasing this future capital of a

rique Septentrionale. A portion of this history is given in French, *Historical Collections of Louisiana*, III., and there is a complete and invaluable translation of the entire work by J. G. Shea, in six volumes, published at New York in 1872 under the title *History and General Description of New France.*

fine and vast country, and to be able to say, not with a sigh, like the hero of Virgil, speaking of his dear native place consumed by the flames, and the fields where the city of Troy had been, but full of a well-grounded hope, this wild and desert place, which the reeds and trees do yet almost wholly cover, will be one day, and perhaps that day is not far off, an opulent city, and the metropolis of a great and rich colony. . . . Rome and Paris had not such considerable beginnings, were not built under such happy auspices, and their founders did not find on the Seine and the Tiber the advantages we have found on the Mississippi, in comparison of which those two rivers are but little brooks."[1] The entire province was declared to have a population of about fifty-five hundred, of which six hundred were slaves.

The year 1722 was marked by the first systematic effort to set up a fixed order of colonial government in Louisiana. In the latter part of May the *Aventurier* arrived at Biloxi with directions from the company to transfer the capital from that place to New Orleans. Within a few weeks the stores of the company were moved to the future seat of government and Bienville there took up his residence.[2] For judicial purposes the colony was divided into nine districts, each under the jurisdiction of a commander. A Superior Council was constituted from the company in France to serve as an appellate court. By an ordinance of May 16, 1722, issued by the commissioners

---

[1] Journal of Father Charlevoix, translated in French, *Historical Collections of Louisiana*, III. 171. See an article by John Dimity on "Charlevoix in New Orleans," in the *Magazine of American History*, X. 140–142.

[2] Shea, *Charlevoix's History of New France*, VI. 67.

of this council, the province of Louisiana was divided into three spiritual jurisdictions.[1] One of these was to be under the control of the Capuchins, another under that of the Jesuits, and the third under that of the Carmelites. Later in the same year, however, by an ordinance of the bishop of Quebec, the Carmelites were deprived of their district, and the parallel of Natchez was made the dividing line between the Capuchins on the south and the Jesuits on the north. Before many years it was discovered that the Capuchins were not sufficiently numerous to attend properly to the spiritual needs of the district assigned them, and Jesuits were gradually admitted. In September, 1726, the company entered into its first contract for the settlement of some Ursuline nuns at New Orleans. It was designed that they should establish a hospital and have charge of the education of the settlers' children. The six women who were first sent over arrived in the summer of 1727 and at once began their work.[2] The convent which was built for them a few years later is still standing, being used as the residence of the archbishop, and is considered by Winsor probably the oldest building in the Mississippi Valley.[3]

With the year 1724 Bienville's governorship came to a temporary close. It seems always to have been his misfortune to be disliked and conspired against by his sub-

[1] Gabriel Gravier's introduction to Marie Madeleine Hachard's *Relation du Voyage des Dames Religieuses Ursulines de Rouen à la Nouvelle Orléans*, p. xli [Paris, 1872].

[2] See the very interesting *Relation* of Marie Madeleine Hachard, one of the six nuns, as above; also Trauchepin, *Relation du Voyage des Premières Ursulines à la Nouvelle Orléans et de leur établissement en cette ville* [New York, 1859]. The official authorization of the work of the Ursulines by the Company of the West is printed in French, *Historical Collections of Louisiana*, III. 79–83, note.   [3] Winsor, *The Mississippi Basin*, 159.

ordinates in office. Probably this is to be accounted for rather more by the jealousies and rivalries that characterized French administration in America than by any unusual combativeness in his own disposition. Be that as it may, after almost a quarter-century of command in the colony, the governor could not save himself from a sharp recall. He was made the scapegoat for many of the blunders and failures of the company, although it must be confessed that by connecting his name with an infamous legal code in the interval between his recall and his embarkation for France he seriously compromised his claims upon the consideration of those interested in a wholesome government in the colony.[1] On his return he defended his course as governor by presenting at court a lengthy memorial, reciting the services he and his numerous brothers had rendered the cause of the French in the American wilderness. But his plea went for nothing, as the Superior Council was convinced that his further control in Louisiana would but perpetuate the evils of the past two decades. From the following report sent to the council by the commander of Dauphin Island and Biloxi after the installation of Bienville's successor, Périer, it appears that the change in the governorship produced no visible effect on the conditions of local politics and administration: "The

[1] This was the so-called *Code Noir* which Bienville drew up from the regulations compiled by the jurists of Louis XIV. for the island of St. Domingo. It was intended primarily to bring within the pale of the law the constantly increasing number of negro slaves in the colony, and for the most part in this direction its provisions were harsh and illiberal, though in perfect accord with the spirit of the times. It continued in effect until after the cession of Louisiana to the United States in 1803. For a full synopsis of the fifty-four articles of the Black Code, see French, *Historical Collections of Louisiana*, III. 89-95, note.

army is without discipline. Military stores and munitions of war are not protected. Soldiers desert at pleasure. Warehouses and store-ships are pillaged. Forgers, thieves, and murderers go unpunished. In short, the country is a disgrace to France, being without religion, without justice, without discipline, without order, without police."[1]

The most important event of Périer's administration was the war with the Natchez. These Indians were the most compactly organized and the farthest advanced of any with whom the French came in contact in the South.[2] They were not numerous, but they held a position of strategic importance on the lower Mississippi. In 1716 Bienville had won their respect by a firm demand for the punishment of some of their number who had murdered a party of French *voyageurs*, and for more than a decade after that time they continued quite friendly toward the French. No one of the French settlements above New Orleans prospered as did Rosalie, which was situated just

---

[1] Quoted in Winsor, *Narrative and Critical History of America*, V. 46.

[2] For a description of the Natchez and an account of the Natchez wars, see Penicaut's journal, in French, *Historical Collections of Louisiana*, New Series, I. 88–95; Le Page du Pratz, *History of Louisiana*, 79–95, 322–376; Shea, *Charlevoix's History of New France*, VI. 80–118; Father Le Petit's narrative, in French, *Historical Collections of Louisiana*, III. 140–158; Dumont, "Historical Memoirs of Louisiana," in French, *Historical Collections of Louisiana*, V. 58–102; King and Ficklen, *History of Louisiana*, Ch. XIV.; Gayarré, *History of Louisiana*, I. 395–450; Gay, Bryant's *History of the United States*, II. 540–542; Winsor, *The Mississippi Basin*, 187–188; Grace King, *Sieur de Bienville*, Ch. XXV.; Wallace, *History of Illinois and Louisiana under French Rule*, Ch. XIV.; Pickett, *History of Alabama*, I. Ch. VII.; Martin, *History of Louisiana*, I. Ch. XI.; and Monette, *History of the Valley of the Mississippi*, I. Chs. VII. and VIII. See also an interesting article by J. H. Walworth on "The Natchez Indians — A Lost Tribe," in the *Magazine of American History*, XI. 300–309.

across the river from the main town of the Natchez. But for the unpardonable effrontery of the French commander, Chopart, the two peoples might have lived long in peace. Chopart was typical of a class of selfish and narrow-minded officials of whom France had far too many in the New World. By his conduct the foundations of peace with the natives, so carefully laid by La Salle, Iberville, and Bienville, threatened to be swept entirely away. His most notorious act, and the one which precipitated the conflict, was his demand that the Natchez abandon the site of their town and their religious shrines in order that he might have it for his private plantation. Argument on part of the incensed Indians proved unavailing, and for the time they appeared to consent to a removal within two months. In secret council, however, they planned a stroke which they hoped would deliver them forever from the intrusions of the French. Other tribes, notably the Choctaws, gladly joined in the prospective enterprise of extermination, and it was arranged that the blow should fall on the day when Chopart had directed the abandonment of the village and temple. That day was November 28, 1729. When it came the work of revenge was accomplished almost without resistance. The Indians entered the homes of the French, and at an agreed signal the massacre began. When it was finished at least two hundred Frenchmen lay dead, among them Chopart. Of the garrison but a single soldier escaped. Most of the women and children were held to be employed as slaves.[1]

---

[1] Dumont, *Mémoires Historiques sur la Louisiane*. See plan of Fort Rosalie in Winsor, *The Mississippi Basin*, 189; also in *Narrative and Critical History of America*, V. 47.

December 3 some fugitives from the slaughter reached New Orleans. Périer lost no time in organizing a little army to advance against the Natchez. The Choctaws who were disgruntled because the Natchez had begun the massacre two days earlier than had been agreed, and had not divided the spoils with their confederates, were won from their alliance and induced to take up arms on the side of the French. In March, 1730, the combined force of French and Choctaws compelled the surrender of the Natchez. The defeated natives then became fugitives. They moved northward and tried to capture the French fort at Natchitoches, commanded by Saint-Denys, but failed. The following year Périer, strengthened by the arrival of three companies of marines from France, made a final movement up the river and completely destroyed the remaining remnant of the Natchez nation. Two hundred were taken as prisoners and sold as slaves on the plantations of St. Domingo. Three hundred escaped and scattered among the tribes who were hostile to the French. It is said that even now, among the Creek Indians who cultivate the fertile lands reserved for them in the upper valleys of the Washita River, there are three hundred or more good citizens who speak the Natchez language and trace their descent back to the vassals of the Natchez "Brother of the Sun."

The Natchez war was the first serious conflict between the French and the Indians in Louisiana. From it the colonists learned the lesson that it was never possible to be too well prepared to resist attack. New Orleans had hitherto been but poorly fortified, but now Périer began to dig a moat around the town and plan forts at several

points on the river to circumvent hostile movements. During the campaign against the Natchez it had been demonstrated that there was need also for defence against internal foes. The absence of the soldiery from New Orleans had all but precipitated a slave insurrection. The number of negroes in the colony was such that their tendency to revolt constituted a very real danger. Only by the prompt execution of a half-dozen of the ringleaders on this occasion was the horror averted.[1]

The net result of the massacre of the inhabitants at Fort Rosalie and the attempted rising of the slaves at New Orleans was to discredit the existing administration of the colony. Within the company itself there was a reaction, and the feeling grew that Louisiana was but a drain upon its resources. Other fields, especially in Asia and Africa, promised vastly more, at least in the way of immediate returns, and the members lost interest in their American investment. At last, convinced that the control of Louisiana was but a dead weight, the company surrendered its charter to the king in January, 1731. The system of commercial monopoly had broken down. The Louisiana situation afforded one more illustration of the folly of intrusting the business of colonization to boards of royal favorites who did not intend to leave the

---

[1] Le Page du Pratz, *History of Louisiana*, 77-79. Accounts of the insurrection differ. Du Pratz says it began in an outbreak of the negroes against a French soldier who insulted a female negro. Charlevoix (*History of New France*, translated by Shea, VI. 119) makes it appear that the rising was instigated by the Chickasaw Indians who sent to New Orleans a trusted negro to notify all his race that "it depended on them alone to recover their liberty and live in quiet and plenty among the English."

comforts of their own homes and cast in their fortunes with the colonies.

May 7, 1732, the king organized a council of government to take the place of the defunct company.[1] Périer was recalled from the governorship of the province, and Bienville restored to his old post. At the time of the change the population of the colony was still not more than 5000, of whom 2000 were negroes. There were eleven distinct settlements and posts. Bienville's second administration began with the migration of considerable numbers of people from France to Louisiana, but unfortunately they came mainly from the pauper and vagabond classes. During the next fifteen years there was no growth in population — rather a decline. In 1745 there were but 1700 white men, 1500 women, and 2020 slaves in the entire province. Fort Rosalie, at one time heralded as the most favored of all the French settlements on the Mississippi, had only eight white men and fifteen negro slaves.

As soon as Bienville was again in full command at New Orleans he began preparations for a war against the Chickasaw Indians, whose country lay between the upper forks of the Mobile River. There were several reasons for such a war. In the first place, the Chickasaws had given refuge to some of the fleeing Natchez, and had encouraged them to maintain a sort of guerilla war with the destroyers of their villages. Moreover, the Chickasaws were prime movers in a growing league of the Indians of the South to destroy French commerce on the rivers emptying into the Gulf, chiefly the Mississippi and

[1] Gayarré, *History of Louisiana*, I. 455.

the Mobile. And finally, the Chickasaws were strongly inclined to an alliance with the English. They received English traders from Carolina with the utmost hospitality, and it was known that several Englishmen lived permanently among them for trading and other purposes. It was likewise understood that the English had not a little to do with prompting the Chickasaws to acts of hostility against French trade. The crusade which Bienville thought it necessary to organize against this tribe partook, therefore, largely of the nature of a movement to check the advance of English influence in the West. The hope of plundering the English traders was not the least of the incentives which impelled the Frenchmen to join the expedition.

Preparations for the campaign were in proportion to its importance.[1] The Choctaws, who lived 160 miles south of the Chickasaw country, were secured as allies, and it was arranged that D'Artaguette, commander at Kaskaskia, with as large a force as he could gather in the Illinois region, should coöperate with the expedition from the south. Bienville himself was to advance by way of the Mobile and Tombigbee rivers. Fort Mobile was left

---

[1] The best contemporary accounts of Bienville's campaigns against the Chickasaws are Le Page du Pratz, *History of Louisiana*, 96-105, and Dumont, "Historical Memoirs of Louisiana," in French, *Historical Collections of Louisiana*, V. 106-118. Modern accounts are in Grace King, *Sieur de Bienville*, Chs. XXVI. and XXVII.; King and Ficklen, *History of Louisiana*, 99-106; Gayarré, *History of Louisiana*, I. 459-492; Martin, *History of Louisiana*, I., Ch. XII.; Winsor, *The Mississippi Basin*, 190-192; Hamilton, *Colonial Mobile*, Ch. XIV.; Monette, *History of the Valley of the Mississippi*, I. Ch. IX.; Pickett, *History of Alabama*, I. Ch. X.; Brown, *History of Alabama*, Ch. VI.; and Wallace, *History of Illinois and Louisiana under French Rule*, Ch. XV.

April 1, 1736. Three weeks later, when the army was at Tombigbee,[1] it was joined by the Choctaw contingent. The French probably numbered about five hundred and the Choctaws from six hundred to one thousand. After a month's travelling up the river they came to the point where it was no longer navigable, and where it was necessary to build a stockade to protect the boats and proceed by land. When the chief village of the Chickasaws was reached the suspicions of the French were confirmed by seeing an English flag flying above the fortification and a number of Carolina traders mingling with the savage warriors. The Chickasaw fort was circular in shape, with three rows of loopholes, and was built of heavy timbers a foot in diameter. The first attack, May 26, resulted in a disastrous repulse of the assailants. It is said that the loss was as high as 50, which number was increased to 120 before Bienville finally decided to abandon the undertaking. The Chickasaw fort was manifestly too strong to be taken by storm. Until the last Bienville hoped for the arrival of D'Artaguette, but in vain. The Illinois commander had been directed to be in the vicinity of the Chickasaw stronghold not later than May 10, at which time Bienville had planned the first attack. D'Artaguette, however, had advanced more rapidly than had Bienville, and had been the first to encounter the foe. With his band of four hundred French and Indians he had engaged unadvisedly in a battle with the northernmost Chickasaws in the hope of defeating them before Bienville arrived, so as to monopolize the credit of the expedition.

[1] The modern Jones's Bluff of the Little Tombigbee River.

At the first onset he was deserted by his Indians and captured. From him the Chickasaws obtained a supply of gunpowder and some despatches from Bienville outlining the plan of attack. These were easily translated by the English traders at the fort, so that everything was in readiness to repel the expedition from the south as soon as it appeared. Having heard only vague rumors of D'Artaguette's proximity, Bienville led his band of discouraged followers back to New Orleans. During the next three years he busied himself with plans for renewing the war, for it was apparent that the French river traffic would never be safe until the power of the Chickasaws was effectually broken.

In 1740 he was again ready. This time the advance upon the Chickasaw country was from a different direction. Fort Assumption, built for the purpose near the site of modern Memphis, was made the mustering place, and an army of thirty-six hundred men was there collected, one-third whites, and the rest Indians and negro slaves. Seven hundred were soldiers newly arrived from France, others were from the Illinois posts, and a few from Canada. All together it was the largest army which the French in America had ever put in the field. So formidable did it appear that the Chickasaws took alarm and declared themselves ready to surrender the English who were among them, and to send their chiefs to Fort Assumption as hostages and peacemakers. Remembering the disasters of the former war, Bienville gladly accepted this offer. By April 1, 1740, he was ready to return to New Orleans. Fort Assumption was abandoned, not to be restored as a military stronghold until the opening of the Civil War. As for the Chickasaws, they were not conquered, and continued almost as regularly as before to jeopardize French trade. They long remained mere tools in the hands of the English, by whom they were constantly encouraged to break their treaty obligations.

Bienville's career in America was now near an end. In 1743 he was succeeded in the governorship by the Marquis de Vaudreuil, a Canadian and a son of a former governor of Canada, after which he went to Europe never to return to the scene of his early labors, though he lived until four years after France had lost her last hold upon the American continent. Conditions in Louisiana at the retirement of Bienville were still extremely unsatisfactory. The colony had succeeded no better under the control of the king than under that of the Company of the West. As we have seen, population actually decreased. Its officers and garrisons entailed on the crown an annual expenditure of 500,000 livres, while the revenues were quite inconsiderable. Louis XV could see in the colony nothing to be proud of, and did not hesitate on numerous occasions to show his contempt for it. The colony was not self-supporting even as to food supplies, being dependent on shipments from the Illinois country and from Europe. Among Governor Vaudreuil's first reports to the home government was one to the effect that if a certain consignment of flour had not arrived at a certain date, the starving garrison would have been beyond his control.

In an anonymous letter written about 1744 by a French officer at New Orleans to a friend in Paris we find the fol-

lowing pessimistic picture of life in the Louisiana capital: "The French live sociably enough, but the officers are too free with the Town's People; and the Town's People that are rich are too proud and lofty; their Inferiors hardly dare speak to them, and here, as every where else (to make Use of a common Proverb), an upstart Fellow thinks that others are not worthy to look at him. Every one studies his own Profit; the Poor labour for a Week and squander in one Day all they have earned in six; from thence arises the Profit of the Publick-houses, which flourish every Day: The rich spend their Time in seeing their Slaves work to improve their Lands, and get Money, which they spend in Plays, Balls and Feasts. What I say of New Orleans, I say of the whole Province, without being guilty of Slander or Calumny. Laws are observed here much in the same Manner as in France, or worse: The rich Man knows how to procure himself Justice of the Poor, if the Affair is to his Advantage; but if the poor Man is in the right, he is obliged to enter into a Composition; if the rich is in the wrong the Affair is stifled. They deal fairly with such as are very sharp-sighted: As the King is at a great Distance, they make him provide Victuals, Arms and Cloathing for the Troops, which those who keep the Offices or Magazines, sell, and put the Money in their own Pockets; the poor Soldier, for whom they were designed, never so much as seeing them. . . . The Country was at first settled by leud good for nothing People, sent from France by Force; afterwards by young People who went thither by Choice, and by young People who had no Fathers, taken, with their own Good-will, out of the Hospitals at Paris and l'Orient. At present no Women are sent there against their Will. Sometimes false Coiners and Smugglers are sent thither, but they are free in the Country, and work for themselves; and even those of them who chose to enter among the Troops, are received there, provided they have not passed thro' the Hands of Justice. The mechanic Arts flourish: The King sends Workmen for building and repairing his Ships: He entertains Seamen there, and Workmen in Wood and Iron. The Youth here are employed in hunting, fishing and pleasuring; very few learn the necessary Sciences, or at best it is what is least attended to. The Children, even of the best Sort, know how to fire a Musket or shoot an Arrow, catch Fish, draw a Bow, handle an Oar, swim, run, dance, play at Cards and understand Paper Notes, before they know their Letters or their God. A Child of six Years of Age knows more here of raking and swearing than a young Man of 25 in France; and an insolent Boy of 12 or 13 Years of Age will boldly insult, and strike an old Man."[1]

The river trade was the most important factor in the life of the colony. The settlers in the Illinois country of whom there were between one and two thousand by 1743, farmed and raised stock during a portion of the year and spent the rest of their time in making trips to

[1] *The Present State of the Country and Inhabitants, Europeans and Indians, of Louisiana on the North Continent of America, by an Officer at New Orleans to his Friend at Paris*, 11-13, 27-29 [London, 1744] There are reasons for believing that the evils of Louisiana life depicted in this letter really existed although the author was certainly far from infallible, since in beginning his epistle he ascribes the local name " English Turn " to a visit by the English to the portion of the Mississippi in question *before* La Salle reached the Gulf in 1682 — certainly an inexcusable error.

New Orleans to dispose of their products. These consisted chiefly of flour and pork, which were transported to market on broad and substantial barges, guided by experienced river navigators. As a rule a large number of such barges went down the river together, from considerations of companionship for the traders as well as immunity from Indian attacks. December was the usual starting time from Kaskaskia and Cahokia and Fort Chartres, and the descent to the New Orleans market would be accomplished by early January. After two or three weeks of bargaining the traders were ready to return, their barges laden this time with sugar, rice, cotton, tobacco, and manufactured articles brought in from France. Naturally the ascent was tedious and wearisome, but thoughts of home and of the joy which their coming would bring in the upper settlements nerved the sturdy rowers to their best efforts.

Vaudreuil assumed the governorship in 1743, with ambitions rather out of proportion to the strength of the colony. He cherished a plan for the maintenance of such a court at New Orleans as would have been nothing less than ridiculous had it ever been realized. As Winsor remarks, "He did not see as well as others saw the rather incongruous exhibition which the manners of Paris made in the swampy little town."[1] About the only life which the place manifested was contributed by the visiting traders, and the occasional arrival of *filles à la cassette*. Instead of being free to organize a social and court system, the new governor found himself under the necessity of devoting his energies mainly to the

[1] Winsor, *The Mississippi Basin*, 260.

checkmating of hostile Indians and the English.[1] One party of the Choctaws persisted in allying themselves with the Carolinians and Georgians, and New Orleans was never quite able to cast off the fear of an English attack by sea. In 1750 the portion of the Choctaws which was attached to the French attacked the smaller portion which supported the English, and by the treaty of Grand Pré effectually repressed them for a time. But the effect was only temporary, for English influence from the East was growing steadily stronger. The Chickasaws offered to conclude a treaty with Vaudreuil, but the governor was suspicious of their motives and preferred to wait until he should have conquered them in war — a consummation which was never attained. The military character of the French occupancy of Louisiana at this time is indicated by the fact that in 1751 Vaudreuil had under his command two thousand troops — probably more than half of the entire white population of the colony.

The location of the French settlements in the Mississippi Valley at this stage of their history is described as follows by Winsor in his *Mississippi Basin:* "By the middle of the century the French in Louisiana were well intrenched outside New Orleans in at least eight districts. Not far from the capital they had a post and settlement at Point Coupée on the Mississippi, below the Red River. They maintained a post at Natchitoches, toward the Spanish frontier in New Mexico. They had another at Natchez, and still another near the mouth of the Arkansas.

---

[1] Several of Vaudreuil's letters on the subject of English and Indian relations are given in the anonymous *Present State of the Country and Inhabitants of Louisiana* before referred to, pp. 31-54.

There were also settlements dependent on Fort Chartres, in the Illinois country, the best compacted of all the occupied regions, numbering at this time, as was computed, eleven hundred whites, three hundred negroes, and about sixty Indian bondmen. This estimate did not include those settlements above Peoria accounted a part of Canada, nor those settlers on the Wabash similarly classed. Besides three native villages near Fort Chartres, with about three hundred warriors, — for the Illinois tribes had been reduced by migrations, — there were, not far away, five distinct French communities: that at Cahokia, below the modern St. Louis; one at St. Philippe, above Fort Chartres; the parent village at Kaskaskia; and another gathering at Prairie du Rocher. Still another, but west of the Mississippi, was that at Ste. Geneviève."[1]

In February, 1753, Vaudreuil was transferred to the governorship of Canada.[2] His place at New Orleans was taken by Captain Kerlerec, an officer of the royal navy, who occupied it during the remaining ten years of French tenure in the valley. Kerlerec quarrelled continually with his subordinates, particularly with Rochemore, the intendant of commerce. Upon his return to Paris in 1763 he was imprisoned in the Bastile on the charge of having misappropriated 10,000,000 livres in four years on a pretence of preparing for an Indian war. The reports sent from the colony during Kerlerec's administration are filled with a wearisome round of complaints against officials, expressions of dissatisfaction with the soldiery, and excuses for inactivity and lack of progress.

---

[1] Winsor, *The Mississippi Basin*, 268.
[2] He did not assume the duties of the new office until two years later.

In the meantime the inevitable conflict between the French and English for possession of the eastern Mississippi Valley was rapidly hastening toward a crisis, and it may be well at this point to cast a backward glance at the results thus far achieved since the rivalry of the two peoples had begun to involve them in open war. The first serious clash had occurred in the year 1690, just after the beginning of the War of the Palatinate in Europe between Louis XIV. on the one hand and the alliance of Protestant sovereigns, headed by William III., of England, on the other. Louis was moved by a great ambition to unite the Spanish and French colonial empires, create a formidable world-monarchy, and bring English colonial enterprise and trading operations within permanently restricted limits. Although this project did not advance as far toward realization as did a similar one formed by Napoleon more than a century later, it was nevertheless a real danger to the English people everywhere, in the colonies as well as at home, and it was only by the most masterly building of coalitions to keep Louis engaged on the continent that William was able to ward off the impending blow. The colonial war, which paralleled that in Europe between 1689 and 1697, took the form mainly of French and Indian raids from Canada upon the settlements of western New England at the instigation of Count Frontenac and retaliatory expeditions of New Englanders against the French posts to the north. Ill feeling between the two peoples was especially strong because of the long-pending dispute over the possession of the Hudson Bay district and because of the conviction of the English that the French had been guilty of stirring up the savages on

the frontiers, notably in the war of King Philip, in 1676. Blow after blow fell upon the bewildered English. In 1690 Schenectady, New York, was burned, and many of its people slaughtered.[1] Salmon Falls and Exeter in New Hampshire, and Fort Loyal (now Portland), Maine, were similarly destroyed. In May, 1690, a meeting of colonial governors was held at New York to discuss the situation and devise measures for prosecuting the war. A threefold attack on the French was projected, but only the movement in charge of Sir William Phips, the energetic governor of Massachusetts, was in any degree successful. With eight small vessels Phips captured Port Royal in Acadia, demolished the French fort at the mouth of the St. John River, and made an attempt, though in vain, to take Quebec. At about the same time an expedition against Montreal failed completely, and in 1691 the French recaptured Port Royal. Throughout the later years of the war the French and Indians continued their raids, meeting with only desultory opposition, until finally the news came as a welcome relief, that in September, 1697, King Louis had found himself hard enough pressed to offer concessions and sign a treaty of peace at Ryswick in Holland.

So far as America was concerned the treaty of Ryswick provided simply for a return to *status quo ante bellum*.[2] "The most Christian King," so runs the seventh article, "shall restore to the said King of Great Britain all countries, islands, forts, and colonies, wheresoever situated,

[1] Letter of Comptroller-General de Monseignat to Madame de Maintenon, in O'Callaghan, *New York Colonial Documents*, IX. 466-469.

[2] The text of the treaty is in Chalmers, *Collection of Treaties*, I. 332-340. The portions relating to America are given in MacDonald, *Select Charters*, 222-223.

which the English did possess before the declaration of this present war. And in like manner the King of Great Britain shall restore to the most Christian King all countries, islands, forts, and colonies, wheresoever situated, which the French did possess before the said declaration of war; and this restitution shall be made, on both sides, within the space of six months, or sooner if it can be done." The Hudson Bay dispute was to be referred to a joint English and French commission, which, however, seems never to have been actually appointed. The war thus closed without settling anything, and its early renewal was practically assured.

Though in Europe the War of the Palatinate ended most disadvantageously for France, Louis's imperial ambitions were not a whit diminished, and no one understood better than the veteran English sovereign that the snake was but scotched, not killed. No sooner was peace declared, therefore, than preparations began to be pushed for a second and more telling bout of the uncompromising duel. William died in 1702, but Queen Anne and her advisers, chief among whom was the Duke of Marlborough, were careful to impose no check upon the rising of the English national spirit against the designs of the Bourbon monarchy, and, ostensibly to prevent the threatened consolidation of France and Spain, war was begun again within a few months. This was the War of the Spanish Succession, made forever memorable by the brilliant exploits of Marlborough and Prince Eugene on the fields of Blenheim, Oudenarde, and Malplaquet, and by the final establishment of English sovereignty at Gibraltar. In America the old war was simply resumed in another series of border forays

by the French and Indians, and another more or less successful English attack upon the French strongholds in Canada. In 1704 occurred the sack of Deerfield, Connecticut, in which sixteen persons were killed and one hundred carried away captive. Numerous other massacres almost as bad fixed more deeply than ever in the minds of the English colonists an undying antipathy to everything French. In 1707 Governor Dudley of Massachusetts sent an expedition of a thousand men under a certain Colonel March for the capture of Port Royal, but it was unsuccessful. Three years later a force of New England troops, aided by a regiment of royal marines, repeated Phips's exploit in 1690, and again for a time the English flag waved over this favored stronghold of the French.[1] In 1711 a large expedition led by an incompetent Englishman by the name of Hill failed to reach its objective point — Quebec — and at the same time a small army sent against Montreal was glad to escape annihilation by a hasty retreat.

In September, 1711, preliminary articles of peace were signed in Europe, and in January of the next year the commissioners of the nations involved began deliberations at Utrecht, in Holland. March 31 (April 11, New Style), 1713, the treaty was definitely concluded. Throughout the war France had been gradually losing in Europe. All the important battles had gone against her, and the country was fast being ruined by the destruction of its people and its wealth. As a consequence King Louis — now near the end of his long and eventful life — was obliged to see peace

---

[1] For an early account of the English attacks on Port Royal during the course of Queen Anne's War, see Shea, *Charlevoix's History of New France*, V. 169-172, 192-201, 225-230.

made on pretty much such terms as the members of the Grand Alliance desired. It has been well said that no previous treaty had changed the map of Europe as did that of Utrecht.[1] The same thing might be said of America. Here, as in Europe, the end of the war was humiliating enough to the French. Not that the English had actually captured and held much American territory; but, as has been indicated, England in 1713 found herself in a position internationally to impose a severe humiliation upon her great rival for the dominance of the western world, and she could be depended on to make the most of a well-earned opportunity. The territorial provisions of the treaty relating to America were as follows: (1) that France should yield to England, "to be possessed in full right for ever," Hudson Bay and all the neighboring lands then under French sovereignty; (2) that the island of St. Christopher and "likewise all Nova Scotia, or Acadie, with its ancient boundaries, as also the city of Port Royal, now called Annapolis Royal, and all other things in those parts which depend on the said lands and islands," should be given over permanently to the English; (3) that Newfoundland should henceforth be wholly English, except that the French should have the right to catch and dry fish on the coast between Cape Bonavista and Point Riche; and (4) that France should retain the island of Cape Breton and all other islands in the Gulf of St. Lawrence. It was further provided that the French population of the territories ceded to England should be allowed to move

[1] James H. Robinson, *History of Western Europe*, 507. The text of the treaty is in Chalmers, *Collection of Treaties*, I. 340-386. Parts relating to America are printed in MacDonald, *Select Charters*, 229-232.

elsewhere at their pleasure within a year, and those who chose to remain and so become British subjects should enjoy complete freedom of religion. In the fifteenth article of the treaty France definitely recognized the sovereignty of Great Britain over the lands of the Iroquois, and thus the established bounds of English jurisdiction were extended pretty well toward the source of the Ohio.

The treaty of Utrecht is of the utmost importance in American history because it clearly marked the first stage in the French decadence in the western world. By it France for the first time was compelled to yield to her rival lands — and lands of no small extent — which she had long claimed by every right known to international law, and had fought for with all the pertinacity of which her scanty colonial forces were capable. Nevertheless she had vast possessions left, larger than even the English had fair right to claim. She still had the St. Lawrence Valley, with entire control of the river and the defences in the Gulf. All the Great Lake country south of the Hudson Bay region and west of the home of the Iroquois was still hers to use as she would. Most of all, the broad valley of the Mississippi which La Salle and Iberville had labored so ardently to fortify with French outposts was as yet but very ineffectively laid claim to by either the Spanish or the English. Discouraging as the loss of Hudson Bay, Acadia, and Newfoundland undeniably was, there was yet abundant opportunity, so far as mere extent and wealth of possessions was concerned, to erect in America a French power against which the English would long be unable to prevail. If this was to be done, however, France would have to exert herself in a manner hitherto unknown. The hard, cold fact of the matter was that if the remaining parts of America were to be insured against future loss, the imperial ambitions of the French monarchs must transfer the scene of their activities from Europe to America — from Spain and Italy and the German principalities to the wilderness country of the St. Lawrence, the Ohio, and the Mississippi. The exhausted finances and depleted military strength of France precluded effective activity in both places. The supreme question was, Would the sovereign authority be wise enough to recognize this truth and far-seeing enough to act upon it?

The events of the next forty years in Europe abundantly demonstrated that as long as the Bourbon monarchy held sway at Versailles the change of base had absolutely no chance of being made. Philip, Duke of Orleans, Regent during the minority of Louis XV., continued the traditional policy; and when Louis himself finally undertook to steer the ship of state, it was with no other idea than that national aggrandizement at the expense of his country's immediate neighbors was above all things else to be desired. By the court the interests of the French in America were systematically neglected, though not so flagrantly as during the later years of Louis XIV. The king and his advisers were exceedingly keen to detect an opening in the maze of European politics and diplomacy for the spreading of Bourbon dominion, but exceedingly blind to the grander, though remoter, possibilities of imperial foundation in America. Looking over the whole field as we now can do, it does not appear likely that any amount

of exertion on part of the French could have established a permanent possession in any considerable part of the western hemisphere. The odds were too heavily against such an achievement. Yet the laxness of the government can hardly be attributed to a discernment of this fact, for until the last the king and ministers boasted loudly of the humbling of the English which they would accomplish in America. The great difficulty was that the distance of America and the many more or less inevitable disappointments connected with all colonial effort blinded the court to the urgency and profitableness of definite concentration of energies upon the transmarine portion of the realm.

During the years from the accession of Frederick the Great in 1740 to the treaty of Aix-la-Chapelle in 1748, France was almost continually involved in the struggle between Austria and the rising power of Prussia regarding the possession of the district of Silesia and the claim of Maria Theresa to the Austrian throne. Of course these issues were inherently of no great concern to France, but King Louis hastened to emulate the example of the doughty Frederick by laying claim to a generous slice of the Austrian dominion, confidently expecting in the end to expand the boundaries of his state quite materially toward the east. Other powers, including Spain, Savoy, Bavaria, and Saxony, came forward with their claims, and erelong the war which had begun simply between two fragments of the German people became a struggle of continental proportions. In fact, it soon became much more than continental, for the imperishable anti-Spanish feeling which had just been displaying itself in the War of Jenkins's Ear and the even more eternal anti-French sentiment which was yet an essential part of every Englishman's inheritance, quickly involved the English nation in the most important portions of the combat. England's interest in the Silesian and Austrian questions was even more remote than that of the French, but the mere fact that France was in the war as an enemy of Maria Theresa determined the English to enter it, together with Holland, as the ally of the Austrians. On the continent England played but a minor rôle, but on the high seas and in the colonies the contest was prosecuted with vigor.

In America the war was designated by the name of England's ruling sovereign, King George II. It began in 1744 with an attack by the French on the English posts in Nova Scotia and an unsuccessful attempt to take old Port Royal, now known as Annapolis. The energies of the British colonies in the north were centred upon the defence of the lands which had been gained in the war of Queen Anne, together with the greatest military enterprise which had yet been executed in America, *i.e.* the capture of Louisburg on the south side of Cape Breton Island. Louisburg was the Gibraltar of the north Atlantic coasts, and with its possession went the control of all the Gulf of St. Lawrence as well as the entrance to the river. It was because the French fully appreciated this that since 1720 they had spent more than $10,000,000 in strengthening its fortifications. As a base of naval operations in the northern Atlantic it was simply invaluable. The reduction of this fortress by the English was the outcome of much careful planning and arduous effort on the part of Governor William Shirley of Massachu-

setts.[1] The large body of 4000 troops, gathered for the undertaking from Massachusetts, Connecticut, and New Hampshire, was put under the command of William Pepperell, a man of resolute character and no small degree of military genius. An English fleet of three ships under command of Commodore Peter Warren coöperated in the attack. After a siege of six weeks the fortress was obliged to capitulate, though defended by a garrison of 560 French regulars and Swiss mercenaries and about 1400 Canadian militia, with at least 150 heavy guns. The surrender occurred June 17, 1745.[2] "When the news was disseminated abroad," writes John Fiske, "the civilized world was dumb with amazement. For the first time it waked up to the fact that a new military power had grown up in America. One of the strongest fortresses on the face of the earth had surrendered to a force of New England militia. Pepperell was at once created a baronet, being the only native American who ever attained that rank. Warren was promoted to the grade of admiral. Louisburg Square in Boston commemorates the victory."[3] As another recent writer says, "The victory was celebrated in many long and sincere prayers of thanksgiving, and in some remarkably bad poetry."[4]

[1] John Fiske regarded William Vaughan, son of a former lieutenant-governor of New Hampshire and a leading proprietor on the Damariscotta River in Maine, as the probable author of the scheme. *New France and New England*, 250.

[2] See Samuel Curwen, *Journal and Letters*, edited by George A. Ward. Curwen was a Salem man who accompanied Pepperell's expedition. An extract from the journal is printed in Hart, *American History Told by Contemporaries*, II. 346–349.

[3] Fiske, *New France and New England*, 256.

[4] Adams and Trent, *History of the United States*, 78.

There was just one other field in which King George's war precipitated hostilities in America. This was at the opposite extremity of the English and French possessions — in the region of Georgia. The granting to James Oglethorpe of the charter of Georgia with its provision for "sea to sea" claims, June 20, 1732,[1] had marked a distinct epoch in the gradual encroachment of the English from the Carolinas in the direction of the French settlements about Mobile and on the lower Mississippi. In 1733 Oglethorpe had concluded treaties of friendship with the Creeks, Cherokees, Choctaws, and Chickasaws, and in 1739 had held an Indian conference at Coweta among the Creeks of Alabama.[2] Throughout the years which followed, the English continued to push around the southern end of the Appalachian ridge in a manner most menacing to the French. Finally, during the course of King George's war, the Georgians actually made a few rather desultory attacks upon the French frontiers. These operations were in themselves of the most insignificant sort, but considered in relation to the pending rivalry on the Gulf, they were weighted with lessons for the future.

The war in Europe, and consequently that in America, was brought to a close by the treaty of Aix-la-Chapelle in

[1] The text of the Georgia charter is in Poore, *Federal and State Constitutions*, I. 369-377, and in MacDonald, *Select Charters*, 236-248.

[2] Hamilton, *Colonial Mobile*, 115. On the English encroachments by way of the Georgia settlements, see Brown, *History of Alabama*, Ch. V. Pickett, *History of Alabama*, Ch. VIII.; and Jones, *History of Georgia*, Vol. I. An interesting contemporary document on the subject is "An Account shewing the Progress of the Colony of Georgia in America from its First Establishment" [London, 1741]. It is printed in the *Force Tracts*, I. No. 5, and in the *Georgia Historical Society Collections*, I. 265-310. The original is in the Harvard College Library.

1748. The end came rather more because everybody was tired of fighting than because any very substantial results had been attained. In Europe Maria Theresa was recognized by the warring powers as the rightful sovereign of Austria, though with the loss of the province of Silesia to Frederick the Great. In America, as at the end of King William's war, there was a return to *status quo ante bellum*. The fifth article of the treaty tells the story: " All the conquests that have been made since the commencement of the war, or which, since the conclusion of the preliminary articles, signed the 30th of April last, may have been or shall be made, either in Europe or in the East or West Indies, or in any other part of the world whatsoever, being to be restored without exception, in conformity to what was stipulated by the said preliminary articles, and by the declarations since signed; the high contracting parties engage to give orders immediately for proceeding to that restitution."[1] Special provisions were made for the deliverance of Cape Breton back to the French, it being given practically in exchange for Madras. It was but natural that the treaty should be received with great disfavor by the English in America. After expending so much money and energy, and achieving so brilliant a feat as the capture of Louisburg, it was exasperating indeed, especially to the people of New England who did the work, to behold their beaten rivals restored to full possession of all they had lost in the war. But if the conduct of the English ministers lent additional force to the ugly suspicion which was already growing up in some parts of

---

[1] Text of the treaty in Chalmers, *Collection of Treaties*, I. 424–442. Portions pertaining to America are printed in MacDonald, *Select Charters*, 252–253.

America that the colonies were regarded as mere pawns by the home government, dependencies to be fostered or thwarted at its will, these same ministers were the last to appreciate the fact.

Still the long-standing rivalry of the English and French in the western hemisphere was in no sense diminished. In fact, with every passing year that rivalry became more intense; and this for two reasons: first, because the tradition of conflict was being all the time strengthened by the actual occurrences of war, and, second, because the natural growth of the two peoples was bringing them into a closeness of relations quite unknown in the time of Louis XIV. In the words of Fiske, the treaty of Aix-la-Chapelle "provided only a short breathing spell before the numerous unsettled questions gave rise to another and far greater war."[1] This greater war was, of course, the so-called French and Indian War, — the contest really decisive of the future control of America. Hitherto the fortunes of the Mississippi Valley had been scarcely at all affected by the wars for dominance in the East and North. The seat of conflict had been far removed, and however many times Acadia and Nova Scotia had been overrun by hostile forces, conquered, tossed back and forth by the diplomats of Europe, reconquered, and rent asunder by conflicting parties, not an acre of French lands in the Middle West had been touched by a martial invader (except, perhaps, for the few desultory movements in the South during the war of King George), and in no one of the treaties in conclusion of the various stages of the struggle had the Mississippi country been so

[1] Fiske, *New France and New England*, 258.

much as mentioned. Now, however, a new era was dawning, and one of immensely wider interests. The French and Indian War was mostly an eastern war, it is true, but it received its main impetus from the desires of both the contending parties to control the great Ohio gateway to the West. In fact, it may be said with truth that the main theatre of the struggle was the valley of the Ohio. On the one hand, the English were attempting to occupy this region, not merely because of its intrinsic value, but also because through it they might enter the wedge which would eventually sever the French possessions in the South from those in the North. On the other hand, the French were jealous of any such extension of Anglo-Saxon control, and resolved to forestall the Englishmen's designs in this direction.

The first important move in the contest was the organization of the Ohio Company in 1748, the year of the close of the inconclusive war of King George.[1] It appears that the tide-water gentry of Virginia, who were the prime promoters of this enterprise, were influenced rather more by the hope of outwitting the Pennsylvanians in the securing of the Ohio trade than by the thought of circumventing the French. But the English Board of Trade, in recommending the project to King George, laid special stress on the serviceableness of such a company in realizing England's transmontane claims. May 19, 1749, a royal

---

[1] Howison, *History of Virginia*, I. Ch. VIII.; Campbell, *History of Virginia*, Ch. LIX.; Moore, *The Northwest under Three Flags*, Ch. III.; and Berthold Fernow, *The Ohio Valley in Colonial Days*, Chs. IV. and V. In Appendix D of the last-mentioned work are papers relating to the Ohio Company taken from the Archives of the Board of Trade and Plantations in London.

order placed at the disposal of the company two hundred thousand acres south of the Ohio and between the Monongahela and the Kanawha, to be rent-free for ten years, on condition that a hundred families should be settled within seven years and a fort built and maintained. It was understood that if these conditions were complied with at the end of the seven years, the full grant of fifty thousand acres which had been asked for would be forthcoming.

The announcement of this enterprise aroused the suspicion and fears of the French. Manifestly the English were ready to begin their long-dreaded expansion beyond the Alleghanies. The "sea to sea" charters would be revived, and no one could tell where the movement would stop. "Every man of sense," writes a contemporary French captain, "who is conversant with the manner in which war can be carried on in that country will agree with me that all the resources of the state will never preserve Canada, if the English are once settled at the heads of these western rivers."[1] The Marquis de la Galissonnière, the new governor at Quebec, was among the first to perceive the import of the Ohio Company's designs,[2] and in June, 1749, he sent Céloron de Bienville from Montreal with instructions to traverse the Ohio Valley, take formal possession of it, ascertain what might be expected from the natives, and drive off such English traders as might be found there. Everything possible was to be done to overcome the disadvantage France incurred by

[1] Dumas, *Mémoire*; quoted in Winsor, *The Mississippi Basin*, 251. Dumas was subsequently in command at Fort Duquesne.

[2] M. de la Galissonnière, "Memoir of the French Colonies in North America," in O'Callaghan, *New York Colonial Documents*, X. 220-232.

being so late to begin operations in this region. Céloron's force included twenty French soldiers, somewhat more than a hundred *voyageurs*, and thirty Iroquois and Abenakis. It was provided with a considerable number of leaden plates, about eleven inches long, seven and a half inches wide, and one-eighth of an inch thick, on each of which an inscription in French was engraved or stamped in capital letters, with blanks left for the insertion of the names of the rivers at the juncture of which with the Ohio they should be deposited, and the dates of their deposit. The party left La Chine on the 15th of June, 1749, reached Fort Niagara July 6, and crossed the portage from Lake Erie by way of Lake Chautauqua to the Allegheny River, arriving there about the end of July. From the Allegheny the travellers passed out upon the Ohio.

Much to his regret Céloron was obliged to recognize that not only the Iroquois, but also the Miamis, Delawares, Shawnees, and other Indians along the way, were much more attached to the English than to the French. This was but natural, inasmuch as they had hitherto had no dealings with the latter, while they had long been visited by English traders who sold goods so cheaply that the natives felt themselves the gainers by every transaction.[1] Nevertheless, while meeting on every hand with rebuffs, Céloron proceeded to take possession at various points and to bury his plates bearing the inscription: "We have placed this plate here as a memorial of the establishment

[1] C. W. Butterfield, "History of Ohio; English Interests Paramount among the Ohio Savages," in the *Magazine of Western History*, VI. 103-117.

of our power in the territory which is claimed by us on the river Ohio and throughout its tributaries to its sources, and confirmed to us by the treaties of Ryswick, Utrecht, and Aix-la-Chapelle."[1] In August two bands of English traders were encountered, and by each of them Céloron sent a warning, to the governor of Virginia in one case and of South Carolina in the other, that if the English persisted in intruding on the upper Ohio it would become necessary for the French to expel them by force. The latter part of Céloron's route lay by way of the Great

[1] "One or two of these plates have since been unearthed. That which was buried near the mouth of the Muskingum was found by some boys in the early years of this [nineteenth] century. It was protruding from a bank which had been washed by the current. The youngsters melted a part of it to make bullets, and the remaining fragment is yet preserved in the collection of the American Antiquarian Society at Worcester, Massachusetts. Another was discovered near the mouth of the Kanawha in 1846." Winsor, *The Mississippi Basin*, 254. It is interesting to observe that one of the plates fell into the hands of the English as early as 1750. In December of that year Governor Clinton of New York wrote to the Lords of Trade in London that he "would send to their Lordships in two or three weeks a plate of lead, full of writing, which some of the upper nations of Indians stole from Jean Cœur [Joncaire], the French interpreter at Niagara, on his way to the river Ohio, which river, and all the lands thereabouts, the French claim, as will appear by said writing. . . . The lead plate gave the Indians so much uneasiness that they immediately despatched some of the Cayuga chiefs to me with it, saying that their only reliance was on me, and earnestly begged that I would communicate the contents thereof to them, which I did, much to their satisfaction and the interests of the English. . . . The contents of the plate may be of great importance in clearing up the encroachments which the French have made on the British Empire in America." O'Callaghan, *New York Colonial Documents*, IX. 604. A facsimile of one of Céloron's plates is given in the *Pennsylvania Archives*, Second Series, VI. 80. It is reproduced in Winsor, *Narrative and Critical History*, V, 9. See also the Dinwiddie Papers, in the *Collections of the Virginia Historical Society*, I. 95, and Parkman, *Montcalm and Wolfe*, I. 62.

Miami, Muskingum, and Maumee to Detroit, which was reached October 6.[1] The report which he made on his return was not very encouraging. As for the Indians, all he could say was that they were nowhere "kindly disposed to the French" and were "wholly friends of the English." The news of the failure of the expedition spread through Pennsylvania, New York, Virginia, and Carolina, where it occasioned general rejoicing. In the meantime Galissonnière had been recalled, believing firmly that war with the English was inevitable, and had been succeeded in the governorship at Quebec by Admiral Jonquière.

[1] Authorities on Céloron's trip are as satisfactory as could be wished — a thing rarely to be said in the history of American exploration. They are: (1) Céloron's journal, preserved in the Archives of the Marine at Paris and published in Orsamus H. Marshall, *Historical Writings*, 237-273, and (2) the journal of Father Bonnecamps, a Jesuit professor of mathematics and hydrography at the College of Quebec, who accompanied the expedition. The latter document is also in the Marine Archives at Paris. Mr. Marshall says that in another department of the Archives he found "a large MS. map, 31½ by 34½ inches square, representing the country through which the expedition passed, including the St. Lawrence westward of Montreal, Lakes Erie and Ontario, the territory south of those lakes as far as the Ohio, and the whole course of that river from the source of the Allegheny to the mouth of the Great Miami. This map forms an important illustration of the expedition. On it are delineated by appropriate characters the points where leaden plates were deposited, where the latitudes and longitudes were observed, and the localities of the Indian villages visited on the route." *Historical Writings*, 240. There is a reproduction of the map in Winsor, *Narrative and Critical History*, V. 569. On Céloron's expedition, see Parkman, *Montcalm and Wolfe*, I. Ch. II.; Winsor, *Narrative and Critical History*, V. Ch. I., and *The Mississippi Basin*, 252-256; O. H. Marshall, "De Céloron's Expedition to the Ohio in 1749," in the *Magazine of American History*, II. 129-150; Hulbert, *Historic Highways of America*, VII. Ch. IV.; C. W. Butterfield, "History of Ohio," in the *Magazine of Western History*, VI. 1-17; and T. J. Chapman, "Céloron's Voyage down the Allegheny," in the *Magazine of Western History*, V. 462-467.

Céloron's trip through the Ohio country, while quite lacking in the results hoped for by Galissonnière, was nevertheless a very effective declaration of the French purpose to establish the rule of the Bourbon on the western slopes of the Alleghanies. As a challenge of possession it was immediately understood and accepted by the English. Even while Céloron was yet on the march, the Virginian council authorized the company recently formed to survey its land grant and proceed with the settlement of colonists. The work of surveying was undertaken in March, 1750, by Dr. Thomas Walker. Leading his party across the Alleghanies from the Shenandoah Valley, he pushed his way along Walker's Creek and Clinch River to Cumberland Gap, and thence up the Cumberland River toward the Ohio. The house which the surveyors built on a cleared spot in the forest was probably the first constructed by Europeans within the present bounds of Kentucky. Maps and charts were prepared and desirable sites marked off for the guidance of future immigrants.[1]

The more important routes into the Ohio Valley lay farther to the north.[2] The main point of departure was

[1] Walker's journal of this expedition was printed at Boston in 1888, under the editorship of William Cabell Rives, with the title, *Journal of an Exploration in the Spring of the Year 1750, by Dr. Thomas Walker of Virginia*. This edition of the journal was incomplete. The document entire is printed in the *Filson Club Publications*, No. XIII. [Louisville, 1898]. This edition was prepared by J. Stoddard Johnston, vice-president of the Filson Club.

[2] On the Ohio Valley routes, see Archer B. Hulbert, *Waterways of Westward Expansion: the Ohio River and its Tributaries;* Ellen C. Semple, *American History and its Geographical Conditions;* A. Huidekoper, "Indian and French History in Western Pennsylvania," in the *Magazine of American History*, I. 683, and II. 52; and Berthold Fernow, *The Ohio Valley in Colonial Days*.

the junction of the Allegheny and Monongahela rivers, where the city of Pittsburg has since risen, but which at the time of the Ohio Company's organization was occupied merely by an Indian village of some fifty or sixty people. In the days when natural routes of travel and trade alone determined the trend of commerce and migration, this river junction was one of the most strategic places of the American interior. As the real head of the Ohio River it commanded the approach to that great waterway, as well as to all the two hundred thousand square miles of territory drained by it and its numerous affluents. This fact of itself was sufficient to make "the Forks" a storm-centre in the French and English conflict for possession of the northeastern part of the Mississippi Valley.

Beginning with 1750, events on the upper Ohio rapidly bore out the prediction of Governor Galissonnière that war must be the early result of such intense international rivalry. Both sides appreciated the significance of the contest and prepared for it with ardor. On their part the English had the advantage of the friendship of most of the Indians, as well as a better acquaintance with the territory in dispute. In a measure this advantage was offset by the fact that the Pennsylvanians were jealous of the Virginians, as were also the Marylanders, and in general there was a notable lack of harmony and unity among the seaboard colonies. The feeling was prevalent that Virginia proposed to monopolize the West, that the Ohio Company was simply a tool in her hands for this purpose, and that the other colonies might after all find themselves deprived of the profit arising from a joint war against the French. Nevertheless, racial pride triumphed over sectional jealousy, and when it came to the supreme test the English stood fairly well together.

Exploration and settlement beyond the Alleghanies progressed rapidly after 1750. In that and the following year Christopher Gist, as an agent of the company, visited the Miamis, Shawnees, and Delawares, in Ohio, with the result that Picktown (or Pickawillany) on the Big Miami, 150 miles from its mouth, was founded and became the westernmost station of the English.[1] The Indians were reported to be "at present very well affected toward the English and fond of their alliance with them." Through scouts sent out about the same time, Governor Hamilton of Pennsylvania had likewise come to the conclusion that the Indians could be depended on as allies in the coming struggle. In April, 1751, the Shawnees and Miamis sent a request to the Pennsylvania authorities to fortify the forks of the Ohio for the protection both of themselves and of the English traders. The dominance of the Quaker element, however, compelled Governor Hamilton to reply to the petition that "those who have the disposition of the public money are entirely averse." In June, 1752, the Indians, in a conference at Logstown

---

[1] R. W. McFarland, "Forts Laramie and Pickawillany," in the *Ohio Archæological and Historical Publications*, VIII. 479–486. For Gist's instructions, see appendix of Pownal, *Topographical Description of North America* [London, 1776]. Gist's journal is published in the *Collections of the Massachusetts Historical Society*, Third Series, V. 101–108, and in the *Filson Club Publications*, No. XIII. Much other original material on the expeditions of Gist and his Pennsylvanian companion, George Croghan, are in O'Callaghan, *New York Colonial Documents*, Vol. VII., and the *Colonial Records of Pennsylvania*, Vol. V.

on the upper Ohio, made the same request of Virginia.[1] The result was that before the end of that year twelve English families had established themselves on the lower Monongahela, and Gist had been instructed to erect a town and fort four miles below the Ohio's forks.

At the same time the French were vigilant and active. In December, 1750, Galissonnière had warned the ministry that Canada and Louisiana were in immediate danger of being wedged apart by the English aggressions on the Ohio. Recognizing the more substantial character of English colonization, he prophesied the early extinction of French power in the Mississippi Valley unless more vigorous measures were adopted, new posts established, agriculture and settled conditions of life fostered, and the friendship of the Indians maintained at any cost. The new governor, Jonquière, acquiesced fully in these views. The two points which the French made most use of as bases of operation in the maintenance of the Ohio Valley were Niagara and Detroit. From Montreal the most direct route into the disputed country was by way of Niagara and the portages between eastern Lake Erie and the Allegheny River; while Detroit commanded the portages between the Maumee, western Lake Erie, and the tributaries of the Ohio. In 1750 the population of the post at Detroit numbered about five hundred, though not fewer than two thousand more of the surrounding Indians were under the immediate control of the French. After becoming governor, Jonquière had adopted a very aggressive policy against the English on Lake Ontario, and by

---

[1] Official records of Governor Dinwiddie in *Virginia Historical Society Collections*, I. 6–22.

threatening the destruction of Oswego had impelled Governor Clinton of New York to call the Albany conference of 1751 to concert measures of defence; but the French administrator died the following year, before hostilities had been commenced, and the prevalence of smallpox and a great scarcity of provisions among the Canadians saved the English yet a while from attack in the East. In the West, however, the post at Picktown was assaulted in 1752 by Céloron's lieutenant, Langlade, at the head of a force of 240 French and Indians from Detroit, with the result that the English were expelled and the valleys of the Maumee and Miami left entirely open to exploitation by the French.[1]

In July, 1752, the Marquis Duquesne de Menneville, the new governor of Canada, arrived at Quebec. The instructions which he carried attested the disposition of the home government to maintain claims at least as large as those set up by Galissonnière, and on the same grounds, *i.e.* the alleged explorations of La Salle on the Ohio in 1670.[2] "The river Ohio," it was declared, "otherwise called the Beautiful River, and its tributaries belong indisputably to France, by virtue of its discovery by Sieur de La Salle; of

---

[1] H. S. Knapp, *History of the Maumee Valley*, Ch. I. Langlade is worthy of note as having been the leader of the first permanent settlement in the present state of Wisconsin, in 1744–1746. See *Wisconsin Historical Collections*, III. 197; M. M. Strong, *Territory of Wisconsin*, 41; and Joseph S. Walton, *Conrad Weiser and the Indian Policy of Colonial Pennsylvania*, Ch. XIII.

[2] Duquesne's instructions are printed in O'Callaghan, *New York Colonial Documents*, X. 242–245. An extract from the document is in Hart, *American History Told by Contemporaries*, II. 354–356. C. W. Butterfield, "History of Ohio; the Ohio Valley invaded by the French," in the *Magazine of Western History*, VI. 413–424.

the trading-posts the French have had there since, and of possession which is so much the more unquestionable as it constitutes the most frequent communication from Canada to Louisiana. It is only within a few years that the English have undertaken to trade there; and now they pretend to exclude us from it. They have not, up to the present time, however, maintained that these rivers belong to them; they pretend only that the Iroquois are masters of them, and being the sovereigns of these Indians, that they can exercise their rights. But 'tis certain that these Indians have none, and that, besides, the pretended sovereignty of the English over them is a chimera. Meanwhile 'tis of the greatest importance to arrest the progress of the pretensions and expeditions of the English in that quarter. Should they succeed there, they would cut off the communication between the two colonies of Canada and Louisiana, and would be in a position to trouble them, and to ruin both the one and the other, independent of the advantages they would at once experience in their trade to the prejudice of ours." The garrisons were therefore to be put in better order, the thirteen thousand militia which Canada was capable of raising were to be systematically drilled, and every preparation was to be made for occupying the contested territory by whatever degree of force might prove necessary. The conditions of European politics portended an early war between England and France, and no time was to be lost in making ready for the conflict in America, where the really main interests of both nations would lie.

A few months after the coming of Duquesne, Governor

Dinwiddie of Virginia appealed to the English Board of Trade for assistance in establishing forts on the Ohio. The junction of the Allegheny and Monongahela, he declared, must be secured without further delay. The French might appear there any day. Cannon were asked for, to be used in the defence of the place, and the two routes of travel thither from the Potomac and from Philadelphia were carefully described. But the race was not destined to be won by the English. Even before Dinwiddie's appeal was transmitted to London Duquesne had sent out a force under Sieur de Marin to begin the work of fortifying the line which Céloron had marked off with his leaden plates three years before. The first establishment was a stockade known as Fort Le Bœuf, on the site of modern Waterford, Pennsylvania. Venango, the Forks, Logstown, and Beaver Creek were other points whose early settlement was embraced in the French plan. It mattered not that the English already had a post at Logstown and a monopoly of trade with the Indian village at the Forks. "I *will* go down the river, and I *will* build upon it," was the unequivocal declaration of Marin when a chieftain by the name of Half-King protested on behalf of the English. The indomitable Frenchman died at his post in October, 1753, but Legardeur de Saint-Pierre took his place, and the ardor of the settlers suffered no diminution.[1]

Believing that the interests of the English demanded an immediate forcing of the issue, Governor Dinwiddie

[1] For a concise statement of the French position relative to the possession of the Ohio Valley about 1752, see the "Royal Ministerial Minutes," in O'Callaghan, *New York Colonial Documents*, X. 242-244.

determined to make a formal demand upon the French to withdraw from the upper Ohio country. Under date of October 30, 1753, instructions were issued to George Washington, then adjutant-general of the Virginia militia, to carry a letter by way of the post at Logstown to the French commander at Fort Le Bœuf, and make a careful study of French strength and numbers on the tributaries of the Ohio.[1] The incidents of the young Virginian's hazardous journey are the commonplaces of schoolboy lore.[2] On the whole the trip was very successful, but the report placed in Dinwiddie's hands after its accomplishment was such as to confirm his worst apprehensions regarding the magnitude of the impending conflict. From Joncaire, in command at the newly established Venango, Washington had received detailed information as to the ambitious plans of the French in the region, and by Saint-Pierre, the commander at Le Bœuf, he had been given a courteous but absolutely uncompromising refusal to consider Dinwiddie's demand for evacuation. The natural conclusion was, therefore, that nothing remained for the English but to yield ignominiously to their rivals or employ force. The first alternative was out of the question — at least it was so considered by Virginia's

[1] The text of the letter is in O'Callaghan, *New York Colonial Documents*, X. 258.

[2] The original authority on it is *The Journal of Major George Washington, sent by the Hon. Robert Dinwiddie, Esq., His Majesty's Lieutenant-Governor and Commander-in-chief of Virginia, to the Commandant of the French Forces in Ohio; to which are added the Governor's Letter and a Translation of the French Officer's Answer* [Williamsburg, 1754]. It is reprinted in Sparks, *Life and Writings of Washington*, II. 432–437. See J. Chapman, "Washington's First Public Service," in the *Magazine of American History*, XIV. 249–257.

proud and ambitious governor; the second must be adopted.

From that moment war was a question of but a few months' time. Letters were sent to all the leading colonies asking for coöperation,[1] and, though intercolonial jealousies rendered the responses very uncertain and in some cases wholly unsympathetic, Dinwiddie pressed forward his war measures as if Virginia were willing to enter the contest quite alone. With remarkable skill he brought his colonial assembly to the point of voting £10,000 for the war and promising land bounties to all who should enlist. In February, 1754, he issued a proclamation in which he agreed to divide among the soldiers not less than two hundred thousand acres of Virginia's western claims. On the 17th of this same month an agent by the name of William Trent began work on the establishment of an English stockade at the Forks.[2] Within a few weeks Colonel Joshua Fry, with Washington second in command, was sent thither with a company of troops to protect the carpenters at their work and subsequently to occupy the fort.[3] "It will be easier to prevent the French settling than to dislodge them when

---

[1] These letters are printed in the *Virginia Historical Society Collections* [Dinwiddie Papers], I. 61-88.

[2] Letter of Governor Dinwiddie to Captain William Trent, transmitting his commission and giving him instructions, in *Virginia Historical Society Collections* [Dinwiddie Papers], I. 55-56. See the *Journal of Captain William Trent from Logstown to Pickawillany in 1752*, edited by Alfred T. Goodman, and published at Cincinnati in 1871.

[3] Governor Dinwiddie's instructions to Major Washington, in *Virginia Historical Society Collections* [Dinwiddie Papers], I. 59; instructions to Fry, *ibid.*, 88. Dinwiddie's call for volunteers for the expedition is in Berthold Fernow, *The Ohio Valley in Colonial Days*, 97.

settled," declared Dinwiddie; and it was to this task of prevention that he was directing his most immediate attention.

But the work had been begun a little too late and, moreover, had to be pursued with exasperating slowness. The advance of the expedition was extremely difficult. Sometimes the mere clearing of the way was such a task that not more than a mile could be covered in a day. When Will's Creek, about 140 miles from the Forks, was reached, Colonel Fry fell sick, and the chief command devolved upon Washington. After several days of delay the undaunted band of Virginians resumed the march. Already too much precious time had been lost, however, for while he was yet on the road the news came to Washington that the uncompleted post at the Forks had been attacked by a detachment of French under Contrecœur and its defenders compelled to surrender. All that Washington could do was to advance into the vicinity of the lost fortification and, with his 150 men, take up what seemed to be a strong position at a place called Great Meadows. From the Indian ally, Half-King, a dependent of the Iroquois, it was learned that a band of Frenchmen was in the vicinity awaiting an opportunity to surprise the Virginians and defeat them. Washington resolved himself to effect the surprise, which he did with such success that ten of the French, including the commander, Jumonville, were killed and the other twenty-two taken captive. The post at the Forks having been lost, Washington proceeded to establish another one — Fort Necessity, at Great Meadows — as a base of operations in the contemplated campaign of recovery. Within a short time 150 more Virginians and Carolinians arrived. An equal number of Indians under Half-King were also at Washington's command. Nevertheless, the French had been rapidly increasing their strength at the head waters of the Ohio and still greatly outnumbered the English. At the Forks there were not fewer than 1400 men. Early in July, 1754, Coulon de Villiers, brother of Jumonville, advanced against Fort Necessity with a force of 600 troops. Against almost double their numbers the English made a stubborn resistance until the exhaustion of their supplies compelled a surrender. On condition that the twenty-two captives of Jumonville's party be set free, Washington's army was allowed to march away with the honors of war. The surrender occurred July 4.[1] The disheartened little army turned to retrace its steps across the Alleghanies, while the victorious French set rapidly about completing the fort at the Forks. The place now received the memorable name, Duquesne, which it was to bear through the few strenuous years of its tenure by the French. Judged by its prologue, the struggle for the possession of the Ohio Valley bade fair to be humiliating indeed for the English. Nevertheless, the most superficial comparison of the resources and possibilities of the two contestants reveals the fact that all that was necessary in order that victory be finally on the side of the English was that they

[1] On the Great Meadows expedition, see Washington's reports to Governor Dinwiddie in *Virginia Historical Society Collections* [Dinwiddie Papers], I. 171 *et seq.*; H. C. Lodge, *George Washington*, I. Ch. III.; and Parkman, *Montcalm and Wolfe*, I. Ch. V. The terms of capitulation at Fort Necessity are in the *Pennsylvania Archives*, II. 146–147.

be awakened to the critical importance of the conflict and constrained for a time to bury their internal jealousies and animosities.

The Great Meadows campaign practically marked the beginning of the so-called French and Indian War — a contest destined in effect to determine the ownership of the Mississippi Valley. It should be observed that there had as yet been no declaration of war by either combatant. The Seven Years' War in Europe, with which the French and Indian War in America was closely parallel, did not begin until many months after Washington's retreat from Fort Necessity, war not being declared, as a matter of fact, until the spring of 1756. For two years this anomalous conflict was waged in America, in India, and on the high seas, while the great powers of Europe were arranging themselves in a new set of alliances. During the single year of 1755 three hundred French vessels and more than seven thousand French sailors were captured and carried into British ports. The prime objects of the British Government, now dictated mainly by Walpole, were to make England's maritime supremacy even more decisive and to increase her colonial empire in both hemispheres at the expense of the French. In the estimation of Walpole these objects could best be attained by the severance of close relations with Austria and by forming an alliance with the aggressive Frederick of Prussia. A treaty between the two powers was therefore made, January 15, 1756. This, of course, practically forced a counter alliance of France and Austria, which was formed by the treaty of Versailles, signed May 1, 1756. With this complete reversal of traditional English and French policies the war in

Europe had its formal beginning. Spain became involved only at a later date.

It should be observed that at the opening of the war in America there was no well-defined plan on the part of even the most aggressive of the English, as Governor Dinwiddie, to drive the French completely from American soil. Such an undertaking would have seemed chimerical in the extreme. The object of the English was simply to prevent the French from acquiring possession of the Ohio Valley, and thus consolidating their hold upon the interior. If the French should gain the Ohio, they would thereby have bridged the chasm between Canada and Louisiana. If, on the other hand, the English should acquire the disputed territory, they would be in a position to enforce the isolation of the two great French quarters of the western world and weaken them proportionally. This, then, was the issue upon which the war was begun.

For a time both sides thought it worth while to appeal to the authority of maps and earlier treaties. In February, 1755, Louis XV.'s agents proposed a compromise whereby all lands east of the Alleghanies should belong to England, and all west of the Allegheny River and north of the Ohio should fall to France. The lands between the crest of the mountains and the Allegheny, and those south of the Ohio, were to be left neutral. The following month England agreed to this, on condition that the French destroy their posts on the Allegheny and the Ohio. Since to do so would break her line of fortifications and at the same time give the English a material advantage in the neutral country, France promptly refused. There was also a good deal of quibbling over

the terms of the treaty of Utrecht, but in the end both parties to the conflict came to recognize that nothing but superior strength in arms would be effectual in maintaining a claim to the Ohio.

From the English point of view the opening years of the French and Indian War were most discouraging.[1] This was due, in the first place, to the military reversals of the period. The failure to secure the site of Fort Duquesne has been mentioned. This turn of fortune revealed in some degree to the English ministry the critical character of the contest in the upper Ohio Valley, and two regiments of five hundred men each, under command of Major-General Edward Braddock, were despatched to the aid of the Virginians.[2] They arrived at the colonial capital, Williamsburg, in February, 1755, where plans were perfected for an early capture of Duquesne. The other source of discouragement was the lack of a coöperative spirit among the colonists, and a disposition to allow petty jealousies and ill-timed policies of economy to defeat the purposes of such far-seeing leaders as Dinwiddie and Washington. It was with the greatest difficulty that the governors could bring their assemblies to the point of appropriating any such sums of money for the impending

---

[1] General accounts of the French and Indian War may be referred to as follows: Bancroft, *History of the United States*, Vol. III.; Lecky, *History of England in the Eighteenth Century*, II. Ch. VIII.; Kingsford, *History of Canada*, Vol. IV.; Woodrow Wilson, *History of the American People*, II. 77-96; Charles C. Smith, *Acadia and Cape Breton;* Fiske, *New France and New England*, 258-359; Winsor, *Narrative and Critical History*, V. Ch. VIII.; and Parkman, *Montcalm and Wolfe*.

[2] Secret instructions to General Braddock, November 25, 1754, in O'Callaghan, *New York Colonial Documents*, VI. 920-922, and in the *Pennsylvania Archives*, II. 203-207.

war as were clearly needed, if success was to be hoped for. The Virginia House of Burgesses hindered Dinwiddie at every turn. "Those canny planters," says Fiske, "were loath to put much money into the governor's hands, lest he should make an improper use of it. At one time they would refuse the appropriation asked for, at another time they would grant a sum too small to be of much use, and yet again they would grant a sufficient sum, while attaching to the bill a rider concerning some long-disputed question, which they knew would elicit an angry veto from the governor. Similarly in Pennsylvania the Assembly refused money for military purposes, in order to wring from the governor some concession with regard to the long-vexed question of taxing proprietary lands. Moreover, the Assembly at Philadelphia was not quite sure that it was worth while to raise troops for taking Fort Duquesne from the French, if it should thereby fall into the possession of Virginia. It was with difficulty that these representative bodies could be made to see anything that required any breadth of vision. Moreover, they were used to contending against their governors; in the eyes of most representatives that was the sole object for which legislatures existed, but they were not accustomed to devote much thought to the French as enemies, nor had they as yet learned very well what it meant to be invaded by Indians."[1] It should be said, however, that in the north — especially in New York and Massachusetts — the horrors of a French and Indian war were very real, and it was there by no means so difficult to organize an effective resistance.

[1] John Fiske, *New France and New England*, 277–278. See also Fernow, *The Ohio Valley in Colonial Days*, Ch. V.

The war which began about the head waters of the Ohio gave promise of being by far the most serious and far-reaching conflict yet waged in America. The struggle was no longer between New England and New France alone; it had assumed continental proportions. Hostilities were begun in an entirely new field, and on such a scale that they could not fail to involve vast regions of the interior country. Nothing could be clearer to the English leaders than that if the great outburst of French energy in the upper valley of the Ohio after 1748 was to be repressed, there must be a union of effort, such as three intercolonial wars had utterly failed to develop. As one means to this end, a congress of all the colonies was called to meet at Albany in the summer of 1754 to treat with the Iroquois, whose friendship must be preserved at all odds, and to consider ways and means for dealing with the French aggressions. Although the situation was so critical only seven of the colonies were represented at the meeting.[1] This was the occasion on which Franklin brought forward his memorable plan of union, — a device which, had it been adopted, would not only have facilitated the prosecution of the French war, but might perhaps, as its author still believed in 1789, have averted the rebellion of the colonies against England in 1775. The plan, how-

[1] For the "Proceedings of the Colonial Congress held at Albany," see O'Callaghan, *New York Colonial Documents*, VI. 853–892; also the "Representations of Certain English Ministers to the King on these Proceedings," *ibid.*, 916–920; Franklin's plan of colonial union is in the *Minutes of the Provincial Council of Pennsylvania*, VI. 105–108. See also Stephen Hopkins, "A True Representation of the Plan formed at Albany, in 1754, for Uniting all the British Northern Colonies," in the *Rhode Island Historical Tracts*, No. IX.; Frothingham, *Rise of the Republic*, 132–157; and Bancroft, *History of the United States*, II. Ch. V.

ever, was not accepted by any one of the colonies, the time for union being not yet ripe, and as a consequence the war was entered upon with a most humiliating lack of harmony and coöperation. It was only by the aid of armies from England that any considerable measure of success was attained. Presumably the war would benefit the colonists more than anybody else, yet they were niggardly alike as to men, money, and supplies. It was on this account mainly that the plan of imposing a tax upon them by the British Parliament now began to grow rapidly in favor among the king's party.

The course of the war lay almost wholly outside the section of the country with which this book primarily deals. It would therefore be wandering too far afield to attempt more than a very brief summary of the military operations by which the cause of the French in America was finally brought to ruin. The English settled themselves to the conflict in 1755, with the design of sending four distinct expeditions against the French, as follows: one against Forts Ticonderoga and Crown Point in New York, and thence against Quebec; another, from New England, by water, against Cape Breton and other French possessions in the northeast; the third, from Albany against Niagara; and the fourth, from Fort Cumberland in Maryland against Fort Duquesne. This last expedition was put in charge of General Braddock, and was begun in June, 1755. Owing to Braddock's personal incapacity, the total lack of acquaintance of the English regulars with the Indian mode of warfare, and the roughness and impenetrableness of the country through which the advance had to be made, the expedition ended in over-

whelming disaster. July 9 the army was set upon by French and Indians who fought from ambush, and Braddock, scorning to allow his men to adopt the mode of fighting employed by their unseen foes, fell on the field with a large proportion of his following.[1] Under Washington's leadership the survivors effected a rapid but orderly retreat. The most important of the four contemplated attacks upon the French had ended in ignominy, and the Bourbon hold upon the valley of the Ohio seemed stronger than ever. The expedition to the northeast was more successful, — eventually effecting an expulsion of the French population from the plundered Acadia. That against Crown Point was also successful, and the French were roundly beaten on the shores of Lake George. The movement against Niagara, however, duplicated that against Duquesne in that the army did not even reach its destination. All in all, the balance of victory lay decidedly with the French during the first two years of the war. Under the superior leadership of the Marquis de Montcalm it seemed that the English were being pretty effectually repelled, and might in the end find themselves rigidly confined to the populated belt of land along the Atlantic coast.

That it did not work out so was due more largely to

[1] On Braddock's expedition and defeat, see Parkman, *Montcalm and Wolfe*, I. Ch. VII. ; Winthrop Sargent, "Braddock's Expedition," in the *Pennsylvania Historical Society Memoirs*, No. V.; a large collection of letters and other documents in the *Pennsylvania Archives* (compiled by Samuel Hazard), Vol. II. ; a body of more formal materials in the *Minutes of the Provincial Council of Pennsylvania*, Vol. VI. ; T. G. Chapman, "Braddock's Defeat," in the *Magazine of American History*, XVI. 446–452; and a collection of letters and reports on the Braddock expedition in the *Virginia Historical Register*, V. 120–141.

the great English statesman, William Pitt, than to any one else. Popular indignation in England at the inefficiency of the Newcastle administration became so strong in 1757 that the cabinet resigned, and by reason of sheer popularity Pitt was elevated to the new ministry as its first secretary of state and actual premier. Pitt was a man of ordinary birth, without fortune, arrogant, and impractical, but he was also enthusiastic, incorruptible, and absolutely the only man of first-rate importance in public life in whom the people had confidence. Most of all, he appreciated as none of his colleagues did, the enormous importance of the wars in progress in India and in America. He perceived the value of a colonial empire, and saw clearly how and when to strike the most effective blows for its preservation. His promotion to the actual direction of England's foreign affairs produced almost immediate results. A new treaty was negotiated with Frederick of Prussia, by which a subsidy of £670,000 was to be paid to Prussia annually to induce her to keep up the war in Europe. Pitt was devoted to this project because, as he declared, he believed England could win America in Germany by helping the Prussians humble the French. The year 1758 marked a complete reversal of the fortunes of war in America. Three powerful expeditions were fitted out, somewhat on the plan of the four which had terminated so indifferently during the past three years. Of these, one was to be led by Amherst against Louisburg; another, under Forbes, was to take Fort Duquesne; and a third, led by Wolfe, was to advance to the capture of Quebec. All these commanders were efficient men, and directly or indirectly all achieved complete success.

Louisburg was captured, July 26, 1758, and possession of the island of Cape Breton assured. Fort Duquesne fell at last into English hands, December 25 of the same year.[1] And after pushing westward from Louisburg and scaling the Heights of Abraham, General Wolfe achieved the greatest success of the war in compelling the unconditional surrender of Quebec, September 18, 1759.[2]

The capture of Montreal, September 8, 1760, — almost precisely a year after the fall of Quebec, — marked the virtual close of the war. On that date the French governor, Pierre François, Marquis de Vaudreuil, who had succeeded Duquesne in 1755, signed capitulations by which not only Montreal, but also all Canada and its dependencies, were given over to the English.[3] Sixty-five thousand people were affected by the change of sovereignty. The privileges of the Catholic religion were guaranteed, but English law was to displace the French code, and all troops were to be transported as prisoners of war to France. The extent of territory transferred was a matter of doubt. Neither Vaudreuil nor the English commander, Amherst, seems to have tried to be explicit upon this point. Doubtless each hoped for a future advantage to his country from such indefiniteness. For more than two years the matter was a prominent one in

---

[1] T. J. Chapman, "The Fall of Fort Duquesne," in the *Magazine of American History*, XVII. 330-336; C. W. Butterfield, "History of Ohio; the English gain the Ohio Country," in the *Magazine of Western History*, VII. 3-16.

[2] The battle on the Plains was fought September 13, five days before the formal surrender. On the fall of Quebec, see especially Parkman, *Montcalm and Wolfe*, II. Chs. XXV.-XXVIII.

[3] The "Articles of Capitulation for the Surrender of Canada" are printed in O'Callaghan, *New York Colonial Documents*, X. 1107-1120.

the diplomatic negotiations between the two powers, and what settlement would have been arrived at had not other factors been brought into the problem to influence the result cannot even be surmised.

From the moment the capitulations were signed, Amherst began to take steps to make them apply to as much territory as possible. A scout by the name of Robert Rogers was despatched with a party of two hundred men in whaleboats to cruise through the Lakes and receive the surrender of all French posts in the region. Orders were issued for garrisons to proceed to these posts, and the most important of them — Detroit — changed masters, November 29, 1760.[1] During the next year Mackinaw, Green Bay, St. Joseph, Sault Ste. Marie, and in fact every French stronghold in the valley of the St. Lawrence and the Great Lakes, had likewise been surmounted with the banner of St. George. With the prospect of peace and undisputed possession, the Ohio Company prepared to enlarge its operations, and individual explorers and land-hunters began to make their way through the wilderness and carry back to the East marvellous reports of the fertility and productiveness of the Middle West. The most illustrious of these adventurers was Daniel Boone, who made his first appearance beyond the Alleghanies in 1760, and (according to the alleged beech-tree inscription) "cilled" his first "bar" in the wilds of the Boone's Creek Civil District,

---

[1] On the operations of Rogers and the surrender of Detroit, see Cooley, *Michigan* (American Commonwealth Series), Ch. II.; Silas Farmer, *The History of Detroit and Michigan*, 234; and Parkman, *The Conspiracy of Pontiac*, Ch. VI.

Tennessee, in that year. The time for the permanent settlement of this region had not yet quite arrived, but the wide publication of its resources, together with the restoring of order in the West, was rapidly preparing the way.

While the English in America, daunted only by the sullen discontent of the natives which broke forth ultimately in the Pontiac War, were taking every advantage of the defeat of the French to enlarge their territorial possessions, the diplomats of Europe were determining the conditions on which French power was to be withdrawn entirely from the western continent. The starting-point of the negotiation was the surrender of Vaudreuil to Amherst. When France found herself utterly unable to prolong the war, and therefore without hope of regaining Canada, she fell back upon the looseness of Vaudreuil's definition of the surrender, and sought to maintain that, as Vaudreuil himself said subsequently, the capitulation included no territory south of the height of land at the head of the streams flowing into the basin of the Great Lakes. The English at least professed to understand, however, that the Canada yielded to them included not only the basin of the Lakes, but also that of the Wabash to the Ohio, and all west to the Mississippi. This interpretation seems to have been quite groundless, for, though at one time the Illinois country had been added to Canada, the arrangement was only a temporary one for administrative purposes, and had been wholly superseded long before 1760.

Nevertheless, when, on July 15, 1761, France offered to cede Canada "as Vaudreuil had surrendered it," she was given to understand that the English must reserve the right of interpreting the terms of Vaudreuil's capitulation. King George's ministers would not admit that any part of the Ohio country was included in Louisiana, or, indeed, that Louisiana and Virginia were anywhere contiguous. Three weeks later the French offered to cede Canada "in the most extensive manner" on condition that a strip of territory running from north to south, just west of the Alleghanies, be declared neutral.[1] This idea of a buffer of neutral lands was similar to the proposal of the French government in 1782 that the region between the Alleghanies and the Mississippi be formed into a protectorate of the United States and Spain. On this earlier occasion, as on the later one, the suggestion met with no favor from the nation most immediately concerned. England maintained that the lands in question were hers in full right. They had been included in the earliest of her chartered colonies, and besides, a long series of treaties with the Iroquois and Southern Indians had given her a well-recognized protectorate over them. There was nothing for France to do but yield, which she did, not very gracefully, September 13, 1761.

While the negotiations were pending, it developed that there was much difference of opinion in English official circles as to the best territorial basis for a treaty. It happened that another of the English conquests during the war was the island of Guadeloupe in the West Indies, of enormous importance in the sugar trade and commercial operations generally. A considerable number of people, mainly

[1] See Jefferys's map of the proposed neutral territory, in Winsor, *The Mississippi Basin*, 416. The map appeared originally in Jefferys, *General Topography of North America and the West Indies* [London, 1768].

of the merchant class, advocated the view that Canada would be of small value to England compared with Guadeloupe, and that the possession of the latter should be rendered doubly secure by returning the former country to its original owner. Numerous pamphlets appeared in support of this contention, among the authors of which were the distinguished brothers, William and Edmund Burke.[1] When the possibility of such a consummation became known in the colonies, a deep spirit of resentment at even the consideration of the plan by the ministry was aroused. In earlier wars with the French colonies the English settlers had been repeatedly disappointed by the return of their hard-won conquests in exchange for English advantages in other parts of the world, and naturally they did not now enjoy the prospect of losing the fruits of all their recent efforts. Happily they had a most able spokesman in Franklin. He, too, turned pamphleteer and with noteworthy effectiveness.[2] The ardor and skill of his arguments for the retention of Canada, and as much other American territory as Eng-

---

[1] The Burke pamphlet appeared in the nature of controversial "Remarks" on the Earl of Bath's *Letter to Two Great Men* [Pitt and Newcastle], in which it was argued that Canada would be more valuable to England than Guadeloupe or any other West India possession.

[2] Franklin's most important pamphlet was entitled, "The Interest of Great Britain Considered with Regard to her Colonies and the Acquisitions of Canada and Guadeloupe." It first appeared anonymously in London in 1760, being prompted primarily by the brochures of the Earl of Bath and his anonymous opponents. The text of the paper appears in Sparks, *Works of Benjamin Franklin*, IV. 1–53. Franklin's representations in the interest of retaining Canada were forcefully answered by the pamphlet, "An Examination of the Commercial Principles of the Late Negotiation between Great Britain and France in 1761," supposed likewise to have been written by Edmund Burke.

land could get, fairly entitle him to be called America's first great expansionist. England, he declared, was insignificant territorially, — "scarcely enough of it to keep one's shoes dry," — and she must compensate for her cramped quarters at home by never losing an opportunity legitimately to enlarge her claims and possessions beyond the seas. Even at the rate at which the population of the seaboard colonies had been increasing, it was not unreasonable to look forward to the time when a surplus population of millions would have to be provided for. The great area between the Alleghanies and the Mississippi could easily be made to support a hundred millions of such people, and England could make no greater mistake than to refuse to possess herself of this region when it was so easily possible for her to insure it for all time to come. "Canada in the hands of the French," declared Franklin "has always stunted the growth of our colonies. To leave the French in the possession of Canada, when it is within our power to remove them, and to depend on our own strength and watchfulness to prevent the mischief that may attend it, is neither safe nor prudent." To the argument of the partisans of Guadeloupe that the retention of Canada would foster a "numerous, hardy, and independent people, who would become useless and dangerous to Britain," Franklin replied that the exigencies of the recent war had certainly demonstrated the difficulty with which the colonists could be brought to act together, and that, except in event of "grievous tyranny and oppression," England had nothing to fear from the growing numbers and strength of her American colonies. "Their jealousy of each other is so great," he declared, "that

however necessary a union of the colonies has long been for their common defence and security against their enemies, and how sensible soever each colony has been of that necessity, yet they have never been able to effect such a union among themselves, nor even to agree in requesting the mother country to establish it for them. Nothing but the immediate command of the crown has been able to produce even the imperfect union, but lately seen there, of the forces of some colonies. If they could not agree to unite for their defence against the French and Indians, who were perpetually harassing their settlements, burning their villages, and murdering their people, can it reasonably be supposed there is any danger of their uniting against their own nation, which protects and encourages them, with which they have so many connections and ties of blood, interest, and affection, and which, it is well known, they all love much more than they love one another? In short, there are so many causes that must operate to prevent it that I will venture to say a union amongst them for such a purpose is not merely improbable, it is impossible. . . . When I say such a union is impossible, I mean, without the most grievous tyranny and oppression. People who have property in a country which they may lose, and privileges which they may endanger, are generally disposed to be quiet, and even to bear much, rather than hazard all. While the government is mild and just, while important civil and religious rights are secure, such subjects will be dutiful and obedient. *The waves do not rise but when the wind blows.*"[1]

[1] "The Interest of Great Britain Considered," Sparks, *Franklin's Works*, IV. 42. See an extract from the *Universal Magazine*, London,

Doubtless these and other expressions from Franklin had their influence upon the ministry and Parliament; but it is probable that, wholly regardless of opinion in America, the decision of the government would finally have been, as it was, to return Guadeloupe to the French and keep a firm grip upon Canada and its alleged dependencies in the Central West.

The course of the negotiations was interrupted by the retirement of Pitt from the ministry, October 5, 1761. Lord Bute, who succeeded to Pitt's office and eventually became nominal as well as real premier, was willing to make peace with France upon much easier terms than Pitt had contended for, but the outbreak of war between England and Spain, three weeks after Pitt's fall, rendered the early conclusion of a treaty out of the question. It was only after the brilliant succession of English victories in the summer of 1762, including the capture of Martinique, Grenada, St. Lucia, St. Vincent, Havana, and the Philippines, that Spain was brought, along with her ally, to the point of humble submission. The English were as tired of the war as were their enemies, and King George and his prime minister were so eager for the restoration of peace that they consented to sacrifice practically all that the last year's triumphs had given them. The preliminaries between England and France were agreed to, November 3, at Fontainebleau, and, despite the fulminations of Pitt against the leniency of the ministry, were approved by Parliament a few weeks later.

1761, urging the government to conquer Louisiana and hold it in preference to Guadeloupe and all other islands, in the *Magazine of American History*, XXVII. 311–312.

NORTH AMERICA AFTER THE TREATY OF PARIS (1762-1763)

February 10, 1763, the terms of the treaty were made definitive at Paris.[1] England's agent in the negotiation was the Duke of Bedford, while France was represented by Choiseul, Spain by Grimaldi, and Portugal by Mello. The ratifications were exchanged among the contracting powers in March, and the treaty was formally promulgated May 4.

Under the treaty of Paris the question as to the extent of Canada dropped out of consideration, for France agreed to yield to the English practically all her lands east of the Mississippi. The seventh article of the instrument provided that, in order to remove forever "all subjects of dispute with regard to the limits of the British and French territories on the continent of America," the boundary between these territories should be "a line drawn along the middle of the river Mississippi from its source to the river Iberville, and from thence by a line drawn along the middle of this river, and the lakes Maurepas and Pontchartrain, to the sea." All French possessions east of the great river were to become English except the city of New Orleans and the island on which it stood. New Orleans, as the capital of the Louisiana territory and essential to its administration, was to remain to the French. Henceforth the navigation of the Mississippi was to be entirely free alike to the subjects of

---

[1] The text of the treaty is in Chalmers, *Collection of Treaties*, I. 467-483. The articles relating to America are printed in MacDonald, *Select Charters*, 261-266. On the treaty, see Lecky, *History of England in the Eighteenth Century*, II. Ch. VIII., and III. Ch. X.; Parkman, *Montcalm and Wolfe*, II. Ch. XXXI.; Winsor, *Narrative and Critical History*, V. Ch. VIII.; and Mahon, *History of England from the Peace of Utrecht*, II. Chs. XXXII.-XXXVIII.

Great Britain and France "in its whole breadth and length, from its source to the sea." Vessels belonging to the subjects of either nation were not to be stopped, visited, or subjected to the payment of any duty whatever. The inhabitants of the ceded territory were guaranteed the liberty of the Catholic religion "as far as the laws of Great Britain permit," and it was further provided that within the space of eighteen months from the ratification of the treaty they might sell their estates, provided it be to subjects of the English crown, and, carrying their personal effects with them, retire "with all safety and freedom" to lands which remained under the Bourbon banner.

The acquisition by war of so vast and desirable a region as the eastern Mississippi Valley without the striking of a blow within its bounds is indeed a remarkable achievement, yet this is precisely what the English had done. By striking straight at the strongholds of French supremacy in northern and eastern America, England rendered the less fortified Bourbon dominions in the interior no longer tenable. Although throughout the war the fate of Louisiana was hanging in the balance, the theatre of conflict was elsewhere, and the Louisianians could not even render any important aid to their fellow-countrymen fighting, in the end so unavailingly, in the north to save them from complete segregation. We hear of proposals at Mobile that Georgia and Carolina should be invaded by Choctaws under French leadership,[1] but nothing of

---

[1] M. Bossu, *Nouveaux voyages aux Indies occidentales* [Paris, 1768]. Translated by J. R. Forster as *Travels through that part of North America formerly called Louisiana* [London, 1771].

note seems to have resulted from such suggestions. Far removed though she was, Louisiana suffered no small inconvenience because of the war. Supply ships from France were continually being captured by English privateers. Money could not be brought from Europe, and the governor was compelled to resort to the issue of a form of paper currency known as *bons*. Commerce was heavily burdened by the levies made upon the colony for the expenses of the war, and the practice of giving yearly presents to the Indian tribes had to be discontinued, — which consideration turned much of the profitable Indian trade into English channels. Moreover, there was always great uncertainty as to whether the Gulf coasts might not become a scene of war. News from the North travelled slowly, and the lower settlements were never very clearly informed regarding the actual state of affairs in Canada and the Ohio country. Fearing an English invasion, the people of New Orleans built a new wall entirely around their city, repaired the batteries at English Turn, and stationed a vessel at the mouth of the river to be sunk, if necessary, to prevent entrance by an English fleet. But though such preparations for defence were the part of wisdom, they proved unnecessary. The English had no purpose to attack the French in the Gulf. They were shrewd enough to see that when Louisburg, Quebec, Montreal, Niagara, Duquesne, and the other northern centres of French power were once wrested from their founders, the power of the French in America would be a thing of the past. There was no need of resorting to such costly expedients as the invasion of the French domain in the West and South, since its fortune must rise and fall precisely with that of Canada and the lower Lake dominion.

When the English authorities agreed to the terms of the treaty of Paris, they were wholly unaware of another and almost equally important move which the French were making. That Spain had become involved in the later stages of the war was due mainly to the efforts of Louis XV.'s minister of foreign affairs, the Duc de Choiseul. During the year 1761, when Pitt, acting on his avowed policy of compassing the annihilation of French naval and colonial power, was making exorbitant demands in the negotiations at Paris, Choiseul had taken advantage of the Spanish king's hostility toward England to demand on behalf of Spain the restoration of some prizes taken by the English, the acknowledgment of Spanish rights to the use of the Newfoundland fisheries, the surrender of Gibraltar, and the withdrawal of English settlements from Honduras.[1] The result of Pitt's prompt rejection of these demands was the formation of a new Family Compact between the two Bourbon powers (August, 1761), by which each guaranteed to the other the territories belonging to it, and Spain agreed to declare war against England if peace was not concluded by May of the following year. When the existence of this arrangement was suspected in England, Pitt at once declared for war with Spain, and though the enemies of his administration took advantage of the issue to secure

---

[1] By the treaty of Paris the Spanish claim to a share in the fisheries was withdrawn, and the British fortifications in the Bay of Honduras were engaged to be destroyed. The possession of Gibraltar was not affected.

his downfall, the succeeding ministry was forced by circumstances to precipitate the conflict in January, 1762. The adherence of the Spanish to the French cause merely delayed for some months the conclusion of the war. It in no wise diminished the superiority of the English, or lessened the losses of France in the final reckoning. In fact, it greatly increased those losses.

By agreement between England and Spain the former, at the close of the war, gave back to the latter all her conquests in Cuba, including Havana, in return for which Spain ceded to England "Florida, with Fort St. Augustin, and the Bay of Pensacola, as well as all that Spain possesses on the continent of North America, to the east, or to the southeast, of the river Mississippi."[1] By this acquisition the sovereignty of the English was established over all the remaining territory (except the island of New Orleans) east of the Mississippi, which had not been acquired from France. But inasmuch as France was responsible for Spain's participation in the war, and consequently for her losses at its close, Grimaldi, the Spanish ambassador at the court of Versailles and Spain's representative in the negotiation, suggested that compensation be made by the ceding of the western portion of the Mississippi Valley to his master, King Charles III. Having lost everything in the New World but this, the French considered it scarcely worth while to risk the forfeiture of Spanish friendship for the sake of retaining Louisiana. The province had long been a financial burden upon the crown, and aside from the humiliation involved in the complete retirement from the American

[1] Treaty of Paris, Article XX.

continent, there was probably not much reluctance in official circles in parting with it. Accordingly, on the same day that the treaty of Paris was signed, Choiseul and Grimaldi agreed to a secret understanding by which the French king "ceded to his cousin of Spain, and to his successors, forever, in full ownership and without any exception or reservation whatever, from the pure impulse of his generous heart, and from the sense of the friendship and affection existing between these two royal persons, all the country known under the name of Louisiana."[1] The territory transferred included New Orleans and all the French claims west of the Mississippi. Ten days later the cession was approved at the Escurial, and ten days later still it was ratified by King Louis. The transaction was not known to the world for fifteen months, and in the meantime the French king continued to exercise the sovereignty of the province.

Thus the close of the Seven Years' War brought the complete subversion of the French colonial empire in America. Though the great Pitt had not been able to maintain himself at the British helm all through the contest, the outcome in America was substantially what he had planned and hoped for — except that he might have contrived to secure all the Mississippi Valley at once for people of English speech and blood instead of allowing the western half of it to fall for a time to the Spaniards. By the treaties of 1763 the plans and achievements of

---

[1] "Preliminary Convention between the Kings of France and Spain for the Cession of Louisiana to the Latter" and the "Definite Act of Cession of Louisiana by the King of France to the King of Spain," in French, *Historical Collections of Louisiana*, V. 234–239.

scores of patriotic and ambitious Frenchmen — La Salle, Iberville, Bienville, Cadillac, Crozat, Galissonnière, Céloron, and many of lesser fame — were brought to naught. Missionaries, *coureurs-de-bois*, fur traders, explorers, and colonists had labored, in all more than a hundred years, with greater or lesser skill and ardor, to build a great French dependency in the heart of the continent. They had been the pathfinders of the Mississippi Valley; they had borne the brunt of the conflict with hostile natives and primeval nature; they had revealed to the world the resources and prospective value of the great region; but in the laying of foundations for an abiding political power they failed. Their numbers had always been too scant, and support from the home government too "penny wise and pound foolish." They could have maintained themselves quite well as against the Spaniard or any other possible European competitor except the very one with whom they had to contend. But the Englishman was too hungry for land, and too shrewd in his methods of obtaining it, as well as too strong numerically and financially, to be long resisted with such force as the French could command in America. At the best it was but a question of time until the scattered Gallic settlements between Montreal and the Gulf should be submerged by the Anglo-Saxon advance beyond the Alleghanies in the latter part of the eighteenth century and after.

The war was essentially a conflict of civilizations, and, viewed in this aspect, its result appears no less inevitable than necessary to the future of the country. The late Professor Hinsdale, one of the first and also one of the most suggestive writers on our western history, states the significance of the issue between the English and French in the following striking manner: "The history of French America is far more picturesque and brilliant than the history of British America in the period of 1608-1754. But the English were doing work far more solid, valuable, and permanent than their northern neighbors. The French took to the lakes, rivers, and forests; they cultivated the Indians; their explorers were intent on discovery, their traders on furs, their missionaries on souls. The English did not either take to the woods or cultivate the Indians; they loved agriculture and trade, state and church, and so clung to their fields, shops, politics, and churches. As a result, while Canada languished, thirteen English states grew up on the Atlantic Plain modelled on the Saxon pattern, and became populous, rich, and strong. At the beginning of the war there were 80,000 white inhabitants in New France, 1,160,000 in the British colonies. The disparity of wealth was equally striking. In 1754 there was more real civilization — more seeds of things — in the town of Boston than in all New France. In time these compact and vigorous British colonies offered effective resistance to Great Britain. It is plain that, had they spread themselves out over half a continent, hunted beaver, and trafficked with the Indians, after the manner of the French, independence would have been postponed many years, and possibly forever. We owe a vast debt to the inherited character of those Englishmen who came to America in the first half of the seventeenth century, and no small debt to the Appalachian mountain wall that confined them to the narrow Atlantic slope until, by reason of compression and growth,

they were gotten ready, first to enter the West in force, and then to extort their independence from England."[1]

The overthrow of the French power in Canada and the Mississippi Valley is certainly to be regarded as the prologue to the American Revolution. Choiseul perceived the tendency of the English to overleap themselves in the hour of their success, and declared, after signing the treaty in 1763, "I ceded it [the eastern Mississippi Valley] on purpose to destroy the English. They were fond of American dominion, and I resolved they should have enough of it." On the relation between the French losses in 1763 and the fortunes of the English colonies in their later struggle for independence a careful American writer has the following to say: "Humiliating as the loss of the North American territories was to France, it was productive of much advantage to the United States in their subsequent struggle with the mother country. Had France in 1776 been in possession, not only of Canada, but of the valley of the Mississippi, it is not likely that she would have accepted the policy of freeing the United States from British dominion; nor had she retained Canada and the Mississippi Valley would she have nourished that bitter resentment to Britain which swayed her after the peace of 1763. Burke insisted that the conquest of Canada was of doubtful value to Britain, as by removing France from North America, it would weaken the community of danger which bound Britain to her American colonies and would precipitate the division of the British Empire. Not only was this the case, but had France held in 1782 the valley of the Mississippi, that great country would

[1] B. A. Hinsdale, *The Old Northwest*, 68.

not have either been claimed by the United States or surrendered by France."[1] Still one other noteworthy passage on the historical significance of the expulsion of the French from North America must be quoted. The English historian John Richard Green strikes straight at the truth when he writes: "With the triumph of Wolfe on the Heights of Abraham began the history of the United States. By removing an enemy whose dread had knit the colonists to the mother country, and by breaking through the line with which France had barred them from the basin of the Mississippi, Pitt laid the foundation of the great republic of the west. . . . The presence of the French in Canada, their designs in the west, had thrown America for protection on the mother country. But with the conquest of Canada all need of protection was removed. The attitude of England toward its distant dependency became one of simple possession; and the differences of temper, the commercial and administrative disputes, which had long existed as elements of severance, but had been thrown into the background till now by the higher need for union, started into new prominence. Day by day the American colonists found it harder to submit to the meddling of the mother country with their self-government and their trade. A consciousness of their destinies was stealing in upon thoughtful men, and spread from them to the masses round them."[2] The ties which bound America to England were yet very strong. The colonists fairly scorned the thought of separation, and

---

[1] Francis Wharton, *The Revolutionary Diplomatic Correspondence of the United States*, I. 330.
[2] Green, *History of the English People*, IV. 197, 202.

prided themselves on their loyalty, and the English regarded the American colonies as their choicest possession. Nevertheless, all far-seeing students of political science agreed that there were elements of danger in the situation, and already the young John Adams had prophesied that the only way by which England would be able to prevent the colonies from setting up for themselves was to keep them all the time disunited. The conflict with the French had determined the ultimate supremacy of English-speaking people in North America, but this did not necessarily mean the permanent aggrandizement of the British nation there. The Seven Years' War had been a turning point in English history, when the chief interests of the English people were shifted from the quarrels and rivalries of the continent to questions of empire beyond the seas. "Mistress of North America, the future mistress of India, claiming as her own the empire of the seas, Britain suddenly towered high above nations whose position in a single continent doomed them to comparative insignificance in the after history of the world."[1] But it remained to be seen whether the island kingdom could govern her distant dependents so adroitly as to neutralize the disintegrating power of three thousand miles of salt water.

[1] Green, *History of the English People*, IV. 198.

CHAPTER VIII

ENGLISH AND SPANISH NEIGHBORS AFTER 1763

THE settlement at the close of the Seven Years' War left practically the entire western hemisphere in the possession of the English and the Spanish. By one stroke the empire of France in America had been reduced from all Canada and the Mississippi Valley to two insignificant islands in the Gulf of St. Lawrence and a few posts in the West Indies. The claim of Spain extended all the way from Cape Horn to an indefinite boundary north of the Columbia River, though only a comparatively small portion of this vast territory had even been explored. The possessions of the English included all the lands east of the Mississippi and indefinitely westward from the settlements in Canada. The great line of division was the Mississippi itself; but on account of a total lack of information regarding the uppermost waters of that stream it was quite impossible to prescribe definite limits for the claims of the two powers in the Northwest.

On the 7th of October, 1763, King George, with the concurrence of the Privy Council, began the work of organizing the recent English acquisitions in America by issuing a proclamation providing for the government of the territories in question, defining certain interior boun-

daries, and regulating trade and intercourse with the Indians.[1] By this instrument four distinct governmental provinces were constituted from the ceded lands — Quebec, East Florida, West Florida, and Grenada. Quebec, as now defined, was considerably less extensive than the country which Vaudreuil had governed. Its southern boundary was described as a line due east from Lake Nipissing which, "crossing the river St. Lawrence and the lake Champlain in 45 degrees of North latitude, passes along the High Lands, which divide the rivers which empty themselves into the said river St. Lawrence, from those which fall into the sea." The forty-fifth parallel is the present northern boundary of New York and Vermont; but the incongruity of this and other descriptions of the line occasioned frequent diplomatic negotiations in later times between England and the United States, until the final settlement of the issue by the Webster-Ashburton treaty in 1842. The provinces of East and West Florida were bounded on the north by the thirty-first parallel and from each other by the Appalachicola River, being simply the territory which had been received from Spain and France, except that by the deflection of the boundary line southward along the course of the St. Mary's River, Georgia received a small strip of land whose possession she had long been

---

[1] The text of the proclamation of 1763 is in the *Annual Register* (1763), 208-213, and Sparks, *Works of Franklin*, IV. 374-379. It is reprinted in MacDonald, *Select Documents*, 267-272, and in Hart and Channing, *American History Leaflets*, No. 5. For discussions of the proclamation, see B. A. Hinsdale, *The Old Northwest*, Ch. VIII., and "The Western Land Policy of the British Government from 1763 to 1775," in the *Ohio Archæological and Historical Quarterly*, I. 207-229; Winsor, *Narrative and Critical History*, VI. Ch. IX.; and Roosevelt, *The Winning of the West*, I. Chs. I. and II.

disputing with the Spanish.[1] Grenada was to be made up of the island of that name, together with the Grenadines, Dominica, St. Vincent, and Tobago. Authority was issued to the governors of the new provinces to call general assemblies as soon as circumstances would permit, which were to have full power to make laws agreeable to the statutes of England for the government of the inhabitants of the respective colonies. The governors were likewise authorized to reward veterans of the French and Indian War by grants of land ranging from fifty acres for privates to five thousand acres for field officers; but it was strictly enjoined that no governor should grant any patent for lands beyond his province, and that no official of an Atlantic colony should allot lands farther west than the sources of the rivers flowing to the eastern seaboard. The great area between the Alleghanies and the Mississippi was to be held in reserve for the use of the Indians. "We do hereby strictly forbid," ran the proclamation, "on pain of our displeasure, all our loving subjects from making any purchases or settlements whatever, or taking possession of any of the lands above reserved, without our special leave and licence for that purpose first obtained."

[1] The following year the northern boundary of West Florida was moved to the parallel of the mouth of the Yazoo (32° 30′), which modification was subsequently the source of no little trouble to both England and the United States. This first West Florida — the British province — is to be distinguished from the later Spanish West Florida and the independent state of West Florida. Henry E. Chambers, "West Florida and its Relation to the Historical Cartography of the United States," in the *Johns Hopkins University Studies in Historical and Political Science*, XVI. No. 5; and B. A. Hinsdale, "The Establishment of the First Southern Boundary of the United States," in the *Report of the American Historical Association for 1893*, 331–334.

If any had already trangressed in this direction they were ordered "forthwith to remove themselves." Officers were to be stationed throughout the reserved territories to preserve friendly relations with the Indians and see that fugitives from justice in any of the colonies were properly apprehended and returned. The natives were to be protected to the utmost in their primeval rights, and the possession of the country by the English was intended to retard rather than facilitate settlement by Europeans.

It appears that several motives controlled in the shaping of this remarkable proclamation. That it was designed primarily, as Franklin considered it, to conciliate the Indians admits of little doubt. Even before the war closed evidences were fast accumulating that the redskins of the West were unusually restless and threatening, and that, in fact, a great insurrection was imminent. By turning the eastern Mississippi Valley into crown lands in which the dispossession of the natives was strictly forbidden, the king and council vainly hoped to forestall any hostile movement which was being projected and to assure a perpetual peace. The proclamation was designed also to limit the old colonies by the mountains and invalidate the sea-to-sea charters, establish more firmly the control of the royal agents over the movements of the colonists, keep the English population in America from diffusing itself, as the French had done, through the vast interior wilderness, and promote British commercial interests by concentrating wealth on the Atlantic seaboard.[1] These latter

---

[1] William F. Poole, in Winsor, *Narrative and Critical History*, VI. 687, regards the limitation of the seaboard colonies as the main purpose of the proclamation. See the Report of the Lords Commissioners for Trade

objects were so commonly understood in the colonies, even when the proclamation was issued, that there was an almost universal expression of dissatisfaction with it. Men charged that the English government was conspiring to rob the colonies of the fruits of the late war and put a check upon the inalienable right of pioneers in a new world to seek out for themselves such homes and possessions as they desire. The policy outlined in the proclamation seemed to sound the death-knell of all colonial schemes, such as that of the Ohio Company, for expansion in the West. The tide which had begun to flow in recent years out of Virginia and Pennsylvania and the Carolinas, across the mountains into the valleys of the Ohio and Cumberland, was to be forcibly turned back by royal edict. Even the most ardent of the government's supporters in the colonies viewed with much regret the adoption by England of a policy of repressive paternalism such as the English settlers had long been accustomed to ridicule in the French imperial system. The measure, like all others encroaching upon colonial rights, was not without opponents at home, and Edmund Burke characterized it as "an attempt to keep as a lair of wild beasts that earth which God, by an express charter, has given to the children of men." As a means of conciliating the western Indians it failed absolutely; and as a harbinger of England's selfish policy in America, now that the question of defending the colonies was no longer a vital

and Plantations, in 1772, on the petition of Thomas Walpole and others for a grant of land on the Ohio, printed in Sparks, *Works of Franklin*, IV. 303-323; also Franklin's elaborate answer to this report, *ibid.*, 324-374.

one, its most obvious result was to widen the breach which was as yet only beginning to appear, but which was destined to grow into a yawning chasm in little more than a single decade. Theodore Roosevelt, in his *Winning of the West*, very well states the issue created by England's opposition to the spread of her people in America as follows: "In the northwest she [England] succeeded to the French policy as well as the French position. She wished the land to remain a wilderness, the home of the trapper and the fur trader, of the Indian hunter and the French *voyageur*. She desired it to be kept as a barrier against the growth of the seaboard colonies towards the interior. She regarded the new lands across the Atlantic as being won and settled, not for the benefit of the men who won and settled them, but for the benefit of the merchants and traders who stayed at home. It was this that rendered the Revolution inevitable; the struggle was a revolt against the whole mental attitude of Britain in regard to America, rather than against any one special act or set of acts. The sins and shortcomings of the colonists had been many, and it would be easy to make out a formidable catalogue of grievances against them, on behalf of the mother country; but on the great underlying question they were wholly in the right, and their success was of vital consequence to the well-being of the race on this continent."[1]

It is quite impossible to ascertain the number of French people living east of the Mississippi at the time the country was ceded to England. Estimates ranging as high as four or five thousand have been ventured by various writ-

[1] Theodore Roosevelt, *The Winning of the West*, I. 36.

ers, though one of the best informed, Justin Winsor, thought it probable that north of the Ohio there were only about 1200 adults and 800 children, together with perhaps 900 negro slaves.[1] There were very few Frenchmen south of the Ohio and east of the Mississippi. The majority of these settlers were traders more or less permanently established, and it will be recalled that by the treaty of Paris they were guaranteed their rights to their homes and lands, with the privilege of selling their possessions to the English and retiring from the country within eighteen months. A considerable number of the settlers north of the Ohio chose to follow the latter course, particularly as the cession of western Louisiana to Spain remained for some time unknown, and it was supposed by them that by merely crossing to the other side of the river they could continue to live under the banner of their native land. A general exodus occurred, and some of the most important posts in the Ohio and Illinois country were all but abandoned. It may be observed that this movement decided the location of the city of St. Louis; for in 1764, when Pierre Laclède Liguest and a company of followers, representing a French fur company, reached the vicinity of the Missouri's mouth with the intention of establishing a new trading-post, they heard of the recent cession and decided to build on the western rather than the eastern bank of the stream, so that, at all events, the sovereignty of Great Britain might be evaded. The site chosen was one which two Frenchmen, Chouteau by name, had occupied the previous winter,

---

[1] Winsor, *The Mississippi Basin*, 432. On the French population of the Ohio Valley, see Roosevelt, *The Winning of the West*, I. Ch. II.

and within a few months a third of the whites and more than half of the negroes who had lived east of the Mississippi had gathered there and given the new town a very respectable population.[1]

The migration of the French had no small weight in determining the Indians upon a general rising against the English. By the natives it was understood that the French were fleeing because they feared the constraints of English rule, and it was reasoned that if the Frenchmen had ground for such alarm, the red men had even greater cause for apprehension. The French had long posed as the friends and protectors of all the tribes west of the Iroquois; but now the helpless natives were to be left to the mercy of the land-grabbing Englishman, and they must either submit to the destruction of their hunting grounds or unite in a desperate campaign of extermination. As soon as the restlessness of the western Indians was brought to the attention of the British government, gifts to the value of four or five thousand pounds were sent to Charleston to be used in placating the tribes of the South. But no such policy was followed in the North, where the greatest danger lay, and it is doubtful anyway whether bribery could have availed more than to postpone for a time the trial at arms which the chieftains of the Northwest had firmly resolved upon. At the very moment when Amherst was declaring that it was of no consequence

---

[1] Elihu H. Shepard, *The Early History of St. Louis and Missouri*, Ch. I.; Frederic L. Billon, *Annals of St. Louis in its Early Days under the French and Spanish Dominations*, Part I.; Reynolds, *The Pioneer History of Illinois*, 82; E. N. Lauder, "Liguest, the Founder of St. Louis," in the *Magazine of American History*, V. 204–210; and Anon., "The Founding of St. Louis," in the *Magazine of Western History*, II. 302–321.

what the Indians thought of the displacement of French by English sovereignty in the West, Pontiac's runners were summoning warriors from all the nations of the Great Lake region to a council for the planning of the war.

In May, 1763, the blow fell by a simultaneous attack upon all the forts from Pennsylvania to Lake Superior.[1] The struggle which ensued was the most terrible in the annals of Indian history. The redskins threw themselves into it with the spirit of desperation. In less than a month two thousand settlers were killed on the frontiers outside the armed posts. The inhabitants on the Ohio and its upper tributaries were all massacred or driven in flight toward the eastern colonies. Every post remaining from the French War was destroyed, and Fort Pitt (old Fort Duquesne) was left awhile the sole sentinel of English authority in the Ohio Valley. In the West everything was lost in the first year of the war except Detroit. But with the year 1764 the tide turned. The

[1] On the Pontiac War, see Bancroft, *History of the United States* (ed. 1883), III. Ch. IV.; Parkman, *The Conspiracy of Pontiac;* Winsor, *Narrative and Critical History*, VI. Ch. IX.; Dillon, *History of Indiana*, Ch. IX.; Moses, *Illinois, Historical and Statistical*, I. Ch. VII.; Cooley, *Michigan*, Ch. III.; Silas Farmer, *History of Detroit and Michigan*, Ch. XXXVIII.; Fernow, *The Ohio Valley in Colonial Days*, Ch. IX.; Reynolds, *The Pioneer History of Illinois*, Ch. IV.; and Moore, *The Northwest under Three Flags*, Ch. IV. The most important original authority is the so-called "Pontiac Manuscript," a journal written in French and probably by a French priest. It was discovered in the roof of a Canadian house which was being torn down, and presented to the Michigan Historical and Pioneer Society. Translations of it are in the *Collections*, VIII. 266–339, of this society, and in the Parkman Mss. in the library of the Massachusetts Historical Society. Other contemporary statements regarding the rebellion, especially the siege of Fort Detroit in 1763, are in the *Michigan Pioneer and Historical Society Collections*, VIII. 340–368.

English authorities, somewhat recovered from the shock, set about the organizing of carefully planned expeditions against the Senecas, Delawares, Ottawas, Ojibways, and other peoples who had been most aggressive in the war, and, largely through the efforts of Colonel Henry Bouquet, success crowned their undertakings. During the autumn of 1764, Bouquet advanced into the very heart of the hostile country, administering defeats and terrifying the savages into subjection.[1] Late in November peace was concluded, but not until after all the whites held in captivity had been surrendered. The Pontiac rebellion failed as much because of the jealousies of the participants in it as because of the measures pursued by the English to suppress it. Although the proclamation of 1763 had come too late to avert the war, the consequent adoption of French methods by the British agents and the published intention of the king and council to hold the western country in reserve for the Indians were not without influence in inducing a lasting conciliation. As time went on Pontiac and his followers came to understand that it was not so much the British government

---

[1] William Smith, "An Historical Account of the Expedition against the Ohio Indians, in the year 1764, under the command of Henry Bouquet," in the *Ohio Valley Historical Series* [Cincinnati, 1868]. The papers and despatches of Colonel Bouquet are reprinted in the *Collections of the Michigan Pioneer and Historical Society*, XIX. 27-296. See Parkman, *The Conspiracy of Pontiac*, Chs. XX.-XXVII., especially a report of General Gage to Lord Halifax on the success of Bouquet's expedition, December 13, 1764, Appendix F; C. W. Butterfield, "History of Ohio; Bouquet's Expedition," in the *Magazine of Western History*, VII. 560-575; Moore, *The Northwest under Three Flags*, Ch. V.; and J. T. Headley, "Colonel Bouquet," in *Harper's Magazine*, XXIII. 577 (October, 1861).

that was their foe as the English colonies on the seaboard. The former promised protection and non-interference; the latter were undeniably greedy for conquest and western settlement — in other words, the extermination of the native population; for that was invariably the sequel of English colonization. During the interval between Pontiac's war and the outbreak of the Revolution this feature of the situation came to be so clearly appreciated by the ten thousand or more native warriors of the West that it is not difficult to explain their almost uniform adherence in that later struggle to the cause of King George.

One very important result of the Pontiac War deserves special mention. To all appearances the effort of the English government to conciliate the discontented Indians by guaranteeing the immunity of their lands had failed to produce its intended effect. The bringing of the natives to a full appreciation of England's motives was a matter of years, and in the meantime sentiment in the colonies adverse to the mother country's western policy had grown materially stronger. The reluctance with which the Indians brought the war to a close was urged by the colonial authorities as ground sufficient to warrant the removal of every governmental restriction upon westward migration. Therefore the preliminary treaty which Bouquet negotiated with the representatives of Pontiac at Fort Stanwix, on the site of Rome, New York, practically abrogated that portion of the proclamation of 1763 which reserved the western lands from settlement by the whites.[1] The Indians were encouraged under this compact to withdraw from the country south

[1] Parkman, *The Conspiracy of Pontiac*, Ch. XXVI.

of the Ohio, and the way was thus prepared in part for the settling a few years later of what are now the states of Kentucky and Tennessee. Sir William Johnson of New York[1] sent George Croghan to England to recommend to the king and council that a line be drawn from the head of the Delaware to the mouth of the Ohio, and that the lands north of this line be reserved for an Indian hunting ground. After considerable delay the necessary authorization for the conclusion of a treaty to this effect was received, and in the autumn of 1768 more than three thousand Indian deputies from the Iroquois and their dependents were assembled at Fort Stanwix for the establishing of definite boundaries for the red man's and the white man's possessions. The Indians were hospitably entertained by Sir William Johnson, and the feasting and speech-making lasted more than seven weeks. "I was much concerned," Sir William subsequently wrote, "by reason of the great consumption of provisions and the heavy expenses attending the maintenance of these Indians, each of whom consumes daily more than two ordinary men amongst us, and would be extremely dissatisfied if stinted when convened for business."[2] The treaty which was finally effected — one of the most notable of its kind in American history — for a consideration of six thousand dollars in money and goods, transferred to the British crown the Indian title to what is now the state of Kentucky, east of the Tennessee River

---

[1] Because of his great influence with the Iroquois, Johnson had been an important figure in the late war. See William E. Griffis, *Sir William Johnson and the Six Nations*, and W. L. Stone, *Life and Times of Sir William Johnson*.

[2] Sir William Johnson to the Earl of Hillsborough, October 23, 1768. O'Callaghan, *New York Colonial Documents*, VIII. 105.

(then known as the Cherokee), and a large part of western Virginia. It also added a large tract of Indian land to western Pennsylvania. In general the line of demarcation between the territory for English use and that reserved for the natives was quite distinctly drawn.[1] Nevertheless, the conviction was strong among the English on both sides of the sea that the Indians by their rebellion had forfeited whatever claim they may have had to the trans-Alleghany country, and that their rights should hereafter be a negligible quantity in the problems of westward expansion. The English government continued to treat the Indians most liberally, but it ceased to pretend that its conduct was guided by motives other than those of good policy.

The Pontiac War represented the last concerted attempt of the red men during the century to save their country from the intrusion of the whites, and the last such uprising of any importance at any time except that led by Tecumseh and his brother, the Prophet, in 1811. Upon this effort they had staked their all. One may sympathize, in a way, with their motives; but all history teaches that the outcome was inevitable, and there are not wanting many and good arguments why it should have been so.[2] Time and time again the settlers in the

---

[1] For Johnson's account of the meeting at Fort Stanwix, with the text of the treaty which was concluded, see O'Callaghan, *New York Colonial Documents*, VIII. 111-157. The treaty and a map to illustrate it are also in the same volume of this collection, pp. 135-137. See Winsor, *Narrative and Critical History*, VI. Ch. IX.

[2] Probably the fairest statement of the right and wrong involved in the displacement of the Indian by the white man is to be found in the pages of Theodore Roosevelt's *Winning of the West*.

West were to be disturbed by isolated outbreaks of the natives; but at the most, these hostile demonstrations caused only temporary lulls in that great westward movement which could not have been withstood had the inhabitants of the country been thrice as numerous and powerful as they were. In the final analysis the conflict between the Indian and the white man in the Middle West was prompted by the utmost contrariety of ideas and practice on the subject of landholding. The native population of the Mississippi Valley was very small, but according to the Indian's way of thinking and acting there was not room for more, especially of an alien race. Great areas of utterly uninhabited country, like the larger part of the present state of Kentucky, were required for hunting expeditions and for battle-grounds of the rival tribes. Indian agriculture was of the most primitive type, and the ties which bound the people to their habitations were correspondingly loose. Had the Indians been gathered in settled communities, in which land was held by a fixed tenure, their dispossession against their will would have been well-nigh indefensible. But under the system which prevailed, the taking of territory unused, if not actually misused, and the devoting of it to the service of the expanding civilization of the East, can hardly be reprobated by even the most extreme humanitarians. The methods of conquest sometimes pursued by the frontiersmen may be heartily condemned, but the ultimate aim of these hardy home-seekers must meet quite generally with approval.

By the time peace was again thoroughly restored in the West, the period of great migration was near its opening.

The strongest impulses of the sort came from Virginia, where the rapid exhaustion of the soil by unscientific tobacco-growing created a perennial hunger for new lands. Many of the Virginians turned southward into the Carolinas for relief, but many more of them looked rather to the West, where were millions of acres of lands awaiting their first opportunity to produce food supplies and other marketable commodities. Among the pioneers were also numerous bands of naturalized foreigners, especially of the Moravian faith. In 1763 the British Parliament had provided by law for the naturalization of all Protestants of foreign birth who had served in the royal army in America, and had purchased lands and settled. The Moravian missionaries had long been active in some of the eastern colonies, especially Pennsylvania, but the unfriendly disposition of their neighbors led them gradually to push farther west into the valley of the Muskingum and other tributaries of the upper Ohio.[1] After the close of the war the routes which had been opened for military purposes were kept in service by streams of emigrants, and it is estimated that between the years 1763 and 1768 not fewer than twenty thousand whites settled across the mountains, although it is to be understood, of course, that but very few of these people got far beyond the eastern brim of the Mississippi Basin. Strong protest

[1] Loskiel, *History of the United Brethren* [London, 1794]. The missionaries called themselves United Brethren, though to people outside their church they were known as Moravians. Winsor considers the house built by the missionary, Christian Frederic Post, on the north side of Tuscarawas Creek, in what is now Starke County, in 1761, to be " probably the first white man's house in the wilds of Ohio." *The Mississippi Basin*, 445. See Fernow, *The Ohio Valley in Colonial Days*, 173, and Parkman, *The Conspiracy of Pontiac*, 128.

was entered by the British authorities against such extensive migration, but quite without effect.[1] The proclamation of 1763 had not been avowedly annulled by the crown, and the colonial governors were admonished to enforce its provisions regarding the settlement of the crown lands. But though threats were repeatedly made, and even soldiers sent in a few cases to expel settlers from the lands they had chosen, the royal prohibition remained substantially a dead letter. Even Washington, who was yet as loyal and law-abiding a subject as King George had, did not scruple to send out his agents and surveyors through the Ohio country to mark out specially desirable tracts, and indicate, by blazing the trees on their bounds, that they had been laid claim to for future patenting.[2]

It was not until the early part of 1765 that the first successful efforts were made by the English to take possession of the left bank of the Mississippi. In February, 1764, Major Arthur Loftus, with a company of perhaps four hundred soldiers who had recently been employed in establishing English authority at Mobile and other points in the Floridas, had attempted to ascend the river from New Orleans for the purpose of supplanting the French with the British flag at Fort Chartres and other posts to the north. But the expedition was attacked and repulsed by Indians, possibly incited by the French,

---

[1] Moses, *Illinois, Historical and Statistical*, 138.
[2] On Washington's speculations in western lands, see Herbert B. Adams, "Maryland's Influence in Founding a National Commonwealth," in the *Maryland Historical Society Publications*, No. XI., Appendix, pp. 72-92, and in the *Johns Hopkins University Studies in Historical and Political Science*, III. 55-77.

when it had gone only so far as Davion's Bluff, or Fort Adams, 240 miles from New Orleans.[1] At the end of his campaign in the Muskingum Valley the following summer, Colonel Bouquet sent a party under Lieutenant Fraser from Fort Pitt to prepare the inhabitants of the Illinois country for transfer to English sovereignty. But this expedition also failed. The French conspired to put Fraser to death, and, strangely enough, it was only by the intervention of Pontiac that he was able to escape down the Mississippi by way of New Orleans and reach the safety of the seaboard colonies.[2] A year later (May, 1765), Sir William Johnson, acting on the recommendation of Bouquet, despatched George Croghan with two boats and several white companions to attempt the task at which Loftus and Fraser had failed.[3] Croghan was a man of such experience and tact that success might well be expected to attend his efforts. He began by preparing to explore and plot the entire course of the Ohio, and though the drawings which he made are not very

[1] D'Abbadie, the French director-general at New Orleans, was said by the commandant Aubry, in a letter to the French government, to have "caused the Indians to be harangued in favor of the English," and to have done all that he could to insure the success of Loftus's expedition. This may very well be true, and yet the suspicion of Loftus that other French officials tampered with the Indians be well founded. Gayarré, *History of Louisiana*, II. 101; Parkman, *The Conspiracy of Pontiac*, 531.

[2] *Michigan Pioneer and Historical Collections*, X. 216.

[3] On the mission of Croghan, see Parkman, *The Conspiracy of Pontiac*, Ch. XXX. The materials for its history are three of Croghan's journals, as follows: (1) the official journal sent to Sir William Johnson, printed in O'Callaghan, *New York Colonial Documents*, VII. 779-788; (2) a topographical journal which appeared in the *Monthly American Journal of Geology and Natural Science*, December, 1831; and (3) a general narrative printed in S. P. Hildreth, *Pioneer History*. These journals are fully characterized in Winsor, *Narrative and Critical History*, VI. 704.

accurate, his account of the fauna and flora of the river's banks is extremely interesting and valuable. Friendly Indians were sent out to bring in all the French traders who remained in the upper part of the valley, and these, when gathered at the mouth of the Scioto, were compelled to take an oath of allegiance to the English government. Their eighteen months of grace had long since expired, and by remaining east of the river they had put themselves inevitably in the way of English citizenship. On the 6th of June Croghan reached the mouth of the Wabash, near which point the expedition was attacked two days later by a band of Kickapoos and Mascotins. The Englishmen had been joined on the upper Ohio by several Delawares, Shawnees, and Iroquois, and the attack by the lower tribes was made on the pretence that they believed the redskin companions of Croghan to be unfriendly Cherokees from the South. The entire party was taken captive and carried within a week to Vincennes, — at this time, according to Croghan, a squalid village containing about eighty Frenchmen and several times as many Indians.[1] Croghan's men became separated, but the commander himself, after being sent up the river to the French post, Ouiatanon, at the Maumee portage, was given his freedom. At this point a great conference was held with the Indian leaders of the West, including Pontiac, with the result that more harmonious relations were established, and Pontiac, appreciating the inevitable-

[1] For the early history of this important French settlement, see Jacob P. Dunn, Jr., "The Founding of Post Vincennes," in the *Magazine of American History*, XXII. 143-158, and the same author's *Indiana*, Ch. II.; William H. Smith, *History of Indiana*, I. Ch. I.; and John B. Dillon, *History of Indiana*, Chs. VI. and VII.

ness of English dominance, made it understood that if plenty of powder, lead, and rum were furnished, the English would thereafter have nothing to fear from his people and their allies. After making promises as safely guarded as possible, Croghan continued his journey down the Maumee, and on the 17th of August reached Detroit, where the allegiance of the assembled Indians was similarly secured. He then went on to Niagara and reported to Johnson that conditions in the West were ripe for the establishment of English supremacy. He had failed in the primary object of his trip, but he had prepared the way for some later comer.

As soon as the report was received, Captain Thomas Stirling was despatched from Fort Pitt with 120 soldiers to complete the work. The expedition met with no resistance, and early in October Fort Chartres, the last to fly the tricolor, was reached. On the 10th of the month the French flag was hauled down, and the commandant, Louis Saint-Ange, gave up his authority.[1] A large proportion of the inhabitants took up their abode

[1] "Minute of the Surrender of Fort Chartres to the English," in O'Callaghan, *New York Colonial Documents*, X. 1161-1165; Correspondence of M. de St. Ange, "Commandant at the Illinois," and M. d'Abbadie, governor of Louisiana, *ibid.*, 1157-1161. On the surrender, see W. L. Stone, *Life and Times of Sir William Johnson*, II. 252; Mason, *Chapters from Illinois History*, 232-238; and Moses, *Illinois, Historical and Statistical*, I. Ch. VIII. On page 134 of the last-named book is a plan of the settlements and Indian villages in the Illinois country, prepared in 1771 by Thomas Hutchins, a captain in the British army. In 1772 Fort Chartres was wholly abandoned by reason of a flood, which washed away a portion of its defences. Its site does not now form part of the bed of the Mississippi, though this is affirmed by both Parkman and Winsor. It is more than a mile from the stream. See Mason, *Chapters from Illinois History*, 242.

across the river at St. Louis where Saint-Ange established his new headquarters,[1] and in 1767 it was estimated that not more than two thousand people of French descent were left on the east side of the Mississippi. More recent investigation, however, seems to warrant us in believing that there never had been many more than that number of Frenchmen in the territory in question. While still at Fort Chartres Captain Stirling was reënforced by a regiment under Major Farmer, which ascended the river from New Orleans, propitiating the natives as it advanced, and using every influence to counteract the French inducements held out to the Chickasaws and Choctaws to cross to the western side and so deprive the English of the benefits of their trade.

Although during the years between the suppression of the Pontiac rebellion and the outbreak of the Revolution the French population remaining east of the Mississippi was nominally subject to English authority, the conditions of frontier life nevertheless allowed the creoles to live on very much as they had done in times before the change of sovereignty. Under the old régime such small measure of political independence as they enjoyed had been due exclusively to their isolation, and they had never learned what it is to exercise by natural or constitutional right the functions of self-government. Hence, despite their first apprehensions, they changed masters with comparative facility. Toward the scarlet-uniformed British officer they were distrustful, and toward the crude backwoodsman from Virginia or Carolina disdainful; but as long as they were undisturbed in property and privileges

[1] Frederic L. Billon (compiler), *Annals of St. Louis*, 25.

of trade they were inclined to make the best of their new political relation. Their resignation was fostered also by the policy of the British commandants on the Illinois and at Vincennes in continuing the old laws and usages, and in general adopting the French system of control in the West. The French language was used in the courts along with the English, and all important documents and records of public transactions were translated into it for the convenience of the creoles. In respect to land allotments also the English followed the practice of the French, *i.e.* that the commandants should exercise the power of granting demesne lands in such quantities as were petitioned for, on the one condition that a portion of the grant be cultivated within a year.[1] The creoles, however, rarely became thrifty agriculturists. They vastly preferred the more exciting pursuits of the trader and trapper. Their half-savage manner of life was fostered by frequent intermarriage with the Indians, and in time their language became a mere corrupt jargon of French and the native dialects. There was much of hardship and peril in their lives; yet with music, dancing, and numerous holiday festivities, they contrived to crowd more pleasure into a year than the average English pioneer got in a lifetime.

Late in June, 1763, Kerlerec, after serving as governor of Louisiana for about ten and a half years, was recalled in disgrace and thrown into the Bastile. He was charged with various indiscretions and crimes in the administra-

---

[1] B. A. Hinsdale, "The Western Land Policy of the British Government from 1763 to 1775," in the *Ohio Archæological and Historical Quarterly*, I. 207-229.

tion of his office, especially with extravagance and embezzlement, and there seems little doubt that he was guilty. From papers preserved in the Archives of the Marine Department it appears that the moral debasement which infected the provincial government was at this time generally characteristic of the populace of Louisiana. Slavery, bribery, drunkenness, brawling, duelling, and prostitution were rife. Fevers and other diseases added greatly to the horrors of life in and around New Orleans. The new governor, Sieur d'Abbadie, was a man of upright character and considerable ability, but his position was indeed an unenviable one. The finances of the province were in hopeless chaos, the subordinate officials were firmly wedded to a system of bribery and plunder, the people were poor and in many cases thriftless.[1] And scarcely was the new administration begun before the treaty of Paris compelled a complete readjustment of relations on the east.

This latter circumstance prevented D'Abbadie from concentrating his efforts upon the settlement of domestic questions as he would have liked to do. Read from its English side the story of the transfer of the eastern Mississippi Valley from France to England differs materially from the French version of it. The English annalists tell us only how irritating and selfish and obnoxious was the conduct of the New Orleans authorities, while the records left by these authorities are fairly

[1] The most important contemporary treatise on Louisiana history, after 1760, is Chevalier de Champigny, "Memoir of the Present State of Louisiana," in French, *Historical Collections of Louisiana*, V. 129-233; on the period from 1762 until the arrival of the Spanish authorities at New Orleans in 1766, *ibid.*, 139-148.

crowded with impeachments of the character, motives, and conduct of the agents of the English. At every point there was controversy, and in all the English were little less than two years in acquiring the possession guaranteed them by the treaty. D'Abbadie's opinion of their methods of procedure is indicated by his declaration that "they never fail on every occasion to harass me with innumerable objections and artifices of the pettiest and most groundless chicanery." Nyon de Villiers, who had forced Washington to surrender at Fort Necessity in 1756 and who was subsequently in command of the Illinois country, wrote as follows to D'Abbadie concerning the dealings of the English with the Indians in that region: "The English, as soon as they became aware of the advantages secured to them by the treaty of cession, kept no measure with the Indians, whom they treated with the harshness and the haughtiness of masters, and whose faults they punished by crucifixion, hanging, and every sort of torments. They wish to wipe away from the minds of the Indians the very recollection of the French name; and, in their harangues to these people, in order to induce them to forego their old attachment for us, they use, in reference to our nation, expressions which are very far from being respectful, not to say gross and rude. I will, however, endeavor to dispose the Indians favorably towards the English, although their hostility to them is very great, and although they refuse to listen to words of peace on this subject."[1] The historian Gayarré well says, "When it is considered that, in the opinion of Villiers, his brother

[1] Gayarré, *History of Louisiana*, II. 98.

Jumonville had been basely assassinated by the English,[1] it must be admitted that his letter, as recorded here, is a monument of his moderation and magnanimity, and is one of the proofs of the more than good faith with which the treaty of cession was executed by the French officers, and another demonstration that the complaints of the English about the obstacles thrown in their way by those officers were not well founded."[2]

Regarding the state of the Louisiana country the new governor wrote to the French ministry, June 7, 1764, as follows: "I have the honor to submit my observations on the character and dispositions of the inhabitants of Louisiana. The disorder long existing in the colony, and particularly in its finances, proceeds from the spirit of jobbing which has been prevalent here at all times, and which has engrossed the attention and faculties of the colonists. It began in 1737, not only on the currency of the country, but also on the bills of exchange, on the merchandise in the king's warehouses, and on everything which was susceptible of it. It is to this pursuit that the inhabitants have been addicted in preference to cultivating their lands, and to any other occupation, by which the prosperity of the colony would have been promoted. . . . If the inhabitants of Louisiana had turned their industry to anything else beyond jobbing on the king's paper and merchandise, they would have found great resources in the fertility of the land and the mildness of the climate. But the facility offered by the country to live on its natural productions

---

[1] During Washington's Great Meadows campaign in 1754.
[2] Gayarré, *History of Louisiana*, II. 99.

has created habits of laziness. Hence the spirit of insubordination and independence which has manifested itself under several administrations. I will not relate the excesses and outrages which occurred under Rochemore and Kerlerec. Notwithstanding the present tranquillity, the same spirit of sedition does not the less exist in the colony. It reappears in the thoughtless expressions of some madcaps, and in the anonymous writings scattered among the public. The uncertainty in which I am, with regard to the ultimate fate of the colony, has prevented me from resorting to extreme measures, to repress such license; but it will be necessary to come to it at last, to reëstablish the good order which has been destroyed, and to regulate the conduct and the morals of the inhabitants."[1]

The more clearly these conditions became understood in France the more determined were the French officials not to let pass the opportunity which the close of the Seven Years' War brought to thrust the burden of governing the province upon the Spanish. However humiliating to national pride, the cession of Louisiana meant only the disencumbering of the national treasury. The undeveloped character of the country, the difficulties of colonization, the constant necessity of bribing the Indians against the English, and the indifferent character of a large part of the inhabitants, rendered the land so profitless that frequently men who had received large grants gave them up as entailing more expense than the income would cover. Louisiana had proved a dead weight in the hands of the great merchant Crozat, and

[1] Gayarré, *History of Louisiana*, II. 104.

he had been glad to rid himself of the burden as early as possible. The Company of the West had buried more than 20,000,000 livres in the wilderness, without a shadow of profit. The French government had squandered between 40,000,000 and 50,000,000 livres in colonization schemes, with only the most discouraging results. And not only had such great capital been consumed uselessly, but from every quarter it was borne in upon the French that if they were even to retain possession of the western Mississippi Valley they must at once devote enormous sums to the increasing of fortifications, strengthening of garrisons, buying the goodwill of the Indians, and the establishing of more satisfactory trade relations between the American interior and Europe. The province itself was financially impotent. At the very time when it was being ceded to Spain by the secret treaty of November 3, 1762, the local officials were repeatedly despatching to the home government that the colony was "in a state of complete destitution," that it was "a chaos of iniquities," and that to reëstablish order therein "it would be necessary to have recourse to measures of an extreme character." It was therefore with slight regret that King Louis wrote to D'Abbadie a letter, April 21, 1764, containing an official communication of the cession of Louisiana to Spain. D'Abbadie was commissioned to "deliver up into the hands of the governor, or of the officer appointed to that effect, the said country and colony of Louisiana, with the settlements or posts thereto appertaining, together with the town and island of New Orleans, such as they may be found on the day of said delivery, it being my will that, for the future, they belong to his Catholic Majesty, to be governed and administered by his governors and officers, as belonging to him, fully, and without reserve and exception."[1] Upon the arrival of a duly accredited agent of Spain the French soldiers and governmental employees were to be immediately withdrawn. D'Abbadie was directed to collect all papers relative to the finances and administration of the colony and carry them in person to Paris, except that papers whose character would render them serviceable to the new magistrates were to be deposited with properly authorized persons at New Orleans.

The king's letter was published in October, 1764. By the colonists the news it contained was received with extreme disfavor. For two years they had alternated between hope and fear, but at last the blow had fallen. Resentment at the transfer of the eastern Mississippi Valley to the English had been strong; but the colonists understood as well as anybody that France had been forced to this move, and besides, as we have seen, the number of Frenchmen east of the river was inconsiderable. But the alienation of Louisiana proper — the main body of the colony — was an event almost wholly unexpected. Unsatisfactory as conditions were, the Louisianians still greatly preferred that the French régime be continued. "As Frenchmen, they felt that a deep wound had been inflicted on their pride by the severing in twain of Louisiana, and the distribution of its mutilated parts

---

[1] "Louis the Fifteenth to M. d'Abbadie," April 21, 1764, in French, *Historical Collections of Louisiana*, V. 143-144. See Gayarré, *History of Louisiana*, II. 110, and Martin, *History of Louisiana*, I. 346.

between England and Spain. As men, they felt the degradation of being bartered away as marketable objects; they felt the loss of their national character and rights, and the humiliation of their sudden transformation into Spaniards or Englishmen without their consent. As colonists, as property owners, as members of a civilized society, they were agitated by all the apprehensions consequent upon a change of laws, manners, customs, habits, and government."[1] D'Abbadie was much chagrined at the turn affairs had taken. No one understood better than he the weaknesses of the colony and the financial outlay that would be necessary to defend it; yet he still conceived it to be possible for France to build up a great self-sustaining dependency between the Mississippi and the Rockies, and he regarded the cession to Spain as not only grossly unjust to Louis XV.'s loyal subjects in America, but as an inexcusable attempt of the court to save money for the time at the expense of future national wealth and prestige. But it was worse than useless to argue the question. The Spaniards were very slow in preparing to take possession, and D'Abbadie died, February 4, 1765, while yet retaining the governorship. He was succeeded in office by Aubry, who for some time had been commander of the royal troops in the colony.

By the English the substitution of Spanish for French dominance west of the Mississippi was hailed with unfeigned delight. The French had long blocked the way to the fullest development of English trade in the West, and as a consequence the feeling between the two peoples along the frontier lines was far from friendly. The wars

[1] Gayarré, *History of Louisiana*, II. 113.

and the removal of the French had considerably thinned the population east of the river, and it was highly important that free access be had to the more numerous peoples on the other side. It was well understood that the Spaniards were less devoted to commerce than the French, and that under their government the English would meet with little rivalry in the control of the Indian trade. "The English," wrote Governor Dobbs of North Carolina, "can now extend their trade beyond the Mississippi and reach the Spaniards of New and Old Mexico, by pushing on our discoverers and traders by the Missouri and the rivers west of the Mississippi, and so secure an open trade to the westward American ocean."[1] Nevertheless, the Spaniards subsequently proved not so easy to deal with as had been expected, and they even succeeded in detaching traffic from the English as far north as Kaskaskia and Detroit; while the question of the right of the English to navigate freely the Mississippi became one of extreme difficulty in the time of the American Revolution.

As soon as the inhabitants of Louisiana became aware of the cession to Spain, they resolved to bring every possible influence to bear on the king to retract the bargain. A convention, in which every parish was represented and which contained many of the ablest men of the colony, was assembled at New Orleans, and a resolution was unanimously adopted supplicating the king not to allow his people thus to be cast off by their mother country. A special committee, headed by Jean Milhet, was despatched to present the colonists' petition to the crown. Milhet's first act after arriving at Paris was to seek out Bienville,

[1] Winsor, *The Mississippi Basin*, 455.

now an old man of eighty-five, but the best friend the colony had in Europe, and secure his coöperation in the representations that were to be made to the Court. Bienville was deeply grieved at the prospect of the alienation of the province which he had done so much to secure for France, and readily consented to join Milhet in an interview with the prime minister, the Duc de Choiseul. When an audience was obtained, Milhet presented the petition and sought with every argument he could command to win a favorable reception for it. Afterwards Bienville made a long and eloquent plea, "like a father suing for the life of his child." But, though Choiseul received the petition with extreme courtesy, he declared it quite impossible to change the course affairs had taken. The tears and entreaties of the broken-hearted Bienville moved the minister to deep sympathy, but he could only close the interview by saying: "Gentlemen, I must put an end to this painful scene. I am deeply grieved at not being able to give you any hope. I have no hesitation in telling you that I cannot address the king on this subject, because I myself advised the cession of Louisiana. Is it not to your knowledge that the colony cannot continue its precarious existence, except at an enormous expense, of which France is now utterly incapable? Is it not better, then, that Louisiana should be given away to a friend and faithful ally, than be wrested from us by an hereditary foe? Farewell, — you have my best wishes. I can do no more."[1] The mission had failed. Milhet waited vainly about the court for some months and then embarked for Louisiana. During his few remaining years the veteran Bienville kept up his

[1] Gayarré, *History of Louisiana*, II. 129.

interest in the colony, but could do nothing to save it from alienation.

The delay of the Spaniards in taking possession at New Orleans encouraged the Louisianians for a year and more to believe that after all the treaty of cession would not be put into effect. Even after Milhet's rebuff this delusion continued to be cherished. But about the middle of July, 1765, the Superior Council received a letter from Don Antonio de Ulloa, containing the information that he had been commissioned by the Spanish king to proceed to New Orleans and assume possession, and that he was already at Havana.[1] The summer and autumn months of 1765 slipped past, and as still Ulloa did not arrive, many of the colonists were again led to believe that the treaty was only a sham intended to cover some diplomatic manœuvre. At last, however, March 5, 1766, the Spanish agent appeared with two companies of infantry and a number of persons who had been commissioned to fill the offices of commissary of war, intendant, comptroller, and treasurer. By the inhabitants he was received respectfully, but sullenly, and without the least show of enthusiasm. Aubry drew up the local militia on the levee and showed the new governor such attention as he could; but the storm of rain and wind which accompanied the landing of the Spaniards was popularly considered a fit inauguration of the new régime. The Superior Council demanded that Ulloa produce evidence of his authority to act for the Spanish king; but he curtly refused, declaring that he proposed to deal only with Governor Aubry, and moreover that he did not intend to assume possession

[1] Champigny, "Memoirs of Louisiana," in French, *Historical Collections of Louisiana*, V. 150.

until satisfactory arrangements should have been made for the passing of a part of the French troops under his command for the continued defence of the colony. However, he proceeded to visit the various posts and settlements of the province and to take a census of their population. The result showed that Louisiana contained 5562 white people, with approximately an equal number of slaves.

The Spanish king could hardly have selected a man of stronger character or more brilliant attainments than Ulloa for the establishment of the Spanish régime in Louisiana. His career had been long and varied, and he had won almost equal laurels in the two great fields of science and administration. At the time of his appointment to the Louisiana post he was commander of the fleet of the Indies and was considered to be better informed on naval affairs than any other Spaniard. His master, Charles III., was above the average of Spanish monarchs in intelligence and force of character, and under the guidance of two such men there was some reason to expect that the change of sovereignty in Louisiana would be accomplished without menace to the inhabitants. In his instructions to Ulloa, King Charles emphasized the fact that Louisiana was not to be subjected to the harsh and restrictive colonial system elsewhere prevailing in the Spanish dominions. "I have resolved," he writes, "that, in that new acquisition, there be no change in the administration of its government, and therefore, that it be not subjected to the laws and usages which are observed in my American dominions, from which it is a distinct colony, and with which it is to have no commerce. It is my will that it be independent of the ministry of the Indies, of its council, and of the other tribunals annexed to it; and that all which may be relative to that colony shall pass through the ministry of state, and that you communicate to me, through that channel alone, whatever may be appertaining to your government."[1] But the inhabitants of the colony continued to be suspicious, and even openly hostile. Every possible obstacle was thrown in the way of the new governor. His plan to redeem the worthless paper currency with which the Louisianians had long been cursed was thwarted. The French soldiers whose services had been promised by their government flatly refused to pass under the command of the Spanish officers. Wherever the proud representatives of the majesty of Castile appeared they were frowned upon and scoffed at.

All this came by way of surprise to Ulloa. In the language of Miss Grace King, "He seems to have approached Louisiana in the same cool, calm, critical spirit of scientific investigation that had actuated him in his recent expedition to determine the configuration of the earth at the equator, and he was about as much prepared to hear that the equator had risen up and protested against the results of his commission, as to find that other purely theoretical factor, the will of the people of Louisiana, in opposition to his presence and functions. He expected the country to change its flag and allegiance, the soldiers their service, the people their nationality, as a thing of the most commonplace of course."[2] Ulloa's whole

---

[1] Gayarré, *History of Louisiana*, II. 258.
[2] Grace King, *New Orleans*, 97. See Champigny's striking characterization of Ulloa, French, *Historical Collections of Louisiana*, V. 152.

political training had been such as to lead him to ignore absolutely in all such transactions the factor of popular sentiment. He had been accustomed to regard the disposition of empires and populations as a divinely bestowed prerogative of monarchs, and under this theory the people were supposed to conduct themselves with due submissiveness, whatever fortune was meted out to them. But even if the Louisianians had possessed the *right* to call in question the decree of their sovereign, Ulloa was at a loss to understand why they should care to do so. The colony, weak and destitute, had been cast off by its mother country without a show of compunction. For half a century the tenure of the French king had conferred no benefit. The burden of administration was understood to be such that Spain, in assuming control, was really bestowing a favor upon the French court. The coming of the Spaniards could certainly not make conditions worse than they had long been, and there was every prospect of a change for the better. The specie of Spain was to be substituted for the stamped paper rags which had long since served their day as currency in the colony. Immediately upon his arrival Ulloa had hastened to make public his instructions to the effect that no changes would take place in the civil organization, or in the laws, customs, and usages, of the province. He had repeatedly asserted that it was both his duty and his most ardent desire to do all in his power to be useful and agreeable to the people. To remove national prejudices he had put the Spanish troops on the same footing with the French, with regard to pay and promotion, and he had endeavored to the best of his ability to conduct himself always as a benevolent governor of the colony and in no sense as a conqueror or despot. In view of all these considerations he could not but feel keenly the open contempt and hostility of the inhabitants. The general aspect of neglect and thriftlessness which was to be observed on every hand tended greatly to increase the new governor's disappointment. With a people suspicious, resentful, indolent, and a country swampy, fever-haunted, undeveloped, he could not look forward to either immediate prosperity or the early inauguration of a more wholesome régime. "From the bottom of my heart I pity you for having been sent to such a country," wrote Kerlerec from the Bastile; and from every other French official who knew from observation the state of the colony came condolences hardly more reassuring.

The refusal of the French troops to enter the Spanish service rendered Ulloa unable to take actual possession of the colony. His own soldiers numbered but ninety, and there was no immediate prospect of gaining reënforcements from Spain. Knowing that his presence at New Orleans but fomented the populace, he withdrew in September, 1766, to the Balize, at the mouth of the Mississippi. His ostensible purpose was to establish a Spanish post in that vicinity, but this done, he remained there more than half a year. The creoles at first believed that he had gone to meet the Spanish troops who were to garrison the colony after its change of masters; but as this proved not to be the case, they concluded that he so despised the people of New Orleans that out of contempt for them preferred to live in the uncouth quarters provided for him at the Balize. As a matter of fact Ulloa was busily engaged with his studies in astronomy and mathematics

and, with characteristic scholarly instincts, was almost lost to the world of politics around him. It may be added, too, that while at the Balize he was awaiting the coming of his affianced bride, the Marquise d'Abrado, a rich and beautiful heiress from Peru, who arrived and became his wife in March, 1767.

During Ulloa's sojourn at the Balize he was frequently visited by Aubry. For several months there had been an understanding between the two to the effect that while the latter should retain the governorship nominally, because of his command of the soldiery, Ulloa should give instructions from time to time and even issue decrees which the French magistrate should enforce. Late in 1766 Ulloa proposed that he should take possession of Louisiana at the Balize, and that the French flag be displaced there as elsewhere by the Spanish. Aubry thought such a course unwise, urging that the ceremony ought to be an impressive one, and should take place nowhere but in New Orleans, in the presence of the masses of the people to be affected by it. Upon Ulloa's insistence, however, Aubry yielded so far as to sign a document by which the Spaniard was put in possession of the province, with the right to substitute the Spanish flag for the French whenever it should please him to do so. The public ceremony of transfer was to be postponed until the arrival of the Spanish troops.[1]

After Ulloa's return to New Orleans the tide of public opinion set in more strongly against him than ever. His manner of living, his tastes, his habits, his conversations,

[1] Champigny in his "Memoir" gives Aubry's account of this arrangement. French, *Historical Collections of Louisiana*, V. 157.

the most trivial matters of his household, were held up public scorn. His wife pursued a course of hauteur an arrogance toward the creole ladies, refused to have any thing to do with New Orleans society, attended mass onl in her private chapel, and by every word and look in creased the jealousy and malignity with which, from he first appearance in the colony, she had been regarded Ulloa was a man of amiable disposition, but withal of rather hasty and nervous temperament; and it was quit impossible for him to conceal his surprise and disgust a the turn affairs had taken. The opposition of the Louisi anians was certainly of a most petty and irritating charac ter. It was not based on any fundamental consideration of right and wrong, but was a matter largely of whim and malicious spite. Under the circumstances Ulloa seems to have held his temper remarkably well.

The crisis was reached with the return of Milhet from Paris in 1768. His long absence had encouraged the people to believe that, despite the first news of failure, he might yet be successful in his mission of saving the colony from alienation. At last he came, however, with nothing more to report than that repeated attempts to present the colonists' petition at court had, without exception, been repulsed. This was the last straw. "Popular disappointment and chagrin flamed into a fury of passion, which swept discretion and judgment before it. There was to be heard in the streets nothing but loud voicings of the hatred of Spain, and the loathing of the yoke about to be put upon them. Calm was completely destroyed from one end of the colony to the other; the wildest excitement prevailed, meetings were held everywhere, in

which heated addresses inflamed still more the violence of feeling."[1] The outcome was that a band of conspirators, which had probably long been organizing in New Orleans, was put directly in the way of executing its deep-laid purpose of expelling the Spaniards from the colony by force. The leaders in the plot were among the most influential men of the city, including Lafrénière, plebeian by birth, but of indomitable energy and ambition; Foucaut, the intendant commissary; Masan, a retired captain of infantry and a wealthy planter; Marquis, a captain in the Swiss troops enlisted in the service of France; Noyan and Bienville, both nephews of the elder Bienville; Doucet, a distinguished lawyer recently from France; and a considerable number of principal merchants. The rendezvous of the conspirators was the elegant villa of Madame Pradel in the upper outskirts of the city, about where Common and Carondelet streets cross to-day. Their first move was to call another meeting of representatives from the parishes. This body formulated an address to the Superior Council, calling upon it to proclaim Ulloa an usurper and order his departure from the colony. This paper was signed by more than five hundred citizens and was scattered throughout the entire country. The Superior Council, stirred by the convention's appeal, issued a decree to the effect that unless Ulloa should produce his credentials before the civil tribunal of the colony within one month, he should be ordered to depart as a public enemy.[2] The Spaniard's sense of dignity and honor

---

[1] Grace King, *New Orleans*, 99.

[2] The decree of the Superior Council is printed in French, *Historical Collections of Louisiana*, V. 164-177, note.

did not permit him to comply with the request, and he at once began preparations to withdraw.

The popular uprising met with no favor from Aubry. In protesting against the action of the Superior Council he declared that, notwithstanding the small force at his disposal, he would, with all his might, oppose Ulloa's departure, had he not been "apprehensive of endangering his life, as well as the lives of all the Spaniards in this country." Although he regretted as much as any one the prospect of Spanish domination, his ideas of military and political subordination were such as to lead him to disapprove thoroughly any attempt of the people by force to escape their doom. He remonstrated with the citizens, portrayed the direful punishments Spain would mete out to them, and endeavored as best he could to incline them to a more submissive course. But his well-intended efforts were in vain. The people were not in a mood to be reasoned with. Perceiving this, Aubry then did what he could to relieve Ulloa's expulsion of its harsher features, — even, indeed, to attach some degree of dignity to it. He assembled all the military strength of the city and escorted the rejected Spanish governor to the levee. A salute was fired in honor of those about to depart, and sentries were stationed to guard Ulloa's ship. All this, however, did not prevent a band of young Frenchmen from hastening the voyage by stealing to the levee in the darkness of the following night and cutting the cables by which the vessel was moored. Ulloa and his suite dropped down the river to await developments.

The committee of citizens which had addressed the Superior Council now drew up a manifesto to their con-

stituents, explaining what they had done and justifying their course.[1] A copy of this document was despatched to the French prime minister, in the hope that such conclusive evidence of the loyalty of the colony would influence a reversal of the mother country's disposal of it. At the same time the new deputies, St. Lette and Lesassier, were ordered to present to Choiseul a formal petition for relief.[2] Ulloa also sent to his government a copy of the Memorial of the Merchants and Planters, accompanied with various imprecations against the leaders in the movement by which he had been banished. "A momentary calm, like the still pause between the blasts of a hurricane, fell over Louisiana and the Louisianians while awaiting a response from France. Surely the king would now reconsider! They had proved their mettle, shown that they would not, could not, pass under Spanish rule. They had committed no violence, but in an orderly, legal manner expelled the intruder. France, at any rate, could not but stand by her sons."[3] Nevertheless, there was much uncertainty as to the result of the appeal. Repeated failures in the past had discouraged even the most sanguine. At this juncture there were not lacking those who favored bidding defiance to both the European powers and transforming Louisiana into an independent republic, and Noyan de Bienville made a secret journey to Pensacola to sound the British agent there on the probable atti-

---

[1] "Memorial of the Merchants and Planters of Louisiana on the Events of the 29th of October, 1768," French, *Historical Collections of Louisiana*, V. 218-230, note.

[2] This so-called "Petition of the Colonists and Merchants to the King" is printed in French, *Historical Collections of Louisiana*, V. 178-179, note.   [3] Grace King, *New Orleans*, 105.

tude of his government in event of such action. But the project met with such discouragement from this quarter as to end it without further question. The Englishman rebuffed the republican emissary with scant courtesy, and lost no time in transmitting to Spain the facts concerning the movement which he had gathered from Bienville.[1]

On the morning of July 24, 1769, the whole town of New Orleans was thrown into a commotion by the arrival of a messenger who came post haste from the Balize with the news that a great armament, under command of Count Alexander O'Reilly, lieutenant-general of the armies of Spain, had just made its appearance at the mouth of the Mississippi and was ready to advance to the conquest, if necessary, of the province. This meant that the last hope of the Louisiana French that the treaty of cession would be abrogated was shattered. Petitions, entreaties, speeches, memorials, manifestoes, conspiracies, theories of government — all had gone for nothing, and the defenceless city of three thousand people lay awaiting whatsoever retribution the angered Spaniard might wish to visit upon her. "But whence," writes the chronicler Champigny in his *Memoir*, "comes this general murmur throughout the city? They [the inhabitants] whisper, they dare not raise their voice, they come and go without knowing what they do. Pallor sits on every face, and tears soon begin to flow. Sobs stifle cries of grief. I share in the general fright. I ask the cause of this public alarm, of the frightful evil with which each seems overpowered. 'We are lost,' says a citizen to me; 'our king abandons us; the Spaniards are at

---

[1] Champigny's "Memoir," in French, *Historical Collections of Louisiana*, V. 178-183.

the Balize, and are coming to take possession of the colony.'"[1] A hurried consultation among the late conspirators was held, and it was decided that, in view of the overwhelming strength of the Spanish fleet, the only practicable course was to submit as gracefully as possible, and by good conduct atone for the indignities shown Ulloa and his companions.[2] On the advice of Aubry, Lafrénière, Milhet, and Marquis accompanied the Spanish messenger down the river in order to obtain an early interview with O'Reilly, and present due apologies for the recent acts of insubordination in the colony. The three men were received with extreme courtesy, and Lafrénière as spokesman was encouraged by O'Reilly's apparent fair-mindedness to place the blame for Ulloa's expulsion on the Spaniards rather than on the men who had really been responsible for the uprising. O'Reilly was given to understand that the Louisianians were now unanimous in their loyalty to their new master, the king of Spain, and that, but for Ulloa's high-handed conduct, possession might have been taken long before.

The Spanish fleet of twenty-four vessels arrived at the New Orleans levee August 18. Already Aubry had assembled the terrified citizens in the open square, or Place d'Armes, and urged prompt and complete submission, with the result that, when the Spaniards appeared, there

---

[1] Champigny's "Memoir," in French, *Historical Collections of Louisiana*, V. 182.

[2] The most notable advocate of this policy was the Attorney-General Lafrénière. Champigny gives an interesting sketch of a speech by Lafrénière to the people of New Orleans, in which the plan of conciliation was recommended. French, *Historical Collections of Louisiana*, V. 184–190.

were no demonstrations whatever of opposition. At noon of the 18th all the militia and royal troops of the city were gathered in the Place d'Armes, facing the river, in order that their presence might lend dignity to the ceremony about to occur. The proceedings which followed are thus admirably sketched by Miss King in her valuable book on New Orleans: "Count O'Reilly, in all the pomp of representative majesty, heralded by music, preceded by silver maces, and followed by a glittering staff, descended the gangway from his ship to the levee, and, advancing to Aubry, presented his credentials from the king of Spain, and his orders to receive the colony. Three thousand Spanish soldiers filed after him from the other vessels to the levee, and formed on the three sides of the Place. The credentials and powers were read aloud to the citizens assembled, an anxious, nervous crowd. Aubry, after a proclamation releasing the colonists from their allegiance to France, presented the keys of the city to O'Reilly. The French flag was lowered, the Spanish raised; the Spanish vessels saluted with their guns, the soldiers fired off their muskets and shouted '*Viva el Rey.*' The French guards were relieved by Spanish guards. The Spanish and French officers, then in procession, crossed the open space to the cathedral, where a *Te Deum* was celebrated. The ceremonies terminated with a grand parade of the Spanish troops, whose stern bearing, rigid discipline, and glittering equipments awed the crowds on the banquettes of the streets through which they passed."[1]

[1] Grace King, *New Orleans*, 109. For other accounts of the inauguration of the Spanish régime, and the administrative work of O'Reilly, see

The inauguration of Spanish sovereignty was now an accomplished fact; it remained but to be seen what would be the effect upon the colony. O'Reilly established himself in one of the most commodious houses in the city, where great numbers of the inhabitants sought him to tender their submission. For the most part, his demeanor was genial, and for a few days the people dared hope that no notice would be taken of their recent insubordination. But O'Reilly was not the man to pass by such offences lightly. As a mere youth he had abandoned his native country, discouraged by the disabilities suffered by Catholics there, and had sought fame and fortune in the service of Spain. He was a man of courage, resolution, and administrative ability, but all his education, military and political, had been Spanish; and he came to Louisiana in 1768 with a firm determination to bring order by force out of the chaos which had there existed during the past three years. The speedy submission of the colonists saved them from violence, but it was far from O'Reilly's intention that Ulloa's expulsion should go unavenged.

On the 21st of August the new governor held a grand levee, to which Lafrénière, Masan, Marquis, Doucet, and the other ringleaders of the conspiracy were invited. As soon after the arrival at the viceregal hotel as opportunity was afforded, O'Reilly asked them to follow him into an adjoining room, where he immediately threw off the disguise of hospitality, denounced his guests as rebels

King and Ficklen, *History of Alabama*, 121-128; Martin, *History of Louisiana*, II. Ch. I.; and Champigny's "Memoir," in French, *Historical Collections of Louisiana*, V. 191-233.

and traitors, and gave orders to the guards for their imprisonment. Twelve men, in all, were arrested. In a few days the trials began. Two of the prisoners were released on the ground that at the time of the conspiracy they held commissions under the French government and were therefore accountable for their deeds only to that government. The other ten attempted no defence. They refused to recognize the lawful jurisdiction of the tribunal before which they were arraigned, claiming that as they were French citizens at the time when the alleged misdemeanor was committed they should be tried, if at all, only in French courts. The Spanish officers refused absolutely to admit their plea, and three days after the arrest O'Reilly was ready to pronounce sentence.[1] Five of the conspirators, including Lafrénière and Noyan de Bienville, were condemned to be hanged; one was to be imprisoned for life, two were to be imprisoned for twelve years, and three for six years. One of the twelve, Villieré, had already been killed by his prison guards. The property of all was confiscated for the benefit of the king's treasury. Every appeal of the citizens in behalf of the condemned men was received by O'Reilly with cold courtesy, but with absolutely no favor. On the 25th of October the sentence was carried into effect in the barracks yard. In the presence of several Spanish officers and soldiers the five who had been condemned to death by hanging were shot instead, for the lack of an official hangman.

[1] Champigny gives a good account of the arrest and trial of the unfortunate Frenchmen, French, *Historical Collections of Louisiana*, V. 194-216. The sentence of O'Reilly's court, *ibid.*, 210-212, note.

By this tragedy the worst fears of the people of the colony were confirmed. The suave, affable O'Reilly was after all but a kind of gracious-appearing fiend who might be expected to wreak his vengeance upon any one at any hour. Not only horror for what had happened, but dire terror of what was likely to follow, everywhere prevailed. No one felt safe, business was almost wholly suspended, and the citizens were almost afraid to speak to each other lest they be accused of plotting insurrection. The city lay helpless in the hands of the soldiery, by whom it was guarded at every point of possible outbreak. It was only by slow degrees that the people recovered from the blow and turned sorrowfully again to their wonted occupations. Even to this day the 25th of October, 1769, is remembered by the creole population of the South as the darkest ever experienced by the city of New Orleans. The heroic devotion of the Louisianians to their mother country, and the cruel fate to which they were so heartlessly abandoned, inspired the keen-tongued Vergennes at a later time to address King Louis with cutting sarcasm: "Ah, Sire! perhaps the names of these five unfortunate Frenchmen who were executed never came to the ears of your Majesty; deign to throw a few flowers on their tomb; deign to say, 'Lafrénière, Noyan, Caresse, Villeré, Marquis, and Milhet, were massacred by the orders of barbarous O'Reilly for having regretted leaving my service and for having wished to sustain my laws.'"

In the following vigorous passage François-Xavier Martin, one of Louisiana's earliest and best historians, has pronounced upon O'Reilly's execution of the Frenchmen a judgment which still stands without manifest need of revision: "Posterity, the judge of men in power, will doom this act to public execration. No necessity demanded, no policy justified it. Ulloa's conduct had provoked the measures to which the inhabitants had resorted. During nearly two years he had haunted the province as a phantom of dubious authority. The efforts of the colonists to prevent the transfer of their natal soil to a foreign prince originated in their attachment to their own, and the Catholic king ought to have beheld in their conduct a pledge of their future devotion to himself. They had but lately seen their country severed, and a part of it added to the dominion of Great Britain; they had bewailed their separation from their friends and kindred; and were afterwards to be alienated, without their consent, and subjected to a foreign yoke. If the indiscretion of a few of them needed an apology, the common misfortune afforded it." [1]

To his government O'Reilly justified his course on the ground that the disaffected state of the colony called for some such severe exercise of discipline. He even urged that by terrifying the inhabitants into submission he was performing an act of mercy, since he might thereby discourage them from emulating the example, and ultimately incurring the fate, of those recently put to death. If his purpose was to reduce the colony to abject submission, he had undeniably succeeded. Henceforth the people endured their wrongs in silence. Sadly but unresistingly they saw the Spanish yoke fastened upon them. The Superior Council was swept away, and in its stead was established a "cabildo," with all the accompanying offices and insti-

[1] Martin, *History of Louisiana*, II. 7-8.

tutions characteristic of Spanish administration.[1] The Spanish language was made the official medium of communication, and even the Ursuline nuns were compelled to use it in their devotions. The judicial system was reconstructed, and in fact every phase of governmental activity and public life underwent change. The province of Louisiana was destined to be handed back and forth among the nations yet several times before it should find its permanent place under the flag of the United States, but on no similar occasion was there as complete and speedy a revolution in the political and administrative system as now.

Notwithstanding acts of ferocity which cannot be excused on any ground, O'Reilly gave the colony a fairly good government. He never ceased to be extremely unpopular, and between his people and the creoles only the scantiest social relations were maintained. Nevertheless, the new governor studied the interests of Louisiana and in many ways advanced her material prosperity. Especially were the finances of the colony benefited. Emigration from Spain set in, and there was a considerable increase of population. At the end of a year and three months O'Reilly fell into disgrace with the home government and was removed from his office. Don Luis de Unzaga became the successor in August, 1770. By this time the affairs of the province had become quite

---

[1] For the political and administrative features of the new Spanish system, see the "Ordinances and Instructions of Don Alexander O'Reilly," under date of November 25, 1769, in French, *Historical Collections of Louisiana*, V. 254-268; for the judicial system, "Instructions as to the Manner of instituting Suits, Civil and Criminal, and of pronouncing Judgments in General," *ibid.*, 269-288.

well adjusted to the new régime, and for some years its people enjoyed a much-needed era of quiet prosperity.

Meanwhile England's acquisition of the eastern half of the Mississippi Valley had inaugurated a new epoch in the westward advance of the seaboard population. Possession, hitherto uncertain by reason of French counterclaims, was now entirely secure. In 1769 Daniel Boone, with five companions, passed through Cumberland Gap and opened up the way to the blue grass region of Kentucky. The adventures of Boone were so characteristic of English pioneering in the West during the decade preceding the Revolution that it may be of interest to quote from what purports to be an autobiographical journal kept by this most interesting of all explorers in the lands on the further Ohio. "It was on the first of May, in the year 1769," he tells us, "that I resigned my domestic happiness for a time, and left my family and peaceable habitation on the Yadkin River in North Carolina, to wander through the wilderness of America, in quest of the country of Kentucke, in company with John Finley, John Stewart, Joseph Holden, James Monay, and William Cool. We proceeded successfully, and after a long and fatiguing journey through a mountainous wilderness, in a westward direction, on the seventh day of June following, we found ourselves on Red-River, where John Finley had formerly been trading with the Indians, and, from the top of an eminence, saw with pleasure the beautiful level of Kentucke. . . . In this forest, the habitation of beasts of every kind natural to America, we practised hunting with great success until the twenty-second day of December following.

"This day [December 22] John Stewart and I had a pleasing ramble, but fortune changed the scene in the close of it. . . . In the decline of the day, near Kentucke River, as we ascended the brow of a small hill, a number of Indians rushed out of a thick cane-brake upon us, and made us prisoners. The time of our sorrow was now arrived, and the scene fully opened. The Indians plundered us of what we had, and kept us in confinement seven days, treating us with common savage usage. During this time we discovered no uneasiness or desire to escape, which made them less suspicious of us; but in the dead of night, as we lay in a thick cane-brake by a large fire, when sleep had locked up their senses, my situation not disposing me for rest, I touched my companion and gently awoke him. We improved this favourable opportunity, and departed, leaving them to take their rest, and speedily directed our course towards our old camp, but found it plundered, and the company dispersed and gone home. About this time my brother, Squire Boon, with another adventurer, who came to explore the country shortly after us, was wandering through the forest, determined to find me, if possible, and accidentally found our camp. . . . We were then in a dangerous, helpless situation, exposed daily to perils and death amongst savages and wild beasts, not a white man in the country but ourselves.

"We continued not in a state of indolence, but hunted every day, and prepared a little cottage to defend us from the winter storms. We remained there undisturbed during the winter; and on the first day of May, 1770, my brother returned home to the settlement by himself, for a new recruit of horses and ammunition, leaving me by myself, without bread, salt or sugar, without company of my fellow-creatures, or even a horse or dog. I confess I never before was under greater necessity of exercising philosophy and fortitude. . . . Thus, through an uninterrupted scene of sylvan pleasures, I spent the time until the 27th day of July following, when my brother, to my great felicity, met me, according to appointment, at our old camp. Shortly after, we left this place, not thinking it safe to stay there longer, and proceeded to Cumberland River, reconnoitring that part of the country until March, 1771, and giving names to the different waters. Soon after, I returned home to my family with a determination to bring them as soon as possible to live in Kentucke, which I esteemed a second paradise, at the risk of my life and fortune. I returned safe to my old habitation, and found my family in happy circumstances. I sold my farm on the Yadkin, and what goods we could not carry with us; and on the twenty-fifth day of September, 1773, bade a farewell to our friends, and proceeded on our journey to Kentucke, in company with five families more, and forty men that joined us in Powel's Valley, which is one hundred and fifty miles from the now settled parts of Kentucke."[1]

[1] While the substance of this narrative is undoubtedly Boone's, its literary form was given it by John Filson, a Pennsylvania school-teacher and surveyor who settled in Kentucky just after the Revolution. The book in which the account appears is known as Filson's *Discovery, Settlement, and Present State of Kentucke* [Wilmington, 1784]. The above quotation is taken from a revised edition of 1793, pp. 324–362 *passim*. It is reprinted in Hart, *American History Told by Contemporaries*, II. 383–385. On the career of Boone, see Thwaites, *Daniel Boone;* Emerson Hough, *The Way to the West*, and the *Lives of Three Early Americans* [Boone,

In the autumn of 1770, about the time that Boone and his five comrades were exploring the region of the river Cumberland, Washington, with Croghan as a guide, and accompanied by a surveyor named Crawford, made his way down the Ohio to the mouth of the Kanawha, observing most carefully all the resources and possibilities of the country brought under view.[1] More and more was he becoming interested in the exploitation of the fine western lands which had been won in 1763. Unlike Boone, the McAfee brothers, Simon Kenton, and the many other daring men who were now pressing rapidly into the wilderness, Washington was a man of strong home attachments, and there is no reason to think that he ever contemplated migration beyond the Alleghanies. But, though his great field of labor lay distinctly in the extreme East, no American statesman of the early period, except perhaps Benjamin Franklin and Thomas Jefferson, served the true interests of the back country nearly so well, or used his unreserved influence half so intelligently to foster English expansion beyond the Alleghany barrier.

Close in the wake of the explorers and surveyors came

Crockett, and Carson]; Roosevelt, *The Winning of the West*, I. Ch. VI.; Winsor, *The Westward Movement*, Ch. IV.; N. S. Shaler, *Kentucky*, Ch. VI.; John P. Hale, "Daniel Boone," in the *Southern Historical Magazine*, I. 205-222; Cecil B. Hartley, *Life and Times of Boone;* J. H. Perkins, "Pioneers of Kentucky," in the *North American Review*, January, 1846; J. M. Peck, *Daniel Boone* [Sparks's Library of American Biography, XIII.]; and Timothy Flint, *Daniel Boone*. See William H. Miner's *Contribution toward a Bibliography of Writings concerning Daniel Boone*, published by the Dibdin Club, New York, 1901.

[1] See C. W. Butterfield (ed.), *The Washington-Crawford Letters concerning Western Lands*. An extract from the journal of the tour to the Ohio in 1770 is printed in the *Old South Leaflets*, No. XLI.

the settlers. A hardy, dauntless race of men they were, and such, indeed, they needed to be, — "men," as Mr. Hosmer has well written, "of sinews of iron and invincible spirits, matching the Indians in forest prowess, becoming sometimes as cruel, but constituting the effective cutting edge with which the wilderness was to be cleft and cleared."[1] Indians were to be fought and driven from their lands, forests were to be hewn down, homes were to be established, and the rudimentary functions of society developed. Government, too, was to be provided for; and in 1772, on the banks of the Watauga, a tributary of the Tennessee, was framed the first written constitution drawn up in the Mississippi Valley. The Watauga settlers occupied a tract of land which had been yielded to them by the friendly Cherokees. The leading spirits of the colony were James Robertson, a Scotch-Irishman (as were very many of these early pioneers of the West), and John Sevier, a Huguenot of gentlemanly birth. Robertson was illiterate, until his wife taught him to read and write, but Sevier had a good education, and was a friend and correspondent of no less important personages than Franklin and Madison. Both Robertson and Sevier had the one sort of ability absolutely indispensable to men in their positions — they knew how to preserve peace with the Indians as long as it was possible, and when it became impossible, they knew equally well how to make every iota of the fighting force of the settlers count for success. The Watauga constitution provided for an elective legislature which met at Robertson's cabin on an island in the Watauga River. It provided, too, that

[1] James K. Hosmer, *Short History of the Mississippi Valley*, 65.

this legislature should choose a committee of five men, including Robertson and Sevier, to exercise a variety of delegated judicial and executive powers. There was a clerk to keep records and a sheriff to serve warrants and make arrests. The duties of all these functionaries were carefully and simply prescribed, with a view purely to practical efficiency. The constitution continued in force six years. At the end of that time the state of North Carolina, by virtue of her claim to the Watauga territory, dissolved the independent Watauga government and set up in its stead a dependency known as Washington County. In effect the change was hardly noticeable for many years, even the board of five executors being a long time continued as before. Such events as the forming of the Watauga Association by the voluntary consent of a group of Tennessee pioneers, cast for the time being upon their own resources, testify in a striking manner to the deep-rooted political instinct of the Anglo-Saxon and Scotch-Irish peoples, and likewise to their peculiar fitness for the establishing of civilization in the wilderness places of the earth.[1]

In 1774 there came on what was generally known in the West as Lord Dunmore's war, a conflict which, though

---

[1] On the Watauga settlement, see Winsor, *The Westward Movement*, Ch. VI.; Roosevelt, *The Winning of the West*, I. 170-193; G. C. Broadhead, "Settlements West of the Alleghanies prior to 1776," in the *Magazine of American History*, XXIX. 332-337; F. J. Turner, "Western State-Making in the Revolutionary Era," in the *American Historical Review*, I. 76-78; Hosmer, *Short History of the Mississippi Valley*, 68-69; John Haywood, *Civil and Political History of the State of Tennessee*, Ch. II.; J. G. M. Ramsey, *Annals of Tennessee to the End of the Eighteenth Century*, Ch. II.; C. L. Hunter, *Sketches of Western North Carolina* [Raleigh, 1877]; and James Phelan, *History of Tennessee*, Ch. III.

begun ostensibly in the interest of the settlers in the Ohio country, was so conducted that it had not a little to do with determining the hostility of the western Indians toward the colonists in the forthcoming Revolution. The trouble had its origin in the jealousies of certain eastern states, especially Pennsylvania and Virginia, regarding the possession of domains in the West and the control of lines of communication with them. The point most hotly contested by the rival colonies was old Fort Duquesne, now known as Pittsburg, at the head of the Ohio.[1] In 1774 the place was held by the Virginians, though Pennsylvania roundly contended that it and all the neighboring country was justly hers. In 1767 a company promoted by Sir William Johnson of New York, Benjamin Franklin of Pennsylvania, the latter's son, Governor Franklin of New Jersey, and Thomas Walpole, a London banker, had been organized to obtain control of the territory lying between the Alleghanies and the Ohio with the ultimate purpose of establishing a settlement. The king and Lord Hillsborough, head of the Board of Trade and Plantations, had objected to the scheme on the ground that such an enterprise would attract too many people from Ireland, entail new expenses on the crown, and constitute a departure from the favorite policy of discouraging colonization beyond the Alleghanies.[2] After

[1] On this controversy, see James Tilghman, "Thoughts on the Situation of the Inhabitants on the Frontier," in the *Pennsylvania Magazine of History*, X. 316 ; Daniel Agnew, *History of the Region of Pennsylvania North of the Ohio and West of the Allegheny River* [Philadelphia, 1887] ; and William P. Palmer, *Calendar of Virginia State Papers*, I. 375.

[2] Sparks, *Franklin's Writings*, IV, 236, 303, and 324, and *Writings of Washington*, II, 483. See George H. Alden, *New Governments West of the Alleghanies before 1780* [Bulletin of the University of Wisconsin], Ch. II.

the conclusion of the treaty of Fort Stanwix, however, and the consequent pushing back of the Indian frontier from the Alleghanies to the Ohio, the government was finally brought to the point of making the desired concession, which was done, August 14, 1772. The Walpole Grant, as it was called, resulted in no settlement, but it aroused no little anxiety on part of the royal governor of Virginia, Lord Dunmore, who saw in it an attempt to carve a new province out of the territory claimed to be within his own jurisdiction. At Pittsburg feeling was so bitter that the Pennsylvanians and Virginians were on the point of plunging into civil war. To a man as intensely partisan to Virginia's interests as was Dunmore, the necessity for action was obvious. Besides being jealous, however, Dunmore was shrewd and diplomatic. Instead of striking directly at the encroachments of the northern colonists upon the Ohio, he cast about for a less audacious but equally effective method of attaining his ends. It was not necessary to search far. For some years the Virginia settlers in the West had been clamoring for aid against the Indians. Pittsburg was an obvious base of operations for the entire Ohio Valley, and Dunmore quickly framed the policy of making it the headquarters and starting-point of a large expedition for the reduction of the western Indians to submission. If he could achieve the brilliant success in this campaign for which he hoped, the very use of Pittsburg as its base would go far toward determining the English government to look with favor upon the Virginian claim. Moreover, such a campaign might still further ingratiate its leader and participants with the government, if perchance it should have any tendency to divert the thought of the colonists from their grievances against the mother country and put a check upon their growing talk of resistance.

The story of Lord Dunmore's war cannot be told in detail here.[1] It contains some of the darkest and most grewsome pages in all the history of the American frontier. The immediate pretext upon which it was begun was an attack by some Cherokees, in April, 1774, upon three rangers employed by an obscure backwoods trader by the name of Butler. Dr. John Connally, the representative of Lord Dunmore, at once ordered all the frontiersmen to prepare for a war of extermination. Captain Michael Cresap, son of a bushranger friend of Washington, and leader of a considerable band of explorers on the Ohio, stirred up bad blood in a most reckless manner by killing two Shawnee agents of Butler, and then making his way to the camp of Logan, an influential Iroquois ally of the English, with the evident intention of attacking it. Though the latter plan was abandoned, it was not long until another party of twenty men, led by a certain Greathouse, murdered ten Indians, including a number of Logan's relatives, and war broke upon the frontier without further delay. Pennsylvania coolly held aloof, while Virginia was forced to bear the brunt of it all.

[1] For accounts of Lord Dunmore's war, see Winsor, *The Westward Movement*, Ch. V.; Moore, *The Northwest under Three Flags*, 185–194; Caleb Atwater, *History of Ohio*, 110–125; Roosevelt, *The Winning of the West*, I. 211–239; Winsor, *Narrative and Critical History*, VI. 707–715; Monette, *History of the Mississippi Valley*, I. 368–385; Charles Whittlesey, *Discourse relating to the Expedition of Dunmore* [Cleveland, 1842]; and the *American Archives*, 4th Series, I. *passim*.

The main incident of the campaign which ensued was the exceedingly destructive battle fought October 10 by one of Dunmore's armies, commanded by General Andrew Lewis, and the Indians, led by the Shawnee chief, Cornstalk, at Pleasant Point, at the junction of the Kanawha with the Ohio. The forces engaged were about equal — eleven hundred to the side — and the result was indecisive. The Indians withdrew from the conflict, but only by reason of their characteristic policy of saving their men in preference even to winning a pronounced victory, if costly. After the battle a council was held for the purpose of concluding peace. The Iroquois Logan flatly refused to take any part in the proceedings, and when specially summoned by Dunmore, sent the following striking reply, described by one writer as the greatest of Indian prose elegies:[1] "I appeal to any white man to say if ever he entered Logan's cabin hungry and he gave him not meat, if ever he came cold and naked and he clothed him not. During the course of the last long and bloody war Logan remained idle in his cabin, an advocate for peace. Such was my love for the whites that my countrymen pointed as they passed, and said, 'Logan is the friend of white men.' I had even thought to have lived with you, but for the injuries of one man. Colonel Cresap, last spring, in cold blood and unprovoked, murdered all the relations of Logan, not even sparing my women and children. There runs not a drop of my blood in the veins of any living creature. This called on me for revenge. I have sought it. I have killed many. I have fully glutted my vengeance. For my country I rejoice at the

[1] Moore, *The Northwest under Three Flags*, 191.

beams of peace; but do not harbor a thought that mine is the joy of fear. Logan never felt fear. He will not turn on his heel to save his life. Who is there to mourn for Logan? Not one!"[1]

Nevertheless, Logan as well as Cornstalk gave consent to the terms of peace arranged by the majority of the council, and the conflict was at an end. Dunmore returned to Virginia, making it appear at least that he had won all the laurels that could be obtained in a frontier war. But the almost immediate outbreak of the Revolution precluded the realizing of any of his deep-laid plans regarding the Ohio country; and in truth it was not long until the doughty British governor became so obnoxious to the belligerent colonists that he was unceremoniously expelled from the commonwealth.

By the year 1775, when war began between England and her American colonies, conditions on the frontier had become, if anything, more confused than ever before. The conclusion of Lord Dunmore's war was followed by a considerable increase in migration to the West, the most notable incident of which was the founding of the colony of Transylvania in Kentucky. Early in 1775, Colonel Richard Henderson, by the treaty of Watauga, acquired from the Cherokee Indians for a consideration of £10,000 in goods, a fine tract of land between the

---

[1] This message is given in Jefferson, *Notes on the State of Virginia* [London, 1787], 105, and in Moore, *The Northwest under Three Flags*, 191. It is now understood that Cresap was not directly responsible for the death of Logan's relatives, but Logan himself evidently thought he was. See Brantz Mayer, "Logan the Indian and Cresap the Pioneer," *Maryland Historical Society Publications* for 1857, and O'Callaghan, *New York Colonial Documents*, VIII. 459–477.

Kentucky and Cumberland rivers.[1] Though the Cherokee chieftain declared the territory to be very "dark and bloody ground," certain to bring disaster to its inhabitants, Henderson was quite undaunted. Daniel Boone, who had been employed in the negotiation of the cession, was despatched with thirty men "to mark out a road in the best passage from the settlement through the wilderness to Kentucke,"[2] the result being the clearing of the so-called Boone's, or Wilderness, Road. In a short time four new settlements were made—Boonesborough at a salt lick on the south side of the Kentucky River, April 1,[3] and shortly after it Harrodsburg, Boiling Springs, and Logan's Station. As described by Mr. Hosmer, these posts were "in each case a little group of cabins under the shelter of a blockhouse. Rows of palisades sometimes connected house with house about a square, so that all were enclosed, each door opening upon a central space, a little stronghold which it was quite certain would need to be defended."[4] A government

---

[1] William P. Palmer (ed.), *Calendar of Virginia State Papers*, I. 282-287.

[2] John Filson, *The Discovery, Settlement, and Present State of Kentucke* (ed. 1793), 335. See Thomas Speed, "Wilderness Road, a Description of the Route of Travel by which the Pioneers and First Settlers First came to Kentucky," in the publications of the Filson Club of Louisville, No. II.

[3] See James T. Moorehead, *Address in Commemoration of the First Settlement at Boonesborough* [Frankfort, 1840], with illustrations, and George W. Ranck, "Boonesborough; its Founding, Pioneer Struggles, Indian Experiences, Transylvania Days, and Revolutionary Annals," in the *Filson Club Publications*, No. XVI.

[4] James K. Hosmer, *Short History of the Mississippi Valley*, 72. On the Transylvania colony, see Roosevelt, *The Winning of the West*, I. 248-267; F. J. Turner, "Western State-Making in the Revolutionary Era,"

was set up on a plan quite similar to that of Watauga, with courts, laws, a militia, and executive and judicial officers. But like Watauga, the little commonwealth of Transylvania was doomed to a very brief independent existence. The land on which it was located was a part of the vast western claims of Virginia, and in 1778 the authority of that state formally annulled the Transylvania constitution and substituted for it a dependent relation similar to that which North Carolina in the same year imposed upon Watauga. There was this difference, however, that while Watauga desired continued autonomy, or in lieu of that, annexation to Virginia, the Transylvanians, through their agents, Gabriel John Jones and George Rogers Clark, actively sought the extension of Virginian authority over them as a measure of defence against the treacherous Cherokees. From Transylvania was created the new county of Kentucky, and through her able governor, Patrick Henry, the successor of Dunmore, Virginia engaged herself to do all that the exigencies of the war with the British would allow to foster and protect so promising a stronghold of her interests in the West.

Meanwhile the course of the Revolutionary War was gravely influencing conditions on the frontiers. Though population there was sparse, there were representatives of all the important factors in the great contest — British soldiers holding the posts like Kaskaskia, Cahokia,

in the *American Historical Review*, I. 77–82; George W. Ranck, "Boonesborough," in the *Filson Club Publications*, No. XVI.; George H. Alden, *New Governments West of the Alleghanies before 1780*, Ch. IV.; Ramsey, *Annals of Tennessee*, Chs. II. and III.; and Winsor, *The Westward Movement*, 97–100. For official documents pertaining to Transylvania, see Palmer, *Calendar of Virginia State Papers*, I. 304–311.

Vincennes, and Detroit, which had been obtained from the French in 1763; American immigrants from Virginia and the Carolinas, mostly hostile to the British and ready to take sides with the seaboard states against them; and, finally, the French *habitans*, who had preferred to remain on English soil after 1763 rather than remove to the western bank of the Mississippi. The number of these peoples is very uncertain, but it is estimated that at the beginning of 1775 there were about three hundred whites in Kentucky, with probably as many more in Tennessee. Exclusive of Spanish New Orleans, there were probably not more than twenty-five hundred French east of the Mississippi. By this time the Indians had come to understand that it was not the English government and its agents, but the restless people of the eastern colonies, that were responsible for the great encroachments of the past decade upon the hunting-grounds of the West; and therefore from the earliest intimation of war between the British and the colonists, the native population, almost without exception, avowed its sympathy with the cause of the former. From 1775 on, the Indians became increasingly hostile, and massacres and raids occurred with distressing frequency.

It was in this phase of the western situation that George Rogers Clark, one of the most active men of the time, saw the necessity of a great campaign in Indiana and Illinois, for the double purpose of stripping the British of their Indian allies and supplementing in a very real manner the larger efforts which were being made in the East. Clark was a Virginian who had figured in Lord Dunmore's war, and in 1776 had settled in the Transylvania colony in

Kentucky. He, with Gabriel Jones, had been elected to the Virginia legislature to represent Transylvania and, though not allowed to vote in the body, had been able, against the wish of Colonel Henderson, but in accord with the desires of his other constituents, to secure the organization of Kentucky as a county of Virginia. This service was rendered in the year 1777. When Clark returned to the West, he found that the Indian problem had recently been greatly aggravated. British agents had set themselves deliberately to stir the natives to outbreaks against the frontiersmen, and to reward them with presents in proportion to the number of scalps they were successful in securing. Governor Henry Hamilton, in command at Detroit, had already won the epithet "hair-buyer" by reason of his complicity with the Indians in their scalping raids, and other agents of the British at Kaskaskia, Vincennes, and Cahokia — not necessarily cruel men in themselves, but acting under orders from above — had gained an almost equally dubious reputation. Throughout the whole country, from the Lakes to Tennessee, there was a veritable reign of terror. Most of the French, and even a few of the English-speaking pioneers, were constrained to save themselves by taking the British side, in the case of the French there being the further consideration that the liberties extended to them by the Quebec Act of 1774 had much influence to reconcile them to the existing régime.[1] For the most part it was a war to the death between the Indians under British incitement on the one hand, and the

[1] Victor C. Coffin, "The Quebec Act and the American Revolution," in the *Annual Report of the American Historical Association for 1894*, 273–281.

settled white population on the other. Until Clark came forward with his audacious enterprise, the settlers were acting wholly on the defensive. From his station at the Falls of the Ohio (modern Louisville), however, Clark studied the situation with characteristic sagacity, and arrived speedily at the conclusion that as long as the British continued to hold the Northwest posts, they would be able to keep up a continuous frontier war, which at the rate things were going would eventually mean the utter ruin of the western settlements. Learning through spies that the French were growing weary of the struggle and lukewarm toward the British, a plan of action began to take tangible form.

Hastening again to the Virginia capital, in December, 1777, Clark presented to his friend, Governor Henry, a definite scheme for the conquest of the Northwest, to be undertaken with such western troops as could be raised for the purpose, but expected to be successful in the end more by reason of the defection of the French from the British cause than on account of any actual military achievement. Clark's proposal was submitted at an opportune time. Burgoyne's surrender at Saratoga had occurred less than three months before, and throughout the East there was a feeling that ultimate success in the war was now well within the bounds of reasonable hope. Already Congress had begun to consider the necessity of taking possession of the Northwest. Governor Henry and the Executive Council were easily persuaded of the feasibility of Clark's plan, and on January 2, 1778, two sets of instructions were issued, one, for public use, authorizing the ambitious young colonel to raise seven companies of fifty men each for militia service in Kentucky, the other, private, directing him to make use of this force in an expedition for the capture of Kaskaskia.[1] Troops were to be recruited west of the Blue Ridge, and the commandant at Pittsburg was ordered to supply boats and ammunition. A grant of £1200 in the depreciated Continental currency was secured for the launching of the enterprise, and Thomas Jefferson, George Mason, and George Wythe pledged themselves to use their influence to secure a bounty of three hundred acres of land for each soldier in Clark's army, provided the attack upon Kaskaskia proved successful.

The next problem was to secure the troops for the campaign. This was not so easy as might be supposed. Almost none could be obtained at Pittsburg. Agents were sent out into various parts of the trans-Alleghany country, but the enemies of Clark, of whom there seem to have been not a few, did what they could to discourage people from enlisting, and by the most persistent efforts only about two hundred men could be gathered together. However, as Clark was advancing down the Ohio with these, there came the news of the French alliance — a turn of fortune no less favorable to the Virginian's designs in the West than to the general cause of the new nation in the East. The *habitans*, already wavering in their allegiance to the British, would now be all the more ready to ally themselves with the Americans, and thus a new and most valuable source of strength in the Mississippi Valley

---

[1] Governor Henry's public and private instructions are given in full in Clark, *Campaign in the Illinois*, 95–97, an edition of Clark's letter to George Mason. They are quoted in W. H. English, *The Conquest of the Northwest*, I. 92–104.

would be obtained. The real object of Clark's expedition was not revealed to the soldiers until the falls of the Ohio had been reached. When it became understood that the plan was to attack Kaskaskia, there was a good deal of murmuring, and several Tennesseeans attempted to escape service in such a prolonged and hazardous expedition by running away in the night. Some were captured and brought back, others made good their defection; but thereafter such discipline was enforced that there was no opportunity for desertion.

June 24, 1778, Clark left his blockhouse at the Falls with a force variously estimated at from 150 to 200 men.[1]

---

[1] By far the most important sources of information on Clark's Illinois campaign of 1778-1779 are the various letters and narratives written from time to time by the leader. These are: (1) a letter to the governor of Virginia, April 29, 1779, on the capture of Vincennes (in Jefferson's *Works*, Washington's ed., I. 222-226); (2) a letter to George Mason, November 19, 1779, printed in the *Ohio Valley Series*, No. III. [Cincinnati, 1869]; (3) a "Memoir." composed at the request of Jefferson and Madison, many years after the campaign, printed (with omissions) in Dillon, *History of Indiana*, 127-184; and (4) a journal, dated at Vincennes, February 24, 1779, printed from the Canadian Archives at Ottawa in the *American Historical Review*, I. 91-96, and (in part) in Hart, *American History Told by Contemporaries*, II. 579-582. All of these accounts, written by Clark, are conveniently included in W. H. English, *The Conquest of the Northwest*, Vol. I. Appendix. One other important original authority is the report of Governor Hamilton to General Haldimand, July 6, 1781, printed from the Canadian Archives in the *Michigan Historical and Pioneer Collections*, IX. 489-516. Important general accounts are Winsor, *The Westward Movement*, Chs. VIII.-XI.; Thwaites, *How George Rogers Clark won the Northwest;* Roosevelt, *The Winning of the West*, II. Chs. II. and III.; W. H. English, *Conquest of the Country Northwest of the Ohio*, Vols. I. and II.; Jacob P. Dunn, *Indiana*, Ch. IV.; Winsor, *Narrative and Critical History*, VI. 716-742; Hinsdale, *Old Northwest*, Ch. X.; "Colonel George Rogers Clark's Sketches of his Campaign in the Illinois in 1778-1779," in the *Ohio Valley Historical Series*, No. III; Hosmer, *Short History of the Mississippi Valley*, 80-95; W. H. Smith,

The Ohio was descended to the mouth of the Tennessee, and then, rather than run the risk of betraying his purposes by appearing on the Mississippi, the wily commander started to lead his troops north through the present state of Illinois by an overland route. The journey was long, but, the season being favorable, not exhausting, and from being lukewarm, the men became quite ardent in their devotion to the enterprise. The Kaskaskia River, three miles from the fort, was reached July 4, and both the fort and town were quickly taken possession of without opposition.[1] The British were not numerous enough to make any resistance, it never having occurred to any of their authorities that such an expedition as that of Clark could possibly be made, or was in any danger of being attempted. The fort was in command of a creole by the name of Rocheblane, who, though faithful to his trust, was quite unable to cope with the audacious presumption by which Clark disarmed opposition. At first the French population was much alarmed for its safety, but Clark speedily announced that there was absolutely no danger, the expedition having been avowedly intended to relieve the creoles as well as the Americans from the rule of the obnoxious British. Father Gibault, the priest, was assured that the Catholic religion would not suffer under the new régime, whereupon he induced the people generally to submit, and the latter proceeded to give expression

History of Indiana, I. Ch. IV.; Mann Butler, *History of Kentucky*, Chs. III.-V.; and John Reynolds, *The Pioneer History of Illinois*, Ch. IV.

[1] There is a plan of "Cascaskies" (Kaskaskia) in Winsor, *Narrative and Critical History*, VI. 717. It is reduced from a plate in Philip Pittman, *Present State of the European Settlements on the Mississippi* [London, 1770].

to their joy, in the words of Clark, by "addorning the streets with flowers and pavilians of different colours, compleating their happiness by singing, etc."[1] In their enthusiasm the jubilant Frenchmen volunteered to bear the good news of their relief from British rule to the neighboring town of Cahokia, and within a short time this place also was in the possession of the Americans. The Illinois country had been conquered without the shedding of a drop of blood.

But one important stronghold in the Northwest, aside from Detroit, remained to be secured. That was Vincennes. Again the French came forward with offers of assistance, which were the more acceptable because Clark's force was small, and he could not be assured that the Indians might not at any time be incited by British agents to cut him off from his military base. Father Gibault declared his willingness to undertake a mission to the post on the Wabash for the purpose of converting its inhabitants to the new régime, and the offer was gladly accepted. Vincennes, like Kaskaskia and Cahokia, had been intrusted by the British to creole agents, and the latter were easily influenced to cast aside the obligations of their position. Gibault argued eloquently against the subservience of the French to the British, especially in view of the recent alliance of France with the United States, and before two days had elapsed Vincennes was added to the growing number of American posts in the West. There was no garrison to offer resistance, and the people simply gathered in the village church and took the oath of their new allegiance. The astonished

[1] Jacob P. Dunn, *Indiana*, 135.

Indians were given to understand that their former great Father, the king of France, had returned to life, and that only a prompt compliance with his wishes could save them from the wrath he felt at their having given aid to the despised British.

Throughout the remainder of 1778 Clark stayed at Kaskaskia, giving his attention to the organization of the conquered territory. Captain Williams was placed in command of the Kaskaskia fort. Captain Bowman was stationed at Cahokia. Captain Helm was given the management of Vincennes and the Wabash country. Colonel Linn was sent to build a post on the present site of Louisville.[1] The term for which his men had enlisted being at an end, Clark recruited new companies from his Virginia veterans and the creoles, who were attracted by his promises of rewards. Strict discipline was enforced, and the new army acquired an efficiency superior even to that of the old one. In recognition of all these services, Virginia proceeded to create the new County of Illinois, embracing all her territorial claims west and north of the Ohio, and to set up in this important portion of the Far West the earliest form of American civil government.[2]

Meanwhile, a determined effort was being planned for the undoing of Clark's audacious work. Late in 1778 Governor Hamilton, who had been greatly surprised but not in the least daunted by the fall of the Indiana and Illinois posts, set out from Detroit by way of the Maumee

---

[1] Benjamin Casseday, *Louisville* [Louisville, 1852].
[2] Carl E. Boyd, "The County of Illinois," in the *American Historical Review*, IV. 623–635, and W. H. English, *The Conquest of the Northwest*, I. Ch. IX.

portage with a force of thirty-six British regulars, fifty creoles, and about four hundred Indians, with the purpose of retaking Vincennes, and if all went well, Kaskaskia and Cahokia also. The primary aim of the expedition was accomplished with ease. The Vincennes fort was found to be defended by Captain Helm and just one other man, the French having deserted their new masters as readily as they had been persuaded a few months before to fraternize with them. Helm was captured December 17, and once more Vincennes was British.[1] An expedition sent out in the direction of Kaskaskia to capture Clark failed, but the creoles of Illinois were thrown into a panic by the fear of future vengeance at British hands, and for a time it seemed that all the efforts of Clark and his Virginians would prove to have been entirely for naught.

January 29, 1779, while Clark was still at Kaskaskia in harassing uncertainty as to the movements of the enemy, he was greatly relieved by the unexpected appearance of Colonel Francis Vigo, a Sardinian by birth, who had long been engaged in trade among the Mississippi towns, and who, at his own suggestion, had been sent to Vincennes to report from time to time upon the conditions prevailing at the place. On the way thither he had been captured by Indians and carried before Hamilton, who had kept him in prison, so that nothing had been heard of him for several weeks. Largely through the intervention of Father Gibault, however, he managed to secure a release, and sought the earliest opportunity to present himself at Kaskaskia and inform Clark that Hamilton's garrison num-

[1] W. H. English, *The Conquest of the Northwest*, I. Ch. VIII.

bered but eighty, and that the earlier an attack upon it was made the better the chance of success, as no one could tell how soon it would be strengthened by reënforcements, which were expected to arrive for the conquest of Illinois the following summer. Clark was a leader of indomitable resolution, and his men by this time had the utmost faith in him. Had it been otherwise, the campaign which was now planned and executed to the minutest detail would not have been possible. Though the winter season was at its worst, Clark resolved to make an immediate expedition against Vincennes and take the garrison of the place at unawares. February 4 a boat known as the *Willing*, carrying six guns, was placed under command of Lieutenant Rogers and ordered to advance to within ten leagues of the Wabash post. The following day, with a band of 170 men, Clark set out upon the toilsome march of more than 200 miles across the water-soaked prairies of southern Illinois. Ten days brought the expedition to the "drowned lands" of the Wabash, which are described by Mr. Hosmer as "a tract low and flat, which, as the snow melted in the breaking up of winter, had become transformed into shallow lakes, stretching sometimes for miles, with only here and there a protruding patch of earth."[1] Progress through such a country was of course extremely slow and perilous. The men were under the necessity of marching for hours in freezing water up to their waists, and sometimes to their shoulders. Nights had to be spent where there was no opportunity to secure warmth and sleep, cook food, or dry frozen clothing. The men kept at their uncomfortable task bravely, however, and at last, on the

[1] Hosmer, *Short History of the Mississippi Valley*, 90.

23rd of February, by a final supreme effort which carried them across the four miles of the Horseshoe Plain, breast-deep in water, they arrived upon high ground on the outskirts of Vincennes. Here Clark addressed his followers, complimenting them upon their loyalty, and everything was done to provide food and warmth for those whose sufferings had been greatest.

From creoles taken captive it was learned that Clark's approach was utterly unexpected by the British and that the French in the village were willing enough to go back to their American allegiance, if only they be given ample protection. Without loss of time one of the captives was sent to warn the creoles that an "army" was about to besiege the town, and that safety could be obtained only by remaining carefully within doors. By skilfully using flags and banners and marching and countermarching his men, Clark made it appear that his forces were several times more numerous than they really were. He was well aware that the fort must be taken more by braggadocio than anything else, and in that he was an adept. As soon as Hamilton became aware of his danger he sent out a party to reconnoitre, but the floods compelled it to turn back. The fickle French went over to the American side in a body, and the British found it useless to offer much resistance. An effort was made to defend the fort, — Sackville, the British called it, — but the marksmanship of the frontier sharp-shooters was of such a quality that Hamilton and his men soon came to the conclusion that it was inexpedient to continue the fight. Hamilton proposed a surrender on condition that the British troops be allowed to go to Pensacola on parole, but Clark insisted upon a surrender unconditionally, and there was nothing left for the defender of Fort Sackville but to comply. Hamilton and twenty-five of his best men were sent as prisoners to Virginia, while the remaining captives, after taking an oath of neutrality, were set at liberty, March 16. Hamilton was subsequently released at the suggestion of Washington.[1]

This second capture of Vincennes was by far the most memorable incident in the hazardous process by which, during the years 1778 and 1779, the great Northwest was secured for the Americans. It was followed in good time by the quelling of the Indian allies of the British, the defeat of the reënforcements on their way from Detroit for the conquest of Illinois, and the establishing of permanent control by the state of Virginia and ultimately by the government of the United States. Hostilities on the frontier were by no means at an end, but hereafter the trend was decidedly against the British. Vincennes was no sooner taken than Clark began to consider the feasibility of an expedition against Detroit, the real British capital and stronghold in the Northwest. Fort Sackville became Fort Patrick Henry, Captain Helm was placed in charge of affairs on the Wabash, and Clark embarked on

[1] *Writings of Washington*, VI. 317, 407, and Moore, *The Northwest under Three Flags*, 237. On Clark's notable capture of Vincennes, see Dunn, *Indiana*, 138-151; W. H. Smith, *History of Indiana*, I. Ch. IV.; John B. Dillon, *History of Indiana*, Chs. XII.-XV.; Law, *History of Vincennes;* Roosevelt, *The Winning of the West*, II. Chs. II. and III.; E. A. Bryan, "Indiana's First Settlement; Clark's Important Conquest of Post Vincennes," in the *Magazine of American History*, XXI. 386-403; W. H. English, *The Conquest of the Northwest*, I. Chs. X. and XI.; and Governor Hamilton's report to General Haldimand in the *Michigan Historical and Pioneer Collections*, IX. 489-516.

the *Willing* for Kaskaskia. The conquest of Detroit had to be postponed, however, and it was in fact destined never to be accomplished by the victor of the Wabash and the Illinois. That important post was one of those which remained in British hands until after the close of the war. Instead of carrying his conquests farther, for the present Clark was employed by Thomas Jefferson, now governor of Virginia, in the establishment of a fort on the Mississippi below the mouth of the Ohio with the purpose of clinching the hold of the Americans upon the great river and ensuring the freedom of its navigation as against the French and Spanish, who might some day be enemies even as they now were friends. On a tract of ground purchased of the Cherokees, as near the mouth of the Ohio as the character of the country would permit, was forthwith constructed a well-built and fully equipped outpost of American authority, receiving as its name that of Virginia's far-seeing and statesmanlike governor.

While all these things were occurring in the North there were also developments on the Gulf which were of vast importance, if not in determining the outcome of the American struggle for ind pendence, at least in fixing the conditions upon which peace would be concluded at the end of the war. In 1777 Don Bernardo de Galvez, a brilliant young officer whose father was viceroy of Mexico and president of the Council of the Indies, became the governor of Louisiana. Like his predecessor, Unzaga, Galvez was an enlightened administrator, careful always to promote the interests of his people, and especially vigilant to reconcile the French population of the province to the rule of the Spaniard. It was just at the time when the

American Revolution was well under way that Galvez became Louisiana's governor, and his martial disposition made it inevitable that he should be strongly inclined to have a share in the movement against the common British foe. As early as December 30, 1776, the Continental Congress had passed a resolution to the effect that a treaty ought to be negotiated with Spain, and that if the Spaniards could be induced to join in the war against Great Britain, the United States would declare her readiness to aid them in recovering possession of the important harbor of Pensacola, provided the inhabitants of the United States should have the free navigation of the Mississippi and the use of the Pensacola harbor.[1] It was not until June 16, 1779, however, — more than a year after the French alliance, — that Spain could be brought to the point of declaring war against the British, and then the step was taken solely because the British cause appeared to be weakening and the Spaniards believed the opportunity to be at hand to repossess themselves of parts of the old colonial empire which had been lost to England in 1763. The terms of the Family Compact bound the Spaniards to take up any war in which the French became involved, but this consideration had small weight in determining the Spanish policy.[2] The greatest loss

---

[1] *Secret Journals of Congress*, II. 40.

[2] For a year and a half the French foreign minister, Vergennes, had been urging the Spanish secretary, Florida Blanca, to join with the Americans against the British, but it was not until April 12, 1779, that a treaty was concluded between the two Bourbon powers with a view to that end. In the treaty it was specified that the Spanish objects in entering the war were to regain Gibraltar, to acquire the river and fort of Mobile, Pensacola, and all the coast of Florida along the Bahama Channel, the expulsion of the English from the Bay of Honduras, and the resti-

suffered by Spain by the treaty of Paris had been the Floridas, exchanged with the British for Havana, and the hope was now strong for their recovery. It was possible, too, that the Floridas thus to be regained might be much more extensive than the provinces yielded in 1763. The Spaniards had once used the name "Florida" to describe the entire region between the Gulf and the Ohio, and by the pursuit of a sufficiently vigorous diplomatic and military policy it was thought that this great territory might once more come to be recognized as appurtenant to the flag of Castile.

As soon as Governor Galvez became aware that a state of open hostilities existed between the Spanish and the British, and that two months after the declaration of war the king of Spain had authorized his subjects in the Indies to take part in it, he began active preparations to drive the enemy from all the region about the Gulf. A military force of fourteen hundred men, composed of local militia, Indians, negroes, and American volunteers, was raised in New Orleans and drilled for the service. The two-year war in the South which followed resolves itself into a series of three campaigns, which can be but summarized here. The first of these, in 1779, was against the British posts on the lower Mississippi. The most important place reduced was

---

tution of the island of Minorca. The allied powers promised not to lay down their arms without having at least obtained Gibraltar for Spain and Dunkirk for France, or, in default of this, some other acquisition at the option of Spain. The treaty was not made known to the Americans. Its text is believed never to have been printed in English, except an abstract in the Sparks Mss., No. XCII., in the Harvard College Library. A Spanish version of it is in *Del Cantillo Tratados de Paz* [Madrid, 1843], 552.

Fort Bute which had been built at Bayou Manshac, the southernmost station belonging to England, lying on the river. Baton Rouge was also taken, as well as Fort Panmure on the site of old Fort Rosalie, or modern Natchez. Three other smaller garrisons near Baton Rouge were likewise compelled to surrender. The second of Galvez's campaigns, in 1780, was against Fort Charlotte and the settlement at Mobile. Two thousand troops were embarked at the Balize, and though badly storm-tossed on the passage, succeeded in landing at an advantageous position, and quickly effecting a conquest of the entire Mobile district.[1] The third and most important of the campaigns for driving the British from Florida was directed against Pensacola. Galvez recognized that this post would be able to offer resistance very different from that which he had hitherto met, and therefore made preparations accordingly. The captain-general of Cuba promised reënforcements, and when they failed to arrive Galvez went to the island in person to secure them. The first armament with which he started to return was broken up by a hurricane, but with indomitable perseverance he returned to Havana and equipped a new one. From Cuba he sailed directly to Pensacola with fourteen hundred troops. A landing was effected on the island of St. Rosa, and a battery was constructed to protect the frigates and transports while crossing the bar into the Gulf. The town was deserted by the British, who took refuge in the neigh-

---

[1] For an excellent account of this campaign, see Hamilton, *Colonial Mobile*, Ch. XXXI. Other discussions of Galvez's conquests in Florida are in Martin, *History of Louisiana*, II. Ch. III., and Gayarré, *History of Louisiana*, III. Ch. III.

boring fort and there endeavored to make effective resistance. The storming of the stronghold by the Spaniards was probably the severest military operation of the sort which had ever occurred on the Gulf shore. The siege continued for a month, and the outcome was by no means certain, until an accident occurred which turned the tide of victory. This was the explosion of the English powder magazine by which a breach was opened in the wall and the valiant defenders compelled to run up the flag of truce. As a result of the capitulation which ensued, not only Pensacola, but also all West Florida, was definitely surrendered to Spain. This was in May, 1781, and, though the war was still in progress on the Atlantic seaboard, nothing really remained for Galvez to do in the South. By a series of the most brilliant successes he had expelled the British and reëstablished Spanish supremacy all along the Gulf coast, precisely as the king and ministry had desired. The young general's services were highly appreciated at Madrid, and as an evidence thereof he was honored with the Cross of the Royal Order of Charles III., the title of Count, promotion to lieutenant-general in the army, and captain-general of Florida and Louisiana.[1] Within a few weeks after the fall of Pensacola he went to Havana to take command of a Spanish attack on Jamaica, while the government at New Orleans was left with Don Estevan Miro, a colonel of the Spanish regiment of Louisiana.

In connection with the conquest of Florida it should be noted that the Spaniards, during the Revolution, engaged also in a remarkable campaign far to the north. In the

[1] King and Ficklen, *History of Louisiana*, 133.

winter of 1780–1781 the commandant at St. Louis sent out an expedition to capture British posts in northern Indiana and southern Michigan, with the undoubted object of winning a Spanish title to the Great Lake region, as was being done at the same time in the lower Mississippi Valley. Fort St. Joseph, located on the river of that name, was taken by storm, its garrison compelled to surrender, and its colors carried away as a trophy of victory.[1] Possession of the country was formally proclaimed in the name of the Spanish king, though no serious effort seems to have been made to prevent the British at Detroit from regaining the captured post. This movement in behalf of Spanish sovereignty in the American interior was the more audacious because of the fact that more than a year before it was made, George Rogers Clark had won the whole intervening Illinois country for Virginia.

The successes of Galvez in his Florida campaigns presaged that when the time came to conclude a general peace, Spain would be found possessed of all the territory east of the Mississippi which she had lost in 1763, if not considerably more. For it was well understood that, though the conquest of the Floridas was a severe blow to British interests in America, the Spaniards were not guided by motives any more charitable toward the United States than the reëstablishing of their own supremacy on the Gulf shore. The truth is that the Americans were pretty generally displeased with the results of Galvez's operations, for by them the British garrisons taken at Pensacola and other points were left free to join Cornwallis's army in Virginia, and so

[1] Edward G. Mason, "The March of the Spaniards across Illinois," in the *Magazine of American History*, XV. 457–470.

have a considerable part in the campaign which culminated at Yorktown.[1] In view of the growing possibility that when peace should be made, Spain would be left in control of both the Floridas and Louisiana, and therefore of the lower course of the Mississippi, the Continental Congress, as early as September, 1779, began definitely to consider the steps necessary to be taken to safeguard for the people of the West the free use of the Mississippi which had been guaranteed by the treaty of 1763. September 9, 1779, John Dickinson, of Delaware, introduced in Congress a proposition to the effect that if Spain should decide to take an active part in the war as an ally of France and the United States, a treaty should be concluded with that power assuring to the Americans the possession of the Floridas, " and also the free navigation of the Mississippi into the sea "; but that if " his Catholic Majesty shall positively insist upon the Floridas being ceded to him and upon the exclusive navigation of the Mississippi from that part thereof which lies in latitude thirty-one degrees north from the equator to its mouth, in such cases the minister be instructed to agree to such propositions, to assent to mutual guarantees, to wit, of the Floridas and the navigation aforesaid to the king of Spain."[2] In event that the freedom of navigation must be given up, it was suggested that commercial privileges as favorable as possible be obtained instead. The next day Samuel Huntington, of Connecticut, introduced a resolution to the effect that if the king of Spain should continue active in the war against

[1] Washington, however, subsequently declared himself satisfied with the conquest of the Floridas. He believed Galvez to be a real friend of the American cause. *Washington's Works*, VIII. 176.

[2] *Secret Journals of Congress*, II. 242.

Great Britain, he should not be precluded from regaining the Floridas, "*provided* always that his Catholic Majesty shall grant to the United States the free navigation of the river Mississippi into the sea, and establish on the said river, at or somewhere southward of the thirty-first degree north latitude, a free port or ports," and should pay to the United States an annual subsidy to be agreed upon.[1] September 11 this resolution was adopted as an expression of the attitude of Congress, though on further consideration, six days later, the matter of a subsidy was dropped. At this time (September 17) a committee of three was appointed to draw up instructions for the negotiation of a Spanish treaty upon the basis thus outlined.[2] September 26 Merewether Smith, of Virginia, moved that a minister plenipotentiary be appointed for the undertaking; and the motion being adopted, three nominations were made — Arthur Lee, John Adams, and John Jay.[3] The following day Jay was elected, while Adams was chosen to begin negotiations of a peace with Great Britain. Jay was really the third American appointee to the court of Madrid. Franklin had been selected for the post January 1, 1777, but had found it more expedient to devote his time to affairs at Paris. After him Arthur Lee had tried his hand at negotiating with the Spanish ministers, only to withdraw in a short time in disgust with their parsimony and duplicity. The post was therefore not an enviable one, but Jay accepted it, and pledged himself to give his country the best service of which he was capable.

September 28 the committee appointed eleven days be-

[1] *Secret Journals of Congress*, II. 244.
[2] *Ibid.*, 249.   [3] *Ibid.*, 255.

fore reported a set of instructions for the Spanish negotiations.[1] Among their provisions were the following: that if the king of Spain "shall obtain the Floridas from Great Britain, these United States will guaranty the same to his Catholic Majesty: provided, always, that the United States shall enjoy the free navigation of the Mississippi into and from the sea;" and "You are particularly to endeavor to obtain some convenient port or ports below the thirty-first degree of north latitude, on the river Mississippi, for all merchant vessels, goods, wares, and merchandises belonging to the inhabitants of these states."[2] During the next three or four weeks there was considerable discussion of various details regarding Jay's prospective mission, and October 13 John Witherspoon, of New Jersey, proposed that the minister be privately instructed to recede from the claim of a free navigation of the Mississippi below the parallel of 31°, provided an insistence upon such right should be found an insuperable bar to the conclusion of a treaty of amity and commerce.[3] By a vote of six states to four Congress decided against such a policy. October 16 Jay's instructions, supplemented by an article on various minor matters, were transmitted to him,[4] and four days later he embarked for France on the government frigate *Confederacy*, which also carried the returning French minister, Gérard.

[1] Printed in Pitkin, *History of the United States*, II. 511-512.
[2] *Secret Journals of Congress*, II. 262-263.   [3] *Ibid.*, 275.
[4] The instructions are printed in Henry P. Johnston's edition of the *Correspondence and Public Papers of John Jay*, I. 248-250; Wharton, *The Revolutionary Diplomatic Correspondence of the United States*, III. 472-474; and in Sparks, *Diplomatic Correspondence of the American Revolution*, VII. 169. Sparks's version is not complete.

As soon as a landing was effected at Cadiz, whither the *Confederacy* was driven by an English man-of-war, Jay sent his secretary of legation, William Carmichael, in advance to Madrid to learn the attitude of the court and especially to discover how closely the Spaniards proposed to follow the French in their dealings with America. In Carmichael's instructions, dated at Cadiz, January 27, 1780, Jay said: "In speaking of American affairs, remember to do justice to Virginia and the western country near the Mississippi. Recount their achievements against the savages, their growing numbers, extensive settlements, and aversion to Britain for attempting to involve them in the horrors of an Indian war. Let it appear also from your representations that ages will be necessary to settle those extensive regions."[1] When spring came, Jay advanced to Madrid and prepared to open active negotiations with the first Spanish secretary of state, Count Florida Blanca. The American minister found the diplomatic path by no means smooth; in fact, he could not even obtain official recognition at any time during his two years' stay, and was always rigidly excluded from the court and shamelessly neglected by the ministry and nobility. Not much time was required to ascertain that the Spaniards had no love for the Americans and that they were especially jealous of the prospective expansion of the United States westward to the Mississippi. Even before Jay had appeared at Madrid the new French minister at Philadelphia, Luzerne, was informing a committee of Congress that Spain would not consent to an alliance with the United States except on condition that the latter power

[1] *Correspondence and Public Papers of John Jay*, I. 266.

declare her willingness not to make settlements to the west of the line established by the British king in the proclamation of 1763, and not to insist upon the right to navigate the Mississippi.[1] And this was precisely the position which Jay found the Spanish court to have assumed. In May, 1780, Count Florida Blanca declared to him that the United States had relinquished all right to the use of the Mississippi and had no reason now for attempting to reëstablish it.[2] Jay protested that he was quite ignorant of any such action on the part of his country, but Blanca hastened to sweep away such trivial objections by a bald declaration that it was his determination to keep the Mississippi entirely out of the control of the Americans, just as he intended to prevent further influence of the British in the Floridas. "The question of the navigation of the Mississippi," says the biographer of Jay, "was a novelty in international diplomacy. The United States was the first power to insist on the right of a people who live along a river to sail through the dominion of other powers to its mouth; they also claimed the same right under the reservation to Great Britain in the treaty of Paris, of the right of navigation. But it was the mediæval policy of Spain to keep the Gulf of Mexico a closed sea from Florida to Yucatan. Florida Blanca, indeed, in September, went so far as to say that the exclusive navigation of the Mississippi was the principal object of the war, and more important than the capture of Gibraltar."[3] This latter fairly astounding statement actually appears in Jay's notes of a conference

[1] *Secret Journals of Congress*, II. 310.
[2] Callahan, *Cuba and International Relations*, 57.
[3] Pellew, *John Jay*, 118.

with Blanca, under date of September 23, 1780. "The Count made several observations," says Jay, "tending to show the importance of this object to Spain, and its determination to adhere to it, saying, with some degree of warmth, that unless Spain could exclude all nations from the Gulf of Mexico, they might as well admit all; that the king would never relinquish it; that the minister regarded it as the principal object to be obtained by the war, and *that obtained*, he would be perfectly easy whether or no Spain procured any other cession; that he considered it far more important than the acquisition of Gibraltar, and that if they did not get it, it was a matter of indifference to him whether the English possessed Mobile or not."[1]

Nevertheless, Jay continued with characteristic earnestness to defend the claims of the people he had been sent to Madrid to represent. Perhaps the most remarkable expression given by him upon the subject during this stage of the controversy was that addressed to Don Diego de Gardoqui, a member of a wealthy firm at Bilbao, who acted occasionally as Blanca's official representative, and in this capacity had several interviews with the American minister. "In the evening," writes Jay under date of September 3-15, 1780, "M. Gardoqui again paid me a visit, and pointedly proposed my offering the navigation of the Mississippi as a consideration for aids. I told him that object could not come in question in a treaty for a loan of one hundred thousand pounds, and Spain should consider that to render alliances permanent, they should be so formed as to render it the interest of both parties to

[1] *Correspondence and Public Papers of John Jay*, II. 424.

observe them; that the Americans, almost to a man, believed that God Almighty had made that river a highway for the people of the upper country to go to the sea by; that this country was extensive and fertile; that the general, many officers, and others of distinction and influence in America, were deeply interested in it; that it would rapidly settle, and that the inhabitants would not readily be convinced of the justice of being obliged either to live without foreign commodities, and lose the surplus of their productions, or be obliged to transport both over rugged mountains and through an immense wilderness, to and from the sea, when they daily saw a fine river flowing before their doors, and offering to save them all that trouble and expense, and that without injury to Spain."[1] To all this Gardoqui simply replied that as yet there was not sufficient American population in the West to create such a demand, and that future generations should be left to manage their own affairs. This emphatic utterance of Jay was fully in accord with his instructions and also with the opinion of American leaders of the time. From Passy, near Paris, October 2, Franklin wrote: "But I hope, and am confident, that court [the Spanish] will be wiser than to take advantage of our distress, and insist on our making sacrifices by an agreement which the circumstances of such distress would hereafter weaken, and the very proposition can only give disgust at present. Poor as we are, yet as I know we shall be rich, I would rather agree with

[1] *Correspondence and Public Papers of John Jay*, I. 394-395. In Wharton, *Revolutionary Diplomatic Correspondence*, IV. 112-150, is a very valuable collection of Jay's correspondence and notes on conferences at Madrid during the summer of 1780. It comprises the envoy's report to the President of Congress, transmitted under date of November 6, 1780.

them to buy at a great price the whole of their right on the Mississippi than sell a drop of its waters. A neighbor might as well ask me to sell my street door."[1] Franklin here foreshadowed the method of adjusting the controversy by purchase, which Jefferson twenty years later was compelled to adopt as the only way to settle the long-standing difficulty.

The delay of the negotiation, ostensibly caused for the most part by the Mississippi question, led to a renewal of discussion in Congress as to the advisability of instructing Jay, as some members had thought wise at the outset, to abandon the contention for free navigation. The yielding point had not yet been reached, however, and on the 4th of October, in a supplementary body of instructions adopted for Jay's guidance, it was provided that "the minister adhere to his former instructions respecting the right of the United States of America to the free navigation of the river Mississippi into and from the sea; which right, if an express acknowledgment of it cannot be obtained from Spain, is not by any stipulation on the part of America to be relinquished. . . . The river Mississippi being the boundary of several states in the union, and their citizens, while connected with Great Britain and since the Revolution, having been accustomed to the free use thereof, in common with the subjects of Spain, and no instance of complaint or dispute having resulted from it, there is no reason to fear that the future mutual use of the river by the subjects of the two nations, actuated by friendly dispositions, will occasion any interruption of that harmony

---

[1] *Correspondence and Public Papers of John Jay*, I. 433, and Sparks, *Franklin's Writings*, VIII. 501.

which it is the desire of America, as well as of Spain, should be perpetual."[1] October 17 a committee which had been appointed to prepare a letter to the ministers at Versailles and Madrid, explaining the grounds for the recent instructions to Jay, brought in an elaborate document in which the whole question of the American claims to the western territory conquered from Great Britain, and to the freedom of navigating the Mississippi throughout its entire course, was discussed with remarkable vigor and dignity.[2] Speaking of the Ohio Valley and the country lying to the south, the committee declared: "In a very few years after peace shall take place, this country will certainly be overspread with inhabitants. In like manner as in all new settlements, agriculture, not manufactures, will be their employment. They will raise wheat, corn, beef, pork, tobacco, hemp, flax, and in the southern parts, perhaps, rice and indigo, in great quantities. On the other hand, their consumption of foreign manufactures will be in proportion, if they can be exchanged for the produce of their soil." At this point the committee saw an opportunity to add a new argument to Jay's almost exhausted stock. There would be just two possible routes for all this vast commerce — southward by the Mississippi, and northward by way of rivers and portages to the Great Lake system. Of these the former was by all odds preferable. Yet if the Spaniards should be so foolish as to close the lower Mississippi against the traffic of the Americans, the route to the north could and would be made

[1] *Secret Journals of Congress*, II. 323–325, and *Correspondence and Public Papers of John Jay*, I. 434–436.
[2] The letter is in the *Secret Journals of Congress*, II. 326–339. It is reprinted in Pitkin, *History of the United States*, II. Appendix IX.

use of; in which case "France and Spain, and the other maritime powers, will not only lose the immediate benefit of it themselves, but they will also suffer by the advantage it will give to Great Britain." Such a prospect, it was hoped, would be not without influence in bringing the court of Madrid to terms.

During the winter of 1780-1781 the exigencies of the war became such that the aid of the Spanish power seemed more than ever indispensable to the American cause. It was inevitable therefore that propositions should be brought forward with a view to securing such aid by the quickest possible means. Jay's reports of the negotiations with Florida Blanca clearly conveyed the idea that the Spanish alliance was being thwarted almost wholly by the attitude of the United States on the Mississippi question. The obvious thing to do, therefore, was to relinquish the claim, and so clear the way for an early treaty of alliance. February 1, 1781, the delegation from Virginia, acting under the instructions of their state legislature,[1] came forward

---

[1] James Madison, one of the Virginia delegates, wrote a letter to the editor of *Niles's Register*, January 8, 1822, in which he threw much desired light upon the change of base in 1781 regarding the Mississippi question. He says that the delegates from Georgia and South Carolina became alarmed at the progress the British were making in the South, and feared especially that peace might suddenly be made on the basis of *uti possidetis*, leaving the British in possession of large portions of these Southern states. It was proposed first of all by the Georgia and South Carolina delegates that Spain be won definitely to the American side by an immediate abandonment of all claim to the navigation of the Mississippi below 31°. Virginia having more western territory than any other state, the matter would be of such importance to her that her delegates, Madison and Bland, whose opinions differed, agreed to ask the legislature of their state for instructions as to how to vote on the proposition in Congress. In response the legislature expressed its will by the following

with a proposal, by no means new on the floor of Congress, but carrying now a peculiar force imparted by the dire extremity to which the country had been reduced. The proposal was, simply, that Jay be authorized to yield the navigation of the Mississippi below 31°, if only free ports near the mouth of the river could be definitely assured for the use of American traders. For the first time such a policy was received with favor, reluctant though quite general, in Congress, and two weeks later Jay was instructed to recede from the Mississippi claim, and not only that, but also from the contention for free ports, "provided such cession shall be unalterably insisted upon by Spain."[1] In the United States there seems to have been a general feeling that this sacrifice of valuable rights in the West would at once overcome all difficulties in the way of a Spanish treaty. Samuel Huntington, President of Congress, wrote to Jay: "On the receipt of this latter instruction Congress have little doubt that the great obstacle to your negotiations will be removed, and

---

resolution: "That the navigation of the river Mississippi ought to be claimed by Virginia only as co-extensive with our territory, and that our delegates in Congress be instructed to procure for the other states in the Union the free navigation of that river only as extensively as the territorial possessions of the said states reach respectively. And that every further or other demand of the said navigation be ceded, if insisting on the same is deemed an impediment to a treaty with Spain. *Provided*, that the said delegates use their endeavors to obtain, on behalf of this state, or other states having territory on said river, a free port or ports below the territory of such states respectively." This explanation by Madison is printed in the *Madison Papers*, I. Appendix, pp. xix-xxii. See *Correspondence and Public Papers of John Jay*, II. 206-207, note, and Pellew, *John Jay*, 123.

[1] *Secret Journals of Congress*, II. 393-395, and *Correspondence and Public Papers of John Jay*, I. 460-461.

that you will not only be able without further delay to conclude the proposed alliance with his Catholic Majesty, but that the liberality and friendly disposition manifested on the part of the United States by such a cession will induce him to afford them some substantial and effectual aid in the article of money."[1]

Such confidence, however, did not rest upon any adequate appreciation of the complexities of Spanish diplomacy. Jay knew from observation how difficult it would be to bind the Spaniards to any specific agreement with the United States. By an American alliance Spain had little to gain, much to lose. Thus far her arms had been victorious in Florida; she held the key to the navigation of the Mississippi; the Gulf of Mexico was fast becoming a mere Spanish sea; and, while it was desirable that the Americans continue by their revolt to give Great Britain trouble, it was not especially important that they gain their independence, particularly since it was beginning to appear that they were many fold more aggressive in their western pretensions than the British authorities had ever been. All these factors in the situation Jay perceived, and while he could not tell how they would work out, he at least understood that it would be by no means so easy a matter to bring the Spanish court to the point of giving any considerable aid "in the article of money" as the members of Congress supposed. The intricacies of the whole matter were such that Jay did not even profess to understand them. "This court," he writes, April 25, "continues pertinaciously to insist on

[1] Huntington to Jay, May 28, 1781, *Correspondence and Public Papers of John Jay*, II. 35. *Secret Journals of Congress*, II. 407.

our ceding that navigation; nor will they, as yet, listen to any middle line. Whether this be their real motive for declining a treaty with us at present, or whether the bills drawn upon me have inspired an expectation of profiting by our necessities, or whether they flatter themselves with a future majority of Congress on that point, or whether they choose, by continuing free from engagements with us, to be better enabled to improve to their advantage the casualties of war, are questions which still remain undecided. Indeed, the movements of this court in general, when compared with the great rules of national policy applicable to their situation, are so inexplicable that I should not be surprised if it should appear in future that they had no fixed system whatever."[1]

Despite Jay's poor opinion of Spanish administration and diplomacy, however, and his chagrin at being able to accomplish nothing toward the conclusion of the desired treaty, he was much displeased with the instruction to yield the navigation of the Mississippi. One reason for this feeling was of a personal nature. Jay recognized that Congress had thrown upon him the entire burden of deciding whether the sacrifice of the Mississippi rights was indispensable to the making of a treaty. Such responsibility was likely in any event to bring him into more or less disrepute at home. If he deemed it necessary to abandon the American right, and proceeded to do so, there would be people who would say that he had been frightened or duped, if not actually bribed. On the other hand, if he refused to yield and in the end failed to get a

[1] Jay to the President of Congress, April 25, 1781. *Correspondence and Public Papers of John Jay*, II. 21.

treaty, "it would soon be whispered what rich supplies and golden opportunities the United States had lost by my obstinacy."[1] This embarrassing test which Jay feared never came, for as time went on the Spanish court became less and less disposed to make a treaty with the United States on any terms. Having the lower course of the Mississippi actually in her possession, Spain was under no necessity of negotiating regarding it. The advances had to come from the American side, and the Spanish could easily afford to repel them. For all practical purposes the Mississippi was not open to the Americans, because the Spanish were in a position at New Orleans to control the river traffic absolutely. Spain considered that she had nine points of the law in the fact of her possession, and the other point in her undoubted ability to make that possession effective — so, why negotiate? Still, Jay believed that if Congress had shown less anxiety regarding the whole matter, the problem would have been much simplified. In those days communication across the ocean, especially in matters of state, was exceedingly hazardous. Vessels carrying papers and instructions were constantly being captured and their diplomatic as well as other valuables confiscated. Jay had been much annoyed by delays and other irregularities in the correspondence which passed between him and Congress. Intimations of the instructions to yield the navigation of the Mississippi, for example, had been received by various parties at Versailles and Madrid before he was himself aware of the change. The Spaniards knew surprisingly well that

[1] Jay to the President of Congress, October 3, 1781. *Correspondence and Public Papers of John Jay*, II. 85.

Congress was weakening in its attitude on the Mississippi question, and the effect upon their willingness to negotiate may easily be imagined. "It has uniformly been my opinion," wrote Jay to the President of Congress, October 3, 1781, "that if after sending me here Congress had constantly avoided all questions about the Mississippi, and appeared to consider that point irrevocable, Spain would have endeavored to purchase it by money, or a free port; but as her hopes of a change in the opinion of Congress were excited and kept alive by successive accounts of debates on that question, and as Congress by drawing bills without previous funds had painted their distress for want of money in very strong colors, Spain began to consider America as a petitioner, and treated her accordingly."[1]

Throughout the remainder of the year 1781 the negotiation, on various pretexts, continued to be postponed. Even when Jay informed Florida Blanca that he was authorized, in case of necessity, to abandon the contention for the navigation of the Mississippi, the wily Spaniard only made reply that "he earnestly desired to see all difficulties on this point removed, but that the treaties subsisting between Spain and other nations, as well as the particular policy and determination of Spain, rendered it necessary that she should possess the exclusive navigation of the Gulf of Mexico."[2] Under date of September 22 Jay had placed in the Spanish minister's hands certain propositions as the basis of a treaty, the sixth of which provided that the United States should "relinquish to his Catholic Majesty, and in future forbear to use, or

[1] *Correspondence and Public Papers of John Jay*, II. 87.
[2] Jay to the President of Congress, October 3, 1781, *ibid.*, 91.

attempt to use, the navigation of the river Mississippi from the 31° of north latitude — that is, from the point where it leaves the United States — down to the ocean."[1] With the proposal on this subject went a warning that if Spain neglected to take advantage of the present opportunity to settle the question of the Mississippi, she need not expect, after the restoration of peace, to find the United States in any wise disposed to make such a concession. Much stress was laid upon the sacrifices which the United States was making in this offer — sacrifices which could be compensated only for the time by even the most liberal aid from Spain in bringing the war to a successful close. These advances were recognized to the extent of a brief note from Florida Blanca, acknowledging the receipt of the plan, and promising that in due time a person would be designated to undertake the negotiation on the side of his Catholic Majesty. Within a few days M. Del Campo, the confidential secretary of Blanca, was appointed, but there matters came to an end. Time after time Jay approached Del Campo, only to be informed that no instructions for the negotiation had yet been given him. In fact, on a plea of illness, the deputy secretary managed to escape an interview for more than three months. "Delay is and has long been the system," wrote Jay to Adams, December 15, "and when it will cease cannot be divined."[2] "To this day," he wrote again to the President of Congress the following February, "the minister has found it convenient to continue the system of delay."[3]

---

[1] *Correspondence and Public Papers of John Jay*, II. 124.
[2] Jay to Adams, December 15, 1781, *ibid.*, 165.
[3] Jay to the President of Congress, February 6, 1782, *ibid.*, 176.

Thus in "expectation, suspense, and disappointment," as the disheartened envoy expressed it, month after month was passed, and though Count de Montmorin, the French minister at Madrid, urged a more considerate treatment of the Americans, the end of the war came with matters standing practically as Jay had found them when he had first appeared at the Spanish court. April 30, 1782, Congress formally voted its approval of Jay's conduct at Madrid, at the same time expressing the keenest surprise that the offer to yield the navigation of the Mississippi below 31° had not "produced greater effects on the counsels of the Spaniards."[1] The minister was urged again to sound the warning that, unless a treaty of alliance be speedily forthcoming, the United States would recede from her offer. Finally, on the 7th of August, Congress adopted the significant resolution that "the American minister at Madrid be instructed to forbear making any overtures to that court, or entering into any stipulations in consequence of overtures which he has made; and in case any proposition be made to him by the said Court for a treaty with the United States, to decline acceding to the same until he shall have transmitted them to Congress for approbation."[2] Thus, despite the fact that when war was ended a Spanish alliance would be of comparatively little value to the United States, Congress left open for more than eight months after the surrender of Cornwallis at Yorktown the possibility of an amicable arrangement con-

---

[1] *Secret Journals of Congress*, III. 98; *Correspondence and Public Papers of John Jay*, II. 208.

[2] *Secret Journals of Congress*, III. 149; *Correspondence and Public Papers of John Jay*, II. 209.

ferring upon Spain the unrestricted sovereignty of the lower Mississippi. As one writer has suggested, "both Jay and Congress retired from the atmosphere of the Spanish court with greater dignity and self-respect than would have been possible had that body [Congress] changed its policy and professions with the changes in the military situation."[1] When the instructions of August 7 were signed, Jay was already busily engaged in the work which Congress had assigned him June 13 of the previous year, *i.e.* the coöperating with Franklin, Jefferson, Laurens, and Adams at Paris in the negotiation of the peace treaty with Great Britain. April 22, 1781, Franklin had written to Jay that he was greatly needed at Paris,[2] and as it was very evident that nothing was being gained at Madrid, the removal to the more important scene of diplomatic activity was made a month or more later. Jay's secretary of legation, Carmichael, was to remain in Spain, and it was understood with Florida Blanca that negotiations might be continued with Aranda, the Spanish ambassador at Paris.

For present purposes the only phase of the peace negotiation at Paris with which we are concerned was that respecting the establishment of the western and southern boundaries of the newly independent nation, and its corollary, the question of the free navigation of the Mississippi. As early as March 19, 1779, — three months before Spain became a party to the war against Great Britain, — Congress

---

[1] Henry P. Johnston, in *Correspondence and Public Papers of John Jay*, II. 209.

[2] Franklin to Jay, April 22, 1781; William Jay, *Life of John Jay*, II. 94; *Correspondence and Public Papers of John Jay*, II. 300–312 *passim*.

undertook to make a statement of the territorial limits which the United States would attempt to assure for herself in event of a Spanish alliance and a successful conclusion of the war which was expected speedily to follow.[1] Even at this time, before Galvez's campaigns had begun, it was proposed that Florida be committed to Spain. The western boundary of the United States was to be the Mississippi; the northern, not south of parallel 45°; and the southern, the parallel 31°. The question of the navigation of the Mississippi was left unmentioned, though probably it was assumed that the river trade would be free and open. August 14 of the same year, in compliance with the urgent advice of the French minister Gerard, Congress drew up definite instructions for the guidance of John Adams, who had already been selected as minister plenipotentiary to negotiate a peace with Great Britain. On the subject of a western and southern boundary the instructions traced a limit as follows: "Thence [from Lake Nipissing] to the source of the river Mississippi: west, by a line to be drawn along the middle of the river Mississippi from its source to where the said line shall intersect the thirty-first degree of north latitude: south, by a line to be drawn due east from the termination of the line last mentioned . . . to the middle of the river Appalachicola, or Catahouche; thence along the middle thereof to its junction with the Flint River; and thence down along the middle of St. Mary's River to the Atlantick Ocean."[2] The final instructions under which the treaty was concluded were issued June 15, 1781 — immediately after Franklin, Laurens, Jefferson, and Jay were joined with

[1] *Secret Journals of Congress*, II. 138. [2] *Ibid.*, 226.

Adams in the negotiation. On this occasion Congress simply declared that, so far as boundaries were concerned, the instructions to Adams in 1779 still "expressed its desires and expectations." With the exception of the explicit injunction to consult France on every portion of the proposed treaty, the commissioners were to be at liberty "to secure the interest of the United States in such manner as circumstances may direct, and as the state of the belligerent and disposition of the mediating powers may require."[1]

At many points in the course of the Revolution it had been apparent that both France and Spain were fearful lest the revolting British colonies should achieve too great a measure of success. France had allied herself with the colonies in 1778 with the primary purpose of revenging herself upon England by ensuring the loss of the latter power's American possessions; but she did not approve of the prospective extension of the new nation all the way westward to the Mississippi. As early as 1779 Luzerne was making a vigorous effort at Philadelphia to induce Congress to abandon the claim of navigating that river. Gerard, before him, had declared that unless this claim was given up Spain would very likely cast in her fortunes on the British side of the war. That Spain had no idea of such a course is perfectly obvious, for she was bent almost solely upon the recovery of Gibraltar and the Floridas, both of which had to be taken from the British. But it has already been made clear that the Spanish, though allies of the French, were far from standing in that relation to the Americans, and that they were keenly hostile to every

[1] *Secret Journals of Congress*, II. 446.

proposition looking to the inclusion of the eastern Mississippi Valley in the American nation.

When the negotiations were opened at Paris in 1782, the Spanish, French, and English were still engaged in hostilities, though the war in America had come entirely to a close. This in itself was enough to complicate matters. But France, on the one hand, was an ally of the United States, and on the other, of Spain — which two powers had been proved to be utterly irreconcilable. Moreover, by the treaty of 1778, the Americans had bound themselves not to conclude peace with Great Britain without the concurrence of France; and by the treaty of 1779 the French had obligated themselves not to make peace with the English until the Spanish should have taken Gibraltar. All together the situation was a perplexing one, and it is little to be wondered at that the more enthusiastic of the American commissioners, Adams and Jay, finally decided to cut the Gordian knot by throwing the treaty of 1778 and the instructions of Congress to the winds, and addressing themselves to the securing of the best terms possible from Great Britain independently of the continental powers.

This policy had its immediate origin in the suspicions of the commissioners, particularly of Jay, that the French ministry proposed to lend its hearty support to the scheme of the Spanish to deprive the United States of all territory west of the Alleghanies. For the most part, these suspicions can be shown very clearly to-day to have been well-founded, and it was only by the shrewdest diplomatic manœuvring, coupled with the coöperation of America's nominal foe, Great Britain, that the ulterior designs of the

Bourbon monarchies failed of realization. Not long after Jay had arrived at Paris to participate in the negotiations, he had an interview with the Spanish ambassador, Aranda, who proceeded to declare for the Spanish control of the Mississippi as emphatically as Florida Blanca had ever done at Madrid, and further, to argue that the western territory, so far as it was not in the possession of the Indians, belonged of right to Spain by virtue of her conquest of West Florida and her posts on the Mississippi and the Illinois. Some weeks subsequently Rayneval, the confidential secretary of the French foreign minister, Count de Vergennes, confessed to Jay that his master proposed to support the Spanish contention, and that he favored giving Spain both sides of the Mississippi below 31°, while agreeing that the territory east of the river and lying between 31° and the Ohio should be left an Indian country, half under a Spanish and half under an American protectorate. The division line between the two "spheres of influence" was to start at the mouth of the Cumberland River, follow that stream nearly to the present site of Nashville, run thence southward to the Tennessee, curve eastward almost to the Alleghanies, and descend through what is now eastern Alabama to the Florida line. A further part of the scheme was that the country north of the Ohio should remain in the possession of the British.[1] Thus the

[1] Gérard Rayneval, "Idea on the Manner of Determining and Fixing the Limits between Spain and the United States on the Ohio and on the Mississippi," in the *Secret Journals of Congress*, IV. 74–80. This paper was not an official communication, but as Jay declared, "it was not to be believed that the first and confidential secretary of the Count de Vergennes would, without his knowledge and consent, declare such sentiments and offer such propositions, and that, too, in writing."

THE PARTITIONING OF THE WEST
PROPOSED BY THE COURT OF FRANCE IN 1782.

young American nation would from the outset find itself limited to the belt of land between the Atlantic and the Alleghanies, while the powers of Europe would be left to dispose at will of the larger part of the great interior. The country which had been explored by the Boones and McAfees, conquered by Clark, settled by the Seviers, Robertsons, and Kentons, and long regarded as belonging by every conceivable right to the people of the seaboard states, was to remain an Indian reserve over which the United States could exercise only the most general jurisdiction.[1] Such a plan to rob the Americans of the fruits of their victory betrayed the essential selfishness of the French court, while it had been understood almost from the beginning that the Spaniards were wasting no ardor on behalf of the American cause. It was the laying bare, in a considerable measure at least, of this double-dealing policy that gave the American commissioners their best justification for breaking the instructions of Congress and ignoring their nominal European ally in the later stages of the negotiation.[2]

The preliminary treaty of peace between the United

---

[1] For maps showing the boundaries of the United States, Canada, and the Spanish possessions, according to the proposals of the court of France in 1782, see Fiske, *Critical Period*, 20, and Foster, *A Century of American Diplomacy*, 60.

[2] On the breaking of the instructions, see Pellew, *John Jay*, Chs. VII. and VIII.; Trescot, *Diplomacy of the United States*, I. 100-106, 118-128; Wharton, *Revolutionary Diplomatic Correspondence*, I., Introduction, §§ 109-111; John Adams, *Works*, I. 340-342, 363-376; Lecky, *History of England in the Eighteenth Century*, IV. 255-264; Winsor, *Narrative and Critical History*, VII. Ch. II.; Hall, *International Law* (4th ed.), 347; Wheaton, *International Law* (ed. by Dana), §§ 257-262; *Correspondence and Public Papers of John Jay*, II. *passim*.

States and Great Britain was signed at Paris, November 30, 1782, and the definitive treaty, September 3, 1783, the interval of eight months having been taken up with the adjustment of relations between England and France. One result of the Revolution had been to add the newly created United States to the number of nations interested in the disposition of the lands in the Mississippi Valley, and the British having lost in that quarter, it was the natural thing that the American negotiators at Paris should insist with uncompromising energy upon the establishment of the Mississippi as the western boundary of the young nation whose interests they represented. As a consequence of Rayneval's revelations it was strongly suspected by Jay, with whom Adams concurred after his arrival upon the scene, that the French government was planning nothing less than to recover possession of the eastern half of old Louisiana, and it was chiefly because of this suspicion that the Americans proceeded to make a treaty with the British commissioner, Oswald, without consulting the French ministry, as they were under obligation to do by the treaty of alliance in 1778 as well as by their instructions from Congress. Franklin was loath to charge the French with such designs; but there can no longer be doubt that Adams and Jay were not far wrong, though it is to be believed that their suspicions proceeded from the general principle of distrust on which they acted throughout the negotiation, rather than from any considerable amount of specific and incriminating evidence in their possession. England preferred that the disputed inland territory belong to the new and comparatively isolated nation rather than that it should fall again

under the rule of either of her continental enemies; and the American representatives, therefore, found no great difficulty in securing their demands upon this point.

By the treaty, the western boundary of the United States was declared to be "a line to be drawn along the middle of the said river Mississippi until it shall intersect the northernmost part of the thirty-first degree of north latitude." The southern boundary was defined by "a line to be drawn due east from the determination of the line last mentioned, in the latitude of thirty-one degrees north of the equator to the middle of the river Appalachicola or Catahouche; thence along the middle thereof to its junction with the Flint River; thence straight to the head of St. Mary's River; and thence down along the middle of St. Mary's River to the Atlantic Ocean." This was precisely the boundary which Congress, in the successive instructions issued to the commissioners, had declared to be desirable. It was further specified that the navigation of the Mississippi throughout its entire course should "remain forever free and open to the subjects of Great Britain, and the citizens of the United States."[1] By a subsequent treaty between

[1] The text of the treaty is in the Revised Statutes relating to the District of Columbia etc. (ed. 1875), 266–269, and in MacDonald, *Select Documents of United States History*, 15–21. Probably the best general discussion of the treaty and its negotiation is that by John Jay, in Winsor, *Narrative and Critical History*, VII. Ch. II. Other accounts deserving mention are Lecky, *History of England in the Eighteenth Century* (Amer. ed.), IV. 218–289; Bancroft, *History of the United States* (ed. 1874), X. Chs. XXVI.–XXIX.; Foster, *A Century of American Diplomacy*, Ch. II.; Lyman, *The Diplomacy of the United States*, I. Ch. IV.; Pellew, *John Jay*, Ch. VIII.; Morse, *John Adams*, Ch. IX., and *Benjamin Franklin*, Ch. XI.; Fiske, *The Critical Period*, Ch. I.; John Jay,

Spain and Great Britain the Bahama Islands were ceded by the former power to the latter in return for the two Floridas — East and West — which went back to Spain after remaining in English possession just twenty years.[1]

Three nations instead of two again shared the American continent. Great Britain possessed the region north of the Great Lakes. Spain continued in possession of the territory west of the Mississippi, and once more also held sway over the Floridas, extending from New Orleans eastward to the Atlantic. The remainder of the continent, about 827,800 square miles, constituted the United States. The population of the latter was not far from three and a half millions — one person to every four square miles, or a total of less than the number of people now gathered within the boundaries of Greater New York. Considered from the standpoint of overcrowding, at least, it was not to be supposed that the young nation would care to enlarge her boundaries for many a generation to come. Men were already saying, both in Europe and in America, that a territory so vast as that stretching from the Atlan-

---

"The Peace Negotiations of 1782-1783," in the *American Historical Association Papers*, III. 79-100, and "Count de Vergennes," in the *Magazine of American History*, XIII. 31-38; Wharton, *Digest of International Law* (ed. 1887), III. 892-956; and Trescot, *The Diplomacy of the Revolution*, Ch. IV. The more important original sources of information are Sparks, *Diplomatic Correspondence*, VI. VII.; Wharton, *Diplomatic Correspondence*, V. VI.; *Secret Journals of Congress*; *Correspondence and Public Papers of John Jay*; Franklin, *Works*; John Adams, *Works*; and the *Annual Register*.

[1] Chalmers, *Collection of Treaties*, I. 495. It should be observed that except for vague claims on the basis of early exploration along the Gulf coast the Spaniards cannot be said ever hitherto to have possessed that part of Florida lying west of the Perdido River. Between 1699 and 1763 this district was held by the French.

TERRITORIAL DIVISION AFTER THE AMERICAN REVOLUTION.

tic to the Mississippi and from the Great Lakes to Florida could not long be held together under a single national system. But even while they were speaking, events were hastening forward which were not merely to set at naught all speculations of this sort, but were to create an inexorable demand that the national domain be yet further enlarged and the possessions of European powers in America still further restricted. The Spanish Count d'Aranda, at the conclusion of the peace of 1782, saw more clearly into the future than did most of his contemporaries when, in a letter to his royal master, he uttered the notable prophecy concerning the United States: "This federal republic is born a pigmy. A day will come when it will be a giant, even a colossus, formidable in these countries. Liberty of conscience, the facility for establishing a new population on immense lands, as well as the advantages of the new government, will draw thither farmers and artisans from all the nations. In a few years we shall watch with grief the tyrannical existence of this same colossus."[1]

[1] Among other notable prophecies upon this occasion was that of Signor Dolfin, the Venetian ambassador at Paris, who declared, "If the union of the American provinces shall continue, they will become by force of time and of the arts the most formidable power in the world." Winsor, *Narrative and Critical History*, VII. 152.

CHAPTER IX

THE NAVIGATION OF THE MISSISSIPPI, 1783–1795

DURING the eight years between the outbreak of the Revolution and the treaty of Paris a remarkable increase had occurred in the population of the eastern Mississippi Valley. It is estimated that in 1783 there were in Kentucky and Tennessee alone not fewer than thirty thousand English-speaking people, and after the restoration of peace and the establishing of national independence the tide of westward migration from the seaboard states set in more strongly than ever. To men of hardy courage and thrifty enterprise the vast and as yet almost wholly undeveloped territory across the mountains offered many inducements. Land was there to be had in the most generous quantities for little more than the asking. There might he who had failed to prosper in the more crowded East find new and better opportunities, if not for the amassing of great wealth, at least for the securing of an ample competence. There also might he whose fortunes had been broken by the war most quickly and most surely recuperate. In many cases, too, the natural impulse to migrate was strengthened by specific grants of land under the authority of the state governments, particularly to men who had served as soldiers in the war, but whom the state was unable to pay in any other fashion.

Prior to the close of the Revolution — in fact, until the beginning of the national period — westward migration was mainly from the Southern states, and hence it was the region south of the Ohio rather than that north of it that was most rapidly settled. Three of these Southern states had very extensive western claims, based for the most part upon royal charters. Virginia asserted a right of control over the entire region between her present southern boundary prolonged to the Mississippi and the present Canadian boundary from Lake Erie to the west end of Lake Superior and thence to the northwest as far as the Lake of the Woods, — in other words, more than a third of all the country between the Alleghanies and the Mississippi. This extensive claim, however, was disputed in the region of Lakes Erie and Michigan by both Massachusetts and Connecticut, and farther south by New York. North Carolina had a western claim representing substantially the present state of Tennessee, and several years before the close of the Revolution she had taken formal possession of the country in question. Georgia had a similar claim to the territory now included in the states of Alabama and Mississippi. Professor McMaster is authority for the statement that by 1783 less than twenty thousand acres of these immense domains had been surveyed and mapped. "It may be doubted," continues this writer, "whether as many as ten thousand acres were under cultivation. Less was known of the country than of the heart of China. There the Indians hunted the buffalo and the deer, and the trappers, unmolested, laid snares for the beaver and the mink. The inhabitants of the eastern part, a gaunt, rawboned, poverty-stricken race, were as much objects of curiosity to the refined and polished natives of Boston and New York as an Esquimau or Turk. They dwelt in the rudest kind of log cabins, and knew no other money than whiskey and the skins of wild beasts. They yielded no revenue to the states claiming their allegiance, and were, in truth, but nominally under the authority of the legislatures. No troops were stationed among them to enforce obedience to the laws of the land. No judges ever journeyed to them to correct abuses, to mete out justice, to vindicate the majesty of the law. But, left to themselves, the people administered prompt and rude justice with the knife and the gun. Up to 1784 these lands had been little more than a source of contention and strife."[1]

In the meantime, during the course of the war, the exigencies of the formation of a united government had pretty largely determined the control of all the land west of the Alleghanies. The conquest of the Northwest by George Rogers Clark in 1778-1779 under the immediate auspices of Virginia had given rise to a general alarm among states, such as Massachusetts and Connecticut, whose western claims conflicted with hers, and also among states, such as Rhode Island, New Jersey, and Delaware, which had no western claims at all, lest when peace was restored Virginia should be left so large and wealthy that she would completely overshadow her sister commonwealths. This feeling was especially strong in Maryland, long the jealous rival of the Old Dominion, and it was from the delegation of this state that there came the earliest proposition advanced in Congress to the effect

[1] McMaster, *History of the People of the United States*, I. 140.

that the United States in Congress assembled should have "the sole and exclusive right and power to ascertain and fix the western boundary of such states as claim to the Mississippi, or South Sea, and lay out the land beyond the boundary so ascertained into separate and independent states, from time to time, as the numbers and circumstances of the people may require."[1] This motion was made October 15, 1777, two days before Burgoyne's surrender at Saratoga, and just when the Articles of Confederation were on the point of being submitted to the states for ratification. For the present the proposition was considered too radical, and no delegation except that from Maryland voted for it. As time went on, however, the idea grew in favor that instead of the western lands remaining under the control of five or six of the more lucky states they should be thrown together as the common possession of all the states which by united effort were winning from the British the right of independent nationality. Maryland in particular adhered without compromise to her original proposal, and though by February, 1779, all the other states in one way or another had been induced to accede to the Articles, she steadfastly stood out against a union on any terms other than the nationalizing of all the western claims of the individual states. This ultimatum forced a general discussion of the whole question in Congress, through newspapers, and in state legislatures. The urgency of the perfecting of the union was great, and that union, even under the loose system contained in the Articles, was possible only by the accession of every one of the thirteen states. Since Maryland made it emphati-

[1] *Journals of Congress*, II. 290.

cally understood that she would not ratify the pending constitution until Congress should give assurance that the Northwest Territory would be "parcelled out into free, convenient, and independent governments," there was no hope of union except by a surrender on part of the landholding states.[1]

The first of these to act was New York, whose legislature, February 19, 1780, voted to cede all western claims to the national government. This broke the ice, and thereafter the states which hesitated to take a similar step were put upon the defensive. September 6, 1780, Congress recommended that the example of New York be universally imitated.[2] The next month, by the notable resolution of October 10, Congress definitely pledged itself against permanent colonization in the West by promising that all unappropriated lands ceded to the United States by any state should be disposed of for the common benefit, and should be "settled and formed into distinct republican states, which shall become members of the federal union, and have the same rights of sovereignty, freedom, and independence as the other states."[3] This unequivocal announcement of policy brought the desired effect. Within the same month Connecticut offered to cede all her claim except three and a quarter millions of acres on the southern shore of Lake Erie — the so-called "Western Reserve." — which she wished still to hold for educational purposes. Despite its incomplete character,

[1] Herbert B. Adams, "Maryland's Influence in Founding a National Commonwealth," in the *Maryland Historical Society Publications*, No. XI., and the same paper under a slightly different title in the *Johns Hopkins University Studies in Historical and Political Science*, 3rd Series, 7-54. [2] *Journals of Congress*, III. 516.

[3] *Ibid.*, 535; Joseph Blunt, *Formation of the Confederacy*, 74.

the cession was gladly accepted by Congress. January 2, 1781, Virginia offered to yield all the territory north of the Ohio on condition that Congress guarantee her the possession of Kentucky.[1] There was much objection, however, to continuing the practice of conditional cessions, and during the three years of discussion which followed Congress manifested no small measure of unwillingness to receive the Virginia grant unless it included all that state's transmontane claims. With the understanding that Kentucky should soon be elevated to the dignity of statehood, the conditional cession was finally accepted March 1, 1784.[2] In the meantime, a month after Virginia had made her original offer, it had become sufficiently apparent to Maryland that her plans for a national domain was to prevail, and she had forthwith instructed her delegates in Congress, February 2, 1781, to accede to the Confederation. On the first day of the following March the new constitution went into effect.[3] The cession of state claims in the Northwest was completed April 19, 1784, when Massachusetts hastened to imitate Virginia's magnanimity during the previous month.[4]

---

[1] *Journals of Congress*, IV. 265.

[2] The act of the Virginia assembly and the deed of cession are in Poore, *Federal and State Constitutions*, I. 427-428.

[3] *Journals of Congress*, III. 582.

[4] On the cessions of western lands by the states, see McMaster, *History of the People of the United States*, I. Ch. II.; Winsor, *Narrative and Critical History*, VII. Appendix I., entitled "Territorial Acquisitions and Divisions"; H. B. Adams, "Maryland's Influence in Founding a National Commonwealth," in the *Maryland Historical Society Publications*, No. XI.; F. J. Turner, "Western State-Making in the Revolutionary Era," in the *American Historical Review*, I. 251-258; Shosuke Sato, "The Land Question in the United States," in the *Johns Hopkins University Studies in Historical and Political Science*, 4th Series, Nos. VII.-IX.; Henry Gannett, *Boundaries of the United States and of the Several States and*

The transfer of the western territory from the sovereignty of the individual states to that of the nation imposed a new burden upon Congress. From the outset the theory upon which that body proceeded was that the territory acquired from the states was as completely subject to its authority as it had been a decade before to that of the king of Great Britain. Throughout the troubled period of the Confederation, Congress was strong at this point, if at no other, and would never for a moment concede the right of the frontier populations to set up their own governments. Governments were established, but they were either in defiance of the national authority or else constituted by its express permission. When the cessions by Virginia and Massachusetts, early in 1784, brought the entire Northwest Territory under the jurisdiction of Congress, it was at once perceived that sooner or later there would have to be some sort of recognized system of administration for the dependent territory. Thomas Jefferson, therefore, set himself to work to devise such a system. The result was the Ordinance of 1784, which provided for the ultimate division of the territory into ten states under conditions to be strictly imposed by the national government.[1] This ordinance was never really in force,

Territories; Thomas Donaldson, *The Public Domain* (House Misc. Doc. 47th Cong., Second Sess., Pt. 4, No. 45); Joseph Blunt, *Historical Sketch of the Formation of the Confederacy.* The most important original source of information is the *Journals of Congress,* from 1777 to 1789. A vast quantity of material is contained in the biographies and writings of Madison, Jefferson, Washington, Arthur St. Clair, Manasseh Cutler, Patrick Henry, and George Mason.

[1] The text of the Ordinance of 1784 is printed in the *Old South Leaflets,* No. CXXVII. In Winsor, *Narrative and Critical History,* VII. 529, there

however, because for some years to come the English-speaking population north of the Ohio was too insignificant to warrant the establishment of even temporary local governments. In 1787 the notable Northwest Ordinance was adopted by Congress as a means of encouraging settlement in the Ohio Valley, and this colonial charter — for in effect that is about what it amounted to — subsequently reaffirmed by the Congress of the Constitution, long continued to be the basis of law and politics in the Northwest.[1] It provided distinctly for three stages of progress — the temporary territorial, the more fixed territorial, and that of ultimate statehood. Under the first stage the government to be established by Congress closely resembled that of modern crown colonies in the British Empire, though when the growth of population should permit, a more liberal system was to be established, embracing a general assembly in two houses, considerable legislative powers, and a delegate in Congress to be allowed to speak, but not to vote. Even at this status, however, and especially when application should be made for the dignity of statehood, Congress was to stand ever

is a map of the proposed division of states by this ordinance. See Sparks, *Writings of Washington*, IX. 48, and Morse, *Thomas Jefferson*, 68.

[1] The text of the Northwest Ordinance of 1787 is in the *Revised Statutes* (ed. 1878) and MacDonald, *Select Documents*, 21–29. For discussions of the Ordinance, see W. F. Poole, "The Ordinance of 1787" in the *North American Review*, CXII. 229–265; Cutler and Perkins, *Life, Journals, and Correspondence of Rev. Manasseh Cutler*; Edward Coles, *History of the Ordinance of 1787*; Jay Amos Barrett, *The Evolution of the Ordinance of 1787* (Univ. of Nebraska, Departments of History and Economics Seminary Papers); Hinsdale, *Old Northwest*, Ch. XV.; McMaster, *History of the People of the United States*, I. Ch. V.; Dunn, *Indiana*, Ch. V.; and Israel W. Andrews, "The Northwest Territory," in the *Magazine of American History*, XVI. 133–147.

ready with conditions and restrictions to determine what the political rights and practices of the people should be. And it should be observed in passing that the rigid system thus applied by Congress to the territory acquired by conquest during the Revolution has been pretty generally perpetuated thoughout the later dealings of the United States with dependencies acquired under other and varied conditions.

For some years immediately after the Revolution by far the most important part of the western country was that south of the Ohio; and of this the most interesting was the region known as Tennessee. Kentucky had been almost abandoned by English-speaking people for a time in the year 1775, but Tennessee had been continuously settled since the founding of the Watauga commonwealth in 1772,[1] and had come to include a population of considerable number — perhaps as many as ten thousand souls.[2] In June, 1784, this territory was ceded by North Carolina to the nation, though it was not until 1790 that the transfer was finally made complete. At the time of the cession it was understood that Congress should have two years in which to accept, and in the meantime the jurisdiction of North Carolina was to be continued as before. In the splendid pasture lands lying between the Holston, the Cumberland, and the foot-hills of the Blue Ridge, however, during the past decade had gathered a population of hardy and independent people whom the experiences of frontier life had brought to the conclusion that nothing

---

[1] The first settler on the Watauga, William Bean, crossed the mountains from North Carolina in 1769.
[2] Albach, *Annals of the West* [Pittsburg, 1858], 507.

was gained by attempting to keep up a political attachment with the East. They had petitioned the North Carolina legislature time and again for protection against the tomahawks of the Cherokees, but always in vain, and now the state was ready to cast them off entirely. There was little ground, it was believed, for expecting that the United States would extend the desired relief or authorize the coveted local self-government. Therefore these people of the backwoods proceeded to hold a convention in a log cabin at Jonesborough and adopt a resolution of secession from North Carolina. The three counties — Washington, Greene, and Sullivan — which participated in the movement were organized into a new political body to be known as the state of Franklin, with a written constitution, a two-house legislature, and a full corps of executive and judicial officials. The choice for governor fell upon John Sevier, one of the founders of the Watauga Association, whose long and notable career in the West had won him the significant name of "the lion of the border." While the Tennesseeans proposed to insure for themselves a considerable degree of autonomy, however, they did not care to attempt the impossible task of maintaining absolute independence. Hence a delegate was despatched to request of Congress that the new state of Franklin be admitted as the fourteenth in the Union.

In the meantime the legislature of North Carolina was not by any means disposed to acquiesce in the turn matters were taking. The act of cession was hastily repealed, and the work of reducing the rebels to order commenced. It was recognized that the secessionists had not a few real grounds of complaint, and the assembly addressed itself first of all to the work of removing these excuses for refractory conduct. Courts were ordered to be organized, an attorney-general for the back country to be appointed, the Tennessee militia to be formed into a brigade, and Sevier was commissioned to take command of the defences of the territory. The result of these conciliatory measures was the utmost confusion in the seceding counties. The people were split into two factions, the one wishing to persevere in the effort to acquire statehood on a footing equal with the mother state, the other advocating the policy of yielding because grievances had been redressed. In 1786 one party elected delegates to the North Carolina legislature, the other chose members to sit in the legislature of Franklin. Two complete sets of officials claimed authority, and for two more years civil strife was incessant. In the end the party of reconciliation won and, like other self-constituted commonwealths of the period, the state of Franklin came to an ignominious end. Sevier was arrested on a charge of high treason, but escaped, and subsequently was so fully restored to public favor that in 1796, when Tennessee became a state of the Union, he was enthusiastically chosen to be her first governor.[1]

The corner-stone principle of our first generation of statecraft was that the newly created United States should jealously guard against becoming involved in the tangles of European politics. Washington warned against "quit-

[1] The history of the short-lived state of Franklin is related in Ramsey, *Annals of Tennessee*, Chs. III.–V.; Phelan, *History of Tennessee*, Chs. X.–XII.; F. J. Turner, "Western State-Making in the Revolutionary Era," in the *American Historical Review*, I. 258–261; McMaster, *History of the People of the United States*, I. 156–163; James R. Gilmore, *John Sevier as a Commonwealth-builder*; and George H. Alden, "The State of Franklin," in the *American Historical Review*, VIII. 271–289.

ting our own to stand on foreign ground." John Adams declared it to be "very true that we ought not to involve ourselves in the political system of Europe, but to keep ourselves always distinct and separate from it." Jefferson repeatedly urged the sentiment of his first inaugural, "Peace, commerce, and honest friendship with all, entangling alliances with none." Considering the resources and ideals of the people this was all very wholesome, but as a matter of fact it was early discovered that no civilized nation, not even one three thousand miles from Europe under eighteenth-century conditions, could possibly maintain a steadfast course of isolation. Endeavor as they might, the people of the United States from the outset could not abstain from interest or influence in the councils of European powers. This was the more true because certain of these powers were vitally interested in the disposition of affairs in America.

On the establishing of her independence the United States was left with two European neighbors — England on the northern border and Spain on the southern and western. It was a matter of common knowledge, too, that France was extremely desirous of repossessing herself of the great region between the Mississippi and the Rockies which she had lost to Spain twenty years before. Only the poverty of her treasury was preventing such a consummation. The truth is, therefore, that in these early days we had no need to cross the Atlantic to become involved in European affairs; we were hemmed in on every side but one by European possessions with which we were compelled to maintain some sort of relations, and instead of two, it seemed not at all improbable that soon three alien flags would float over soil contiguous with our own. During the first quarter-century of independence the diplomacy of the United States with Europe was concerned in a very large degree with the settlement of our border-line relations with the Spanish, French, and English. Except for the question of the Northwest posts, with the English we managed, on the whole, to get on fairly well; but on the west and south trouble was well-nigh perennial. By the westward movement the pioneers from the United States were brought face to face in constantly greater numbers with the Spaniard across the Mississippi and the Florida border, and in neither place did the relations between the two peoples long continue to be even presumptively harmonious. The more fundamental causes of conflict were the abiding differences in race, religion, government, and general manner of life — the same that had organized the Armada and impelled Cromwell to a Spanish war. The immediate occasions of ill feeling were two in number — the dispute over the Florida boundary line and the navigation of the Mississippi.

It will be remembered that by the treaty of peace between Great Britain and the United States, negotiated in 1782 and issued in definitive form in 1783, it was provided that "the navigation of the river Mississippi, from its source to the ocean, shall remain forever free and open to the subjects of Great Britain, and the citizens of the United States." This would doubtless have been an abiding settlement of the matter had not Spain, then hostile to both Great Britain and the United States, possessed all the lands west of the river, as well as the Floridas on the eastern side. Spain had had nothing to

do with the making of the treaty in question, and it was at least very uncertain whether she would consider herself obligated to observe its stipulations concerning the use of the Mississippi. By the same instrument the southern boundary of the new nation was fixed at the thirty-first parallel east from the Mississippi as far as the Appalachicola River, and thence by a slightly irregular line (the present northern boundary of Florida) to the sea. When this arrangement was first made Great Britain still considered herself in possession of both East and West Florida, and hoped to be able to retain these provinces permanently under her control. In pursuance of this hope the British commissioner had secured the insertion of a secret article in the treaty to the effect that if Great Britain should continue to hold the Floridas, the boundary between West Florida and the United States should not be 31° but 32° 30′. This line would intersect the Mississippi at the mouth of the Yazoo River, near the present site of Vicksburg, instead of at the mouth of the Yassous, nearly fifty miles below Natchez, as would the former line. Thus Great Britain and the United States virtually recognized the northern boundary of West Florida to be 32° 30′ so far as they were themselves concerned, but agreed that if any other power was to have the Floridas such power must be content with the region south of 31°.[1]

Ere the end of another twelvemonth the Floridas again belonged to Spain. As will be recalled, the retrocession came by way of compromise. The Spanish government

[1] See the American commissioners' defence of this secret article, July 18, 1803, in John Adams, *Works*, I. 375, Appendix F. The text of the secret article is in the *Treaties and Conventions concluded between the United States of America and Other Powers*, 373.

had been demanding persistently that the English yield Gibraltar, and just before peace was effected with America the Shelburne ministry had been on the point of acceding to the demand. The end of the war with America and the French, however, emboldened the ministry in its dealings with Spain, and the latter power was given to understand that in no case would England yield more than the Floridas. Inasmuch as the Spanish already held the western province by reason of Galvez's conquests during the war, it was only the eastern that was ceded outright.

But no sooner was Spain restored to her former possession in this quarter than the very pertinent question arose as to what were "the Floridas"—or rather what was "West Florida," for east of the Appalachicola there was no doubt on the subject of boundaries. The United States claimed all lands southward to 31°.[1] On the ground that England in 1763 had established a province of West Florida which extended northward to 32° 30′, and further that in the treaty of retrocession in 1783 the name "Florida" was used without qualification, Spain, with very good grace, maintained that 32° 30′ was properly to be considered her division line from the United States. And when a little later she became aware of the secret article in the Paris treaty by which 32° 30′ was distinctly recognized as the northern limit of West Florida, her

[1] On the general subject of the Florida boundary, see B. A. Hinsdale, "The Establishment of the First Southern Boundary of the United States," in the *Annual Report of the American Historical Association for 1893*, 331-366; Charles H. Haskins, "The Yazoo Land Companies," in *Papers of the American Historical Association*, V. 395-437; H. E. Chambers, "West Florida and its Relation to the Historical Cartography of the United States," in the *Johns Hopkins University Studies in Historical and Political Science*, 16th Series, No. V.

indignation at the ruse of the contracting powers knew no bounds. By their own admission, the strip of land between 31° and 32° 30' belonged to West Florida; and West Florida now belonged to Spain. England was guilty in that she had played Spain false in ceding her a region which had in part already been given to another power. But the United States was doubly guilty in having received willingly the land which she knew was a part of West Florida, and which therefore, by reason of Galvez's conquests, was not England's to give away. Such was the light in which the Spaniards, at least, chose to regard the matter. The war spirit ran at high tide, and, as John Fiske remarks, once more "Castilian grandees went to bed and dreamed of invincible armadas."[1]

So far as the United States was concerned, Spain had at her disposal a very easy and effective means of retaliation. The peace treaty of 1783 had guaranteed to the subjects of Great Britain and to the citizens of the United States unrestricted freedom of navigation of the Mississippi throughout its entire course. But Spain had not been a party to that treaty and, since the territory on both sides of the mouth of the river was hers, she was in a position to exercise absolute control over all river trade below 31°, — indeed, by virtue of her Yazoo claims, below 32° 30'. When, therefore, the alleged double dealing of the United States with regard to the Florida boundary became known, the Spanish government proceeded to threaten. Unless the territory in dispute should be promptly and unconditionally yielded by the United States, Spain would make absolutely no treaty on commercial and kindred

[1] Fiske, *Critical Period of American History*, 209.

subjects with the young nation, and, moreover, the Mississippi below Natchez would be closed to all American trade, and any vessel that should venture across the forbidden line would be liable to capture and confiscation.

To the people of the West and Southwest this latter threat presaged a direful contingency. The regions now occupied by the states of Kentucky, Tennessee, Alabama, and Mississippi[1] already counted their population by the thousands, and settlement from the East was all the while increasing. These people were engaged almost entirely in agriculture, and their prosperity was dependent upon the facility with which they could dispose of their products in the eastern states and in Europe. Such sales constituted their only means of procuring necessary manufactured articles and of accumulating wealth. Transportation by land, however, was so slow and so expensive that trade between the East and West by way of the Alleghany routes was all but impracticable. Even the high prices which western products — grain, pork, tobacco, etc. — commanded in the eastern markets did not permit of much profit to the producer after expenses of carriage were paid.

There was, however, one way by which this difficulty could be largely overcome, and that was by sending the products in barges down the Mississippi to New Orleans or the vicinity, reloading them there upon sea-going vessels, and thus making shipment by an all-water route to the various Atlantic ports. This was the expedient

---

[1] It should be observed that Georgia's cession of western lands was not made until 1802, so that at the time of which we are speaking this state owned a vast domain bordering on the Mississippi — the present states of Alabama and Mississippi.

which the western people had come by 1784 almost exclusively to employ. The free and unrestricted use of the Mississippi, confirmed by the treaty of 1783, was therefore a matter of vital consequence. The fact that Spain held New Orleans had long been a source of considerable chagrin on part of the Westerners, and the acquisition of West Florida by the same power in 1783 had occasioned general alarm. Yet it was not until the dispute arose over the northern boundary of Florida that any real inconvenience was suffered. Thereafter trade upon the lower Mississippi was entirely at the mercy of the Spanish authorities. At Natchez was established a custom-house whose officials boarded every American vessel that deigned to pass the town, and while the threat of confiscation was not usually put into effect, the traders were subjected to the payment of heavy tolls and were frequently delayed and annoyed in ways almost intolerable. Besides the inconveniences and losses suffered at the hands of the rapacious Spaniards, there was always the consciousness, so utterly repugnant to the freedom-loving Westerner, that his trade, his gains, indeed, his very livelihood, were entirely at the mercy of a Bourbon king and his emissaries. There was no way of escape. It was not merely the Mississippi's mouth that the Spaniard held, but the entire Gulf coast, with all its ports, river-mouths, and harbors. Trade by way of Pensacola or Mobile would have been no freer than by way of New Orleans.

The consequence of all this was that, before a year had elapsed after the reëstablishment of Spanish power in Florida, the trade of the Kentuckians and Tennesseeans was wrecked. The element of risk was so great and the losses so numerous by the Mississippi route, that it had become scarcely more practicable than that through Cumberland Gap. By reason of its enforced isolation, the Southwest stood in immediate danger of becoming commercially stagnant. Tobacco which was worth $9.50 in Virginia would bring but $2 in Kentucky. Corn, pork, flour, and other food products, so abundant in the West and so much in demand in the East, were almost valueless because of the difficulty of transportation. From the people of the Southwest there went up to the Congress of the Confederation a ringing appeal for help. The whole power of the nation, it was urged, should be directed to the task of bringing Spain to terms. The people of the West were citizens of the United States just as much as were the inhabitants of Massachusetts and New York, and as such they must be equally protected. Indeed, most of the western people had only recently come from the eastern states, and were closely bound to the eastern people by many ties even stronger than the political. They were now blazing the way of civilization, bearing the brunt of the struggle with the wilderness, Indians, and jealous European powers. Surely they were not to be cast off by the people of the home states and denied the protecting vigilance of the government to which they professed the utmost loyalty.

But the cry thus raised fell for the most part on ears that were deaf. The people of the states had interests of their own to subserve, and many of them were not greatly concerned about the prosperity or the tribulations of the Westerners. At least, they were not concerned enough to sacrifice their own interests for those of Kentucky and Tennessee; and such a sacrifice it would undoubtedly have

required to undertake at the time to open the Mississippi again to western trade. By the majority of the people of the East the right to use the great river was regarded as properly belonging to the Westerners, and the opinion generally prevailed that such right should not be hastily or needlessly abandoned; but it was likewise held that peaceable relations with Spain were too indispensable to be endangered by undue persistency with regard to a matter which, after all, affected only a relatively small number of people.

The critical character of the situation created in the West by the Spanish closure of trade was discussed with keen perception by Washington in a notable letter to Governor Benjamin Harrison, of Virginia, October 10, 1784, in which were set forth observations made during a tour of the western country during the preceding September. The trip, covering a distance of six hundred and eighty miles, had been made on horseback, and though somewhat curtailed by a threatened Indian uprising, it had been extensive enough to render possible an estimate of conditions based on carefully authenticated facts. "I need not remark to you, sir," says the letter, "that the flanks and rear of the United States are possessed by other powers, and formidable ones, too; nor how necessary it is to apply the cement of interest to bind all parts of the Union together by insoluble bonds, especially that part of it which lies immediately west of us, with the middle states. For what ties, let me ask, should we have upon those people? How entirely unconnected with them shall we be, and what troubles may we not apprehend, if the Spaniards on their right, and Great Britain on their left, instead of throwing stumbling-blocks in their way, as they now do, should hold out lures for their trade and alliance? What, when they get strength, which will be sooner than most people conceive (from the emigration of foreigners, who will have no particular predilection toward us, as well as from the removal of our own citizens), will be the consequence of their having formed close connections with both or either of those powers, in a commercial way? It needs not, in my opinion, the gift of prophecy to foretell.

"The western states (I speak now from my own observation) stand as it were upon a pivot. The touch of a feather would turn them any way. They have looked down the Mississippi, until the Spaniards, very impolitically I think for themselves, threw difficulties in their way; and they looked that way for no other reason than because they could glide gently down the stream, without considering, perhaps, the difficulties of the voyage back again, and the time necessary to perform it in, and because they have no other means of coming to us but by long land transportations and unimproved roads. These causes have hitherto checked the industry of the present settlers; for, except the demand for provisions, occasioned by the increase of population, and a little flour, which the necessities of the Spaniards compel them to buy, they have no incitements to labor. But smooth the road, and make easy the way for them, and then see what an influx of articles will be poured upon us; how amazingly our exports will be increased by them, and how amply we shall be compensated for any trouble and expense we may encounter to effect it."[1]

[1] Washington to Benjamin Harrison, October 10, 1784. Sparks, *Washington's Writings*, IX. 62-63. The letter is reprinted in the *Old South*

In the early summer of 1785 Don Diego de Gardoqui, the trusted agent of Florida Blanca, arrived as the first envoy to the United States from Spain. He presented his credentials July 2, and declared that he had been fully commissioned to conclude a treaty of amity and commerce.[1] After a delay of some months, negotiations were opened between him and John Jay, who, since the conclusion of the Paris treaty, had returned to the United States, only to find that he had been chosen by Congress some months before to succeed Robert R. Livingston in the very important office of secretary for foreign affairs.[2] It was a curious coincidence by which the same two men who, five or six years earlier, at Madrid, had wrestled unavailingly with the problem of a treaty, were thus again pitted against each other in the diplomatic arena. It had previously been the purpose of Congress to send Jay to Spain on a second mission to arrange a commercial treaty, but the coming of Gardoqui rendered such a course unnecessary. Full discretionary powers were at first given Jay to treat on all subjects of interest to the two nations in whatever manner might seem to him advisable;[3] but August 25, 1785, he was more specifically enjoined to secure a treaty which should "stipulate the right of the United States to their territorial bounds, and the free navigation of the Mississippi from the source to the ocean, as established in their treaties with Great Britain."[4]

Leaflets, No. XVI., with other significant extracts illustrative of Washington's intense interest in the West.

[1] *Secret Journals of Congress*, III. 563–570.
[2] *Correspondence and Public Papers of John Jay*, III. 126.
[3] Commission of July 21, 1785. *Secret Journals of Congress*, III. 571.
[4] *Secret Journals of Congress*, III. 586.

Probably Congress could not with dignity have asked for less, yet it must have appeared exceedingly doubtful, even before the negotiations commenced, whether Spain could be brought to yield at the same time on both these fundamental matters of dispute any more easily than during the course of Jay's labors at Madrid in 1780-1782. At the outset Gardoqui represented that his sovereign, Don Carlos III., was well disposed toward the United States and sincerely desired amicable relations with her. But at the same time it was declared with emphasis that the Spanish government would not accede indiscriminately to every demand the young nation might care to make. Aside from the territorial claim in northern Florida, there were two things for which the people of the United States, or at least portions of them, were clamoring — a treaty of commerce and the reopening of the Mississippi to free trade. Of these, said the envoy, Spain would grant one, but not both. Between the two the United States might choose. A satisfactory treaty of commerce she might have, but upon one condition, and one only, *i.e.* that all claim to the right of navigating the Mississippi below Natchez be definitely abandoned. The alternative thus offered was declared to be absolutely final. A year of painstaking negotiation on the subject effected not the slightest change in the envoy's position.

In this proposition from Spain lay all the elements of a disastrous conflict between the East and the West. The New England states in particular, being interested primarily in commerce, zealously urged the making of a commercial treaty with Spain, even if such a course should involve a sacrifice of trading rights on the Missis-

sippi. It is doubtful whether the sore straits in which such an abandonment of the western people would have left them were appreciated at all adequately by the New Englanders. The clamor for relief and for protection by the nation was commonly supposed to arise from a few malcontents, and to be greatly exaggerated as an expression of real western sentiment. But it is equally certain that the consideration which chiefly guided the men who were so willing to thwart the Westerners' only hope of prosperity was the thought that in so doing they were filling their own pockets. At a time when the states, on account of boundary disputes and commercial rivalries, were on the point of plunging into war among themselves, it was hardly to be expected that any great amount of sacrifice would be made by the people of New England for the benefit of the inhabitants of Kentucky and Tennessee.

Of course, on the merits of the case the people of the East generally considered the Westerners quite right in their contention for the use of the Mississippi, but they also regarded it highly inexpedient under existing circumstances to press the claim too far. Our present dealings with Spain were but a matter of choice between the greater and lesser of two evils. Since it appeared that either the majority's demand for a commercial treaty or the minority's demand for the opening of the Mississippi must be abandoned, men in high station who counted themselves friends of every enterprise looking to the prosperity of the West were yet constrained to take the extreme eastern view. Secretary Jay was one of these. In his responsible position he could not but desire the continuance of peace and the establishment of close commercial relations with all the European powers. He was apprehensive lest, if the question of the navigation of the Mississippi be allowed to force itself prominently into the negotiations with Spain, that question and its kindred issue, the Florida boundary, might involve the two nations in war; and all risk of war must be avoided at any cost.

Accordingly, on the 3rd of August, 1786, Congress was definitely advised by the secretary to consent to the closing of the Mississippi for a period of twenty-five years, in the hope that by such a concession the desired treaty of commerce might be secured. In his speech on this occasion Jay enumerated many reasons for concluding an amicable settlement with Spain, even if involving terms unsatisfactory to the United States. Among them were that France, the ally of the United States, was also an ally of Spain, and as between the two the latter alliance was probably the stronger; that England would be glad to take advantage of a struggle between Spain and the United States; that commercial interests demanded friendship with Spain; that Spain was at the time "sincerely disposed to make friends of us"; that the navigation of the Mississippi was not then important nor likely to be so during the period of the proposed treaty; and that by insisting too strongly on their rights at this juncture the United States might lose all claim to the navigation of the river in the future. Jay made it clear that he did not regard his proposal as an ideal solution, but merely as the only one which could be deemed at all practicable. Nor did he consider it in any sense final. "My letters written from Spain," he asserted, "when our

affairs were the least promising, evince my opinion respecting the Mississippi, and oppose every idea of our relinquishing our right to navigate it. I entertain the same sentiments of that right, and of the importance of retaining it, which I then did. Mr. Gardoqui strongly insists on our relinquishing it. We have had many conferences and much reasoning on the subject, not necessary now to detail. His concluding answer to all my arguments has steadily been, that the king will never yield that point, nor consent to any compromise about it; for that it always has been, and continues to be, one of their maxims of policy to exclude all mankind from their American shores. I have often reminded him that the adjacent country was filling fast with people; and that the time must and would come when they would not submit to seeing a fine river flow before their doors without using it as a highway to the sea for the transportation of their productions; that it would therefore be wise to look forward to that event, and take care not to sow in the treaty any seeds of future discord. He said that the time alluded to was far distant, and that treaties were not to provide for contingencies so remote and future. For his part he considered the rapid settlement of that country as injurious to the states, and that they would find it necessary to check it."

The conclusion to which all these considerations brought the secretary was that, under existing conditions, it "would be expedient to agree that the treaty should be limited to twenty-five or thirty years, and that one of the articles should stipulate that the United States would forbear to use the navigation of that river [the Mississippi] below their territories to the ocean." Whether

Gardoqui would be disposed to agree to such an arrangement Jay was unable to state, since of course his instructions from Congress had not afforded him the liberty of advancing such a proposition. He, however, thought the experiment worth trying, and this for several reasons. In the first place, unless the Mississippi question could in some way be settled, there was not the slightest possibility of a treaty being concluded. In the second place, as Jay put it, "as that navigation is not at present important, nor will probably become much so in less than twenty-five or thirty years, a forbearance to use it while we do not want it, is no great sacrifice." Thirdly, said Jay, "Spain now excludes us from that navigation, and with a strong hand holds it against us. She will not yield it peaceably, and therefore we can only acquire it by war. Now as we are not prepared for a war with any power; as many of the states would be little inclined to a war with Spain for that object at this day; and as such a war would for those and a variety of obvious reasons be inexpedient, — it follows that Spain will, for a long space of time yet to come, exclude us from that navigation. Why, therefore, should we not (for a valuable consideration, too) consent to forbear to use what we know is not in our power to use?" Lastly, Jay asked, if Spain and the United States should "part on this point," what were the latter to do? They were not capable of war; there was only the remotest possibility that they could gain their end through any new international arrangement; and experience impressed strongly the fact that diplomatic opportunities lost in dealing with the Spaniards were practically gone forever. It was much to be wished that the whole controversy

could have been postponed for years, but that was clearly out of the question. It must somehow be settled now. If it were not, and the United States continued to rebuff the Spanish advances by insisting too strongly on their rights, unmistakable as they were, the result might be to drive Spain into a permanently hostile position where all manner of ill treatment would be heaped upon the young and defenceless nation. In this case "the Mississippi would continue shut; France would tell us our claim to it was ill founded; the Spanish posts on its banks, and even those out of Florida in our country, would be strengthened; and that nation would there bid us defiance with impunity, at least until the American nation shall become more really and truly a nation than it at present is. For, unblessed with an efficient government, destitute of funds, and without public credit, either at home or abroad, we should be obliged to wait in patience for better days, or plunge into an unpopular and dangerous war with very little prospect of terminating it by a peace either advantageous or glorious."

The strong feature of Jay's whole contention was that, while failing to appreciate the present importance of the Mississippi navigation, he recognized diplomatic conditions as they actually existed, and proposed to deal with the Spaniards on that basis. If he could not secure what he wanted, he would nevertheless take what he could get. His declarations had a very pessimistic sound, to be sure, but they were only such as might have been expected from a man whose acquaintance with both the strength and weakness of the American position was as thoroughgoing as was Jay's. When one takes into account the state of the country in 1786, — the weakness of Congress, the breakdown of the Articles of Confederation, the utter wreck of finances, and the despicable jealousies and enmities of the states, — the reasonableness of the secretary's policy becomes more apparent. It was quite impossible that he should foresee that nearly a decade later the whole question of the navigation of the Mississippi should reach its first satisfactory settlement amicably through the pressure brought to bear upon the Spaniards by a treaty which he was himself destined to negotiate with Great Britain in 1794. In the course of his remarkable address to Congress Jay, recurring to his tortuous experiences as a diplomat and foreign minister, expressed the opinion that "courts never admit the force of any reasoning or arguments but such as apply in their favor," and ventured the assertion that "even if our right to that navigation [of the Mississippi], or to anything else, was expressly declared in holy writ, we should be able to provide for the enjoyment of it no otherwise than by being in capacity to repel force by force."[1]

In Congress Jay's proposition to yield the Mississippi for twenty-five years aroused a storm of debate.[2] By the New England members it was received with unfeigned delight, because it foretokened the desired treaty of commerce, while the representatives from the South were generally opposed. The party lines drawn and the arguments employed were of a purely sectional character. The New Englanders demanded that the Spanish treaty be negotiated immediately on the terms Jay suggested, or in

[1] *Secret Journals of Congress*, IV. 51–52.
[2] For the numerous motions and proposals which the consideration of Jay's report elicited in Congress, see the *Secret Journals*, IV. 81–127.

truth upon any others that might prove necessary. By them it was contended with good reason that the evil conditions so prevalent throughout the country were in a large measure due to the stagnation of trade. To energize trade, treaties were essential, and a treaty with Spain was especially to be desired. If, as Jay said, in order to secure such a treaty the navigation of the Mississippi must be given up, why so let it be. On the other hand, the members from the southern states, who were more interested in the "back country," expressed a decided unwillingness to accept such a solution of the matter. They saw visions of Spanish power in the West which were at least not reassuring. Commercial treaties were not of so great importance to the people south of the Potomac, and therefore the policy advocated by the Northerners in their own interest met with scant support outside New England and New York. " Was it reasonable, such was the language of some noted Southerners, to demand so great a sacrifice from one section of the country for the benefit of another? Massachusetts seemed to think it very hard that the South would not fall in with Spain; would not sell the affections of her western colonies; throw away her richest possessions; distrust an ally able and willing to befriend her; and court, by the most precious sacrifices, an alliance with a power whose impotency was notorious. But what would Massachusetts say to a proposition to give up to Great Britain her right of fishery as the price of some stipulation in favor of tobacco?"[1]

The culminating point of the discussion in Congress elicited by Jay's proposal for the temporary closure of the

[1] McMaster, *History of the People of the United States*, I. 378.

Mississippi was reached August 30, when as a result of much debate and repeated voting upon motions and amendments, the following definite resolution was brought before the body for its acceptance or rejection: "Resolved, that the secretary to the United States for the department of foreign affairs be and hereby is instructed to propose, and if possible to obtain the following stipulations, viz., That the citizens of the United States shall not be interrupted in transporting the *bona fide* productions of the United States upon the Mississippi River, from thirty-one degrees north latitude to the city of New Orleans, where they shall be allowed to land the same, and permission be granted them to occupy storehouses and other necessary buildings for the reception thereof. That the boats or other vessels, on board of which the said productions shall have been transported to New Orleans, shall have free leave to return up the Mississippi River to any place within the territory of the United States; provided that so far as they navigate below thirty-one degrees north latitude, they shall not load any species of goods, wares, or merchandise whatsoever, but by permission of the Spanish government in Florida. That American merchants or factors shall have free leave to reside at New Orleans for the purpose of receiving such American productions as may be brought down the said river Mississippi, and for exporting the same from thence in American or Spanish bottoms under the regulations of the respective countries. That a duty not exceeding two and a half per cent *ad valorem* shall be paid to the crown of Spain, upon all American produce shipped from the same city of New Orleans, in American bottoms, within six months after

such exportation, for which good and sufficient bonds shall be given previous to the departure of any vessel on board of which such produce shall be laden. That American vessels may freely navigate up the said river Mississippi, from the mouth to the said city of New Orleans, but shall not carry any species of goods, wares, and merchandise whatever, contrary to the regulations of the crown of Spain, under pain of seizure and confiscation. That if in the course of his negotiation with the *encargado de negocios*[1] of his Catholic Majesty, it shall be found indispensable for the conclusion of the same, that the United States and their citizens, for a limited time, should forbear to use so much of the river Mississippi as is south of the southern boundary of the United States, the said secretary be and hereby is authorized and directed, on behalf of the United States, to consent to an article or articles stipulating on their part and that of their citizens, a forbearance of the use of the said river Mississippi, for a period not exceeding twenty years, from the point where the southern boundary of the United States intersects the said river to its mouth or the ocean; provided, that such stipulation of a forbearance of the use of the said river for a limited time, as aforesaid, shall not be construed to extinguish the right of the United States, independent of such stipulation, to use and navigate the said river from its source to the ocean."[2] It was further provided in the resolution that in no case should the exclusive Spanish navigation of the river below 31° be conceded if the

---

[1] This was Gardoqui's official title. It was more modest than that of minister, though its bearer was vested with practically all the powers of a minister. [2] *Secret Journals of Congress*, IV. 120–121.

Spaniards should attempt to hinder American trade above that parallel, and that no treaty should be signed by the secretary which did not expressly yield the Spanish claim to the belt of land between 31° and 32° 30′ along the north Florida border.

Upon this proposition, Pinckney, of South Carolina, demanded the yeas and nays, with a result which shows in a most conclusive manner the purely sectional character of the controversy. When the vote was taken there were upon the floor of Congress twenty-nine delegates, representing all of the thirteen states except Delaware. Voting was of course by states, and in order that the proposed new instructions be issued, nine of these must concur in their favor. The vote stood seven affirmative and five negative. Massachusetts, New Hampshire, Rhode Island, Connecticut, New York, Pennsylvania, and New Jersey — all the New England and middle states represented — made up the majority; while Virginia, Maryland, Georgia, and the two Carolinas, under the peculiar system of the Confederation, were able to defeat the measure. It is further worthy of note that the states voted solidly; that is, there was not a single instance in which the vote of a state was dissented from by a minority member of the delegation.[1] The general result might have been prophesied with considerable assurance, but the clear-cut character of the division was one more revelation of that startling dominance of sectional over national interests which threatened the complete subversion of the tottering Union.

In the West Jay's proposition was received with an outbreak of righteous indignation. During the two years

[1] For the vote, see *Secret Journals of Congress*, IV. 122-123.

since the arrival of the Spanish minister the western hatred of the Spanish power had been steadily increasing. Only a few weeks before Jay's recommendation was made, an incident had occurred which more than anything else thus far operated to swell the grievance of the Westerners beyond the point of endurance. Thomas Amis, an enterprising and reckless North Carolina trader, ventured down the Mississippi below the Spanish line with a flatboat laden with a cargo of flour, domestic utensils, and agricultural implements, which he expected to dispose of to the Spanish settlers near the river's mouth. When he reached Natchez, however, he was stopped by the authorities, and his goods brought to land. Both boat and cargo were confiscated. With what they characterized as rare generosity, the officials permitted Amis to return in freedom to the states.[1] After a long and exhausting journey overland, the unfortunate trader at length found himself again among the settlers of Kentucky. It may be assumed that the tale which he had to recount lost nothing in the telling. Wherever he went he was at once the object of boisterous sympathy, and the occasion of a violent burst of wrath against the Spaniard. As a recent writer has said, "No pilgrim returning from the Holy Land, showing the stripes which had been inflicted on him by the Turks, aroused more indignation than did

---

[1] The pass given to Amis by the lieutenant-colonel at Natchez, Don Carlos de Grandpri, is given in the *Secret Journals of Congress*, IV. 326. It was dated August 29, 1786, and declared that during Amis's detention he had "behaved himself as a gentleman and man of the strictest honour." Amis's oath "on the holy evangelist of Almighty God," in which he declared his losses before a North Carolina justice of the peace, is in the *Secret Journals*, IV. 325.

Amis with his story." And occurrences of the sort were all the time becoming more frequent.

Little is it to be wondered at, therefore, that when the news was borne to the West that Congress was meditating an acceptance of the closure of the Mississippi for twenty or twenty-five years (if indeed a treaty to that effect had not already been made)[1] the Westerners were not long in arriving at the conclusion that it was useless longer to trust to national protection, and that the time had come for them to take the matter into their own hands. George Rogers Clark was placed in command of some hastily raised troops, and a general policy of reprisal upon the Spanish was adopted. Under Clark's order a store belonging to a Spaniard at Vincennes was looted and the owner forced to flee down the river.[2] The Indians were everywhere exhorted to seize and hold any Spanish property they might find. The Kentuckians petitioned the Virginia legislature for relief, and anonymous letters setting forth the sad state of the Westerners were circulated throughout the East. Many of these letters threatened the reëstablishment of British control in the West unless the government of

[1] For quite a while it was believed in the West that a treaty had been concluded. See an extremely interesting letter by Thomas Green to the governor, council, and legislature of Georgia, written at Louisville, December 23, 1786, in which the indignant Kentuckian goes on to say: "The commercial treaty with Spain is considered to be cruel, oppressive, and unjust. The prohibition of the navigation of the Mississippi has astonished the whole western country. To sell us and make us vassals to the merciless Spaniards, is a grievance not to be borne. Should we tamely submit to such manacles, we should be unworthy the name of Americans, and a scandal to the annals of its history." *Secret Journals of Congress*, IV. 315–317.

[2] For Jay's report to Congress on the subject of Clark's reprisal, see the *Secret Journals of Congress*, IV. 301 et seq.

the United States should speedily perform its duty of protection.

One of these anonymous letters, written by a gentleman at the falls of the Ohio (Louisville) to his friend in New England, under date of December 4, 1786, is so striking as to have won a place in the *Secret Journals of Congress*, and as an intelligent expression of western sentiment at the time is worthy of very careful consideration. The writer of it shared the belief, very prevalent in the back country in the latter part of 1786, that Congress had actually concluded a commercial treaty with Spain, and at the behests of the New Englanders had paid for it by an abandonment of the navigation of the Mississippi. "Dear Sir," begins the letter, "Politicks, which a few months ago were scarcely thought of, are now sounded aloud in this part of the world, and discussed by almost every person. The late commercial treaty with Spain, in shutting up, as it is said, the navigation of the Mississippi for the term of twenty-five years, has given this western country a universal shock, and struck its inhabitants with an amazement. Our foundation is affected; it is therefore necessary that every individual exert himself to apply a remedy. To sell us and make us vassals to the merciless Spaniards, is a grievance not to be borne. The parliamentary acts which occasioned our revolt from Great Britain were not so barefaced and intolerable. To give us the liberty of transporting our effects down the river to New Orleans, and then be subject to the Spanish laws and impositions, is an insult upon our understanding. We know by woful experience that it is in their power, when once there, to take our produce at any price they please. Large quantities of flour, tobacco, meal, etc., have been taken there the last summer, and mostly confiscated. Those who had permits from their governor were obliged to sell at a price he was pleased to state, or subject themselves to lose the whole. Men of large property are already ruined by their policy."[1]

The writer then proceeds vigorously to upbraid the New Englanders who are considered primarily responsible for the government's supposed abandonment of the West. "What benefit can you on the Atlantick shores receive from this act? The Spaniards from the amazing resources of this river can supply all their own markets at a much lower price than you possibly can. Though this country has been settling but about six years, and that in the midst of an inveterate enemy, and most of the first adventurers fallen a prey to the savages, and although the emigration to this country is so very rapid that the internal market is very great, yet the quantities of produce they now have on hand are immense. Flour and pork are now selling here at twelve shillings the hundred; beef in proportion; any quantities of Indian corn can be had at nine pence per bushel. Three times the quantity of tobacco and corn can be raised on an acre here that can be within the settlement on the east side of the mountains, and with less cultivation. It is therefore rational to suppose that in a very few years the vast bodies of waters in those rivers will labor under immense weight of the produce of this rich and fertile country, and the Spanish ships be unable to convey it to market. Do you think to prevent the emigration from a barren

[1] *Secret Journals of Congress*, IV. 320–321.

country loaded with taxes and impoverished with debts, to the most luxurious and fertile soil in the world? Vain is the thought, and presumptuous the supposition. You may as well endeavor to prevent the fishes from gathering on a bank in the sea which affords them plenty of nourishment. Shall the best and largest part of the United States be uncultivated, a nest for savages and beasts of prey? Certainly not. . . . Shall all this country now be cultivated entirely for the use of the Spaniards? Shall we be their bondmen as the children of Israel were to the Egyptians? Shall one part of the United States be slaves, while the other is free? Human nature shudders at the thought, and freemen will despise those who could be so mean as to even contemplate on so vile a subject."

And now comes the point of the whole argument — the threat of an armed uprising, and the consequent possibility of a separation of the West from the United States. "We can raise twenty thousand troops," says the writer, "this side the Alleghany and Appalachian mountains; and the annual increase of them by emigration from other parts is from two to four thousand. We have taken all the goods belonging to the Spanish merchants of post Vincennes and the Illinois, and are determined they shall not trade up the river, provided they will not let us trade down it. Preparations are now making here (if necessary) to drive the Spaniards from their settlements at the mouth of the Mississippi. In case we are not countenanced and succored by the United States (if we need it) our allegiance will be thrown off, and some other power applied to. Great Britain stands ready with open arms to receive and support us. They have already offered to open their resources for our supplies. When once reunited to them, 'farewell, a long farewell, to all your boasted greatness.' The province of Canada and the inhabitants of these waters, of themselves, in time, will be able to conquer you. You are as ignorant of this country as Great Britain was of America. These hints, if rightly improved, may be of some service; if not, blame yourselves for the neglect."[1]

The negotiations with Gardoqui went steadily forward, but yet with slight show of real progress. With every passing month it was clearer that the cause of the Westerners was gaining in the states. The Virginia legislature, while condemning Clark's reprisal at Vincennes, voted unanimous sympathy with the people of the back country.[2] Madison's great influence had been won over to their side. While the New Englanders were as persistent as ever, the people of the middle states were turning toward the southern view. Under the Articles of Confederation the consent of nine states was necessary to the ratification of any treaty, and by the middle of April, 1787, when Jay made another comprehensive report to Congress on the state of the negotiation with Spain, it was evident that such a majority could never be secured in support of any agreement to yield the navigation of the Mississippi River, even for a limited term of years. Jay had drawn up an article making such a concession, but it was never in any great

---

[1] *Secret Journals of Congress*, IV. 320–323. The letter is printed in Lyman, *Diplomacy of the United States*, I. 232–234, note.

[2] Documents pertaining to Virginia's action are in the *Secret Journals of Congress*, IV. 305–328.

danger of being accepted.[1] With respect to the navigation of the Mississippi, Jay said in his report that he and Gardoqui had "had repeated conversations which produced nothing but debate, and in the course of which we did not advance one single step nearer to each other. He continued, and still continues, decided in refusing to admit us to navigate the river below our limits on any terms or conditions, nor will he consent to any article *declaring our rights in express terms, and stipulating to forbear the use of it for a given time.*"[2] Jay made it clear that in his proposal to compromise with Spain by yielding the navigation of the lower Mississippi for a specified number of years his purpose was "to save the *right* and only suspend the *use*" during the term of the treaty. But the problem of bringing Congress to the adoption of this plan was rendered quite irrelevant by the fact that when it was laid before Gardoqui he flatly rejected it, and once more declared emphatically that the Spanish policy was to exclude Americans, as well as all other peoples, from the Gulf of Mexico, absolutely and permanently. "A variety of circumstances and considerations which I need not mention," says Jay in concluding his report, "render this negotiation dilatory, unpleasant, and uncompromising; and it is much to be wished that the United States could jointly and unanimously adopt and pursue some fixed and stable plan of policy in regard to Spain, especially during the residence of Mr. Gardoqui, who, I do verily believe, is

[1] This proposed article is in the *Secret Journals of Congress*, IV. 298-299.

[2] Report dated April 11, 1787, *Correspondence and Public Papers of John Jay*, III. 240. *Secret Journals of Congress*, IV. 297-301. The report was read before Congress, April 13.

sincerely disposed to do everything useful and acceptable to America that his instructions and the essential interests of his country, as understood by him and his master, will permit."[1]

Seven days after Jay's report was made, Madison moved in Congress that Jefferson be sent from Paris as minister plenipotentiary to Spain to "enter into commercial stipulations" and to "make representations" on the questions of Florida and the Mississippi.[2] One of the most heated controversies in the history of Congress ensued. But nothing tangible came of it — except still more conclusive proof that a treaty with Spain was at the time wholly impossible.[3] Spain still contended for the closure of the Mississippi as a *sine qua non*, and the number of states which would any longer support a treaty on that basis was steadily decreasing. During the next two years the interests of all the states was centred upon the making and the ratification of the Constitution. In the hope of increased powers of the central government and of added facilities for the conduct of foreign relations, the question of the Spanish treaty, along with many other kindred matters, was allowed to fall into abeyance. Conditions in the West continued as unsettled as ever; but the prospect of a reorganized government served to eke out the patience of the people somewhat, and loyal relations with the Union were fairly well maintained. By vote of Congress, September 16, 1788, Jay's commission to negotiate was revoked, and the

---

[1] *Correspondence and Public Papers of John Jay*, III. 243.

[2] *Secret Journals of Congress*, IV. 339.

[3] See Jay's argument against transferring the negotiations back to Madrid, *ibid.*, 338–342.

settlement of the whole affair was passed on to the new government under the Constitution. At the same time a resolution was enthusiastically adopted that "the free navigation of the river Mississippi is a clear and essential right of the United States, and the same ought to be considered and supported as such."[1] This final expression of opinion by the old confederate Congress marked an advance in national sentiment which augured well for the new government to be organized the following March.

Meanwhile an unscrupulous adventurer by the name of James Wilkinson, a Marylander who had settled in Kentucky in 1784, was working out a solution of the problem in a method peculiarly his own. The failure of Clark in the so-called Wabash expedition for the capture of Vincennes in 1786 had left Wilkinson probably the most popular and influential man in the West. No one understood better than he, however, that in order to retain popularity among the Westerners incessant activity and bold deeds were all the time necessary. No possible achievement would go so far in this direction as the opening of the Mississippi to the trade of the Kentuckians and their fellows, and with the most consummate ambition Wilkinson proceeded to address himself to this great task, which even the government of the nation had thus far failed to accomplish. His first step was to test the temper of the Spanish authorities by sending a flatboat loaded with food-stuffs down the river to Natchez. When the barge reached this point it was stopped and examined, but when the commandant learned whose craft it was, he decided to allow it to pass without tolls or confiscation.

[1] *Secret Journals of Congress*, IV. 447.

He knew something of Wilkinson's influence in the West and was afraid of war if the soldier-merchant should be treated with disrespect. At New Orleans, however, the intendant, Martin Navarro, knew nothing of Wilkinson and little of the temper of the Kentuckians, and was on the point of confiscating the cargo when an influential merchant of the city who was aware of Wilkinson's reputation besought the governor, Miro, to intervene lest a war with the Americans be precipitated. The merchant gave Miro to understand that the Kentuckians were on the verge of making an expedition against New Orleans to open the Mississippi, and urged that no action be omitted to ward off such a calamity. The strong influence of Wilkinson was alleged to be a reason why he should be treated with peculiar consideration. Miro was fully persuaded of the wisdom of this view, and gave orders that Wilkinson's goods be allowed to be sold free of duty. In a short time Wilkinson presented himself at New Orleans, sought out his merchant advocate and obtained an interview with Miro, represented with the most consummate bravado that he was the specially commissioned agent of Congress, and brought the Spanish authorities to believe that only by yielding to him whatever he might ask could they avert certain war with the United States. The result was that Miro and Wilkinson struck a bargain by which the latter was to do all that he could to win the people of Kentucky to friendship with the Spanish, and in return he was to be afforded a safe market at New Orleans for all the flour and tobacco he could send thither. Soon after Wilkinson's return to Kentucky he was approached by Colonel Connally, of the

British army, a man who had gained a most unsavory reputation in the war of Lord Dunmore in 1774, with a plan to join the Kentuckians with the British in an expedition for the conquest of Spanish Louisiana.[1] But the prospect of wealth which the recent compact with Miro had opened up was too tempting to be thus thrust aside, and Connally was frightened into withdrawing to his post at Detroit.

Wilkinson now prepared a great trading expedition to New Orleans. Enormous quantities of flour, bacon, tobacco, butter, and hams were collected at Louisville and stored on twenty-five flatboats, each bearing the Kentucky colors and carrying a swivel gun or a three-pounder for defence, ready for the voyage. Early in January, 1789, "amid the shouts and blessings of the whole town," the flotilla started. The popularity of Wilkinson was at its highest pitch. "He was looked on as a great deliverer. He had opened the Mississippi. He had made a market, and emptied countless rude warehouses and barns, where for three years the kindly fruits of the earth had been stored up, and where, but for him, they might have stayed till they were eaten by rats and worms, or become foul from decay."[2] No sooner was Wilkinson's expedition well under way than dozens of other traders hastened to follow his example. Indeed, so many barges were fitted out for the lower Mississippi trade that by the spring of 1789 the price of food in some of the Kentucky counties had risen sixty per cent.[3] But despite all this

[1] Letter of Arthur St. Clair to John Jay, December 13, 1788, in William H. Smith, *St. Clair Papers*, II. 101.

[2] McMaster, *History of the People of the United States*, I. 523.

[3] Letter dated Marietta, March 10, 1790, *Freeman's Journal*, May 12, 1790.

the question of the navigation of the Mississippi was by no means settled. Because of Miro's pledge, Wilkinson's cargoes were treated considerately, but those of the other traders met their accustomed fate. Miro's promise of protection was merely a personal one to Wilkinson, and carried absolutely no immunity for the merchandise of other Westerners. And as time went on and the chicanery by which Wilkinson had wrung his concession from the Spanish governor came to be understood at New Orleans, even his prerogatives passed into airy nothingness. Within a twelvemonth the status of trade on the lower Mississippi was precisely what it had been before Wilkinson appeared on the scene.[1]

It must always be remembered to the credit of Thomas Jefferson that he was one of the first public men, not himself a Westerner, to appreciate the real importance, not merely to the West, but to the nation at large, of maintaining inviolate the right to navigate the Mississippi. As early as August 2, 1790, after the Washington administration was well under way, and when the work of adjusting our foreign relations was seriously undertaken, Jefferson, as secretary of state, wrote a letter to William Carmichael, the American *chargé d'affaires* at the court of Madrid, instructing him to impress the Spanish ministry thoroughly "with the necessity of an early and even an

---

[1] On Wilkinson's operations in the Southwest at this time, see Roosevelt, *The Winning of the West*, III. 123-152; McMaster, *History of the People of the United States*, I. 520-524; Gayarré, *History of Louisiana*, III. Ch. V.; and Martin, *History of Louisiana*, II. 91-110. By far the most important original source of information on the career of Wilkinson is his *Memoirs of my Own Times* [Philadelphia, 1816], in three volumes. The period under present consideration, however, is passed over very lightly.

immediate settlement of this matter." Negotiations were not to be opened, however, unless as a preliminary consideration the complete freedom of navigation of the Mississippi should be conceded. The securing of this concession was to be followed by a demand for "a port where the sea and river vessels may meet and exchange loads, and where those employed about them may be safe and unmolested." The immediate urgency of the matter was thus emphasized: "It is impossible to answer for the forbearance of our western citizens. We endeavor to quiet them with an expectation of an attainment of their ends by peaceable means. But should they, in a moment of impatience, hazard others, there is no saying how far we may be led; for neither themselves nor their rights will ever be abandoned by us."[1] In 1787 Jefferson had written to Madison, "The act which abandons it [the Mississippi] is an act of separation between the eastern and the western country."[2] The acknowledged purpose of Jefferson, now that he stood at the head of the foreign department of the new government, was to secure New Orleans, together with the island on which the city is located, as the desired place of deposit. His opinion was, however, that Spain should not be asked at the outset to make so great a concession, but should rather be gradually familiarized "by reason and events" with the nature and force of the American demand.

In December, 1791, it was intimated to the secretary of state by a Spanish commissioner that his Catholic Majesty

---

[1] Jefferson to Carmichael, August 2, 1790, *American State Papers, Foreign Relations*, I. 247; *Jefferson's Works* (ed. by Washington), III. 173.

[2] Jefferson to Madison, January 30, 1787, *Jefferson's Works*, II. 87.

had become willing to make some arrangement with the United States respecting the use of the Mississippi, provided the negotiation be carried on at Madrid.[1] Jefferson strongly recommended to the President that advantage be taken of this overture without delay, and that Carmichael and some other capable man be designated to undertake the task of securing a favorable treaty on behalf of the United States. The suggestion appealed favorably to Washington, and under date of January 11, 1792, Carmichael and William Short, American *chargé d'affaires* at Paris, were nominated "to be commissioners plenipotentiary for negotiating and concluding, with any person or persons who shall be duly authorized by his Catholic Majesty, a convention or treaty concerning the navigation of the river Mississippi by the citizens of the United States."[2] On the further recommendation of Jefferson, the scope of the negotiation was widened to include the two other cardinal issues between the United States and Spain — the Florida boundary and the regulation of commerce.[3] In a remarkable state paper transmitted by Jefferson to the President, March 18, 1792, embodying "observations on the subjects of negotiation, to be communicated to the commissioners of the United States," the American argument in behalf of the free navigation of the Mississippi was stated with rare cogency under three distinct heads, *i.e.* the treaty of Paris of 1763, the treaty at the close of the Revolution, 1782–1783, and the law of nature and nations.[4] To summarize his points in the brief-

---

[1] Jefferson to Washington, December 22, 1791, in the *American State Papers*, I. 251.   [2] *Ibid.*, 131.   [3] *Ibid.*, 134.
[4] This significant document is in the *American State Papers*, I. 252-

est possible way, Jefferson maintained, (1) that the people of the English colonies in America, as British subjects, acquired by the treaty of 1763 unrestricted rights on all parts of the Mississippi's course, and that these rights were held in common by all the colonies; (2) that Galvez's conquests during the Revolution could not legally affect the conditions of navigation on the lower Mississippi, since New Orleans had all the time been in Spanish hands since 1763, and, furthermore, that the continuous rights of the English-speaking Americans could not be interrupted by the mere fact that they had seen fit to throw off the sovereignty of Great Britain; and (3) that, on broad grounds, the law of nature and nations prescribed that the ocean should be free to all men, and the rivers to all who dwelt upon them. This last point, being more vague and disputable than the others, was fortified with copious references to Grotius, Pufendorf, and other recognized authorities on international law. It was finally recommended as a *sine qua non*, and Carmichael and Short were so instructed, that the American "right be acknowledged of navigating the Mississippi, in its whole breadth and length, from its source to the sea, as established by the treaty of 1763."

The American commissioners were received at the court of Madrid early in February, 1793. From the outset, however, the prospect of a successful negotiation was dark, and this for two reasons. In the first place, Count d'Aranda had been succeeded in the office of prime minister by Don Manuel Godoy, the Duke of Alcudia, who at

257. Considerable portions of it are quoted in Lyman, *The Diplomacy of the United States*, I. 236–241.

this stage was by no means so conciliatory as he was to be a few years later, and who appointed as the Spanish commissioner that veteran in the business of tantalizing the Americans — Diego Gardoqui. Moreover, a change in the status of Spanish foreign relations in Europe operated against the negotiation. Better feeling existed between Spain and England, while, on the other hand, all possibility of French intervention on behalf of the interests of the United States was ruined by an early declaration of war by the French republic against Spain. After acquainting themselves with every aspect of the situation, the commissioners came to the conclusion that at such a time by pressing for a hearing they would but work injury to their cause. Their instructions bound them to certain definite and pretty rigid lines, and they were not long in perceiving that the new Spanish ministry was in no mood for considering with the least degree of favor the only terms they had been empowered to offer. They therefore adopted a general policy of procrastination, from which there was no danger whatever of their being stirred by the temporizing Gardoqui. In the course of time the home government, aroused by Spanish intrigues in the Southwest, sought to energize its representatives at Madrid; but, though the latter once got so far as to lay the American claims before Godoy, absolutely no progress was made in respect to the great objects of their mission. The only point gained was a vague statement from Godoy to the effect that the Spanish had no intention of interfering with the operations of the United States to reduce the Southwestern Indians to order. The commission was finally dissolved by the return of Carmichael from Madrid

to the United States. Short remained as *chargé d'affaires*, but was disliked by Godoy and had no chance to render his country any service of importance.[1]

Meanwhile Jefferson's favorite policy of "familiarizing" the Spaniards gradually with the new American régime and its greater efficiency in international affairs was occupying a good deal of time, and the people of the West were again becoming very restive under their commercial restraints. The swarm of officials with whom it was necessary to deal in order to use the Mississippi grew both larger and more arrogant. They were spoken of by the tradesmen as worse than the subjects of the Dey of Algiers — a comparison particularly expressive in the last decade of the eighteenth century. Every packet which sailed down the river with goods for an Atlantic port ran the risk of being confiscated entire as soon as it crossed the line 32° 30'. If it escaped this, the gauntlet which had to be run was yet formidable. The vessel was sure to be stopped at New Madrid,[2] boarded, and searched, and the captain compelled to purchase a pass on which he might proceed to New Orleans.[3] This place reached, the entire cargo must be

[1] Much documentary material on the mission of Carmichael and Short is contained in a communication by President Washington to Congress, April 15, 1794, in the *American State Papers*, I. 432-446. For general accounts, see Trescot, *The Diplomatic History of the Administrations of Washington and Adams*, 226-233; Lyman, *The Diplomacy of the United States*, I. 236-251; and Schuyler, *American Diplomacy*, 271-274.

[2] This was a small settlement on the Mississippi which was the sole representation of a fantastic scheme entered into by Colonel George Morgan, a New Jersey trader, and the Spanish envoy, Gardoqui, to set up an elaborate Spanish principality in the territory above Natchez. See Roosevelt, *The Winning of the West*, III. 140.

[3] An interesting description of one of these passes is in the *American Daily Advertiser*, August 24, 1793.

landed on the levee and a duty of fifteen per cent *ad valorem* paid. The goods could not be sold at the port, but must be reloaded, and for this another duty of six per cent was charged. Thus more than one-fifth of the value of the cargo had to be paid in duties to the Spanish officials, not to mention the great loss of time and other annoyances involved.

Just at the time when these troubles became most acute the West was thrown into a state of fomentation by the outbreak of the French Revolution. The new Spanish governor at New Orleans, Baron de Carondelet, soon had all he could do to restrain the enthusiasm for "liberty, equality, and fraternity" which broke out among the French population of Louisiana in consequence of the fall of the Bastile and the revolutionary events which followed in such bewildering succession in the French capital. The conditions with which Carondelet had to contend in order to prevent an uprising against the rule of the Bourbons are indicated by a letter to his home government in which he says, "By extreme vigilance, and by spending sleepless nights, by scaring some and punishing others, by banishing a number, particularly some newcomers from France who were debauching the people with their republican teaching, by intercepting letters and documents suspected of being incendiary, and by prevaricating with everybody, I have done better than I had expected, as the province is now quite orderly and quiet."[1] To the inhabitants of Kentucky and Tennessee, however, the disturbed conditions in Louisiana and the difficulty which Carondelet was having in keeping down the excitable French seemed

[1] Gayarré, *History of Louisiana*, III. 830.

to designate this as the most fitting occasion for a demonstration of force in defence of their rights on the Mississippi. To take advantage of the preoccupation of the Spanish authorities and compel an unequivocal recognition of commercial privileges hitherto denied seemed obviously the part of wisdom. In 1793 Citizen Genet landed in the United States as the representative of the recently established French Republic, and at once proceeded to fit out privateers for the war against England and in numerous other ways violate the neutrality which President Washington had so wisely proclaimed. The wild enthusiasm with which Genet was received by the more democratic element of the country spread like wildfire across the Alleghanies, and very soon the people of the Southwest were burning anew with indignation at the neutral policy of the Administration in the war, and at the failure of the government thus far to relieve their commercial situation, and with hatred, too, for both England and Spain, who were in alliance now against France. Emissaries sent out by Genet made capital of the commercial question and easily determined the Westerners to wage war at once upon the Spaniards in Louisiana.[1]

The leader for the movement was easily found in George Rogers Clark, who now proposed to expatriate himself and turn his back upon the government which he felt, with some justice, had been unappreciative of his earlier efforts. Clark was commissioned major-general in the service of the French Republic, and at once proceeded to raise troops, under the additional title of "Com-

[1] Frederick J. Turner, "The Origin of Genet's Projected Attack on Louisiana and the Floridas," in the *American Historical Review*, III. No. 4.

mander-in-Chief of the French Revolutionary Legions on the Mississippi." His avowed purpose was to capture the Spanish posts on the Mississippi and open the river to free trade. There was no attempt to conceal the preparations, and knowledge of them soon reached both the Spanish at New Orleans and the United States authorities at Philadelphia. It would be difficult to determine in which quarter the news caused the greater alarm. Washington and the Federalist leaders were greatly concerned because the movement, headed by Clark, seemed to be so entirely spontaneous, so unmistakably representative of the stand which the western people as a whole were ready to take. Democratic societies throughout the West were busy passing resolutions condemning the government for its inactivity, and declaring that the time had indeed come for the people of the West to take the whole matter of dealing with the Spaniards into their own hands. Governor Shelby, of Kentucky, when requested by the Administration to prevent the carrying out of Clark's plans, was forced by public sentiment to evade the order and to cause as much delay as possible by entering into a tedious consideration of the constitutional powers involved.

After all, though, there was vastly more talk than action. The number of actual volunteers was small. To leave home and other interests and go on a crusade of extermination against the Spaniard was a very different matter from assembling in Democratic clubs, and, under the spell of wild enthusiasm, passing inflammatory resolutions against "the wicked Dons." Governor St. Clair, of the Northwest Territory, forbade the citizens of that region to take part in any sort of filibustering

expedition; and Governor Blount, of Tennessee, made it understood that any persons under his jurisdiction who should join Clark's force would "lay themselves liable to heavy Pains and Penalties, both pecuniary and corporal, in case they ever returned to their injured country." When, in 1794, Genet was recalled in disgrace, the movement in the West, for which he had been so largely responsible, was greatly discredited. The firm attitude of Governors St. Clair and Blount, and the building of a fort near the mouth of the Ohio by General Wayne, to prevent the Clark expedition by force, caused the final collapse of the whole affair.[1]

The Spaniards seem not to have been long alarmed by the threatened invasion of Clark. They were too well pleased with the prospect of a final separation of Kentucky and Tennessee from the United States greatly to deprecate the movement, even though directed against themselves. They probably felt that, while Clark's expedition would temporarily embarrass them, yet it would lead in the end to the extension of Spanish power to the Ohio — a consummation to be attained the more readily because Spain had the free navigation of the Mississippi to hold out as a bribe to the inhabitants of

---

[1] On the threatened war with the Spaniards, see W. H. English, *The Conquest of the Northwest*, II. Ch. XX.; Gayarré, *History of Louisiana*, III. Ch. VI.; Winsor, *The Westward Movement*, Ch. XXIII.; Roosevelt, *The Winning of the West*, IV. Chs. III. and IV.; Thomas M. Green, *The Spanish Conspiracy: a Review of Early Spanish Movements in the Southwest;* and N. P. Langford, "The Louisiana Purchase and Preceding Spanish Intrigues for Dismemberment of the Union," in the *Minnesota Historical Society Collections*, IX. 453–508. Documentary materials are in the *American State Papers, Foreign Relations*, I. 454–460, and the *American Historical Review*, II. No. 3 and III. No. 3.

those regions. At any rate, the Spaniards by no means appreciated the efforts of the United States government to prevent the execution of Clark's plans. Carondelet even ordered Wayne's fort on the Ohio to be destroyed.

When the confusion incident to Genet's mission and its western sequel was cleared away, relations between the Westerners and the Spaniards became substantially as they had been before. The people of the West had most fortunately been saved from the complication that must have resulted had they played into the hands of the French, but their good fortune in this respect was not yet very apparent. One thing was settled, as the Westerners felt. The government had refused to allow them to vindicate their rights, hence now it was the undeniable obligation of the government itself to do the work. In the cry for relief which now arose louder than ever, it was by no means difficult to detect an undertone of threat. The Democratic Society at Lexington resolved to *demand* that the federal government adopt such means as would instantly give to the people of Kentucky the free use of the Mississippi. The population south of the Ohio represented a confused medley of economic and political views, but upon one point it was solidly united, *i.e.* that the Mississippi must be opened and kept open. And by 1794 the further sentiment had come to be very generally concurred in that the government must meet the Westerners' demands in this matter as the price of their continued allegiance.

The impatient and uncompromising tone of the western appeal warned the Administration that, if redress were not speedily forthcoming, the anti-Spanish crusade which had

been so seriously threatened under the inspiration of Genet's agents might actually be undertaken. To avert the direful consequences of such a contingency, the efforts which had been making toward a diplomatic adjustment were redoubled. In November, 1794, Thomas Pinckney, of South Carolina, was nominated by Washington for the post of envoy extraordinary to the Spanish court.[1] He was instructed to make every possible effort to secure a settlement of the Mississippi question on such terms as would conciliate the disaffected Westerners. When, in June, 1795, Pinckney arrived in Spain, he found conditions more favorable for the negotiation than they had been at any previous time. Spain had been unsuccessful in the war with France, and the alliance with England was unpopular. Through the strategy of the prime minister, Don Manuel Godoy, the Spanish government had unexpectedly extricated itself from the struggle by a peace signed at Bâle in July, 1795. This peace was so popular that the people immediately hailed Godoy with the title by which he was ever afterward known — the Prince of Peace. The reputation given him by the treaty of Bâle made Godoy covetous of more glory of the same character. Among better-informed Spaniards the feeling had become strong that a war with the United States was almost inevitable, but the Prince of Peace now set himself to the task of relieving his country from any such danger. The arrival of Pinckney offered the desired opportunity, and Godoy let it be known at once that Spain was at least willing to negotiate on all the subjects in dispute with the United States. After some

[1] *American State Papers, Foreign Relations*, I. 469.

weeks of discussion, and only after he had demanded his passports, October 24, in disgust with the evasive, delaying policy of the Spanish government, Pinckney finally secured the surprisingly liberal treaty of San Lorenzo el Real, signed October 27, 1795.[1]

This treaty was properly a treaty only of boundaries and navigation; it contained no commercial stipulations. The northern limit of Florida was fixed, as the United States demanded, by a line "beginning on the river Mississippi, at the northernmost part of the thirty-first degree of latitude north of the equator, which from thence shall be drawn due east to the middle of the river Appalachicola, or Catahouche; thence along the middle thereof to its junction with the Flint; thence straight to the head of St. Mary's River, and thence down the middle thereof to the Atlantic Ocean." The fourth article of the treaty yielded full rights of navigation of the Mississippi, as follows: "It is likewise agreed that the western boundary of the United States, which separates them from

[1] The text of the treaty is in *Treaties and Conventions between the United States and Other Powers* (revised edition), 776-784, and Lyman, *Diplomacy of the United States*, I. 253-258. Pinckney's successive reports on the course of the negotiation, including a copy of the treaty, are in the *American State Papers, Foreign Relations*, I. 533-549. The seventh chapter of Lyman's book contains an excellent account of the negotiations. See also Schuyler, *American Diplomacy*, 265-281; Winsor, *The Westward Movement*, Ch. XXIV.; B. A. Hinsdale, "The Establishing of the First Southern Boundary of the United States," in the *Annual Report of the American Historical Association for 1893*, 331-366; H. E. Chambers, "West Florida and its Relation to the Historical Cartography of the United States," in the *Johns Hopkins University Studies in Historical and Political Science*, 16th Series, No. V.; Trescot, *The Diplomatic History of the Administrations of Washington and Adams*, Ch. IV.; Pitkin, *History of the United States*, II., Ch. XXIII.; Charles C. Pinckney, *Life of General Thomas Pinckney;* and George E. Rives, "Spain and the United States in 1795," in the *American Historical Review*, IV. 62-80.

the Spanish colony of Louisiana, is in the middle of the channel, or bed, of the river Mississippi, from the northern boundary of the said states, to the completion of the thirty-first degree of latitude north of the equator. And his Catholic Majesty has likewise agreed that the navigation of the said river, in its whole breadth, from its source to the ocean, shall be free only to his subjects and the citizens of the United States, unless he should extend this privilege to the subjects of other powers by special convention." Concerning the desire of the United States for a place of depositing goods brought down the river on flatboats, and awaiting shipment on ocean-going craft, the treaty contained the following (Article XXII.): "And, in consequence of the stipulations contained in the fourth article, his Catholic Majesty will permit the citizens of the United States, for the space of three years from this time, to deposit their merchandises and effects in the port of New Orleans, and to export them from thence without paying any other duty than a fair price for the hire of the stores; and his Majesty promises either to continue this permission, if he finds, during that time, that it is not prejudicial to the interests of Spain; or if he should not agree to continue it there, he will assign to them, on another part of the banks of the Mississippi, an equivalent establishment."

Probably the main consideration which prompted Godoy to make a treaty with the United States, and to agree to terms which were liberal beyond expectation, was his desire to offset the treaty which Jay had negotiated with England during the preceding year. That treaty was regarded with great disfavor, not only by European powers, but by a very large element of the people of the

United States, because it was represented, however wrongfully, as having been made in a spirit of abject subservience to England. Nevertheless, Godoy feared that since the Jay treaty was so vigorously upheld by the Federalist Administration it would lead to an alliance of the United States and England, which might in turn mean the reëstablishment of British control in the Mississippi Valley. Besides, just at the time that the news of the Jay treaty reached Godoy, Spain's relations with England were very much strained, and the wily prime minister felt that the good will of the people of the United States was eminently to be desired. Had he foreseen the storm of disapproval which the Jay treaty was yet to arouse in the United States, or had he really understood the Administration's position in the matter, he would have felt under less constraint to neutralize the treaty's British propensities by a shower of Spanish favors. It was fortunate for the long-wearied Kentuckians and Tennesseeans that he did not wait longer to watch developments before seeking actively to win their friendship.[1]

The Spanish treaty was so acceptable that it was ratified by the United States Senate practically without opposi-

[1] In anticipation of what will be said in a later chapter it may be observed here that the Spanish government soon came to regret the liberality of the treaty of 1795. On one pretext or another Natchez, and other Mississippi posts between 31° and 32° 30′, were held by Spanish troops more than two years longer. Curiously enough, the Jay treaty, which had gone so far toward insuring the success of Pinckney's negotiation, became ostensibly the main obstacle to the execution of the treaty which it had rendered possible. The third article of the Jay treaty contained the provision that "the river Mississippi shall, . . . according to the treaty of peace, be entirely open to both parties," *i.e.* England and the United States. In May, 1797, the Spanish government made formal protest against this clause, on the ground that according to her own treaty with the United States in 1795 the right of free navigation of the Mississippi

tion. After more than a decade of border quarrels, incipient invasions, and fruitless negotations, the Spanish restrictions upon western trade were removed. The question had, indeed, been a most serious one, perilously involving the very integrity of the Union. For a time the diverse economic interests of the East and West threatened as direful a disaster as similarly diverse interests of North and South occasioned three-quarters of a century later. The merits of the controversy between Westerner and Spaniard are not so easily determined as might appear. Of course the Spanish attempt to monopolize the lower Mississippi would be thoroughly reprehensible if judged by standards of to-day. But conditions a hundred years ago were different. Barring cruel and unnecessarily annoying methods employed, the Spaniards, in forbidding free navigation of that part of the Mississippi which lay wholly within their territories, were well within the bounds of the international practice of their time. In Europe the Rhine tolls were not abolished until 1804, and the Congress of Vienna in 1815 opened the other great rivers of western Europe to free navigation. The Danube was not opened until 1856. International jurists are not yet at all agreed as to the right of closing river navigation in cases similar to that of the Mississippi, and it may be of interest to observe that it was not until the treaty of Washington, as late as 1871, that the lower St. Lawrence opened unreservedly to the free use of United States citizens.

belonged exclusively to her own subjects and the citizens of the American nation. England was declared to have lost all right to such navigation in 1783, and after that date no nation except Spain could confer it upon another. The question of British navigation of the river, however, was no longer a crying one, and the Spanish objection was allowed to lapse.

CHAPTER X

NAPOLEON AND THE LOUISIANA COUNTRY

THE signing away of her colonial empire in 1763, although accompanied by an outward show of indifference, was really the deepest humiliation France had ever experienced. That England was the chief gainer by the transaction was hardly calculated to reconcile the loser. Turgot's aphorism to the effect that colonies are like fruits which cling to the stem only until they are ripe, with its implied prediction that the newly acquired possessions of England would in due season establish their independence, was after all rather barren of solace for a people whose imperial ambitions had been as great as those of the eighteenth-century French. Except negatively, the contingent dissolution of England's empire could not compensate France for the loss of hers. The increasing evils of the Bourbon régime, the impoverishment of the people, the exhaustion of the national resources, and the traditional inferiority of the French upon the sea seemed utterly to preclude an early regaining of any of the forfeited possessions. Certainly France would not soon again enjoy the prestige in India which had formerly been hers; and it was even more sure that she would experience the greatest difficulty in winning for

herself a second time the magnificent region between the Alleghanies and the Mississippi in America.

However, it was not the yielding of possessions in India or the eastern Mississippi Valley that occasioned the keenest regret. The arbitrament of war had rendered these cessions to England wholly unavoidable. To lament their loss and to dream of their recovery were equally idle. Under pressure considerably less imperative, however, the vast territory west of the Mississippi and east of the Rocky Mountains had been given to Spain in this same year in recognition of her alliance in the recent struggle and in compensation for her loss of the Floridas to England. And it was this act that the French government, almost before the treaty had been signed, began to regard as violable and to plan to undo.

Hope for the speedy recovery of the Louisiana territory was rendered the more reasonable by the close relationship of the Bourbon monarchs of the two nations and by the comparative subservience of the Spaniard. It was known, moreover, that Spain was not yet very strongly attached to her recent acquisition and that she had no definite plan for its exploitation and settlement. It was but natural to conclude that, the Spanish court being more greedy for gold than for lands, a sufficient financial consideration would easily induce a retrocession. Unfortunately, however, the payment of the cash, such as would have been tempting to the Spaniard, was positively forbidden by the condition of the French treasury. Scarcely could current expenses be met, without any such appropriation as the regaining of Louisiana would demand. During the closing years of the reign of Louis XV, conditions in this respect grew worse rather than better, and it was not until the Count de Vergennes became Louis XVI.'s minister of foreign affairs that it was deemed worth while to make an avowed effort toward the recovery of Louisiana. This was in the days of the American Revolution, when France was enjoying sweet revenge at England's expense, and when her relations with Spain were once more those of a close ally. At the end of the war the two powers endeavored jointly to rob the Americans of the full fruits of their success by limiting the possessions of the states to the lands east of the Alleghanies. Due to American vigilance and England's preference for neighbors of her own blood and speech along the Great Lake frontier, France and Spain were frustrated in this scheme. Vergennes tried at this time to purchase Louisiana for the French, but he could not offer a sum satisfactory to the Spanish king. There can be little doubt that, failing in this, the French ministers then became so ardent in championing the aggressive territorial schemes of their southern neighbor in America, chiefly because they still expected their country some day to fall heir to the Spanish dominions along the Mississippi.

Years passed, and the Revolution came on in France. Throughout that terrible struggle the project of the revival of the empire, and particularly of the recovery of Louisiana, was never wholly lost to view. In the summer of 1795, when the treaty of peace was signed at Bâle between the French Republic and the Spanish king, the commissioners of the Republic endeavored to secure a retrocession of the coveted territory, but failed — again only because of inability to pay the price asked. By this

same treaty, however, Spain ceded to France the eastern part of St. Domingo (Hayti).[1] The western part of the island had been possessed by the French since 1697, and under the Bourbon monarchy had constituted their most important foreign colony. The importance of the island, aside from its abundant natural resources, and the fact that two-thirds of the commercial interests of the French prior to the Revolution had centred there, lay in the fact that it constituted the most practicable base of operations in enterprises affecting the American continent. In view of the English supremacy in the seas in that quarter, and also because of the threatened rebellion of the natives under the chieftain Toussaint Louverture, French tenure promised for a time to be so hazardous in Hayti that only the name of sovereignty was assumed in 1795.[2]

Within six months after the treaty of Bâle the constitution of 1795 had been put in operation, and the government had been organized under the executive control of the five Directors. It was the ambition of the Directory, not merely to conserve the domestic results of the Revolution, but also to realize the fond dream of a revived colonial empire. To this latter end the Louisiana negotiations were earnestly renewed. In 1797 Don Carlos IV., king of Spain, was made a tempting offer — not indeed in the shape of gold, but in that of very valuable

[1] Martens, *Recueil des Principaux Traités conclus par les Puissances de l'Europe*, VI. 124–128.

[2] On conditions prevailing in St. Domingo, see Adams, *History of the United States*, I. 378 *et seq.*, and E. W. Gilliam, "The French Colony of San Domingo: Its Rise and Fall," in the *Magazine of American History*, XX, 471–479.

lands.[1] It was proposed that in payment for Louisiana three fair districts recently wrung by French arms from the Pope should be united with the Duchy of Parma, and the whole should be given under the name of a principality to a son of the present Duke of Parma, who was also the son-in-law of the Spanish king. The proposition was of course in the nature of a bribe whereby Don Carlos was to secure the advancement of his daughter's interests by simply resigning the sovereignty of Louisiana to France. Had the lands thus offered represented the losses of any other power than the papacy the bargain would probably have been closed at once. But Don Carlos was an earnest devotee of the church. Virtuous in private life, unostentatious in manners, and industrious beyond any of his courtiers, he stood far above the average of his people in the finer qualities of character, and exhibited a combination of religious profession and genuine piety altogether too rare among those by whom he was surrounded. The Directors had miscalculated their man. With so sacrilegious a bargain as they proposed he would have nothing to do. Much as he cared for his daughter, and ready as he would have been under other circumstances to part with Louisiana for her sake, he declared he could never be betrayed into bargaining for the lost possessions of St. Peter. Having nothing else to offer, the Directors were forced temporarily to acknowledge their plans thwarted.

In July, 1797, the foreign policy of the Directory was given a fresh stimulus by the elevation of Charles Maurice de Talleyrand to the office of minister of foreign affairs.

---

[1] *Mémoires du Prince de la Paix*, III. 23. The "Prince of Peace" was Don Manuel Godoy, prime minister of Spain from 1792 to 1798.

Talleyrand was in many respects a remarkable man and had before him a remarkable, if not a very admirable, career. Trained for the church, he had from early life indulged such laxity of morals that the only ground upon which he can be said to have won his way to the bishopric of Autun was his unexcelled administrative ability. He had been prominent in the early days of the Revolution, being despatched to England in 1792 to secure recognition for the new Republic; but before returning he was warned that his name had been placed on the list of those "disposed to serve the king" — or, in other words, that he had unwittingly become an *émigré*. He remained in England until February, 1794, when the Alien Bill forced his departure. He went thence to the United States, where he spent about a year in travel and study of American republicanism. The result of this visit was to strengthen him in the conviction that France had nothing to expect from the United States, and that the regaining of Louisiana was her only hope of preventing the growth of another great English nation across the Atlantic. At the end of the Reign of Terror he returned to France to become in time the chief coadjutor of Napoleon and altogether the shrewdest, subtlest, and most unprincipled diplomat of his day.[1]

---

[1] There are numerous biographies of Talleyrand, and editions of his voluminous correspondence. Among these the most noteworthy are Lady Charlotte Julia Blennerhassett, *Life of Talleyrand*, 2 vols., translated from the German by Frederick Clarke; Charles K. McHarg, *Life of Prince Talleyrand, with Extracts from his Speeches and Writings;* A. Marcade, *Talleyrand, Prêtre et Évêque;* Bernard de Lacombe, *Talleyrand, Évêque d'Autun;* the Duc de Broglie, *Mémoires du Prince Charles Maurice de Talleyrand*, 5 vols., translated by Raphaël Ledos de Beau-

When Talleyrand assumed the office of foreign secretary his course of action, so far as America was concerned, was already determined. He would at all hazards restore French authority in the valley of the Mississippi. His first approaches to the Spanish government on this subject were made through Citizen Guillemardet, whom he sent as minister to Madrid in May, 1798. Guillemardet was instructed first of all to upbraid the Spanish for evacuating certain posts on the Mississippi (Natchez was the most important), as they had engaged themselves to do by their treaty with the United States in 1795. "The court of Madrid," wrote Talleyrand in his instructions, "ever blind to its own interests, and never docile to the lessons of experience, has again quite recently adopted a measure which cannot fail to produce the worst effects upon its political existence and on the preservation of its colonies. The United States have been put in possession of the forts situated along the Mississippi which the Spaniards had occupied as posts essential to arrest the Americans in those countries."[1]

Guillemardet was instructed to urge upon Don Carlos and his ministry that every consideration rendered it extremely ill-advised to make any concession to the Americans, whose undoubted aim it was ultimately to control the entire continent themselves. "Moreover," continued Talleyrand, "their conduct ever since the moment of their independence is enough to prove this

fort; G. Pallain, *Le Ministère de Talleyrand sous le Directoire;* and Pierre Bertrand, *Lettres Inédites de Talleyrand à Napoleon, 1800-1809.*

[1] "Instructions données au Citoyen Guillemardet, Prairial, An VI." (May 20-June 19, 1798), Archives des Affaires Étrangères. Quoted in Adams, *History of the United States*, I. 356.

truth: the Americans are devoured by pride, ambition, and cupidity; the mercantile spirit of the city of London ferments from Charleston to Boston, and the Cabinet of St. James directs the Cabinet of the Federal Union. . . . There are no other means of putting an end to the ambition of the Americans than that of shutting them up within the limits which Nature seems to have traced for them." And now the writer came to the point. "But Spain is not in a condition to do this great work alone. She cannot, therefore, hasten too quickly to engage the aid of a preponderating Power, yielding to it a small part of her immense domains in order to preserve the rest. . . . Let the court of Madrid cede these districts [*only* Louisiana and the Floridas were asked] to France, and from that moment the power of America is bounded by the limit which it may suit the interests and the tranquillity of France and Spain to assign her. The French Republic, mistress of these two provinces, will be a wall of brass forever impenetrable to the combined efforts of England and America. The court of Madrid has nothing to fear from France."

But this splendidly audacious demand was thwarted by a series of events beyond the power of Talleyrand to control. About the same time that Citizen Guillemardet began to interview the Spanish ministry Napoleon set out for Egypt with the intention of establishing French control in that quarter and thus threatening England's intercourse with India and the East. Lord Nelson followed with the English fleet, and on the 1st of August, 1798, attacked and totally destroyed the French fleet at Abukir Bay. Napoleon's connections with France being now entirely cut off, the Egyptian campaign was an acknowledged failure. No one realized this as keenly as did Napoleon himself. He won a brilliant victory over the Mamelukes in the battle of the Pyramids, gained control of the basin of the Nile, and invaded Syria, but in the face of all his successes loomed up the fact that his army was imprisoned without hope of escape. Napoleon was not the man to waste time in such a situation, and therefore, since the army could not be transported back to France, he resolved to leave it in Egypt and return alone to the field of action in Paris, where discontent with the failures of the Directory was reported to be daily increasing. August 22, 1799, he managed to run the English blockade, and on October 9 landed with a few attendants at Fréjus.[1]

The Egyptian disaster only reënforced the policy of delay adopted by the Spanish ministry in dealing with the Louisiana question. Already Spain had been practically driven by France to declare war against England, and it was becoming all the time more apparent that the Directory's plans involved the continued use of Spain as a tool both in Europe and America. The liberality of the Spanish treaty with the United States in 1795, together with Spain's efforts to execute its terms in good faith, so exasperated Talleyrand and the Directors that war between France and Spain was for a while imminent. To avert such a casualty the Spanish prime minister, Don

[1] On Napoleon's Egyptian campaign, see the Duc de Broglie, *Memoirs of Prince Talleyrand*, I. 198; R. W. Phipps (ed.), *Memoirs of Napoleon Bonaparte, by Louis Antoine Fauvelet de Bourrienne*, I. Chs. XV.–XXI.; W. M. Sloane, *Napoleon Bonaparte*, II. Chs. V.–IX.; and Pierre Lanfrey, *History of Napoleon the First*, Chs. X. and XI.

Manuel Godoy, retired temporarily from the foreign office in March, 1798. The vexatious delay in securing the treaty of San Lorenzo el Real has all but obscured from American eyes the honorable but perilous efforts which Spain made during the following two or three years to fulfil her part of the contract. When Napoleon returned to France, in 1799, it could not be disguised that Guillemardet's mission to procure Louisiana had failed completely.

Meanwhile the Directory had been on the verge of war with the United States. As the eighteenth century drew to an end the strong friendship which had been engendered between America and France during the former's war for independence fast melted away. At the outbreak of the French Revolution in 1789 the sympathies of the people of the United States were quite generally with the revolutionists. But when the movement for liberty so soon degenerated into a mere carnival of crime and bloodshed, the sensibilities of the Americans, as indeed of sane and law-abiding people everywhere, suffered a rude shock. Sympathy gave place in many quarters to burning indignation. Presuming unduly on the friendship of the American people, and professing to believe that the young nation was bound irrevocably to her by the treaty of alliance of 1778, France had shown no hesitancy in demanding open assistance from the United States in the war which she declared against England early in 1793; and finding no aid forthcoming and meeting only with an official proclamation of neutrality, she had thereafter maintained such irritating relations with the United States that by the time the Adams Administration was well under way war between the two powers seemed inevitable. Incensed by the Jay treaty with England, the French government had refused, early in 1797, to receive Charles C. Pinckney, appointed by Washington to succeed Monroe as minister at Paris. Then followed the sending of the commission composed of Pinckney, Marshall, and Gerry, the well-known incident of the X. Y. Z. papers, the suspension by Congress of the French treaties, the hastening of preparations for war, and finally a considerable number of captures of French vessels by the *Constellation*, the *Boston*, the *Enterprise*, and other American ships.[1] The spirit manifested by the Americans was so determined that the Directory, having already on its hands in Europe more military enterprises than it could properly attend to, promptly backed down and humbly communicated to President Adams that, if another minister should come to Paris, he would be fittingly received. Contrary to the popular desire and the advice of such men as Washington, Hamilton, and Secretary Pickering, Adams at once resolved to stay the course of war by sending another commission of three — Oliver Ellsworth, William Vans Murray, and W. R. Davie. When they arrived at Paris they found a new government in power and one disposed to meet them more than halfway in negotiating a peace.

Bearing the blame for the Directory's failure to prosecute the American war, Talleyrand was forced to retire from the foreign office July 20, 1799. His favorite scheme of recovering Louisiana from Spain had received

---

[1] McMaster, *History of the People of the United States*, II. Ch. X.; Morse, *John Adams*, Ch. XI.; Magruder, *John Marshall*, Ch. VIII.; Schouler, *History of the United States*, I. Ch. IV.

a severe blow. The fiasco in Egypt and the virtual surrender to the United States had robbed France for a while of the prestige upon which the wily minister had been depending to overcome Don Carlos. When Talleyrand left the foreign office there seemed little reason to expect that within less than fifteen months the whole Louisiana territory would have become once more French. But such was to be the case, largely because a greater than Talleyrand was about ready to put his hand to the enterprise.

Upon his return from Egypt Napoleon was received with the wildest enthusiasm. His recent failure was forgotten, and only his earlier victories and his promises of future successes were remembered. Borne up by popular adoration, he lost little time in setting aside the feeble Directory by the *coup d'état* of the eighteenth Brumaire (November 9, 1799) and having himself created First Consul.[1] It was with this government, headed by Napoleon, that the second commission appointed by President Adams was called to treat. Already the young Corsican's plans were large, but they did not embrace a war with the United States. Accordingly a treaty, that of Morfontaine (more commonly known as the convention of 1800), was negotiated, whereby the United States was released from all obligations under the French alliance of 1778, in return for which France was impliedly relieved from all responsibility for captures of American vessels and goods during the pending conflict with England.[2]

---

[1] The Duc de Broglie, *Memoirs of Prince Talleyrand*, I. 203-210; Bourrienne, *Memoirs of Napoleon Bonaparte* (ed. by R. W. Phipps), I. Ch. XXIV.; Lanfrey, *History of Napoleon the First*, I. Ch. XII.; and Sloane, *Napoleon Bonaparte*, II. Ch. X. and XI.

[2] Martens, *Recueil des Principaux Traités conclus par les Puissances*

By the summer of 1800 Napoleon was well established in the office of First Consul, which meant that he was well started on the road to imperial supremacy. The victory over the Austrians at Marengo in June of that year had amply vindicated those who even in the midst of the Egyptian disappointment had still protested that France had not for many a day seen such a military genius as Napoleon. Great plans and magnificent visions were then being entertained by the young man of thirty-one, and the policies of the most remarkable career of modern times were rapidly taking shape. Methods of internal administration for France, schemes for the consolidation of Europe under French control, and ambitions for the revival of a world-wide French colonial empire were all busying the Consul's indefatigable brain. We may be assured that among these varied interests the last occupied no subordinate position. Although affairs in France and in Europe were naturally more immediately urgent, it appears that throughout the earlier portion of his career

de l'Europe, VII. 96 *et seq.* The text of the treaty, in English, is in *Treaties and Conventions concluded between the United States of America and Other Powers* (first printed as Senate Exec. Doc. No. 36, 41st Cong., third sess.), 266-275. On the treaty and the circumstances leading to it, see Lyman, *The Diplomacy of the United States*, Ch. VIII.; McMaster, *History of the People of the United States*, II. Ch. X.; Schouler, *History of the United States*, I. Ch. IV.; Morse, *John Adams*, 265-287, and *Thomas Jefferson*, 173-193; Winsor, *Narrative and Critical History*, VII. Ch. VII.; Trescot, *Diplomatic History of the Administrations of Washington and Adams*, Ch. III.; Lodge, *Alexander Hamilton*, 194-221; and Emanuel Spencer, "Napoleon Bonaparte and Peace with America," in the *Magazine of American History*, XXVI. 298-301. Among numerous original sources may be mentioned the *Annals of Congress*, VII.-X.; the *American State Papers, Foreign Relations*, II.; John Adams, *Works*, VIII., IX.; *Life and Correspondence of Rufus King*, II.; and Thomas Jefferson, *Writings*, IV.

Napoleon was always stirred to his mightiest efforts by his dreams of a great French dominion beyond the seas.[1] Probably not the least consideration which induced him to restore Talleyrand, after the eighteenth Brumaire, to the office of secretary of foreign affairs was the latter's well-known sympathy with the policy of colonial revival.[2]

In July, 1800, Napoleon began his efforts at French aggrandizement in America by ordering Talleyrand to despatch to Citizen Alquier, the French minister at the court of Spain, authority to make a treaty for the recovery of Louisiana. This proposition, as we have seen, was by no means a new one. It had been repeated in sundry forms and at varying intervals ever since 1763. But never before had the demand for retrocession been backed by a man of such force as Napoleon, and with his attempt in this direction it seemed not at all improbable that the time for a reëstablishment of French power in America had come. By way of compensation for Louisiana, Alquier was directed to renew the promise of an aggrandizement of the Duchy of Parma which Talleyrand on his own initiative had made three years before.[3]

In obedience to his instructions, Alquier hastened to confer with the Spanish foreign minister, Señor Urquijo, and to lay before him Napoleon's offer in such a manner as to make it very plain that a prompt and unconditional acceptance was expected. In fact, Urquijo was boldly

[1] William M. Sloane, "Napoleon's Plans for a Colonial System," in the *American Historical Review*, IV. No. 3.

[2] In view of Talleyrand's unpopularity Napoleon deemed it best not to offend the public by restoring him at once to the position "naturally due" him. Reinhard, the foreign secretary at the time of the *coup d'état*, was retained in office for a short time. *Correspondance de Napoléon Premier*, XXX. 330.

[3] *Ibid.*, VI. 415.

told to reject the offer "if he dared." Under the pressure of Alquier's threats the cautious Spaniard speedily signified his willingness that the retrocession be made, but explained also that his own attitude in the matter would count for little unless the king could be won over to the plan.[1]

Alquier was not lacking in certain elements of shrewdness so becoming in the diplomat at all times, and particularly when working in the service of a Napoleon. He knew full well that the queen, Doña Maria Luisa, herself from Parma, would be strongly appealed to by the prospect of an increase of her daughter's titles and dominions, and therefore it was to the queen rather than to the king that he first addressed Napoleon's offer. Sure enough, Doña Maria was greatly pleased, and all her influence was readily thrown on the side of Alquier in bringing the king to the point of acceptance. The desired result was achieved sooner than could have been expected. For the sake of his daughter, and at the entreaties of his wife, Don Carlos agreed to give up Louisiana — and with it, presumably, the religious scruples which had troubled him on the former occasion. It was even with enthusiasm that the project was approved. Both king and queen were loud in their praises of the generosity of Napoleon, and that the wily First Consul was entirely sincere in his verbose protestations that the bargain was primarily for Spain's good, neither seems for a moment to have doubted. Don Carlos gave every evidence of being entirely convinced that the representation which Alquier made in the following note was sound: "The progress of the power

[1] Adams, *History of the United States*, I. 364–365.

and population of America, and her relations of interest always maintained with England, may and must some day bring these two powers to concert together the conquest of the Spanish colonies. If national interest is the surest foundation for political calculations, this conjecture must appear incontestable. The court of Spain will do, then, at once a wise and great act if it calls the French to the defence of its colonies by ceding Louisiana to them, and by replacing in their hands this outpost of its richest possession in the New World."[1]

Before Alquier could reach the point of making a definite treaty, however, he was displaced by a special commissioner, General Berthier. The reason for the change was that the First Consul believed he could impose more implicit confidence in the new appointee.[2] Berthier arrived in Madrid late in August, 1800, bearing the *projet* of a treaty which had been prepared by Talleyrand. According to the terms of this instrument, France was to add to Parma a territory containing not fewer than one million inhabitants, and was to secure the consent of Austria and such other powers as might be interested in this shifting of boundaries. In return for these considerations, Spain was to cede Louisiana to France, and also the two Floridas. Spain was to yield possession of these American territories whenever the promised increase of Parma should be actually realized. And the two

---

[1] Note addressed by Alquier, August 3, 1800, Archives des Affaires Étrangères. Quoted in Adams, *History of the United States*, I. 365.

[2] Bonaparte to Talleyrand, 9 Thermidor, An VIII. (July 28, 1800). *Correspondance de Napoléon Premier*, VI. 426. Berthier was Napoleon's "right hand in matters of secrecy and importance." Adams, *History of the United States*, I. 366.

powers were to make common cause against any who might oppose these arrangements.[1]

Throughout September Berthier pushed the negotiation with much vigor. Several difficulties arose which operated to delay matters. Napoleon had originally asked for only Louisiana, whereas he was now asking also for the Floridas, and six war-ships besides. Moreover, through Talleyrand's indiscretion, the object of Berthier's mission had been published in Paris, and had, of course, become known to the American minister at Madrid, who, in the interest of his country, now proceeded to hinder the negotiation by asking some very pointed and embarrassing questions. Berthier, however, encouraged Don Carlos in the anticipation that Tuscany was to be the Parmese acquisition, and it was not long until the old king was sending post-haste for his former prime minister and favorite, Godoy, and was receiving him in an ecstasy of joy, crying: "Congratulate me on this brilliant beginning of Bonaparte's relations with Spain! The Prince-presumptive of Parma, my son-in-law and nephew, a Bourbon, is invited by France to reign on the delightful banks of the Arno over a people who once spread their commerce through the known

---

[1] "Instructions au Général Berthier, 8 Fructidor, An VIII." (August 26, 1800); "Projet de Traité préliminaire et secret, 10 Fructidor, An VIII." (August 28, 1800), Archives des Affaires Étrangères. Cited in Adams, *History of the United States*, I. 367. "In the history of the United States hardly any document, domestic or foreign, to be found in their archives has greater interest than this *projet;* for from it the United States must trace whatever legal title they obtained to the vast region west of the Mississippi. The treaties which followed were made merely in pursuance of this engagement, with such variations as seemed good for the purpose of carrying out the central idea of restoring Louisiana to France." Adams, I. 367-368.

world, and who were the controlling power of Italy, — a people mild, civilized, full of humanity; the classical land of science and art."[1]

On the 1st of October, not twenty-four hours after the treaty of Morfontaine in settlement of the strained relations of France and the United States had been signed at Paris by Napoleon's brother Joseph, Berthier and Godoy signed the treaty of San Ildefonso, by which Louisiana was retroceded to France.[2] The two treaties were essentially inconsistent, so far as the disposal of American affairs was concerned, and no one was more keenly aware of this than the crafty Talleyrand himself. No one supposed, certainly not Talleyrand, that the people of the United States would view with complacency the transfer of Louisiana from decadent Spain to aggressive France, and it was folly to expect that, if the transfer were actually made, the recently established peace between the French and the Americans would long endure.

By the treaty of Lunéville, signed February 9, 1801, after Austria's humiliation at Hohenlinden, the Grand Duke of Parma was dispossessed of his lands, and it was provided that the young duke, his son and Don Carlos's son-in-law, should be established in the government of Tuscany.[3] This was a step, of course, toward the execution of the treaty of San Ildefonso. In order

---

[1] Godoy's *Memoirs*, III. 20. Translation in Adams, *History of the United States*, I. 369.

[2] "Traité préliminaire et secret, Octobre 1, 1800," *Recueil de Traités de la France*, par De Clercq, I. 411, and Martens, *Recueil des Principaux Traités conclus par les Puissances de l'Europe*, X. 467.

[3] Koch, *Histoire Abrégée des Traités de Paix entre les Puissances de l'Europe* (edition continued by Schoell), V. 357-358.

fully to complete the arrangements, Napoleon's brother Lucien was sent to Madrid as ambassador. This move was doubtless a mistake, at least as Napoleon subsequently had reason to regard it, for Lucien had a will of his own, and in his dealings at the Spanish court ignored his brother's orders right royally. It should be noted, however, that it was with Godoy that he had to treat, and Godoy was a very different man from Urquijo. Since the adding of the Floridas to Napoleon's demand, the king's enthusiasm for the retrocession had fast ebbed away, and he had persuaded Godoy again to assume the duties, though not the title, of minister of foreign affairs, because he could find no one else who was shrewd enough to hold his own with Napoleon and his agents.[1] With Godoy, Lucien made a treaty, March 21, 1801, providing for the creation of the kingdom of Tuscany and for the immediate transfer of Louisiana.[2] But, being bribed heavily by the Spanish minister, he subscribed to another treaty — that of Badajos — June 6, which thwarted Napoleon's designs upon Portugal and aroused no small indignation on the part of the First Consul.[3] The loss of the Russian alliance, however, the victory of Nelson's fleet at Copenhagen, and the

[1] This explanation of the quasi-restoration of Godoy to his former position comes from his own *Memoirs*, III. 76–78, but is clearly proved to be correct by facts known from other sources.

[2] Martens, *Recueil des Principaux Traités conclus par les Puissances de l'Europe*, VII. 336–339. Text and English translation in the *American State Papers*, II. 511. Translation in the *Annals of Congress* (1802–1803), 1018.

[3] Martens, *ibid.*, VII. 348–351. The treaty of Badajos was an agreement primarily between Don Carlos IV. and Don Juan, prince regent of Portugal.

imminent surrender of the French army in Egypt forced Napoleon for a little time to resign himself, albeit with very ill grace, to the disposition of Spanish and Portuguese affairs made by his self-willed brother.

On the 27th of July Talleyrand was definitely instructed to demand of the Spanish government the authority to take possession of Louisiana.[1] The First Consul was growing impatient. The San Ildefonso bargain, made almost a year before, must be put into effect and that without further delay. Godoy, however, had now almost supplanted the king in dictating Spain's foreign policy; and Godoy had no mind to yield Louisiana as long as that territory could be retained — certainly not until the execution of the French side of the bargain should have been made entirely secure. Through Godoy's influence the Spanish king had been kept from affixing his signature to the various treaties concerning Louisiana, and without his doing so the treaties could not be regarded as absolutely binding. It was not until October 15, 1802, — more than a year after the time of which we are speaking, — that Don Carlos thus formally committed himself to the retrocession. In Godoy were exhibited the very same qualities of suavity, shrewdness, and duplicity, which so markedly characterized the French First Consul and his foreign minister. So that when these men were pitted against one another in the diplomatic arena, the world might well attend closely in anticipation of interesting developments.

Resolved to meet Napoleon on his own ground and frus-

[1] Bonaparte to Talleyrand, 8 Thermidor, An IX. (July 27, 1801), *Correspondance de Napoléon Premier*, VII. 210.

trate his suspected design of securing possession of Louisiana without really making the promised compensation, Godoy represented to Talleyrand that in the present state of affairs the authority demanded by the First Consul could never be granted. For while Don Carlos's son-in-law, the young king of the newly created and newly christened Etruria, had been called to Paris with his queen and had been magnificently entertained there and given every assurance that he was in very truth the sovereign of the goodly Italian kingdom, French garrisons were still maintained in that kingdom, French generals ruled it, no European power had yet recognized it, and so far as yet appeared the royal title was an altogether empty one. There was certainly much ground for suspecting the French of insincerity. Just what was Napoleon's actual intention at this juncture cannot be definitely ascertained. Such things under the Napoleonic system of diplomacy were not committed to paper. But that as matters then stood Godoy was fully warranted in refusing to relinquish Louisiana admits of no doubt whatever.

Of course Godoy's refusal incensed the First Consul. He himself wrote the scathing note which Talleyrand was directed to send through Azara, the Spanish minister at Paris, to Don Carlos. "It is at the moment," so ran the message, "when the First Consul gives such strong proofs of his consideration for the king of Spain, and places a prince of his house on a throne which is fruit of the victories of French arms, that a tone is taken toward the French Republic such as might be taken with impunity toward the Republic of San Marino. The First Consul, full of confidence in the personal character of his

Catholic Majesty, hopes that from the moment he is made aware of the bad conduct of some of his ministers, he will look to it, and will recall them to the sentiments of esteem and consideration which France does not cease to entertain for Spain. The First Consul will never persuade himself that his Catholic Majesty wishes to insult the French people and their government at the moment when these are doing so much for Spain. This would suit neither his heart nor his loyalty, nor the interest of his crown."[1] To Lucien was intrusted the task of letting the Spanish sovereigns know that Napoleon was highly indignant at the "extravagant and insolent" conduct of the Prince of Peace, "*ce misérable*." "I am long-suffering," wrote the First Consul, "but already I am warmly affected by this tone of contempt and disregard which is taken at Madrid; and if they continue to put the Republic under the necessity either of enduring the shame of the outrages publicly inflicted on it, or of avenging them by arms, they may see things they do not expect."[2]

Godoy, however, refused to be moved in the least by the menacing attitude thus exhibited. He felt that the facts of the case justified him in the stand which he had taken, and his distrust of the motives of the First Consul was only confirmed by the latter's importunity and bravado. It was not for Godoy to yield on the order of even the victor of the Pyramids and Marengo. The truth is that Napoleon had come nearer finding his match in the wily Spanish minister than in any general with whom he had

---

[1] *Correspondance de Napoléon Premier*, VII. 225.
[2] Bonaparte to Talleyrand, 27 Thermidor, An IX. (August 15, 1801); *ibid.*, 226–227.

yet measured strength on the field of battle. That he was sorely piqued was not unnatural.

And yet one way was left open for the accomplishment of the desired end. That was the occupation of Louisiana by force. Spain was comparatively weak, the Spanish population in Louisiana was relatively small, and there seemed to be no good reason why the territory in question might not be brought under French control regardless of Godoy's stubborn opposition. By way of preparation for the seizure of the Louisiana country Napoleon undertook to crush the revolution in St. Domingo led by Toussaint Louverture. Louverture was a negro who, within the narrow confines of St. Domingo, was playing essentially the same part that Napoleon himself had begun to play in Europe. Since St. Domingo was the recognized base of operations against Louisiana, Napoleon resolved to subdue the insurrection, reëstablish negro slavery, and make the island the chief stronghold of French power in the western Atlantic. On the 22nd of November, 1801, the combined French and Spanish fleets left Brest for the conquest of Toussaint's kingdom.[1] Late in January, 1802, the war was begun under the direction of Napoleon's brother-in-law, Leclerc, and after a three months' struggle Toussaint, largely because of the treachery of his generals, was forced to surrender. He was carried to Europe and imprisoned in a fortress on the Swiss frontier, where he died, April 7, 1803.[2]

---

[1] For a brief sketch of the French preparations to take possession of Louisiana through the reduction of St. Domingo, see James K. Hosmer, *History of the Louisiana Purchase*, Ch. III.

[2] For an excellent account of Louverture's career, and of his influence upon the history of the United States, see Adams, *History of the United States*, I. Ch. XV. Other works which may be referred to in this connec-

The sailing of the fleet for St. Domingo had occurred just ten days after the arrival of Robert R. Livingston, the new American minister to the French court. A few weeks subsequently Livingston wrote to Rufus King, who was then the American minister at London, that he was authoritatively informed that the armament would proceed to Louisiana in case no serious opposition was met in the island. The task of reducing the revolutionists to subjection proved too great, however, to admit of any further conquest by Leclerc's troops, and accordingly we find Napoleon, in June, 1802, ordering his minister of marine to prepare estimates for a special expedition to Louisiana. It was announced that it was his intention "to take possession of Louisiana with the shortest delay," and to send this expedition "in the utmost secrecy under the appearance of being directed on St. Domingo."[1]

The prospect of losing Louisiana after this fashion was hardly pleasing to Spain — least of all to Godoy. It was well understood that Napoleon would prefer to secure the territory without the necessity of fighting for it, since he had other uses for his men and money. This determined Godoy to make the best of a bad situation and forestall the proposed expedition by a definite cession, on terms as favorable to Spain as possible, of the territory that now seemed quite certain to be lost in any event. He there-

---

tion are Jean François Dubroca, *La vie de Toussaint-Louverture, chef des noirs insurgés de Saint-Domingue;* C. W. Elliott, *St. Domingo, its Revolution and its Hero;* Pierre Laffitte, *Toussaint-Louverture;* Marcus Rainsford, *St. Domingo;* James Stephen, *Buonaparte in the West Indies;* and Wendell Phillips, *The St. Domingo Insurrection.*

[1] Bonaparte to Contre-Amiral Decrès, 15 Prairial, An X. (June 4, 1802), *Correspondance de Napoléon Premier,* VII. 485.

fore made Talleyrand an unequivocal promise that Louisiana should be promptly delivered on two conditions: first, that Austria, England, and the dethroned Grand Duke of Parma be induced to recognize the young king of Etruria; and second, that the territory thus transferred from Spain to France be never alienated by the latter power. Through General Gouvion St.-Cyr, the new French minister at Madrid, Talleyrand hastened to make emphatic promises that on both these points the terms proposed by Godoy should be strictly observed. That France would never sell or in any other way dispose of Louisiana was made the subject of a written pledge signed on behalf of the First Consul by St.-Cyr, in July, 1802.[1] Napoleon was still asking for the Floridas also, though Talleyrand strongly advised that East Florida, at least, be left in the hands of the Spaniards as a sort of buffer against the United States. The king was heavily bribed to allow the cession of the Floridas and the queen easily won over to support it. In the pledge just mentioned it was specified that the French should obtain the entire coast of the Gulf of Mexico westward to the mouth of the Rio Grande — which meant the inclusion of the Floridas with Louisiana. But St.-Cyr's statement was far from being a reciprocal agreement, and Godoy adroitly contrived to prevent its becoming such, so far as the Floridas were concerned. In the hurry of later events France was

[1] When, more than a year later, Marquis de Yrujo, the Spanish minister at Washington, was protesting against the transfer of Louisiana from France to the United States, he used this pledge of St.-Cyr as an argument that a sale of the territory in question by France could not be binding. Yrujo to Madison, September 4, 1803, *American State Papers*, II. 569.

given no time in which to make good Napoleon's extensive claim. The question of sovereignty in Florida remained to vex the relations of Spain and the United States long after the possession of Louisiana had been permanently settled. Meanwhile, due to lack of resources and also to the better prospect of a peaceable occupation of the Louisiana territory, the proposed French expedition for its conquest was indefinitely postponed.

When Jefferson assumed the presidential office March 4, 1801, it was with the conviction that our foreign relations, particularly with France and Spain, were destined long to be peaceful and free from serious complications. In giving expression to the famous aphorism, "Peace, commerce, and honest friendship with all nations; entangling alliances with none,"[1] the new President little realized how severely the national policy thus outlined was to be tested by a situation already rapidly assuming form. Much less did he foresee that our traditional course of isolation was in most imminent danger of interruption by France, with whom a very satisfactory treaty had just been concluded, and toward whose people he had always been most friendly. And least of all did he conceive that any possible contingency of his administration could result in the adding of more than 875,000 square miles to a national domain which, in the first inaugural, was declared already to be "large enough for our descendants to the thousandth and thousandth generation." "With respect to Spain," the new President wrote to William C. C. Claiborne, the recently appointed governor of the Mississippi territory,

[1] In the first inaugural address, March 4, 1801. The address is printed in Richardson, *Messages and Papers of the Presidents*, I. 321–324.

"our disposition is sincerely amicable, and even affectionate. We consider her possession of the adjacent country as most favorable to our interests, and should see with an extreme pain any other nation substituted for them. . . . Should France get possession of that country, it will be more to be lamented than to be remedied by us, as it will furnish ground for profound consideration on our part, how best to conduct ourselves in that case."[1] Though his admiration for Napoleon had suffered a rather severe shock by reason of the acts of the eighteenth Brumaire, Jefferson still expected to have the confidence of the First Consul and anticipated only the pleasantest relations with him. As to this he was soon to be disillusioned; and as time went on the more he came to know of the Consul and later emperor the more he was compelled to distrust him.

It was not until June, 1801, that the rumors of the treaty of retrocession were deemed worthy of official notice in the United States, though as early as the preceding March, King had reported to Secretary Madison that there was no little evidence that they were true.[2] News travelled across the Atlantic slowly enough a hundred years ago, and the people of America were kept only very imperfectly informed of contemporary events in Europe, — particularly when there was any effort, as in this case, to conceal the facts. June 1, King wrote to Madison that Lord Hawkesbury, the British minister of

[1] Jefferson to William C. C. Claiborne, July 13, 1801, *Writings of Thomas Jefferson* (Ford's ed.), VIII. 71.

[2] King to Madison, March 29, 1801, *American State Papers*, II. 509, and Charles R. King (ed.), *The Life and Correspondence of Rufus King*, III. 414.

foreign affairs, had interviewed him on the subject of Louisiana, and had very unreservedly expressed the reluctance with which the English government would acquiesce in the displacement of Spanish by French power on the Mississippi. "The acquisition," Hawkesbury had declared, "might enable France to extend her influence, and perhaps her dominion, up the Mississippi and through the Great Lakes even to Canada. This would be realizing the plan to prevent the accomplishment of which the Seven Years' War took place; besides, the vicinity of the Floridas to the West Indies, and the facility with which the trade of the latter might be interrupted, and the islands even invaded, should the transfer be made, were strong reasons why England must be unwilling that the territory should pass under the dominion of France." King reported that he had given his lordship to understand that the United States would certainly oppose the transfer. The two had agreed that, in the facetious *mot* of Montesquieu, "it was happy for the trading powers that God had permitted Turks and Spaniards to be in the world, since of all nations they are the most proper to possess an empire with insignificance."[1]

During the summer of 1801, Secretary Madison wrote mild letters on the subject of the retrocession to our ministers at London, Paris, and Madrid, setting forth the almost universal feeling in America that the passing of Louisiana into the hands of the French would be detrimental to the interests of the United States.[2] Trouble

[1] King to Madison, June 1, 1801, *American State Papers*, II. 509, and *Life and Correspondence of Rufus King*, III. 469.

[2] Madison to Charles Pinckney, June 9, 1801; to Robert R. Livingston, September 28, 1801, *American State Papers*, II. 510–511, and the *Annals of Congress* (1802–1803), 1014–1015.

enough had been experienced during the last two decades with the Spanish on the southwest, but there was abundant reason to expect much greater annoyance if the French should become our neighbors in that direction. Spain was at best but a decadent power, while France, under the aggressive leadership of Napoleon, was rapidly becoming the dominant nation of Europe. It was the earnest desire of the people and of the Administration that the Spaniards should continue in possession of the trans-Mississippi country.

"The whole subject," Madison wrote to Pinckney at Madrid, "will deserve and engage your early and vigilant inquiries, and may require a very delicate and circumspect management. What the motives of Spain in this transaction may be are not so obvious. The policy of France in it, at least as relates to the United States, cannot be mistaken. Whilst she remained on the footing of confidence and affection with the United States, which originated during our Revolution, and was strengthened during the early stages of her own, it may be presumed that she adhered to the policy which, in the treaty of 1778, renounced the acquisition of continental territory in North America; and was more disposed to shun the collisions threatened by possessions in that quarter, coterminous with ours, than to pursue objects to which the commanding position at the mouth of the Mississippi might be made subservient. Circumstances are not now the same. Although the two countries are again brought together by stipulations of amity and commerce, the confidence and cordiality which formerly subsisted have had a deep wound from the occurrences of late years. Jealousies

probably still remain, that the Atlantic states have a partiality for Great Britain, which may, in future, throw their weight into the scale of that rival. It is more than possible, also, that, under the influence of these jealousies, and of the alarms which have at times prevailed, of a projected operation for wresting the mouth of the Mississippi into the hands of Great Britain, she may have concluded a preoccupancy of it by herself to be a necessary safeguard against an event from which that nation would derive the double advantage of strengthening her hold on the United States, and of adding to her commerce a monopoly of the immense and fertile region communicating with the sea through a single outlet. . . . She [France] must infer, from our conduct and our communications, that the Atlantic states are not disposed to enter, nor are in danger of being drawn, into partialities toward Great Britain unjust or injurious to France; that our political and commercial interests afford a sufficient guaranty against such a state of things; that without the coöperation of the United States, Great Britain is not likely to acquire any part of the Spanish possessions on the Mississippi ; and that the United States never have favored, nor so long as they are guided by the clearest policy, ever can favor, such a project. She must be led to see again, and with a desire to shun, the danger of collisions between the two republics, from the contact of their territories, and from the conflicts in their regulations of a commerce involving the peculiarities which distinguish that of the Mississippi."[1]

[1] Madison to Pinckney, June 9, 1801, *Annals of Congress* (1802–1803), 1014.

While declaring that the establishment of French sovereignty in that quarter would be "ominous" and would "occasion extreme pain" on the part of all Americans, President Jefferson was loath to recognize the import of Napoleon's policy and reluctant to acknowledge the wisdom of making open and vigorous opposition to it. Although possessed of intense convictions and guided invariably by great enthusiasms, Jefferson was essentially a man of peace; and in the face of the serious situation which he felt was certain to develop in the Mississippi region if Napoleon prosecuted the plans credited to him, he was determined at all honorable hazards to prevent the young nation from becoming involved in war. Godoy kept delaying the consummation of the treaty, and Toussaint's rebellion continued to call for all the strength the First Consul could muster. Otherwise possession could have been taken in Louisiana before the President had even become convinced of the French plan, much less devised a means of thwarting it.

But by the spring of 1802 not even Jefferson could longer persuade himself that Napoleon's designs upon Louisiana were only gross misrepresentations. There were too many evidences that these designs were quite real, and this despite the fact that at Paris, Talleyrand, when quizzed by Livingston late in December, 1801, had roundly denied the existence of any such thing as a treaty of retrocession. "It had been a subject of conversation," admitted the smooth-tongued secretary, "but nothing [had been] concluded." The trustworthiness of this denial was rather seriously compromised by the fact that at precisely the same time that it reached Jefferson, there

came also from King a full copy of the treaty itself,[1] setting forth all the terms of the retrocession as arranged by Lucien Bonaparte and Godoy.[2] This was proof positive that Talleyrand was attempting to deceive the United States. Both Madison and Livingston were thrown into a bad temper by such a revelation of duplicity, and the outlook for a peaceful adjustment seemed correspondingly darkened.

The President now resolved to avail himself of the services of a French gentleman of high standing and ability, Dupont de Nemours by name, in whom he had implicit confidence, and who was just on the point of returning home from an extended visit in America. To Dupont Jefferson expressed an earnest desire that he use his influence, unofficially of course, with the First Consul, and convince him if possible of the disastrous effects which must follow a French attempt to possess Louisiana. A letter was also placed in Dupont's hands which was to be carried to Livingston, but which the bearer was asked to read in order that he might have the arguments it contained for use on Napoleon. One portion of this letter in particular has become famous as indicating the seriousness of a situation which could drive Jefferson to such emphatic expressions of anti-French, pro-English sentiment. "The cession of Louisiana and the Floridas by Spain to France works most sorely on the United States. . . . It completely reverses all the political relations of the United States, and will form a new epoch

[1] Not the original treaty of San Ildefonso, but the one negotiated by Lucien Bonaparte and Godoy, March 21, 1801.
[2] *Life and Correspondence of Rufus King*, IV. 15-20.

in our political course. . . . There is on the globe one single spot, the possessor of which is our natural and habitual enemy. It is New Orleans, through which the produce of three-fourths of our territory must pass to market. France, placing herself in that door, assumes to us the attitude of defiance. Spain might have retained it quietly for years. Her pacific dispositions, her feeble state, would induce her to increase our facilities there, so that her possession of the place would be hardly felt by us, and it would not, perhaps, be very long before some circumstance might arise which might make the cession of it to us the price of something of more worth to her. Not so can it ever be in the hands of France; the impetuosity of her temper, the energy and restlessness of her character, placed in a point of eternal friction with us, and our character, which, though quiet and loving peace and the pursuit of wealth, is high-minded, despising wealth in competition with insult or injury, enterprising and energetic as any nation on earth: these circumstances render it impossible that France and the United States can continue long friends, when they meet in so irritable a position. They, as well as we, must be blind if they do not see this; and we must be very improvident if we do not begin to make arrangements on that hypothesis. The day that France takes possession of New Orleans fixes the sentence which is to restrain her forever within her low-water mark. It seals the union of two nations, who, in conjunction, can maintain exclusive possession of the ocean. From that moment we must marry ourselves to the British fleet and nation. We must turn all our attention to a maritime force, for which

our resources place us on very high ground; and having formed and connected together a power which may render reënforcement of her settlements here impossible to France, make the first cannon which shall be fired in Europe the signal for the tearing up of any settlement she may have made, and for holding the two continents of America in sequestration for the common purposes of the united British and American nations. This is not a state of things we seek or desire. It is one which this measure, if adopted by France, forces on us as necessarily as any other cause, by the law of nature, brings on its necessary effect."[1]

Coming as it did, just when Toussaint's rebellion seemed to have been crushed and the way thus opened to Louisiana, Dupont's influence upon Napoleon, though wielded with much skill and tact, counted at the time for little or nothing.[2] Yet the French successes in St. Domingo were only apparent. The carrying away of Toussaint in no sense ended the struggle. The tenure of the island continued to be as uncertain as before. One army of seventeen thousand men had been consumed in suppressing the negroes. Another was even now being swept out of existence by a scourge of yellow fever. The call for money and men was incessant, else — so ran the despatches — "St. Domingo will be forever lost to France." November 1, 1802, Leclerc himself fell a victim to the

[1] *Jefferson's Works* (Washington's ed.), IV. 431-434.
[2] See J. H. Hollander, "Du Pont de Nemours and American Affairs," in the *Johns Hopkins University Studies in Historical and Political Science*, 21st Series, No. VI.; J. G. Rosengarten, "Du Pont de Nemours," in the *Magazine of American History*, XXI. 234-240; and Adams, *History of the United States*, I. Ch. XVI.

fever. Unwittingly the negroes by their stubborn rebellion were postponing the establishment of French authority in Louisiana until the arrival of a day when European conditions were to force an abandonment of the whole project. In this indirect sense, at least, the United States owes no small debt of gratitude to Toussaint and those who struggled with him in what they understood to be the cause of liberty.

CHAPTER XI

THE LOUISIANA PURCHASE

THE summer of 1802, in respect to the Louisiana situation, was a time of suspense. The Spaniards were still in possession of the territory and were giving no indication of an intention to withdraw. Napoleon's designs were well understood, but his preoccupation with St. Domingo rendered his immediate course extremely uncertain. The war between England and France had been brought to a close by the treaty of Amiens, and it was not unreasonable to suppose that, being thus relieved from the pressure of European affairs, Napoleon might now find himself able to establish order quite speedily in St. Domingo and proceed without further delay to take possession of Louisiana. There was but one ground for hope in the United States that events would not thus shape themselves. This was the strong probability of an early renewal of the European war. Although the treaty of Amiens was avowedly conclusive in the settlement of the issues at stake between England and France, there could really never be an abiding peace as long as Napoleon was at the helm in the latter country. President Jefferson clearly perceived this, and thought the resuming of the struggle a question merely of a few years. If there could but be enough delay in Napoleon's American proceedings to prevent the taking of Louisiana before the renewal of hostilities with England, the problem of the lower Mississippi might be solved without any positive action on part of the United States. The exigencies of another European war would certainly stay the course of French aggressions in the western hemisphere. It was quite within the range of possibility that such a war would render the treaty of San Ildefonso nugatory and leave the Spaniards in undisputed possession of the Louisiana territory.

Just as the Administration was beginning to feel fairly comfortable in this anticipation, there came a piece of news which marked a wholly unexpected move in the great game. From Natchez, Governor Claiborne, of the Mississippi territory, sent word to the secretary of state that the Spanish intendant, Don Juan Ventura Morales, had withdrawn the right of deposit at New Orleans, which had been granted Americans by the treaty of San Lorenzo el Real in 1795.[1] It will be remembered that this right, so critically important to the population beyond the Alleghanies, had been secured only after long and bitter contention. Pinckney's hard-won treaty had redeemed from industrial stagnation the finest region and the hardiest people that the United States contained, and with every passing year the prosperity of the West be-

[1] W. C. C. Claiborne to Secretary Madison, October 29, 1802, *American State Papers*, II. 470. The date of the intendant's decree was October 16. "The late act of the Spanish government at New Orleans," wrote Claiborne, "has excited considerable agitation at Natchez and its vicinity. It has inflicted a severe wound on the agricultural and commercial interests of this territory, and will prove no less injurious to all the western country." See Gayarré, *History of Louisiana*, III. 456-458.

came a matter of larger national importance. This prosperity was absolutely dependent on the free use of the Mississippi and of New Orleans as a post for the exchange of goods from river barges to ocean-going craft. Morales's order in 1802 cancelled by one stroke all that had been gained in behalf of the Westerners by more than a decade of diligent diplomacy.

It is not at all improbable that the responsibility for the order lay with Napoleon, and that the retrocession treaty had been accompanied by a secret agreement on the subject. At least there was a strong feeling in the United States at the time that this was the case — particularly in the West, where the closure was regarded as simply a foretaste of French administration. The alleged reason for Morales's order was the necessity under which the intendant found himself of increasing the revenues from New Orleans. In a despatch he stated that these revenues for the year 1802 amounted in all to only $121,041 — a sum which would have been "greatly increased but for the contraband trade carried on by the flatboats which come down the river."[1] The treaty of 1795 had specified that for three years New Orleans should constitute a place of deposit for American traders, and that at the end of this time either the right should be renewed at New Orleans or some other place should be designated for the purpose. At the expiration of the three years, in 1798, nothing had been done concerning the renewal. Both nations seem to have assumed that

---

[1] Gayarré, *History of Louisiana*, III. 577. See Franklin S. Riley, "Spanish Policy in Mississippi after the Treaty of San Lorenzo," in the *Annual Report of the American Historical Association for 1897*, 175–193.

the existing arrangement would be allowed to stand indefinitely. In withdrawing the right Morales now asserted that it was long since forfeit, that the treaty which established it had been a mistake on Spain's part from the outset, and that the river should no longer be open to American commerce except on the payment of heavy tolls. He further declared that the retrocession of Louisiana was to be made the occasion for a reopening of the whole question of Spain's relations with the United States. The Spanish governor at New Orleans, Don Juan de Salcedo, protested vigorously against the intendant's action as freighted only with danger to Spain, and likewise the Spanish minister at Washington, Don Carlos Martinez de Yrujo, hastened to characterize the closure as merely a piece of high-handed despotism on the part of Morales; but under the clumsy colonial and diplomatic system of Spain the opinion of governors and ministers counted for little or nothing.

When Congress convened in December it was expected by many that decisive steps would be taken, both to reopen the Mississippi, and to circumvent the reëstablishment of French authority at New Orleans. From the West arose an uncompromising demand for action of this sort. That there was not much excitement, however, on part of the legislators is evidenced by the fact that more than a week elapsed before the Senate could muster a quorum. The President's message was read on the 15th. Those who expected it to take radical ground on the Louisiana question were sorely disappointed. That subject seemed to have been studiously avoided. Much was said about the carrying trade,

relations with the Barbary powers, Indian affairs, national finances, the army, and the navy; but on the subject which, in view of its intrinsic importance and the President's well-known appreciation of it, might have been expected to receive most attention, only the following extremely colorless statement was to be found: "The cession of the Spanish province of Louisiana to France, which took place in the course of the late war, will, if carried into effect, make a change in the aspect of our foreign relations which will doubtless have just weight in any deliberations of the legislature connected with that subject."[1] And as for Congress, the same conservative disposition was manifested by a resolution passed in January, 1803, to "wait the issue of such measures as that department of the government [the Executive] shall have pursued for asserting the rights and vindicating the injuries of the United States."[2]

Nevertheless, while Jefferson was not saying much officially, he was thinking a great deal, and also employing every available means to bring influence to bear upon Napoleon to relinquish his schemes for aggrandizement in America. The President's policy was confessedly one of delay, in regard both to France and Spain. He was not sure to what extent the one was responsible for the acts of the other. Keenly conscious, too, that the Federalists were secretly desiring his discomfiture and even his failure in the management of the nation's affairs, he was led to be the more cautious, lest a mistake should create

---

[1] Richardson, *Messages and Papers of the Presidents*, I. 343.
[2] Resolutions of January 7, 1803, *Annals of Congress* (1802-1803), 339.

political capital for the party opposed to him. Under existing conditions, war would not merely exhaust the nation's limited resources, but would also inevitably have a reactionary effect at the polls. Jefferson, indeed, owed his own election in part to the popular dissatisfaction aroused by increased taxation during the recent threatened war with France. "Peace is our passion," he therefore declared, and to maintain peace he was as willing to bear and forbear as Washington had been in 1793 and as Madison was to be in 1811.

Out of the West, however, continued to arise a clamor such as would not be stilled. It was the people of this section who suffered by the closure of the Mississippi, and it was they also who had most reason to fear the transfer of the western bank of the river to France. Their demand for national protection was rapidly assuming a very determined tone, and the threat of secession, now by no means unfamiliar, aroused the Administration to the danger of pursuing an apparently indifferent policy too far. The actual disruption of the Union must not be risked, even for the sake of external peace.

To meet this phase of the situation the President resolved upon the expedient of sending a special envoy to France and Spain. Not much would probably be gained by such an envoy that could not just as well be gained by the resident ministers, but this manifestation of interest on part of the Executive would at least do no harm abroad and might have a salutary effect upon the discontented elements at home. The man for the mission was not hard to find. Without a moment's hesitation Jefferson selected James Monroe, who had just retired from the governorship

of Virginia. Monroe had many qualities to recommend him for the task. He was genial, conscientious, patriotic, and well versed in the art of diplomacy. A lifelong friend of Jefferson, he was well informed as to the Administration's principles and in hearty sympathy with its policy. He was as popular with the Westerners as any man who could have been chosen, and his appointment was well designed to soothe the ruffled spirits of these long-suffering people. His former residence in Paris, while not of wholly glorious memory, had nevertheless prepared him in no small degree for the work now committed to him.

On the 10th of January, 1803, Monroe was notified of the President's intention,[1] and on the day following his nomination was sent to the Senate, where it was speedily confirmed, though not without Federalist opposition.[2] Jefferson expressed the fear that peace was about to be overborne by the Westerners and the Federalists, and called upon Monroe to make a "temporary sacrifice" of himself "to prevent this greatest of evils in the present prosperous tide in our affairs." "The circumstances are such," it was urged, "as to render it impossible to decline, because the whole public hope will be rested on you." Even while the Senate was acting upon the appointment, the President wrote again to Monroe: "The agitation of the public mind on the occasion of the late suspension of our right of deposit at New Orleans is extreme. In the western country it is natural and grounded on honest motives. In the seaports it proceeds from a desire for

[1] Jefferson to Monroe, January 10, 1803, *Writings of Jefferson* (Ford's ed.), VIII. 188.

[2] Richardson, *Messages and Papers of the Presidents*, I. 350.

war which increases the mercantile lottery; in the federalists generally and especially those of Congress the object is to force us into war if possible, in order to derange our finances, or if this cannot be done, to attach the western country to them, as their best friends, and thus get again into power. Remonstrances, memorials, etc., are now circulating through the whole of the western country and signing by the body of the people. The measures we have been planning, being invisible, do not satisfy their minds. Something sensible therefore was become necessary."[1]

The "something sensible" was, of course, the sending of a special envoy. And the object for which he was to be sent was the effecting of an agreement which Jefferson had become convinced was the only adequate solution of the difficulty, *i.e.* the purchase of New Orleans and the Floridas. Better by far, argued the President, spend a few millions outright in securing an independent title to the mouth of the Mississippi than go to war to regain a right of deposit which must always be a source of friction and liable to withdrawal. Livingston had already been instructed to feel his way in respect to this matter at the French court. Livingston's usefulness for the purpose, however, was much impaired by the fact that prior to receiving this instruction he had been very emphatic in assuring the French government that the United States cared not at all who possessed New Orleans, so long as the right of her citizens to navigate the Mississippi freely was guaranteed. On the day of Monroe's nomination General

[1] Jefferson to Monroe, January 13, 1803, *Writings of Jefferson* (Ford's ed.), VIII. 190.

Smith, of Maryland, had introduced a resolution in the House appropriating $2,000,000 "to defray any expenses which may be incurred in relation to the intercourse between the United States and foreign nations";[1] and the following day a House committee, on the ground that New Orleans must either be fought for or bought, reported in favor of applying the money to the purchase of West Florida and New Orleans.[2] It was the execution of this project which was now intrusted to the special envoy.

"Having determined on this," continued Jefferson in his letter to Monroe, "there could not be two opinions among the republicans as to the person. You possess the unlimited confidence of the Administration and of the western people; and generally of the republicans everywhere; and were you to refuse to go, no other man can be found who does this. The measure has already silenced the Feds. here. Congress will no longer be agitated by them; and the country will become calm as fast as the information extends over it. All eyes, all hopes, are now fixed on you; and were you to decline, the chagrin would be universal, and would shake under your feet the high ground on which you stand with the public. Indeed, I know nothing which would produce such a shock, for on the event of this mission depend the future destinies of this republic." Jefferson candidly expressed the opinion that by the intended purchase alone could the United States secure herself against an early war, and that in default of it no time should be lost in making overtures to England with a view to assuring herself of an ally in the coming struggle.

[1] *Annals of Congress* (1802–1803), 370.   [2] *Ibid.*, 371–374.

Monroe was urged to make ready for the trip as speedily as possible, "for the moment in France is critical." An absence of at least a year was to be anticipated. A deep sense of the personal inconvenience this appointment might carry with it was expressed by the President, but the envoy was consoled with the suggestion that "some men are born for the public." It was a matter of regret to Jefferson that the "eagle eyes" of the public would not allow the providing of a special frigate for Monroe's use. But that honor had been denied Pinckney, Livingston, and King, and the economical policy which constituted the Administration's strongest claim to popular support could not be broken over in the case of one whom the opposition already chose to regard as the object of gross favoritism by the President and secretary of state. Monroe was therefore to take ship like any other passenger, with the right of reserving a cabin for his own comfort and convenience. His remuneration was to be $9000 per year in addition to travelling expenses.

To Governor Garrard, of Kentucky, Jefferson wrote, January 18, that the people of the Southwest need have no fears as to the future of their trade, since Monroe was then on the point of setting out for France "to secure our rights and interests on the Mississippi, and in the country eastward of that."[1] To smooth the way for Monroe in France the President wrote to Dupont de Nemours, February 1, explaining the urgency of the Mississippi question, commending Monroe as qualified in every respect to treat upon the subject, and requesting Dupont to exert

[1] Jefferson to James Garrard, January 18, 1803, *Writings of Jefferson* (Ford's ed.), VIII. 203.

all his influence in behalf of a speedy and satisfactory conclusion of the negotiation. Monroe went, declared Jefferson, "to aid in the issue of a crisis the most important the United States have ever met since their independence, and which is to decide their future character and career." The use of the Mississippi was asserted to be "so indispensable that we cannot hesitate one moment to hazard our existence for its maintenance. If we fail in this effort to put it beyond the reach of accident, we see the destinies we have to run, and prepare at once for them. Not but that we shall still endeavor to go or in peace and friendship with our neighbors as long as we can, *if our rights of navigation and deposit are respected;* but as we foresee that the caprices of the local officers, and the abuse of those rights by our boatmen and navigators, which neither government can prevent, will keep up a state of irritation which cannot long be kept inactive, we should be criminally improvident not to take at once eventual measures for strengthening ourselves for the contest."[1]

The purchase of more than New Orleans and the Floridas was not for a moment contemplated. The United States was still too poor to buy territory for which she had absolutely no need. Her debt was large and her ability to borrow was limited. The reduction of the debt and the lessening of the national expenses were among the cardinal features of the Administration's programme. The territory which was really desired, and which Monroe and Livingston were authorized to pur-

[1] Jefferson to Dupont de Nemours, February 1, 1803, *Writings of Jefferson* (Ford's ed.), VIII. 203–208.

chase, was described by Jefferson as merely "a barren sand 600 miles from east to west, & from 30 to 40 & 50 miles from north to south, formed by deposition of the sands by the Gulf Stream in its circular course round the Mexican Gulf."[1] The only portions of the tract that were at all valuable had already been preëmpted by Spaniards, whose titles would not of course be interfered with in event of the prospective purchase, so that the United States could anticipate no financial returns for the money expended. Jefferson persistently contended in letters to citizens, both of the United States and of France, that it was the interests of peace and nothing else that made the purchase expedient and, in fact, quite necessary.

In expressions of confidence in the two men charged with the negotiation, Jefferson was profuse. To Livingston he wrote: "The future destinies of our country hang on the event of this negotiation, and I am sure they could not be placed in more able or more zealous hands. On our part we shall be satisfied that what you do not effect, cannot be effected."[2] It was not unnatural that Livingston should feel just a bit piqued at the appointment of a special envoy, since, to some, it might seem to indicate a lack of confidence in his own ability to deal with the situation. To forestall any such feeling and secure complete harmony between the two ministers, Jefferson, in his correspondence, laid much emphasis on the fact that Monroe's appointment had been intended primarily to

[1] Jefferson to Dupont de Nemours, February 1, 1803, *Writings of Jefferson* (Ford's ed.), VIII. 206.
[2] Jefferson to Robert R. Livingston, February 3, 1803, *ibid.*, 209-210.

calm the Westerners, and, at the same time, to hasten the settlement of an issue which the Federalists had "caught as a plank in a shipwreck." It was also urged that only by sending a special minister could all the necessary information and instructions be safely transmitted.

In a letter to the President, March 7, written at New York just before his departure for Europe, Monroe gave expression at some length to his views on the issues at stake and the probabilities of the forthcoming negotiation. Adopting as his starting point the resolution introduced by Senator Ross, of Pennsylvania, February 15, requiring the President to take possession of New Orleans at once by an armed force, Monroe declared: "The resolutions of Mr Ross prove that the federal party will stick at nothing to embarrass the adm^n and recover its lost power. They nevertheless produce a great effect on the publick mind and I presume more especially in the western country. The unanimity in the publick councils respecting our right to the free navigation of the river, and its importance to every part of the U States, the dissatisfaction at the interference of Sp^n which will not be appeased while the power of a similar one exists, are calculated to inspire the hope of a result which may put us at ease forever on those points. If the negotiation secures all the objects sought, or a deposit with the sovreignty over it, the federalists will be overwhelmed completely: the union of the western with the Eastern people will be consolidated, republican principles confirmed, and a fair prospect of peace and happiness presented to our country. But if the negotiation compromises short of that, and leaves the management of our great concerns in that river, which comprize every thing appertaining to the western parts of the U States, in the hands of a foreign power, may we not expect that the publick will be disappointed and disapprove of the result. So far as I can judge, I think much would be hazarded by any adjustment which did not put us in complete security for the future. It is doubtful whether an adjustment short of that would be approved in any part of the union; I am thoroughly persuaded it would not to the westward. ... It therefore highly merits consideration whether we should not take that ground as the ultimatum in the negotiation which must in every possible event preserve the confidence & affection of the western people. While we stand well with them we shall prosper. ... I hope the French gov? will have wisdom enough to see that we will never suffer France or any other power to tamper with our interior; if that is not the object there can be no reason for declining an accommodation to the whole of our demands."[1]

On the 8th of March, the next day after the foregoing letter was written, Monroe set sail.[2] The instructions which he bore, while general rather than specific in nature, provided for three contingencies: (1) Should Napoleon be willing to sell New Orleans and the Floridas, any sum not exceeding ten millions might be offered, besides commercial privileges for ten years, a speedy extension of citizenship to the population of the regions acquired, and in case of urgent demand, an absolute guarantee of the

[1] Monroe to Jefferson, March 7, 1803, Monroe's *Writings*, IV. 5-7.
[2] For Monroe's preparations for the voyage, see his letter to George Clinton, March 6, and to Jefferson, March 7, in his *Writings*, IV. 3-8.

west bank of the Mississippi to the French. (2) Should Napoleon refuse to sell any territory whatsoever, even a few square miles on which a post might be built, a renewal of the right of deposit under the most favorable terms possible was to be secured. (3) Should even this be refused, communication of the fact to the President would be followed by special instructions — probably an order for Monroe to cross the Channel to England.[1] It thus appears that Napoleon might have met the demands Monroe and Livingston were empowered to make — the minimum demands at least — by merely renewing the *entrepôt* at New Orleans, or by selling a few square miles for the establishment of a new place of deposit. Such a transaction would have involved in no sense the loss of French prestige in America, and indeed such a settlement had already been promised Livingston by Talleyrand.

In reality Jefferson did not expect immediate compliance by Napoleon with even the most modest of these requests. In private conversations he continued to admit that his only hope was to delay matters until war should again break out between France and England. That such a war was coming he clearly foresaw, although it came much sooner than he expected, and the results which flowed from it were such as he had hardly given a passing thought. If the people would only be patient enough to allow him to "palliate and endure" until that event, he believed that under its stress France might be constrained to yield to the American demands as the

---

[1] Instructions of Secretary Madison to Livingston and Monroe, March 2, 1803, *American State Papers*, II. 540; and *Annals of Congress* (1802–1803), 1095–1107.

price of American neutrality. In the meantime Napoleon would probably take possession of Louisiana and might hold it for some years.

The French minister at Washington, M. Pichon, discerned the President's policy and continued to send home the most discouraging reports of the outlook for the French in America. Secretary Madison was artfully confirming Pichon in his fears, and Napoleon was strongly advised by his American representative to yield at once the territory desired. Although unable to complain of any lack of consideration shown himself, yet Pichon did report that at the President's table he noticed that civilities and attentions to the British *chargé* were redoubled.[1] That a British alliance was on the point of being formed he had not the slightest doubt. Monroe himself, before sailing, had assured the frightened Frenchman that in event of such an alliance the two powers "would not stop half way." In his report to the First Consul Pichon said that Monroe had given him to understand that if the negotiation for New Orleans failed, "the Administration had made up its mind to act with the utmost vigor, and to receive the overtures which England was incessantly making;" also that he could "only imperfectly imagine the extent of those overtures." It must be said that if Monroe actually represented, as Pichon's statements strongly imply, that England had made overtures, he overstepped the truth. Only one or two un-

---

[1] Pichon to Talleyrand, 4 Pluviôse, An XI. (January 24, 1803), Archives des Affaires Étrangères. Quoted in Adams, *History of the United States*, I. 437.

authorized suggestions of an alliance from the British minister, Thornton, had been received. Nevertheless, Pichon was well warranted in taking the toast which had recently been proposed by General Smith at a banquet — "Peace, if peace is honorable; war, if war is necessary" — as a conclusive expression of the American position.

Some of Secretary Madison's affirmations regarding the question at issue and its future bearings sound so strange to-day that it is difficult to appreciate how generally they were concurred in a hundred years ago. New Orleans, he urged, was in itself of no value to the United States; the location was bad and would doubtless be abandoned for another east of the river. The United States had no disposition whatever to acquire territory beyond the Mississippi, or to take the slightest step in that direction. This river was clearly designated by nature to be the permanent boundary between the French possessions and the United States. It would be far from the interest of the United States to acquire lands west of the river, or to suffer her people to emigrate thither. For settlement in that region would inevitably result in the birth of a rival nation, since it was not to be thought of that the United States could ever govern territory beyond the Mississippi. This would mean endless strife between the two English-speaking nations on opposite sides of the river. All in all, it was highly desirable to the United States that the French continue in their western possessions, although Spain would have made the better neighbor.

The departure of Monroe had its anticipated effect. The country became more quiet than for two or three years. The disposition patiently to await the outcome was all but universal. For more than a month the matter was not mentioned officially at Washington. Then Jefferson broke the silence by asking the Cabinet what should be done in case Napoleon refused to accede to any of the envoy's demands. The consensus of opinion was that in such event they should "use all possible procrastination" with France, and enter as expeditiously as possible into an alliance with the British, though care should be exercised to postpone the war, at least until the following spring, to allow the United States time to prepare. Jefferson reached the high tide of his new British proclivities in proposing that England be allowed to take Louisiana for herself — a suggestion which, however, was unanimously rejected by the Cabinet.

Had Jefferson, Madison, and the other Republican leaders only known the real purposes of Napoleon, they would have been spared this exhibition of gross inconsistency between their present foreign policy and that of ten years before. Napoleon had absolutely no thought of engaging in a war with the United States, except as a very remote possibility after his European plans should have been realized. In fact, he was finding it quite out of the question even to take possession of the American territory secured to him by the treaty of San Ildefonso. The kingdom of Etruria which he had engaged himself to create and bestow on Don Carlos's son-in-law was still in a very inchoate condition, and Godoy, strongly suspecting the First Consul of treachery, was proceeding on the theory that the treaty had not been kept and that Louisiana therefore still rightfully belonged to Spain. The Missis-

sippi question was considered by the Spanish authorities as one which it would remain with them to settle. On the 19th of April Yrujo, who was always more of a friend to Jefferson than to Napoleon, exultingly informed Secretary Madison that Don Carlos had repudiated Morales's action, and that the right of deposit at New Orleans would be forthwith restored.[1] The governor of the latter place had been ordered from Madrid to make adequate provision for the accommodation of the western traders. Deep regret was expressed at the inconvenience occasioned by the intendant's order, and the President was tendered a flattering statement of gratitude for his careful and considerate course in the recent breach.

Had the continuance of Spanish possession at New Orleans been assured to the satisfaction of the President and his advisers, this turn of affairs would have ended the whole matter, and Monroe's mission would have been brought to a sudden stop. Why negotiate with Napoleon for territory that belonged to another power, or for commercial rights which were already possessed at the hand of another government? But that Napoleon would eventually take possession of Louisiana the Administration did not for a moment doubt, and therefore, while pleased with the conciliatory course of the Spanish, it was not supposed that the reversal of Morales's order would mean anything a year or two hence, when the French flag should be flying over New Orleans. The negotiations at Paris were accordingly to be maintained. And it is well that they were; for otherwise the splendid opportunity which was

[1] Madison to Livingston and Monroe, April 18, 1803, *American State Papers*, I. 556.

soon to be offered for the only permanent adjustment of the question might have been lost.

Although about the time of Monroe's appointment Napoleon was gathering a fleet for the reduction of the Spanish power at New Orleans, and was declaring his purpose to raise Louisiana to a degree of strength which would make the province easily capable of self-defence in time of war, he was already being forced to acknowledge to himself that French prospects in America were anything but bright. News came that the campaign in St. Domingo had utterly failed, that Leclerc was dead, and that the pacification of this indispensable base of operations against Louisiana would require efforts more gigantic and costs more appalling than even those of the past two or three years. Within a twelvemonth fifty thousand men had been consumed in the island like water on a thirsty desert. Such waste of men and money not even Napoleon could afford — not to mention the stigma attached to defeat by a handful of disorganized negroes. The soldiers murmured ominously at the suggestion of another St. Domingan campaign, with its inevitable end of death, and probably inglorious death by fever at that. It was one of the elements of strength of Napoleon, although several times he was brought thereby into popular discredit, that he knew when to abandon an enterprise whose disastrous end he foresaw. St. Domingo could not be conquered. It must be abandoned. The question was, How could it be abandoned and yet the world be blinded to the fact that defeat forced the move?

With characteristic stolidity Napoleon worked out the answer. No one was taken into his confidence, not even

Talleyrand, until the plan was complete. The earliest manifestation of a change of policy was a message sent to the Corps Législatif, February 20, in which England was referred to in terms so bitter that it was at once suspected by many that the First Consul's intention was to reopen the war with that nation. Livingston scented the new line of action, and rightly surmised that it meant an abandonment of the St. Domingan and Louisiana projects. And when, on the 12th of March, he was himself a witness of the famous scene in Madame Bonaparte's drawing-room where Napoleon declared excitedly to the British ambassador, Whitworth, that he "must either have Malta or war," there could no longer be doubt as to what was coming.[1] This was only four days after Monroe's departure from the United States. The contingency for which Jefferson had been waiting was at hand, though of course he knew it not for many a day after. Both powers commenced promptly to prepare for the titanic struggle. The taking possession of Louisiana was indefinitely postponed, as Napoleon felt now it could be without loss of prestige, in view of the larger undertaking in which he was about to engage. It was just at this point that Godoy, who hated Napoleon and took unfeigned delight in discomfiting him, secured the overruling of Morales's closure of the Mississippi. This was the earliest moment that Spain had dared take such action, but thereafter the attitude of the Spaniards toward the United States continued to be most flattering.

Before they were made public Napoleon's new plans came to involve nothing less than the alienation of

[1] Livingston to Madison, March 12, 1803, *American State Papers*, I, 547.

Louisiana. Even if the territory could be made French, it could not be defended against England's navy in the war now about to begin. That the English ministry was bent even more intensely upon the defeat of Napoleon's scheme of colonial revival than his ambition for dominance in Europe was plainly understood. "If you can obtain Louisiana — well," Prime Minister Addington had said to Rufus King; "if not, we ought to prevent its going into the hands of France."[1] To lose Louisiana gracefully, and without losing it to England, was now the clearly determined policy of the First Consul.

On Sunday, April 10, while Monroe was on his way from Havre to Paris, Napoleon summoned Talleyrand and Barbé-Marbois, ministers of foreign affairs and finance respectively, to meet him in secret council after the Easter services at St. Cloud. It was on this occasion that the plan which had heretofore been barely suggested to Talleyrand was explained in detail. With unusual force the First Consul dwelt upon the reasons for such a step — how that St. Domingo was lost, and without St. Domingo Louisiana could not be reduced; how, even if Louisiana could be made French, it could not be defended against the superior naval strength of the English; and how it was very well known that the subversion of the French colonial scheme was to be England's chief aim in the struggle just begun. To his ministers Napoleon declared: "I think of ceding it [Louisiana] to the United States. I can scarcely say that I cede it to them, for it is not yet in our possession. If, however,

[1] Rufus King to Madison, April 2, 1803, *American State Papers*, II. 551.

I leave the least time, I shall only transmit an empty title to those republicans whose friendship I seek. They ask of me only one town in Louisiana; but I already consider the colony as entirely lost; and it appears to me that in the hands of this young power it will be more useful to the policy, and even to the commerce, of France, than if I should attempt to keep it."[1]

Marbois, who was an ardent republican and very friendly to the United States, thought well of the plan, though Talleyrand was rather skeptical. To Napoleon, of course, it really mattered very little what his ministers thought. On the following day Marbois was called at early dawn into the presence of the First Consul, where he heard the following characteristically laconic and expressive deliverance: "Irresolution and deliberation are no longer in season; I renounce Louisiana. It is not only New Orleans that I cede; it is the whole colony, without reserve. I know the price of what I abandon. . . . I renounce it with the greatest regret; to attempt obstinately to retain it would be folly. I direct you to negotiate the affair. Have an interview this very day with Mr. Livingston."[2]

It was not Marbois, but Talleyrand, however, who first broached the matter to the American minister. On the day of Marbois's commission Talleyrand took occasion to inquire of Livingston whether the United States would care to purchase all of Louisiana, and what they would be willing to pay for it, explaining that he did not "speak from authority, but that the idea had struck him."[3]

---

[1] Barbé-Marbois, *Histoire de la Louisiane*, 286.   [2] *Ibid.*, 298.
[3] Livingston to Madison, April 11, 1803, *American State Papers*, II. 552.

Livingston was naturally somewhat taken aback by the suggestion. He had asked for a mere crumb and had been tendered the whole loaf. After pleading so long and earnestly, and withal so ineffectually, for "barren sands and sunken marshes," "a small town built of wood," and "an insignificant strip of land valuable to the United States but only a drain of resources from France,"[1] it was somewhat disconcerting to be asked complacently whether he would care to have all the region between the Mississippi and the Rockies.

After regaining his composure, Livingston bethought himself that, if the credit of achieving such a consummation was to be exclusively his own, the transaction must be effected without delay. For Monroe was hourly expected — had indeed arrived at Saint-Germain late Monday night, April 11. At one o'clock the next day he was at his Paris hotel. Still there was a little time in which an agreement might be reached before the envoy should be ready to take part in the negotiation. On Tuesday, the day of Monroe's arrival, Livingston labored hard to get Talleyrand to commit himself to some definite statement regarding the sale of at least New Orleans and the Floridas. But the foreign minister was not of the sort to make a bargain so readily. Duplicity, subtle awakening of hopes without confirmation, contempt for the feelings of others, were his stock in trade. As soon as he perceived Livingston's sudden anxiety he assumed the most tantalizing indifference on the whole subject. He knew nothing, had heard nothing, had said nothing, could

[1] Livingston to Napoleon, February 27, 1803, *American State Papers*, II, 539.

promise nothing. He even declared emphatically that Louisiana did not belong to France. That the making of a treaty of retrocession between France and Spain had been talked about he admitted, but that such a treaty had never been made he was quite sure.[1] Livingston had seen the treaty with his own eyes and told Talleyrand so. But the latter was not affected in the least by such testimony and insisted that no such treaty was in existence. Considering the impatience of Livingston to effect the purchase without Monroe's aid, this brazen conduct on the part of Talleyrand must have been almost too much to be endured with equanimity.

The chance was lost, for by Tuesday evening Monroe was ready to begin work. On that evening he called on Livingston, and the two decided to spend the next day in arranging papers preparatory to the joint negotiation, which was to begin as soon as Monroe could be presented at court.[2] The following afternoon,—Wednesday,—after the papers were arranged, a party was entertained at dinner in Livingston's apartments. During the dinner Livingston saw Marbois whiling away the time in an outer garden, and sent an invitation to the genial Frenchman to become one of the party. The invitation was accepted, and over the coffee-cups Livingston detailed to Marbois

[1] Livingston to Madison, April 13, 1803, *American State Papers*, II. 552. In a letter to Madison, April 15, Monroe wrote, "I was informed on my arrival here, by Mr. Skipwith, that Mr. Livingston, mortified at my appointment, had done everything in his power to turn the occurrences in America, and even my mission to his account, by pressing the government on every point with a view to show that he had accomplished what was wished without my aid." Monroe's *Writings*, IV. 9.

[2] Livingston to Madison, April 13, 1803, *American State Papers*, II. 552.

his recent interview with Talleyrand and particularly the latter's exasperating conduct when the Louisiana question was raised.[1] Marbois in a rather non-committal way gave Livingston to understand that he was himself possessed of some information relative to the First Consul's plans for Louisiana, and intimated that if the American minister would call at his residence after the dinner party had broken up, he might learn something of interest.

After the guests had departed, Monroe with them, Livingston hastened to Marbois's quarters, and in the course of the midnight interview which followed the first definite proposition for the sale of Louisiana was made. The finance minister's price, to which Napoleon had assented, was about 125,000,000 francs, of which one-fifth was to be paid to citizens of the United States who had claims against France. Despite the fact that he had been empowered to give as much as $10,000,000 merely for New Orleans and the Floridas, Livingston did not at once assent to the idea of purchasing all Louisiana, although even at Marbois's price it was of course absurdly cheap. He had learned by his experience with Talleyrand not to display too much anxiety on the subject. Being assured that the United States did not care to acquire the region west of the Mississippi, and would not in any case pay the price asked, Marbois lowered his figure to 80,000,000 francs, including the claims. Livingston still protested that the United States did not want Louisiana, that they would be perfectly satisfied with New Orleans and the Floridas, and that it was useless for the French ministers to make offers of the

[1] Monroe to Madison, April 15, 1803, Monroe's *Writings*, IV. 10.

territory beyond the Mississippi. With the emphatic assertion that the United States could not and would not pay any such sums as had been named for Louisiana, Livingston brought the conference to an end.

Nevertheless, he was greatly pleased with the turn affairs had taken. And it was at least no matter for regret that the turn had occurred before Monroe had been able to take any active part in the negotiation. That this important feature might not be overlooked by the government at home, Livingston sat down about three o'clock in the morning and wrote to Secretary Madison a detailed account of the interview which he had just had with Marbois, and expressed the opinion that the United States could well afford to make the purchase at the price named, though every means would be employed to reduce it. The money might be raised, he thought, by the sale of the territory to some European power whose proximity the United States would have no reason to fear.[1]

Delay in dealing with Napoleon was always hazardous, but for more than two weeks Monroe and Livington risked a withdrawal of the offer in an effort to reduce the price demanded. Any one of a score of possible contingencies might have impelled the First Consul to show an entirely different front. Had the commissioners been aware of incidents which were daily occurring in the Tuileries, they would doubtless have seized the first opportunity to close the bargain. For to purchase Louisiana they in a very short time became pretty well resolved.

---

[1] Livingston to Madison, April 13, 1803, *American State Papers*, II. 552.

There seemed, indeed, to be but one alternative. Napoleon had determined to sell; they must either buy or incur his extreme displeasure. Instructions from America for the larger negotiation could not be awaited. By effecting the purchase as speedily as possible the commissioners could secure all that the United States was asking and vastly more besides. The additional acquisition could be sold to pay the cost of the whole. Thus the United States would drive a shrewd bargain which would at once gain her immediate ends in New Orleans and the Floridas, and at the same time free her from fear of a French power in the West — and all at absolutely no expense financially. Verily, it was a scheme to be proud of, and the realization of it was to be the crowning act of political sagacity and patriotic endeavor on the part of the American ministers.

Among the French people the project of alienating Louisiana was far from popular. By many it was regarded as a base betrayal of his country's interests by the man who, it was beginning to be suspected, had already been guilty of such an offence on the famous eighteenth Brumaire. Napoleon's position was now so secure, however, that he had small occasion for deference to popular opinion. Under the veiled monarchical system of the day such opinion had scant means of expression. So that, though the threatened retrenchment in America was regarded with keen regret by that large element of the people whose heart was set upon the revival of the old colonial empire and who had trusted Napoleon to realize their hopes, little was said openly against the sale.

In the First Consul's own household the situation was

far otherwise. The brothers, Lucien and Joseph, were thrown into a storm of passion by Napoleon's proposal. Particularly was Lucien enraged, because it was he who had negotiated the treaty of San Ildefonso, by which France had regained Louisiana and had solemnly bound herself not to alienate it. Although the fact was not known to Monroe and Livingston, the bare suggestion of the sale induced a desperate quarrel among the three brothers and for a while greatly endangered the project. It is probable, however, that Napoleon finally became only the more determined upon the execution of his plan as an illustration to his brothers of the uselessness of their opposition. Lucien and Joseph insisted that the Legislative Chambers would never allow the cession. Napoleon gave them to understand that the Chambers were not to be consulted.

The story of the most picturesque incident in the quarrel of the three brothers over the Louisiana question is well told in the *Mémoires* written by Lucien nine years after the occurrence.[1] Coming home one evening to dress for the theatre, Lucien found Joseph awaiting him with the news of Napoleon's purpose — news which, as Joseph rightly guessed, would hardly make Lucien feel like amusing himself. Instead of going to the theatre, the two brothers spent the evening in formulating a plan whereby to thwart the intended action. It was agreed that an interview should be sought with the First Consul the next morning. Lucien was to seek an audience first, and Joseph was to

[1] Théodore Jung, *Lucien Bonaparte et ses Mémoires* [Paris, 1882], II. 128–154 *passim*. Reproduced in Adams, *History of the United States*, II. 33 *et seq*.

present himself somewhat later, as if without any previous understanding. It was agreed to await Napoleon's mention of the subject, lest he be angered by his brothers' audacity. Lucien tells us that during the night he carefully rehearsed all the arguments at his command against the proposed sale, and determined at least to persuade Napoleon to consult the Chambers on the subject, which, as Lucien knew, would result in an adverse vote. This, it may be said, was just as well known to Napoleon, and to incur opposition in that quarter was no part of his plan.

The next morning, according to agreement, Lucien sought the First Consul. That august personage was found in an excellent humor, enjoying the luxuries of his perfumed bath. Various matters were talked of, but not one word was ventured concerning the thing uppermost in the minds of both. "It was almost time to leave the bath, and . . . we had not discussed Louisiana any more than we had the year forty," writes Lucien. "I was vexed at it, but the nearer the last moment of speaking of it approached, the more I put off doing so. The body-servant was already holding the sheet prepared to wrap his master in; I was about to leave the place, when Rustan [one of the Consul's lackeys] scratched at the door like a cat."

The arrival of Joseph was announced. Napoleon called out that his brother might enter and that he would remain in the bath a quarter of an hour longer. Lucien indicated to the newcomer by a sign that the Louisiana question had not been mentioned. While Joseph was manifesting extreme perplexity as to how best to broach the subject, Napoleon himself relieved the situation by addressing to

him the question, "Well, brother, so you have not spoken to Lucien?"

"About what?" asked Joseph.

"About our plan in regard to Louisiana, you know," was the reply.

Joseph hastened to amend the answer by suggesting that the plan was none of his.

Designating Joseph as "preacher" and "mister grumbler," Napoleon said he would talk further of the matter after he had left the bath, but that he might as well state that he had "decided to sell Louisiana to the Americans." Lucien, who was supposed to be in ignorance of the entire project, endeavored to express by a simple "Ah! Ah!" such mild surprise as might be expected of one in that position. Napoleon, however, professed to understand the exclamation as indicating a definite approval, and proceeded to contrast Lucien's submissiveness with Joseph's pugnacity. Joseph hastened to explain that Lucien's views were identical with his own. This forced an open acknowledgment from Lucien, and also the confession that he flattered himself the Chambers would not give their consent to the sale of Louisiana.

"You flatter yourself!" cried Napoleon, with cutting irony; "that is fine, in truth."

Upon Joseph's inquiring whether or not it was the purpose of the First Consul to make the sale without consulting the Chambers, the latter replied, "Precisely; that is what I have taken the great liberty of saying to Mr. Joseph, and what I repeat here to Citizen Lucien, begging him to tell me his opinion about it also, himself, apart from his paternal tenderness for his diplomatic conquest."

Then once more preparing to leave the bath, the First Consul declared suddenly in a tone "loud enough to make us turn round": "And then, gentlemen, think what you please about it, but give this affair up as lost, both of you; you, Lucien, on account of the sale in itself, you, Joseph, because I shall get along without the consent of any one whomsoever, do you understand?"

Lucien believed subsequently that the smile which inevitably forced itself to his face at the deliverance of these words was the real cause of "the tempest which was brewing, not in a tea-pot, according to the proverb, but rather in the bath-tub of him who was beginning to make all the sovereigns of Europe quake." The most immediate provocation, however, was given by Joseph, who, approaching the bath, exclaimed with much force, "And you will do well, my dear brother, not to expose your plan to parliamentary discussion, for I declare to you that I am the first one to place himself, if it is necessary, at the head of the opposition which cannot fail to be made to you."

Lucien was prevented from making a similar declaration by the "more than Olympian bursts of laughter" of the First Consul. Flushed with anger, Joseph cried: "Laugh, laugh, laugh, then! None the less I will do what I say, and, although I do not like to mount the tribune, this time they shall see me there."

Napoleon was ready with a rejoinder. "You will have no need," he asserted, "to stand forth as orator of the opposition, for I repeat to you that this discussion will not take place, for the reason that the plan which is not fortunate enough to obtain your approbation, conceived

by me, negotiated by me, will be ratified and executed by me all alone, do you understand? by me, who snap my fingers at your opposition."

The quarrel was becoming fast and furious. Lucien declares he wished to leave the scene but dared not do so. To another of Joseph's fierce denunciations Napoleon attempted an enraged reply: "You are an insolent fellow! I ought—" The rest of the sentence, if indeed it was spoken, cannot be reported, for just at that moment the First Consul made a violent motion in the water which resulted in a drenching of all the surrounding objects, including Joseph. Lucien tells us that he was luckily protected from this aquatic explosion by the greater distance at which he was standing. "I observed only then," he continues, "that following the difference existing between the two characters, exasperated, as it seemed to me, to the same pitch, the paleness of the Consul contrasted singularly with the redness of Joseph; and finding myself by my sort of silent neutrality in the midst of sharp or offensive remarks, which had been exchanged, as it were raised to the height of the rôle of peacemaker, and yet not wishing to pose as one, I tried to attain this end by seeming to take what was going on as a sort of joke, and I quoted rather gayly, with a bombastic accent, the famous '*Quos ego*' . . . of Virgil; for in fact the image of Neptune rebuking the waves let loose in spite of him had seemed to my mind just a little ludicrous, and the 'I ought' of the Neptune of the bath-tub alone reaching my ear completed for me in action, at least in parody, the literary translation of the celebrated reticence, the first subject of admiration for young Latinists."

Anger was overcome in the ludicrous aspects of the situation. Dripping and sputtering, Joseph beat a hasty retreat to secure a change of clothing, while the First Consul surrendered himself into the hands of the valet who, according to some accounts at least, had fainted from fright at one stage of the altercation. Subsequently, in a calmer conversation with Lucien, Napoleon expressed the conviction that recent experience in St. Domingo had demonstrated that national glory would never come to France from the marine, that Louisiana was certain to be lost in any event, and that it was highly expedient to dispose of the territory while it was yet possible to secure thereby some funds with which to prosecute the war with England. For Lucien's continued recurrence to the question of constitutionality Napoleon cherished only the supremest contempt. "Constitution! unconstitutional! republic! national sovereignty!—big words! great phrases! . . . Ah, it becomes you well, Sir Knight of the Constitution, to talk so to me! You had not the same respect for the Chambers on the eighteenth Brumaire." This thrust was a keen one, inasmuch as Lucien had been President of the Council of Five Hundred on the occasion referred to, and had betrayed that body to his brother without a show of compunction. "If I were not your brother, I would be your enemy," declared Lucien in conclusion of the interview. To which Napoleon replied by flinging his snuff-box on the floor and exclaiming: "You my enemy! I would break you, look, like this box."

Such scenes in the Tuileries were frequent. On one occasion, we are told, the controversy between Joseph and

Napoleon became so violent that the latter fled for refuge to the private apartments of Josephine. But of all this Monroe and Livingston were ignorant. The negotiations dragged. Marbois's lowest price had been refused, and each side waited for the other to move. Monroe was hindered by illness. Livingston was growing impatient. Both were yet in a mood to be persuaded, if necessary, to strike a reasonable bargain for New Orleans and the Floridas and let go the Louisiana proposition. At the end of two weeks after Monroe's arrival the desired settlement seemed in some respects farther from realization than at any time since Marbois's first advances were made to Livingston. Yet in truth the making of the treaty was near at hand.

There is considerable uncertainty about the exact sequence of events during the closing days of the negotiation, but it seems that it was Napoleon who broke the deadlock, and that he did so by placing in the hands of Marbois, April 23, the *projet* of a secret convention with the United States, to be communicated at once to the American commissioners.[1] This *projet* provided for the cession of Louisiana, in return for the granting of several concessions by the United States, including the free navigation of the Mississippi, perpetual right of deposit at six points on the river, the payment to France of 100,000,000 francs, and the liquidation of American claims left unprovided for by the Convention of 1800. On the 27th of April Marbois met Livingston and Monroe at the latter's lodgings and laid before them Napoleon's *projet*. Monroe had recovered from his illness only sufficiently to be able

[1] *Correspondance de Napoléon Premier*, VIII. 289.

to recline on a sofa. Marbois and Livingston took their position at a table near by and the work began. Marbois admitted at the outset that Napoleon's terms were rather high and, instead of insisting upon these as indispensable, brought forward another *projet* of his own devising which he believed his master would accept.[1]

After several hours' discussion Marbois took his departure, and Monroe and Livingston were free to canvass the matter between themselves. The result was the drawing up of a *contre-projet*, which fixed the price of Louisiana at 70,000,000 francs — 50,000,000 to be paid directly to France and the remainder to French creditors in the United States.[2] This proposition was submitted to Marbois on the 29th. He declared emphatically, however, that it was useless to offer less than 80,000,000 francs for the territory, including the claims, and the Americans at last yielded. The next morning their modified *projet* was laid before Napoleon. May 1 Monroe and Livingston dined at the Tuileries. Nothing was said by the First Consul on this occasion respecting Louisiana, except that the question should be promptly settled.[3] That evening the commissioners had their final interview with Marbois on the subject. The day following, May 2, the treaty of cession was signed. It specified that 60,000,000 francs be paid direct to France.[4] Within the next week the amount of American claims was estimated definitely at 20,000,000 francs; so that the total purchase price of Louisiana was 80,000,000 francs, or practically $15,000,000. All documents per-

---

[1] Monroe's Memoranda, *Writings*, IV. 12–13.
[2] *Ibid.*, 14.
[3] *Ibid.*, 15.
[4] *Ibid.*, 17.

taining to the treaty were antedated to the 30th of April.[1]

After Livingston had set his name to the treaty he rose and shook hands with Monroe and Marbois. "We have lived long," he exclaimed, "but this is the noblest work of our lives. . . . The treaty we have signed has

[1] The text of the treaty is in the *American State Papers*, II. 507-509; the *Annals of Congress* (1802-1803), 1004-1007; *Treaties and Conventions between the United States and other Powers*, 266-286; *United States Statutes at Large*, VIII. 200-206; and MacDonald, *Select Documents*, 160-165. The literature on the subject of the Louisiana Purchase is very extensive. Among source materials should be mentioned the *American State Papers, Foreign Relations*, II. 525-544; the *Annals of Congress* (1802-1803), 1007-1210; Jefferson's *Account of Louisiana, being an Abstract of Documents in the Offices of the Departments of State and of the Treasury* [Philadelphia, 1803]; Jefferson's *Works* (Ford's ed.), Vol. VIII.; Monroe's *Writings*, Vol. IV.; the *Correspondance de Napoléon Premier;* and Théodore Jung, *Lucien Bonaparte et ses Mémoires*. A convenient collection of original materials is the "State Papers and Correspondence bearing upon the Purchase of the Territory of Louisiana," 57th Cong., second sess., House Document No. 431. General accounts of the Purchase are as follows: Adams, *History of the United States*, I. Chs. XIII.-XVII. and II. Chs. I.-VI. (the best); James K. Hosmer, *History of the Louisiana Purchase;* McMaster, *History of the People of the United States*, II. 621-635; Binger Hermann, *The Louisiana Purchase;* Lyman, *The Diplomacy of the United States*, I. Ch. IX.; Gilman, *James Monroe*, 77-96; Morse, *Thomas Jefferson*, Ch. XIV.; Barbé-Marbois, *Histoire de la Louisiane, et de la cession de cette colonie par la France aux États-Unis de l'Amérique* [Paris, 1829]; Gayarré, *History of Louisiana*, III. Ch. VIII.; Roosevelt, *The Winning of the West*, IV. Ch. VI.; Thomas M. Cooley, "The Acquisition of Louisiana," in the *Indiana Historical Society Publications*, II. 65-93; Daniel R. Goodloe, "The Purchase of Louisiana," in the *Publications of the Southern History Association*, IV. 149-172; C. F. Robertson, "The Louisiana Purchase in its Influence upon the American System," in the *Papers of the American Historical Association*, I. 253-290; and N. P. Langford, "The Louisiana Purchase and Preceding Spanish Intrigues for Dismemberment of the Union," in the *Minnesota Historical Society Collections*, IX. 453-508. There is a good bibliography of the Louisiana Purchase, prepared by Professor J. F. Jameson, in Gilman's *James Monroe*, Appendix.

not been brought about by *finesse* nor dictated by force. Equally advantageous to both the contracting parties, it will change vast solitudes into a flourishing country. To-day the United States take their place among the powers of the first rank. . . . The instrument we have signed will cause no tears to flow. It will prepare centuries of happiness for innumerable generations of the human race. The Mississippi and the Missouri will see them prosper and increase in the midst of equality, under just laws, freed from the errors of superstition, from the scourges of bad government, and truly worthy of the regard and care of Providence." Napoleon was likewise pleased with the outcome. "The negotiation leaves me nothing to wish," he declared. "Sixty millions for an occupation that will not perhaps last a day! The sale assures forever the power of the United States, and I have given England a rival who, sooner or later, will humble her pride." The 60,000,000 francs received for the territory, intended at one time to be devoted to the construction of canals in France, were eventually consumed in the First Consul's vain preparations for an invasion of England.

The actual extent of the territory thus acquired by the United States long remained a matter of dispute. The subject of boundaries was one with which Napoleon and his agents refused to deal except in the most vague terms. When Livingston had asked Talleyrand to designate the eastern boundaries of Louisiana the latter simply replied that he did not know what they were — that the United States must take the territory as France received it from Spain. When asked further as to what France had meant

THE LOUISIANA PURCHASE.

to receive from Spain, the crafty minister only replied that he did not know. "I can give you no direction," he declared; "you have made a noble bargain for yourselves, and I suppose you will make the most of it." Napoleon, when appealed to by Marbois for a definite understanding on the subject, made answer that the Americans should be left in the dark in this matter, and that "if an obscurity did not already exist, it would perhaps be good policy to put one there." The First Consul had long ago decided what the boundaries were, and Talleyrand at the time of his conversation with Livingston had his chief's written explanation of them in his desk; but not a word was vouchsafed the Americans to save them from weary years of uncertainty, wrangling, and threatened war along the disputed borders of Louisiana.[1]

Certain it is that the Floridas were not included in the

[1] Article I. of the treaty, which alone dealt with the matter of boundaries, was as follows: "Whereas, by the article the third of the Treaty concluded at St. Ildefonso (the 9th Vendémiaire, An 9), October 1, 1800, between the First Consul of the French Republic and His Catholic Majesty, it was agreed as follows: His Catholic Majesty promises and engages on his part to cede to the French Republic, six months after the full and entire execution of the conditions and stipulations herein, relative to his Royal Highness the Duke of Parma the Colony or Province of Louisiana, with the same extent it now has in the hands of Spain, and that it had when France possessed it; and such as it should be after the treaties subsequently entered into between Spain and other States: And whereas, in pursuance of the Treaty, particularly of the third article, the French Republic has an incontestable title to the domain and to the possession of the said territory, the First Consul of the French Republic, desiring to give to the United States a strong proof of friendship, doth hereby cede to the said United States, in the name of the French Republic, for ever and in full sovereignty, the said territory, with all its rights and appurtenances, as fully and in the same manner as they might have been acquired by the French Republic, in value of the above-mentioned treaty, concluded with His Catholic Majesty."

purchase, though, as we shall see, there was no small amount of doubt concerning the boundary between Louisiana and West Florida. The Floridas were still Spanish, having been rescued by Godoy from the final treaty of San Ildefonso which received the signature of Don Carlos in October, 1802. It was the Floridas, rather than Louisiana, which Monroe and Livingston had been commissioned to purchase. But, finding that these territories still belonged to Spain, all that the American representatives could do in negotiating at Paris was to seek the aid of the French in bringing Spain to the point of making a cession of the desired lands to the United States. Livingston upon one occasion stipulated as a necessary condition of the purchase of Louisiana that France give the United States assistance of this sort.[1] Napoleon refused, however, to pledge himself upon the subject in the treaty. A verbal promise to use his influence for the transfer of Florida to the United States was as far as he would go.

Although Louisiana had exchanged owners not fewer than three times, no one pretended to know its actual boundaries. Napoleon had decided what he would claim them to be, but this decision was wholly arbitrary, as his decisions generally were. It was commonly understood that the territory extended northward to the source of the Mississippi, but the location of this was yet a matter of mere conjecture. By some it was believed that Texas westward to the Rio Grande belonged to the purchase, on the strength of La Salle's accidental landing at the bay of St. Louis in 1684. But this view did not generally

---

[1] Livingston to Madison, April 13, 1803, *American State Papers*, II. 552.

prevail.[1] Until recent years it was thought that the purchase included all the territory between the forty-second parallel and the British lands on the north, west to the Pacific, thus embracing the present states of Idaho, Oregon, and Washington. Even as late as 1897 the Government Land Office was publishing maps based on this conception. After a very careful investigation of the whole subject, Mr. Binger Hermann, recently Commissioner of the Land Office, has shown conclusively that no one supposed at the time the purchase was made that it extended beyond the Rocky Mountains, and, further, that under the terms of the treaty itself no transmontane territory could be considered as changed in ownership.[2] France, when first in possession of Louisiana, prior to 1763, never regarded her claims as reaching farther than the head waters of the tributaries of the Mississippi. And by the first article of the treaty it was this original Louisiana which was ceded by France in 1803. The Oregon territory was acquired by the United States in 1846, but on grounds wholly aside from the Louisiana Purchase. Nevertheless, the impression lingered until our own day that this region had really been included in the cession from France.

[1] See John R. Ficklen, "The Louisiana Purchase vs. Texas," in the *Publications of the Southern History Association*, V. 351–388. By the treaty of 1819 the United States forfeited to Spain whatever claim to Texas she may have had on the basis of the Louisiana Purchase. The agitation which finally resulted in the incorporation of Texas with the United States in 1845 was enlivened by the popular cry for the reannexation of Texas, — as if it were a matter merely of getting back territory that had once belonged to us.

[2] Binger Hermann, *The Louisiana Purchase and our Title West of the Rocky Mountains*, 70.

The area of the purchase, definitely understood at last, was 875,025 square miles. The total area of the United States at the time was but slightly greater, *i.e.* 909,050 square miles. The lands acquired may be defined in general as including New Orleans, the island on which the city stands, and the entire Mississippi Valley west of the river, together with the north shore of the Gulf of Mexico westward to the Sabine. By its acquisition a region was added which is more than seven times as large as Great Britain and Ireland, more than four times the size of the German Empire, or of Austria, or of France; more than three times that of Spain and Portugal; more than seven times that of Italy; nearly ten times that of Turkey and Greece. It is larger, in fact, than Great Britain, Germany, France, Spain, Portugal, and Italy combined.[1] Concerning it Mr. James K. Hosmer well says: "Tales regarded as absurdly extravagant were told of the resources of the new country, but the facts have surpassed all that was fancied. It is probable that scarcely a square mile of the great region will ultimately prove unavailable for human uses, desert through much of it was long believed to be. There is no soil in the world more fertile than that bordering the Mississippi and its great affluents. Where the farmer fails of a chance, the ranchman can often find opportunity; if flocks and herds are out of the question, the lumberman is accommodated; while in the absolute waste the miner finds coal, oil, and almost every metal that can be useful to man."[2]

It is certainly quite unnecessary to dwell upon the his-

---

[1] Binger Hermann, *The Louisiana Purchase*, 36.
[2] James K. Hosmer, *The History of the Louisiana Purchase*, 183–184.

torical importance of the Louisiana Purchase, both to the buying and the selling nation. As the most dignified way of escape from an embarrassing situation it seemed for a time to have been a happy move on the First Consul's part. It doubled the territory of a nation whose friendship he desired to maintain, and at the same time forestalled the aggrandizement of his arch-enemy, England, in the western world. Nevertheless, it is certain that Napoleon's high-handed manner in alienating the territory without consulting the Chambers, and in flagrant violation of the wishes of the people generally, wrought no little injury to his credit with the French. And it may not be too much to affirm, as some of the best students of the period do, that the sale of Louisiana marked the turning-point in the First Consul's career, the place where the reaction against his plans and policies really began.

Few events, if any, since the adoption of the Constitution, have influenced the history of the United States as has the purchase of Louisiana. As Mr. John W. Foster well says in his *Century of American Diplomacy:* "It made the acquisition of Florida a necessity. It brought about the annexation of Texas, the Mexican War, the thirst for more slave territory to preserve the balance of power, the Civil War, and the abolition of slavery. It led to our Pacific coast possessions, the construction of the transcontinental lines of railway and our marvellous Rocky Mountain development, the demand for the Isthmus Canal, the purchase of Alaska, the annexation of Hawaii. It opened up to us the great field of commercial development beyond the Pacific in Japan, China, and the islands of the sea. It fixed our destiny as a great world power, the effects of which we are to-day, just beginning to realize."[1] One has only to conceive, if he can, the history of our country with the Louisiana Purchase and its long chain of resultant events left out, to understand, in some degree at least, the cardinal significance of "the largest transaction in real estate which the world has ever known."

[1] John W. Foster, *A Century of American Diplomacy*, 204.

CHAPTER XII

CONGRESS AND THE PROBLEMS OF NATIONAL EXPANSION

THE purchase of all Louisiana was a consummation wholly unexpected in the United States. In the instructions issued by President Jefferson and Secretary Madison to Monroe and Livingston this possible turn in the negotiation had not received the barest mention. Jefferson had hardly expected the commissioners to be able to secure New Orleans and the Floridas, much less the great region between the Mississippi and the Rockies. Even if it had been supposed by the Administration that such an extensive acquisition could be made, there would have been little or no disposition to urge a settlement on such a basis. For it was generally agreed that the United States had absolutely no need for territory beyond the natural boundary of the Mississippi. It may almost be said that Louisiana was forced on the United States. Napoleon was certainly the aggressive party in the negotiation. The greatest credit is due Jefferson for his statesmanlike conduct in connection with the entire affair, but it was rather as the organizer of Louisiana than as its purchaser that he achieved his best distinction.

After the purchase had been concluded, Monroe and

Livingston could not but wonder how their work would be received in the United States. Deeply conscious that they had far exceeded their instructions, and yet just as certain that they had been serving their country's best interests, they sent an elaborate joint despatch, May 13, containing the following noteworthy justification of their course: "An acquisition of so great an extent was, we well know, not contemplated by our appointment; but we are persuaded that the circumstances and considerations which induced us to make it will justify us in the measure to our Government and country. Before the negotiation commenced, we were apprised that the First Consul had decided to offer to the United States, by sale, the whole of Louisiana, and not a part of it. We found, in the outset, that this information was correct, so that we had to decide, as a previous question, whether we would treat for the whole, or jeopardize, if not abandon, the hope of acquiring any part. On that point we did not long hesitate, but proceeded to treat for the whole. . . . We found, as we advanced in the negotiation, that M. Marbois was absolutely restricted to the disposition of the whole, that he would treat for no less portion, and, of course, that it was useless to urge it. On mature consideration, therefore, we finally concluded a treaty on the best terms we could obtain for the whole. By this measure we have sought to carry into effect, to the utmost of our power, the wise and benevolent policy of our government, on the principles laid down in our instructions. The possession of the left bank of the river, had it been attainable alone, would, it is true, have accomplished much in that respect; but it is equally true that it would have left much still to

accomplish. By it our people would have had an outlet to the ocean, in which no Power would have the right to disturb them; but while the other bank remained in the possession of a foreign Power, circumstances might occur to make the neighborhood of such Power highly injurious to us in many of our most important concerns. A divided jurisdiction over the river might beget jealousies, discontents, and dissensions, which the wisest policy on our part could not prevent or control. With a train of colonial governments established along the western bank, from the entrance of the river far into the interior, under the command of military men, it would be difficult to preserve that state of things which would be necessary to the peace and tranquillity of our country. A single act of a capricious, unfriendly, or unprincipled subaltern might wound our best interests, violate our most unquestionable rights, and involve us in war. By this acquisition, which comprises within our limits this great river, and all the streams that empty into it, from their sources to the ocean, the apprehension of these disasters is banished for ages from the United States. We adjust by it the only remaining known cause of variance with this powerful nation; we anticipate the discontent of the great rival of France, who would probably have been wounded at any stipulation of a permanent nature which favored the latter, and which it would have been difficult to avoid, had she retained the right bank. We cease to have a motive of urgency at least, for inclining to one Power, to avert the unjust pressure of another. We separate ourselves in a great measure from the European world and its concerns, especially its wars and intrigues. We make, in fine, a great stride to real and substantial independence, the great effect whereof will, we trust, be felt essentially and extensively in all our foreign and domestic relations. Without exciting the apprehension of any Power, we take a more imposing attitude with respect to all. The bond of our union will be strengthened, and its movements become more harmonious, by the increased parity of interests which it will communicate to the several parts which compose it."[1]

Despite his surprise at the outcome, Jefferson at once grasped the essential justice of this argument. Louisiana had been bought, and now the United States must make the best of the new situation in which she found herself. The treaty of cession must be duly ratified, the necessary appropriations for its execution must be made, steps must be taken to establish the authority of the United States at New Orleans and throughout the territory, and some fashion of government must be devised for the people thus to be taken under American control. The task was appalling in magnitude, particularly in view of the fact that it must be undertaken in the face of the most bitter and uncompromising opposition from the party out of power. From the beginning of the Mississippi trouble the Federalists had clamored for war with Spain, or France, or both — anything indeed but the peaceable settlement which Jefferson had been bent upon effecting. Even before Monroe had started for France, Ross, a leading Federalist of Pennsylvania, had moved in the Senate that fifty thousand men be raised and $5,000,000 be appropriated

[1] Monroe and Livingston to Secretary Madison, May 13, 1803, *American State Papers*, II. 558–559.

for an expedition to advance at once upon New Orleans.[1] Numerous other proposals of a similar nature were made, more or less officially. It was charged by the Republicans that the Federalists were posing as the champions of the Westerners merely in order to win their political support and so regain control of the government at the next election. Whatever degree of truth there may have been in this accusation, it cannot be denied that large numbers of them opposed the Administration in the spirit of sheer factiousness. It was their hope that Jefferson's party would prove unequal to the successful management of the government, and they rejoiced with but ineffectual attempts at concealment at every discomfiture of the "upstart" Republicans.

The announcement of the purchase of the Louisiana territory was the signal for a new outbreak of the Administration's foes. In this project the Federalists believed they had found the shoal upon which the Jeffersonian party might be stranded. It goes without saying that they could be trusted to make the most of the opportunity. Throughout New England and the other Federalist states a storm of ridicule and indignation began at once to brew. All manner of invectives were heaped upon the new enterprise and upon those who were held to be responsible for it. Every conceivable ill result of the purchase was magnified into an inevitable calamity. Much was made of the fact that the administration leaders had only so recently declared themselves strongly against the

[1] Resolution of February 16, 1803, *Annals of Congress* (1802–1803), 95. See Monroe's letter of March 7, 1803, quoted in the preceding chapter (p. 507).

acquisition of territory beyond the Mississippi. Inconsistency, vacillation, duplicity, and numerous other charges of the sort were hurled with telling effect upon the President and his secretary of state.

If this territory were added to the United States, said the opposition, the East would be depopulated, the West would grow up into a rival nation, civil war would result, and eventual separation of the sections. In urging these considerations the Federalists could quote almost literally from the reports of Madison's interviews with the Frenchman Pichon. Especially was the public exhorted to consider the expense in which the United States would be involved by the purchase. Newspaper writers vied with each other in devising schemes whereby to make the sum to be paid for Louisiana seem enormous. Fifteen million dollars for a wilderness — when Maine had been sold by Ferdinando Gorges for £1250 and Pennsylvania had cost William Penn but little over £5000! The purchase price of Louisiana would make 433 tons of pure silver. It would load 866 wagons, which would form a procession (each occupying three rods) five and a third miles in length. It would take a man two months to load the wagons at the rate of sixteen a day. This sum, in the form of silver dollars piled in a column, would extend upward a distance of three miles. It would pay an army of 25,000 men eight dollars a week for twenty-five years, or support forever, by interest, 1800 free schools, allowing $500 a year per school, and accommodating 90,000 pupils. It would supply every man, woman, and child in the country with three dollars apiece. In truth, it was a larger amount than could be amassed by bringing together

every piece of specie currency in the land.[1] By thus artfully stating the expense in which the purchase would involve the United States, in terms literally true but yet producing a greatly exaggerated effect, the Federalists contrived to create the impression in many quarters that the Administration was about to impose an intolerable financial burden on the people. Numerous other arguments were brought forward, some of which will appear presently in our consideration of the congressional debates on the subject.[2]

The news of the purchase reached the United States on the 30th of June. Within a week Jefferson had canvassed the matter sufficiently to have placed his finger upon the main objections to the acquisition, and also to have devised at least a partial means of obviating them. It was not the dangers of migration, or the expense, or the prospective loss of the East's preponderance in the nation, that troubled the President. He was concerned only with what he conceived to be the constitutional obstacles in the way. As early as January, 1803, he had submitted to Secretary Gallatin the question as to whether the territory which Monroe and Livingston had been authorized to purchase could be acquired by the United States without an amendment to the Constitution.[3] His

[1] McMaster, *History of the People of the United States*, II. 630.

[2] The objections to the treaty are well summarized in Albert Bushnell Hart, *Foundations of American Foreign Policy*, 203.

[3] With his inquiry Jefferson transmitted to Gallatin a letter from Attorney-general Lincoln, who doubted the constitutionality of a "direct independent purchase." Lincoln to Jefferson, January 10, 1803, Jefferson, Mss. Cited in Adams, *History of the United States*, II. 78. Gallatin, in his reply, dissented from the necessity of an amendment. "To me it would appear," he wrote, "(1) that the United States, as a nation,

own opinion was that it was "safer not to permit the enlargement of the Union" except by such amendment. Jefferson's view of the Constitution was that it conferred upon the national government only the right to exercise specifically delegated powers and such other powers as were very manifestly demanded for the execution of those delegated. Under this interpretation it was at least a question whether foreign territory could be acquired without an amendment, for the Constitution certainly did not provide for such action, either expressly or by obvious implication. When Jefferson found that the country to be annexed was not a small strip at the mouth of the Mississippi, but rather a vast domain of unknown extent and resources beyond the river boundary, the question took on added importance. He was now more sure than before that the Constitution must be amended, if not before, at least after, the transfer had been made. In a letter to his close friend, Senator Breckenridge, of Kentucky, August 12, Jefferson declared that the treaty must be ratified and Congress, when convened, must take the necessary action to carry it into effect. "But I suppose," he adds, "they [Congress] must then appeal to *the nation* for an additional article to the Constitution, approving and confirming an act which the nation had not previously authorized. The Constitution has made no provision for our holding foreign territory, still less for our incorporating foreign

have an inherent right to acquire territory; (2) that whenever that acquisition is by treaty, the same constituted authorities in whom the treaty-making power is vested have a constitutional right to sanction the acquisition." Gallatin's *Works*, I. 112. The doctrine of national powers thus advanced was precisely that which had long been contended for by the Federalists.

nations into our Union. The executive, in seizing the fugitive occurrence which so much advances the good of their country, has done an act beyond the Constitution. The legislature, in casting behind them metaphysical subtleties and risking themselves like faithful servants, must ratify and pay for it, and throw themselves on their country for doing for them unauthorized what we know they would have done for themselves had they been in a situation to do it. It is the case of a guardian, investing the money of his ward in purchasing an important adjacent territory, and saying to him when of age, I did this for your good; I pretend to no right to bind you; you may disavow me, and I must get out of the scrape as I can; I thought it my duty to risk myself for you."[1] It was entirely proper, under the circumstances, to stretch the power of the national government even to the extent of buying Louisiana; but — so ran the argument — the strain must be relieved as quickly as possible by an amendment of the fundamental law. "Our peculiar security," wrote Jefferson to Senator Wilson Cary Nicholas, of Virginia, "is in the possession of a written Constitution. Let us not make it a blank paper by construction."[2]

Soon after the arrival of the treaty the President drew up an amendment whereby the province of Louisiana was "incorporated with the United States and made part thereof," and submitted it to the Cabinet.[3] The territory

[1] Jefferson to John C. Breckenridge, August 12, 1803, Jefferson's *Works* (Washington's ed.), IV. 498, and (Ford's ed.), VIII. 242-244, note.
[2] Jefferson to Wilson C. Nicholas, September 7, 1803, Jefferson's *Works* (Washington's ed.), IV. 505, and (Ford's ed.), VIII. 247-248, note.
[3] *Writings of Thomas Jefferson* (Ford's ed.), VIII. 241-249. Two drafts of an amendment are here given in parallel columns.

north of the thirty-second parallel was to be held as an Indian reserve until a subsequent amendment should open it to settlement by the whites; that south was to be organized under a territorial government, with the same rights of citizenship as were enjoyed by the inhabitants of the Northwest and Mississippi territories. The opinion generally prevailed in the Cabinet, however, as throughout the country, that an amendment was unnecessary. The Federalist view that the sovereignty of the nation constituted ample basis for territorial expansion became the popular one. The devotion of the Federalists to the theory of strong national powers precluded them from attacking the purchase at the point which Jefferson considered most vulnerable, — the constitutional, — and threw them back upon arguments of expediency and national interests. The country at large did not share the President's misgivings, and though Jefferson seems never to have abandoned the idea that an amendment would have been well in order, no serious effort to secure one on this subject was ever made. Late in the year Senator John Quincy Adams submitted a proposed amendment, but it was not even seconded.

Meanwhile despatches from Livingston and Monroe gave the Administration to understand that delay in ratification of the treaty was perilous. Such opposition to the cession had developed at the French court that Napoleon might be constrained to annul the bargain. In this event the whole negotiation would have to be conducted over again, with extreme uncertainty as to the outcome. "I most solemnly press you," wrote Livingston, "to get the ratification as soon as possible, and to do

all that on our part remains to be done. . . . How happy, my dear sir, are we to have concluded a treaty which will forever exclude us from the politics of this stormy quarter of the globe. I hope that you will not let it pass totally through your hands."[1]

Spurred by this advice, Jefferson proceeded to throw his constitutional doubts to the winds and take the requisite steps for making the purchase irrevocable. Congress was called to meet in special session October 17. Both houses were convened, because not merely was the treaty to be ratified, but certain general legislation would be necessary to provide for the execution of its terms. In his message, October 17, Jefferson said not a word concerning the constitutional aspects of the purchase. "Congress witnessed at their late session," he wrote, "the extraordinary agitation produced in the public mind by the suspension of our right of deposit at the port of New Orleans, no assignment of another place having been made according to treaty. They were sensible that the continuance of that privation would be more injurious to our nation than any consequences which could flow from any mode of redress, but reposing just confidence in the good faith of the government whose officer had committed the wrong, friendly and reasonable representations were resorted to, and the right of deposit was restored. Previous, however, to this period we had not been unaware of the danger to which our peace would be perpetually exposed whilst so important a key to the commerce of the western country remained under foreign power. . . .

[1] Livingston to Madison, June 3, 1803, *American State Papers*, II. 563.

Propositions had therefore been authorized for obtaining on fair conditions the sovereignty of New Orleans and of other possessions in that quarter interesting to our quiet to such extent as was deemed practicable, and the provisional appropriation of $2,000,000 to be applied and accounted for by the President of the United States, intended as part of the price, was considered as conveying the sanction of Congress to the acquisition proposed. The enlightened government of France saw with just discernment the importance to both nations of such liberal arrangements as might best and permanently promote the peace, friendship, and interests of both, and the property and sovereignty of all Louisiana which had been restored to them have on certain conditions been transferred to the United States by instruments bearing date the 30th of April last. When those shall have received the constitutional sanction of the Senate, they will without delay be communicated to the Representatives also for the exercise of their functions as to these conditions which are within the powers vested by the Constitution in Congress."[1] Already Jefferson had written to Breckenridge, "The less we say about constitutional difficulties respecting Louisiana, the better. . . . What is necessary for surmounting them must be done *sub silentio*."[2] In parting with his private convictions on this matter Jefferson well understood that the principle of strict construction, which, as he declared, was the very "breath of his political life," was receiving a severe blow, and that in later times, if the nation

[1] Richardson, *Messages and Papers of the Presidents*, I. 358.
[2] Jefferson to John C. Breckenridge, August 18, 1803, *Writings of Jefferson* (Ford's ed.), VIII. 245, note.

should come to dominate despotically over the states, he might well be reprobated by succeeding generations of Virginians as the first high traitor to their interests. Nevertheless, the securing and organizing of the Louisiana Purchase now appeared incomparably the greatest concern of the nation, and to it the President addressed himself with a fervor which would have been impossible in a less broad-minded patriot. His final word on the constitutional question, written more than five weeks before the assembling of Congress, was that while he believed an amendment would serve as a wholesome safeguard against broad construction, yet if "our friends shall think differently, certainly I shall acquiesce with satisfaction, confiding that the good sense of our country will correct the evil of construction when it shall produce ill effects."[1]

In his message the President carefully rehearsed the steps which had been taken to relieve the western traders and which had culminated in the unexpected purchase treaty. He commended the liberality of the French government and expressed the hope that the United States would not be dilatory in giving effect to the arrangement. The advantages to be derived from it were set forth with true discernment. "Whilst the property and the sovereignty of the Mississippi and its waters secure an independent outlet for the produce of the western states, and an uncontrolled navigation through their whole course, free from collision with other powers and the dangers to our peace from that source, the fertility of the country, its climate and extent, promise, in due

[1] Jefferson to Wilson Cary Nicholas, September 7, 1803, Jefferson's *Works* (Washington's ed.), IV. 505.

season, important aids to our treasury, an ample provision for our posterity, and a wide spread for the blessings of freedom and equal laws."[1] The wise utilization of this splendid acquisition would now fall to the legislative branch. "With the wisdom of Congress it will rest to take those ulterior measures which may be necessary for the immediate occupation and temporary government of the country; for rendering the change of government a blessing to our newly adopted brethren; for securing to them the rights of conscience and of property; for confirming to the Indian inhabitants their occupancy and self-government, establishing friendly and commercial relations with them; and for ascertaining the geography of the country acquired."

In this connection it is interesting to note the disposition of the Louisiana territory which Jefferson had outlined some months before in a letter to Horatio Gates. "With respect to the territory acquired," he wrote, "I do not think it will be a separate government as you imagine. I presume the island of N. Orleans and the settled country on the opposite bank, will be annexed to the Mississippi territory. We shall certainly endeavor to introduce the American laws there & that cannot be done but by amalgamating the people with such a body of Americans as may take the lead in legislation & government. Of course they will be under the Governor of Mississippi. The rest of the territory will probably be locked up from American settlement, and under the self-government of the native occupants."[2] It was evidently some such general

---

[1] Richardson, *Messages and Papers of the Presidents*, I. 358.
[2] Jefferson to Horatio Gates, July 11, 1803, *Writings of Jefferson*

policy as this that the President expected the legislative department of the government forthwith to inaugurate.

Within four days after the convening of Congress the treaty had been ratified by the Senate by a vote of 24 to 7, and publicly proclaimed. There was little time to spare, for by the terms of the instrument ratification was to be exchanged within six months after the signing by the plenipotentiaries. The six months would expire October 30. The Federalists opposed, but with no hope of success. With unabated ardor they then entered upon a vigorous campaign against the legislation necessary for the execution of the treaty. First of all there was the purchase money — $11,250,000, exclusive of the claims — to be provided for. Then the treaty contained an article (III.) to the effect that "the inhabitants of the ceded territory shall be incorporated in the Union of the United States, and admitted as soon as possible, according to the principles of the Federal Constitution, to the enjoyment of all the rights, advantages, and immunities of citizens of the United States; and, in the meantime, they shall be maintained and protected in the free enjoyment of their liberty, property, and the religion which they profess." This meant that provision must be made at once for the maintenance of law and order and security of individual rights after the territory in question should have come under American control.

The debates on these subjects were brief,[1] but, as Mr. Henry Adams has declared, none ever took place in the

(Ford's ed.), VIII. 250-251. See a letter advancing similar ideas, written to John Dickinson, August 9, *ibid.*, 262-263.

[1] In the House, October 25-27; in the Senate, November 2-3,

Capitol which better deserved recollection.[1] They began with the resolution introduced in the House October 24 by Gaylord Griswold, of New York, calling upon the President to lay before Congress a copy of the treaty of San Ildefonso, together with a copy of the deed of cession from Spain to France under that treaty, and all other papers which would go to show how well founded had been the French title to Louisiana.[2] It was generally understood that the Spanish government was enraged at the conduct of Napoleon in violating the pledge of non-alienation given through Gouvion St.-Cyr, and that Godoy and his associates were proclaiming loudly that, France having failed to keep her part of the contract, in respect to the Parmese acquisition, as well as the pledge of non-alienation, Louisiana still belonged of right to Spain. The Spanish minister, Yrujo, was plying Madison with repeated protests against the acceptance of the territory by the United States, affirming that it was not Napoleon's to sell.[3] The fact that the Spaniards were still in control at New Orleans was construed to lend considerable color to this representation. At any rate, it supplied the Federalist opposition with a useful weapon. What folly, they contended, to pay $15,000,000 for territory which the United States would some day awake to find still belonging to an alien power! Spain declared Louisiana still to be hers, and Spain ought to know. The

---

[1] Adams, *History of the United States*, II. 96. For the debates, see *Annals of Congress* (1803–1804), (House, 386–515 *passim;* Senate, 31–74).

[2] *Annals of Congress* (1803–1804), 386.

[3] Yrujo to Madison, Sept. 4, Sept. 27, Oct. 12, 1803, *American State Papers*, II. 569, 570.

purchase was but a shrewd trick on the part of Napoleon whereby to wheedle the United States out of money enough to maintain his European wars.

By the close vote of 59 to 57 the Republicans defeated Griswold's resolution.[1] The next day the House went into Committee of the Whole to consider measures for carrying the treaty into effect.[2] Following the precedent of the Jay treaty debate in 1796, the House now proceeded to discuss the general aspects of the treaty and pass judgment upon its merits and defects as freely as if it were not already the supreme law of the land beyond their legitimate power to annul. Mr. Griswold again led the assault upon the measure — this time directing his eloquence against the article providing for the incorporation of the ceded territory into the United States. His arguments upon this point expressed the views of numerous opponents of the purchase. It was not possible under the Constitution, he said, for the President and Senate to alter the character of the Union by contracting for the admission of new states into it. The Union was a "copartnership," and the national government, as the mere agent of the members, could not admit a new partner. That could be done only by the express sanction of each state. "The incorporation of a foreign nation into the Union, so far from tending to preserve the Union, is direct inroad upon it; it destroys the perfect union contemplated between the original parties, by interposing an alien and a stranger to share the powers of government with them." In obligating the nation to so incorporate Louisiana, declared

[1] *Annals of Congress* (1803–1804), 419.   [2] *Ibid.*, 432.

Griswold, the Administration had greatly exceeded its powers, and the people of the United States could not be regarded as bound by the treaty to redeem the promise. Objection was made also to the seventh article, providing in substance that the ships of France and Spain, under prescribed conditions and for a period of twelve years, should be admitted to the ports of the ceded territory on the same terms, in respect to duties, as American ships. Under laws then existing the ships of France and Spain were liable to an extra tonnage duty, and their cargoes to a duty of ten per cent advance, when arriving in the Atlantic ports. The granting of exemption from these charges in the ceded territory was urged to be a violation of the constitutional provision that "all duties, imposts, and excises, shall be uniform throughout the United States;"[1] also that "no preference shall be given, by any regulation of commerce, or revenue, to the ports of one state over those of another."[2] Other speakers followed, for the most part but paraphrasing the arguments of Griswold. It was generally conceded by the opposition that the United States could acquire territory, but only to hold as a perpetual colony or dependency, not to be brought into the Union as a state. As Roger Griswold, of Connecticut, put it, "a new territory and new subjects may undoubtedly be obtained by conquest and by purchase; but neither the conquest nor the purchase can incorporate them into the Union. They must remain in the condition of colonies, and be governed accordingly."[3]

[1] Art. I. Sect. 8. *Annals of Congress* (1802–1803), 434.
[2] Art. I. Sect. 9.
[3] *Annals of Congress* (1803–1804), 460–462.

The counter arguments of the Republicans were various, and on the whole conclusive. Beginning with the sovereign power of the nation to acquire territory, which the Federalists could not deny, the supporters of the purchase advanced to the view that the power must carry with it the right to stipulate whatever terms seemed necessary — even the admission of new states or the establishing of preferential import duties. Thomas Randolph, of Virginia, clearly stated the view of his party when he declared that "the alleged preference given to New Orleans over the other parts of the Union did not present a constitutional difficulty, because it was to be considered as the price paid for the ceded territory; that by the treaty no preference was given to one *state* over another, because Louisiana was a territory and not a state."[1] Joseph H. Nicholson, of Maryland, put it thus: "Louisiana is a territory purchased by the United States in their confederate capacity, and may be disposed of by them at pleasure. It is in the nature of a colony whose commerce may be regulated without any reference to the Constitution." After a day's earnest discussion a vote was taken on the question of making provision for carrying into effect the treaty of purchase. The result showed 90 in favor and 25 opposed.[2] On the 29th a bill enabling the President to take possession of Louisiana and establish such temporary government in the territory as he thought most adequate, was passed by a vote of 85 to 7.[3] The nature of the act is apparent from its title: "An act authorizing the creation of a stock to the amount

---

[1] *Annals of Congress* (1803–1804), 438. [2] *Ibid.*, 488.
[3] *Ibid.*, 548, and Appendix, 1245.

of $11,250,000, for the purpose of carrying into effect the convention of the thirtieth of April, 1803, between the United States of America and the French Republic, and making provision for the payment of the same." With this comprehensive piece of legislation the House completed its labors, for the time being, on the Louisiana question.

The debate in the Senate may be said to have begun November 2, although on the 26th of October this branch, by a vote of 26 to 6, had passed a bill to enable the President to take possession of Louisiana.[1] When the debate opened, the matter under immediate consideration was the bill authorizing the appropriation for the purchase, which had been passed by the House four days before. The arguments in the Senate followed largely the same course as in the lower house, except that much more extreme views were expressed on both sides. James White, of Delaware, for example, declared himself in favor of the acquisition of New Orleans and such other posts on the Mississippi as might be necessary to insure the complete and uninterrupted navigation of that river. "But as to Louisiana," he declared, "this new, immense, unbounded world, if it should ever be incorporated into this Union, which I have no idea can be done but by altering the Constitution, I believe it will be the greatest curse that could at present befall us." The reasons for this belief Mr. White set forth as follows: "You had as well pretend to prohibit the fish from swimming in the sea, as to prevent the populating of that country [Louisiana, par-

[1] *Annals of Congress* (1803–1804), 26.

ticularly the northern portion] after its sovereignty shall become ours. To every man acquainted with the adventurous, roving, and enterprising temper of our people, and with the manner in which our western country has been settled, such an idea must be chimerical. The inducements will be so strong that it will be impossible to restrain our citizens from crossing the river. Louisiana must and will become settled, if we hold it, and with the very population that would otherwise occupy part of our present territory. Thus our citizens will be removed to the immense distance of two or three thousand miles from the capital of the Union, where they will scarcely ever feel the rays of the general government; their affections will become alienated; they will gradually begin to view us as strangers; they will form other commercial connections, and our interests will become distinct. These, with other causes that human wisdom may not now foresee, will in time effect a separation, and I fear our bounds will be fixed nearer to our houses than the waters of the Mississippi. We have already territory enough, and when I contemplate the evils that may arise to these States from this intended incorporation of Louisiana into the Union, I would rather see it given to France, to Spain, or to any other nation of the earth, upon the mere condition that no citizen of the United States should ever settle within its limits, than to see the territory sold for $100,000,000, and we retain the sovereignty. . . . And I do say, under the circumstances, even supposing that this extent of territory was a desirable acquisition, $15,000,000 was a most enormous sum to give."[1]

[1] *Annals of Congress* (1803-1804), 34.

Pickering, of Massachusetts, expressed the opinion that the treaty was unconstitutional because it stipulated pledges which there was no power to make good. He referred particularly to the incorporation of the Louisianians provided for in the third article. This he believed could be legitimately accomplished only by securing the express consent of every state in the Union — a thing which was manifestly out of the question.[1] Tracy, of Connecticut, concluded an able presentation of his side of the case in the following language: "I have no doubt but we can obtain territory either by conquest or compact, and hold it, even all Louisiana, and a thousand times more, if you please, without violating the Constitution. We can hold territory; but to admit the inhabitants into the Union to make citizens of them and states, by treaty, we cannot constitutionally do; and no subsequent act of legislation, or even ordinary amendment to our Constitution, can legalize such measures. If done at all, they must be done by universal consent of all the states or partners of our political association; and this universal consent I am positive can never be obtained to such a pernicious measure as the admission of Louisiana, of a world — and such a world — into our Union. This would be absorbing the northern states, and rendering them as insignificant in the Union as they ought to be if, by their own consent, the new measure should be adopted. . . . The principle of admission, in the case of Louisiana, is the same as if it contained ten millions of inhabitants; and the principles of these peoples are probably as hostile to our government, in its true construction, as they can

[1] *Annals of Congress* (1803–1804), 44.

be, and the relative strength which this admission gives to the southern and western interest is contradictory to the principles of our original Union as any can be, however strongly stated."[1]

In his frank avowal of fear that the states to be carved out of the purchase, together with those already forming on the eastern bank of the Mississippi, would some day dominate the nation and draw the balance of power from the East to the West, Senator Tracy was at the same time betraying the secret of much of the opposition to the purchase, and indulging in a prophecy which subsequent generations have seen abundantly fulfilled. Even as early as the Constitutional Convention at Philadelphia in 1787, no little jealousy on part of the eastern — especially the New England — states as against the West was beginning to display itself. By 1803 this feeling had grown sufficiently to impel of itself a general anti-expansion policy in some quarters of the seaboard. Eight years later, by the time the admission of Louisiana as a state was under contemplation, it had developed in New England into an almost uncontrolled passion, inducing open threats of secession in event of the investment of any more western territory with the prerogatives of statehood.[2] As Senator White had so forcefully declared,

[1] *Annals of Congress* (1803–1804), 58.

[2] In his speech upon the question of admitting Louisiana, January 14, 1811, Josiah Quincy, a leading member of Congress from Massachusetts, used the following remarkable language: "I address you, Mr. Speaker, with an anxiety and distress of mind with me wholly unprecedented. To me it appears that this measure would justify a revolution in this country. I am compelled to declare it as my deliberate opinion that, if this bill passes, the bonds of this Union are virtually dissolved; that the states which compose it are free from their moral obligations; and that, as it

Louisiana, once brought under the American flag, was certain to fill rapidly with emigrants from the United States. Unless a man believed, as White did, that this newly populated land would establish its independence from the United States, he could not well close his eyes to the enormous possibilities of an industrial and political overbalancing of the East. In the troubles regarding the navigation of the Mississippi, the interests of New England and the West had been diametrically opposed, and the two sections, to state it mildly, had not been increased in their respect for each other. The antipathy thus forced upon the attention of the public was taken by not a few New Englanders, as well as many people in other parts of the country, to forecast the bitter antagonism which westward expansion must inevitably produce.

Probably the ablest speech made in the Senate in support of the purchase was that of John C. Breckenridge, of Kentucky, in answer to the opposition's arguments in general, and those of Senator Tracy in particular.[1] He began by characterizing the purchase, not only as to the manner of its negotiation, but also as to the result achieved, as one of the most splendid transactions which the annals of any nation could exhibit. "To acquire an empire of perhaps half the extent of the one now possessed,[2] from the most powerful and warlike nation on earth, without

---

will be the right of all, so it will be the duty of some, to prepare definitely for a separation — amicably if they can, violently if they must." *Annals of Congress*, 11th Cong., third sess., 525.

[1] *Annals of Congress* (1803–1804), 58–65.

[2] The employment of this phrase by Breckenridge shows how little even the friends of the purchase policy understood the extent and value of the lands acquired from France. As a matter of fact, the Louisiana terri-

bloodshed, without the oppressing of a single individual, without in the least embarrassing the ordinary operations of your finances, and all this through the peaceful forms of negotiation, and in despite, too, of the opposition of a considerable portion of the community, is an achievement of which the archives of the predecessors, at least, of those now in office, cannot furnish a parallel."

In answering the arguments of Senators White, Pickering, and others, to the effect that the acquisition would prove destructive of the Union, Mr. Breckenridge spoke with genuine eloquence. "This is an old, hackneyed doctrine — that a republic ought not to be too extensive. But the gentleman [Senator Pickering] has assumed two facts, and then reasoned from them: first, that the extent is too great; and secondly, that the country will soon be populated. I would ask, sir, what is his standard extent for a republic? How does he come at that standard? Our boundary is already extensive. Would his standard extent be violated by including the island of Orleans and the Floridas? I presume not, as all parties seem to think their acquisition, in part or in whole, essential. Why not, then, acquire territory on the west, as well as on the east, side of the Mississippi? Is the goddess of liberty restrained by watercourses? Is she governed by geographical limits?

---

tory lacked but 34,025 square miles of being as large as the United States, with all her territories, prior to the purchase. It should be noted, however, that Jefferson appreciated the Louisiana acquisition at its full worth. In a letter to Horatio Gates, July 11, 1803, he wrote: "The territory acquired, as it includes all the waters of the Missouri & Mississippi, has more than doubled the area of the U. S., and the new part is not inferior to the old in soil, climate, productions, & important communications." *Writings of Jefferson* (Ford's ed.), VIII. 249.

Is her dominion on this continent confined to the east side of the Mississippi? So far from believing in the doctrine that a republic ought to be confined within narrow limits, I believe, on the contrary, that the more extensive its dominions, the more safe and more durable it will be. In proportion to the number of hands you intrust the precious blessings of a free government to, in the same proportion do you multiply the chances for their preservation. I entertain, therefore, no fears for the Confederacy, on account of its extent." [1]

It may well be that this view was rather more optimistic than conditions a hundred years ago seemed to warrant. Without the railroad, telegraph, and steamship, it is small wonder that men doubted the ability of any government to maintain efficiency throughout such an extent as the purchase now gave the United States. Geographical limitations upon government were then very real items to be reckoned with. Nevertheless, it must be admitted that Senator Breckenridge in his speech entered a most forceful protest on behalf of the western people against the narrowness and provincialism still so dominant between the Alleghanies and the seaboard. The strongest point that he made was that while, as Senators White and Tracy had said, the people of the United States, in event of the annexation of Louisiana, would migrate thither in large numbers, they would inevitably do so anyway, even if Spain or France continued in control. The Louisiana population was certain to be drawn mainly from the United States. Neither the French nor the Spanish showed disposition to migrate to America in any consider-

[1] *Annals of Congress* (1803–1804), 60.

able numbers, while the restless westward advance of the English-speaking peoples from the Alleghanies to the Mississippi betokened that the river would not long continue to mark the limits of their enterprise. The question then, said Breckenridge, was simply this: "Is the Confederacy more in danger from Louisiana, when colonized by American people under American jurisdiction, than when populated by Americans under the control of some foreign, powerful, and rival nation?" To his mind there could be but one answer. This aspect of the matter was of great weight in influencing the senators to acquiesce in the terms of the treaty. Even John Quincy Adams, who had voted against the bill enabling the President to take possession of Louisiana, declared in speaking of these terms: "I trust they will be so performed [*i.e.* "punctually and faithfully"], and will cheerfully lend my hand to every act necessary for the purpose. For I consider the object as of the highest advantage to us; and the gentleman from Kentucky himself [Breckenridge], who has displayed with so much eloquence the immense importance to the Union of the possession of the ceded territory, cannot carry his ideas further on that subject than I do."[1] The speedy conversion of Adams may have been due not more to Breckenridge's eloquence than to the activity of Pickering in opposing the treaty; for the relations of the two Massachusetts senators were notoriously hostile. Adams continued to believe in the efficacy of a constitutional amendment, however, and while approving the incorporation of Louisiana found much fault with the means adopted to that end.

[1] *Annals of Congress* (1803–1804), 68.

Support of the Louisiana project involved an almost complete abandonment of the time-honored doctrines of the Republicans. The tenets of the Kentucky and Virginia Resolutions were being violated by the Administration at every turn.[1] The implied powers under the Constitution were being exploited as they had never been during the Washington and Adams administrations. Only five years before Breckenridge so ardently championed the Louisiana transaction in the Senate he had led the legislature of Kentucky in declaring itself determined "tamely to submit to undelegated, and consequently unlimited, powers in no man or body of men on earth;" and in affirming that submission to the exercise of such powers "would be to surrender the form of government we have chosen, and to live under one deriving its powers from its own will, and not from our authority." "Nothing could be more interesting," says Mr. Henry Adams, "than to see the discomfort with which the champions of state rights tossed themselves from one horn to the other of the Federalist dilemma. The Federalists cared little on which horn their opponents might choose to impale themselves, for both were equally fatal. Either Louisiana must be admitted as a state, or must be held as a territory. In the first case the old Union was at an end; in the second

---

[1] The Kentucky Resolutions, of November 10, 1798, are given in N. S. Shaler, *Kentucky*, 409-416; those of November 22, in Elliot, *Debates* (ed. 1836), IV. 570-572. The text of the Virginia Resolutions of December 24, 1798, is in Madison's *Writings* (ed. 1865), IV. 506-507. All of these are reprinted in MacDonald, *Select Documents*, 148-160. See Hermann Von Holst, *Constitutional History of the United States*, I. Ch. IV.; E. D. Warfield, *The Kentucky Resolutions* of 1798; and Alexander Johnston, in *Lalor's Cyclopædia of United States History*, II. 672-677.

case the national government was an empire, with inherent sovereignty derived from the war and treaty-making powers — in either case the Virginia theories were exploded."[1]

On the second day of the debate, November 3, the bill appropriating the purchase money was passed by a vote of 26 to 5. The senators voting in the negative were Pickering, of Massachusetts, Hillhouse and Tracy, of Connecticut, and Wells and White, of Delaware.[2]

Another question which demanded an early settlement was the relation which the newly acquired territory should bear to the United States. Did Louisiana now belong to the central government at Washington, or to the states? And, in either case, how should the territory be governed? By a curious reversal of positions the Federalists maintained that while the general government might, by reason of its inherent sovereignty, rule the territory as England or France ruled dependencies, it could not be brought into the Union as a state without the consent of the states already existing; the Republicans held that Louisiana now became merely a part of the general territory mentioned in the Constitution, and might be admitted as a state, or as several states, solely at the discretion of Congress. One thing was certain, — the annexation foreboded a change in the character of the old Union. Whether the imperial policy of the Federalists, or the assimilative plan of the Republicans, was followed, the nation could not go on the same. The one meant a radical transformation in the underlying re-

[1] Adams, *History of the United States*, II. 112.
[2] *Annals of Congress* (1803–1804), 73.

publican theory of the government; the other meant, at the very least, an early overbalancing of the East by the West in the councils of the nation.

In his message, October 17, Jefferson had called upon Congress to take measures "necessary for the immediate occupation and temporary government" of the newly acquired country. In a special message, October 21, he again besought the legislative branch to make "such temporary provisions as the case may require."[1] This request was followed by the appointment of a select committee on the subject in the House, with John Randolph as chairman. The bill which the committee soon reported was understood to have emanated from the President.[2] It provided in substance that for the time being there should be no attempt to change the existing institutions of Louisiana, and that until Congress could arrange definitely for a new government the President should administer the affairs of the territory without check or hindrance. This proposition was bitterly attacked by the Federalists, on the ground that it placed entirely too much power in the hands of the President, and that the continuance of the Spanish régime under the American flag amounted to nothing less than "tearing the Constitution to tatters." The Republican claim, however, that the Constitution was made for the states, not the territories, while admittedly capable of producing governmental abuses, came to be generally accepted. It was simply an assertion of the now well-established principle that Congress has power in

[1] Richardson, *Messages and Papers of the Presidents*, I. 363.
[2] The text of the measure is in the *Annals of Congress* (1803–1804), Appendix, 1245.

the territories which it cannot exercise in the states, and that the limitations of power found in the Constitution are applicable only to the states.[1] By a strictly party vote the committee's bill was passed in the House, as likewise in the Senate.[2] It became law October 31.

This measure was, of course, but temporary. A month after its adoption Senator Breckenridge moved for a committee to draw up a definite and permanent scheme for the territorial government of Louisiana.[3] The members appointed were Breckenridge himself, Jackson and Baldwin, of Georgia, and John Quincy Adams, of Massachusetts.[4] December 30 they reported a bill which seems to have been drawn up by Secretary Madison in collaboration with the President.[5] The most cursory examination of the measure revealed the theory upon which it had been constructed. This was that the same sovereign power which had been construed as enabling the national government to acquire the territory, enabled it also to govern the inhabitants of the territory absolutely without restriction. Louisiana was considered clearly outside the pale of the Constitution, in an even more dependent relation than such territories as Indiana and Mississippi. The bill began by dividing the ceded area into two parts on the line of the thirty-third parallel — the boundary between the present states of Arkansas and Louisiana. Henceforth the northern portion alone was to bear the name "Louisiana"

[1] Cf. Thomas H. Benton, *Examination of the Decision of the Supreme Court in the Case of Dred Scott*, 55.

[2] The vote in the House was 90 yeas, 25 nays; in the Senate, 26 yeas, 5 nays.

[3] Motion of November 28th. *Annals of Congress* (1803–1804), 106.

[4] *Ibid.*, 211.   [5] *Ibid.*, 223 et seq.

and was to be subject to the territorial government of Indiana. It contained as yet but few whites, and its affairs were mainly such as related to the Indians. The southern portion was to bear the name of the "Territory of Orleans." The government devised for this region exceeded in despotism anything the United States had yet known, falling but little short in this respect of the systems recently in vogue under the French and Spanish régimes. There was absolutely no provision for popular government in the territory. The governor and secretary were to be appointed by the President, the former for a term of three years, the latter for a term of four. The legislative council of thirteen members was to be appointed annually by the President without even consulting the Senate. The governor was to have unrestricted power of convening and proroguing this council. The judicial officers, also appointed by the President, were to hold their positions for four years only, rather than during good behavior. The right to a jury trial was limited to cases involving the sum of $20 or more, and to capital cases in criminal prosecutions. The slave trade was restricted by the provision that no slave should be imported from abroad, no slave should be brought into the territory from the Union who had been imported from abroad since May 1, 1798, and no slave should be carried into the territory under any circumstances except by an American citizen "removing into said territory for actual settlement, and being, at the time of such removal, *bona fide* owner of such slave."[1]

[1] The text of the act as finally approved by the President, March 26, 1804, is in the *Annals of Congress* (1803–1804), Appendix, 1293–1300.

Unfortunately the Senate debates on this bill were not recorded. We only know that after numerous unsuccessful attempts on the part of John Quincy Adams and others to check the exercise of arbitrary power the measure was passed, February 18, 1804, after six weeks' debate, by a vote of 20 to 5.[1] In the House opinion was widely divergent. On the one hand, there were those who contended, with George W. Campbell, of Tennessee, that the bill "really establishes a complete despotism; it does not evince a single trait of liberty; it does not confer one single right to which they [the inhabitants] are entitled under the treaty; it does not extend to them the benefits of the federal Constitution, or declare when, hereafter, they shall receive them."[2] On the other hand, there were those who joined in the confession of Dr. Eustis, of Boston: "I am one of those who believe that the principles of civil liberty cannot suddenly be engrafted on a people accustomed to a regimen of a directly opposite hue. The approach of such a people to liberty must be gradual. I believe them [the inhabitants] at present totally unqualified to exercise it. . . . I consider them as standing in nearly the same relation to us as if they were a conquered country."[3] The House as a whole was not ready to accept such centralization of authority

---

It appears also in English, and in French in the anonymous *Recueil dans lequel sont contenus la Constitution des États-Unis avec ses amendements, le traite par lequel la Louisiane a été cédé aux États-Unis*, etc. [New Orleans, 1806], 74–102. This compilation is bound in a volume with other documents relating to early Louisiana history under the title, *Louisiane, 1804 à 1807*.

[1] *Annals of Congress* (1803–1804), 256.
[2] *Ibid.*, 1063.
[3] *Ibid.*, 1058.

in the hands of the President as the Breckenridge bill proposed. By a vote of 74 to 23 it struck out the section which vested legislative power in the council to be appointed by the President. An amendment was substituted, providing for an elective territorial legislature after the first year. The restriction on the right of jury trial was rejected, and the entire act was limited to two years. In this altered form it passed the House March 17, though not a few Republicans joined with the Federalists to the end in opposing it.[1]

The Senate refused absolutely to concur in any of the House amendments, except as to the duration of the act, and this was reduced to a single year. Inasmuch as in so short a time not even the alarmists could hope for the inauguration of a better system than the one proposed, the House accepted the Senate's compromise and passed the bill, March 23, in its original form except as to the time limit. The vote was rather close — 51 to 45.[2] The first stage of Louisiana legislation was complete.[3] By the

---

[1] The vote was 66 to 21. *Annals of Congress* (1803–1804), 1199.
[2] *Ibid.*, 1229.
[3] Most of the works referred to in the preceding chapter (especially p. 531), contain more or less elaborate accounts of the Louisiana debate and early Louisiana legislation. By far the best treatment of the subject is Adams, *History of the United States*, II. Chs. IV.–VI. The acquisitions resulting from the Spanish-American war have occasioned, within recent times, a vast amount of discussion of the problems of administration of dependent territory under the law and practice of the United States. A few books and essays in this field, which not infrequently recur to the precedents of the Louisiana Purchase, may be cited as of general interest: A. T. Mahan, *Lessons of the War with Spain*; Whitelaw Reid, *Problems of Expansion;* Max Farrand, *Legislation of Congress for the Government of the Organized Territories of the United States;* Albert Bushnell Hart, *Foundations of American Foreign Policy* (espe-

Breckenridge Act, says Mr. Adams, "Louisiana received a government in which its people, who had been solemnly promised all the rights of American citizens, were set apart, not as citizens, but as subjects lower in the political scale than the meanest tribes of Indians, whose right to self-government was never questioned."[1]

It is certainly true that the measures adopted for the government of the Louisiana territory marked no slight departure from the nation's recognized principles and policies. One has only to compare the Breckenridge Act with the ordinance reported to the Congress of the Confederation by Jefferson, in 1784, for the government of the territory recently ceded by the individual states, or with the even more noteworthy Northwest Ordinance of 1787, to be struck with the illiberality of the system now imposed upon Louisiana. Yet it should be borne in mind that the circumstances of the Louisiana settlement were wholly

---

cially Chs. V. and VI.); Simeon E. Baldwin, "Historic Policy of the United States," in the *Annual Report of the American Historical Association for 1893*, 369-390; J. W. Burgess, "Government of Distant Territory," and "The Constitution and Newly Acquired Territory," in the *Political Science Quarterly*, XIV. 1-18, and XV. 381-398; Benjamin Harrison, "The Status of Annexed Territory," in the *North American Review*, CLXXII. 1-22; E. W. Huffcut, "Constitutional Aspects of the Government of Dependencies," in the *Annals of the American Academy of Political and Social Science*, XIII., Supplement 19-45; Theodore S. Woolsey, "The Government of Dependencies," *ibid.*, XIII., Sup. 3-18; Carl Becker, "Law and Practice of the United States in the Acquisition and Government of Dependent Territory," *ibid.*, XVI., Sup. 404-420; A. Lawrence Lowell, "The Government of Dependencies," *ibid.*, XIII., Sup. 46-59, "The Colonial Expansion of the United States," in the *Atlantic Monthly*, LXXXIII. 145-155, and "The Status of our New Possessions," in the *Harvard Law Review*, November, 1899; and Harry P. Judson, "The Constitution and the Territories," in the *Review of Reviews*, XXI. 451-456. [1] Adams, *History of the United States*, II. 125.

unique. The territories east of the Mississippi were peopled with the frontiersmen who had gone out but recently from the seaboard states, and who, as men largely of Saxon blood and speech, had always been accustomed to more or less participation in the government to which they owed allegiance. On the other hand, the Louisianians presented a variety of French, Spanish, and creole elements — all equally devoid of experience in self-government. Under both the earlier French régime and the later Spanish possession, New Orleans had been the seat of an autocracy as complete within its sphere of operation as that at Paris or Madrid. That the inhabitants of the ceded territory were not capable of passing instantly out of the shadow of absolutism into efficient administration of their own political affairs will hardly be disputed by any one acquainted with conditions prevailing in the province. There may have been, on the part of the Jefferson administration, a greater departure from the general securities of the Constitution than was entirely necessary, but that there was every warrant for governing the territory independently of that instrument has been subsequently affirmed, not only by the authority of the Supreme Court,[1] but by the repeated practice of the nation. For, despite Jefferson's endeavors to set the early Louisiana régime in such a light that it would not, in after years, be regarded as a precedent, the system with which the advent of American control at New Orleans was accompanied has been repeatedly appealed to by expansionists ever since.

[1] Opinion of Chief Justice Marshall, 1828; American Insurance Company and Others *v.* Canter, I. Peters's Reports, 511-546.

CHAPTER XIII

ESTABLISHING THE AMERICAN RÉGIME

THE territory acquired by the purchase of Louisiana was, for the most part, a *terra incognita*. Except for a belt along the western bank of the Mississippi, it was unknown alike to Spaniards, Frenchmen, and Americans. Under the Spanish régime it had been divided vaguely into two great administrative districts — Louisiana and Spanish Illinois — the one comprising the area south of New Madrid (southern Missouri), the other that north. Spanish Illinois, in 1803, included a number of small settlements and trading posts, such as those at Ste. Geneviève, St. Louis, St. Charles, etc., with a total population doubtless increased somewhat over the six thousand which a rude census four years earlier had given the territory. But it was necessarily devoid of any system of general government. It was not until after the Lewis and Clark expedition of 1804–1806 that this northern region came to be appreciated at anything like its full worth. And it was not until still considerably later that it acquired sufficient population to warrant definite territorial organization at the hands of the United States.

Our best source of information regarding the population and resources of Louisiana at the time of the purchase from France is a state paper communicated by President Jefferson to Congress, November 14, 1803.[1] According to statistics cited in this document, the population of the entire territory, in 1769, when O'Reilly took definite possession in behalf of Spain, was between 13,000 and 14,000, including the 3190 people of the city of New Orleans. By the census of 1799, this number had increased to 42,000, of which 6000, as we have said, were north of New Madrid. Only 2000 lived between New Madrid and the Arkansas, leaving 34,000 between that river and the Gulf. Professor McMaster affirms that three-fourths of the population and seven-eighths of the wealth were to be found below Pointe Coupée, fifty miles south of the mouth of the Red.[2] It is estimated that in 1803 the total population was approximately 50,000, exclusive, of course, of the Indians, who were supposed to number not more than 25,000 or 30,000. Some estimates go as high as 60,000, and some, based on apparently good

[1] *American State Papers, Miscellaneous*, I. 344-356. This document covers a very wide range of topics, such as boundaries, territorial divisions, classes and number of population, fortifications, militia, natural and manufactured products, existing system of administration, exports and imports, etc. It is reprinted in the *Old South Leaflets*, No. CV. Among other contemporary descriptions of the Louisiana country are (1) *The Journal of Andrew Ellicott, Late Commissioner of the United States, 1796-1800, for determining the Boundary between the United States and the Possessions of his Catholic Majesty in America* [Philadelphia, 1803]; (2) Amos Stoddard, *Sketches, Historical and Descriptive, of Louisiana* [Philadelphia, 1812]; (3) F. M. Perrin du Lac, *Voyage dans les deux Louisianes et chez les nations du Missouri, par les États-Unis, l'Ohio et les provinces qui le bordent en 1801, 1802, et 1803* [Paris, 1805]; and (4) Berquin-Duvallon, *Vue de la colonie espagnole du Mississippi, ou des provinces de Louisiane et Floride occidentale en l'armée, 1802* [Paris, 1803].

[2] McMaster, *History of the People of the United States*, III. 15.

authority, even higher.[1] The population of New Orleans was placed at 8000 to 10,000. The revenues of the city were $19,278, the expenses hardly $10,000. The yearly produce of the entire province was estimated at 3000 pounds of indigo, 6,000,000 pounds of cotton, 5,000,000 pounds of sugar, and 250,000 gallons of molasses.[2] The annual exports were valued at $2,158,000; the imports at $2,500,000. The revenues accruing to the king's treasury barely averaged $120,000 a year, while the expenses of administering the affairs of the province went above $800,000 in 1802. Financially, at least, Louisiana was a mere encumbrance to Spain. Mr. Charles Gayarré, the careful historian of Louisiana, states it as his conclusion that from March 5, 1766, when Ulloa landed at New Orleans, to November 30, 1803, when the territory was given over to the French, "the ordinary and extraordinary expenses incurred by Spain in relation to Louisiana, over and above the small revenue she derived from that colony, may, without exaggeration, be put down at about fifteen millions of dollars."[3] In other words, Spain paid as much for four decades of hazardous tenure as it cost the United States to secure full, complete, and permanent possession. This she had done in the vain hope of establishing a barrier in the interest of her Mexican possessions against the danger of English aggression through the expansion of the seaboard colonies.

The peoples inhabiting Louisiana, and especially New Orleans, at the time of the purchase were extremely

[1] Gayarré, *History of Louisiana*, III. 622.
[2] Martin, *History of Louisiana*, II. 234.
[3] Gayarré, *History of Louisiana*, III. 624.

heterogeneous — "Anglo-Hispano-Gallo-Americans," as Josiah Quincy called them during the famous debate on the admission of Louisiana in 1811. By far the most numerous were the French creoles, and despite forty years of Spanish tenure the prevailing language, social customs, religious institutions, and political practices were characteristically French. The Spaniards in the colony were generally of the official class. Many Americans had crossed the river and taken up their abode on what at the time was foreign soil, but most of the English-speaking people in the territory were transient traders rather than permanent settlers. So far as the observation of the New Orleans creole went, the typical American was the dashing, swaggering, boisterous flatboatman, who made his way once a year, or oftener, down the river, quarrelling with the Spanish tax officials and threatening all manner of dire vengeance if his precious cargo of pork or grain was molested. Perhaps this may account for the fact, which must be confessed, that Americans were anything but popular at New Orleans, and that the pending establishment of the sovereignty of the United States was regarded with ill-concealed contempt.

Before describing the settling of American authority over Louisiana, late in 1803, it will be of interest to review some phases of the recent history of the province — particularly since the retrocession from Spain to France in 1800. After the death of Leclerc in St. Domingo in 1802, the man whom Napoleon first selected to head the expedition against Louisiana was General Bernadotte. Because of his excessive demands in the way of men and money, however, Bernadotte was given another mission —

that of serving as minister plenipotentiary to the United States.[1] In his stead was substituted for the command of the Louisiana expedition General Victor, with whom was associated Pierre Clement Laussat, who in the capacity of prefect was to administer the civil affairs of the province after its reduction by Victor's forces. That the United States would be stirred by jealousy by the bringing of Louisiana once more under French control was fully expected. Therefore, so ran Victor's instructions from Napoleon, "the arrival of the French forces should be marked there by the expression of sentiments of great benevolence for these new neighbors."[2] Laussat was charged to maintain "sources of intelligence" — in plain English, spies — in the western states, to make all possible alliances with the Indians, and never to forget that "if war takes place, Louisiana will certainly become the theatre of hostilities." The intention of the First Consul was declared to be "to raise Louisiana to a degree of strength which will allow him in time of war to abandon it to its own resources without anxiety; so that enemies may be forced to the greatest sacrifices merely in attempting to attack it."

With instructions of this tenor Laussat sailed for New Orleans January 12, 1803, the next day after Jefferson

---

[1] His instructions were signed by Talleyrand, January 14, 1803. Before Bernadotte could leave France the war with England was renewed, and he remained to serve his master in a military capacity. Barbé-Marbois, *Histoire de la Louisiane*, 223.

[2] "Instructions secrètes pour le Captaine-Général de la Louisiane, approuvées par le Premier Consul le 5 Frimaire, An XI." (November 26, 1802), Archives de la Marine, Mss. Quoted in Adams, *History of the United States*, II. 5.

had sent to the Senate Monroe's nomination as special envoy to France. Victor remained in Holland, laboring to fit out the fleet for the conquest. This work was so prolonged that before preparations were finished the war with England had been renewed. Victor's fleet was diverted from its original purpose, and the Louisiana expedition was never realized. Perhaps it would be better to say that the fleet was diverted from its *alleged* purpose; for within a few weeks after the instructions were issued to Victor and Laussat, Napoleon was definitely committed to the renewal of the war, which no one understood better than he would involve the giving over of Louisiana to another power.

March 23 the cabildo, or city council, at New Orleans completed arrangements for the reception and provisioning of the large body of troops expected soon to arrive with General Victor. The next day a vessel came in from Havre bringing documents which specified the form of government the province was to receive at the hands of the French. There were to be a captain-general at the head with a salary of 70,000 francs; a lieutenant-captain-general, to govern in Upper, or Spanish, Louisiana, with a salary of 20,000 francs; two brigadier-generals, each with 15,000 francs a year; two adjutant-commandants, with 9000 francs each; and a colonial prefect, with 50,000 francs.[1] The captain-general was to be commander-in-chief of the land and naval forces and to have general charge of the relations of the colony with other colonies and powers. The colonial prefect, the second officer in importance, was to administer the

[1] Martin, *History of Louisiana*, II. 182-184.

colony's finances, including taxes and expenditures, control the police system, and oversee trade, agriculture, the public stores, the census, the press, public instruction and worship, and in general the other interests formerly in charge of the Spanish intendant. Another officer of importance was the commissary of justice, who, as his title would indicate, was to superintend the courts and prepare a provisional civil and criminal code. There was, of course, no provision for popular government. Only monarchical institutions were in favor with the originators of the system. But it was rightly judged that the Louisianians, never having known anything but absolutism, would not complain on this score. In truth, the inhabitants of the territory were for a time overjoyed with the prospect of being once more united with the nation whose blood flowed in the veins of nine out of ten of them.

On the 26th of March the colonial prefect, Laussat, arrived at New Orleans. He was received by the Spanish governor and intendant, the clergy of the city, the leading military officials, and a group of other dignitaries, with flattering cordiality; while among the populace his coming was made the occasion of the wildest enthusiasm and excitement. In the course of the ceremonies of his reception Laussat made an address in which he declared that in her prospective control of Louisiana, France would be careful to serve only the interests of the colony. In fact, said he, it was for this alone that Napoleon had secured the retrocession. Order was to be strictly maintained; treaties with the Indian nations were to be observed, laws and customs were to be respected; the clergy were to be protected, and religion and education consistently fostered.[1]

Nevertheless, there were some discordant notes in the pæan of welcome with which the prefect was greeted. The slave owners constituted a large proportion of the inhabitants, and these, remembering how the French had abolished slavery in St. Domingo in 1794, became apprehensive lest a similar course should now be followed in Louisiana. In a despatch to his home government, March 29, the Spanish intendant, Morales, declared that this consideration had largely offset the rejoicing with which Laussat's coming had first been hailed.[2] The reaction speedily went so far as to lead a contemporary writer, quoted by Barbé-Marbois in his account of this period, to say: "Every one will be astonished to learn that a people of French descent have received without emotion and without any apparent interest a French magistrate, who comes to us, accompanied by his young and beautiful family, and preceded by the public esteem. Nothing has been able to diminish the alarms which his mission causes. His proclamations have been heard by some with sadness, and by the greater part of the inhabitants with the same indifference as the beat of the drum is listened to when it announces the escape of a slave or a sale at auction."[3] Nothing could have been more welcome to the majority of Louisianians than the restoration of French authority under the old Bourbon régime. Upon second thought, however, there appeared much doubt as

[1] Gayarré, *History of Louisiana*, III. 580.
[2] *Ibid.*, 581.
[3] Barbé-Marbois, *Histoire de la Louisiane*, 226–227.

to whether the new order in France might not rob the retrocession of its boasted benefits for the colony.

One of Laussat's first acts was to despatch to Decrès, the minister of marine, a detailed account of the state of the retroceded territory. The era of Spanish control was declared to have been a period of decline. New Orleans was pictured as being in a more backward condition than when it became a Spanish colony. "The fortifications," wrote Laussat, "have never been kept up, and are falling into decay; the ditches are filling up; the terraces are crumbling down; the palisades are wanting, or rotten; the bridges have given away, or consist only of one or two beams; the gates are off their hinges, and are lying on the ground. . . . With regard to public edifices, those which we find here are the same which have been left by the French. The Spaniards have not made any solid and permanent constructions."[1]

Having described the shiftlessness and low public spirit which characterized the Spanish régime, Laussat next paid his respects to the Spanish colonial government as existing at New Orleans. "I will now proceed," he writes, "to say how justice is administered here, which is worse than in Turkey. All judgments are given in the name of the governor, except in matters appertaining to the revenue, in which the authority of the intendant is supreme. . . . Suits are so expensive that a good many individuals prefer to sacrifice their interests, however considerable they may be, than maintain them at law. The right of appeal to Cuba and to Madrid is a slow and ruinous remedy."[2]

There is evidence to corroborate Laussat's low estimate

[1] Gayarré, *History of Louisiana*, III. 582.   [2] *Ibid.*, 583.

of Spanish judicial processes. Daniel Clark, the United States consul at New Orleans, wrote to the Department of State at Washington in 1803: "All the officers plunder when the opportunity offers; they are all venal. A bargain can be made with the governor, intendant, judge, or collector, down to the constable; and if ever an officer be displeased at an offer of money, it is not at the offer or offerer, but because imperious circumstances compel him to refuse, and the offerer acquires a degree of favor which encourages him to make a second offer when a better opportunity is presented."[1]

As to the right of deposit, Laussat in his report made suggestions which indicate that he was already planning to nullify the reopening of the New Orleans port by the Spanish government in 1803. Napoleon had been greatly incensed at the overruling of Morales's closure, and was determined, through his agents, to put an end to the freedom of American traffic down the river. Laussat wrote that this purpose might be achieved in either of two ways: first, by withdrawing again the right of deposit and compelling the traders to store their goods in government warehouses; second, by taking advantage of the right reserved by Spain to substitute some other place for New Orleans, and designating some "wholly untenable spot." It is evident that had French tenure long continued in Louisiana after the retrocession, and without the limita-

---

[1] Gayarré, *History of Louisiana*, III. 584. Gayarré comments as follows: "This is a frightful picture. That there were but too many cases of corruption seems to be true, but that it should have been systematically carried to the extent here described by Laussat and Daniel Clark, is somewhat rebutted by other testimony, and not confirmed by living witnesses of great respectability."

tions which Jefferson at first hoped to impose upon it, the use of the lower Mississippi must have become as controverted a matter as during the earlier Spanish occupancy.

To Laussat's proclamation of the good intentions of the French government toward Louisiana a considerable number of leading planters replied in a formal address. They declared that their "most ardent wish had always been to resume the glorious name of Frenchmen," and that the proclamation which announced to them that their long-cherished hope was gratified had "filled their souls with the delirium of extreme felicity." Nevertheless, they went on to make it plain that they were not suffering by reason of the Spanish occupation. "We should be unworthy of what is to us a source of much pride if we did not acknowledge that we have no cause of complaint against the Spanish government. We have never groaned under the iron yoke of an oppressive despotism. . . . We [the French and Spanish] have become bound together by family connections and by the bonds of friendship. Let them have the untrammelled enjoyment of all the property they may own on the soil which has become the land of freedom, and let us share with them, like brothers, the blessings of our new position."[1] At the same time the inhabitants of New Orleans presented also an address to Laussat. It began by declaring: "Thirty-four years of foreign domination have not weakened in our hearts the sacred love of country, and our joy in returning to our national flag is equal in intensity to the grief we felt when we were forcibly separated from it. Happy are the colonists of Louisiana who have lived long enough to see their reunion to

[1] Gayarré, *History of Louisiana*, III. 588.

France, which they had never ceased to desire, and which now satisfies their utmost wishes! In an age so fruitful in astonishing events it is unquestionable that some have occurred which are greater, more imposing and more memorable, but perhaps none offer a spectacle as interesting and as affecting as that of victorious and triumphant France holding out a protecting hand to her children, cast away, of old, from her bosom, in consequence of the weakness and prevarication of a pusillanimous government, and calling them to a share in the fruits of a glorious peace,[1] which has terminated in so brilliant a manner the most bloody and terrible revolution. . . . Perhaps France would attach less value to the homage of our fidelity, if she saw us relinquishing without any regret our allegiance to the sovereign who has loaded us with favors, during all the time he had reigned over us. Such culpable indifference is not to be found in our hearts, in which our regret at our separating from him occupies as much space as our joy in securing the nationality we had lost, and it is by keeping up an eternal recollection of his favors, that we intend to show ourselves worthy of the parental attachment and of the benefits which we expect from the French government."

These two addresses are remarkable testimonies to the satisfaction of the colonists with the Spanish administration in Louisiana. It is not often, as Mr. Gayarré says, that "departing power is greeted with such hosannas, and that the incense of public worship is offered to the setting sun."

---

[1] The peace of Amiens, broken by Napoleon within a few weeks after this address was written. [2] Gayarré, *History of Louisiana*, III. 589–590.

April 10, the Marquis de Casa Calvo, a former governor of Louisiana,[1] arrived from Havana, having been sent by the Marquis of Somoruelos, captain-general of Cuba, to act with the governor, Salcedo, in delivering the control of Louisiana into the hands of the French. He was well remembered in the colony, where numerous anecdotes concerning his haughty disposition, yet courtly manners, were the commonplaces of the street. Perhaps the most characteristic of these anecdotes was the one representing him as exclaiming, when reproached for returning the bow of a negro, "Shall I be outdone in politeness by a negro?" In a letter to Decrès, Laussat described Salcedo as "an infirm old man in his dotage," and expressed the opinion that the Cuban captain-general had sent a special commissioner for the transfer of Louisiana because he considered "old Salcedo not presentable to the French." Because of Casa Calvo's reputation as a hater of the French, Laussat was inclined to think that a better man might have been found for the mission. The coming of the marquis to New Orleans was followed by a time of general festivity among the inhabitants. Neither Spanish nor French proposed to allow the transfer to be made without fitting ceremony. The whole population, but especially the aristocrats of both nationalities, entered upon a bewildering series of fêtes, balls, and theatrical entertainments, which came to an end only after the energies and purses of all were showing unmistakable signs of exhaustion.

The following vivid account of the festivities, written

[1] In 1797–1798. He had previously been in command of Fort Dauphin in St. Domingo.

by an observer of them, is worth quoting: "M. Laussat exhibited in brilliant entertainments, embellished by the graces of his affable and beautiful wife, that fascinating elegance which seems to be one of the attributes of the French character. The Louisianian ladies, who looked upon her as a model of taste, appeared at those entertainments with a magnificence which was a just cause of astonishment in such a colony, and which might have been successfully compared with any efforts of that sort even in the principal cities of France. The Louisianian ladies, who may justly be said to be remarkable for their habitual gravity, are generally tall and exquisitely shaped; the alabaster whiteness of their complexion, which was admirably set off by their light dresses, adorned with flowers and rich embroidery, gave a fairy-like appearance to these festivities. The last one, particularly, astonished me by its magnificence. After tea and the concert were over, the dancing was interrupted at midnight, and the guests went down to a saloon — where, on a table laid for sixty or eighty persons, arose, on the top of rocks, the temple of Good Faith surrounded with columns, and surmounted by a dome, under which was placed the allegorical statue of the goddess. But, farther on, beyond that room, one was attracted by the flood of light which burst from an immense pavilion, in the shape of a gallery. There, forty or fifty tables, covered with a variety of dishes, were spread for the accommodation of four or five hundred guests, who grouped themselves round them in small detached parties. The tendency of these festivities was, no doubt, to spread the taste for pleasure and luxury in a colony which, being in its nascent state, still needs a

great deal of economy and labor; but, nevertheless, these entertainments, under the circumstances in which they were given, were the result of a useful and enlightened policy, because they strengthened the common customs and manners which connected us and the colonists, causing them to cherish what is French, and impressing them with a proper sense of the grandeur of the mother country."[1]

Six weeks after the Marquis of Casa Calvo's arrival a proclamation was issued by the Spanish authorities, formally announcing the intention of their sovereign to surrender the province to the French Republic.[2] All persons employed in any branch of the king's service and wishing to remain under his government were to be free to go to Cuba or any other portion of the Spanish realm. Laussat disliked the inducements held out to the colonists to continue their allegiance to Spain, and reported to Decrès that the marquis had gone so far as to exact a promise of continued allegiance from two companies of negro militia, which included all the mechanics New Orleans possessed. Two of these men declared to Laussat that they had been imprisoned for twenty-four hours to force them to give the desired pledge.

As the weeks went by Laussat became more and more impatient. He found his position an extremely embarrassing one. It was Victor, not Laussat, who had been commissioned by Napoleon to receive the Louisiana terri-

---

[1] Claude C. Robin, *Voyages dans l'intérieur de la Louisiane, de la Floride occidentale, et dans les isles de la Martinique et de Saint-Domingue, pendant les années 1802, 1803, 1804, 1805, et 1806* [Paris, 1807], II., 131–132. Translated in Gayarré, *History of Louisiana*, III. 616–617.

[2] Martin, *History of Louisiana*, II. 188.

tory from the Spanish, and the long-awaited expedition had not yet arrived. Laussat was empowered only to govern the territory as prefect after the transfer had been made. Prior to that he could do little or nothing officially. To Decrès he continued to write, rehearsing the high-handed measures of the Spanish and the generally unsatisfactory conditions which prevailed. "I see these things," he declares, "without daring to take exception, for fear of making them worse. The Spanish authorities have shown themselves exceedingly reserved, more captious, and even almost haughty towards me. To every one of my demands or applications the government has an evasive answer prepared. It shuns, isolates, and watches me. It takes umbrage at the least of my steps or proceedings, or even at my language, however insignificant it may be. It is afraid of complying with my plainest requests. Firmness and dignity are all that I have to oppose to their prejudices and unreasonableness. But, frequently, I am obliged to keep pent up within my breast my feelings of vexation, because the Spanish authorities might take offence at them and revenge themselves, without my being able to prevent it, on the friends of the French."[1]

Vague rumors of the sale of Louisiana to the United States reached New Orleans in the early summer, but no one was at first inclined to give them the least degree of credence. Laussat assured the people that such a move on the First Consul's part was utterly inconceivable. Nevertheless, on the 28th of July he wrote to Decrès that the story was coming from so many sources that the

[1] Gayarré, *History of Louisiana*, III. 595-596.

colonists were beginning to entertain ugly suspicions, and he wished specific authority to declare it a mere calumny. Hardly was this request despatched when a vessel, fresh from Bordeaux, came into the New Orleans port, bearing a letter from Napoleon to Laussat in which the transaction with Monroe and Livingston three months before was fully set forth. Under date of June 6 the First Consul had designated Laussat commissioner both to receive Louisiana from the Spaniards and to deliver it to the commissioners to be appointed by the United States. These instructions came to Laussat "like thunder out of a clear sky." Instead of assuming control of the colony as prefect after Victor should have established a French military occupation over it, he was himself to take it over from the Spaniards, and with the enjoyment of at best but a few weeks' sovereignty pass it on to the Americans. Of course there was nothing to do but obey without a word of protest.

The ceremony of transfer from Spain to France was arranged for November 30th. On that day Casa Calvo, Salcedo, and Laussat, together with all the officials, clergy, and other dignitaries of the colony, both Spanish and French, assembled in the cabildo, or city hall, and proceeded in an elaborate ceremony to execute the instructions of the European governments. Laussat exhibited an order from Don Carlos of Spain for the yielding of the colony and another from Napoleon authorizing him to receive it. The keys of the city were given into the prefect's keeping, and the Spanish commissioners absolved from their former allegiance all the inhabitants of the colony who should prefer to remain under French sovereignty. The three chief dignitaries took up their position on the main balcony of the hall, while the Spanish flag, after being saluted by a discharge of artillery, was drawn down from the staff which stood in the open space now known as Jackson Square, but then as the Place d'Armes, in front of the cabildo, and replaced by the flag of France, which was similarly saluted. The square was occupied by the Spaniards and a squad of local militia, while on all sides the populace crowded together to witness the inauguration of the ephemeral French régime.[1]

The public proclamation with which Laussat followed the ceremony of transfer expressed at the same time his regret that the French restoration was but temporary and his sincere hope that in the rapid succession of governments the people of the colony might continue to prosper and be happy. "The mission which brought me among you across the sea," he declared, "through a distance of seventy-five hundred miles, that mission on which I had long rested so many fond hopes, and so many ardent wishes for your happiness, is now totally changed; and the one with which I am now charged, less gratifying, but still equally flattering to me, offers me one source of consolation — which springs from the reflection that it will, in its results, be more advantageous to you. The Commissioners of his Catholic Majesty, in conformity with the powers and orders which they and I have respectively received, have just delivered me the possession of the province. You

---

[1] Grace King, *New Orleans*, 157–161; King and Ficklen, *History of Louisiana*, 152–154; Gayarré, *History of Louisiana*, III. Ch. X.; Martin, *History of Louisiana*, II. Ch. X.; and Barbé-Marbois, *Histoire de la Louisiane*, 352–355.

see the flag of the French Republic now displayed, and you hear the repeated detonations of her guns, announcing to you to-day, on all sides, the return of French domination. It will be for an instant only, Louisianians, and I am on the eve of transferring the possession of this colony to the Commissioners of the United States. They are near at hand — I expect them soon."

The motive behind the sale was thus adroitly put: "The approaching struggles of a war begun under the most sanguinary and terrible auspices, and threatening the safety of the four quarters of the world, had induced the French government to turn its attention toward Louisiana, and to reflect on her destinies. Considerations of prudence and humanity, connecting themselves with those of a more vast and durable policy — worthy, in one word, of the man whose genius weighs at this very hour in its scales the fates of so many great nations — have given a new direction to the beneficent intentions of France towards Louisiana. She has ceded it to the United States of America."[1]

Laussat endeavored to reconcile the people to the sale by demonstrating how by it alone they were saved from the danger of a British conquest. He called attention to the clause of the purchase treaty guaranteeing the early incorporation of the inhabitants of the ceded territories into the "Union of the United States," and congratulated them upon becoming thus identified with a nation "which by its rapid progress seems destined to the most brilliant rank that a people ever enjoyed on the face of the earth." He declared further that by the transfer the

[1] Gayarré, *History of Louisiana*, III. 600 *et seq.*

colonists — soon to be no longer such — would escape the almost inevitable commercial restriction of the colonial condition, and would, along with the rest of the United States, enjoy boundless freedom of exporting and importing. "Your country will become an immense warehouse or place of deposit, affording you countless profits. The Nile of America, the Mississippi, which flows, not through parched deserts of sand, but through the most extensive and the most fertile plains of the new world, will soon see its bosom darkened with a thousand ships belonging to all nations of the earth, and mooring at the quays of another Alexandria."

The Spanish régime being now at an end, it became necessary for Laussat to establish a temporary government under French control to maintain the colony in order until such time as the commissioners of the United States should be ready to receive it. No attempt was made to set up the elaborate system which Napoleon had outlined before the sale to the United States, yet the provisional administration organized was quite complete. It included an administrator-general, a treasurer, a mayor, two adjuncts, and a municipal council of ten members substituted for the old Spanish cabildo. The militia was re-officered, and it was proclaimed that the famous Black Code given to the province by Bienville under the authority of Louis XV. in 1724, excepting those parts which were inconsistent with the Constitution of the United States, should be considered the temporary law of the land.[1]

[1] Martin, *History of Louisiana*, II. 197. For a synopsis of the Black Code, see Gayarré, *History of Louisiana*, I. Appendix.

Within a few days the Spanish troops were withdrawn, leaving the military posts unoccupied. In or near the city of New Orleans there were four of these posts. The troops of the United States not having arrived to occupy them, there was much fear that in the interim they would be seized by lawless parties, and either destroyed or used as strongholds from which to defy the provisional government. To insure against such danger a number of young Americans in the city, led by Daniel Clark,[1] the consular agent of the United States, and increased in numbers by several French creoles, organized themselves into a battalion of three hundred or more members, and put their services at the disposal of Laussat. The Americans were mostly captains and mates of vessels, merchants, clerks, and seamen belonging to vessels in port. There were as yet few resident Americans in the colony. Says Monette in his *History of the Valley of the Mississippi:* "The French, by their zeal, vigilance, and patriotism during their time of service, proved themselves worthy of American citizenship. Their services were gladly accepted, and detachments from their numbers were detailed upon regular tours of duty in patrolling the city by day and by night."[2]

The commissioners appointed by President Jefferson to receive the Louisiana cession were General James Wilkin-

---

[1] Clark had been for twenty years a resident of New Orleans, and was now a wealthy planter and merchant. Andrew Ellicott, in his *Journal*, p. 174, says that Clark was commissioned to serve as consul at New Orleans primarily for the purpose of preventing injustice to American merchantmen, whose ships were being captured by French privateers in the West Indies and condemned without show of justice in the courts of the Louisiana capital.

[2] Monette, *History of the Valley of the Mississippi*, I. 56.

son, who despite his dubious relations with the Spaniards a decade before had risen to a high position of command in the United States army, and Governor William Claiborne, of the Mississippi territory. A week before the transfer from Spain to France Laussat had held a two-hour interview with Wilkinson, who was then returning from the Florida frontier by way of New Orleans, and had discussed with him various courses of action to be adopted in case the Spanish should resist yielding possession of the colony. In a letter to Decrès, December 10,[1] the prefect declared he had hastened the ceremony of transfer from Spain because he suspected the good faith of the Spaniards, and did not wish to give them time to receive instructions contrary to the execution of the Ildefonso treaty. Laussat well knew how bitterly the Spanish ministry and Yrujo at Washington were upbraiding the United States for accepting a bargain based on Napoleon's breach of faith with Spain. Nor was he alone in his suspicions. Due to Yrujo's activity, the Administration would not have been much surprised had the Spaniards balked in the proceedings at New Orleans. Jefferson proposed to take no risks, and therefore ordered ample military preparations in the Southwest, so that force could be made to supplement diplomacy if necessary. Parts of the militia of Ohio, Kentucky, and Tennessee were to be held in readiness to advance upon New Orleans instantly upon command. Fort Adams, near the intersection of the present southern state line of Mississippi with the river, was made the base of operations in the contemplated campaign, and a considerable force of militia was collected

[1] Quoted in Gayarré, *History of Louisiana*, III. 608–616.

there. Five hundred Tennesseeans under the command of Colonel Dogherty advanced as far as Natchez, while Governor Claiborne had ordered a company of Mississippi cavalry to be ready to march with him to New Orleans, December 10.

The expedition was delayed somewhat, and it was not until the 17th that it reached the vicinity of New Orleans. On the following day Laussat sent two prominent French citizens to conduct Claiborne and Wilkinson into the city. With an escort of thirty of the Mississippi cavalry the commissioners came to the prefect's house and were received with a salute of nineteen guns. On the 19th Laussat returned the courtesy by a visit to the American camp two miles out from the city. Without further delay arrangements for the ceremony of transfer were consummated.

From contemporary letters and papers recent Louisiana writers have been able to piece together a most interesting and detailed account of this notable occasion. The day of the transfer — December 20 — was one of those bright, balmy days so characteristic of the Crescent City in early winter. Those who looked with favor upon the event about to occur contrasted the beauties of the day with the rainy dreariness of the day three weeks before on which the French had assumed their short-lived possession, and took it to augur well for the colony in its newest relation. At nine o'clock, by order of Laussat, the ceremony began by the assembling of all the militia in the Place d'Armes. Already the populace of the city was astir and the streets were thronged. The square was then much more open than now and twice as large, and the view from it included the great sweep of the river as it rounded the crescent which gives the city its second name. The vessels which lay at the levee were decorated with flags, and everywhere there were the signs of a public holiday. "In the centre of the Place d'Armes," says Miss King, "arose the great flagstaff, bearing the flimsiest of fabrics and strongest of symbols that has ever held the hearts of mortals to a coign of earth. About the staff were grouped the military, a vivid spot of steel and color, and around them, and as far as eye could see, human faces, eagerly looking up in the bright December sun, a motley of color and expression, white, black, yellow, red, Frenchman, Spaniard, African, mulatto, Indian, and, most visible of all by his height and boisterous triumph on the occasion, the tall, lanky Westerner, in coonskin cap and leathern hunting-shirt."[1] For many a person in the crowd this was to be the third such occasion he had lived to see. No doubt there were many who hoped it would be the last. It was not altogether agreeable to be tossed about among the nations so promiscuously as the Louisianians had been.

When the American cavalcade started from the camp a cannon was fired as a signal, and when the city had been entered by the Tchoupitoulas gate the fact was announced by a salute of twenty guns from Fort St. Charles. By noon the American troops were in the Place d'Armes, occupying a station on the side of the square opposite the militia. They included a detachment of dragoons in red uniform, two companies of infantry, one of carabineers, four pieces of artillery, and a number of cannoneers.

[1] Grace King, *New Orleans*, 161.

While the American soldiery vied with the local militia in maintaining a dignified presence in the Place d'Armes, Claiborne and Wilkinson were conducted into the presence of Laussat and his suite. The meeting occurred in that historic old structure which under the Spanish régime was known as the cabildo, because in it the municipal council, or cabildo, was accustomed to meet, but which the French had christened the Hôtel de Ville. This building, probably the finest of its kind in America a hundred years ago, is still standing, and is described as a "picturesque, imposing, and dignified meeting place for the Supreme Court of the state" — blackened and worn, but yet elegant in its luxurious architecture and its historical associations. Its council chamber and adjacent balcony have been the scenes of many notable ceremonies, among which the transfer of Louisiana from France to the United States is easily first in interest and importance.

The meeting in the council chamber on this occasion was an especially brilliant one. Besides the suite of Laussat there were present numerous influential citizens — churchmen, Spanish cavaliers, and French officials. The ceremonies were similar to those performed in the same place three weeks before, with a mere change in the parties participating. The treaty of cession was read in both English and French, Laussat read his credentials issued by Napoleon, and Claiborne read his commission from President Jefferson. The prefect then formally proclaimed the cession accomplished and handed over to Claiborne the keys of New Orleans.[1] The inhabitants of

[1] The written instrument of cession, signed by Claiborne, Wilkinson, and Laussat, is in the *Annals of Congress* (1804–1805), 1230–1231.

Louisiana who chose to pass under the new government were declared to be absolved from their oath of fidelity to the French Republic.

This done, the commissioners walked out upon the balcony, in view of the assembled populace, and Claiborne addressed the throng, congratulating them on the event "which irrevocably fixed their political existence and no longer left it open to the caprices of chance." He assured them that the United States received them as brothers, and would hasten to extend to them a participation in the invaluable rights forming the basis of their own unexampled prosperity; and that, in the meanwhile, the people would be protected in the enjoyment of their liberty, property, and religion, that their commerce would be favored and their agriculture encouraged.[2]

All the while the tricolor of France had been floating at the top of the tall staff in the centre of the Place d'Armes. But now the time had come to lower it. With the commissioners still standing at the edge of the balcony and the people crowding below to hear Claiborne's address, — though probably not half could understand a word that was spoken, — slowly the tricolor began to descend and the stars and stripes to ascend. When they met halfway a gun was fired as a signal, and immediately the land batteries began their discharges, which were responded to by the armed vessels in the

[1] Some regard the entire ceremony as having taken place on the balcony, e.g. Dr. Hosmer, in his *Louisiana Purchase*, 169–170. Miss Grace King's view, set forth in her *New Orleans*, 162–165, has been adopted by the writer.

[2] Claiborne's brief address upon this occasion is in the *Annals of Congress* (1804–1805), 1233.

river. According to Miss King, twenty-one days before, when the French flag was flung to the breeze for its last brief reign in Louisiana, a band of fifty old soldiers formed themselves into a guard of honor to act as a kind of death watch to their national emblem.[1] They stood now at the foot of the staff and received in their arms the tricolor as it descended, and while the Americans were rending the air with their shouts, they marched silently away, their sergeant bearing it at their head. The scene was viewed by all with the profoundest marks of respect. The American troops as they passed presented arms to the banner of the departed power, and it was carried to the government house and left in the keeping of Laussat. Never again was it, or any of its kind, to wave as the symbol of established supremacy over any part of the North American continent. No one understood better than the French prefect the far-reaching significance of the occasion. In his despatches to Decrès he recurs again and again to the enormity of the sacrifice which Napoleon had made. "The Americans," he wrote, "have given $15,000,000 for Louisiana; they would have given $50,000,000 rather than not possess it. . . . In a few years the country as far as the Rio Bravo will be in a state of cultivation. New Orleans will then have a population of from thirty thousand to fifty thousand souls, and the country will produce sugar enough to supply America and part of Europe. Let us not blind ourselves; in a few years the existing prejudices will be worn off; the inhabitants will gradually become Americans by the introduction of native Americans and Englishmen — a system

[1] Grace King, *New Orleans*, 163.

already begun. What a magnificent New France have we lost!"[1]

Although the French population could hardly have been expected to join in the cheering with which the lowering of the tricolor was accompanied, there were not a few other evidences that the establishment of the new régime aroused no enthusiasm on part of the majority of the people. Governor Claiborne's speech was listened to respectfully, but sullenly. His "Louisianians, my fellow-citizens" fell flat. After the American troops had defiled out of one side of the square and the militia out of another, and the crowds had returned to their labors and amusements, the new governor must have been fairly appalled at the magnitude of the task before him. He had been commissioned, not only to receive Louisiana, but also to administer its affairs until Congress should decide upon the proper government for it. The ill-concealed indifference, and even hostility, of large portions of the inhabitants augured not well for the future. And the storm of controversy which was sweeping the country as the result of the purchase rendered congressional action extremely uncertain. A less conscientious and patriotic man would have hesitated to transfer his labors from the quiet Mississippi to the petulant Louisiana territory.

Receiving from Laussat the command of the militia, Claiborne at once took measures to increase its efficiency, though he was careful to man the posts and guard-houses with his own troops. On the same day of the transfer he supplemented his address from the cabildo balcony with a proclamation reiterating the good intentions of the

[1] Martin, *History of Louisiana*, II. 244.

United States and exhorting all the inhabitants to faithful allegiance to their new flag.[1] The laws and municipal regulations which were in force at the time of the cession were to continue unchanged, pending the action of Congress.

The latter phase of the situation was the most pregnant with trouble. It was truly an anomalous position in which Claiborne found himself. In him were vested all the powers of the defunct government, a curious Gallo-Spanish hybrid; and combining as he did the prerogatives of governor-general, intendant, and what not, was possessed of vastly more power than had been enjoyed by any official in the employ of either the French or Spanish monarchies. His position as a kind of absolute proconsul seemed absurdly out of harmony with the republican pretensions of the nation he served. Moreover, he was to administer laws which he knew nothing about, — could not even read, — and to enforce Spanish municipal regulations of which he had never heard, and which were thoroughly inconsistent with all that his political training and experience had taught him to consider just and right. Much to the increase of his perplexities, he recognized the fact that most of the inhabitants were suspicious and inclined to be rebellious. The few Americans in the territory were hopelessly lost in the mass of creoles, Spaniards, negroes, and other discontented elements. A score of traits were possessed by the French and Spanish in common, and both alike hated the Americans. Especially indignant were they at the idea of being bought by

[1] Gayarré, *History of Louisiana*, III. 620. The text of the proclamation is in the *Annals of Congress* (1804–1805), 1232.

the Americans. "Every American," says Miss King, "who walked the streets of New Orleans, did it with the air of a personal purchaser of the province, an arrogance unbearable to the Creoles, who resented it with an arrogance still more galling to the Americans."[1] As far as possible they ignored the existence of the new government. In not a few cases they even spurned to take office under it. English having become the governmental language, the creoles steadfastly refused to learn it, or to use it if they happened to be able to do so. Claiborne knew no French or Spanish, and naturally surrounded himself with advisers and officials appointed from the Americans, who began to come in greater numbers into the province. This only increased the jealousy of the older population, who foresaw their complete eclipse politically by the newcomers. Not only was the government of Claiborne despised, but the future settlement by Congress was dreaded. Would the United States fulfil her obligations as set forth in the third article of the purchase treaty, or would she continue the high-handed régime instituted under Claiborne? The notorious division of opinion throughout the country and the prolongation and heat of the Louisiana debates in Congress gave much ground for apprehension. "A Creole and an American could not meet without a dispute and an affray. The animosity involved all; the governor himself and the United States general, Wilkinson, actively participated in it. At night, insurrectionary placards posted on the corners of the street attracted crowds around them, preventing their being torn away, reading them aloud, copying

[1] Grace King, *New Orleans* 164.

them. Every day produced its crop of duels; the governor's private secretary and brother-in-law, attempting to refute a slander, was killed in one. The old militia was disorganized, and there was too much jealousy and distrust, too distinct a line drawn between the two populations, to hope for any new, common, efficient force."[1]

To make matters worse, Caso Calvo and his suite lingered, and continued by their social graces to emphasize the uncouthness of the Americans. The Spaniards now took pleasure in reversing the situation of ten or twelve years before. By subtle hints of Spanish invasions, or French and Spanish designs jointly to recover Louisiana from the United States, they managed to keep Claiborne in as apprehensive a state of mind as Carondelet and other Spanish governors had suffered in the days before the treaty of San Lorenzo el Real.

At last came news from Congress. March 23, 1804, an act (the Breckenridge Act) had been passed, dividing the province into two parts and providing for the administration of the new Territory of Orleans. The proclamation of this measure, however, only added to the discontent of the Louisianians. Scarcely a feature of it met with approval. The division of the territory was bitterly resented as being evidence of the intention of Congress to diminish its importance and postpone as long as possible the execution of the third article of the treaty. The prohibition of the importation of slaves, except by new immigrants into the territory, was regarded as a blow aimed at the prosperity of the older inhabitants. And the provision of the act which declared certain land concessions

[1] Grace King, *New Orleans*, 165.

made by the Spanish government null and void was looked upon as but an entering wedge for a general policy of confiscation and dispossession. Altogether there appeared small reason to hope for an early incorporation into the Union with "the rights, advantages, and immunities of citizens of the United States."

Laussat, who like Casa Calvo (though with better motives) had lingered for a while at New Orleans, communicated to the French ministry a lively description of the first four or five months of the American régime and the state of feeling which prevailed among the people of the territory. He declared that while the creoles had at first scorned the idea of a transfer to the United States, yet as the time of the change of dominion approached they became pretty well reconciled to it and rather hospitable toward the prospective government. "But," he continues, "hardly had the agents of that government taken the reins in hand, when they accumulated errors on errors, and blunders on blunders." He then proceeded to enumerate a long list of these errors and blunders — many of which seem to us to have been quite unavoidable, and hence not rightly styled errors, but all of which certainly did have a part in producing the local disaffection which Laussat considered so serious. Among the acts enumerated were the introduction of the English language, the preference shown American over French dances at public balls, the partiality shown Americans in the offices and courts, the "arbitrary mixture of old usages with new ones," the intemperate speeches, the "injurious precautions," the bad advisers, the "savage manners and habits," etc. "It was hardly possible that

the government of the United States should have a worse beginning." Laussat considered Claiborne and Wilkinson as bad men as could have been selected for the administration of the affairs of the territory. Claiborne he characterizes as having "estimable qualities as a private man, but possessing little intellect, a good deal of awkwardness, and being extremely beneath the position in which he had been placed." Wilkinson was described as a mere "rattle-headed fellow, full of odd fantasies." Probably the judgment of Claiborne was much too severe. He was ill-fitted for the post, it is true, but his long experience as governor of Mississippi had given him such an acquaintance with southwestern life and conditions as was possessed by very few Americans at the time. Laussat's estimate of Wilkinson was, if anything, too mild.

All in all, however, Laussat believed that, despite her bad beginning, the United States would yet win the attachment of the Louisianians. Only the continuance of a grossly blundering policy on the part of the Administration could long keep the hostility of the creoles alive. "There are advantages inherent to the Constitution and to the situation of the United States, of which it is impossible to prevent these people from experiencing the salutary influence." Laussat did not share the belief of some that in the event of Napoleon's triumph over England he would once more bring Louisiana under the tricolor by purchase or by conquest. Nevertheless, he did predict the eventual detaching of the territory from the Union, after it should have become well populated, and thought that France might then establish with it such commercial relations as would approximate to the old colonial system.

CHAPTER XIV

THE TERRITORY OF ORLEANS AND THE NEW LOUISIANA

JUNE 1, 1804, there was held a mass-meeting at New Orleans, called by a number of influential merchants of the city and planters of the vicinity, for the purpose of taking steps to secure better terms from Congress than were contained in the Breckenridge Act of the previous March. In the meeting it was unanimously resolved to petition Congress to repeal those portions of the act which provided for a division of the territory and placed restriction upon the importation of slaves. It was decided also to ask for the immediate admission of Louisiana, with its original boundaries, into the Union as a state. Two larger meetings in July heard and approved a committee's draft of a memorial to Congress on these subjects, and three men — Derbigny, Sauvé, and Destréhan, all French — were constituted a deputation to carry the petition to Washington. In late summer they set out upon their long journey.

The day upon which Congress had decreed that the new territorial government should go into effect was October 1, 1804. The occasion was marred by the fact that four of the thirteen members of the legislative council appointed by the President flatly refused to serve. Some

of the other appointees were awed into adopting a practically similar course. It was not until December 4, and only after Claiborne had taken it upon himself to appoint substitutes for the refractory four, that the legislative council was ready to begin its work. During the two months' session which ensued, attention was devoted mainly to the organization of a judicial system. The territory was divided into twelve counties, with an inferior court for each composed of one judge. Two orders that must have been puzzling and provoking to the non-English people of the territory were that all suits at law should be instituted by a petition in the form of a bill in chancery, and that in the definition of crimes and the mode of prosecution in criminal cases the common law of England should be strictly adhered to. A committee was appointed to prepare a civil and criminal code upon this basis. "Bills in chancery" and "common law" were wholly foreign to anything the Louisianians had known hitherto in legal procedure, and when it was explained that common law was "unwritten law, drawing its binding force from immemorial usage and universal reception in England," it is small wonder that the bewildered inhabitants quickly suspected its adoption to be a mere subterfuge on the part of the United States authorities whereby to govern Louisiana by a purely arbitrary system.

Both Casa Calvo and Morales, with their retinues of officials, continued to loiter at New Orleans. As early as August 28 Secretary Madison had written to Claiborne that the presence and conduct of the Spaniards justly excited attention, and that the day on which the new government was to go into effect (October 1) might well be made the occasion of giving the officers to understand that their immediate departure would be heartily approved by the United States.[1] Believing that the discontent which prevailed in the territory was augmented by the influence of these men, Claiborne very gladly acted on Madison's suggestion, October 9, and communicated to Casa Calvo the Administration's desire that such Spaniards as did not intend to become American citizens should not longer remain on American soil. On the plea, however, that he expected shortly to be employed in defining the boundary line between the United States and Mexico, Casa Calvo refused to leave the territory.[2] The undoubted effect of his course in this particular was to strengthen the impression which prevailed among many of the inhabitants that Spain was planning a reacquisition of Louisiana. It was well known that the United States was extremely desirous of securing the Floridas — that indeed it was the Floridas, and not the territory west of the Mississippi, that Monroe and Livingston had been commissioned to purchase in 1803. It was also known that the only terms upon which the Spanish government would even consider the alienation of the Floridas was the retrocession of Louisiana by the United States.[3] And it was confidently believed by many that just as soon as the war between Spain and England should be brought to a close, Spain and the United States would effect an exchange of the two territories. "So general

---

[1] Madison to Claiborne, August 28, 1804, *Writings of James Madison*, II. 203.

[2] Claiborne to Madison, *Executive Journal*, I. 102.

[3] Claiborne to Madison, April 5, 1805, *ibid.*, I. 120.

has been this impression," wrote Claiborne to Madison, "that many citizens have been fearful of accepting any employment under the American government, or even manifesting a respect therefor, lest at a future time it might lessen them in the esteem of Spanish officers."[1]

The Spanish forces in Pensacola and West Florida amounted to nine hundred effective men. Two hundred were stationed at Baton Rouge, about eighty at Mobile, and according to common report the number of troops in Texas had been considerably augmented. It was even believed by some that at a point distant only 240 miles from the mouth of the Sabine two thousand troops had been concentrated by the Spaniards in anticipation of a movement against Louisiana if diplomacy should fail.[2] When called upon, April 19, 1805, to tell what he knew of the increase of the Spanish armaments, Casa Calvo declared that the increase was only apparent, the number of troops at the points named being occasioned solely by concentration there preparatory to a withdrawal from the country. Still he expressed surprise at the desire of the United States to hold territory west of the Mississippi, bringing forward the time-worn argument that a republican government could not endure throughout so large a realm. The net result of several conferences was only yet further to convince Claiborne that "the great object of the Spanish government will be to limit the possessions of the United States westwardly by the Mississippi," and that until the result of Monroe's mission to purchase the Floridas, of which we shall speak

[1] Claiborne to Madison, December 11, 1804, *Executive Journal*, I. 55.
[2] Claiborne to Madison, *ibid.*, I. 118.

presently, should be known, "the Louisianians will not consider their political destiny as fixed."[1]

By the autumn of 1805 it had become understood at New Orleans that the effort of Monroe to buy the Floridas had been unsuccessful. Spain would entertain the idea of ceding the territory in question only on condition of the recovery of Louisiana. Although the closing of such a bargain was unthought of at Washington, the news of Spain's ultimatum naturally increased the belief among the Louisianians that before the passage of many months their country would again be brought under the flag of Castile. Casa Calvo, when appealed to for his opinion, declared that Don Pedro Cevallos, the Spanish minister of foreign affairs, had informed him definitely that the desire of the court of Spain was to make the Mississippi the boundary, and that their expectation was to obtain this object in due time. This confession did not come by way of surprise to Claiborne, but it certainly made him feel far from easy in his position. Little wonder that he wrote to Madison that, next to a final adjustment of limits with the Spanish government, he most desired to see every Spanish officer removed from the ceded territory. "There must certainly be a power existing, somewhere vested, to cause to be executed the clause in the treaty which directs the Spanish forces to be withdrawn within three months from the ceded territory,[2] and I should be pleased to have

[1] Claiborne to Madison, *Executive Journal*, I. 128.

[2] The clause of the treaty (the last of Article V.) to which Claiborne referred reads as follows, "The troops, whether of France or Spain, who may be there, shall cease to occupy any military post from the time of taking possession, and shall be embarked as soon as possible, in the course of three months after the ratification of the treaty." Of course it

it hinted to me that, in my character as commissioner or governor, I could, on this occasion, take, if necessary, compulsory measures."[1]

While the conduct of the officers at New Orleans was extremely irritating and in plain violation of the spirit of the treaty of purchase, Spain was yet much further from cherishing aggressive ambitions in respect to Louisiana than Governor Claiborne thought. Of course the alienation of the territory by Napoleon had been bitterly resented by the Spanish authorities, and there was at first a strong disposition to blame the United States for being a party to so fraudulent a bargain. Since the First Consul had not fulfilled the terms of his contract with Spain, argued the ministers, Louisiana had never been rightfully his to sell, and therefore properly belonged yet to Spain. Yrujo, the Spanish minister at Washington, made formal protest, September 4, 1803, against the cession.[2] However, war with England clearly precluded Spain from taking any steps to nullify Napoleon's sale, and the wiser counsel prevailed that Spain would better make the best of the situation and not endanger a war with the United States in the midst of her other troubles. In the course of some months, therefore, Minister Yrujo informed Secretary Madison that he had received orders to declare that his Catholic Majesty "had thought fit to renounce his opposition to the alienation of Louisiana made by France, notwithstanding the solid reasons on which it was founded,

should be remembered that Spain was very far from being a party to this treaty.

[1] Claiborne to Madison, *Executive Journal*, I. 253.
[2] Yrujo to Madison, September 4, 1803, *American State Papers*, II. 569.

thereby giving a new proof of his benevolence and friendship toward the United States."

Due to this assurance, repeated frequently by Yrujo, the Administration did not worry greatly over alleged Spanish intrigues to regain Louisiana. There were many issues between Spain and the United States which the President and his Cabinet considered more pregnant with peril. The chief of these were the boundaries of the Louisiana territory, the injuries done to American commerce jointly by the Spanish and French, and the ownership of the Floridas; and these were the issues upon which Monroe and Pinckney, after the conclusion of the purchase treaty with France, were commissioned to negotiate at Madrid. In his instructions to Monroe, Secretary Madison expressed the belief that, while certain important issues collateral with the Louisiana Purchase had lately arisen, there was nothing in the avowed sentiments or policy of Spain "to justify the inference that she wishes to be no longer at peace with us."[1] Monroe was directed to proceed from London by way of Paris in order to ascertain the attitude of the French government upon the questions at issue. Numerous expressions from Napoleon and Talleyrand had already given strong indication that, with respect to Florida, the boundaries, and the claims, France would unhesitatingly take the part of Spain; and of this Monroe quickly assured himself during his brief stay in Paris.

The negotiations at Madrid, which were not begun until nearly a year after the American commissioners

[1] Madison's instructions, April 15, 1804, are in the *American State Papers*, II. 627–630.

were appointed, were from the outset extremely unsatisfactory. French influence was evidently at work, setting the Spanish more firmly against the American claims. Throughout the spring of 1805, Monroe and Pinckney continued to appeal for a fair, speedy, and conciliatory settlement of the matters in dispute, letting it be understood, however, that the United States was not "unprepared for or unequal to any crisis which may occur."[1] May 12 they submitted to Cevallos an ultimatum to the effect that if Spain would cede the Floridas the United States would yield on her part "her claim to territory west of a line to be drawn from the mouth of the Colorado to its source, and from thence to the northern limits of Louisiana, in such a manner as to avoid the different rivers and their branches which empty into the Mississippi." It was offered also that the United States would establish a territory of thirty leagues on both sides of this line, which should "remain forever unsettled," or of thirty leagues on her own side only, if Spain desired to extend her settlement to the Colorado.[2] This project cannot be said to have embodied much of a concession, except as to the territory in the region of the Columbia River, known as the Oregon country. The claims of the United States in that quarter, while disputed by both Spain and England,

---

[1] Very full records of the negotiation are in the *American State Papers*, II. 627–669. An excellent general account is in Adams, *History of the United States*, III. Ch. II. See also Gilman, *James Monroe*, Ch. IV.; McMaster, *History of the People of the United States*, III. Ch. XIV.; and Charles C. Pinckney, *Life of General Thomas Pinckney*.

[2] Pinckney and Monroe to Cevallos, May 12, 1805, *American State Papers*, II. 665.

were at least as good as those of the former nation, and the commissioners were now proposing to relinquish these claims just as they were on the point of being so materially strengthened by the explorations of Lewis and Clark.

But the ultimatum failed. Cevallos replied on the 15th that Spain saw no gain that could come to her by accepting the proposed terms, and that therefore the king had rejected them outright.[1] Three days later, Monroe, whose duties as resident minister at London would not permit a longer stay at Madrid, asked for his passport, and on the 21st had his final audience with the king. On the 23rd he and Pinckney despatched a joint note to Secretary Madison, informing him of the failure of the negotiation.[2] The message which Jefferson sent to Congress, December 3, expressed the fear that war would be inevitable between the two nations, or that at least it would be necessary " to join in the unprofitable contest of trying which party can do the other most harm."[3] The year 1805 closed for the United States with a lowering horizon.

Meanwhile there had been certain developments in the policy of the United States toward Louisiana. During the session of 1804–1805, Congress was absorbed more by the question of a government for Louisiana than by any other topic. In both Houses the debates were able and prolonged. It was understood that the temporary system which had gone into effect the past October was

[1] Cevallos to Monroe and Pinckney, May 15, 1805, *American State Papers*, II. 666.

[2] Monroe and Pinckney to Madison, May 23, 1805, *ibid.*, II. 667.

[3] Richardson, *Messages and Papers of the Presidents*, I. 382.

to continue one year only. The great problem was as to the more permanent system to be substituted for it. On the 4th of January, 1805, the petition of the "Merchants, Planters, and Other Inhabitants of Louisiana" was read in the Senate. Coming directly from the people, it expressed unmistakably what they thought of their new national relations and what they desired for the improvement thereof. The idea which had been advanced so often on the floor of Congress, that the Louisianians were unfit for freedom and self-government, was scouted by the petitioners, and it was sarcastically inquired whether the authorities of the United States now considered them less capable politically than a year before, when by the treaty they had been promised incorporation as soon as possible into the Union. The prohibition of the slave trade, the imposing upon the territory of an English, and therefore alien, judicial system, and partiality shown new settlers in the distribution of offices and favors, were all brought forward as grievances. But the main contention was for the early execution of the third article of the treaty. "The inhabitants of the ceded territory," asserted the petition, "are to be incorporated into the Union of the United States. . . . To be incorporated must mean to form a part of it. But to every component part of the United States the Constitution has guaranteed a republican form of government, and this,[1] as we have already shown, has no one principle of republicanism in its composition. It is therefore not in compliance with the letter of the treaty, and is totally inconsistent with its

[1] That is, the existing system under the Act of March 26, 1804.

spirit, which certainly intends some stipulations in our favor. For if Congress may govern us as they please, what necessity was there for this clause, or how are we to be benefited by its introduction? If any doubt, however, could possibly exist on the first member of the sentence, it must vanish by a consideration of the second, which provides for our admission to the rights, privileges, and immunities of citizens of the United States. But this territorial government, as we have shown, is totally incompatible with those rights. Without any vote in the election of our legislature, without any check upon our executive, without any one incident of self-government, what valuable privilege of citizenship is allowed us? What right do we enjoy, of what immunity can we boast, except, indeed, the degrading exemption from the cares of legislation and the burden of public affairs?" With very good grace the members of Congress were called upon to prove true to "the principles of your Revolution, the sacred, self-evident, and eternal truths on which your governments are founded." [1]

Three weeks after the presenting of this memorial John Randolph, chairman of the House committee on that portion of the President's message which dealt with Louisiana,[2] and also on the Louisianians' petition, made a

---

[1] The text of the petition appears in an anonymous book, *Louisiane, 1804 à 1807*, in the Harvard College Library [see p. 571]. It is printed in the *Annals of Congress* (1804–1805), 1597–1608, and in part in Hart, *American History Told by Contemporaries*, III, 377–380. There are extensive quotations from it in Gayarré, *History of Louisiana*, IV. 58–64.

[2] In his message of November 8, 1804, the President had called the attention of Congress to the advisability of ameliorating the territorial government of Louisiana. Richardson, *Messages and Papers of the Presidents*, 371.

report in which it was held that only "under torture" could the third article of the treaty be construed to mean what the petitioners said it did.[1] Nevertheless, the committee considered the Louisiana situation susceptible of radical improvement, and the report was supplemented by a resolution to the effect that "provisions ought to be made by law for extending to the inhabitants of Louisiana the right of self-government." The outcome of several weeks' debate upon the subject was the passage of an act, approved March 2, providing for the government of the Territory of Orleans by authorizing the President to establish a government in all respects similar to that of the Mississippi territory, and in conformity with the ordinance of the Congress of the Confederation in 1787, except in respect to descent and distribution of estates and the prohibition of slavery. As soon as the free population of the territory should reach sixty thousand the people were authorized to form a constitution and a state government, so as to be admitted into the Union upon the footing of the original states "in all respects whatever." Congress reserved the right in the meantime to modify boundaries, as seemed expedient. Instead of thirteen legislators appointed by the President, there were to be twenty-five, elected for a term of two years by the people. The upper house, or legislative council, was to be composed of five members chosen by the President and Senate out of ten nominees selected by the house of representatives of the territory. They were to serve a term of five years, but could be removed by the President at any time.[2]

---

[1] The report is printed in the *Annals of Congress* (1804–1805), 1015–1017.
[2] The text of the act is in the *Annals of Congress* (1804–1805), 1674–1676.

This system represented a great improvement over that then prevailing. Yet it was far from satisfactory to the people of the territory. April 21 Governor Claiborne wrote to Madison that the people had been "taught to expect greater privileges, and many are disappointed."[1] He believed, however, that as great powers had been given them as they "could manage with discretion," and that "an early introduction of the entire representative system in Louisiana would be a hazardous experiment." Of course many of the grounds for discontent were not at all affected by this second measure for the settlement of Louisiana affairs. The restriction on slave importation was not removed, the operation of the English common law was in no wise limited, the arbitrary powers of the governor were but very slightly curtailed. Some reasons for complaint, as the introduction of the English language in the conduct of the government, were of such a nature that only a long lapse of time could take away their force.

Throughout the year 1805 the presence of the Spanish officials in the territory was growing all the time more obnoxious. President Jefferson had, indeed, authorized Governor Claiborne to urge their final departure, but to do this in a manner which would not occasion undue offence was not so easy. Casa Calvo did not spend all his time at New Orleans, but made several tours through the surrounding country, ostensibly for the purpose of indulging his love of the chase and acquiring geographical knowledge, though the United States authorities were convinced that his real object was to sound the

[1] Claiborne to Madison, *Executive Journal*, II. 145.

attachment of the planters to the new government. January 10, 1806, Governor Claiborne despatched a certain Captain Ross to intercept the marquis on his travels and inform him that the President had directed him and all other persons remaining in the Spanish employ to leave the Territory of Orleans as soon as possible. "I repeat to your Excellency," declared the letter which Ross was instructed to place in Casa Calvo's hands, "that this is only a measure of precaution dictated by the circumstances of the times, and not intended as an act of offence toward your nation, or of rigor against yourself and the other gentlemen attached to the service of his Catholic Majesty."[1] The "circumstances of the times" referred to were the failure of Monroe's mission, the current rumors of a reëstablishment of Spanish authority at New Orleans, the reënforcements lately arrived at Pensacola, and the reported increase of Spanish forces on the western frontier.

The next day a similar communication was sent to the ex-intendant, Morales, who was then at New Orleans, and who bitterly resented the governor's action. He declared that he was tarrying on business connected with the closing of his former administration — that he was expecting from the viceroy of Mexico the sum of $400,000, with which he was to pay debts of the Spanish government to certain citizens of the territory, and that these payments could be made only through him personally. Claiborne at once spoiled the force of this plea by promising to send him a passport as soon as the money should arrive. On the 25th of January Morales

[1] Gayarré, *History of Louisiana*, IV. 128.

was told flatly that his departure would be expected before the end of the month. Left without argument or resource, the ex-intendant started for Pensacola February 1. Three days later Casa Calvo appeared at New Orleans, despite the fact that Major Porter, in command of the district of Natchitoches, had been authorized to use force if necessary to prevent his coming again to the city.[1] February 6 Claiborne politely but forcibly informed the Spaniard that his departure must not be delayed beyond a few days. Remonstrances and arguments proved of no avail. While expressing regard for the comfort and welfare of Calvo and his followers, Claiborne made it very clear that the President had given his orders, and that they were expected to be obeyed. To Calvo's retort that he looked upon the government's treatment of him as "a shameful act of violence" and an insult to the king, his master, Claiborne replied, "On the contrary, the residence of so many Spanish officers in this territory having been permitted by the President so long beyond the time prescribed by the treaty for their departure, is a proof of his respect for his Catholic Majesty, and of his liberal indulgence toward those employed in his service; an indulgence which, I am sorry to perceive, is not sufficiently appreciated by all who experience it." As in the case of Morales, a definite date — February 15 — was set, on or before which Casa Calvo would be expected to depart. February 12 the marquis received a passport from the governor, who took occasion to express "his best wishes for the health and happiness of the nobleman whose presence has become so unacceptable." Full of wrath and

[1] *Executive Journal*, II. 40.

resentment, the haughty Spaniard waited until his last day of grace and then set out upon the road to Pensacola.

The dismissal of Morales and Casa Calvo, while entirely justifiable and in the end proved to have been clearly the wise course, for a time produced effects which threatened to culminate in open war. The hostility of the Spaniards toward the Americans became doubly manifest. On the 15th of March Claiborne was informed by Governor Folch, of Florida, that thereafter no mail of the United States would be allowed to pass by land or water through his territory. It was reported on good authority that the Spanish fortifications at Mobile were undergoing repairs, and that Spanish agents were circulating among the various Choctaw nations with the purpose of securing their alliance in event of a war against the United States. The navigation of the Alabama and Tombigbee was prohibited to the Americans resident in the upper valleys of these rivers, and the situation there became quite analogous to that prevailing on the Mississippi during the time of the Spanish closure. It was so critical, indeed, that Claiborne wrote to Secretary Madison that in his opinion, unless the free navigation of those rivers and the right of deposit at Mobile should be restored within six months, the settlements on the rivers would be ruined, perhaps abandoned. Claiborne believed that not fewer than twelve hundred troops should be maintained in the territory. "The presence of such a force," he urged, "would not only deter the Spanish agents in our vicinity from venturing on acts which are calculated to irritate, but, what is infinitely of more importance, it would give our new fellow-citizens a confidence in the American government which, I am sorry to say, many of them, at this time, do not possess. . . . The native Americans declare that the government neglects them, and the ancient Louisianians, seeing no military preparations, are impressed with an opinion that the United States are either unable, or unwilling, to contend with the power of Spain."[1]

As a matter of fact, the Spanish government was very far from contemplating a war with the United States. Already Spain was involved in a joint war with France against England, and all her failing energies were required for the exigencies of that great contest. Her attitude toward the United States during the years following the purchase of Louisiana was certainly irritating in the extreme, but there is no reason to believe that the high-handed conduct of her agents in America was expressly authorized by the government. A more efficient and scrupulous government would not have permitted such acts as those of Morales and Casa Calvo, but at the most Spain's offence was of a negative rather than a positive character. After the first impulsive outbreak at Napoleon's perfidy, the king and ministry had quickly come to their senses and agreed to recognize the purchase of Louisiana by the United States as binding and permanent. By the Administration at Washington it was thought that war was not probable as long as Spain should be engaged in the great Napoleonic conflict. According to this view, it would be only by some decided turn in the European struggle, whereby Spain would be left free to pursue her ends in America, that immediate danger could be created. As we know now, the progress of that struggle within a

[1] Claiborne to Madison, March 27, 1806, *Executive Journal*, II. 104.

very few years had reduced Spain to such a position of national humiliation that independent action was for a long time out of the question. By the time that Spain, after the final banishment of Napoleon from European politics was once more a sovereign nation, a score of circumstances rendered the reacquisition of Louisiana well-nigh unthinkable. The inhabitants of the territory had in the meantime become loyally attached to the United States, Spain's American colonies were engaged in a wholesale revolt with every prospect of eventual success, Spain had been reduced by wars, extravagance, and non-productiveness to the position of a third-rate power, while the United States had been steadily waxing greater in all the qualities that were needed to make her formidable. But of course, within Governor Claiborne's limited range of vision in the early years of his administration at New Orleans, these things could not in any wise be foreseen; and it need occasion no surprise, therefore, that during the long interval which witnessed the gradual Americanizing of the Louisianians, he, and others with him, took frequent alarm at the high-handed measures by which the Spanish agents were accustomed to keep a war cloud always peering above the horizon.

During the first decade of their territorial existence, Louisiana and Orleans were threatened with disruption through the machinations, not only of resentful Spanish officials, but also of disaffected Americans. The most remarkable of these attempts to sever the Mississippi Valley from the nation with which it had become politically identified was that instituted by the man who had failed by but one electoral vote of succeeding John Adams in the Presidency — Aaron Burr.[1] As early as 1804, while yet Vice-President, Burr had begun his treasonable career by communicating to Anthony Merry, the British minister at Washington, a scheme for the separation of the country west of the Alleghanies from the United States and the erection of it into an independent nation. The precise nature of Burr's plans has never been clearly ascertained. Probably he himself had not projected his scheme very far into the future. But he realized that his political career in the East was ended, that the better class of men believed him bankrupt in both private and public character and would no longer trust or tolerate him, and that the West afforded the only remaining field for the gratification of his inordinate ambitions. Because of the misunderstandings which were making the sojourn of Merry at Washington uncomfortable no less for himself than for the Administration, Burr evidently expected to be able to secure the concurrence of the English government in his plans, and perhaps even its open support. Merry, being much disgruntled with the President and Cabinet, listened quite willingly to Burr's proposals — so

---

[1] Original materials for the study of the Burr conspiracy are: James Wilkinson, *Memoirs of my Own Time*, Vol. II.; John Marshall, *Writings*, 33-111; Matthew L. Davis, *Memoirs of Aaron Burr*, II. Chs. XVIII.-XIX.; W. H. Safford, *The Blennerhassett Papers*; Thomas Jefferson, *Writings* (Washington's ed.), Vols. IV.-V. *passim*; the *American State Papers, Miscellaneous*, Vol. I.; and the *Annals of Congress*, Appendices to Vols. XVI. and XVII. Among general accounts may be mentioned: Adams, *History of the United States*, III. Chs. IX.-XIV. and XIX.; McMaster, *History of the People of the United States*, III. Ch. XV.; Morse, *Thomas Jefferson*, Ch. XVI.; Magruder, *John Marshall*, Ch. XI.; W. H. Safford, *Life of Herman Blennerhassett*; James Parton, *Life of Aaron Burr*; Walter F. McCaleb, *The Aaron Burr Conspiracy*; and Sumner, *Andrew Jackson*, Ch. I.

much so that the conspirator was induced to promise "to lend his assistance to his Majesty's government in any manner in which they may think fit to employ him, particularly in endeavoring to effect a separation of the western part of the United States from that which lies between the Atlantic and the mountains, in its whole extent."[1] Colonel Williamson, a British army officer, was enlisted in Burr's service, and despatched to London to lay all the details of the plan before the ministry and receive its answer.

Burr was well informed as to the disaffection which existed in Louisiana and the Territory of Orleans, and represented to the British that the detachment of that region from the United States would meet with no opposition from the creoles. He had ascertained this from several sources, but chiefly from Sauvé, Derbigny, and Destréhan, the deputies who had borne the Louisiana petition to Washington in the latter part of 1804, and who had been introduced to the then Vice-President by General Wilkinson. "Mr. Burr," wrote Merry to the British foreign secretary in March, 1805, "has mentioned to me that the inhabitants of Louisiana seem determined to render themselves independent of the United States, and that the execution of their design is only delayed by the difficulty of obtaining previously an assurance of protection and assistance from some foreign power, and of concerting and connecting their independence with that of the inhabitants of the western part of the United States, who must always have a command over them by the rivers which com-

---

[1] Merry to Harrowby, August 6, 1804, Mss. British Archives. Quoted in Adams, *History of the United States*, II. 395.

municate with the Mississippi. It is clear that Mr. Burr means to endeavor to be the instrument of effecting such a connection."[1] The aid for which Burr asked the British government was a fleet to be despatched to the mouth of the Mississippi, and a loan of $500,000 with which to pay soldiers and put the new state in running order. Merry was cognizant of Burr's dubious reputation, but was yet constrained to write, "I have only to add that if a strict confidence be placed in him, he certainly possesses, perhaps in a much greater degree than any other individual in this country, all the talents, energy, intrepidity, and firmness which are required for such an enterprise."

It was part of the plan that while the project was being considered by the British ministry Burr should make a visit to New Orleans and identify himself effectively with the dissatisfied creole population. Leaving Philadelphia in April, 1805, the would-be empire builder set out on his long journey down the Ohio and the lower Mississippi, during the course of which a detour was made to Nashville, Tennessee, and Andrew Jackson added to the rapidly growing list of influential men who were more or less in sympathy with Burr's western scheme. June 6, General Wilkinson, now governor of Louisiana with headquarters at St. Louis,[2] and the lifelong friend and admirer of Burr, was encountered at Fort Massac — a military

[1] Merry to Harrowby, March 29, 1805, Mss. British Archives. Quoted in Adams, *History of the United States*, II. 403.

[2] It will be remembered that Louisiana was now properly the region north of the Territory of Orleans, though the arrangement stood but for a few years, and we may apply the term "Louisianians" rather loosely (as we have done in the present chapter) to all the people under the flag of the United States west of the Mississippi.

post on the north bank of the Ohio, a few miles above its junction with the Mississippi. After a four days' conference Wilkinson retraced his course to St. Louis, while Burr, provided with letters of introduction, especially to Daniel Clark, the richest and most prominent American in New Orleans, continued on his way toward the Gulf. On the evening of the 25th of June the creoles, gathered for amusement as was their custom at the New Orleans levee, were rewarded with the sight of an unusual spectacle. An elegant ten-oared barge, resplendent with colors and sails, swept proudly round the bend in the river and drew up at the landing. It was the vessel which Wilkinson had presented to Burr, that he might create as favorable an impression as possible when he appeared at the creole city. When the wondering natives learned that the handsome and distinguished gentleman who stepped from the boat was an ex-Vice-President of the United States, they lost no time in rendering him every possible service, for he was by far the most notable personage who had deigned to visit New Orleans since the transfer from France. One of his older biographers writes that Burr was received everywhere in the city as a great man, and was "invited by Governor Claiborne to a grand dinner, given to him, and which was attended by as distinguished a company as New Orleans could assemble."[1] Nevertheless, it appears that the visitor spent most of his time with the enemies of Claiborne and of the Spaniards. During the two weeks he remained in the city he took so little care to keep his machinations secret that his plan of disunion came to be well understood publicly. "The tale

[1] Parton, *Life of Burr* [New York, 1858], 393.

is a horrid one," wrote Clark, in a disapproving letter to Wilkinson. "Kentucky, Tennessee, the state of Ohio, the four territories on the Mississippi and Ohio, with part of Georgia and Carolina, are to be bribed with the plunder of the Spanish countries west of us to separate from the Union."[1] Even before Burr's departure, July 14, the project had become well known to the Spanish population of the territory, who, though not yet reconciled to the rule of the United States, were nevertheless slow to sanction an enterprise which would rob Spain of still more of her declining American empire. And the agents of the Spanish government in West Florida and Texas, when apprised of the plan, were fairly furious. The creoles, however, were stirred to no little enthusiasm by the prospect of independence.

Having accomplished as much as he had expected on this preliminary trip, Burr returned to the East in the fall of 1805, again visiting Andrew Jackson and Governor Wilkinson on the way. In the meantime the latter had met with repeated failure in his efforts to seduce the people of his territory into the plot. Although in later years Wilkinson took a solemn oath that he had never been a party to Burr's disunion scheme, the evidence of his conduct is all against him, and it appears that he grew cold in the cause only when he came to believe that it was doomed to certain failure. Burr returned to Washington late in 1805, only after some weeks to have his hope of British aid dashed. The ministry had

[1] Daniel Clark to William Wilkinson, September 7, 1805, Wilkinson's *Memoirs*, II. Appendix. Quoted in Adams, *History of the United States*, III. 224.

at first been inclined to look with favor upon the project, but Pitt had finally decided that the foreign office had too much business of greater importance to attend to. Through Merry, Burr endeavored to frighten the prime minister into compliance with his schemes by representing that unless England should give the desired aid he and his associates would, " though very reluctantly, be under the necessity of addressing themselves to the French and Spanish governments then at war with England." He added, however, reported Merry, that " the disposition of the inhabitants of the western country, and particularly Louisiana, to separate themselves from the American Union was so strong that the attempt might be made with every prospect of success without any foreign assistance whatever; and his last words to me were that with or without support, it certainly would be made very shortly."

That there was a strong disposition among the people of the Territory of Orleans to throw off the recently established sovereignty of the United States admits of no question. The feeling was even as strong as Burr represented it, though the disaffection among the population of Kentucky, Tennessee, and other regions east of the Mississippi was much exaggerated. "Mr. Burr stated to me—" wrote Merry to his government, "what I have reason to believe to be true from the information I have received from other quarters—that when he reached Louisiana he found the inhabitants so impatient under the American government that they had actually prepared a representation of their grievances, and that it was in agitation to send deputies with it to Paris.

The hope, however, of becoming completely independent, and of forming a much more beneficial connection with Great Britain, having been pointed out to them, and this having already prevailed among many of the principal people who are to become his associates, they had found means to obtain a suspension of the plan of having recourse to France." Nevertheless, Burr well understood that the support of the creoles was entirely dependent upon his success in winning the English ministry to his scheme; and when this failed he was in sore straits.

It may be that had Burr been able to postpone a while the execution of his plans the English ministry would in time have found itself in a position to help him. Relations between England and the United States were growing all the time more strained, and in less than a decade the two nations were destined to be plunged a second time in war with each other. But the conspiracy had gone so far that it could not be delayed with any hope of ultimate success. Mainly through Burr's own indiscretion, its existence had come to be known throughout the country, and even to the Administration at Washington, and the blow must be struck quickly if at all. Despairing of support from the English, Burr made bold to approach the Spanish minister, Marquis Yrujo, with a proposal that Spain take up the work of thrusting back the bounds of the United States to the Alleghanies. Just to what extent Spain was to profit territorially by the adoption of such a course does not appear. But Yrujo, like Merry, was quarrelling with the President and Cabinet, and it did not seem unreasonable to expect him to give his support to almost any project

that would cause the Administration trouble. Ex-Senator Dayton, of New Jersey, one of Burr's leading fellow-conspirators, was chosen to interview Yrujo on the subject. By artfully relating the overtures that had been made to the British, Dayton endeavored to arouse the Spaniard's jealousy and lead him to commit himself to recommend to his government that aid be extended to Burr. Failing in this, Dayton then proceeded to threaten that, if the movement went on without Spanish coöperation, both the Floridas would be seized and added to the new nation, and perhaps also Mexico. But Yrujo knew even better than Merry the essential weakness of Burr's cause, and while he pretended to be much interested and went so far as to contribute a few thousand dollars, he was wary of making promises, and even Burr himself in a personal visit was able to accomplish nothing. Yrujo, who was as keen a diplomat as Washington then contained, could not be blinded to the fact that England had refused aid and that the threats of Dayton and Burr were devoid of any real menace to Spain. He chose to hold aloof from the project, not out of regard for the United States or for his dignity as an accredited minister from a foreign power, but simply because he had no confidence in the success of the disunion scheme.

After this failure Burr had all he could do to keep the conspiracy alive. He advanced with startling boldness from one fantastic plot to another, even going so far as to plan the seizure of the higher officials at Washington, the destruction of the national vessels in the navy-yard, and the confiscation of the public moneys in the Washington and Georgetown banks, all in order to paralyze the opposition of the government and secure the emancipation of Louisiana and the western states. President Jefferson, who was already distracted with the numerous feuds and quarrels which rent the official circles of the nation, proceeded on the theory that the people could be trusted in the end to defeat Burr's intrigues, and gave little heed — none at all officially — to the conspiracy. Burr was encouraged by this to believe that the President was afraid of him and took the less pains to throw the veil of secrecy over his conduct. Knowing that an indictment hung over his head in New York, and that his only possible chance for power and influence in the future lay in the realization of his western schemes, he threw himself with sheer desperation into a cause which his better judgment must already have told him was irrevocably lost. Without foreign aid, the people of the West could not be persuaded to raise the standard of rebellion; and by the spring of 1806 all hope of such aid was withered.

Not the least important of the many reasons for the failure of the conspiracy was the uncompromising loyalty of western leaders like Jackson and Clay, who, though they fell for a time under the spell of Burr's winning personality, recoiled most forcibly from the scheme of severing the western country from the United States. Because of Burr's former high position in the nation, Governor Claiborne had at first received him with every mark of respect and deference; but Claiborne was far too honest and loyal an official to be drawn into any sort of plot against his country, and as soon as he came to understand Burr's direful purposes he became utterly cold and unsympathetic. Even Wilkinson, forseeing the end, played

the traitor to his friend by writing to President Jefferson a detailed account of the plot, with a scathing denunciation of its author, and eventually appearing as leading witness against the accused when he was brought to trial. Wilkinson, commander-in-chief of the United States army though he now was, was a pensioner of Don Carlos IV., receiving $2000 a year for services of a secret character, and had from the outset been averse to Burr's scheme for the dismemberment of Spain's territorial possessions in North America. "Wilkinson," wrote Yrujo to Cevallos, "is entirely devoted to us. He enjoys a considerable pension from the king. With his natural capacity and his local and military knowledge, he anticipated with moral certainty the failure of an expedition of this nature [against the Spanish Southwest, as Burr had planned]. Doubtless he foresaw from the first that the improbability of success in case of making the attempt would leave him like the dog in the fable with the piece of meat in his mouth ; that is, that he would lose the honorable employment he holds and the generous pension he enjoys from the king. These considerations, secret in their nature, he could not explain to Burr ; and when the latter persisted in an idea so fatal to Wilkinson's interests, nothing remained but to take the course adopted. By this means he assures his pension ; and will allege his conduct on this occasion as extraordinary service, either for getting it increased, or for some generous compensation. On the other hand, this proceeding secures his distinguished rank in the military service of the United States, and covers him with a popularity which may perhaps result in pecuniary advantages, and in any case will flatter his vanity.

In such an alternative he has acted as was to be expected; that is, he has sacrificed Burr in order to obtain, on the ruins of Burr's reputation, the advantages I have pointed out."[1] The defection of Wilkinson was a severe blow to the conspiracy and hastened not a little its inevitable end.

Twice during the latter part of 1806 was Burr arrested on a charge of treason, but soon released because of lack of evidence. Kentucky's rising young lawyer, Henry Clay, served as his counsel, though only after exacting from him an oath of loyalty. With a small band of adherents the arch-conspirator, now a refugee, once more made his way down the Mississippi as far as Natchez. Deeming it unsafe to proceed farther in that direction, he abandoned the boats with which the Irishman Blennerhassett had equipped him and set off toward the east. In a short time he was captured, and the whole movement was at an end.

The trial which followed at Richmond, presided over by the great Chief Justice Marshall, was one of the most notable in the history of the country. Despite the fact that Burr's long-continued treasonable conduct was the commonplace of popular report, the verdict of the jury was "Not guilty." The court held that no course was left open to it but that of acquittal, since the evidence introduced was "in its nature merely corroborative and incompetent to prove the overt act of treason in itself," and proof of the overt act by two witnesses was not forthcoming. The dismissal of the case in this manner was far from satisfactory to the large number of people, in-

[1] Yrujo to Cevallos, January 28, 1807, Mss. Spanish Archives. Quoted in Adams, *History of United States*, III. 342–343.

cluding the President, who believed Burr unquestionably guilty, and who hoped that his punishment would long stand as an object-lesson to the unscrupulous and over-ambitious politicians of the country. But perhaps the ignominy and oblivion into which the conspirator now passed constituted punishment as heavy as could be conceived in the case of a man of Burr's aspiring temperament. It is only to be regretted that Wilkinson, who in spirit at least was as great a sinner as the man he betrayed, was allowed to remain at the head of the army of the United States until overwhelmed by successive failures and misdeeds during the War of 1812.

In the meantime the Florida question was nearing a partial solution. In order to make clear the way in which this was coming about, it is necessary briefly to review the cardinal facts of the boundary controversy and the vexed problem as to whether West Florida was rightly to be considered a part of the Louisiana Purchase. When Monroe and Livingston, in 1803, affixed their signatures to the treaty by which Louisiana was ceded to the United States, they were extremely happy at the outcome of their negotiations, and yet they realized keenly that they had not executed their explicit instructions to purchase the Floridas. As soon as the treaty was signed Livingston began to cast about for some means of making it appear that the commissioners *had* fulfilled their orders, even if they had greatly exceeded them. By conjuring mysteriously with the diplomatic records at Paris he finally succeeded in accomplishing the desired object. The startling theory which he evolved was that by the treaty of San Ildefonso France had acquired the ownership of Florida west of the Perdido River without knowing it, and three years later had ceded it, equally unwittingly, to the United States. No one knew better than Livingston that Spain had by no means intended that the status of West Florida should be affected in the least by the retrocession of 1800, but on examining the words of the treaty he found them capable, as he thought, of an ambiguous interpretation. Louisiana had been retroceded "with the same extent that it now has in the hands of Spain, and that it had when France possessed it, and such as it should be according to the treaties subsequently entered into between Spain and other States." When France possessed Louisiana prior to 1763, argued Livingston, it undeniably included West Florida. At the time of the retrocession of 1800 the territory in question was clearly in Spain's possession. What reason was there for alleging that it was not yet a part of Louisiana? And if it was such a part, it must have been ceded by Spain to France and subsequently by France to the United States. Livingston quickly brought Monroe to this opinion and together they wrote to Secretary Madison, "We consider ourselves so strongly founded in this conclusion, that we are of opinion the United States should act on it in all the measures relative to Louisiana in the same manner as if West Florida was comprised within the island of New Orleans, or lay to the west of the river Iberville."[1]

[1] Livingston and Monroe to Madison, June 7, 1803, *American State Papers*, II. 564. For an excellent discussion of this subject, see Henry E. Chambers, "West Florida and the Historical Cartography of the United States," in the *Johns Hopkins University Studies in Historical and Political Science*, 16th Series, 239-252.

There could be no doubt in the mind of any one that if West Florida had really been possessed by France in 1803 as a part of Louisiana, the title to it was now vested solely in the United States. For there had been absolutely no intelligible limitations placed upon the territory ceded, other than that it should include only what had been previously known as Louisiana. The *crux* of the matter lay in the question as to whether West Florida had become a French possession by the treaty of retrocession in 1800. Livingston and Monroe said that it had; that Spain had owned it in 1800; that it had once been a part of Louisiana; that Spain retroceded the whole of Louisiana in 1800; that therefore she ceded West Florida. The flaw in the argument consisted in the fact that the treaty of 1800 was one purely of retrocession, by which Spain clearly intended to give back to France precisely what France had given her in 1762 — nothing more or less. Spain did not acquire West Florida in 1762. The territory which was organized the following year into a province under that name was ceded by France instead to England, and held by that power for twenty years. It must thus be evident that Spain could not have receded it to France in 1800.

If President Jefferson had acted on Livingston's advice, he would have thrown to the winds all further attempt to negotiate for West Florida and proceeded to assume possession as if the question of ownership was no longer an open one. Even Livingston admitted that such a course would very probably mean war with Spain, but he did not consider that a contingency to be feared. Monroe supported this view, and the greater weight of his judgment inclined the President pretty strongly for a time toward an acceptance of the course which Livingston had marked out. But though he most ardently desired the annexation of West Florida and believed this the only desirable solution of the perennial strife with Spain on the Gulf, Jefferson was just as loath to commit the country to a war with Don Carlos as he had been to precipitate a conflict with Napoleon. He therefore chose rather the slower method of diplomacy. "We have some claims," he wrote to John C. Breckenridge in August, 1803, "to go eastwardly to the Rio Perdido, between Mobile and Pensacola, the ancient boundary of Louisiana. These claims will be a subject of negotiation with Spain; and if as soon as she is at war we push them strongly with one hand, holding out a price with the other, we shall certainly obtain the Floridas, and all in good time."[1] Whereas Livingston and Monroe were urging the President to seize West Florida and negotiate for East Florida, his policy was rather to negotiate for West Florida and for the present let East Florida strictly alone. Pinckney, the United States minister at Madrid, was informed by Secretary Madison that the Floridas were not to be considered as certainly included in the Louisiana Purchase, "being, it appears, still held by Spain." Nevertheless, he was instructed to make diligent inquiry concerning the actual status of the territories. The President was at first not greatly impressed with Livingston's theory; but as the summer of 1803 went on he came to consider it well founded, and as early

[1] Jefferson to Breckenridge, August 12, 1803, Jefferson's *Works* (Washington's ed.), IV. 498.

as August 25th of that year he declared himself "satisfied our right to the Perdido is substantial, and can be opposed by a quibble on form only.[1] This conviction, however, did not shake his desire for continued peace. His plan was to push the claim through diplomatic channels as vigorously as was safe, awaiting the outbreak of war between Spain and England to insure success.

Though Jefferson did not approve of Monroe's policy of forcing an immediate contest with Spain, he yet had implicit confidence in his special envoy, and, as we have seen, directed him very soon after the conclusion of the Louisiana Purchase, to proceed from Paris to Madrid to supplant Pinckney in the conduct of the contemplated negotiation for the Floridas. Pinckney had incurred the wrath of Cevallos, the Spanish foreign minister, and had been recalled at the request of the Spanish government, though the recall was not to take effect until some time after. Being informed of the anger of the officials at Madrid at Napoleon's sale of Louisiana to the United States, Monroe tarried at Paris for the storm to blow over. While thus waiting he received the unexpected commission of minister plenipotentiary to England in place of Rufus King, who had resigned and gone home. In July, 1803, he reached London; but before he had been allowed to work a month on the impressment question he was ordered once more to Spain as a special envoy to aid Pinckney in negotiating for the Floridas. The character and outcome of the labors of the two agents during the two years which followed have already been

---

[1] Jefferson to Madison, August 25, 1803, Jefferson's *Works* (Washington's ed.), IV. 503.

related. On the Florida question they had been instructed to do two things: persuade Spain to acknowledge the Perdido as the eastern boundary of Louisiana, and buy for $2,000,000 the rest of her possessions east of the Perdido.[1] On both these points the negotiations failed absolutely, with the result that President Jefferson was brought for the first time in this controversy to the very verge of recommending an immediate declaration of war against Spain and the organizing of expeditions to drive the Spaniard out of both Texas and the Floridas. Letters which came from Governor Claiborne and General Wilkinson, however, told of the strengthening of the Spanish defences on the Gulf, the reënforcement of the Spanish garrisons, and the difficulties, growing greater daily, of wresting from Spain any of the territory in dispute. Consequently the President fell back upon the old plan of negotiation. With consummate craft he contrived to get from Congress an appropriation of the two millions which he thought would suffice eventually to secure both the Floridas, though only after precipitating a quarrel with John Randolph, who led in opposing the appropriation. The bill was signed February 13, 1806.[2] But the appropriation was really useless, as Spain persistently refused either to recognize that the United States had any rights in West Florida or to alienate by sale or cession any of the territory which remained under the flag of Castile.

Thus matters stood until the invasion of Spain by Napoleon in 1807–1808, and the consequent fall of the Spanish monarchy. The establishment of Joseph Bona-

[1] Madison to Monroe, April 15, 1804, *American State Papers*, II. 627.
[2] *Annals of Congress* (1805–1806), 1226, 1227.

parte on the throne of Don Carlos, in the latter year, was the signal for a general revolt of the Spanish-American colonies. The people of Buenos Ayres rose in rebellion and drove out the viceroy appointed by the Supreme Junta of Spain. In a few months the provinces of Venezuela, New Granada, and Mexico were aflame with revolution. Erelong the movement spread to West Florida, where it first manifested itself in the district of New Feliciana, lying along the Mississippi just across the American boundary line of 31°. This district contained a conglomerate population of Englishmen, Spaniards, and renegade Americans, who observed the confusion pervading the Spanish dominions, and considered the occasion opportune to throw off the galling yoke of the Bourbon, and establish a government more to their liking.[1] The leading spirits of the district issued a call for a convention of delegates from all parts of West Florida, and themselves chose four representatives. Three other districts responded, and the royal governor, Don Carlos Dehault Delassus, gave his consent to the meeting. The convention assembled at St. John's Plains in the latter part of July, 1810. As soon as deliberations had begun it appeared that there was much division of opinion as to the best course to pursue. The delegates from New Feliciana favored the establishment of an independent government. Others favored continued resistance to the

---

[1] H. L. Favrot, "Some Account of the Causes that brought about the West Florida Revolution," in the *Louisiana Historical Society Publications*, Part II., and H. E. Chambers, "West Florida and its Relation to the Historical Cartography of the United States," in the *Johns Hopkins University Studies in Historical and Political Science*, 16th Series, No. V.

sovereignty of Joseph Bonaparte, but fidelity to the lately deposed king, Ferdinand VII. The majority of the delegates, and a much greater majority of the people at large, were for annexation to the United States. This latter party was vigorously supported by public opinion and the press of Kentucky, Tennessee, and the Southwest generally. In these quarters it was believed that if the United States did not take West Florida England would do so, and in that case the old trouble regarding the navigation of the Mississippi was more than likely to be renewed. In the convention at St. John's Plains the radicals did not have their way, and when the body adjourned it was found merely to have recommended a provisional government in the name of Spain, and the establishing of courts of justice as nearly like those of the United States as the Spanish law would allow.

But the timid course of the convention did not commend itself to the large element of the people who had become firmly resolved upon the annexation of their country to the United States. Mass-meetings and conventions declared forcibly against further submission to government by Spain in any form. The popular movement gained such momentum that within a few weeks a declaration of independence had been issued, a standing army had been raised and equipped, a lone-star flag had been adopted, a constitution had been drafted, and an American by the name of John Rhea had been elected president of the temporary republic. On the 22nd of September, the convention, which had resumed its sessions, commissioned Philemon Thomas to lead an expedition against the Spanish fort at Baton Rouge. The fort was defended

by twenty indifferent soldiers under command of Louis Grandpré, and was quickly reduced by storm. Among the prisoners taken was Governor Delassus, who had become frightened at the lengths to which the people were going, and had at last aroused himself to check the movement, only to find it entirely beyond his control. Thomas's success at Baton Rouge decided the convention formally to declare West Florida a free and independent state, and to authorize Rhea to open negotiations with the United States with a view to annexation. The terms which Rhea proposed to President Madison[1] were that West Florida should be admitted into the Union as a state, or as a territory, with all the rights of self-government possessed by other parts of the United States, or, if this was not possible, that the province be added to the Territory of Orleans; that it should be left in full possession of its public lands; and that the United States should extend to it a loan of $100,000. The terms were so reasonable that the President and his Cabinet lost no time in deliberation. A proclamation was at once issued taking possession of the territory in the name of the United States and annexing it to Orleans.[2] Governor Claiborne, who was then at Washington, was ordered to see that the proclamation was duly put into effect, and that the new territory was organized as quickly as possible after the American fashion.[3]

By the end of November Claiborne had reached Baton

[1] Rhea's letter was dated October 10, 1810. It was sent to Madison by Governor Holmes, of the Mississippi territory, a week later. The text is in the *American State Papers*, III. 395-396.

[2] For the President's proclamation, see the *American State Papers*, III. 397-398.

[3] *Ibid.*, III. 396-397.

Rouge and was announcing to the people that their offer to the United States had been accepted. For the most part the news was received with every demonstration of joy. There were numerous malcontents, however, who clung to the idea of an independent state, and who had to be dealt with by force before they ceased running up the lone-star flag in defiance of the stars and stripes. By the opening of the year 1811 law and order had been secured in the five important districts of Baton Rouge, New Feliciana, St. Helena, St. Ferdinand, and Tanchipaho — in short, in all the country west of the Pearl River. Beyond that line confusion was to reign supreme yet for many years. The population there was very sparse, being made up chiefly of deserters from the army, fugitives from justice, and men who had fled from the states to escape their debts. Spain had never tried to assert her authority over these people, and the United States did not find it practicable to do so until a considerably later time. The status of the region remained more or less anomalous, in fact, until the final cession of the Floridas by Spain to the United States in 1819.

The outcome of the West Florida dispute proved that Jefferson's policy of delay had been the wise one. Without war, and at very slight expense, the United States had secured the sovereignty of the coveted territory and had thereby established for her western citizens the perpetual free use of their great central trade route to the sea. Livingston's far-fetched contention that West Florida was acquired by reason of the Louisiana Purchase was dropped out of account; the United States could hereafter base her claim on the stronger founda-

tion of a mutual contract entered into by herself and the people of the annexed province.

Meanwhile the legislature of the Territory of Orleans was petitioning Congress for the admission of the territory into the Union as a state.[2] The population had greatly increased during recent years and was fast becoming more homogeneous and American. The creoles had become fairly well reconciled to the prospect of permanent United States citizenship, and the popular cry for statehood came now with much better grace than just after the purchase from France. The question came before Congress during the session of 1810–1811. At its first mention it aroused little interest, but before the bill enabling the territory to frame a state constitution could be passed, a prolonged and notable debate had taken place in both houses.[3] Opposition to the measure came almost wholly from the Federalists — the men who had begun by decrying the Louisiana Purchase in the first place, and then had consistently fought every project of the Jefferson and Madison administrations which was in any way concerned with the organization and government of the new territory. They

---

[1] On the annexation of West Florida, see the excellent monograph of H. E. Chambers entitled "West Florida and its Relation to the Historical Cartography of the United States," in the *Johns Hopkins University Studies in Historical and Political Science*, 16th Series, No. V.; also the same author's "A Short-lived American State," in the *Magazine of American History*, XXVII. 24–29; McMaster, *History of the People of the United States*, III. 369–375; and Gayarré, *History of Louisiana*, IV. Ch. V.

[2] *Annals of Congress*, 12th Cong. first sess., 557 and 585.

[3] See especially the records of the House debate in the *Annals of Congress*, 11th Cong., third sess., 493–542.

now declared that the admission of Orleans as a state was both unconstitutional and inexpedient. The Union, they contended, was one simply of the states which existed at the time of its original formation. The Constitution was framed for the then existing states, adopted by them, and could not legitimately be stretched to cover any other people or territory. Orleans was outside the bounds of the United States as defined by the treaty of 1783; it could not therefore be brought into the confederation of states. If Congress should begin to carve new states of the enormous domain acquired from France, where would the end be? If Orleans were now admitted other districts would present claims just as good in later years. What would become of the old states of the Union, the states that first drew together into a nation under the Constitution, and for whose benefit alone that instrument had been ordained and established? Their independence would be lost, their control of the government would become a thing of the past, they would find themselves completely overbalanced by the new commonwealths of the West. They would find that, "instead of annexing new states to the Union, they had annexed the old Union to a band of foreign states." Such was the alarm which the New England members professed to feel at the Republican policy of admitting Orleans that they unhesitatingly pictured the passage of the bill as practically equivalent to a disruption of the Union. The speech of Josiah Quincy in the House of Representatives, January 14, 1811, is especially memorable in this connection. Quincy declared that no man exceeded him in love for the old Union and the Consti-

tution, but that if the bill to admit Orleans passed, the old Union had ceased to exist and the Constitution had been rent asunder. It would then be the right of all, as it would be the duty of some, to prepare for a separation, peaceably if they could, forcibly if they must.[1] When called to order for employing such language on the floor of the House, he appealed to the assembly and was sustained by a vote of 56 to 53. Thus vindicated, he continued with much vigor to elaborate his views. The Constitution, he said, was made "for ourselves and our posterity," and not for the people of New Orleans, nor for the people of Louisiana. They did not, they could not, enter into the scope of the Constitution, for it embraced only the United States of America. New states might, indeed, be admitted to the Union. But they must be made from the territory within the original limits of the United States. "No power has been delegated to Congress to admit foreigners to a share of political power under the compact. The introduction of a new associate will be followed by a new division of power, and a new division by a lessening of the share held by the old partners. Can this be done without unanimous consent? . . . Does any one suppose that the people of the northern and Atlantic states will with patience behold senators and representatives from states beyond the Missouri and Red rivers pour in on Congress, manage as they see fit the affairs of a seaboard fifteen hundred miles away from their homes, and rule a body into which they have come unconstitutionally? They neither will see it, nor ought to see it."

[1] *Annals of Congress*, 11th Cong., third sess., 525.

Quincy's argument was as forceful as could have been made on his side of the question, but the Republicans had little difficulty in answering it quite effectually. They had only to call up the clause of the fourth article of the Constitution which gives Congress power to dispose of and make all needful rules and regulations respecting the territory of the United States, and show that power to dispose of territory presupposes the power to hold territory, which in turn presupposes the power to acquire it. Moreover, Louisiana had been acquired by treaty — a treaty which contained the provision that the people of the territory should be incorporated into the Union and admitted as soon as possible. By the Constitution itself treaties are declared to be the supreme law of the land. It follows that they must be implicitly obeyed. From this point of view the United States was under obligation to admit the Louisianians to statehood as soon as they were at all worthy of the trust, all considerations of expediency to the contrary notwithstanding. The bill was finally passed in the House by a vote of 77 to 36, and after some minor amendments, likewise in the Senate by a good majority. The President promptly approved it.[1]

It was decided that the new state should bear the name Louisiana rather than Orleans, while the territory north of the thirty-third parallel which had been known as Louisiana since 1804 should hereafter be designated as the Territory of Missouri. The bounds of Louisiana were fixed as

[1] The text of the enabling act is in the *Annals of Congress*, 11th Cong., third sess., 1326–1328. The subsequent act for the admission of Louisiana, approved April 8, 1812, is in the *Annals of Congress*, 12th Cong., second sess., 2264–2266.

the Sabine from its mouth to the thirty-second parallel, thence due north to the thirty-third parallel, eastward along the thirty-third degree to the Mississippi, down the Mississippi to the Iberville, through the middle of the Iberville, Lake Maurepas, and Lake Pontchartrain to the Gulf of Mexico, and along the Gulf shore to the point of beginning. The customary requirements had been enjoined that the constitution of the new state should be republican in form, should be based upon the fundamental principles of civil and religious liberty, and should secure to each citizen trial by jury in all criminal cases and the privilege of the writ of habeas corpus. By a supplementary act, the part of West Florida which lay south of thirty-one degrees and between the Mississippi and the Pearl rivers was added to the new state. A month later the region between the Pearl and the Perdido, still garrisoned by the Spanish at Mobile, was annexed to the Mississippi territory.

Scarcely were the new arrangements completed when the nation found itself engaged in its second war with Great Britain. The trouble had been brewing ever since the close of the Revolution, and unhappily was of such a nature that its course could not be stayed even by the unsatisfactory makeshifts and compromises which for a quarter of a century had kept us from falling into actual armed combat with the Spaniards. During the earlier part of the War of 1812, the people of the Southwest were far more concerned with their home interests than with the conflict which was raging over impressment, neutral rights, and treaty violations. Many troops were recruited from the states and territories of the Mississippi Valley, but until

its very close the war was fought on distant soil and on the high seas. It was only when the British, in 1814, planned a great expedition for the seizure of the mouth of the Mississippi that the inhabitants of Louisiana and Mississippi and Missouri, as well as the Kentuckians and Tennesseeans, were brought to realize that the issue of the war was of extreme moment and might have to be decided by themselves. A fleet of fifty of England's best ships, carrying nearly twenty thousand fighting men, and commanded by Wellington's brother-in-law, Sir Edward Pakenham, made its appearance at Ship Island without having incurred the slightest opposition. The United States, in fact, had nothing to oppose to such an array. The fleet brought numerous civil officials who were to follow up the work of conquest by the organizing of British administration at New Orleans; for the expedition had no less a purpose than the planting of the British flag throughout the Mississippi Valley, and the hemming in of the United States by British possessions, precisely as the British seaboard colonies prior to 1763 had been hemmed in by the possessions of the French.

That this programme was not executed, at least so far as the reduction of Louisiana, was due in the main to two things: the inspiring leadership of General Andrew Jackson, and the sharpshooting abilities of the western companies of militia. Until General Jackson arrived at New Orleans to assume command, December 2, — just eight days before Pakenham's fleet was at Ship Island, — almost nothing had been done to organize resistance to the approaching foe. The composite character of the Louisiana population made it unusually difficult to enlist the

people unanimously in any sort of enterprise in which international lines were drawn. However, practically all elements were more or less antagonistic to the British, and no one knew so well as Jackson how to take advantage of the people's prejudices and turn them to the service of his country. Even the creoles, whose attachment to the United States was yet comparatively feeble, had in their nature no more deep-rooted trait than their hatred of the Englishman and all his works, and Jackson found it no great task to arouse them very effectually against the invader. By the most desperate energy New Orleans was quickly put in a state of defence. Creoles, Spaniards, Americans, negroes — all were pressed into the service and given specific work to do in the coming struggle. Jackson's main reliance, however, was a body of Kentucky and Tennessee riflemen under Coffee and Carroll, whose merits as fighters he well knew from observation. The test came when Pakenham, with eight thousand men, including four regiments fresh from the Peninsular War, attempted a flank attack, by way of Lake Borgne and Pontchartrain, upon the city of New Orleans. Jackson's men were drawn up behind intrenchments fortified with cotton bales, logs, rails, earth, and whatever else the soldiers could lay hands on. Against this line the splendid British army hurled itself time and again, only to have its ranks pitiably thinned by the unrivalled marksmanship of the backwoods sharpshooters. The surprise of the British was no less than their chagrin. With such an army it had not been thought necessary to take the numerous precautions which would otherwise have been deemed advisable. The battle of New Orleans must be added to the long list of such conflicts in which overconfidence of the attacking forces contributed as much to their defeat as the skill and bravery of the attacked. Pakenham was killed in the battle, and with him two other generals, seven colonels, seventy-five officers of lesser rank, and more private soldiers than perished in any battle of the Revolution. The shattered survivors withdrew to their ships, and before any further operations could be planned, news came that already, before the battle of New Orleans, peace between the United States and Great Britain had been arranged by the negotiators at Ghent. So far as determining the issues of the war was concerned, the great American victory had been superfluous. However, it was perhaps worth all it cost in increasing the respect of the Southwestern people for the power and dignity of the United States. Another noteworthy result was the bringing of General Jackson into national prominence and the setting of that strenuous campaigner, for better or for worse, upon the tortuous road to the Presidency.[1]

With the repulse of Pakenham's army at New Orleans the Mississippi River and Valley ceased to be objects of international rivalry and contention. Three nations of the Old World — Spain, France, and England — had been compelled by varying circumstances to yield forever all pretensions of sovereignty in the great American Middle West, and a new nation of western growth, having now

[1] On the New Orleans campaign, see Gayarré, *History of Louisiana*, IV. Chs. IX.-XI.; McMaster, *History of the People of the United States*, IV. Ch. XXVII.; Adams, *History of the United States*, VIII. Chs. XII.-XIV.; and Sumner, *Andrew Jackson*, Ch. II.

twice vindicated its claims to independence, had proved its right to possess and transform into a civilized habitation the country which no European people had yet succeeded in using to either its own or the world's advantage. After the War of 1812 it but remained for the New Englanders and the Virginians and the Carolinians to continue their peaceful migrations toward the West, until the backwoods wilderness was converted into thousands of richly productive farms, with towns and cities, schools and churches, newspapers and libraries, and numerous other distinctive features of a highly civilized mode of life. For three decades after the treaty of Ghent the most characteristic emblem of American development was the canvas-covered wagon, or prairie schooner. On all the roads leading across the mountains from the seaboard states might be seen at almost any time long lines of these picturesque vehicles, moving in stately procession toward the promised land. The wagons were drawn usually by oxen, sometimes by horses, and contained all their drivers' worldly possessions except perhaps a dog or cow chained to the axle behind. Other less fortunate emigrants went all the way on foot, bearing on their sturdy shoulders heavy packs of food and other necessary supplies. Still others travelled on horseback. And after 1810, when the first steamboat made her way successfully down the long path from Pittsburg to New Orleans, much of the emigrant's journey was frequently accomplished by water routes.

The results of this great movement, which had been in progress more or less for over half a century, were at last becoming apparent in the creation of new commonwealths. The present state of Louisiana was admitted to the Union, as we have seen, in 1812. At that time the newly created Territory of Missouri contained a population of more than twenty thousand whites, together with a large number of negro slaves. In 1816 Indiana became a state, in 1817 Mississippi, and in 1818 Illinois. In 1819 Arkansas was separated from Missouri and constituted a territory. To the streams of migration which up to this time had flowed mainly from the southern seaboard states began now to be added others of large importance from more northern, and even New England, sources. The result was a mixing of population which had not a little to do with the intensity of the struggle, first precipitated about 1820, by the great question of slavery in the Mississippi Valley states and territories. But eventually this commingling of national elements proved a signally fortunate phase of our western development; it not only hastened the inevitable convulsion caused by slavery, and the consequent dispelling of the "black shadow," but it has given to the people of the West that wide variety of temperament and energy which must always be conducive to the very best in civic life and growth. If it be true that the typical American is to be found to-day between the Alleghanies and the Rockies, it must be because it is there that the greatest number of American ideas and ideals have been fused together in the making of social, intellectual, and political conditions.

INDEX

Accau, Michel, employed by La Salle to explore the upper Mississippi, 101, 143.

Alaminos, Antonio de, pilot of Córdova's expedition in 1517, 12; visit to Jamaica, 13.

Albany, conference at in 1751, 260; Congress of 1754, 271.

Allouez, Father Claude, founds mission of the Holy Spirit at La Pointe, 59; and of Francis Xavier at Green Bay, 60; reaches the Fox-Wisconsin portage, 60; speech to the Indians at Sault Ste. Marie, 63–65.

Alquier, Citizen, negotiates at Madrid for the retrocession of Louisiana, 474.

Amherst, Baron Jeffrey, receives the surrender of Canada in 1760, 275.

Amichel, name applied to lands discovered by Pineda, 19; lacking in gold, 20.

Amis, Thomas, in the hands of the Spaniards at Natchez, 433.

Apalache, Narvaez at, 23; Soto in the vicinity of, 31.

Aranda, Count d', prophecy concerning the United States, 399.

Arkansas River, reached by Joliet and Marquette, 74; Tonty's post on, 126.

Aubry, Sieur d', succeeds D'Abbadie as governor of Louisiana, 321; relations with Antonio de Ulloa, 324–334.

Augel, Antoine, on the upper Mississippi with Accau and Hennepin, 143.

Bahia de Caballos named by Narvaez, 24.

Balize, Antonio de Ulloa at, 328.

Barbé Marbois, François, Marquis de, approves of Napoleon's plan to sell Louisiana to the United States, 517; interview with Livingston on the subject of Louisiana, 520; concludes treaty for the sale of Louisiana, 530.

Bayagoula Indians, Iberville among, 178.

Beaujeu, Sieur de, companion of La Salle, 121.

Berthier, General Alexandre, employed by Napoleon to negotiate for the retrocession of Louisiana, 475; concludes treaty of San Ildefonso with Godoy, 477.

Bienville, Céloron de, sent by Galissonnière to take possession of the Ohio Valley, 252; report of, 255.

Bienville, Sieur de, brother of Iberville, recovers Tonty's letter, 180; encounters Englishmen on the lower Mississippi, 183; explores the course of the Red River, 187; in charge of colony at Mobile, 193; removed for a time from office, 196; formulates the Black Code, 223; again governor of Louisiana, 228; expeditions against the Chickasaws, 228–232; returns to France, 232; intercedes for Louisiana, 323.

Biloxi, Iberville's colony established at, 181; hardships of the settlers, 182; visited by the governor of Pensacola, 188; abandoned, 190.

Blanca, Count Florida, negotiations with John Jay, 377.

Bonaparte, Joseph, quarrel with Napoleon over the alienation of Louisiana, 523–528.

2 U   657

INDEX

Bonaparte, Lucien, negotiates treaty with Godoy for the transfer of Louisiana to France, 478; opposes the alienation of Louisiana by Napoleon, 523.

Boone, Daniel, first crosses the Alleghanies in 1760, 276; exploration of Kentucky, 342–344; negotiates treaty of Watauga with the Cherokees, 353;. traces the Wilderness Road, 353.

Bouquet, Henry, in the Pontiac War, 303.

Braddock, General Edward, defeat near Fort Duquesne, 273.

Breckenridge, John C., defends the annexation of Louisiana, 563–565; reports bill for the organization of the Louisiana territory, 569.

Burr, Aaron, treasonable relations with Anthony Merry, 626; proposes to take advantage of disaffection in Louisiana, 627; visit to Louisiana and New Orleans, 628–630; solicits Spanish aid, 632; failure of plans, 634; deserted by Wilkinson, 635; trial for treason, 636.

Bute, Lord, directs negotiation of the treaty of Paris, 282.

Cadillac, Antoine de la Mothe, governor of Louisiana, 198; recalled, 203.

Canada, surrendered to the English, 275; question of the extent of, 277.

Carmichael, William, receives instructions from Jefferson, 444; appointed to negotiate treaty with Spain, 446; fruitless efforts at Madrid, 448.

Carondelet, Baron de, governor of Louisiana, restrains enthusiasm aroused by the French Revolution, 450.

Casa Calvo, Marquis de, commissioner to deliver Louisiana to the French, 587; lingers at New Orleans, 609; on the Spanish armaments in Louisiana, 611; requested by Claiborne to depart from Louisiana, 610, 620; goes to Pensacola, 623.

Champlain, Samuel de, employs Nicolet in western exploration, 46.

Charlevoix, Pierre François Xavier de, report on Louisiana, 219–221.

Cherokee Indians, cede lands for the Watauga settlement, 346; yield lands to Richard Henderson for Transylvania, 352.

Chicago River, La Salle on, 106.

Chickasaw Indians, conclude treaties with the French at Mobile, 193; Bienville's expeditions against, 228–232.

China, Sea of, Nicolet's expedition to discover, 46; rumors concerning, 52; speculation regarding, 57; Duluth's proposed search for, 142, 155.

Choctaw Indians, conclude treaties with the French at Mobile, 193; aid Bienville against the Chickasaws, 229.

Claiborne, Governor William, appointed commissioner to receive Louisiana from the French, 596; organizes a military force, 597; receives Louisiana from Laussat, 599–600; proclamation to the people of Louisiana, 602; difficulty of position at New Orleans, 603; forces departure of Casa Calvo and Morales, 610, 622; refuses to be involved in Aaron Burr's schemes, 634; establishes order in West Florida, 645.

Clark, Daniel, leads in the defence of New Orleans, 595.

Clark, George Rogers, agent of Transylvania, 354; commissioned to conquer British posts in the West, 357; preparations for the expedition, 358; receives the surrender of Kaskaskia and Cahokia, 360, and of Vincennes, 364–366; establishes Fort Jefferson on the Mississippi, 367; reprisal on the Spaniards at Vincennes, 434; commissioned to lead expedition against the Spaniards on the lower Mississippi, 451; failure, 453.

Colbert, Jean Baptiste, French minister of marine, appoints Talon to

INDEX

be intendant and Courcelles to be governor of New France, 58.

Columbus, Christopher, fourth voyage of, 10.

Company of the West, organized, 204; relations of John Law with, 206; surrenders Louisiana patent, 227.

Congress, Continental, appoints John Jay to negotiate treaty with Spain, 374; instructs Jay, 375, 380; authorizes Jay to yield the navigation of the Mississippi, 383; Jay displeased with instructions of, 385-387; issues instructions regarding the boundaries of the United States, 391; recommends cessions of western lands, 404.

Congress of the Confederation, approves Jay's conduct at Madrid, 389; instructs Jay to end negotiation, 389; dealings with western lands, 406, 407; adopts the Northwest Ordinance, 407; instructs Jay in 1785 to treat with Gardoqui, 421; advised by Jay to yield the navigation of the Mississippi, 424; debate on Jay's proposal, 428-432; sectional character of the Mississippi question, 432; receives Jay's report on his negotiations with Gardoqui, 438-440; revokes Jay's commission to negotiate with Gardoqui, 440.

Córdova, Francisco Hernandez de, expedition to Honduras in 1517, 12; on the Yucatan coast, 12; death, 13.

Coronado, Francisco Vasquez, explores the American interior from the southwest, 27.

Courcelles, Sieur de, issues patent to La Salle, 85.

Coureurs-de-bois, forbidden to trade with the Indians, 141.

Coxe, Daniel, expedition to the mouth of the Mississippi, 183.

Cresap, Michael, in Lord Dunmore's war, 350.

Croghan, George, expedition to establish English authority in the Illinois country (1765), 310; failure of, 311.

Crozat, Antoine, receives monopoly of Louisiana trade, 199; establishes trading posts on the Mississippi, 201; surrenders his patent, 203.

D'Abbadie, Sieur, governor of Louisiana, 315; description of Louisiana in 1764, 317; commissioned to deliver Louisiana to Spain, 319; death, 321.

Detroit, becomes an important base of French operations, 259.

Dickinson, John, resolution on relations with Spain, 373.

Dinwiddie, Governor Robert, plans to secure the upper Ohio Valley, 262; sends Washington to Fort Le Bœuf, 263; prepares for war on the upper Ohio, 264.

Don Carlos IV., agrees to yield Louisiana to the French, 474, 476.

Douay, Father Anastasius, accompanies La Salle, 1684-1687, 124; with Iberville, 175.

Du Chesneau, M., on the illegal trade of the *coureurs-de-bois*, 141; causes the arrest of Duluth, 157.

Duluth, Daniel Greysolon, commissioned by Frontenac to explore the Sioux country, 138; takes possession of the far Northwest for France, 140; encounters Hennepin on the Mississippi, 154; proposed search for the China Sea, 142, 155; arrested by Du Chesneau at Quebec, 157.

Dunmore, Earl of, war with the Indians, 347-352; jealousy of Pennsylvania, 348.

Duquesne, Marquis, governor of Canada, 260; directs fortification of the upper Ohio, 262.

England, prolonged contest with France in the eighteenth century, 170; policy in the eastern Mississippi Valley after 1763, 296-298; sovereignty established on the Mississippi, 309-313, 316.

English, advance of feared by La Salle, 171; visit the lower Mississippi, 183; traders in the Arkansas

660   INDEX

country, 186; relations with the Choctaws, 236; struggle for the Ohio Valley, 252–275; colonization in America compared with the French, 290; pleased with French cession of Louisiana to Spain, 321.

English Turn, Bienville meets Englishmen at, 183–184.

Espíritu Santo, bay named by Hernando de Sotò, 30.

Espíritu Santo, Rio del, named by Garay, 16; identity of, 16–19.

Falls of St. Anthony, discovered and named by Hennepin, 151.

Family Compact, formed in 1761, 286.

Ferdinand and Isabella, decree of 1495, 11.

Florida, proved not to be an island, 21; ceded by Spain to England in 1763, 287; retroceded by England to Spain in 1783, 398; France negotiates with Spain to obtain, 475; saved from cession to France by Godoy, 484; Jefferson resolves to secure for the United States, 502; Monroe and Livingston authorized to procure, 508; not included in the Louisiana Purchase, 533; Monroe and Pinckney negotiate to secure from Spain, 614–616, 641–642.

Florida, West, province of, defined by Proclamation of 1763, 295; Spain's desire to acquire, 368; Galvez's campaigns in, 369–371; boundary of, by the treaty of Paris 1782–1783, 413–415; English province of, 414; Spanish dispute with the United States concerning boundary, 414–416; boundary established by the treaty of San Lorenzo el Real in 1795, 456; Livingston's theory as to acquisition by the United States in 1803, 638; not a part of the Louisiana Purchase, 639; Jefferson's policy regarding, 639; popular convention in 1810, 643; republic of created, 644; annexed to the United States, 645; Claiborne establishes order in, 645–646.

Fort Chartres, established by the French, 219; surrendered to the English, 312.

Fort Crêvecœur, built by La Salle, 100; Tonty in command of, 101.

Fort d'Huillier, established by Le Sueur, 165.

Fort Duquesne, captured and named by the French, 265, 266; taken by the English, 275.

Fort Frontenac, in charge of La Salle, 90.

Fort La Boulaye, established by Iberville, 186.

Fort Le Bœuf, established by the French, 262.

Fort Necessity, Washington's defeat at, 266.

Fort Rosalie, Indian Massacre at, in 1729, 225.

Fort St. Joseph, Spanish expedition against, 372.

Fort St. Louis (on Mobile River), established by the French, 192; hardships of the colony, 194; removal to new site, 197.

Fort St. Louis (on the Texan coast), La Salle's colony at, 122; Spaniards visit, 129.

Fort Stanwix, Sir William Johnson's treaty with the Iroquois at, 305.

Fox River, Nicolet ascends, 49; Allouez and Dablon on, 60; ascended by Joliet and Marquette, 68.

France, La Salle's plans for, in the Mississippi Valley, 92; takes possession of Louisiana, 111; projected colonization in the American interior, 118; La Salle's settlement a failure, 130; possession of the Sioux country taken by Duluth, 140; prolonged struggle with England in the eighteenth century, 170; first colony on the Gulf of Mexico, 175–182; cedes eastern Mississippi Valley to England in 1762, 283; involves Spain in the Seven Years' War, 286; cedes Louisiana to Spain in 1763, 288; design to limit the bounds of the United States in 1782, 393; disregarded by the Americans

INDEX

in negotiating the treaty of Paris, 393; desire to recover Louisiana from Spain, 461; Directory endeavors to regain Louisiana, 464; threatened war with the United States, 469; convention of 1800 with the United States, 471; reacquires Louisiana by the treaty of San Ildefonso, 477; pledged not to alienate Louisiana, 484; sells Louisiana to the United States, 530.

Francis Xavier, mission of, founded by Father Allouez, 60.

Franklin, Benjamin, plan of colonial union in 1754, 271; pamphlet on the retention of Canada by England, 279-282; views on the navigation of the Mississippi, 379.

Franklin, state of, organized, 409; suppressed by North Carolina, 410.

Franquelin, Jean Baptiste Louis, map of the Mississippi Valley, 112.

French, search of, for the Mississippi, 45; take possession of American interior at Sault Ste. Marie, 62-65; first reach the Mississippi, 70; take possession of Louisiana, 110-115; fail in first attempt to colonize Mississippi Valley, 130; explore the upper Mississippi, 133-168; methods of exploration compared with Spanish, 134; take possession of the Sioux country, 140; establish colony at Biloxi, 181; rivalry with the Spaniards on the Gulf of Mexico, 188, 207; prospects in the West as viewed by Governor Spotswood, 216-218; extent of settlements in the Mississippi Valley in 1751, 236; struggle for the Ohio Valley, 252-275; excluded from the American continent, 283-288; colonization in America compared with English, 290; migration from the eastern Mississippi Valley after 1763, 300; conditions of life in the West, 313-314.

French and Indian War, begun in 1754, 267; English plans at the outbreak of, 268; lack of harmony among the English colonists, 269; the prologue to the American Revolution, 291.

Frontenac, Comte de, appointed governor of New France, 65; employs Joliet to explore the West, 65; commissions Duluth to explore the Sioux country, 138; interested in western traffic, 141.

Galinée, Brehan de, narrative of La Salle's expedition toward the Ohio, 86-88.

Galissonnière, Marquis de la, sends Céloron de Bienville to take possession of the Ohio Valley, 252.

Galvez, Bernardo de, succeeds Unzaga as governor of Louisiana, 367; campaigns against the British in Florida, 369-371.

Garay, Francisco de, obtains grant from the Order of St. Jerome, 13; patent for colonizing northern shore of Gulf of Mexico, 13; sends maps to the Spanish court, 16, 21; failure of expedition to Amichel, 20; death, 20.

Gardoqui, Diego de, represents Florida Blanca in negotiation with Jay, 378; first Spanish envoy to the United States, 421; negotiations with Jay, 1785-1786, 422-438; refuses to allow a time limit upon the Spanish closure of the Mississippi, 439; negotiation with Carmichael and Short in 1793, 448.

Genet, Edmond C., violates Washington's proclamation of neutrality, 451; incites the Westerners against the United States, 451; recalled, 453.

George III., issues Proclamation of 1763, 294-299.

Georgia, colonization of, 248.

Gist, Christopher, establishes Picktown on the Big Miami, 258.

Godoy, Don Manuel, becomes Spanish prime minister, 447; negotiates treaty of San Lorenzo el Real with Pinckney, 455-458; resigns his office, 469; negotiates treaty of San Ildefonso with Berthier, 477;

INDEX

hinders the retrocession of Louisiana to France, 479; exacts pledge from France not to alienate Louisiana, 484; regards treaty of San Ildefonso as null, 512.

Great Meadows, Washington's campaign in 1754, 265.

Green Bay, Nicolet at, 48; Joliet and Marquette visit, 68, 76.

Grelon, Father, story of, 52.

Griffon, built near Niagara Falls, 96; La Salle's voyage in, 97; fate of, 98.

Griswold, Gaylord, opposes the annexation of Louisiana, 554-556.

Grosseilliers, Sieur de, on the shores of Lake Superior, 53.

Guadeloupe, question of retention by the English in 1761, 278-282.

Guillemardet, Citizen, sent by Talleyrand to Madrid in 1798, 466; fails to secure Louisiana, 469.

Hamilton, Governor Henry, incites the western Indians, 356; recovers Vincennes for the British, 363; surrender to George Rogers Clark, 366.

Hawkesbury, Lord, expresses English opposition to the retrocession of Louisiana to France, 487.

Hennepin, Father Louis, on the early life of La Salle, 82; description of Niagara Falls, 95; sent by La Salle to explore the upper Mississippi, 101, 144; descends the Illinois, 145; ascends the Mississippi, 145; captured by the Sioux, 145; description of the Minnesota country, 149; discovers and names the Falls of St. Anthony, 151; encounters Duluth on the Mississippi, 154; returns to France, 158; accounts of his American explorations, 158-161; alleged descent of the Mississippi to the Gulf, 159.

Holy Spirit, Mission of the, founded by Father Allouez, 59.

Huntington, Samuel, resolution on relations with Spain, 374.

Huron Indians, Nicolet among, 47; dispersed by the Iroquois, 51.

Iberville, Sieur d', plan to colonize Louisiana, 174; expedition sails from France, 175; at Ship Island, 177; explores the lower course of the Mississippi, 178; establishes colony at Biloxi, 181; authorizes the abandonment of Biloxi, 190; death, 190; criticism of French colonial policy, 191.

Illinois, conquest by George Rogers Clark, 360; county of, established by Virginia, 362.

Illinois River, Joliet and Marquette on, 76; La Salle on, 99.

Indian land tenure, European attitude toward, 114; character of, 307.

International Law, bearings of, on early French claim to Louisiana, 112-114.

Iroquois Indians, drive the Hurons westward, 51; invade the Illinois country, 103; determine the early French route westward, 135; English treaty with, in 1754, 271; treaty of Fort Stanwix, 305.

Jackson, Andrew, wins the battle of New Orleans, 652-654.

Jay, John, appointed commissioner at Madrid, 374; receives instructions from Congress, 375; instructions to William Carmichael, 376; encounters difficulties at the Spanish court, 376; despair of gaining a treaty, 384; opinion of the Spanish government, 385; displeased with the action of Congress, 385-387; course in the negotiation commended by Congress, 389; takes part in peace negotiations at Paris, 390; suspicion of French designs against the United States, 393; succeeds Livingston as secretary for foreign affairs, 421; empowered to treat with Gardoqui in 1785, 421; advises Congress to yield the navigation of the Mississippi, 424; report to Congress on negotiations with Gardoqui, 438-440; commission to negotiate revoked in 1788, 440.

Jefferson, Thomas, drafts the Ordi-

nance of 1784, 406; instructs Carmichael to guard the interests of the Westerners, 445; contends for the free navigation of the Mississippi, 447; outlines course of isolation for the United States, 485; anticipates pleasant relations with Napoleon, 486; policy of delay in dealing with the Louisiana question, 490, 499, 509; regrets the retrocession of Louisiana to France, 486, 490; letter to Livingston on the retrocession, 491–493; message to Congress, December 15, 1802, 498; nominates Monroe as special envoy to France, 500; letter to Monroe on the Mississippi question, 501–504; resolves to purchase New Orleans and the Floridas, 502; proposes that England be allowed to take Louisiana, 512; surprise at the purchase of Louisiana, 539; favors ratification of the purchase, 542, 549–552; doubts constitutionality of the purchase, 546–548; proposes an amendment to the Constitution, 547; message to Congress, October 17, 1803, 549; suggested disposal of the Louisiana territory, 552; appoints Wilkinson and Claiborne to receive Louisiana from the French, 595; policy regarding West Florida, 639.

Jesuits, relations of La Salle with, 82.

Jogues, Father Isaac, at Sault Ste. Marie, 50; captured by the Mohawks, 51.

Johnson, Sir William, negotiates treaty of Fort Stanwix, 305.

Joliet, Louis, starts for the Mississippi, 66; joined by Marquette, 67; among the Mascotins, 69; on the Wisconsin, 70; reaches the Mississippi, 71; descends to the Arkansas, 72–75; return by way of the Illinois River, 76; loss of records, 77; map of the Mississippi, 77; forbidden to establish a trading post on the Mississippi, 79.

Joutel, Henri, accompanies La Salle in 1684, 124; return to France, 128.

Kankakee River, La Salle's descent of, 98.

Kaskaskia, established by the French, 188; taken by George Rogers Clark, 360.

Kentucky, explored by Dr. Thomas Walker, 256; Daniel Boone in, 342–344; colony of Transylvania established in, 352; county of, created by Virginia, 354; nearly abandoned in 1775, 408; trade revived in 1789 by Wilkinson, 443.

Kerlerec, Chevalier de, governor of Louisiana, 237; recalled in disgrace, 314.

King, Rufus, reports to Secretary Madison rumors of the retrocession of Louisiana, 486.

La Barre, Le Febvre de, hostility toward La Salle, 117.

La Chine, Montreal seigniory of La Salle, 83, 85.

Lake Pepin, named, 148; Perrot builds fort on shores of, 163.

Lake Superior, Nicolet at eastern end of, 47; Grosseilliers and Radisson on the shores of, 53; visited by Ménard, 56; the pathway to the far Northwest, 136; early knowledge of, 137.

La Pointe, Grosseilliers and Radisson at, 53; mission of the Holy Spirit founded by Father Allouez, 59; Father Marquette at, 59.

La Salle, Sieur de, early life, 82; arrives in New France, 83; ambition to explore the West, 84, 91; expedition toward the Ohio, 86–89; in charge of Fort Frontenac, 90; receives letters patent, 93; voyage of the *Griffon*, 96; descends the Illinois, 99, 101; builds Fort Crèvecœur, 100; reaches the Mississippi, 104; descent to the Gulf, 106–110; takes possession of Louisiana, 111; return to the Illinois country, 115; goes to France, 117; commissioned to colonize Louisiana, 119; the settlement at Fort St. Louis, 122; death, 125; estimates of character, 131.

INDEX

Laussat, Pierre Clement, appointed prefect of Louisiana by Napoleon, 579; arrives at New Orleans, 581; attitude of Louisianians toward, 582; description of the Spanish régime, 583; addressed by the people of Louisiana, 585; dislikes conduct of the Spaniards, 590; appointed commissioner to receive Louisiana from Spain and to deliver it to the United States, 591; proclamation to the people of Louisiana, 592–594; establishes temporary French government, 594; transfers Louisiana to the United States, 597–600; regrets the cession, 601.

Law, John, financial operations in Paris, 205; relations with the Company of the West, 206; failure of Mississippi scheme, 212.

Le Sueur, Pierre, searches for copper on the upper Mississippi, 165; account of the Sioux Indians, 166.

Livingston, Robert R., minister to France, 483; letter of Jefferson to, 491–493; Monroe joined with, in negotiation at Paris, 501, 506; purchase of Louisiana by United States proposed to, 517; unsatisfactory relations with Talleyrand, 518; interview with Marbois on the purchase of Louisiana, 520; determines on the purchase, 522; aids Monroe in negotiating the treaty of purchase, 530; despatch to Secretary Madison, 540–542; urges ratification of the purchase, 548; theory of the acquisition of West Florida by the United States in 1803, 638.

Loftus, Major Arthur, attempts to ascend the Mississippi in 1764, 309.

Logan, reply to Lord Dunmore's summons, 351.

Logstown, Indian conference at, 259.

Louis XIV., imposes check on exploration in America, 79; grants letters patent to La Salle, 93; confers monopoly of Louisiana trade on Crozat, 200.

Louisburg, captured by the English, 247.

Louisiana, state of, created from the Territory of Orleans, 650; opposition to the admission of, 647–649; boundaries, 650.

Louisiana, taken possession of by La Salle, 111; extent of, in 1684, 112–115; in 1713, 300; plan of La Salle to colonize, 118; Crozat's monopoly of trade, 201; colonized by Iberville, 177–188; population of, in 1717, 204; in 1732, 228; in 1745, 228; in the hands of the Company of the West, 204; John Law and, 205, 212; New Orleans the capital of, 210; described by Charlevoix, 219–221; under a royal council of government, 228; extent of settlement about 1750, 236; eastern portion ceded by France to England, 283; effects of French and Indian War upon, 285; western portion ceded by France to Spain, 288; condition of, in 1764, 317; feeling in, regarding cession to Spain, 320, 322, 330; Spanish difficulty in taking possession of, 325–335; conspiracy against Spanish sovereignty, 331; petition against cession to Spain, 322, 333; Count O'Reilly takes possession of, 336; France desires to regain after 1763, 461; French Directory negotiates for the retrocession of, 463–467; Napoleon's purpose to regain, 473; Don Carlos IV. agrees to yield, 474; rumor of retrocession to France reported by King to Madison, 486; Madison's letter to Pinckney regarding retrocession of, 488–489; Jefferson's letter to Livingston on same subject, 491–493; Napoleon proposes to sell to the United States, 516; the sale effected, 530; doubt as to the boundaries of, 532–535; area of the Purchase, 536; importance of the acquisition by the United States, 537; purchase of, justified by Monroe and Livingston, 540–542; opposition to the purchase, 543–545,

553; constitutionality of the purchase doubted by Jefferson, 546-548; Jefferson's suggested disposal of, 552; debates in Congress on the organization of, 553-572; act of Congress enabling the President to take possession of, 557-558; influence of the annexation upon political parties, 567; Jefferson requests Congress to provide temporary government for, 568; restricted by the Breckenridge Act to the territory north of 33°, 569; description of, in 1803, 575-578; Spanish régime described by Laussat, 583; address of people to Laussat, 585; rumors of purchase by United States reach New Orleans, 590; transferred from Spain to France, 591; Laussat's proclamation to the people of, 592-594; transferred from France to the United States, 597-602; people petition Congress for a more liberal government, 608; Breckenridge Act goes into effect in, 609; petition considered by Congress, 617-620; operations of Aaron Burr in, 628-631.

Louverture, Toussaint, leader in the St. Domingan insurrection, 482.

Mackinaw, Straits of, Nicolet at, 48; strategic importance of, 48, 136; La Salle discovers Tonty at, 105.

Madison, James, receives report of the retrocession of Louisiana to France, 486; expresses American opposition to the retrocession, 487-489; views on the future of the West, 511.

Marquette, Father Jacques, displaces Allouez at La Pointe, 59; belief concerning the Mississippi, 61; establishes the mission of St. Ignace, 62; joins Joliet, 67; among the Mascotins, 69; on the Wisconsin, 70; reaches the Mississippi, 71; descends the Mississippi, 72-75; reaches the Arkansas, 75; return by way of the Illinois River, 76; at Green Bay, 77; death, 78; burial at St. Ignace, 79.

Maryland, jealous of Virginia on account of latter's western claims, 402; influences cessions by the states, 404.

Mascotins, Nicolet visits, 49; Joliet and Marquette among, 67.

Mavila, Soto defeats the Indians at, 32.

Membré, Zenobius, describes the lower Mississippi country, 109; carries La Salle's report to Paris, 116.

Ménard, René, visit to Lake Superior, 56.

Milhet, Jean, carries Louisiana petition to the French court, 322.

Mille Lacs, visited by Duluth, 140.

Mississippi River, size, 6; historical importance, 7; controversy regarding Pineda's reputed discovery of, 14-19; Narvaez at the mouth of, 25; discovered by Hernando de Soto, 34; descent of, by Luis de Moscoso, 40; possibly reached by Grosseilliers and Radisson, 55; early name of, 59; mention of, by the Jesuit Relation of 1669-1670, 60; question of direction and outlet, 61; discovered by Joliet and Marquette, 71; named La Buade by Joliet, Conception by Marquette, 71; first reached by La Salle, 104; La Salle descends, 106-110; French possession taken at the mouth of, 111; La Salle's plan for a colony upon, 118; ascended from the Illinois by Hennepin, 145-149; Falls of St. Anthony discovered and named by Hennepin, 151; Hennepin and Duluth meet, 154; extent of Hennepin's discoveries, 157; Hennepin's alleged descent of, 159; Perrot on the upper waters of, 163; Le Sueur ascends to the Minnesota country, 165; confusion as to the upper course of, 167-168; lower course explored by Iberville, 178; Englishmen enter the mouth of, 183; posts established on, by Crozat, 201; free navigation by the treaty of Paris (1762), 283; English sovereignty established on eastern bank, 309-313; Continental Congress considers the free navigation of, 375, 380–383; Jay's negotiations at Madrid concerning, 376–390; Continental Congress authorizes Jay to yield the navigation of, 383; free navigation of, guaranteed by the treaty of Paris (1782–1783), 397; closed by Spain against American trade, 417; importance of, to the West, 416, 420, 423; Jay advises Congress to yield the navigation of, 424; West aroused by the closure of, 434–438, 449; Westerners demand that the United States protect their interests, 454; free navigation guaranteed by Spain in the treaty of San Lorenzo el Real, 457; closure of by Morales arouses the West, 500; Monroe and Livingston commissioned to negotiate for the opening of, 509; right of deposit restored by Spain, 513; Napoleon favors closure of, 584.

Mississippi Valley, physical characteristics, 2; area, 3; population, 3–5; importance of, in American history, 6.

Missouri River, mouth viewed by Joliet and Marquette, 73; seen by La Salle, 106.

Mobile River, probably the Spanish Rio del Espíritu Santo, 19; French establish Fort St. Louis on, 192.

Montreal, captured by the English, 275.

Monroe, James, appointed special envoy to France in 1803, 501; letter to Jefferson on the prospects of the negotiation, 507; receives instructions, 508; arrives at Paris, 518; determines on the purchase of Louisiana, 522; aids Livingston in negotiating treaty of purchase, 530; despatch to Secretary Madison, 540–542; negotiation at Madrid for a treaty with Spain in 1805, 614–616, 641.

Morales, Don Juan Ventura, withdraws right of deposit at New Orleans, 496–498; forced to depart from Louisiana, 622.

Moscoso, Luis de, successor of Soto, 40; descent of the Mississippi to the Gulf, 41.

Napoleon Bonaparte, Egyptian expedition, 467; returns to France, 468; *coup d'état* of the eighteenth Brumaire, 471; desire to regain Louisiana, 473; instructs Talleyrand to demand immediate possession of Louisiana, 479; indignation at Godoy's Louisiana policy, 480; prepares to take Louisiana by force, 482, 483; undertakes reduction of St. Domingo, 482; advised by Pichon to sell New Orleans to the Americans, 510; baffled in St. Domingo, 514; prepares to renew war with England, 515; proposes to sell Louisiana to United States, 516; purpose opposed by the French people, 522; and by the members of his family, 523–528; *projet* for the cession of Louisiana to the United States, 529; ratifies the treaty of cession, 532; leaves Louisiana boundaries indefinite, 533; designates Victor and Laussat to take possession of Louisiana, 579; favors the closure of the Mississippi, 584.

Narvaez, Pamphilo de, receives grant from Charles V. in 1526, 22; landing in Florida, 22; perilous expedition to St. Mark's, 22–24; constructs boats at the Bahia de Caballos, 24; starts anew for the Rio de las Palmas, 25; at the mouth of the Mississippi, 25; death, 26.

Natchez Indians, uprising in 1729, 225; dispersed, 226.

Nemours, Dupont de, carries letter from Jefferson to Livingston, 491; Jefferson's letter to, explaining Monroe's mission, 504.

New Orleans, site chosen by Sauvole, 180; founded by the French, 208; laid out by Sieur de la Tour, 209; becomes the capital of Louisiana, 210, 221; described by Charlevoix, 220; Ursuline nuns at, 222; de-

scribed by a French officer in 1744, 233, 234; visits of Illinois traders to, 235; conditions at, about 1763, 315; Ulloa arrives at, 324; Count O'Reilly takes possession of Louisiana for Spain at, 336; right of deposit at, secured by the United States in 1795, 457; right of deposit withdrawn by Morales, 496-498; Jefferson resolves to secure for the United States, 502; Monroe and Livingston authorized to purchase, 508; right of deposit at, restored by Spain, 513; Laussat arrives at, 581; address of people to Laussat, 585; festivities at, in 1803, 587-589; news of purchase of Louisiana by the United States reaches, 591; ceremony of transfer of Louisiana from Spain to France, 591; ceremony of transfer of Louisiana from France to the United States, 597-602; hostility to the sovereignty of the United States, 602-607; visited by Aaron Burr, 629; battle of, 652-654.

New York, cedes western lands, 404.

Niagara Falls, mentioned by Galinée, 87; described by Hennepin, 95.

Niagara River, building of the *Griffon* on, 96.

Nicolet, Jean, employed by Champlain, 46; starts from Three Rivers, 47; at Mackinaw, 48; among the Mascotins, 49; hears of the "great water" (Mississippi), 49; returns to Three Rivers, 49.

Nikampe, speech of, 99.

North Carolina, western claims of, 401; cedes claims to the United States, 408; revokes cession and suppresses the state of Franklin, 409.

Northwest Ordinance, adopted by Congress in 1787, 407; territorial system established by, 407.

Ohio Company, organized in 1748, 251.

Ohio River probably reached by La Salle, 89; beginnings of English-French rivalry on the upper waters of, 257.

Ohio Valley, English settlement in, after 1763, 308; upper portion disputed by Virginia and Pennsylvania, 348.

Oregon, not included in the Louisiana Purchase, 535.

O'Reilly, Count Alexander, arrives at New Orleans to take possession for Spain, 335; punishes conspirators, 337-339; character of, as governor, 341.

Orleans, territory of, created, 569; Breckenridge Act provides government for, 570-573; Act goes into effect, 608; Act of 1805 for the government of, 619; visit of Aaron Burr to, 628-631; petitions Congress for admission as a state, 647; admission opposed by the Federalists, 647-650; admitted under the name of Louisiana, 650.

Ottawa Indians, Nicolet among, 46.

Ottawa Valley, first French route westward, 135.

Pakenham, Sir Edward, expedition to capture New Orleans, 652; defeat and death, 653.

Panuco River, Moscoso's company arrives at, 41.

Pensacola, founded by the Spaniards, 176; governor of, visits Biloxi, 188; captured by the French but recovered by the Spaniards, 207; taken by Bernardo de Galvez, 371.

Perier, Sieur de, governor of Louisiana, 223; war with the Natchez, 224-226.

Perrot, Nicholas, prepares for the ceremony at Sault Ste. Marie, 62; in command of the Sioux country, 163; takes possession of Mille Lacs region, 164.

Peter the Martyr, chronicle of, 11.

Philip, Duke of Orleans, attitude as Regent toward French interests in America, 244.

Phips, Sir William, captures Port Royal, 239.

INDEX

Pichon, M., advises Napoleon to yield to American demands in 1803, 510.

Picktown, established by Gist, 258; captured by Langlade, 260.

Pinckney, Thomas, commissioned to negotiate treaty with Spain, 455; concludes treaty of San Lorenzo el Real in 1795, 456; negotiations at Madrid in 1805, 615, 641.

Pineda, Alonso Alvarez de, in command of Garay's expedition in 1519, 13; meets Cortés, 14; controversy regarding his reputed discovery of the Mississippi, 14–19; importance of his explorations, 21.

Pitt, William, and the Seven Years' War, 274; retirement from the English cabinet, 282.

Pontiac's War, 299–304.

Proclamation of 1763, issued by George III., 295–299.

Quebec, captured by General Wolfe, 275.

Quebec, province of, defined by the Proclamation of 1763, 295.

Quincy, Josiah, speech on the admission of Louisiana, 648.

Radisson, Pierre d'Esprit, visits Lake Superior, 53; *Relation* of, 54.

Randolph, John, defends the purchase of Louisiana, 557.

Raymbault, Father, at Sault Ste. Marie, 50; death of, 51.

Rayneval, Gérard, betrays French designs against the United States, 394.

Recollects, at Fort Frontenac, 91.

Rémonville, Sieur de, memoir on the colonization of Louisiana, 172.

Rhea, John, president of the republic of West Florida, 644; asks for annexation of West Florida to the United States, 645.

Rochelle, La Salle's colonists gathered at, 120.

St. Ange, Louis, surrenders Fort Chartres, 312; at St. Louis, 313.

St. Croix River, Duluth on, 142.

St.-Cyr, General Gouvion, pledges France not to alienate Louisiana, 484.

St.-Denys, Juchereau de, explores the Red River, 202.

St. Domingo, acquired by France, 463; Napoleon's attempt to crush negro insurrection in, 482; French losses in, 493.

St. Ignace, mission of, established by Father Marquette, 62.

St. Louis, founded by the French, 305.

St. Lusson, Sieur, takes possession of the American interior at Sault Ste. Marie, 62.

Salcedo, Don Juan de, protests against Morales's closure of the Mississippi, 498.

Sault Ste. Marie, Nicolet at, 47; mission established by Fathers Raymbault and Jogues, 50; French take possession of the American interior at, 62–65.

Seignelay, Marquis de, minister of marine, favors colonization of Louisiana, 119.

Seneca Indians, La Salle among, 86.

Sevier, John, at the Watauga settlement, 346; governor of the state of Franklin, 409.

Ship Island, Iberville at, 177.

Short, William, joined with Carmichael in negotiations at Madrid in 1793, 446.

Sioux Indians, early contact of the French with, 138; Duluth among, 139–142; Le Sueur among, 166–167.

Soto, Hernando de, receives appointment from Charles V., 28; preparations for his expedition, 29; on the Florida coast, 30; advances into the interior, 30; dealings with the Indians, 31; battle of Mavila, 32; discovery of the Mississippi, 34; relations with Aquixo, 35; on the Washita, 37; discouragement of, 38; death, 39.

Spain, early navigators in the Gulf of Mexico, 9; zeal for American exploration, 21; interest languishes after Soto's failure, 42; compara-

tive unimportance of Spanish explorations, 45; methods of exploration contrasted with the French, 134; rivalry with the French on the Gulf of Mexico, 188, 207; war with England in 1762, 282; cedes Florida to England in 1763, 287; receives western Louisiana from France in 1763, 288; takes possession of Louisiana in 1766, 336; desires to recover the Floridas, 368; negotiations with John Jay regarding the navigation of the Mississippi, 377–390; regains the Floridas from England, 398, 413; closes the Mississippi to American trade, 417; position on the lower Mississippi described by Jay, 424–427; treaty of San Lorenzo el Real with the United States, 455–458; concedes the free navigation of the Mississippi River, 457; yields Louisiana to France by the treaty of San Ildefonso, 477; restores right of deposit at New Orleans, 513; recognizes the purchase of Louisiana by the United States, 613; Monroe and Pinckney negotiate for a treaty with, 614–616; unable to regain lost territory in America, 625; revolt of American dependencies against, 642.

Spotswood, Alexander, journey to the Blue Ridge, 215; on the French in the Mississippi Valley, 216–218.

Starved Rock, fortified by Tonty, 103; taken by the Iroquois, 103; re-fortified, 116.

Stirling, Captain Thomas, establishes English authority in the Illinois country, 312.

Sulpitians, relations with La Salle, 82, 85, 88.

Taensa Indians, La Salle among, 108.

Talleyrand, Charles Maurice de; becomes French minister of foreign affairs, 464; character, 465; effort to secure retrocession of Louisiana, 466; retires from the foreign office, 470; failure to secure Louisiana, 471; restored to office by Napoleon, 473; prepares *projet* of a treaty for the retrocession of Louisiana, 475; demands immediate possession of Louisiana, 479; offers to sell Louisiana to United States, 517; refuses to give Livingston satisfaction, 518; leaves Louisiana boundaries indefinite, 532.

Talon, Jean Baptiste, appointed intendant of New France, 58; plans for western exploration, 58; recalled, 65.

Texas, not included in the Louisiana Purchase, 534.

Three Rivers, Nicolet starts from, 47; Nicolet's return to, 49.

Tonty, Henri, arrives in New France, 94; in command of Fort Crèvecœur, 101; establishes "Rock Fort," 103; flees to Green Bay, 103; found by La Salle, 105; attempts to rescue La Salle's colony on the Gulf of Mexico, 126, 127.

Tracy, Uriah, opposes the annexation of Louisiana, 560.

Transylvania, colony of, established, 352; absorbed by Virginia, 354.

Treaty of Aix-la-Chapelle, 248–250.

Treaty of Bâle, France acquires eastern St. Domingo, 463.

Treaty of Lunéville, 477.

Treaty of Morfontaine, 471.

Treaty of Paris (1762–1763), preliminaries signed, 282; territorial provisions for America, 283, 284.

Treaty of Paris (1782–1783), American commissioners ignore France in negotiating, 396; boundaries of the United States established by, 397, 413; free navigation of the Mississippi guaranteed by, 397, 412; secret article on Florida boundary, 413.

Treaty of Ryswick, 239.

Treaty of San Ildefonso, negotiated by Berthier and Godoy in 1800, 477.

Treaty of San Lorenzo el Real, negotiated by Pinckney and Godoy in 1795, 455; establishes Florida boundary, 456; guarantees free

INDEX

navigation of the Mississippi, 457; Godoy's motives in negotiating, 458; speedily accepted by the United States, 458.

Treaty of Utrecht, 241.

Trent, William, sent by Dinwiddie to establish a fort at the forks of the Ohio, 264.

Ulloa, Antonio de, commissioned to take possession of Louisiana for Spain, 324; character, 325; encounters difficulties at New Orleans, 326; expelled from New Orleans, 332.

United States, impossibility of isolation, 410–412; boundaries of, by the treaty of Paris (1782–1783), 396–398; dispute with Spain regarding southern boundary, 414–416; treaty of San Lorenzo el Real with Spain, 455–458; threatened war with France, 469; convention of 1800 with France, 471; acquires Louisiana from France, 530; annexes West Florida, 645; war with Great Britain in 1812, 651–654.

Unzaga, Luis de, succeeds O'Reilly as governor of Louisiana, 341.

Vaca, Cabeza de, companion of Narvaez, 25; journey to Culiacan, 26; account of his travels, 27.

Vaudreuil, Marquis de, governor of Louisiana, 232, 235; governor of Canada, 237; surrenders Canada to the English, 275.

Velasquez, Diego, sends expedition to Honduras, 12.

Vespucius, Americus, explores the Gulf of Mexico, 9.

Vigo, Colonel Francis, agent of George Rogers Clark, 363.

Vincennes, first surrendered to George Rogers Clark's agent, 361; retaken by Governor Hamilton, 363; captured again by Clark, 364–366.

Virginia, western claims of, 401; cedes claims to the United States, 405; sympathy with the West, 438.

Walker, Dr. Thomas, explores Kentucky, 256.

War of the Austrian Succession, 245.

War of the Palatinate, 238.

War of the Spanish Succession, 240.

Washington, George, journey to Fort Le Bœuf, 263; Great Meadows campaign, 265–267; trip down the Ohio in 1770, 345; letter to Governor Harrison on the western situation in 1784, 419–420.

Watauga, association formed, 346; absorbed by North Carolina, 347.

Western Passage, search for, by the Spaniards, 10, 13, 21; by the French, 46.

White, James, opposes the annexation of Louisiana, 558–559.

Wilkinson, James, secures special concessions on the lower Mississippi, 442; great trading expedition in 1789, 443; immunity lost, 444; appointed commissioner to receive Louisiana from the French, 595; dealings with Aaron Burr, 628, 630, 635; a pensioner of Spain, 635.

Winnebagos, Nicolet among, 48.

Wisconsin River, reached by Fathers Allouez and Dablon, 60; descended by Joliet and Marquette, 70.

Yrujo, Don Carlos Martinez de, on the closure of the Mississippi by Morales, 498; informs Madison of restoration of right of deposit at New Orleans, 513; refuses to accede to Aaron Burr's schemes, 633.

The Foundations of American Foreign Policy

WITH A WORKING BIBLIOGRAPHY

By ALBERT BUSHNELL HART

Professor of History, Harvard University; Author of "American History told by Contemporaries," etc.

Cloth 12mo $1.50 net

"A very good introduction to the whole subject. There are seven chapters comprising as many diplomatic phases: The United States as a World Power, The Experience of the United States in Foreign Military Expeditions, Boundary Controversies, A Century of Cuban Diplomacy, Colonies, What the Founders of the Union thought concerning Territorial Problems, and the Monroe Doctrine. To these is added a working bibliography of American diplomacy, sure to be helpful to those who wish to pursue the subject systematically." — *St. Louis Post-Dispatch.*

"This book is of great value to students and statesmen, editors and politicians, being a complete résumé of the diplomacy of this government from the time it threw off the yoke and took its place as an independent nation. Professor Hart is a very clear, concise, and interesting writer, and he not only recapitulates the facts of history, but arranges and compares them in such a way that his readers can easily follow the trend of American ideas." — *Nebraska State Journal.*

"Lucidly written, and the conclusions reached are indispensable. . . . The book may be commended to 'anti-imperialists' for their instruction. Yet it is not controversial in tone or partisan in its arguments; it contains simply the results of profound historical knowledge. A bibliography adds greatly to its value." — *Providence Journal.*

American Diplomatic Questions

By JOHN B. HENDERSON, Jr.

Cloth 8vo $3.50 net

"Of vast practical service to every American who gives to the great international questions of his country the attention they deserve, nor, indeed, does its usefulness stop there. It will be found as serviceable in Europe, though there, naturally enough, its use will be restricted to diplomatic circles, members of parliaments, editorial writers, and a limited number of students of international affairs, whereas with us it is a book for all the people, for all voters, who may be called upon to take into consideration most of the large issues here involved, which are of the present and the future, as well as of the past. The book deals with the fur seals and the Behring Sea Award; the inter-oceanic canal problem; the Samoan question, now settled to our entire satisfaction, and, therefore, at present, at least, strictly historic; the Monroe Doctrine, with special reference to the Venezuelan boundary dispute; and the northeast coast fisheries — a problem that is gradually adjusting itself without diplomatic interference." — *The Mail and Express* (New York).

THE MACMILLAN COMPANY
66 FIFTH AVENUE, NEW YORK

HISTORY OF THE UNITED STATES
From the Compromise of 1850
By JAMES FORD RHODES. In four volumes.   Cloth   8vo $10.00 net

"It is the one work now within reach of the young American student of to-day in which he may learn the connected story of the great battle that resulted in the overthrow of slavery and the rededication of the republic to unsullied freedom. In no other publication are these facts so concisely, so fully, and so well presented, and the student who makes careful study of this work will fully understand, not only the actual causes that led to the war, but he will know how gradually they were developed from year to year under varying political power, until the nation was ripe for the revolution. . . . Taking the work all together, we regard it as the most valuable political publication of the age, and the intelligent citizen who does not become its careful student must do himself great injustice." — *The Times*, Philadelphia.

THE HISTORY OF SOUTH CAROLINA UNDER THE PROPRIETARY GOVERNMENT, 1670-1719

THE HISTORY OF SOUTH CAROLINA UNDER THE ROYAL GOVERNMENT, 1719-1776

THE HISTORY OF SOUTH CAROLINA IN THE REVOLUTION, 1775-1780

THE HISTORY OF SOUTH CAROLINA IN THE REVOLUTION, 1780-1783

By EDWARD MCCRADY, a Member of the Bar of Charleston, S.C., and President of the Historical Society of South Carolina.
   8vo   Cloth   Gilt top   Each $3.50 net

"Unquestionably a valuable contribution to American historical literature. It covers a field that no one has hitherto attempted adequately to treat of. It evidences a vast amount of research into musty archives and an instinct that guided the author to a discriminating selection of material. . . . The future must surely be indebted to Mr. McCrady in no mean degree." — *St. Louis Globe-Democrat*.

RECONSTRUCTION IN MISSISSIPPI
By JAMES W. GARNER, Ph.M., Member of the Mississippi Historical Society.
   Cloth   8vo $3.00 net

"The latest and one of the most valuable examples of pacific literature which is eradicating the bitterness from our national history. It has taken over 400 pages to enable Mr. Garner to tell the story of that time of distrust and calamity, and even with so generous an allowance of space he has not been able to permit himself much comment, but has packed every page with facts, taking the pains in each instance to give his authorities for statements made. . . . The story that follows is one of arrogance upon both sides, of frailty and passion, indignation, courage, conscience, fanaticism, nobility, and contemptibility. Mr. Garner has made the dry records of the legislature and newspapers tell their dramatic story, and it will be impossible for any American to read it without sympathy. . . . It is a valuable chapter of American history, and should have no lack of readers." — *Chicago Tribune*.

MARYLAND AS A PROPRIETARY PROVINCE
By NEWTON D. MERENESS, sometime University Fellow in History in Columbia University.   Cloth   8vo $3.00 net

"We cannot speak too highly of the way in which this work has been done. Dr. Mereness has studied every point in the light of the original contemporary documents, printed and in manuscript, not only those in the archives of the State, but those in private collections; and references to the authorities confirm every statement. The labor undergone has been great; but the result is a work planned and carried out in the truest historical spirit, and invaluable to the student of American history and institutional development." — *The Nation*.

THE MACMILLAN COMPANY
66 FIFTH AVENUE, NEW YORK